FLYING HIGH

NEW YORK

FLYING HIGH

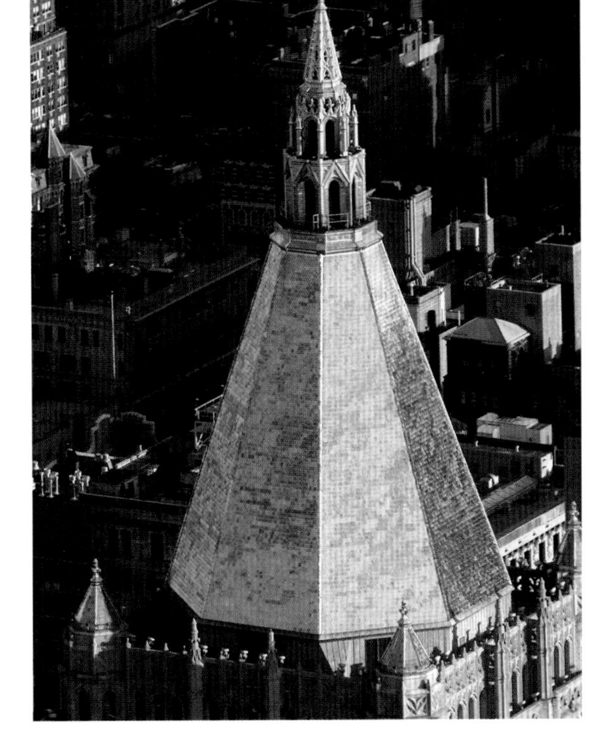

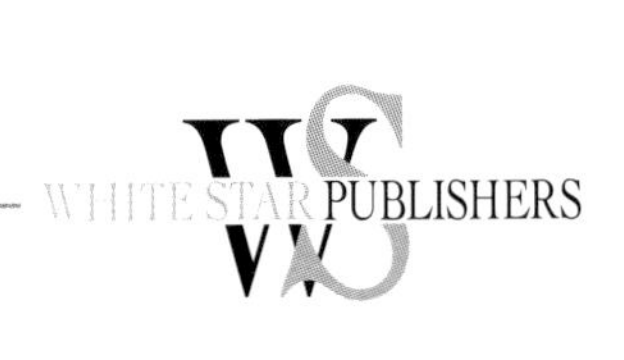

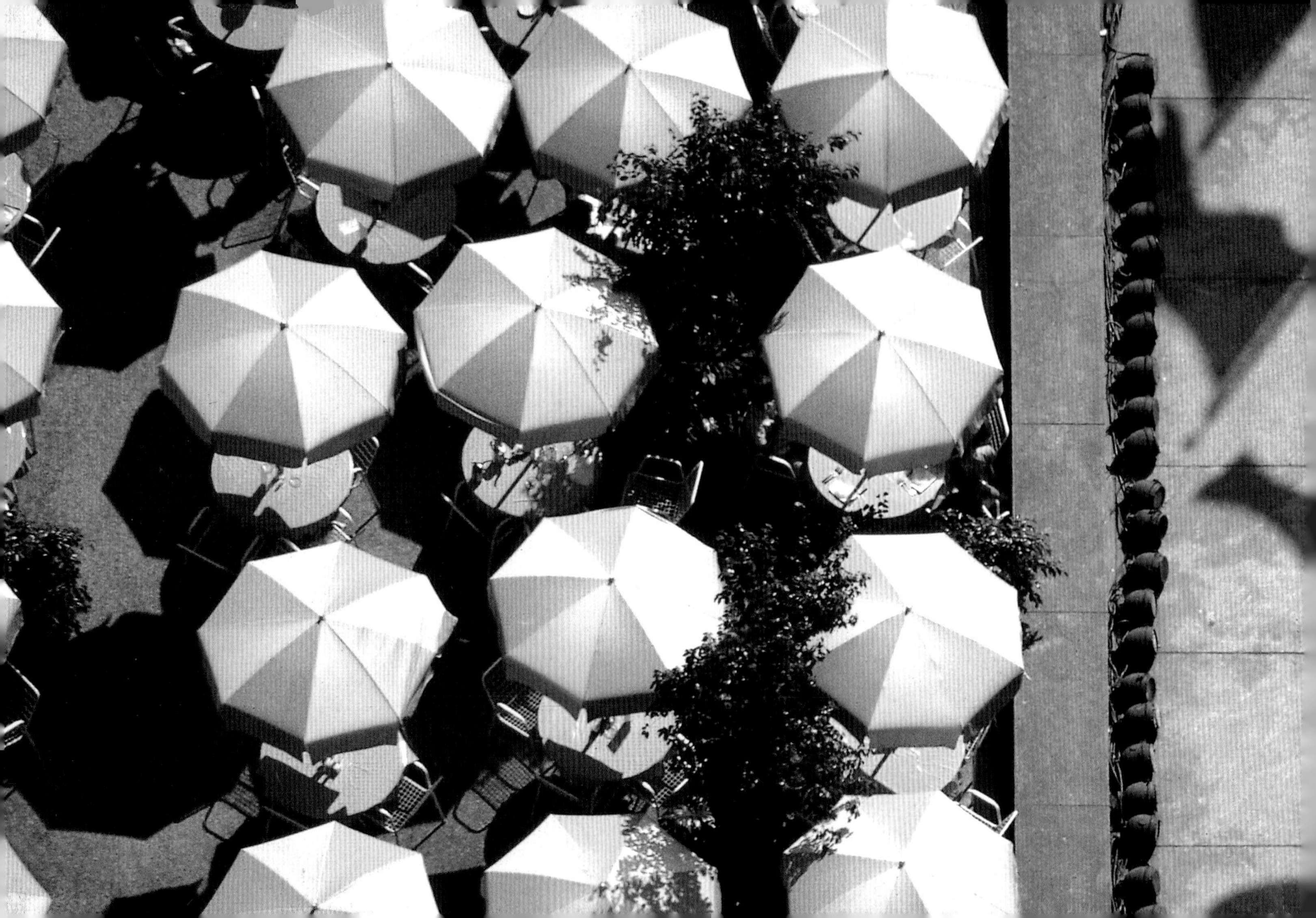

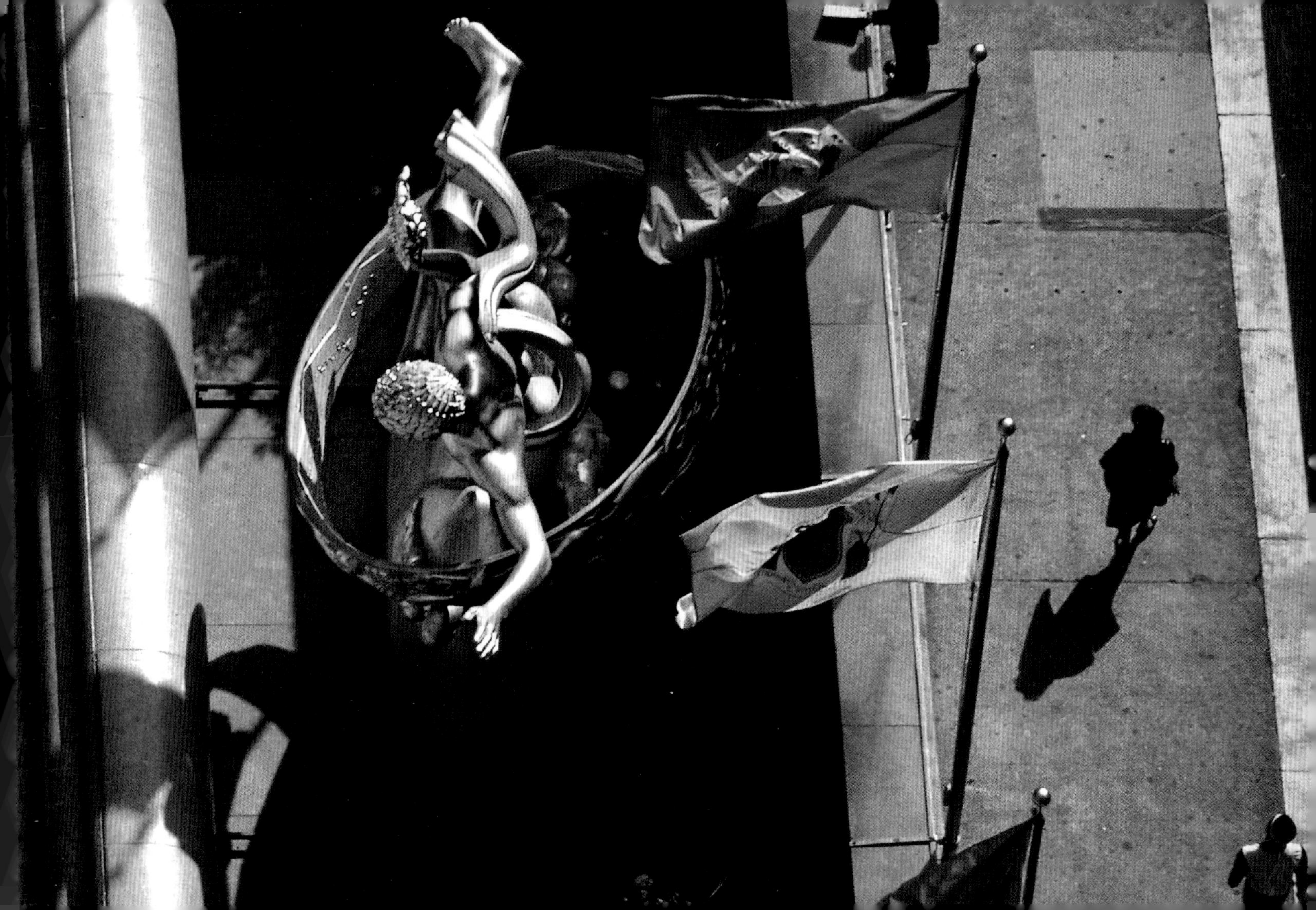

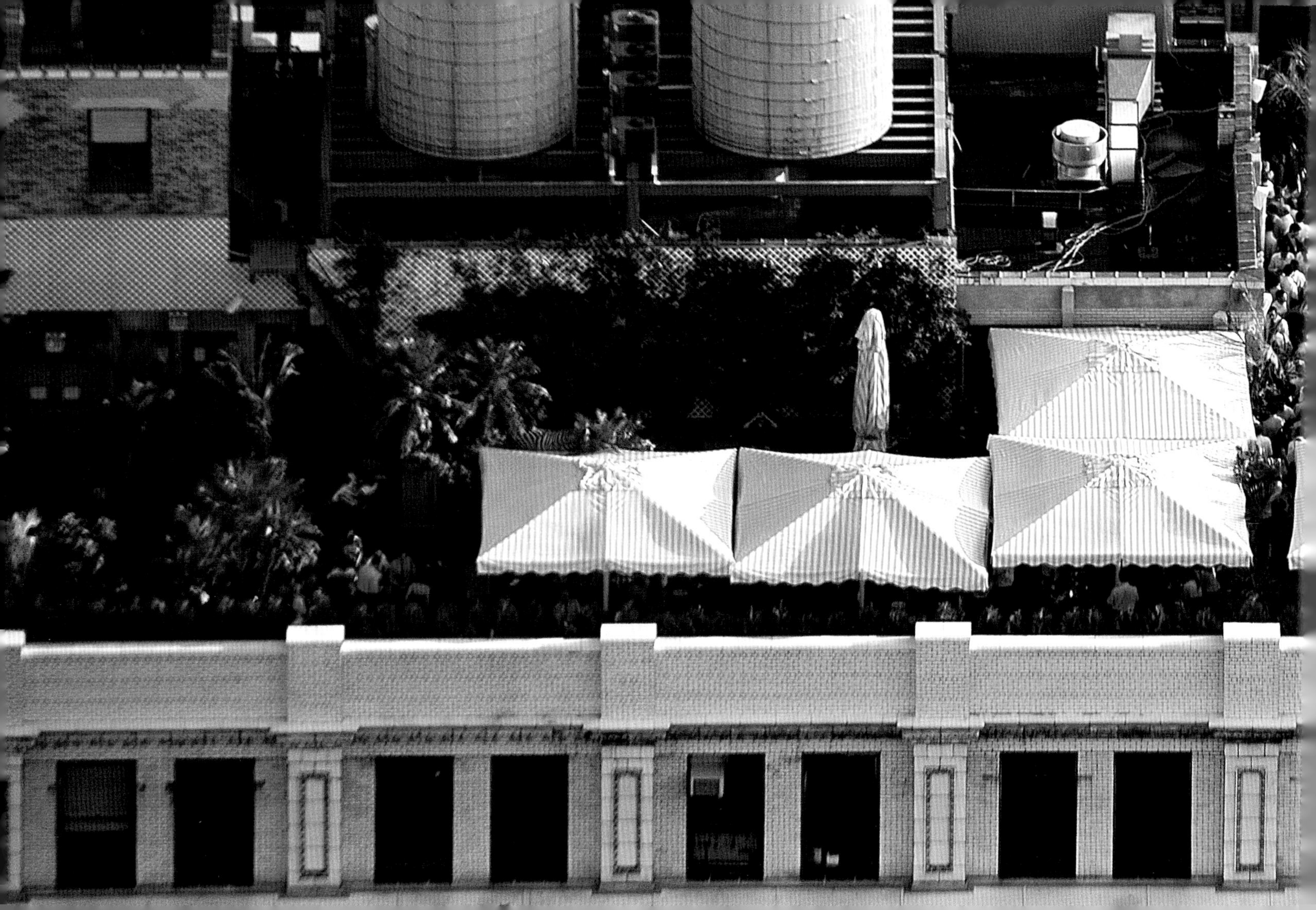

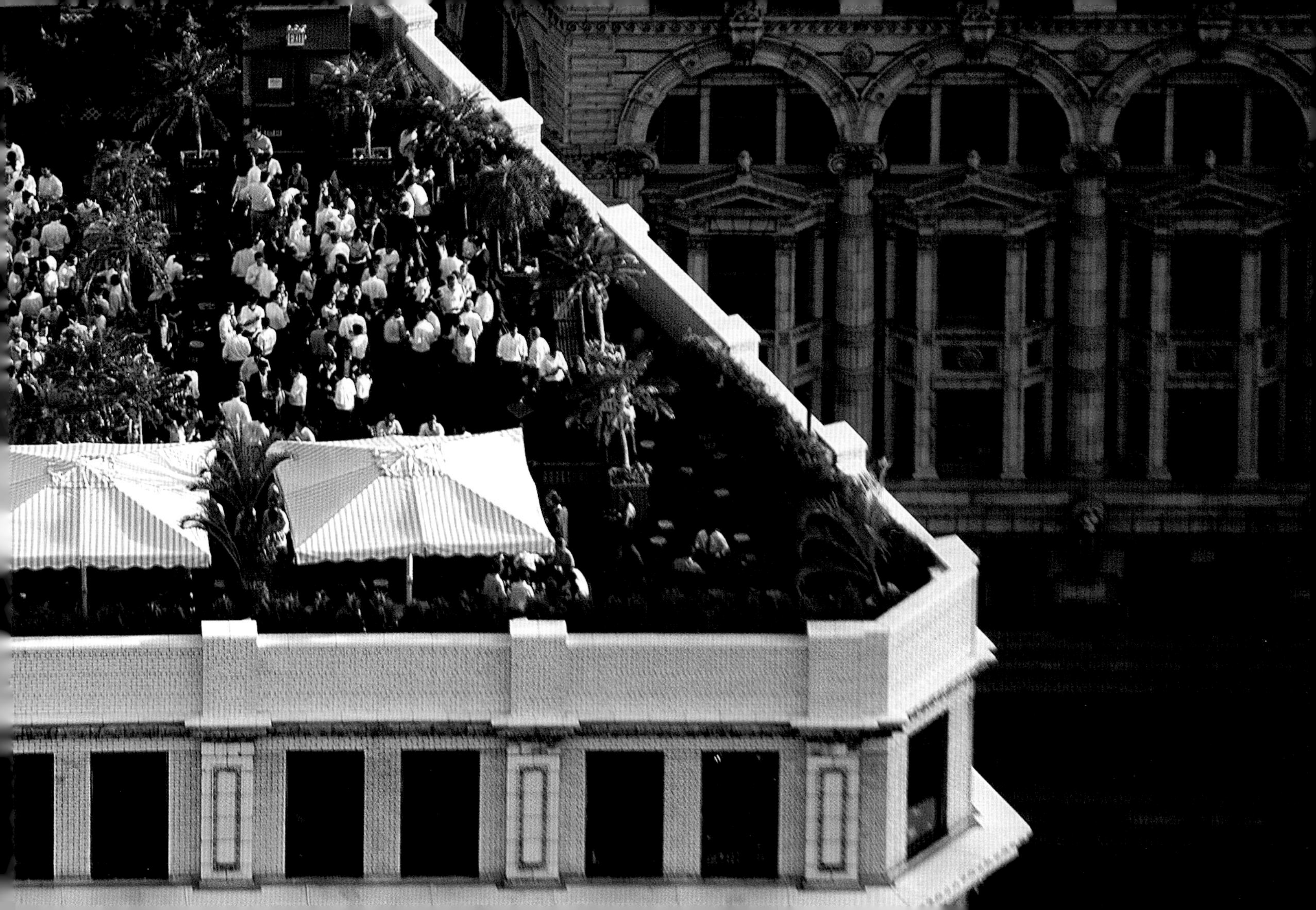
EXIT

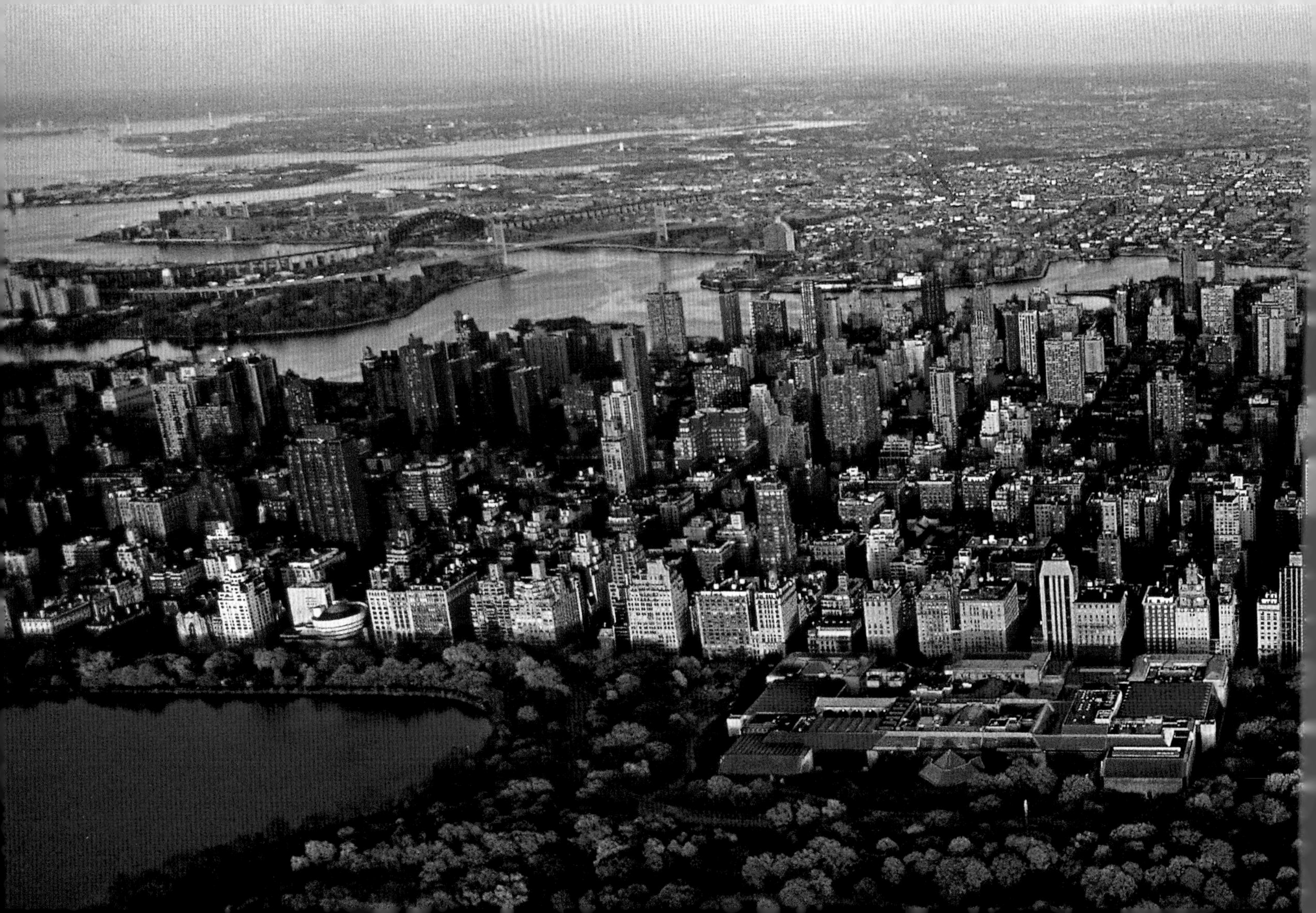

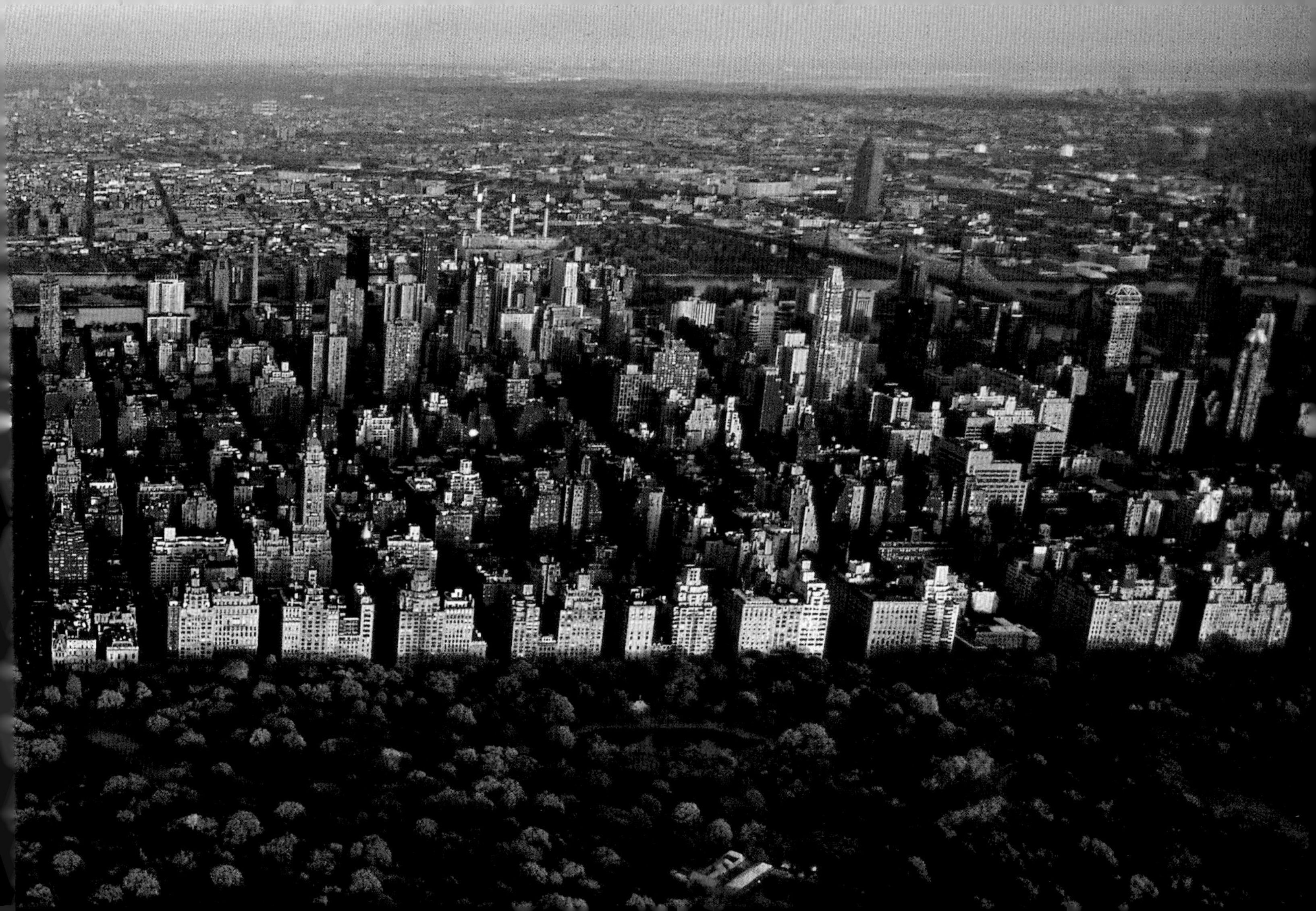

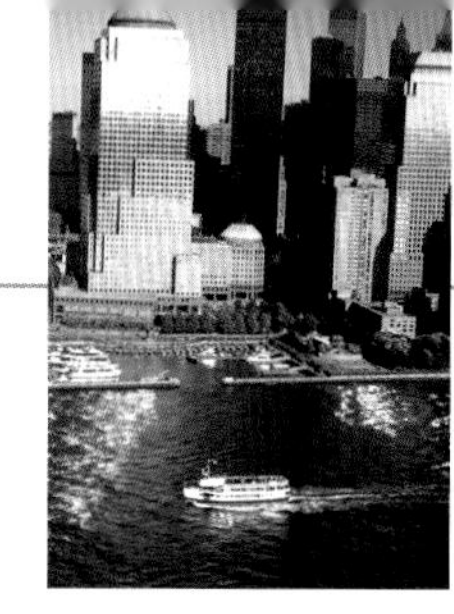

PHOTOGRAPHS

Michael Yamashita

Text
ELIZABETH BIBB

Book coordination
LAURA ACCOMAZZO

Graphic Design
PAOLA PIACCO

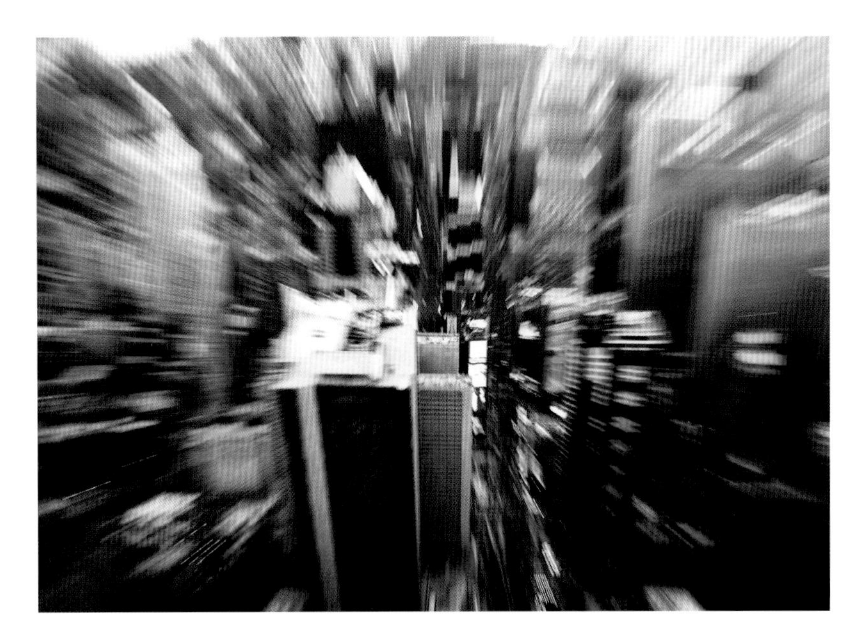

Cover
The Statue of Liberty, New York harbor.

Back cover
Central Park.

1
The New York Life Insurance Building.

2-3
The Prometheus at Rockefeller Center.

4-5
Rooftops in New York hold not only heating and cooling systems, but also summertime revels.

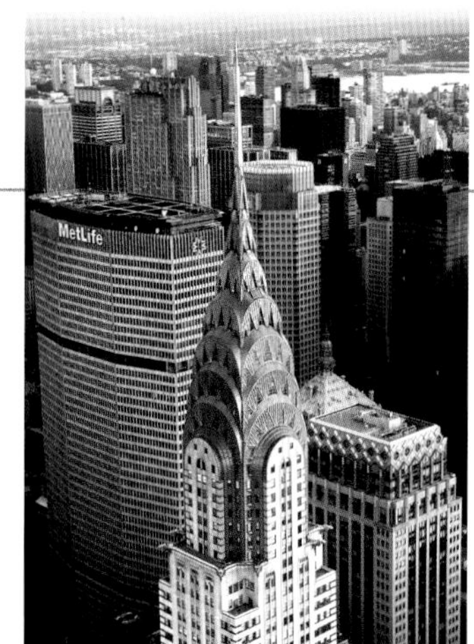

Contents

6-7
Stylish apartments edge Central Park West.

8
The World Financial Center is part of the revival of Lower Manhattan since the tragedy of 9/11/01.

9
The lights of Times Square in the late afternoon.

10
The grace of the Chrysler Building contrasts with MetLife's bulk.

11
The Statue of Liberty keeps a vigilant watch over New York harbor.

12-13
Over 3.8 million people visit the Empire State Building each year.

14-15
Central Park is a 844-acre front yard for some of the most expensive real estate in the world.

16-17
The Great White Way crosses Fifth Avenue at 23rd Street.

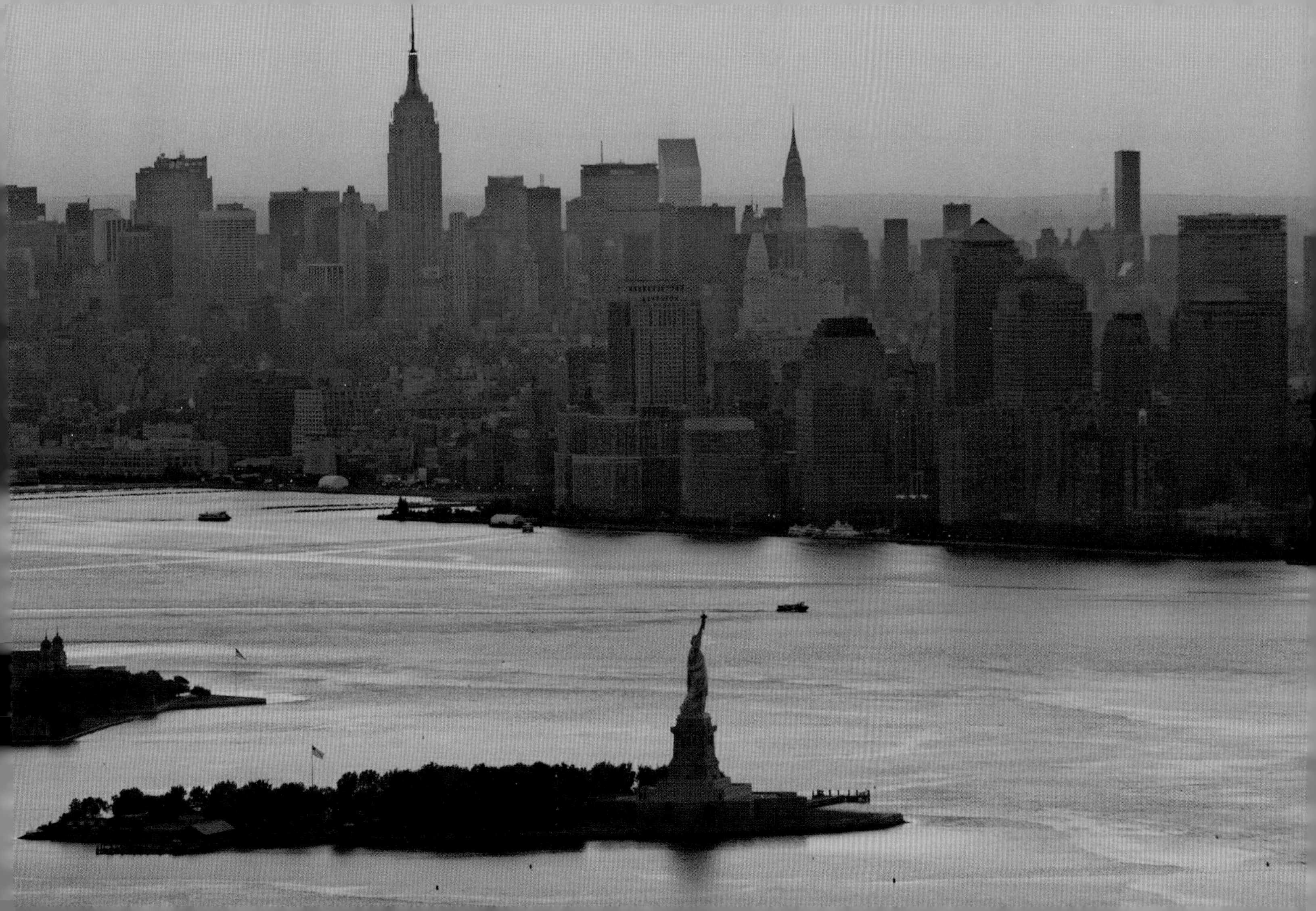

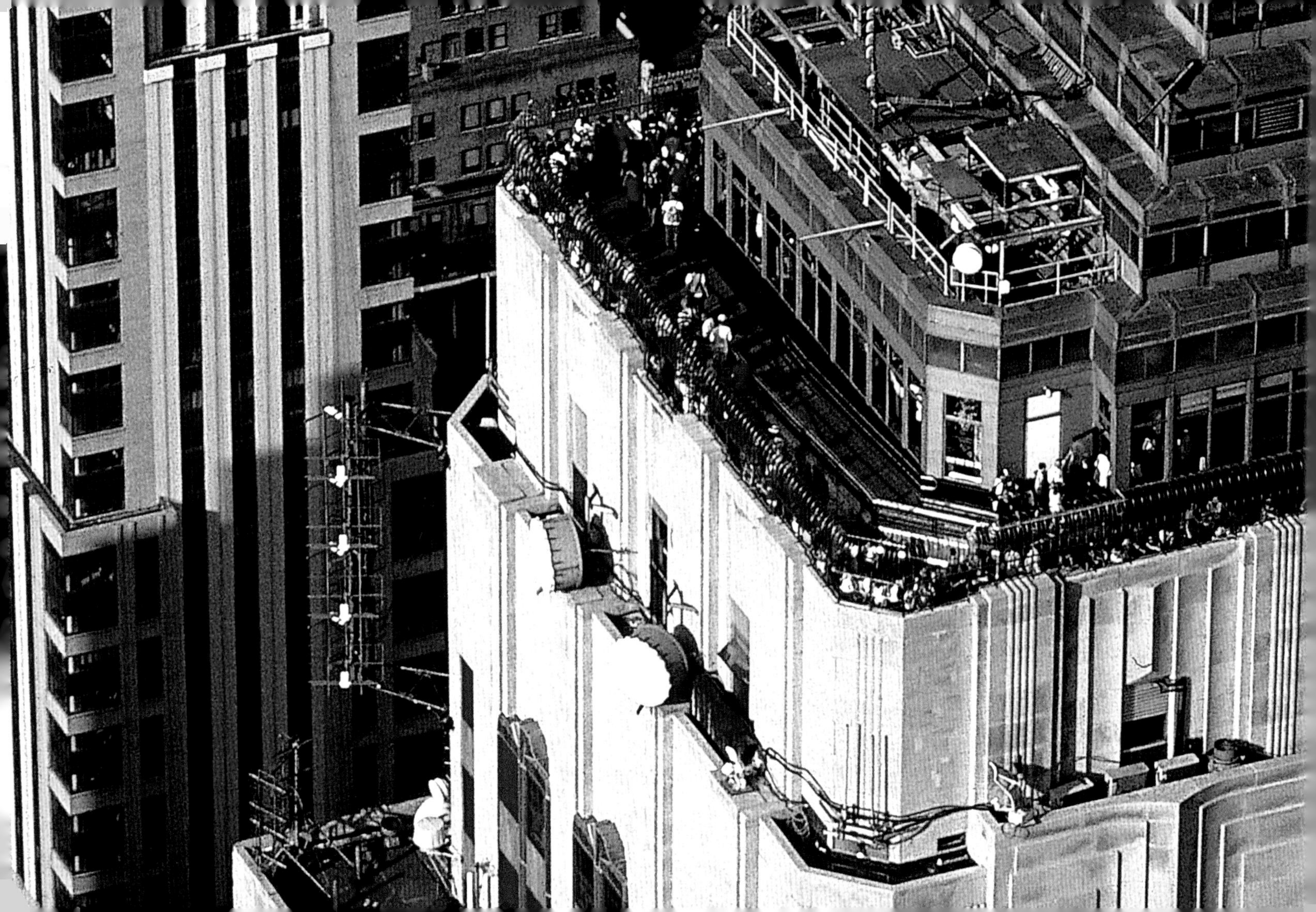

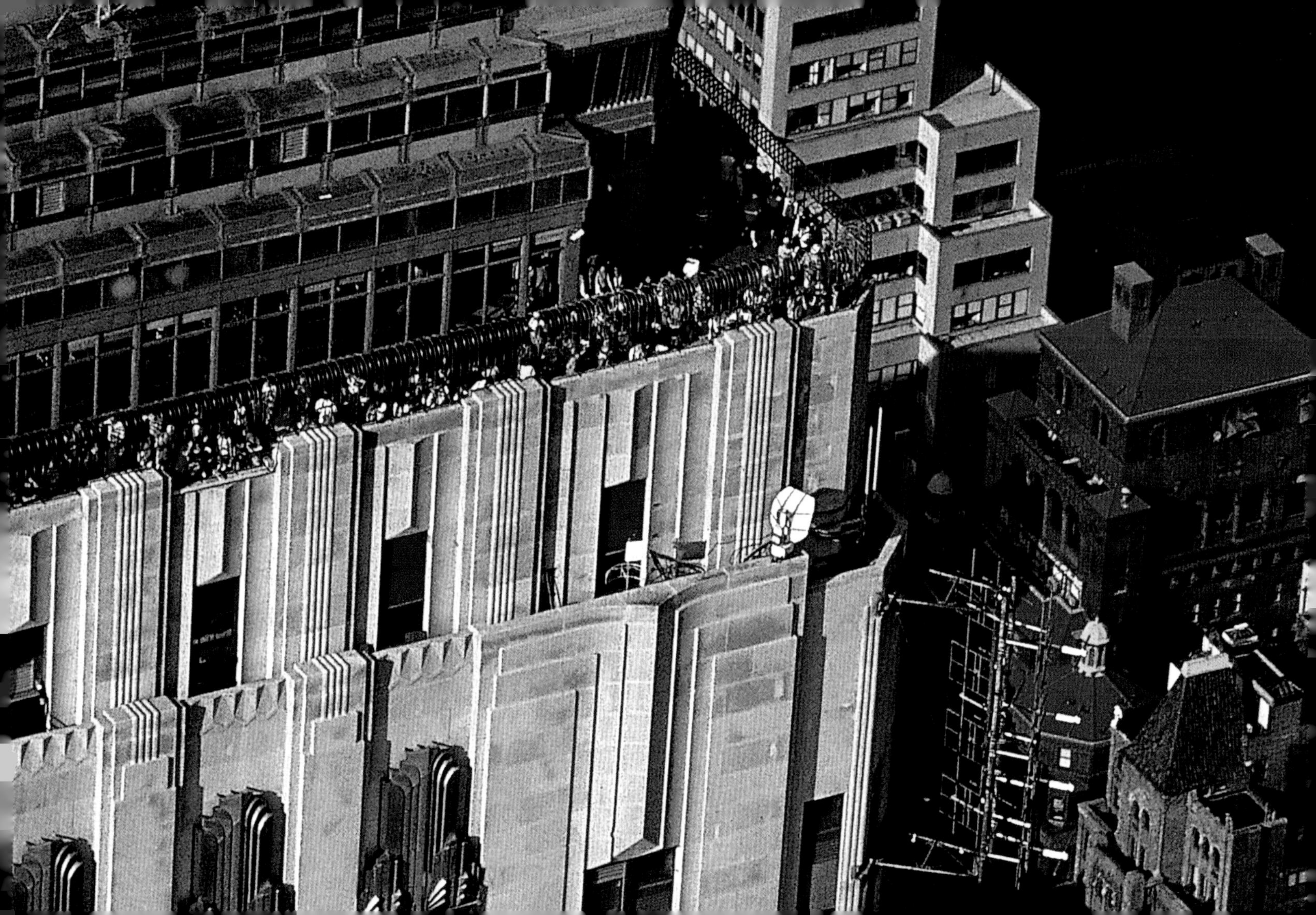

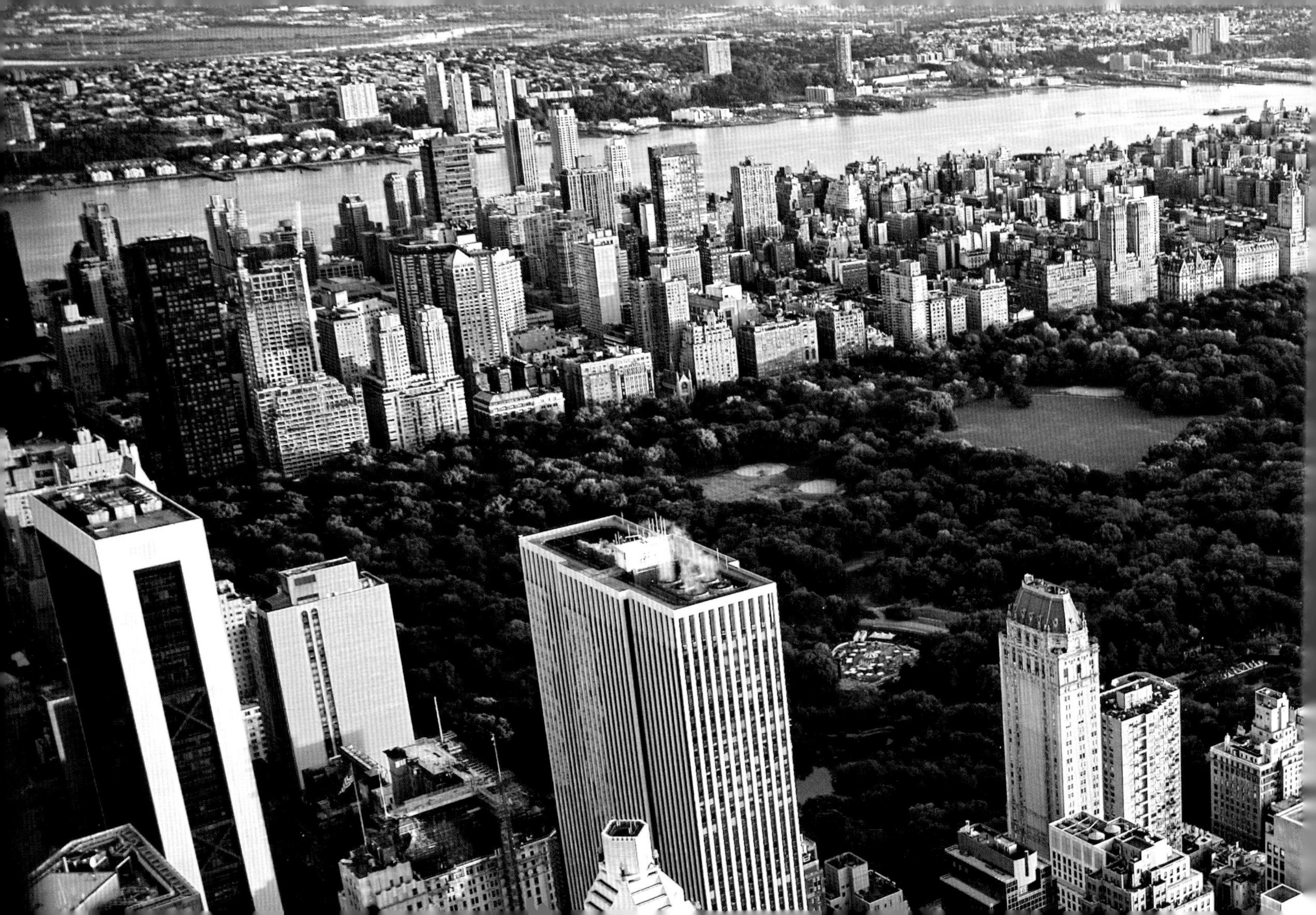

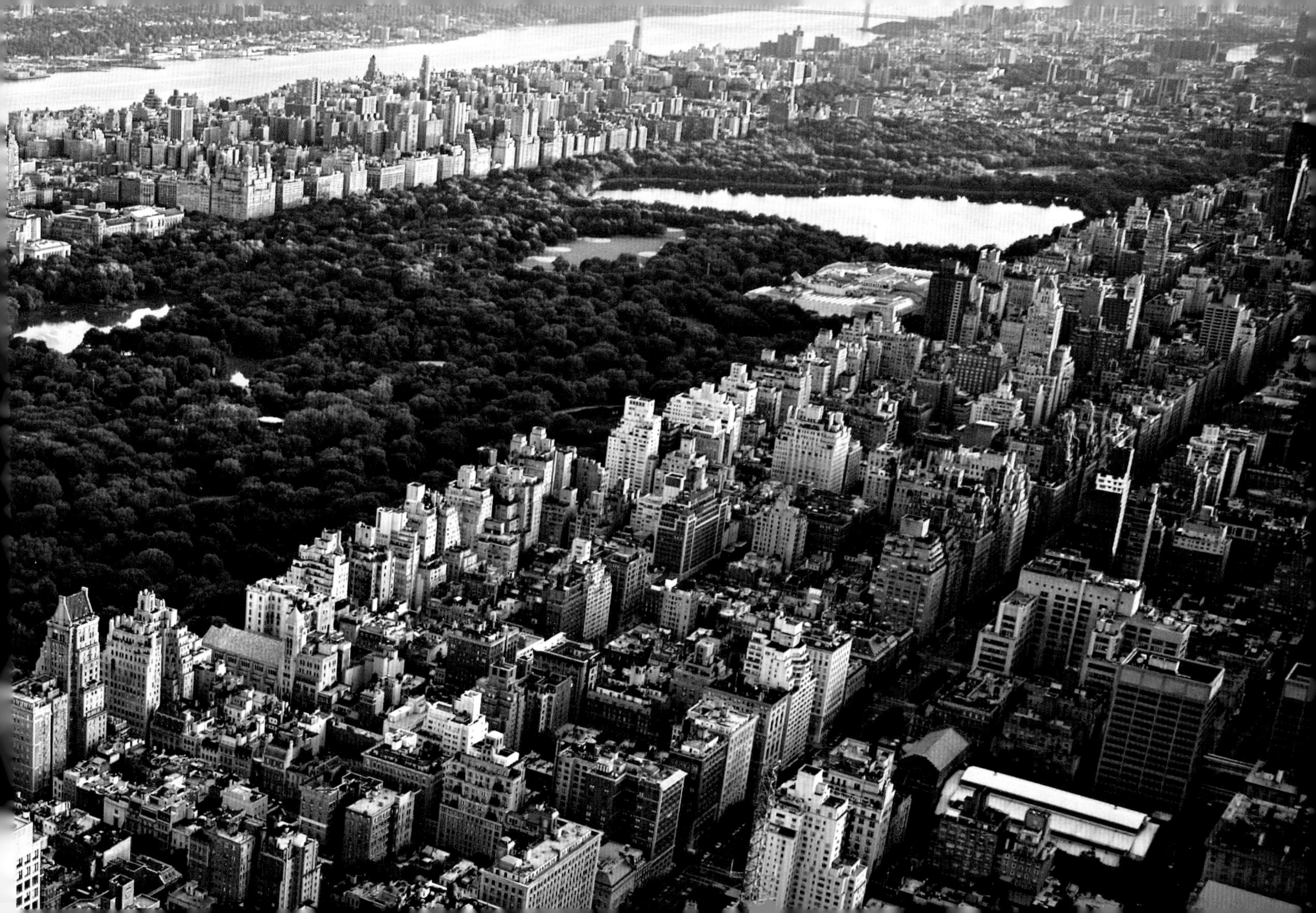

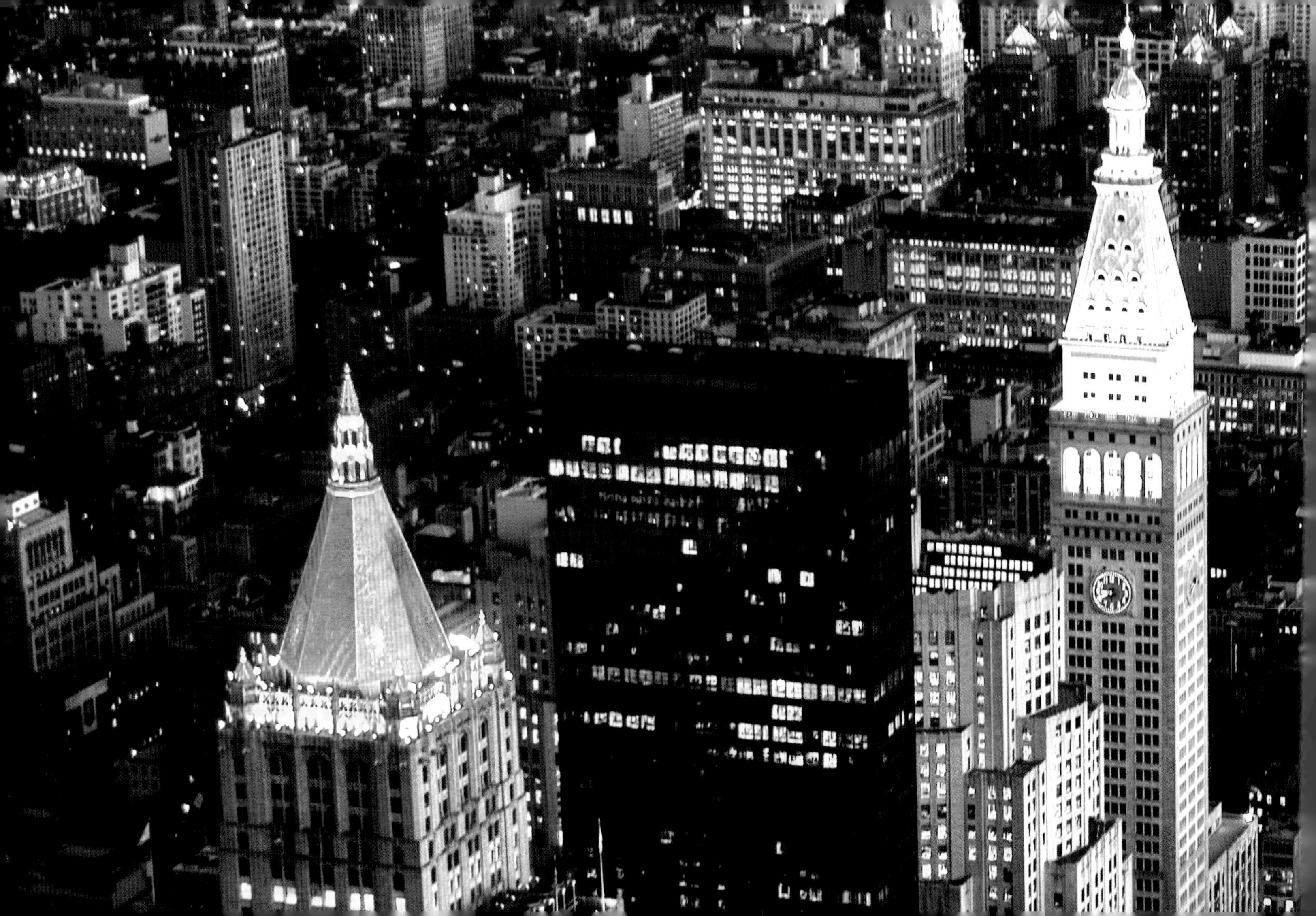

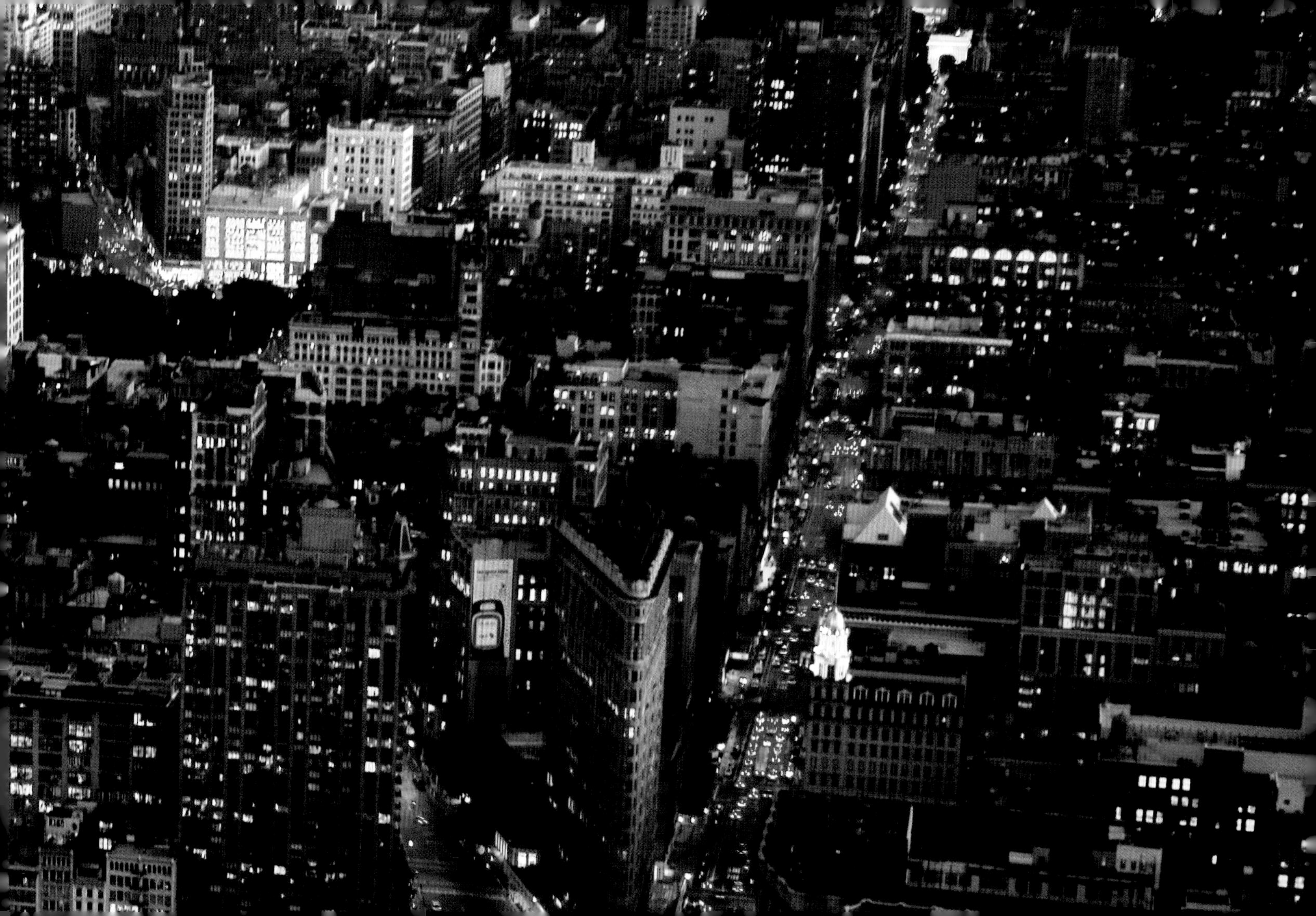

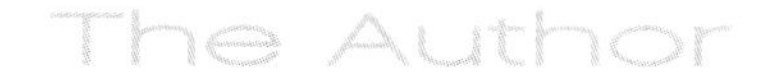

The Author

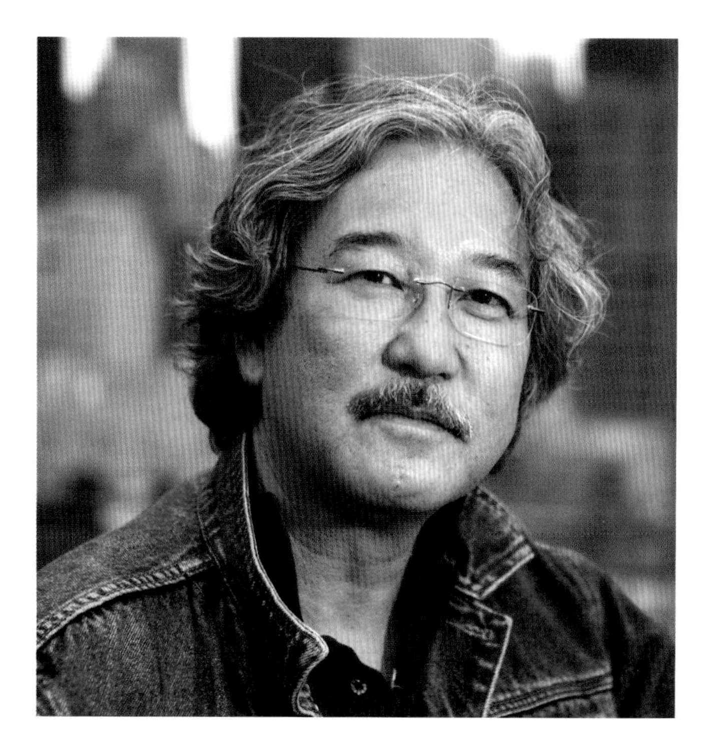

MICHAEL YAMASHITA HAS COMBINED HIS DUAL PASSIONS OF PHOTOGRAPHY AND TRAVEL FOR OVER 25 YEARS WORKING FOR *THE NATIONAL GEOGRAPHIC*. FOR A GEOGRAPHIC PHOTOGRAPHER, SHOOTING AERIALS IS PART OF THE JOB – OFTEN THE MOST EXCITING PART. FOLLOWING THE PHOTOGRAPHER'S AXIOM OF "GO HIGH" TO GET THE BEST OVERVIEW OF A PLACE, YAMASHITA HAS HUNG FROM RUSSIAN HELICOPTERS IN AFGHANISTAN, FLOATED OVER MYANMAR IN A HOT-AIR BALLOON AND FLOWN ABOVE THE MEKONG DELTA. SHOOTING NEW YORK FROM ABOVE WAS A DREAM ASSIGNMENT FOR HIM, A CHANCE TO SHOOT SOME OF THE MOST SPECTACULAR ARCHITECTURE IN THE WORLD, ALL WITHIN AN HOUR OF HIS HOME IN RURAL NEW JERSEY.

YAMASHITA'S MAGAZINE PHOTOGRAPHY HAS LED TO BOTH BOOK AND FILM PROJECTS, INCLUDING AWARD-WINNING FILMS *ZHENG HE, THE GHOST FLEET*, AND *MARCO POLO: THE CHINA MYSTERY REVEALED*. HIS MOST RECENT BOOKS, BOTH PUBLISHED BY WHITE STAR, ARE *ZHENG HE*, AND *MARCO POLO: A PHOTOGRAPHER'S JOURNEY*. HIS BOOK ON THE GREAT WALL OF CHINA IS DUE IN 2007. HIS OTHER TITLES INCLUDE *IN THE JAPANESE GARDEN* AND *MEKONG: MOTHER OF WATER*.

20-21
The steel Chrysler Building commands a central spot in Midtown Manhattan.

22-23
The triangles of the Hearst Tower's exo-skeleton are a stark contrast to the rectangular design of its neighbor, the Time Warner Towers.

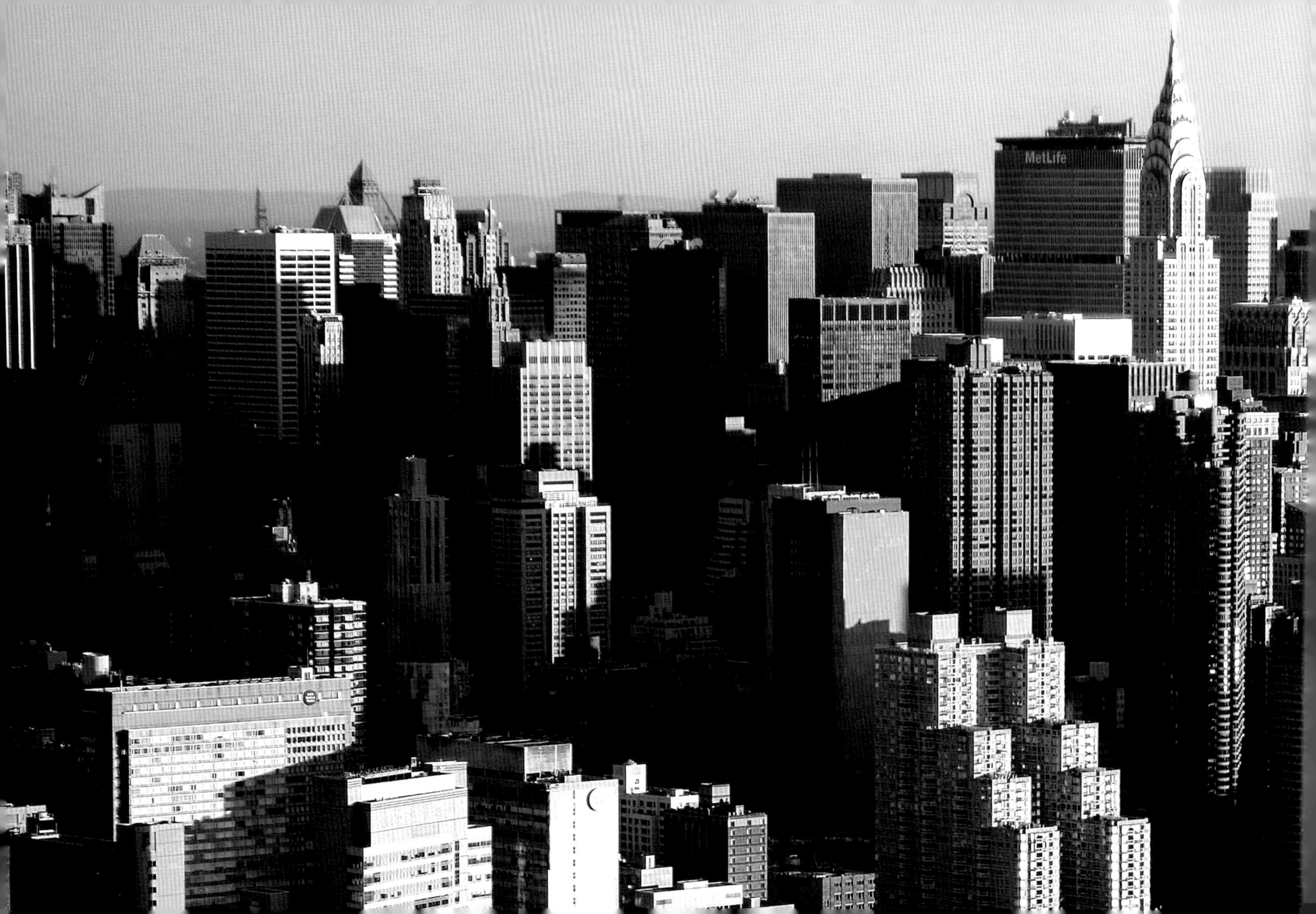
MetLife

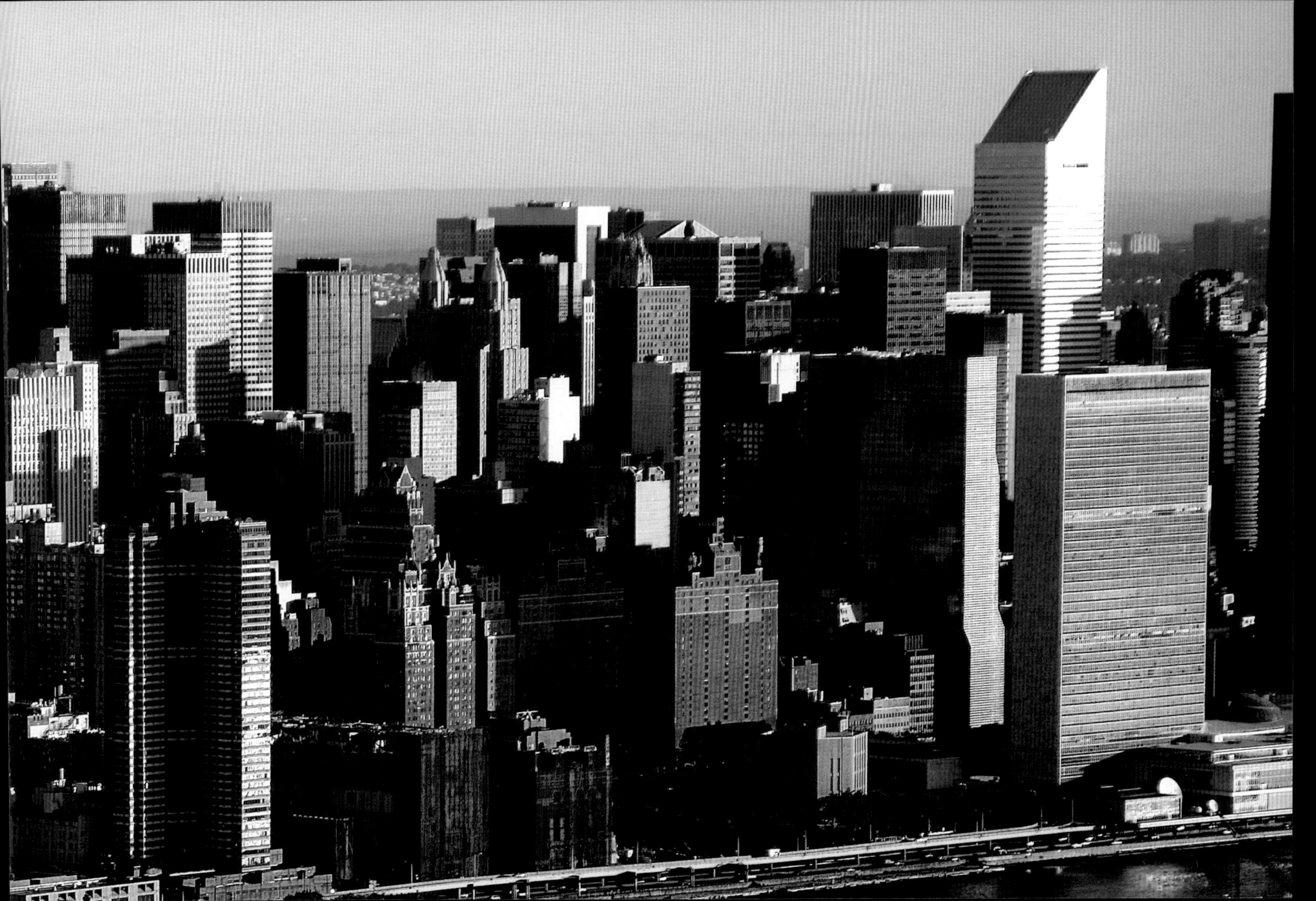

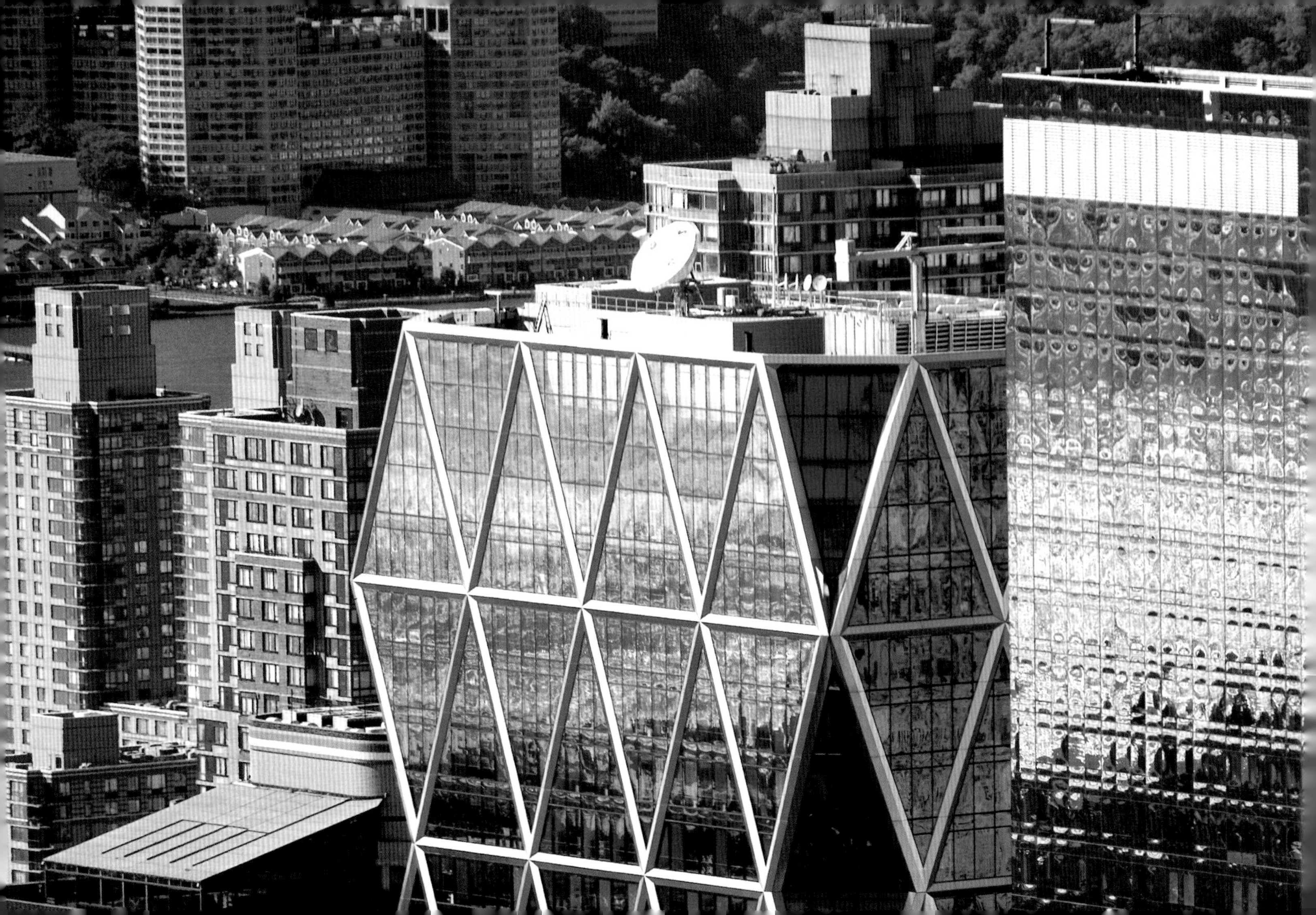

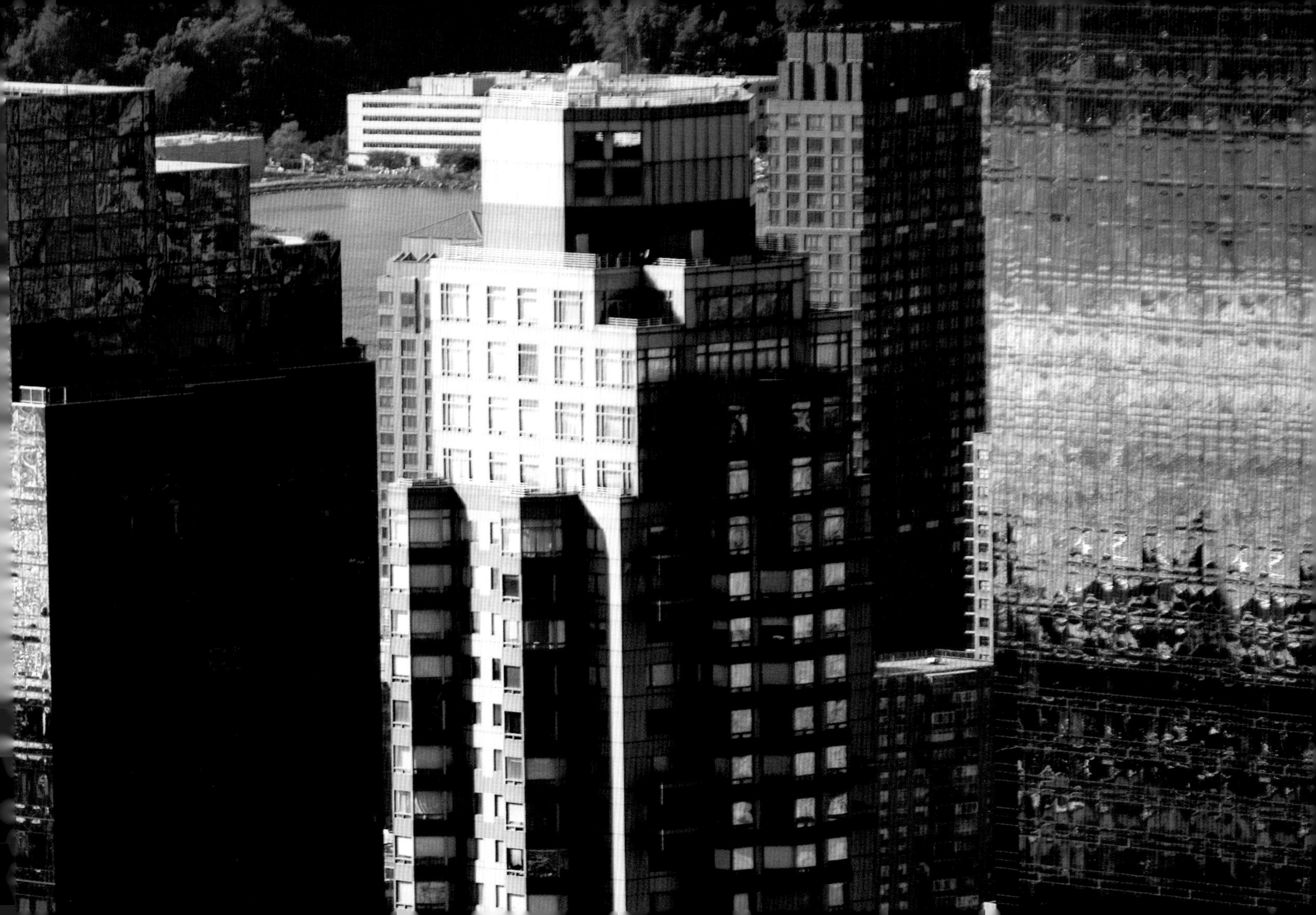

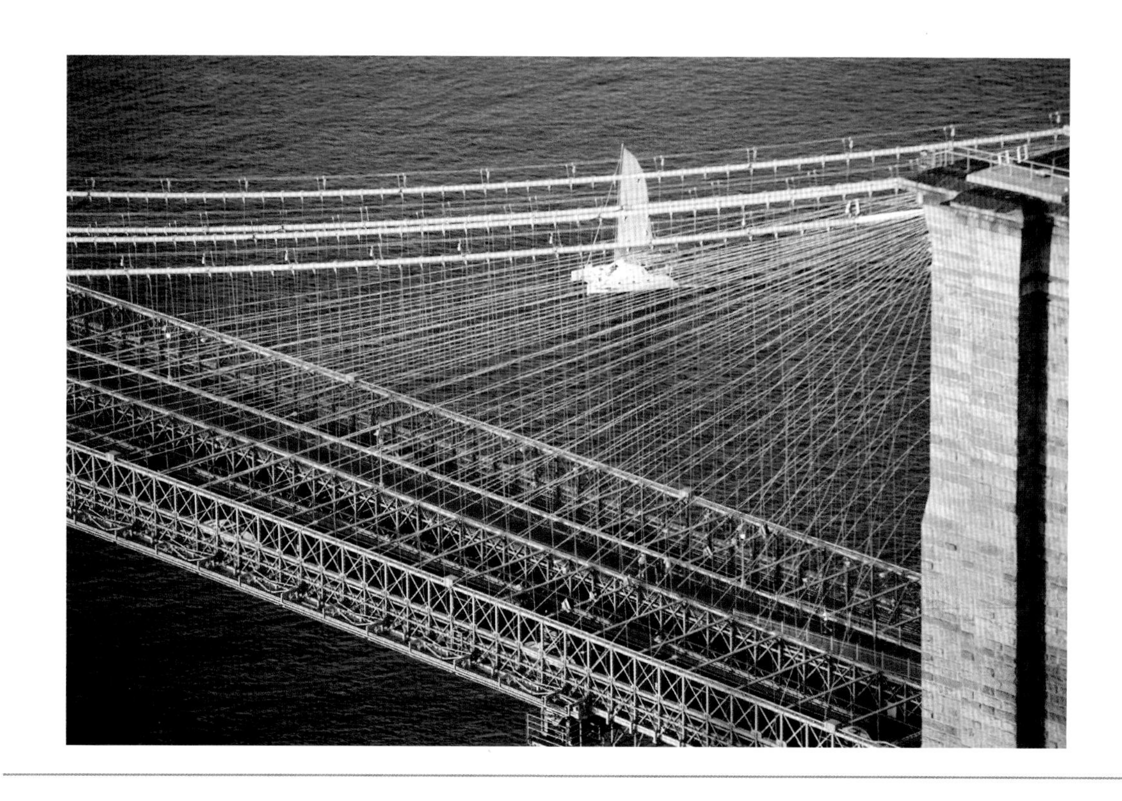

Introduction

NEW YORK, WHEN VIEWED AT GROUND LEVEL, IS A MESSY CITY – IN THE BEST AND WORST SENSES OF THE WORD – A POLYGLOT MIX OF PEOPLES, IN ALL SHAPES, SIZES, AND DRESS, A PLACE THAT DEFIES THE STROLLING THAT MAKES WANDERING THROUGH CITIES SUCH AS PARIS, VENICE OR ROME SUCH A JOY. NEW YORK, MORE SPECIFICALLY THE BOROUGH OF NEW YORK WE CALL MANHATTAN, IS A CLUTTER OF CARS, TAXIS, TRUCKS AND BUSES – ALL PART OF THE "CULTURE OF CONGESTION" AS ARCHITECT REM KOOLHAAS DESCRIBED IT IN HIS BOOK ON NEW YORK, *DELIRIUM*. AT GROUND LEVEL, NEW YORK THROBS, PULSATES, VIBRATES LIKE THE BASS ON A DRIVE-BY BOOM BOX. BUT CLIMB A FEW STORIES TO THE ROOFTOP OF A SIX-FLOOR WALKUP IN CHELSEA OR GREENWICH VILLAGE, AND THE CITY BEGINS TO GET QUIETER, OFTEN SURREALLY SO.

24
"Enfranchising cable, silvered by the sea, of woven wire, grayed by the mist ..." These words by poet Marianne Moore are some of the many inspired by the Brooklyn Bridge.

Introduction

FROM THE OBSERVATION DECK OF THE EMPIRE STATE BUILDING OR THE TOP OF THE ROCK AT ROCKEFELLER CENTER, IT IS QUIETER STILL, AND A CERTAIN ORDER BEGINS TO PREVAIL. NUMBERED STREETS CRISS-CROSS THE CITY; LONG AVENUES RIBBON THEIR WAY FROM NORTH TO SOUTH, WITH VEHICLES AND PEOPLE MOVING SOUNDLESSLY ALONG THEM. AT THIS HEIGHT, EYE TO EYE WITH OTHER SKYSCRAPERS, ONE SEES A RAREFIED WORLD, A WORLD THAT ONLY WINDOW-WASHERS, MONEYED MOGULS AND SOCIALITES, AND CERTAIN HIGH-FLYING CELEBRITIES LIKE PALE MALE, THE RED-TAILED HAWK WHO CREATED A BROUHAHA WHEN HE SET UP CAMP IN THE EAVES OF A TONY FIFTH AVENUE APARTMENT BUILDING, EVER SEE. AT THIS HEIGHT, ONE STARTS TO FEEL AS THOUGH THE CITY, WITH ALL ITS TREASURES ARRAYED BELOW, IS ONE'S OWN.

IN NEW YORK, THIS KIND OF VIEW IS WORTH MILLIONS. ANY REALTOR WILL CONFIRM THAT A ROOM WITH A VIEW IS THE DREAM OF EVERY NEW YORK BUYER. ADD ROOFTOP ACCESS TO THAT VIEW, AND SUDDENLY EVEN THE TINIEST STUDIO APARTMENT ACQUIRES WHAT EVERY NEW YORKER NEVER HAS

Introduction

ENOUGH OF – SPACE. LOOKING DOWN AT THE FRAY FROM ABOVE GIVES ONE A SENSE OF BEING FREE OF THE CONFINES OF STREETLIGHTS AND TRAFFIC JAMS, NOT TO MENTION THE FOUR WALLS OF A CRAMPED RESIDENCE.

GO EVEN FURTHER UP, HIGH ABOVE THE MERCANTILE CATHEDRALS OF WALL STREET AND MIDTOWN MANHATTAN, DETACHED FROM ANY EARTHLY REMINDERS, SAVE FOR THE SOUND OF A HELICOPTER'S BLADES OR A JET-ENGINE'S ROAR, THE CITY GIVES THE IMPRESSION OF BEING A WELL-CALIBRATED MACHINE. ORDERLY, SILENT, NEW YORK FROM THE SKY BECOMES A COLLECTION OF MANAGEABLE GEOMETRIC CHUNKS. THE METHOD TO ITS MADNESS IS REVEALED. FROM ABOVE, MANHATTAN MAKES SENSE. ITS OVER 50 UNIQUE NEIGHBORHOODS, FROM SOHO TO HARLEM, FOLLOW A LOGICAL SCHEMATIC PLAN, LIKE MONDRIAN'S *BOOGIE ON BROADWAY* COME TO LIFE.

IT MIGHT BE ARGUED THAT THE JOYOUS, SOME WOULD SAY NOXIOUS, NOISE OF MANHATTAN IS DILUTED AT 1200 FEET, DISSIPATING INTO THIN AIR AND LEAVING LITTLE BUT A GRID DESIGNED BY 19TH- CENTURY MERCHANTS. BUT FROM AN AERIAL PERSPECTIVE, CITY LIFE – WORKING, FUNCTIONING,

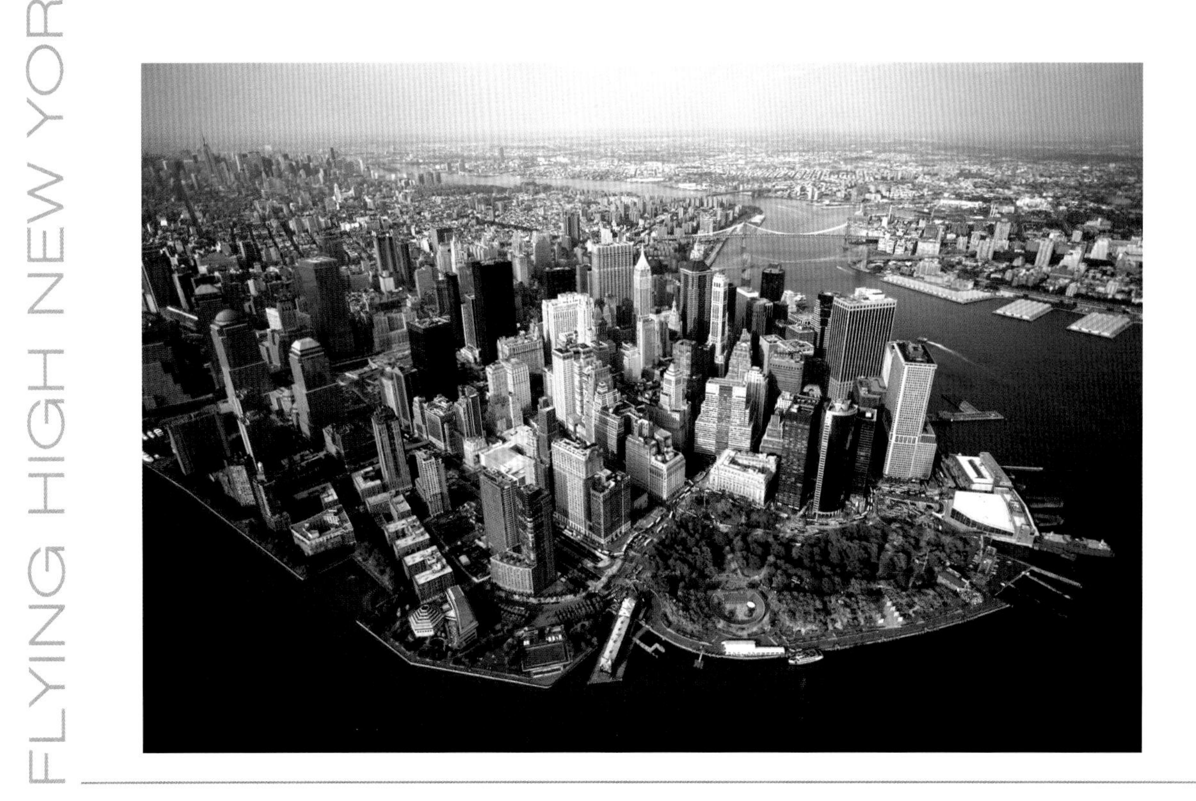

28
The Dutch founded New Amsterdam at the tip of Manhattan in 1625; today it is the center of New York's financial world.

FLOWING IN AND AROUND ALL THE CITY'S HIDDEN POCKETS, CORNERS, AND CANYONS – GIVES ONE A SENSE OF BELONGING THAT IS RARELY POSSIBLE ON THE GROUND.

WHILE THE SCALE OF MANHATTAN'S SKYSCRAPERS AT GROUND LEVEL CAN BE DWARFING, EVEN DEHUMANIZING, FROM ABOVE, THEY SEEM LIKE STURDY ANCHORS, SECURING THE OCCASIONALLY FRAYED EDGES OF THE CRAZY QUILT OF THE CITY TO THE EARTH.

FROM ABOVE, IT REALLY IS POSSIBLE TO SEE THAT THE BRONX IS UP AND THE BATTERY'S DOWN. ONE CAN SEE THE SHAPE OF THE RESERVOIR IN CENTRAL PARK AND WATCH RUNNERS MAKE A GRACEFUL LOOP AROUND IT. ONE CAN SEE TOY-SIZED CABS, BUSES AND FERRIES TAXIING PASSENGERS INTO AND AROUND THE BUSTLING CITY. AND ONE CAN FOLLOW THE TOPOGRAPHY OF THE ISLAND, FROM LOW-LYING BLOCKS OF A DOWNTOWN AREA CREATED BY LANDFILL TO THE ANGLED INCLINES OF MURRAY HILL.

ABOVE IT ALL, IT'S EASY TO SEE THE DEFINING FEATURE THAT MAKES LIFE IN MANHATTAN SO UNIQUE – THE ORIGINAL BOROUGH OF WHAT IS AR-

Introduction

GUABLY THE GREATEST CITY IN THE WORLD IS AN ISLAND UNTO ITSELF. SURROUNDED BY WATER: THREE RIVERS AND THE SEA, COMPLEMENTED BY A DEEP-WATER HARBOR, MANHATTAN IS CONNECTED TO THE MAINLAND BY BRIDGES AND TUNNELS. THE TUNNELS, UNSEEN UNDER THE RIVERS, EMERGE INTO A TANGLE OF CLOVER-LEAF INTERSECTIONS IN MANHATTAN AND NEW JERSEY AND LONG ISLAND. THE BRIDGES, HOWEVER, WHEN VIEWED FROM ABOVE, ARE GRACEFUL, YET STALWART CONNECTORS TO THE OUTER BOROUGHS OF NEW YORK AND THE COUNTIES OF NEW JERSEY.

NEW YORK'S GREAT HARBOR IS WHAT ATTRACTED FIRST THE DUTCH, THEN THE ENGLISH TO THE LAND THE NATIVE ALGONQUIN TRIBES CALLED MANHATTAN. GIOVANNI DA VERRAZANO IS BELIEVED TO BE THE FIRST EUROPEAN TO "DISCOVER" NEW YORK IN 1524, WHILE SEARCHING FOR A NEW ROUTE TO ASIA FOR THE KING OF FRANCE. IT WAS ENGLISHMAN HENRY HUDSON, WHO IN 1609 WHILE IN THE EMPLOY OF THE DUTCH EAST INDIA COMPANY, SAILED INTO THE BAY AND UP THE RIVER THAT WAS TO BE NAMED FOR HIM. DUTCH AND BELGIAN MERCHANTS FOLLOWED, AND IN 1626, PETER MINUIT, WHO WAS

Introduction

THE FIRST DIRECTOR-GENERAL OF NEW AMSTERDAM, AS THE AREA WAS NOW CALLED, PURCHASED MANHATTAN ISLAND FROM THE LOCAL INDIAN TRIBE FOR JEWELRY, TRINKETS AND TOOLS WORTH $24 IN TODAY'S MONEY.

A THRIVING FUR AND TOBACCO TRADE GREW IN WHAT WAS NOW CALLED NEW AMSTERDAM, AND FROM THE ISLAND'S SOUTHERN TIP, THE SETTLEMENT BEGAN TO EMERGE INTO A CITY. AT FIRST, WINDMILLS AND BRICK HOUSES APPEARED, AND FIELDS OF TOBACCO WERE CULTIVATED IN TODAY'S GREENWICH VILLAGE. CHURCHES APPEARED, AS WELL AS CIVIC BUILDINGS. IT DID NOT TAKE LONG FOR THE BRITISH, WHO HAD CLAIMED THE NEW WORLD AS THEIR OWN, TO DECIDE TO GET A PIECE OF THE ACTION IN NEW AMSTERDAM. IN 1653, THE DUTCH ERECTED A WOODEN PALISADE, ON WHAT WAS TO BECOME WALL STREET, TO SECURE THEIR BORDERS, AGAINST THE INTRUSIONS OF THE ENGLISH, AS WELL AS HOSTILE NATIVE AMERICANS. ENGLISH WARSHIPS APPEARED IN THE HARBOR IN 1664, AND THE SETTLERS OF THE CITY, DISGUSTED BY THE IRON FIST OF THEIR GOVERNOR, PETER STUYVESANT, SURRENDERED TO THE BRITISH WITH BARELY A FIGHT.

Introduction

BUT HOLLAND WAS NOT ABOUT TO GIVE UP ITS GEM IN THE NEW WORLD SO EASILY, AND RECLAIMED THE COLONY IN 1672, RENAMING IT NEW ORANGE. EVENTUALLY THOUGH, THANKS TO BRITAIN'S SWAP OF SURINAM IN SOUTH AMERICA FOR HOLLAND'S NEW ORANGE/NEW AMSTERDAM IN 1674, ENGLAND PREVAILED AND THE COLONY BECAME NEW YORK, NAMED AFTER CHARLES II'S BROTHER, THE DUKE OF YORK (LATER JAMES II). THE BRITISH QUICKLY ANNEXED THE ENTIRE ISLAND, FROM THE BUSTLING TRADING CENTER AT THE SOUTHERN TIP ALL THE WAY TO THE RURAL WILDERNESS AT THE NORTHERN END.

WHEN THE COLONISTS REVOLTED IN THE MID-18TH CENTURY, BRITAIN KNEW THAT CONTROL OF THE HUDSON RIVER WAS ESSENTIAL TO THEIR STAKE IN THE NEW WORLD. IN THE FALL OF 1776, THE SAME YEAR THE COLONIES HAD DECLARED THEIR INDEPENDENCE FROM BRITAIN, THE ENGLISH GENERAL HOWE SECURED NEW YORK, DRIVING THE AMERICAN ARMY OF GEORGE WASHINGTON NORTH TO WEST POINT. IT REMAINED A BRITISH BASTION THROUGHOUT THE REVOLUTION, AND IT WAS NOT UNTIL 1783, EIGHT

Introduction

MONTHS AFTER IT HAD ENDED AND THE COLONISTS, WITH THE HELP OF THE FRENCH, HAD WON THE REVOLUTIONARY WAR, THAT THE BRITISH FINALLY RELINQUISHED THE CITY. BY THEN HALF THE CITY HAD BEEN BURNED BY THE BRITISH, INCLUDING TRINITY CHURCH, WHICH HAD BEEN BUILT IN 1697.

BY 1785, MANHATTAN HAD BECOME THE FIRST CAPITAL OF THE NEW UNITED STATES, WITH GEORGE WASHINGTON AS ITS FIRST PRESIDENT. WASHINGTON TOOK HIS OATH OF OFFICE AT FEDERAL HALL, BUT WITHIN FIVE YEARS, THE CAPITAL WAS MOVED TO PHILADELPHIA AND ULTIMATELY WASHINGTON, DC. IT WAS BECOMING CLEAR THAT NEW YORK WAS DESTINED FOR A FUTURE AS A COMMERCIAL, NOT A POLITICAL, HUB.

AS NEW YORK PUSHED PAST ITS NORTHERN BOUNDARIES, THE NEED FOR SOME SORT OF PLAN TO MAKE SENSE OUT OF THE RAPID GROWTH FROM AGRARIAN AND HUNTING OUTPOST TO MAJOR COMMERCIAL CENTER BECAME APPARENT. NEW AMSTERDAM'S FIRST STREETS WERE BASED ON INDIAN TRAILS, AND THEN BY PATHS FOLLOWED BY FARMERS AND LIVESTOCK. THE NATURAL TOPOGRAPHY OF THE ISLAND DETERMINED THE ROUTES THESE PATHS TOOK,

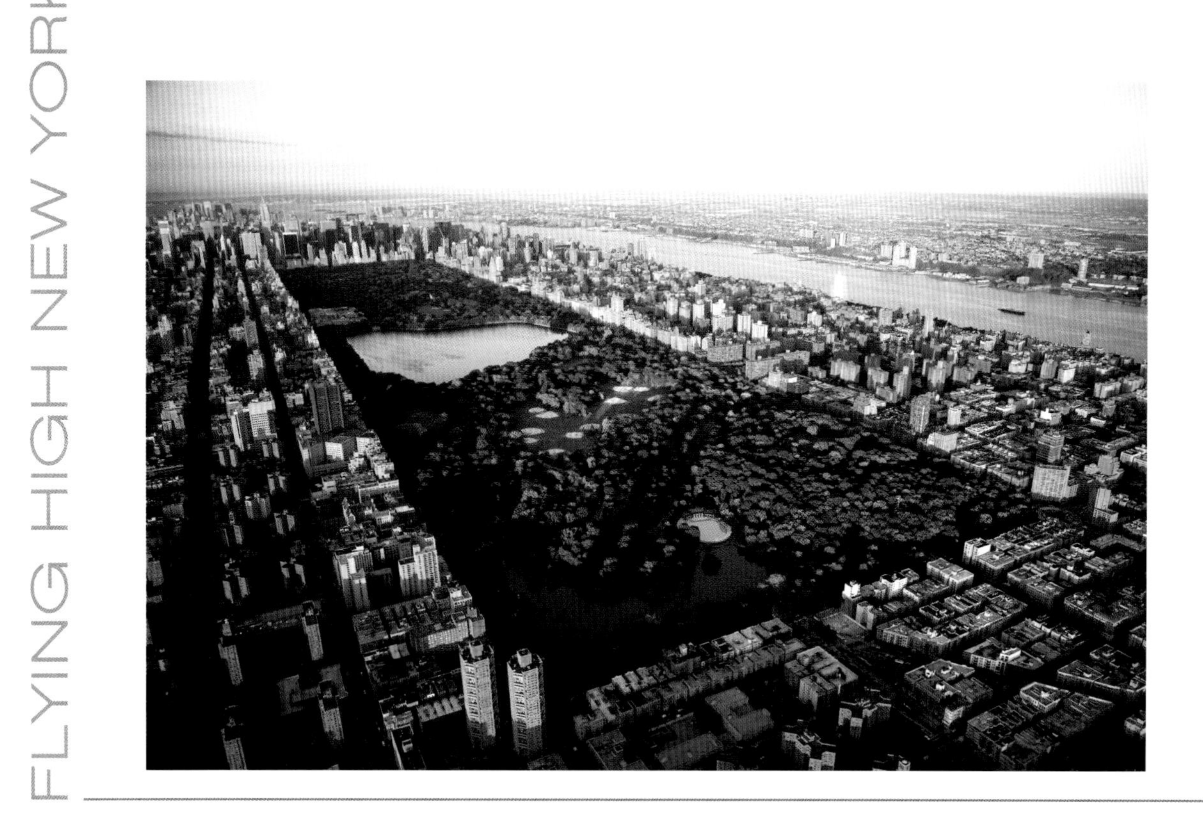

Like a giant's footprint, Central Park, 843 acres in area, makes its mark in the middle of New York.

AROUND SWAMPS AND SPRINGS, CANALS AND TRENCHES. BUT IN 1811 A GROUP OF MERCHANTS WERE COMMISSIONED TO DEVISE A CITY PLAN, WHICH WAS TO BE THE BASIS FOR NEW YORK'S APPEARANCE TO THIS DAY.

ITS GRID PATTERN, STARTING ABOVE CANAL STREET (ONCE AN ACTUAL CANAL), OF 12 NUMBERED AVENUES AND 155 CROSS STREETS RUNNING RIVER TO RIVER WAS DESIGNED FOR BUSINESS. IT IS POSSIBLE TO FOLLOW NEW YORK'S HISTORY BY WALKING NORTH ON FIFTH AVENUE OR EIGHTH AVENUE, OR FOR A CROSS-SECTION OF THAT HISTORY, WALKING FROM THE EAST RIVER TO THE HUDSON ACROSS 42ND STREET.

THE GRID WAS NOT DESIGNED TO PROVIDE BROAD PROMENADES OR BUCOLIC PARKS AND SQUARES; RATHER IT WAS DESIGNED FOR SIMPLICITY AND EFFICIENCY. IN A CITY FILLED WITH RESIDENTS HAILING FROM ALL OVER THE WORLD AND SPEAKING MANY LANGUAGES AND DIALECTS, STREETS WOULD HAVE NUMBERS INSTEAD OF NAMES. THOUGH THERE WERE ABOUT 100,000 PEOPLE LIVING IN MANHATTAN IN 1811, THE GRID ANTICIPATED THE ISLAND'S BURGEONING GROWTH TO OVER 1.5 MILLION TODAY.

Introduction

BUT EVEN AS NEW YORK SPILLED OVER INTO FOUR OTHER BOROUGHS, INTO BROOKLYN AND QUEENS ON LONG ISLAND AND THE BRONX ON THE MAINLAND, LAND BECAME ONE OF THE MOST PRECIOUS COMMODITIES ON THE ISLAND BOROUGH OF MANHATTAN. THOUGH THE NUMBERED STREETS EVENTUALLY EXPANDED TO 255 ON INTO HARLEM, RIVERS AND THE SEA BLOCKED ANY FURTHER HORIZONTAL EXPANSION. THAT LEFT ONLY ONE OPTION – UP.

AT ONE TIME, A TRAVEL ESSAYIST ONCE REMARKED, THE ONLY WAY TO SEE THE TIP OF MANHATTAN WAS TO CLIMB TO THE TOP OF TRINITY CHURCH'S SPIRE; TODAY, YOU HAVE TO GO TO THE TOP OF A MIDTOWN SKYSCRAPER TO SEE TRINITY CHURCH. FROM THE MID-19TH CENTURY ON, NEW YORK BEGAN TO GROW VERTICALLY, AND HAS NOT STOPPED. NEW YORK'S BEDROCK BASE, COMBINED WITH THE DEVELOPMENT OF PASSENGER ELEVATORS AND LIGHT STEEL FRAMES FOR HIGH-RISES, MADE BUILDING SKY-GRAZING TOWERS POSSIBLE. ZONING RULES IN THE EARLY 20TH CENTURY ATTEMPTED TO INSURE THAT AS BUILDINGS WENT UP, THEY WOULD BE CONSTRUCTED WITH

Introduction

ENOUGH SETBACKS TO ALLOW SUN TO REACH BOTH THE SIDEWALKS BELOW AND THE OFFICES WITHIN. ORNAMENTATION THAT ONLY BIRDS COULD SEE COVERED BUILDING EXTERIORS.

BY THE TIME THE 20TH CENTURY WAS IN FULL SWING, SO WAS THE AGE OF THE SKYSCRAPER: FROM THE BAROQUE MASTERPIECES OF THE WOOLWORTH AND (NOW DEMOLISHED) SINGER BUILDINGS, TO THE ART DECO WONDERS OF ROCKEFELLER CENTER, MODERNIST MASTERPIECES OF THE SEAGRAM BUILDING AND THE LEVER HOUSE, AND POST-MODERN TOWERS OF MIDTOWN AND DOWNTOWN. NEW YORK IS SECOND ONLY TO HONG KONG IN THE NUMBER OF SKYSCRAPERS, AND IT HAS THE MOST SKYSCRAPERS IN THE WORLD ON AN ISLAND. FOLLOWING THE COLLAPSE OF THE WORLD TRADE CENTER'S TWIN TOWERS AFTER TERRORIST ATTACKS ON SEPTEMBER 11, 2001, THE EMPIRE STATE BUILDING IS CURRENTLY THE CITY'S TALLEST.

THE WORLD TRADE CENTER LEFT A GAPING HOLE IN THE DOWNTOWN SKYLINE, A HOLE THAT HAS BEEN THE SUBJECT OF CONTROVERSY FOR FIVE

Introduction

YEARS SINCE THE TERRORIST ATTACKS. GROUND WAS BROKEN IN 2006 FOR THE FREEDOM TOWER, A SINGLE ICONIC SKYSCRAPER THAT WILL BE BOTH A MEMORIAL AND A TESTAMENT TO THE REBIRTH OF THE CITY, BUT THE FOOT-PRINT OF THE ORIGINAL TWIN TOWERS WILL REMAIN EMPTY AS A MEMORIAL TO THOSE WHO DIED THERE THAT DAY. AS SEEN FROM ABOVE, THE BLANK SPACE THAT WAS LEFT AFTER THE BUILDINGS WERE DEMOLISHED IS A STARK REMINDER OF THAT TRAGEDY. THIS TEARING DOWN AND BUILDING UP IS REP-RESENTATIVE OF THE WAY NEW YORK HAS AND ALWAYS WILL GROW. OTHER CITIES SPRAWL IN ALL DIRECTIONS, BUT TO NEW YORKERS, THE ONLY WAY TO GO IS UP. SKYSCRAPERS IN NEW YORK SYMBOLIZE THE SAME KIND OF HOPE AND UPLIFT AS A STEEPLE ON A CHURCH, THOUGH THEY ARE DEDICATED TO COMMERCE INSTEAD OF RELIGION (IT COULD BE ARGUED THAT COMMERCE IS A SORT OF RELIGION IN NEW YORK.)

THAT IS WHY THE ONLY WAY TO GET A FULL PICTURE OF WHAT THE CITY LOOKS LIKE IS TO FOLLOW PHOTOGRAPHER MICHAEL YAMASHITA'S AXIOM – "GO HIGH." THERE IS A PREPONDERANCE OF WAYS TO ACCOMPLISH THIS: BY

Introduction

LEG-POWER – SAY, CLIMBING TO THE TOP OF THE STATUE OF LIBERTY FOR A VIEW OF MANHATTAN FROM THE SOUTH OR MOUNTING THE STEPS OF RIVERSIDE CHURCH FOR A VIEW FROM THE NORTH; THE ROOFTOP OBSERVATION DECKS ON THE 86TH AND 102ND FLOORS OF THE EMPIRE STATE BUILDING OR THE TOP OF THE ROCK OBSERVATION DECK ON ROCKEFELLER CENTER. FOR BIRDS-EYE-VIEW THRILLS, A HELICOPTER IS IN ORDER. BUT FAR EASIER IS TO SETTLE INTO A COMFORTABLE CHAIR AND TOUR ALL THE MANY ASPECTS OF MANHATTAN FROM THE AIR IN THESE PAGES. MINUS THE VERTIGO.

40-41
New York City's civic center looms south of Canal Street and Chinatown, with city, state and federal offices and courthouses, as well as the Tombs, Manhattan's infamous jail.

42-43
On the day the Brooklyn Bridge was dedicated in 1883, 150,000 people crossed the bridge.

44-45
The Statue of Liberty's serene face has watched over the New York harbor since 1886.

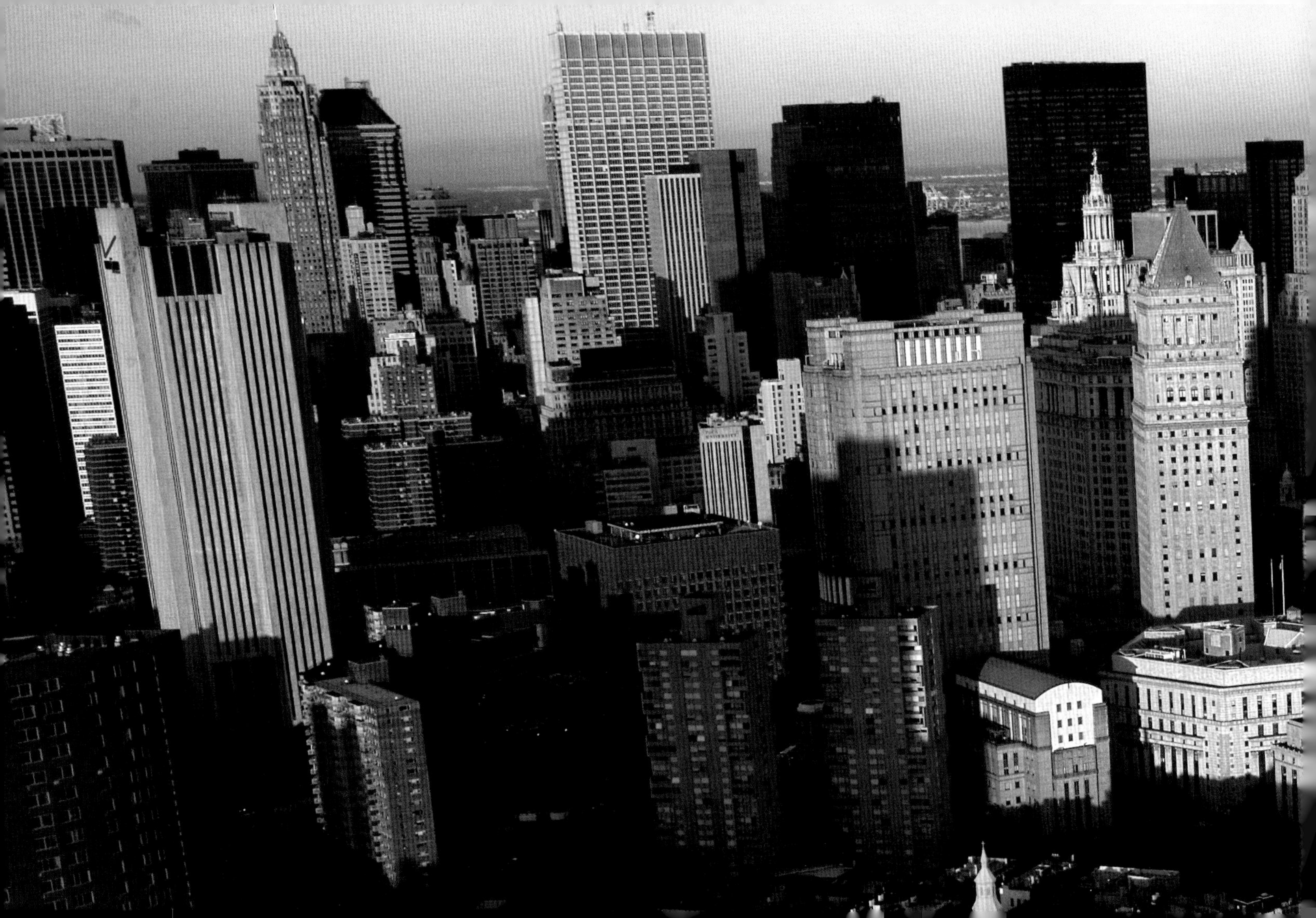

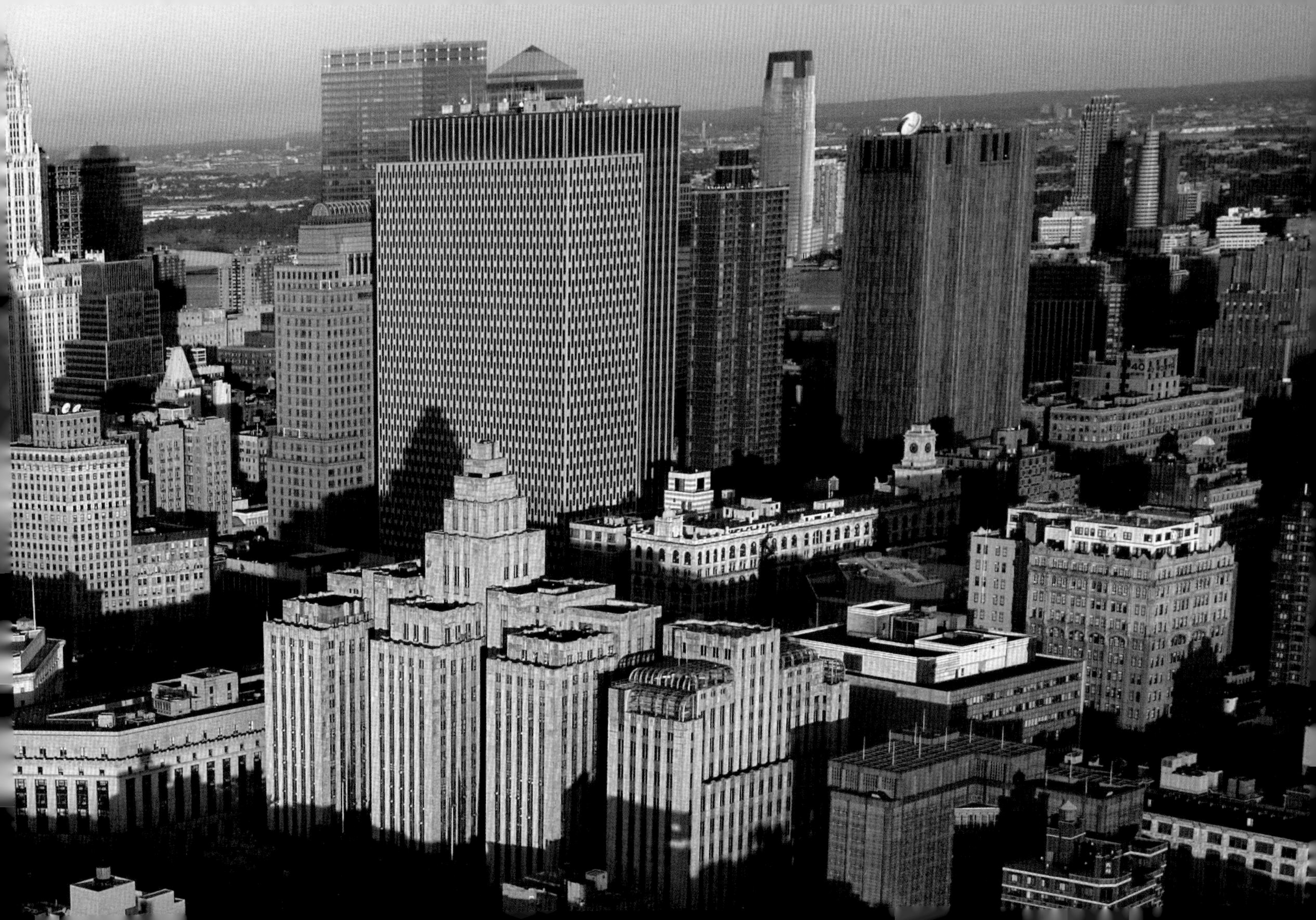

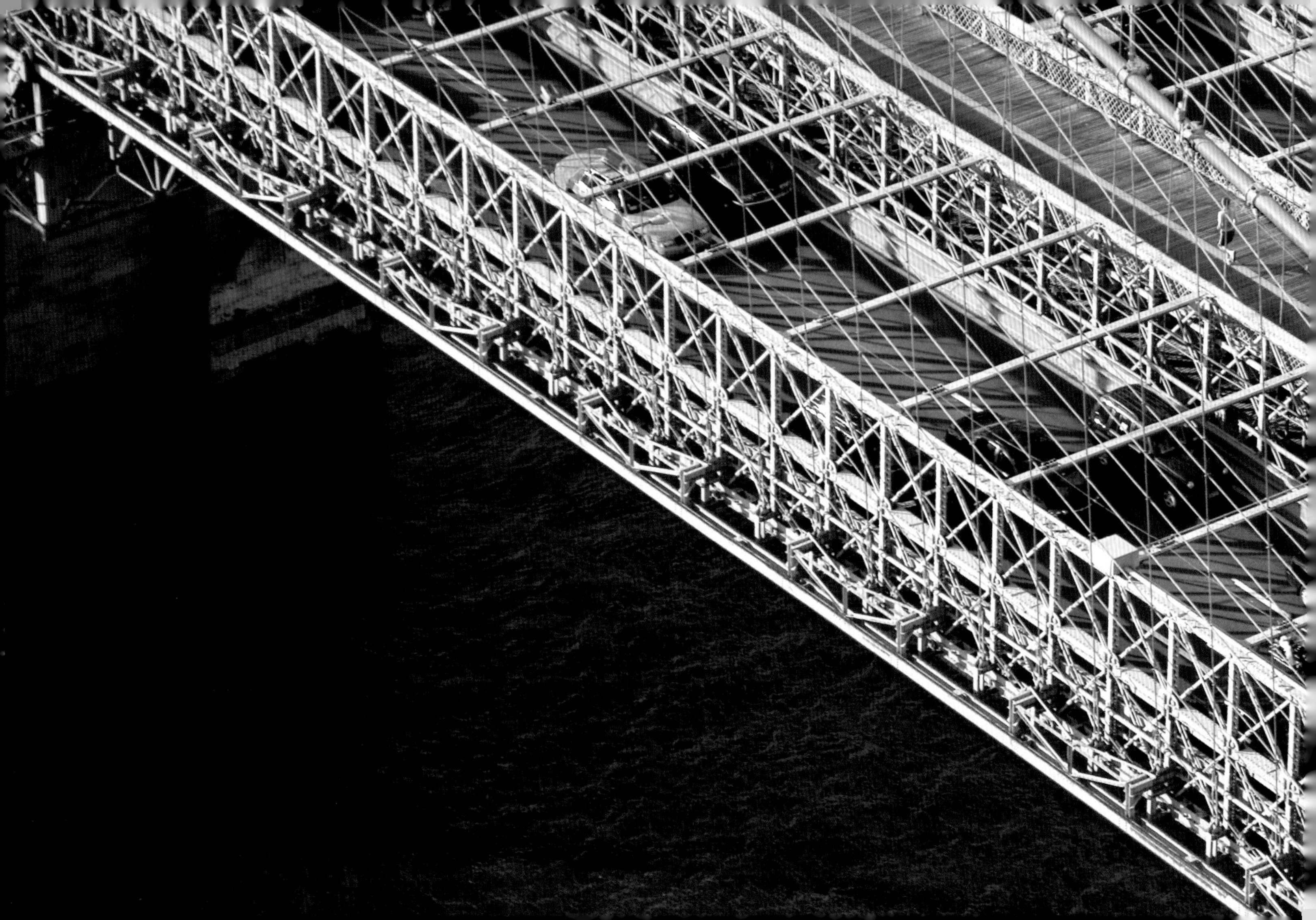

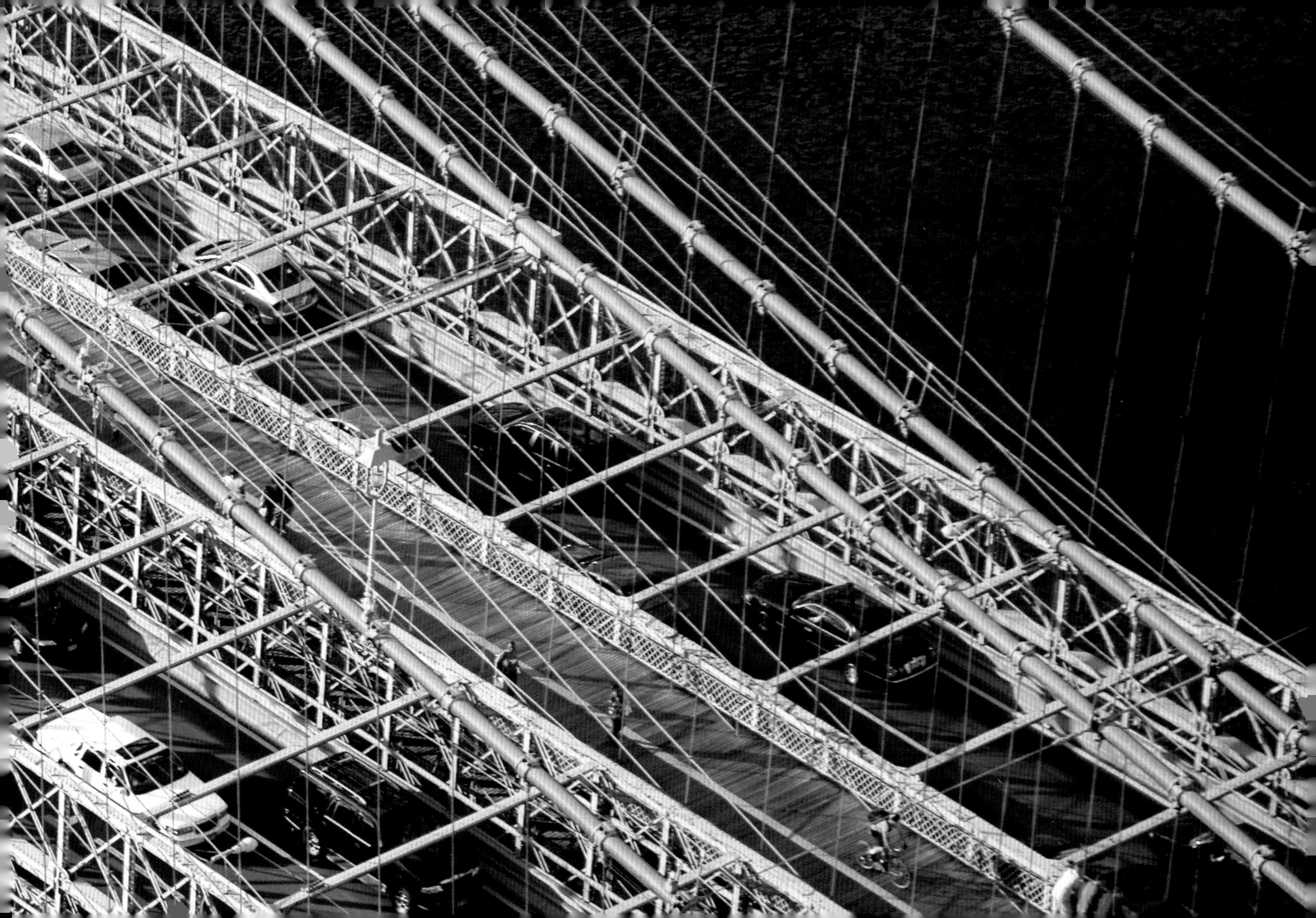

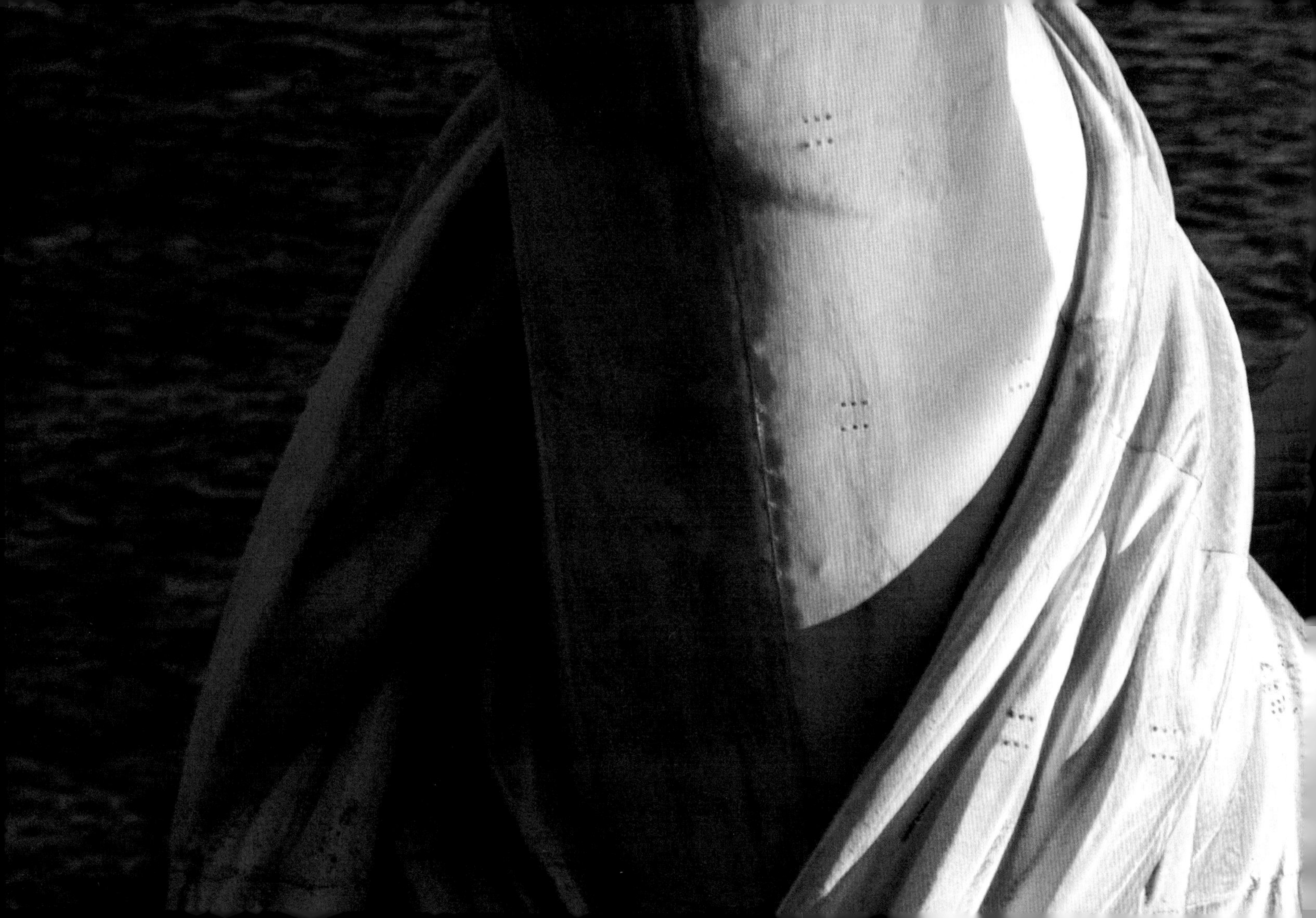

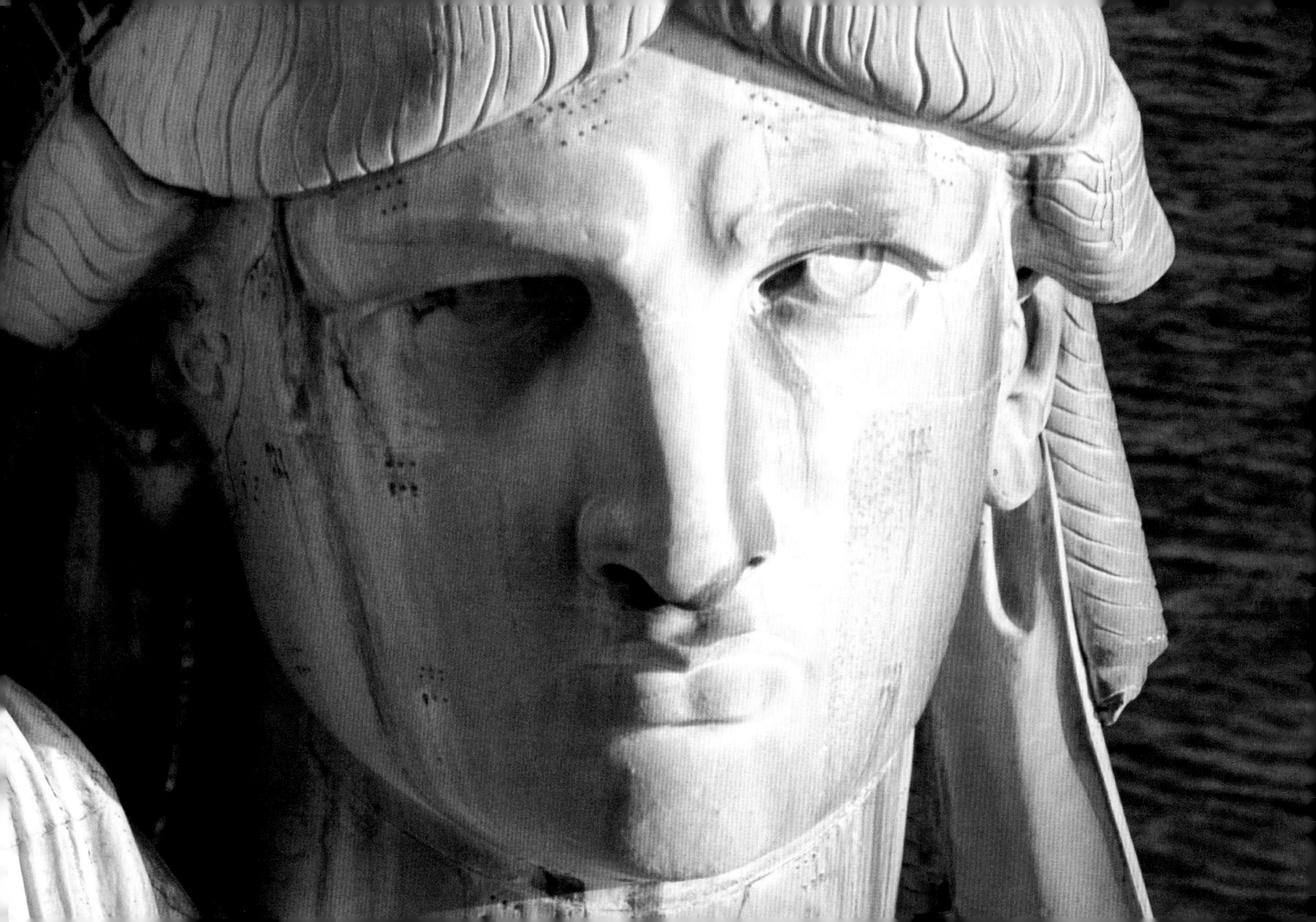

UPTOWN EAST

SILK STOCKINGS AND SKYSCRAPERS

Flying High

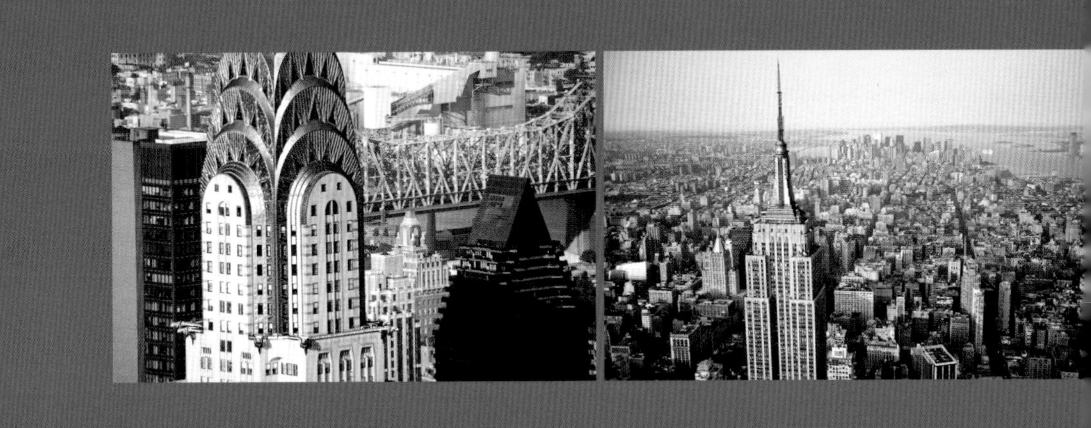

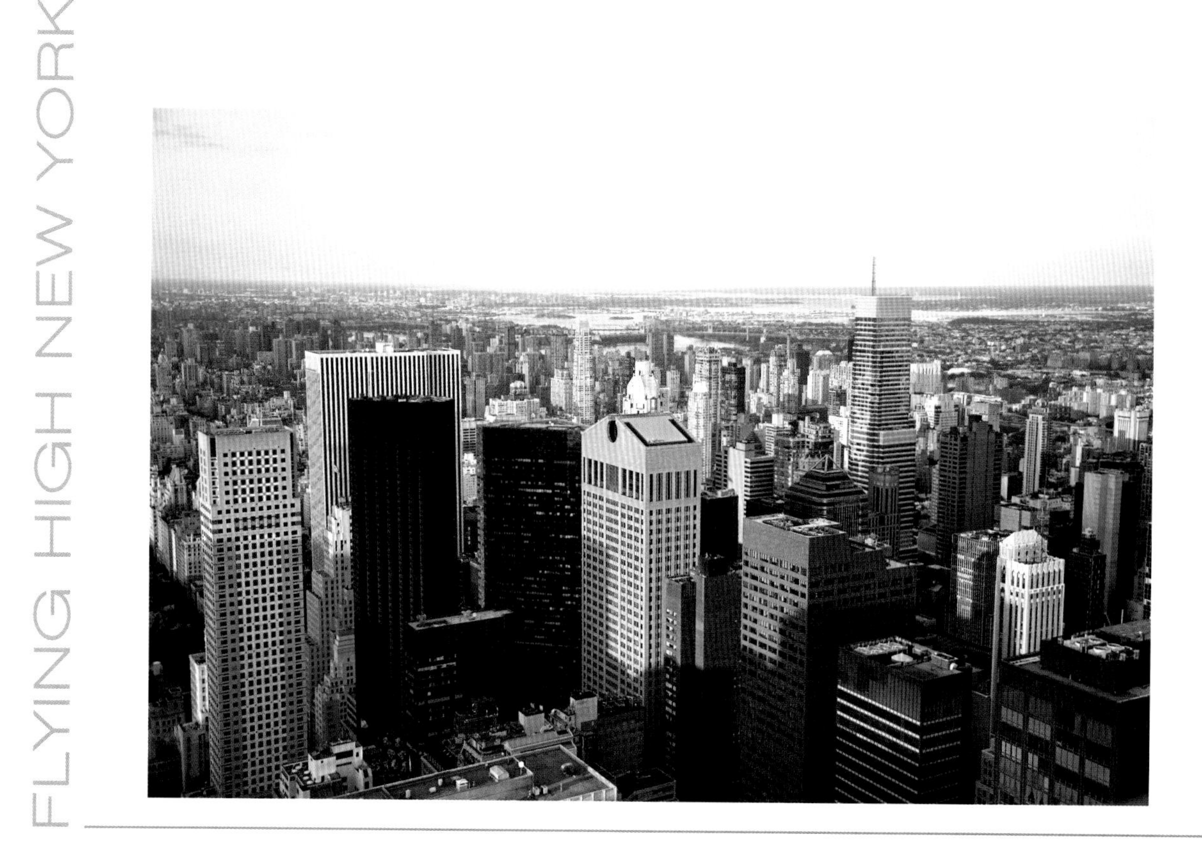

47
The Chrysler Building's dramatic steel arches contrast with the black triangle atop 100 UN Plaza (left). The Empire State Building remains the tallest in the city (right).

As the city below Wall Street grew more and more dense, those with the means moved north in search of more space, cleaner air, and cheaper real estate. Roads were built as needed, and land disputes soon became common. It was soon apparent that some order was needed to control the expansion northward.

In 1811, a master plan for the development of Manhattan was approved, calling for a grid-based design of intersecting north/south and east/west avenues and streets, extending from Houston (pronounced How-ston) up to 155th Street. Fifth Avenue was the dividing line between east and west above Washington Square Park, which at the time was a militia ground.

That same design exists in large part today, although the grid now extends well beyond 155th Street into the Bronx. The planners had no use for the ascetic flourishes of circles and squares seen in Paris and London; New York was all about business, and its design was meant to be practical. Building within the rectangular grid was the easiest and "most convenient" approach for construction of homes and offices, according to the designers. And so, the city grew uptown, in an orderly – on paper, at least – manner, and soon, rather than farms and homesteads, offices and apartment buildings began to dominate. While the west side retained its agrarian character for longer, commerce quickly dominated on the east side.

The Uptown East area is composed of a series of neighborhoods, each with its own character and topography: the Flatiron district, where Fifth Avenue crosses Broadway; Murray Hill/Kips Bay, home to tree-lined streets of brownstones and the huge Bellevue, NYU medical complex; Turtle Bay, where restaurants and apartments cater to the international diplomatic set Sutton Place; fashionable Lenox Hill and Carnegie Hill, an elegant residential enclave; Yorkville on the far

48
This quintet of skyscrapers in midtown includes: the 712 Fifth Avenue, the General Motors, the Trump and former IBM buildings, and the "Chippendale" Sony building.

Uptown East
Silk Stockings and Skyscrapers

east, where the mayor's home, Gracie Mansion, overlooks the East River; Spanish Harlem and East Harlem where the Triboro Bridge, extends from Manhattan, over Randall's Island, and on to the city's outer boroughs of the Bronx and Queens.

By the 1900s, the eastern midsection of the city, from 34th Street to 59th Street, was on its way to becoming the busiest single commercial district in the United States. The early part of the 20th century also became the most productive period of building in New York's history; this was the beginning of the age of skyscrapers. Fabled structures like the Flatiron Building, at the juncture of Broadway and Fifth Avenue, the Empire State Building, at 34th Street and Fifth Avenue, and the Chrysler Building, on 42nd Street, rose skyward, fueled in part by the race to design the tallest building in the world. The race was ultimately won by the Empire State Building, which held the title until the World Trade Towers surpassed it in 1970.

With the mastering of steel-beamed construction, captains of industry realized that the answer to Manhattan's finite acreage was to build up, and up, and up. Proximity to transportation hubs, like Grand Central Station, as well as piers, made the area – especially midtown east, the place where a great majority of the city's skyscrapers were and are concentrated. After both World Wars, the surge in high-rise building continued. From Art Deco gems like the Daily News Building and the Chanin Building to the International-style masterpieces, Lever House and the Seagrams Building, the Upper East Side was where corporate America wanted to be. Soon, foreign investors wanted a piece of the action, and more and more international firms built prominent New York bases. During the boom years of the 1980s, post-modern landmarks like the Sony, Citigroup, and the Bear Stearns Building, were added to the skyline. Today the race is on to build "green" skyscrapers, using environmentally sound and sustainable methods.

New York's identity as a world capital, if not the world capital, after World War II, made it the likely location for the United Nations, which was built east of First

Uptown East
Silk Stockings and Skyscrapers

Avenue near the East River in 1952. The design of the UN combines the International style of architecture, seen in the monolithic Secretariat, as well as utopian concept of the French architect, Le Corbusier, which called for tall buildings and low-lying ones to be linked by open, park-like areas. After the founding of the United Nations, the neighborhood surrounding it grew, and is now dotted with diplomatic residences and offices, and businesses catering to the international clientele. Looming above the UN, like a black exclamation mark, is the 72-floor Trump World Tower, the tallest residential building in the world, developed by Donald Trump.

New York is known for many larger-than-life individuals – from Peter Stuyvesant in the early years of New Amsterdam to John D. Rockefeller and Andrew Carnegie – who have left their marks on the city; Trump, with his entrepreneurial spirit and his zest for risky, often controversial, ventures, is one of them. With prominent projects throughout the city, Trump continues to add his name to the skyline of New York.

As midtown became synonymous with the hustle and bustle of corporate New York, people seeking more sedate environs for their homes took advantage of the city's improved transportation options and headed even farther north. Soon the Upper East Side became known as the fashionable place to live. With Central Park as a front yard, opulent mansions were built along Fifth Avenue. Park Avenue, with its planted islands creating a green pathway straight down to Grand Central Station, became the next exclusive address. Today, many of those mansions are gone, leveled to make way for equally opulent apartment buildings. Others have been preserved as museums, like the Frick and the Cooper-Hewitt.

New York has over 80 museums, and nine of them are located on Fifth Avenue. In fact, Fifth Avenue, from 82nd to 105th street, has officially been dubbed Museum Mile, beginning with the Metropolitan Museum of Art, to the Guggenheim, a bastion of modern art, and extending to the Museo del Barrio and the Jewish Museum and the Museum of the City of New York.

Parallel to Fifth Avenue runs Madison Avenue, syn-

FLYING HIGH NEW YORK

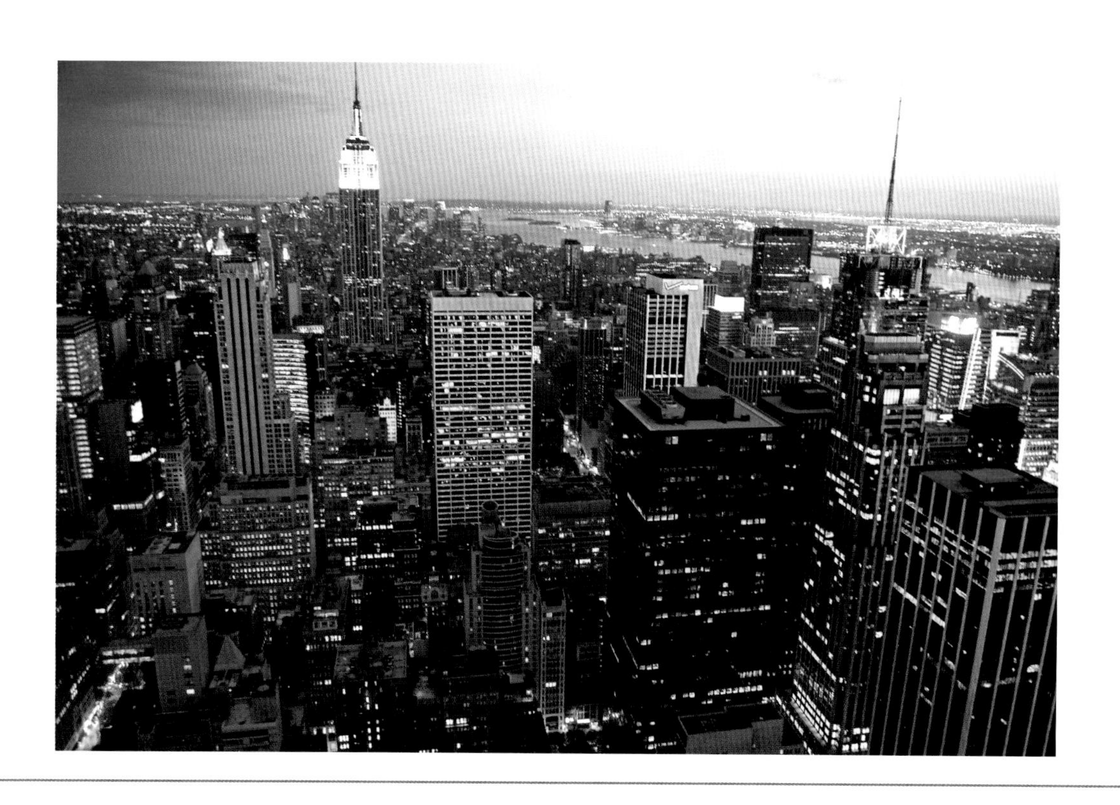

52
In the evening, the top of the Empire State Building is illuminated: white lights for "regular" days and colored lights to mark special events such as the Marathon or Veterans Day.

onymous with advertising in the United States and lined with office towers and elegant boutiques and shops. Lexington Avenue, east of Park, was not a part of the original 1811 grid plan. It, however, is part of the reason the Upper East Side grew so quickly, as a major subway line runs beneath it. Avenues, like First, Second and Third, and their cross streets, farther east of the epicenter of the city retained their early ethnic character longer than the more central avenues. But even there, older buildings are fast disappearing, as properties are gobbled up for development.

Beyond 96th Street, where the Lexington Avenue subway emerges from underground, is Harlem, founded in 1658 as Nieuw Haarlem, by the Dutch. The neighborhood has gone through a multitude of incarnations. In the 17th and 18th centuries, it was the site of country residences of wealthy New Yorkers. When the New York and Harlem Railroad opened, it became a thriving suburb. With the coming of the subway, it became a magnet for immigrants escaping the slums of the Lower East Side. Irish, Italian and Puerto Rican immigrants, as well as African-Americans have called it home. After the Civil War, thousands of former slaves emigrated from the south to Harlem. During the 1920s, dubbed the Harlem Renaissance, many noted African-American musicians, artists and writers were drawn there. The neighborhood's fortunes have risen and fallen over the years, but as always, real estate leads the way in New York. Having endured cycles of crime and violence in the 1960s and 1970s, the area is undergoing a cultural and commercial rejuvenation, as urban pioneers rediscover the space, the history and the many architectural gems (selling and renting for far less than buildings a few blocks south) of Harlem. A flight up the East River and over the Franklin Delano Roosevelt (FDR) Drive, which runs along the eastern edge of Manhattan, is a ride through history. It is along this route that the most recognizable skyline in the world rises. For a closer aerial look at the Upper East Side, the Roosevelt Island Tramway ferries passengers in a Swiss-style gondola over the East River and back, coming to rest under the Queensboro Bridge at 59th.

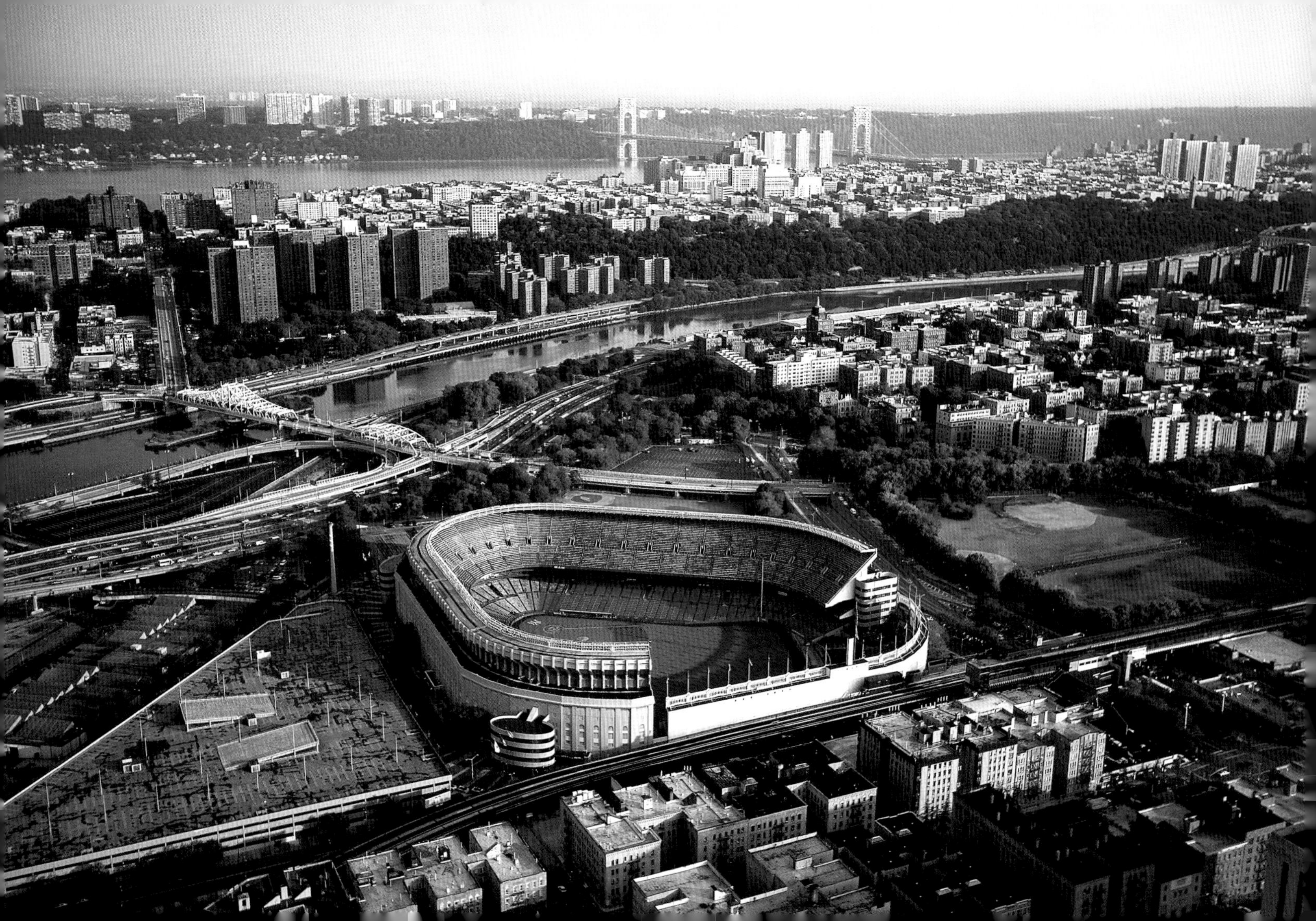

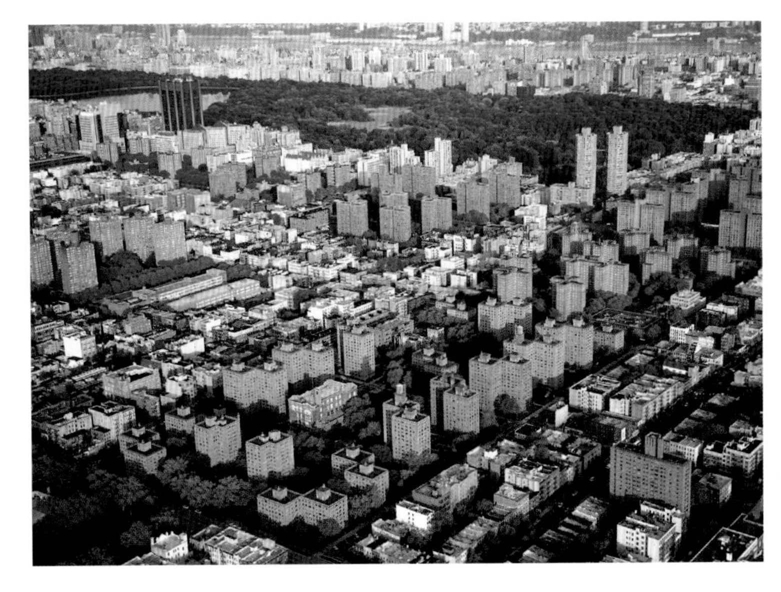

54

Though once housed on Manhattan's Polo Grounds, the New York Yankees have called Bronx-based Yankee Stadium home since 1921.

55

In this view, Manhattan's Upper East Side extends to the edge of Central Park, visible in the upper part of the image.

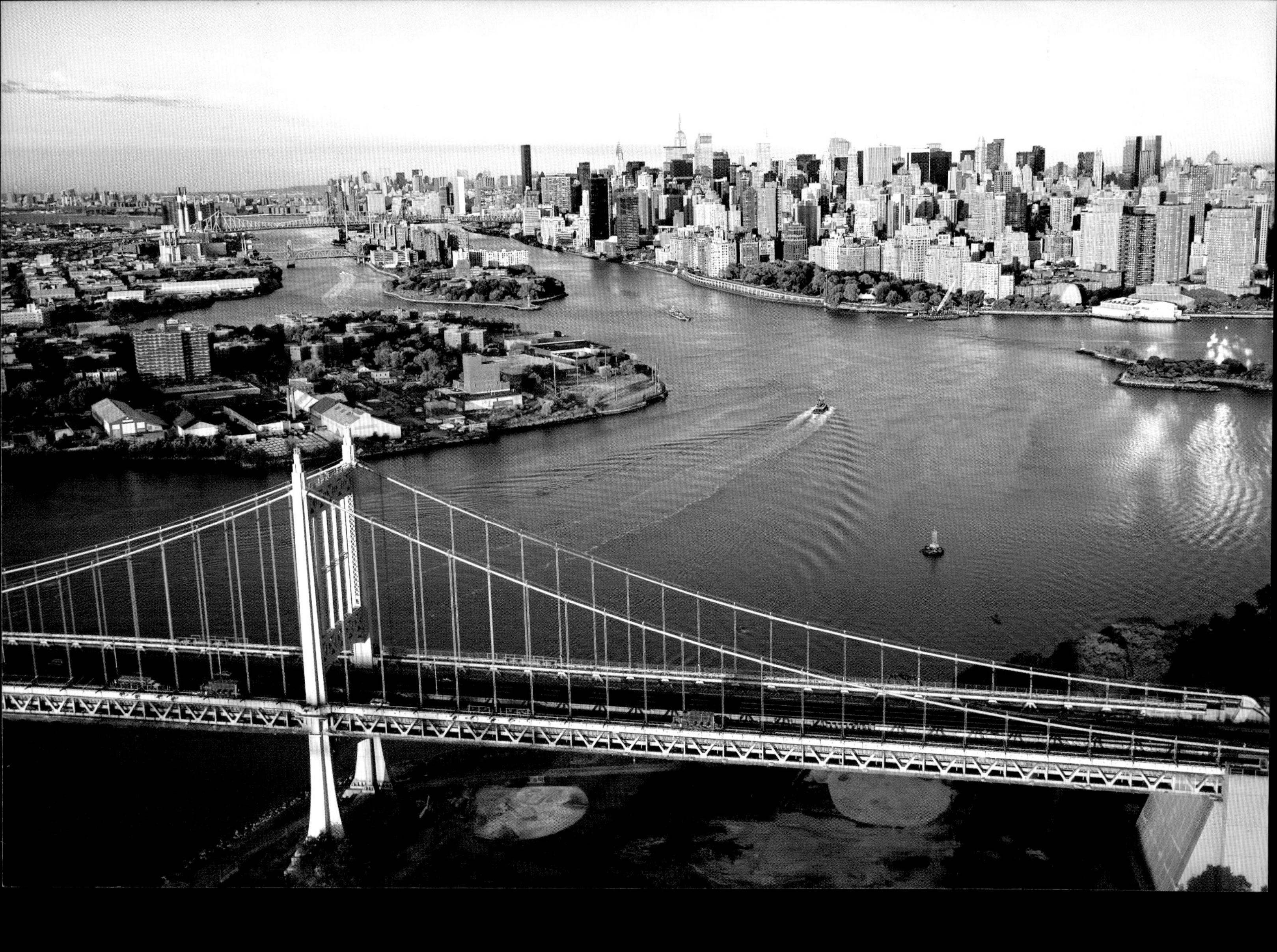

56
The Triborough Bridge has three branches that straddle three boroughs of New York City; here, the East River suspension span links Manhattan to Queens.

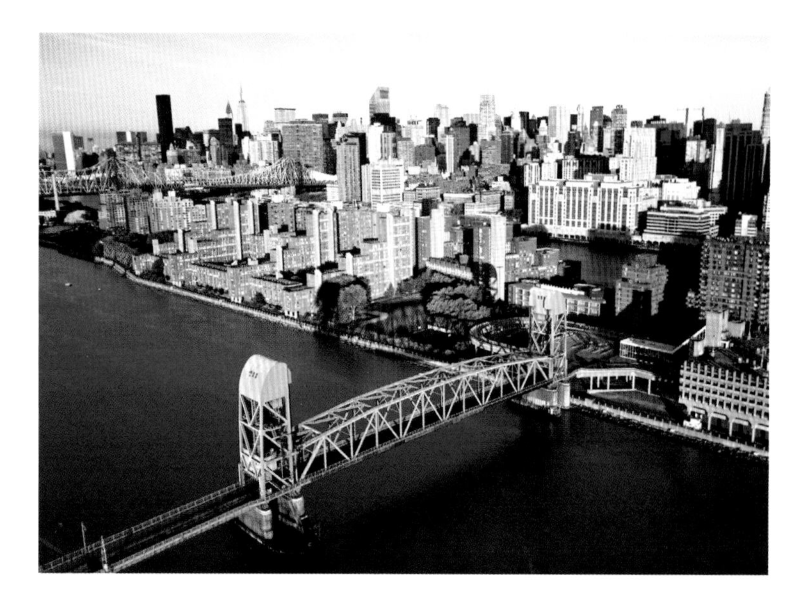

58
The Roosevelt Island Bridge provides the only way for cars to reach the island, which sits in the East River.

59
The Queensborough Bridge is also known as the Fifty-Ninth Street Bridge, made famous in a song by Simon and Garfunkel.

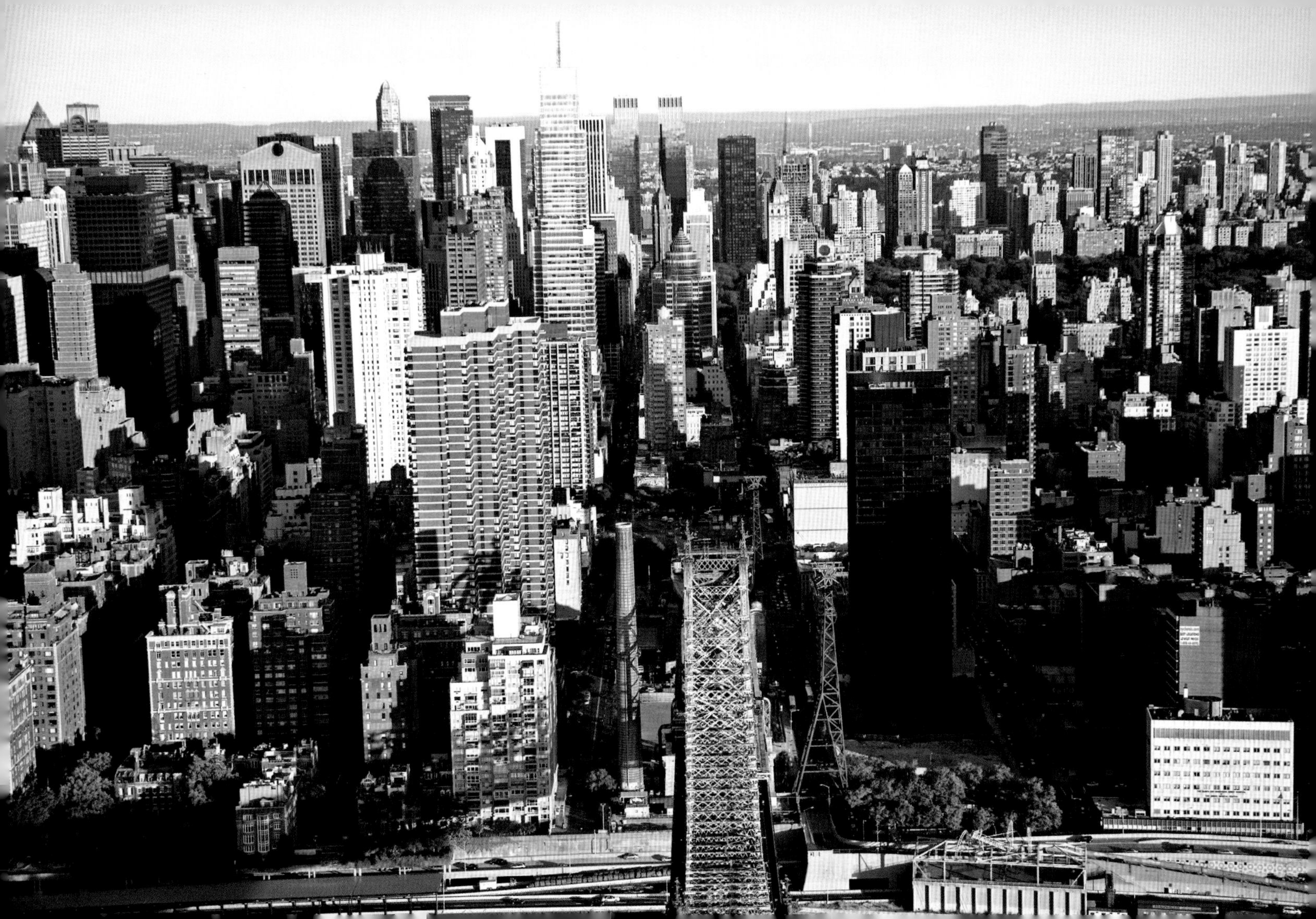

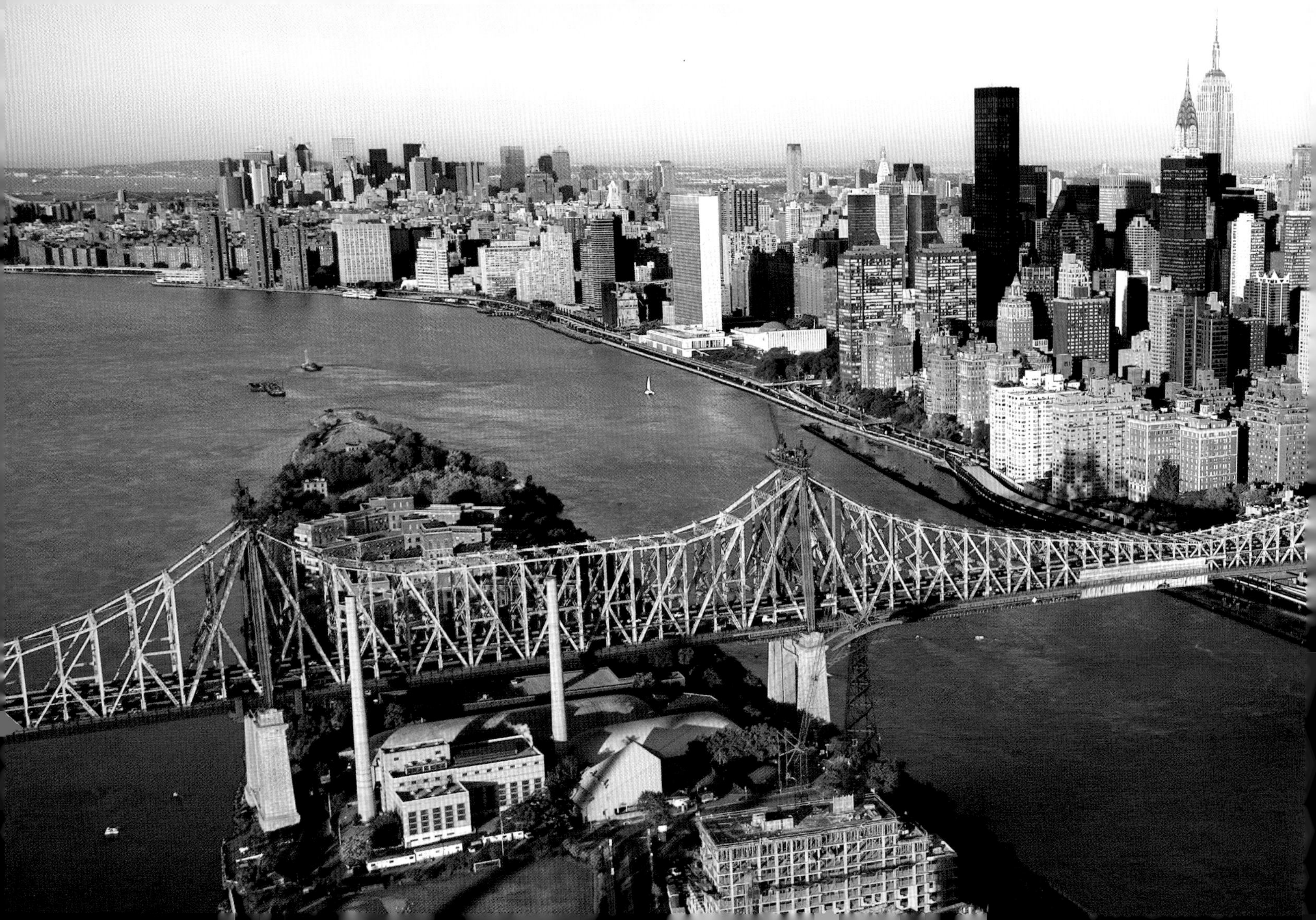

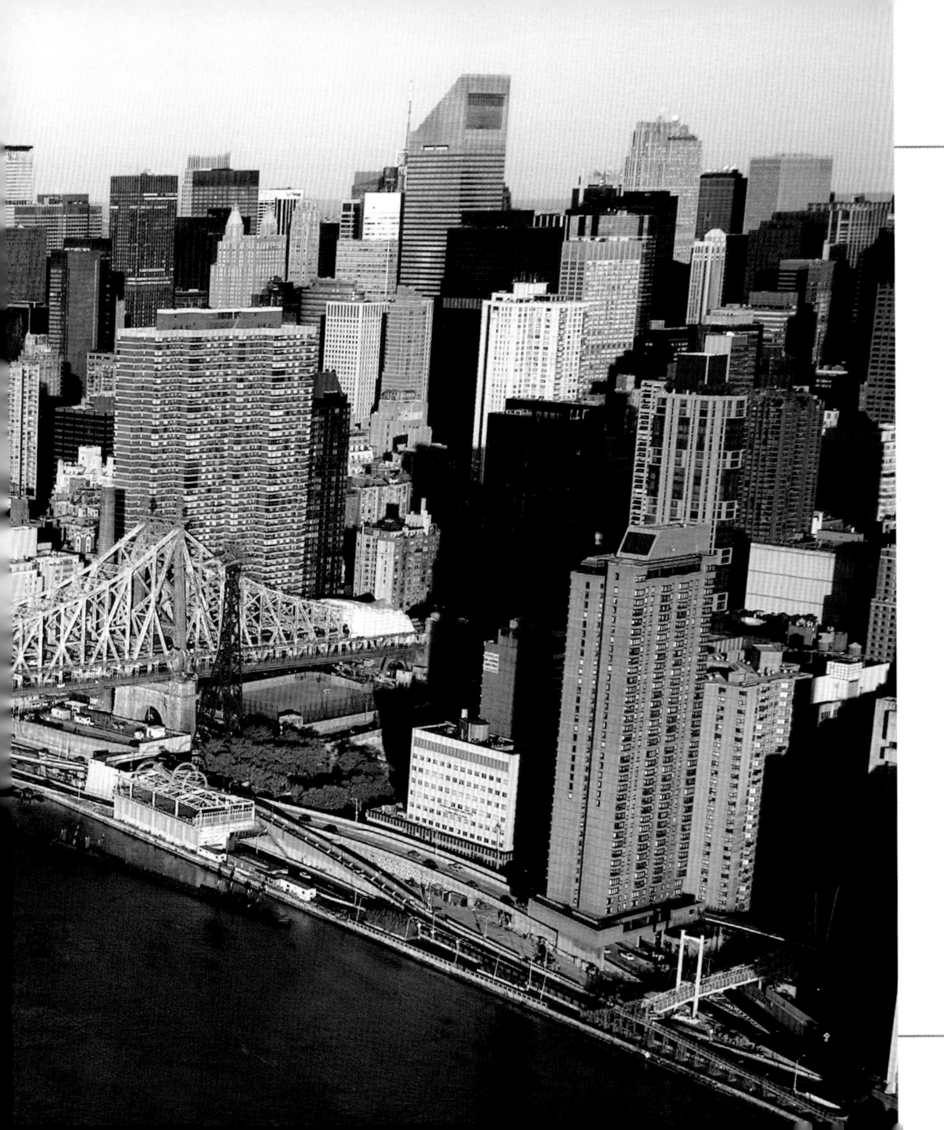

60-61
The Queensborough Bridge spans the East River and crosses over Roosevelt Island, connecting Manhattan to Long Island City, in Queens.

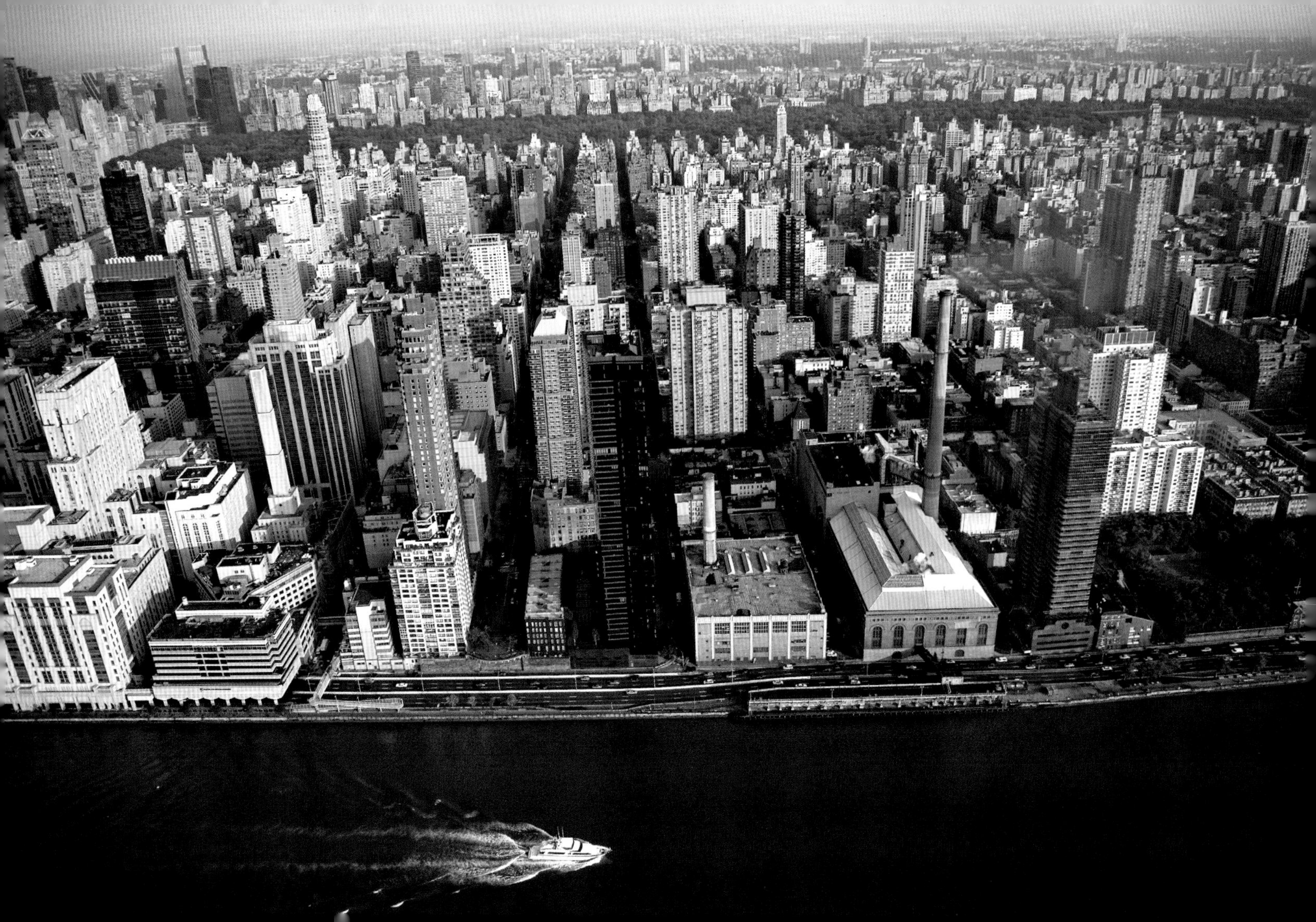

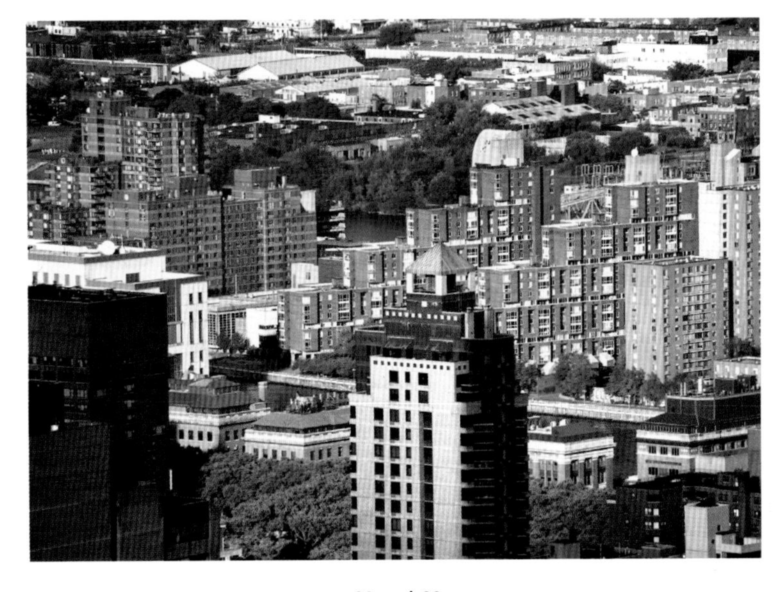

62 and 63
Roosevelt Island, in the East River, sits opposite Rockefeller University and New York Presbyterian Hospital in the East River.

65

The renowned New York Presbyterian Hospital straddles the F.D.R. Drive along the East River.

66-67

The ivy-covered walls of Rockefeller University surround one of the world's pre-eminent centers of scientific research.

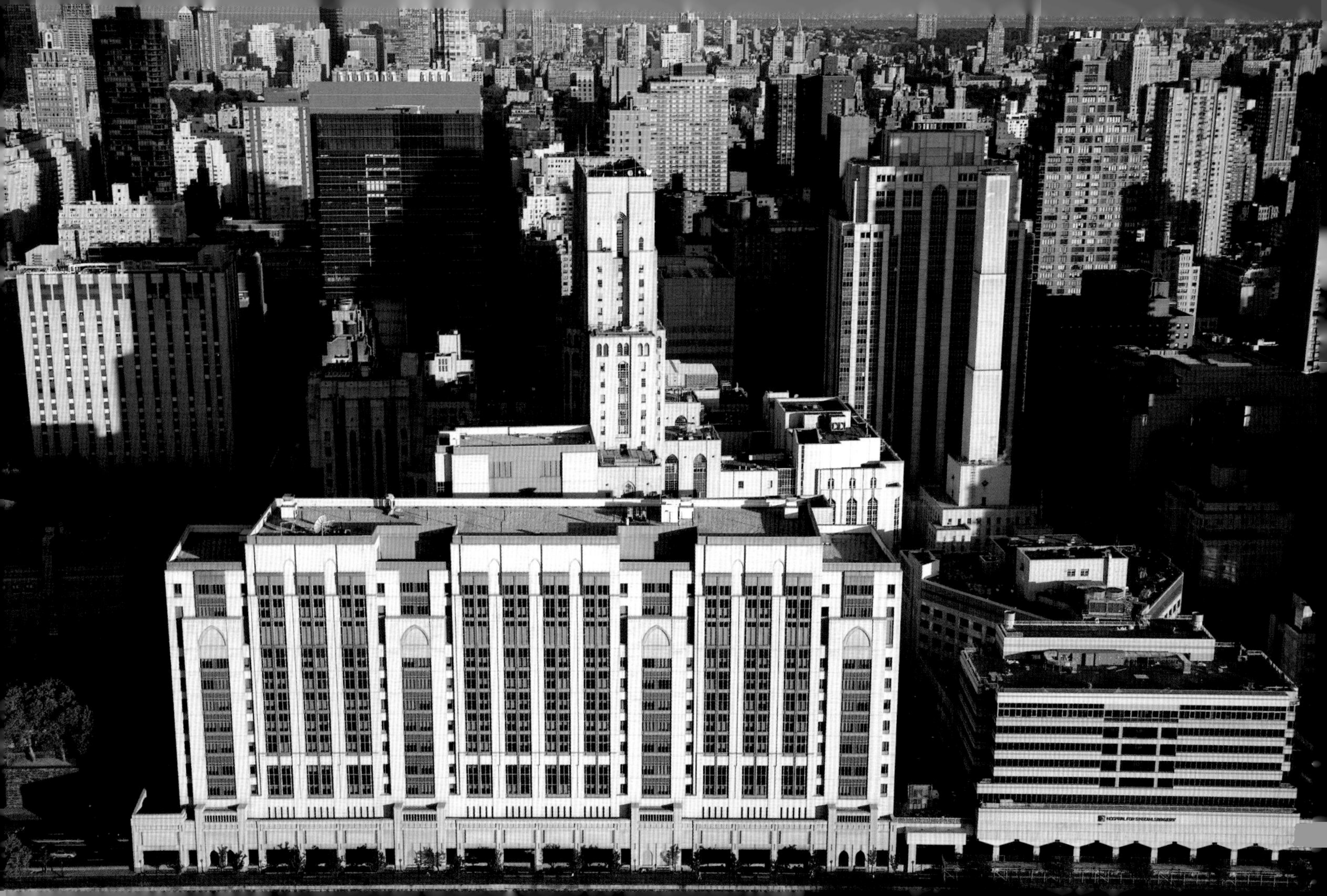

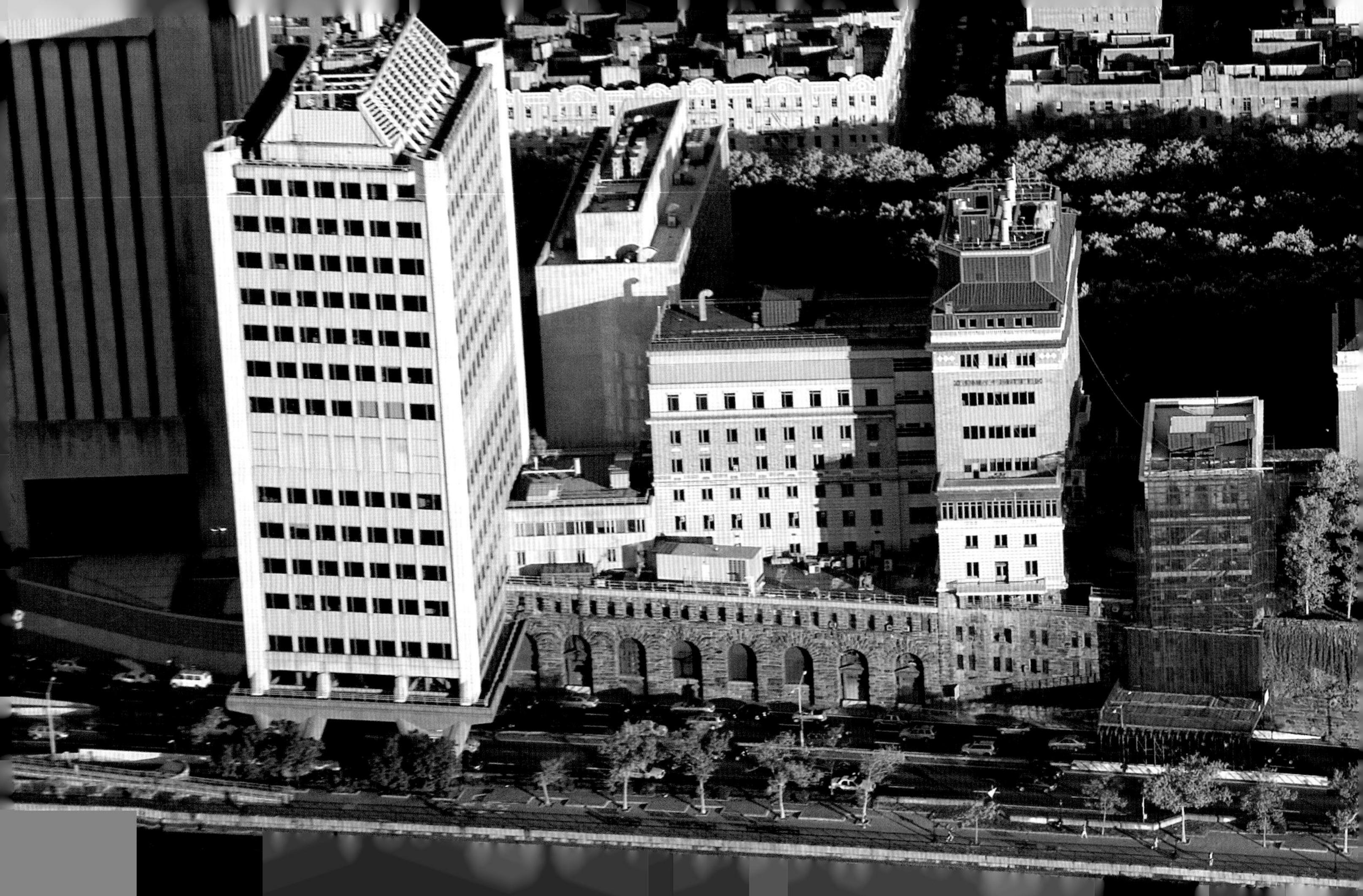

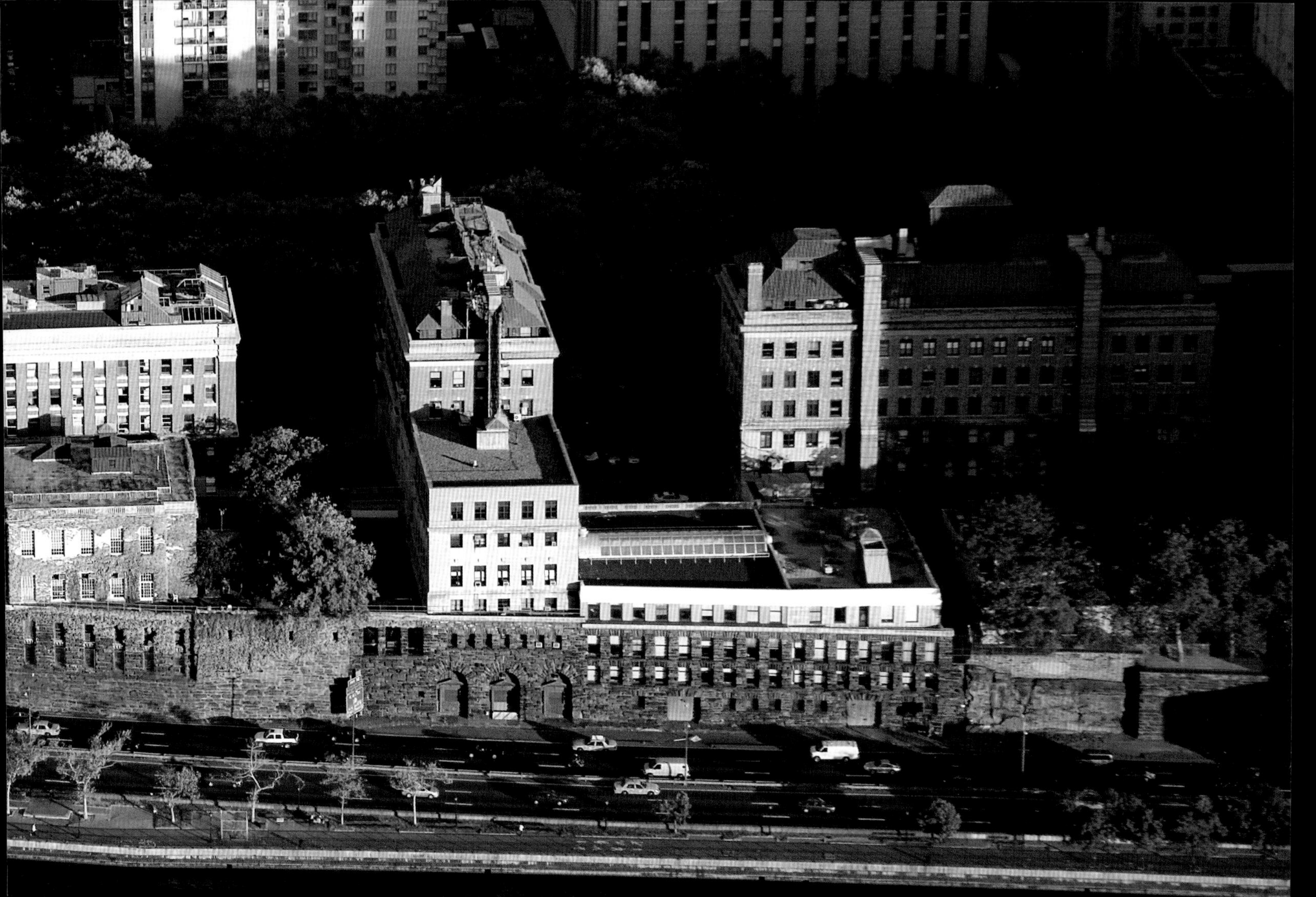

69
The Citigroup Center is like a shimmering icicle in the middle of a snow-covered mid-town. In the foreground is Roosevelt Island.

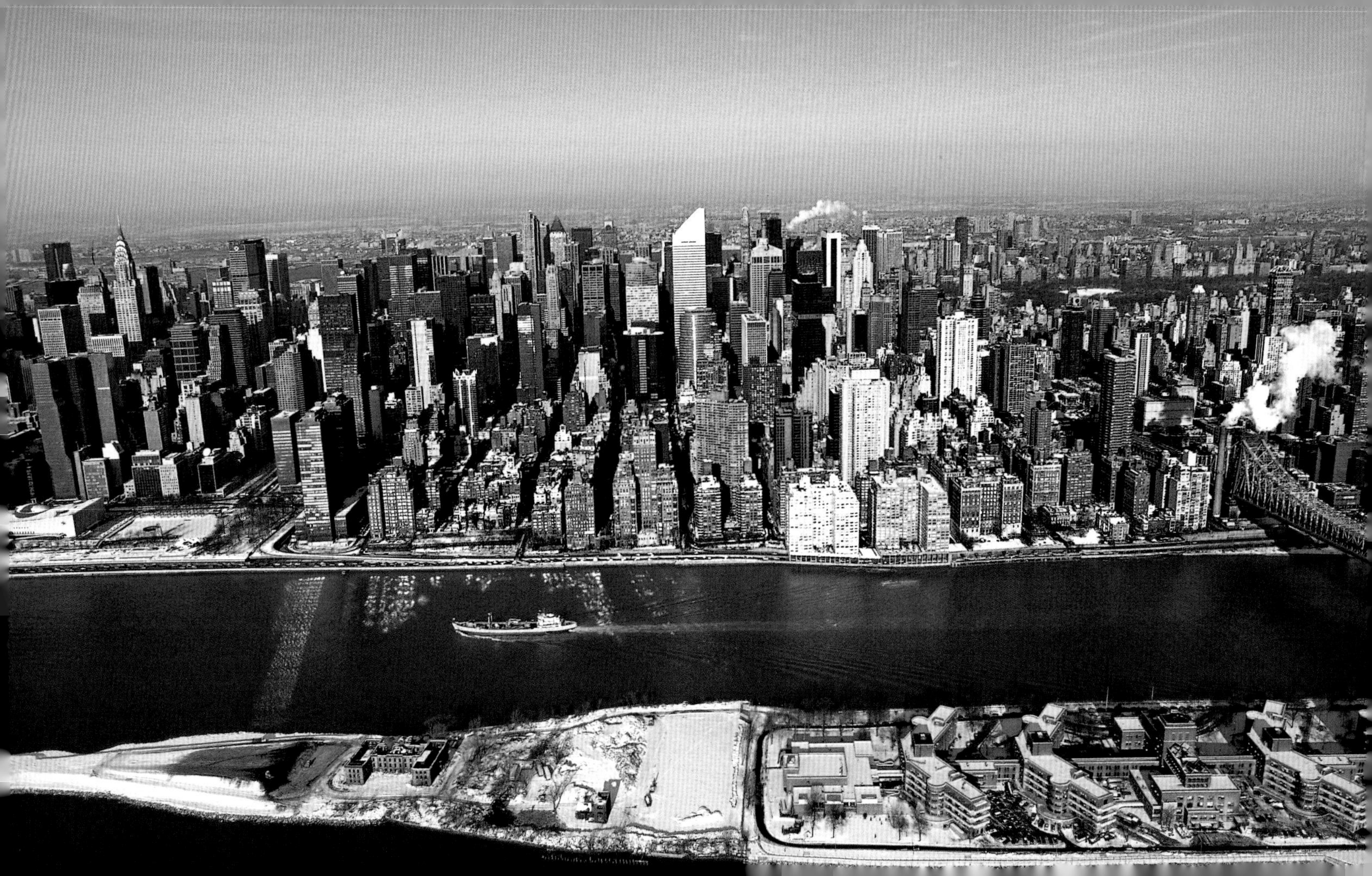

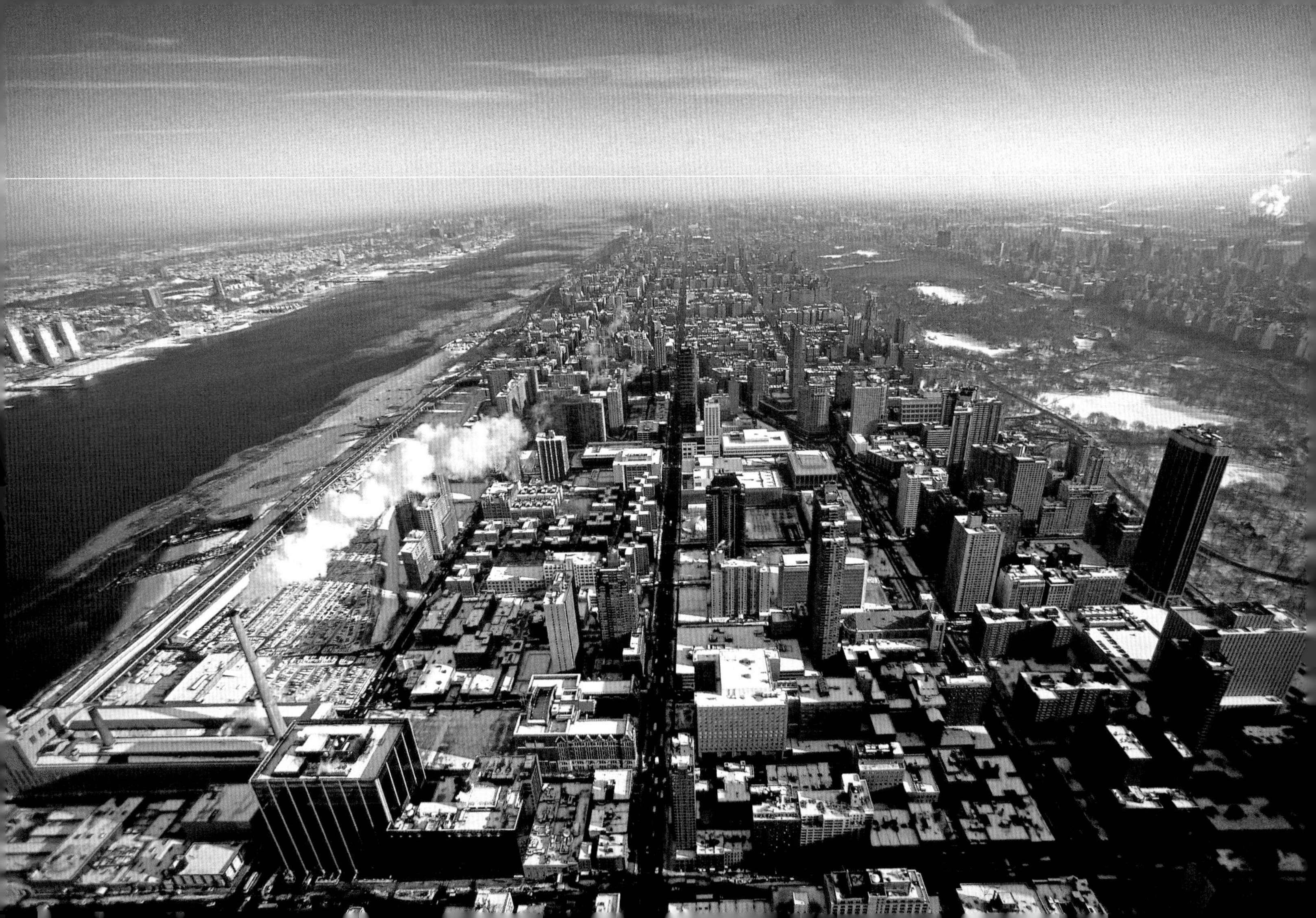

70
Bordering the East River Park are public housing projects and New York City's largest wastewater pumping station.

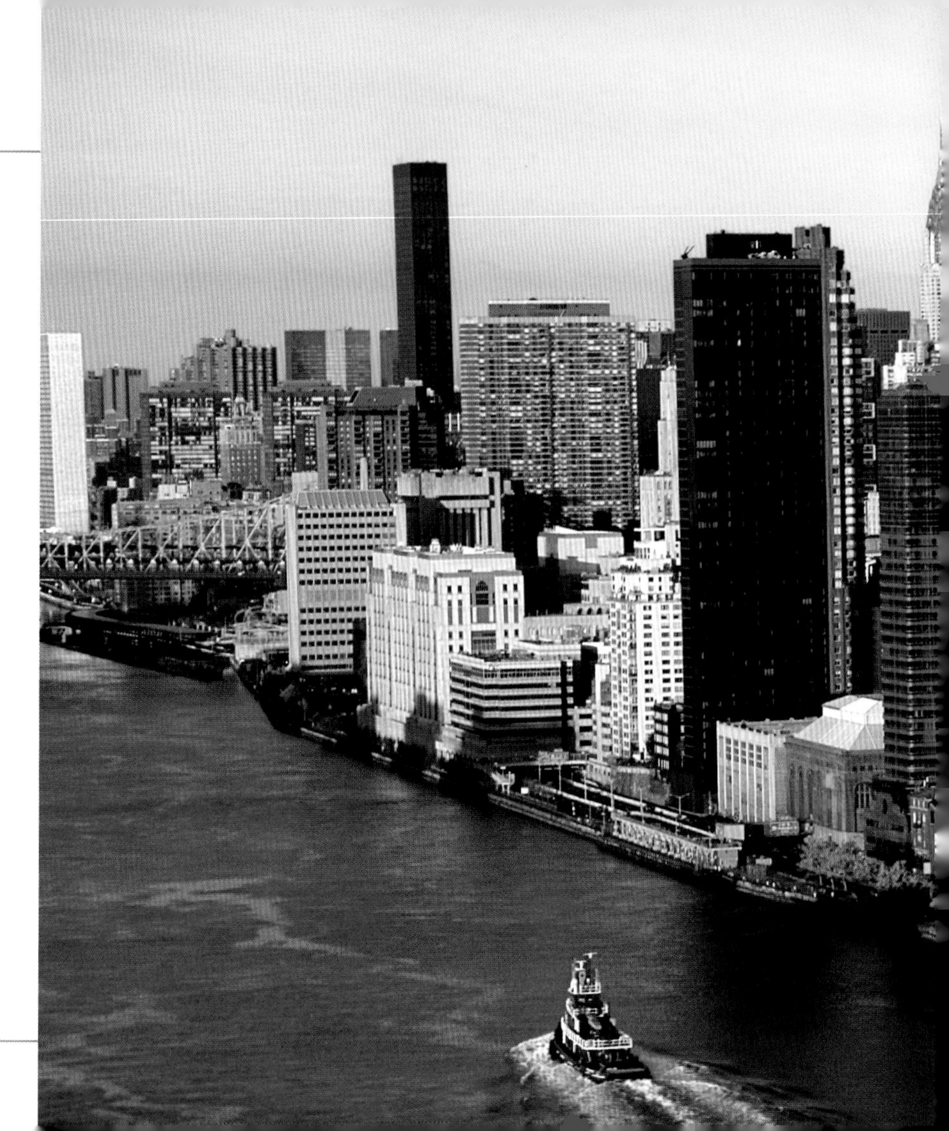

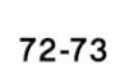

72-73
A tugboat glides toward the New York Presbyterian Hospital, Weill Cornell Medical Complex and Rockefeller University.

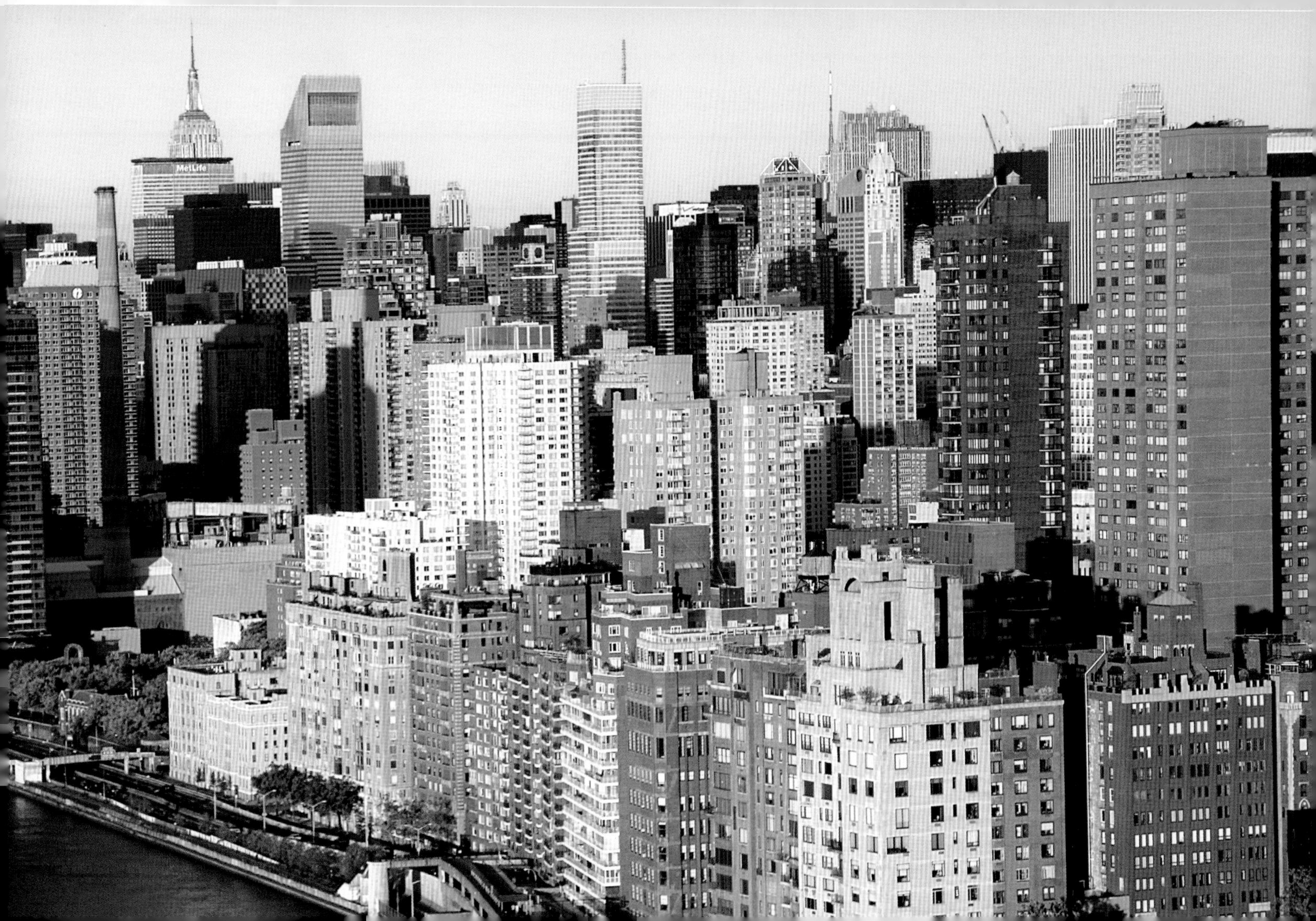
MetLife

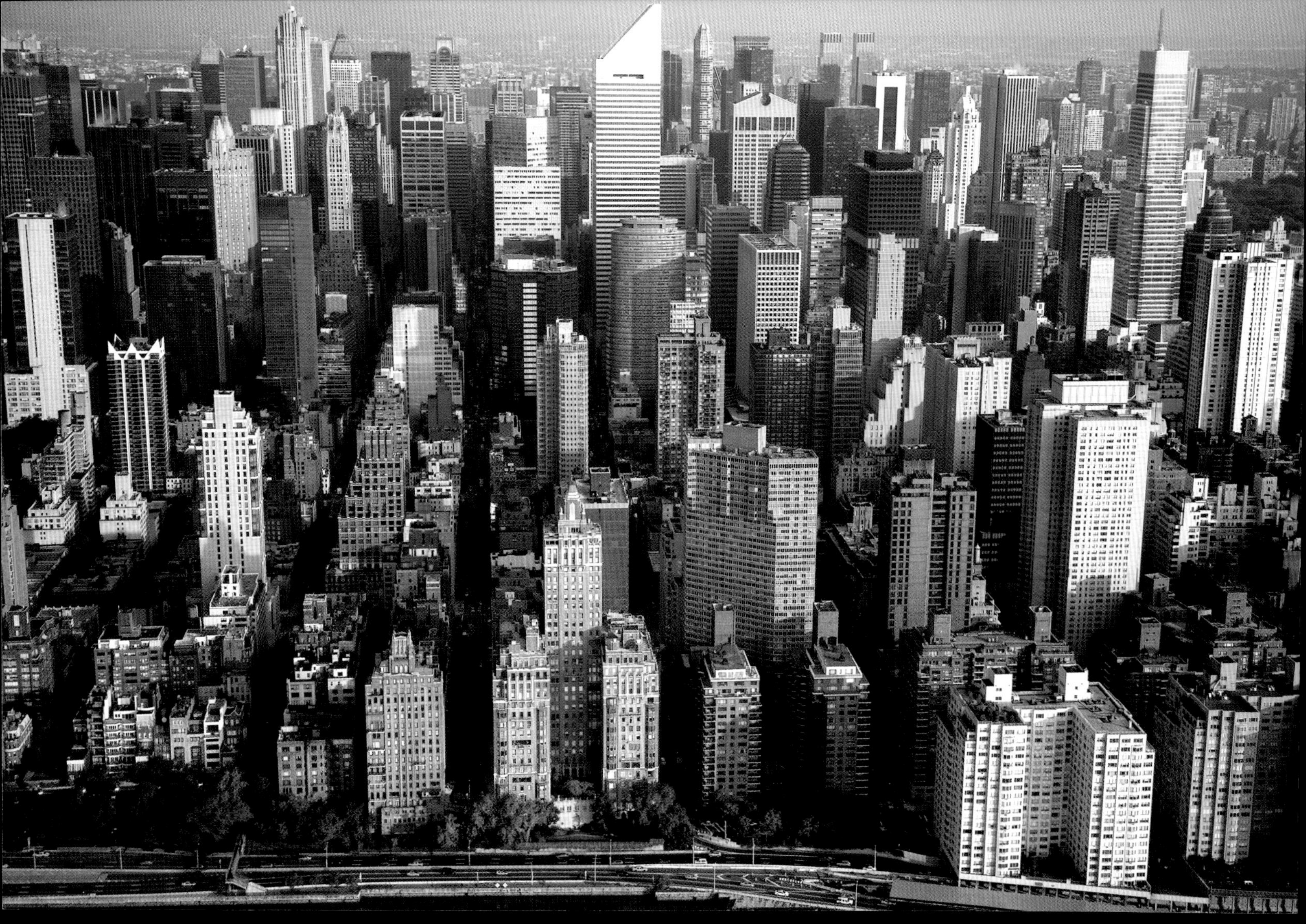

74

This view of midtown from the East River, looking west, shows architectural masterpieces from the early to the late 20th century, including Beekman Place and the wedge-shaped Citigroup Center.

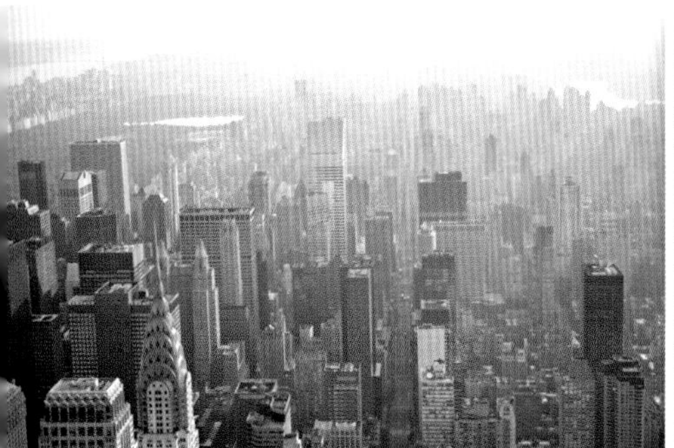

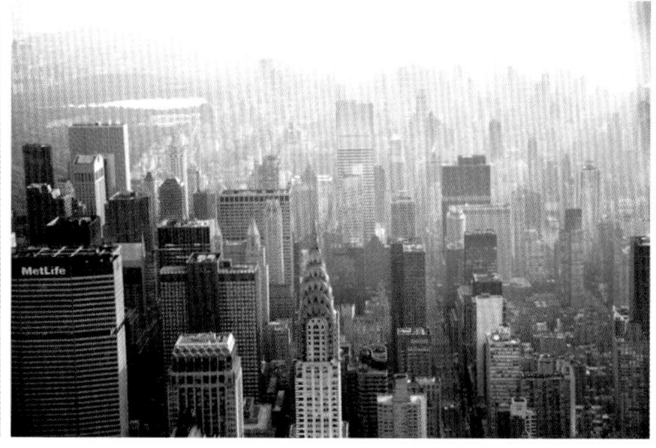

76
Midtown Manhattan has one of the highest concentrations of skyscrapers in the world.

77
Once hilly farmland overlooking a protected bay, the area dubbed Turtle Bay now claims a collection of notable skyscrapers, including (from left to right) Citigroup Center, 100 UN Plaza, and Trump World Tower.

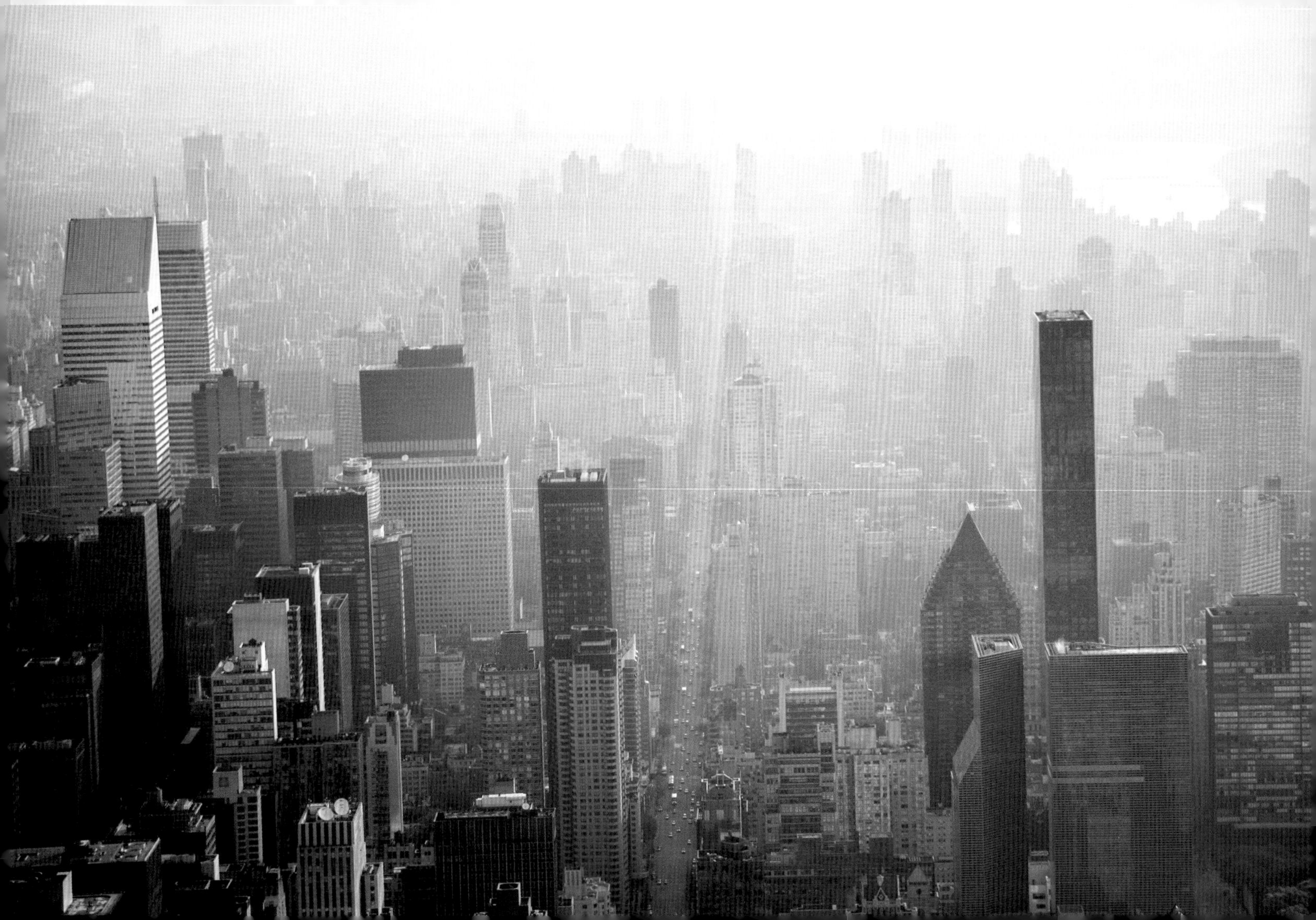

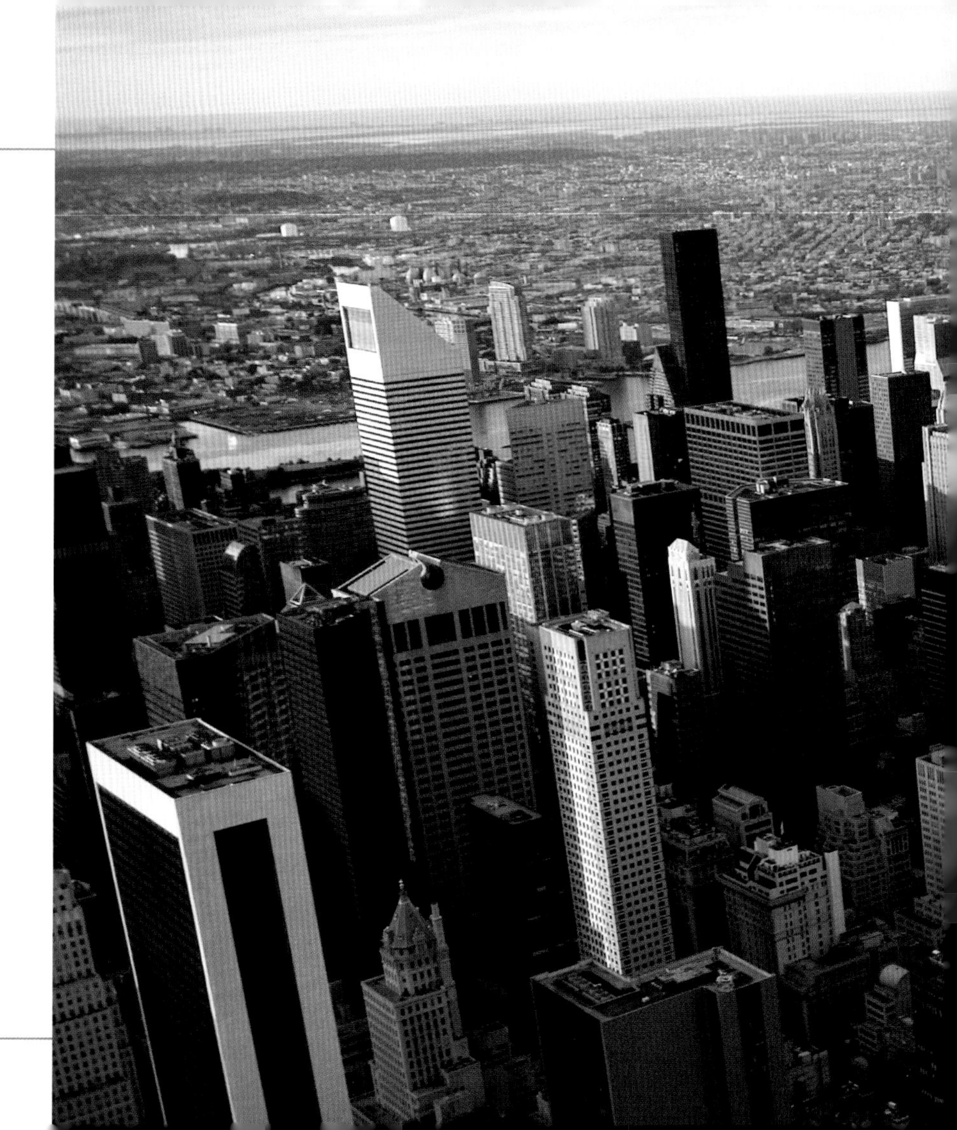

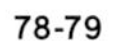

78-79

From the Solow Building on 57th Street (bottom left) to the Empire State Building on 34th Street, midtown Manhattan, is, as architect Rem Koolhaas put it, a frontier in the sky.

80-81

Looking south from the top of the Empire State Building, New Jersey, Staten Island and Long Island, as well as Hudson and East Rivers, are visible.

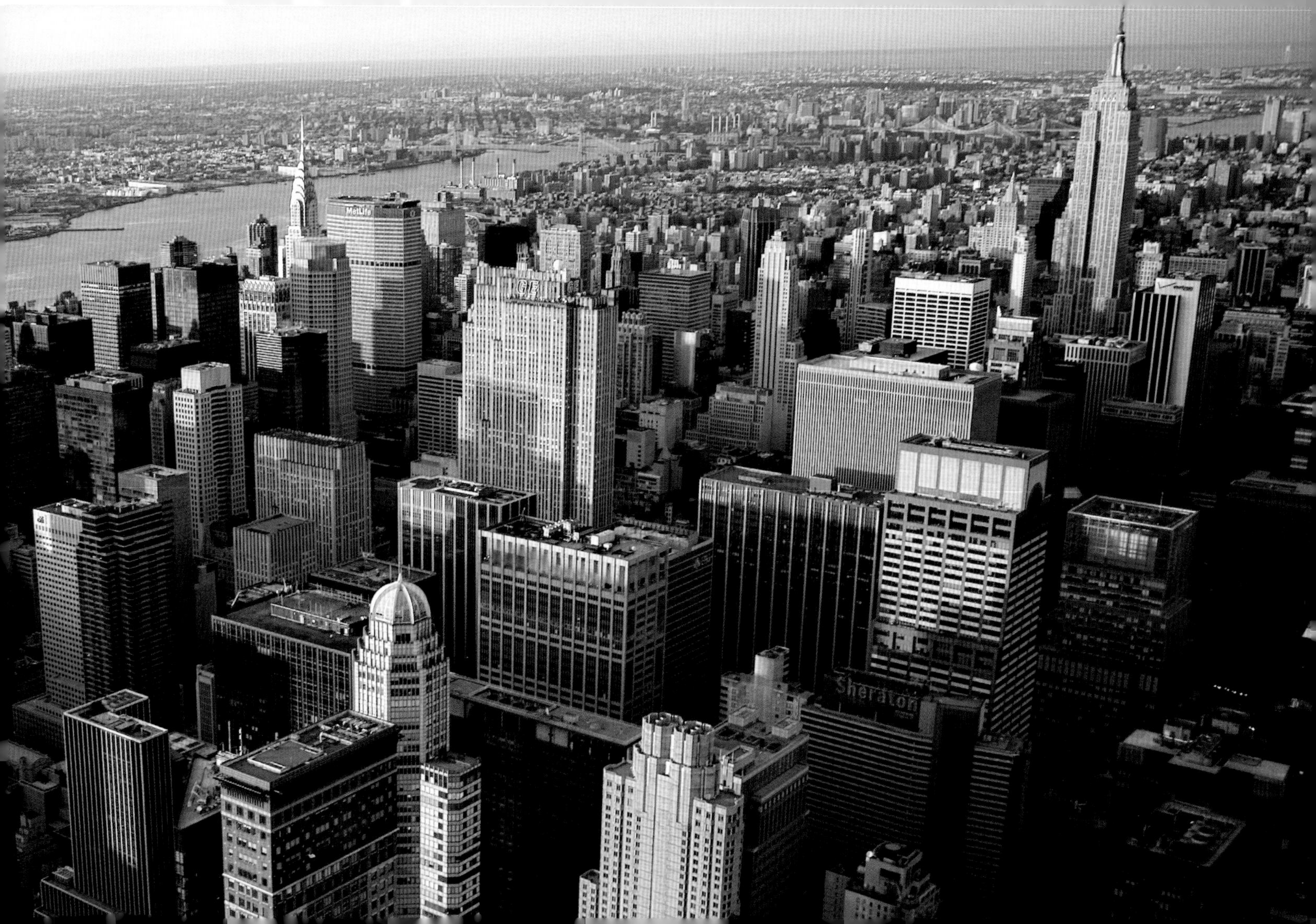
MetLife
GE
Sheraton

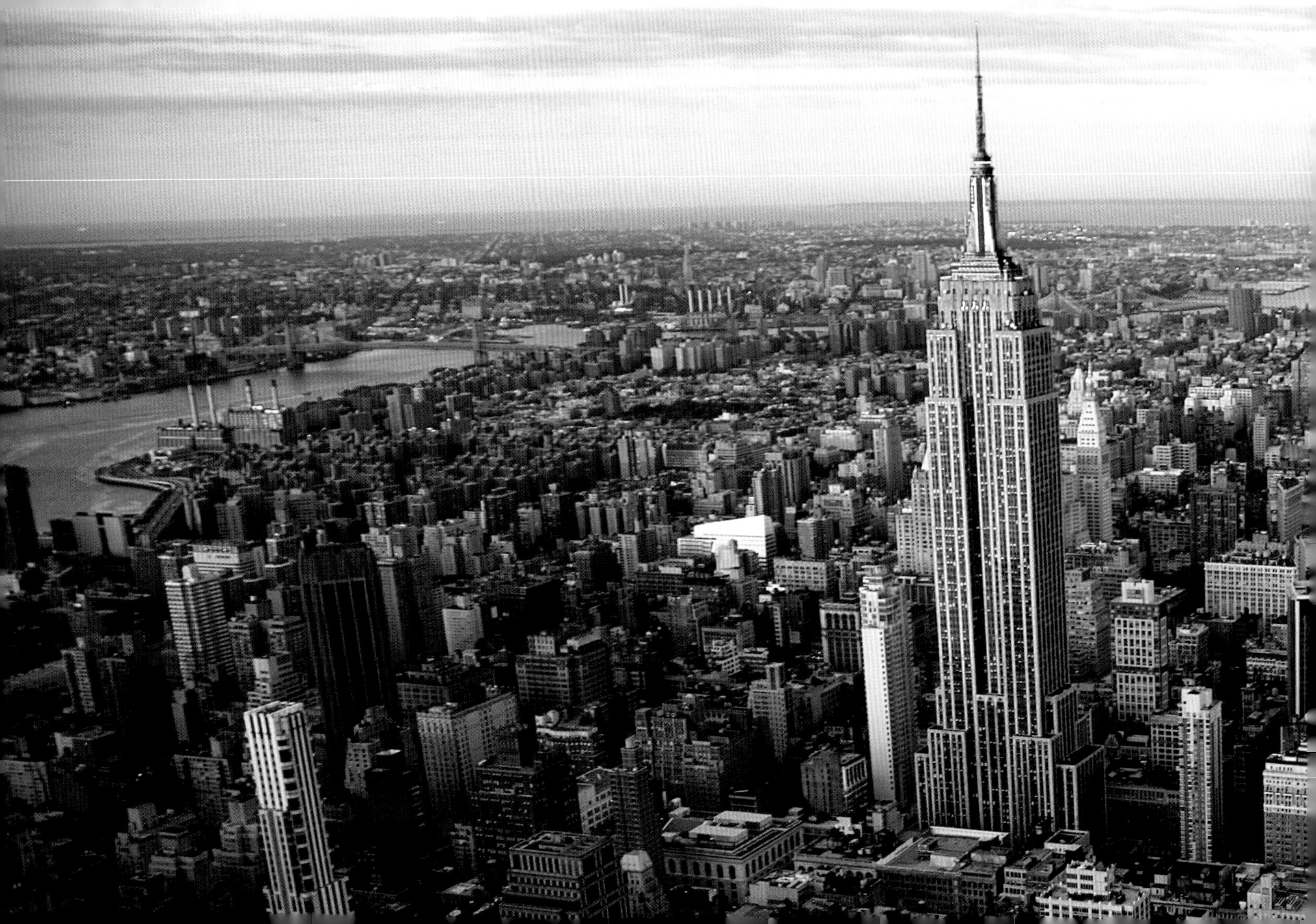

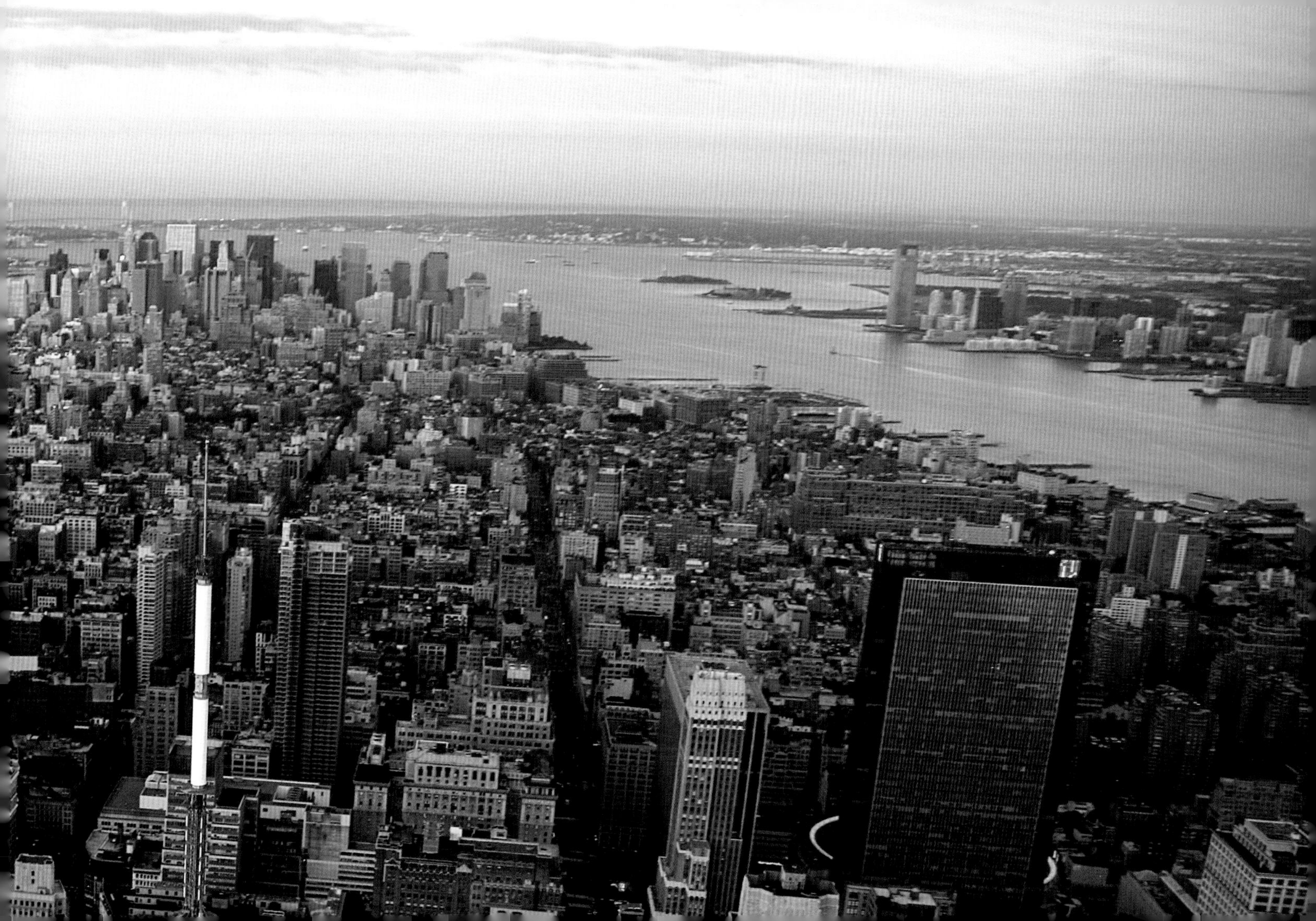

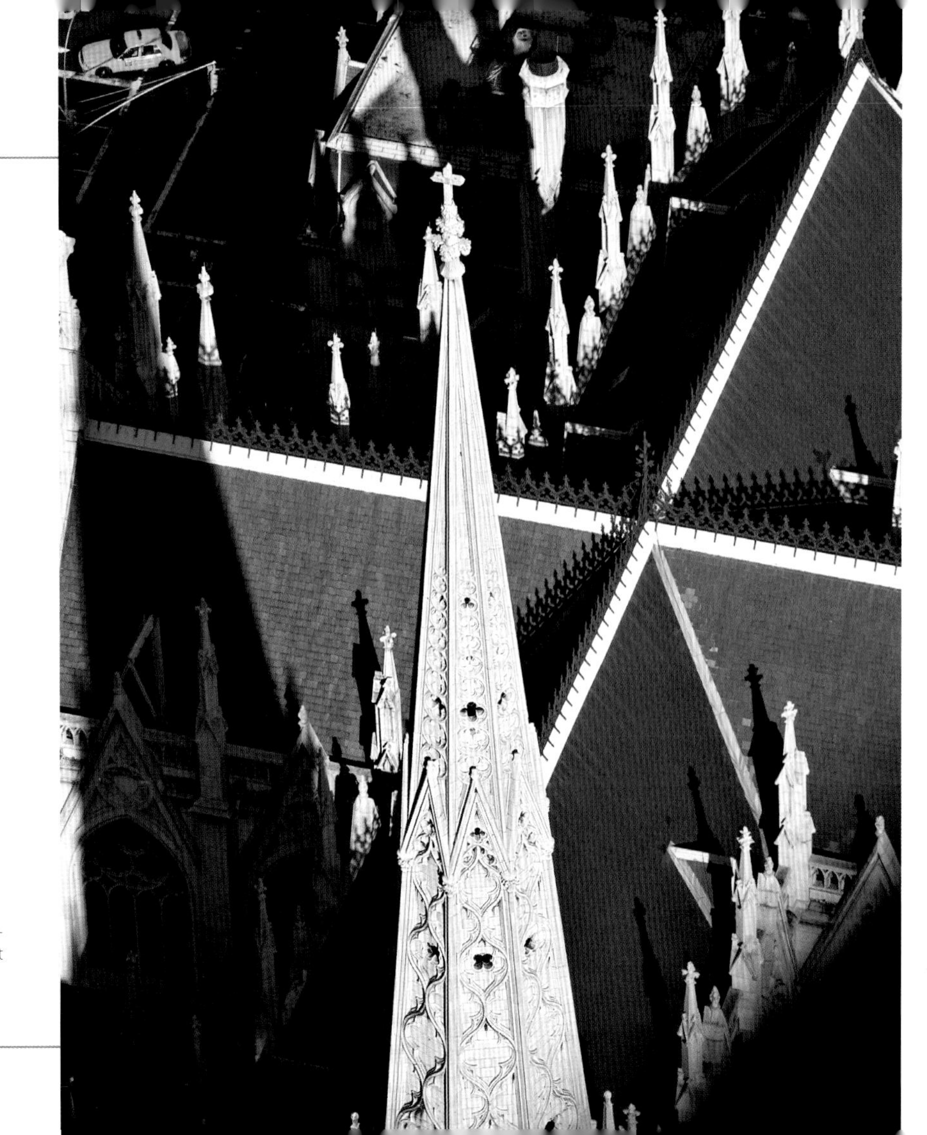

82

The spires of St. Patrick's Cathedral are like sentries standing at attention over Fifth Avenue.

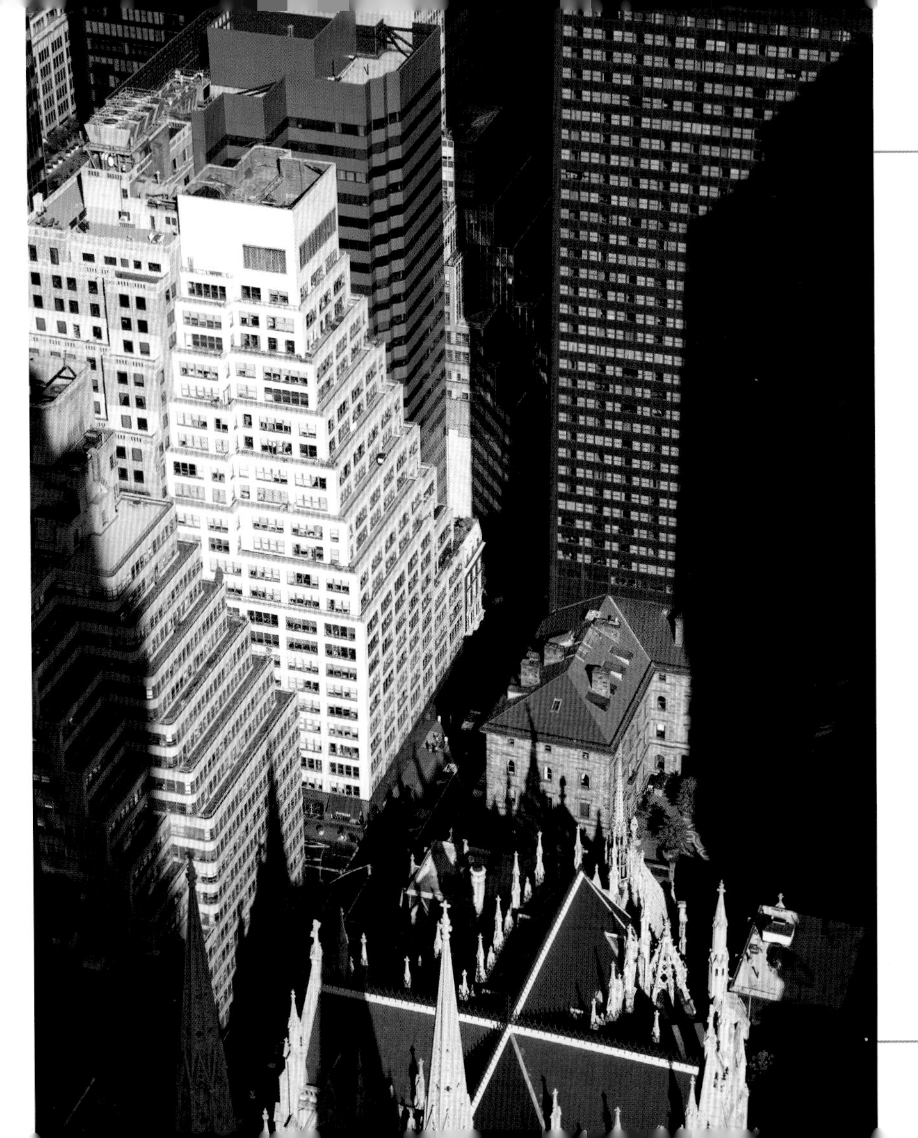

83

St. Patrick's Cathedral, the largest Roman Catholic cathedral in the United States, looms over the Villard Houses on Madison Avenue.

84-85

An American flag flies in front of a bastion of US capitalism, the General Motors bulding, alongside the zig-zag façade of the Trump Building.

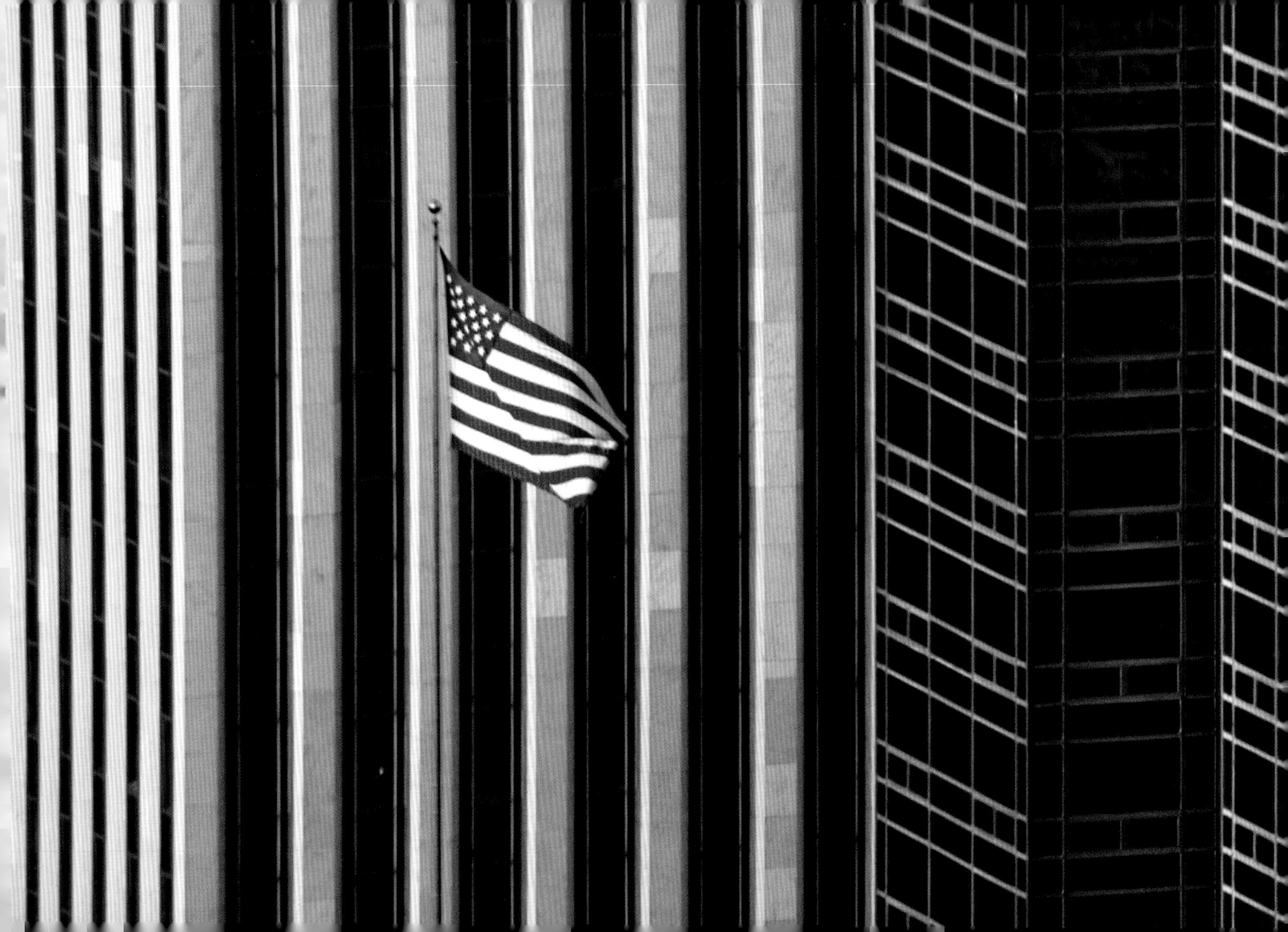

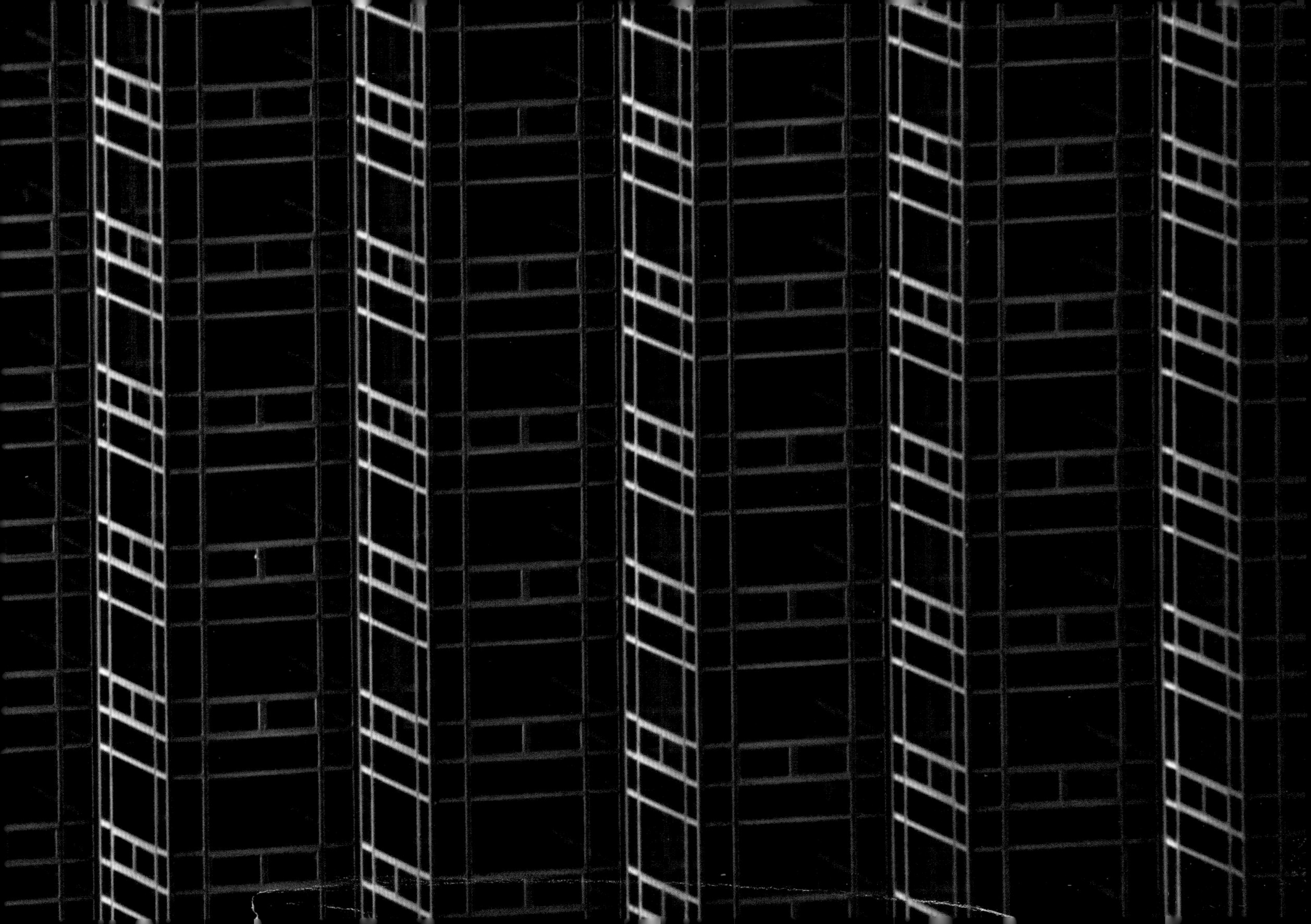

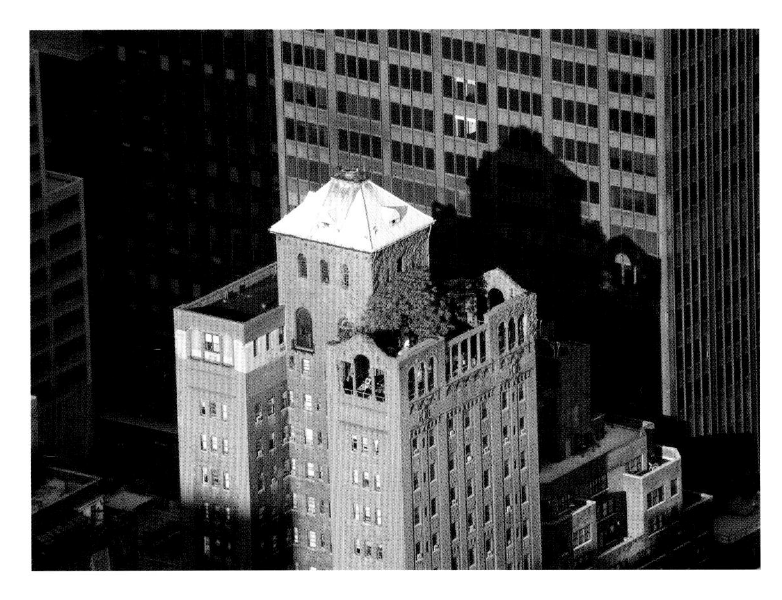

86
Rooftop gardens bring the land to the sky in Manhattan.

87
The Sony Building, 197 meters tall, has an unmistakable perforated façade and has been nicknamed the "Chippendale Building" because of its bizarre design. Its construction was completed in the late Seventies.

88-89
Shades on a midtown office building create changing geometric patterns throughout thc day.

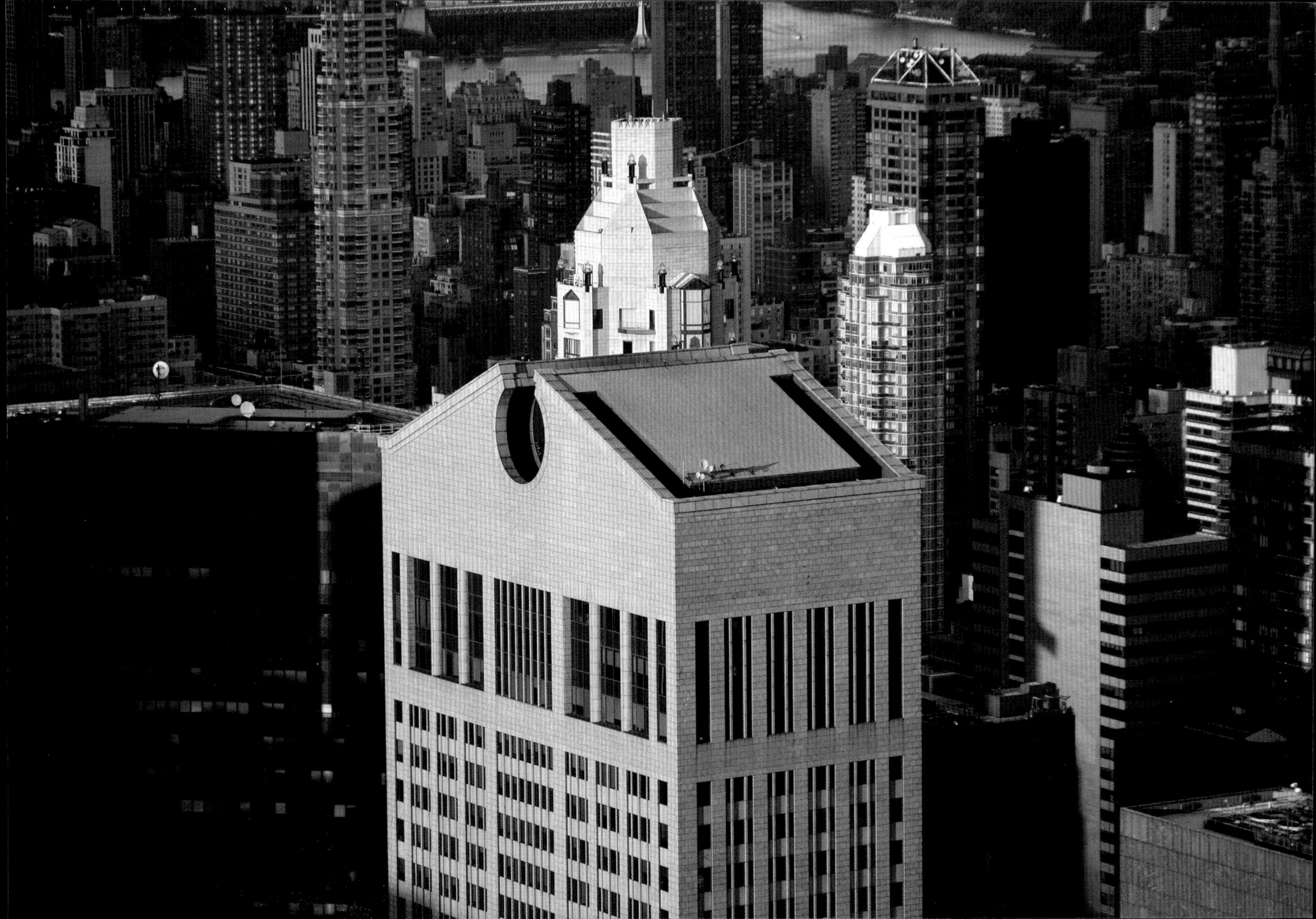

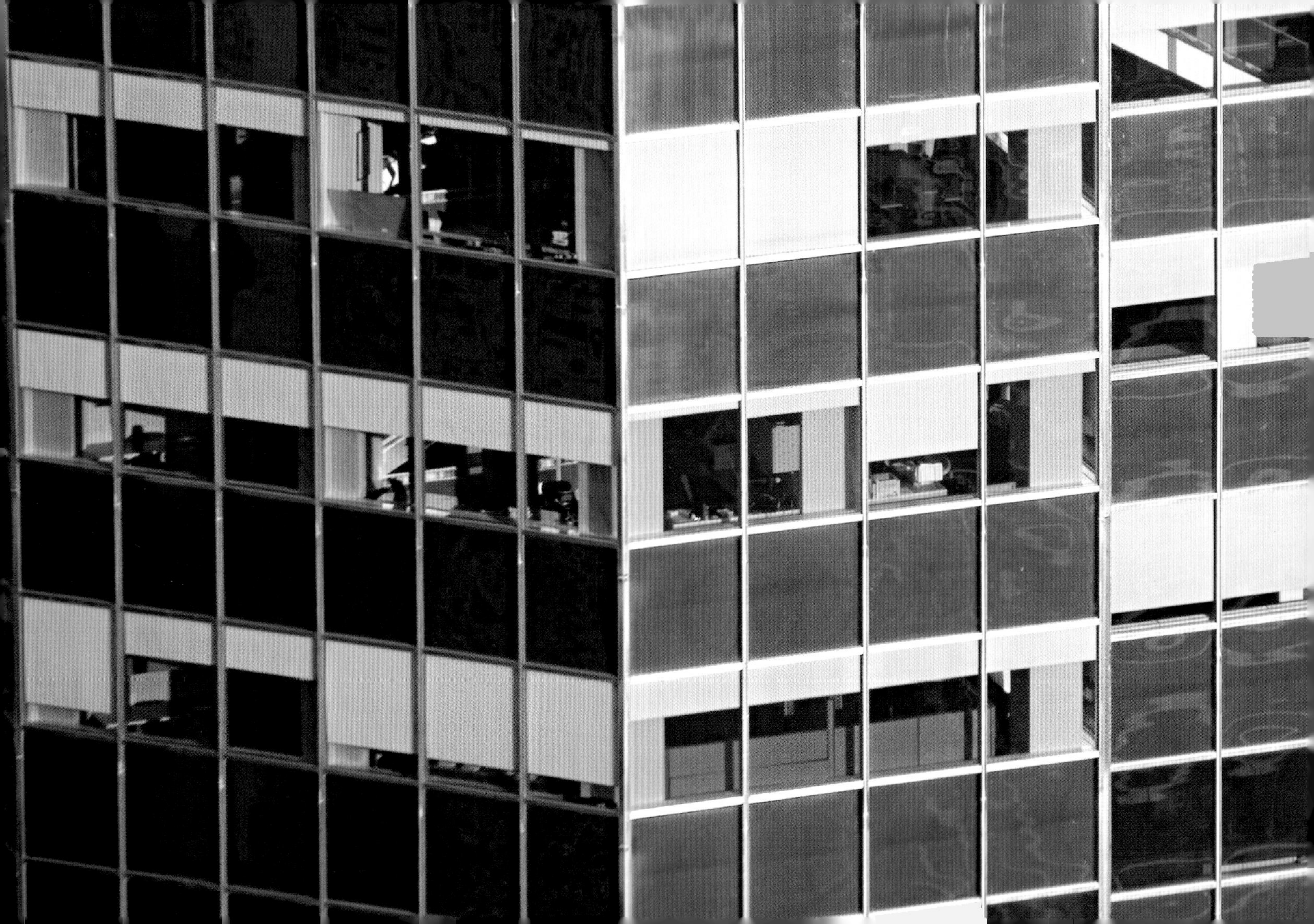

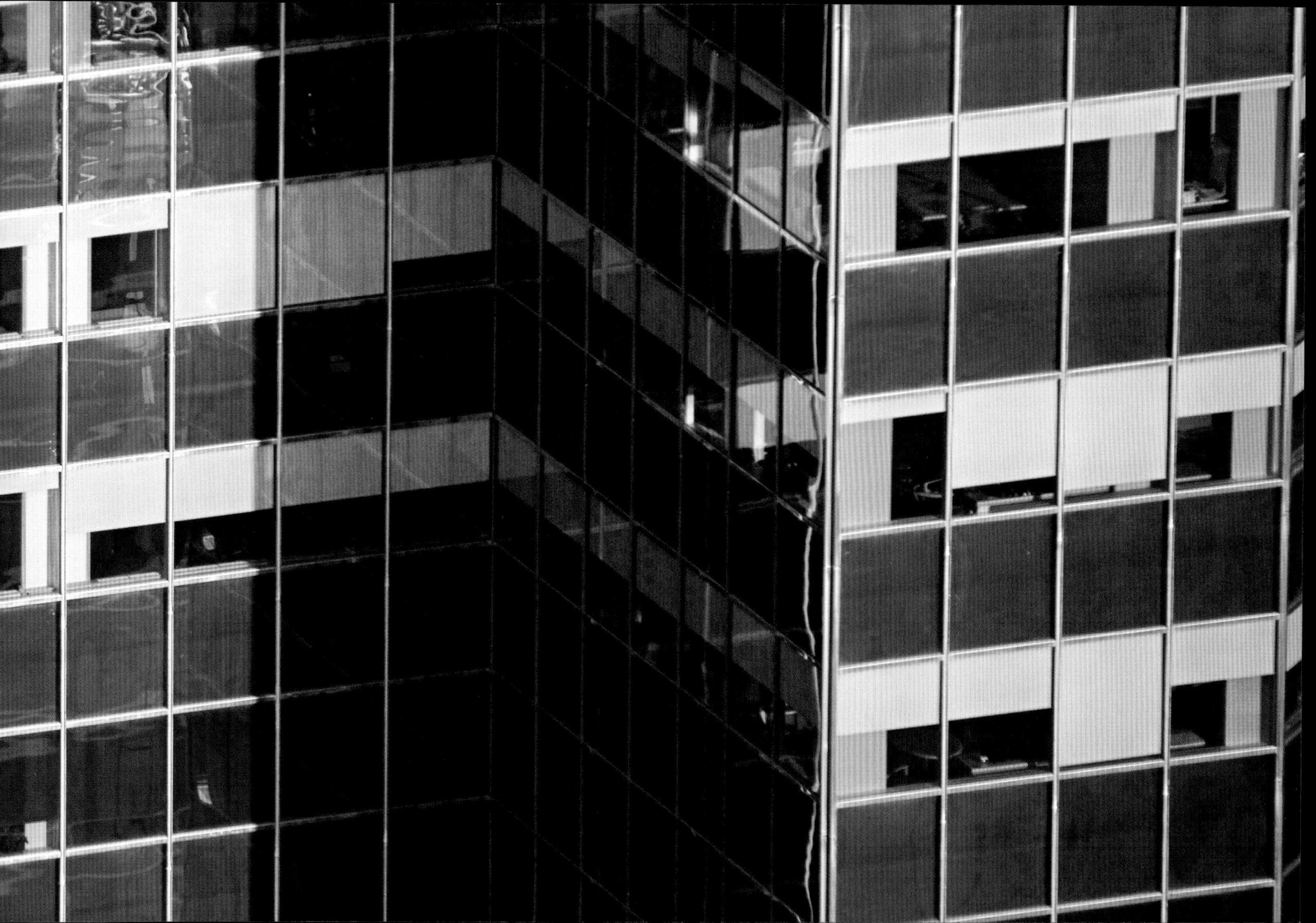

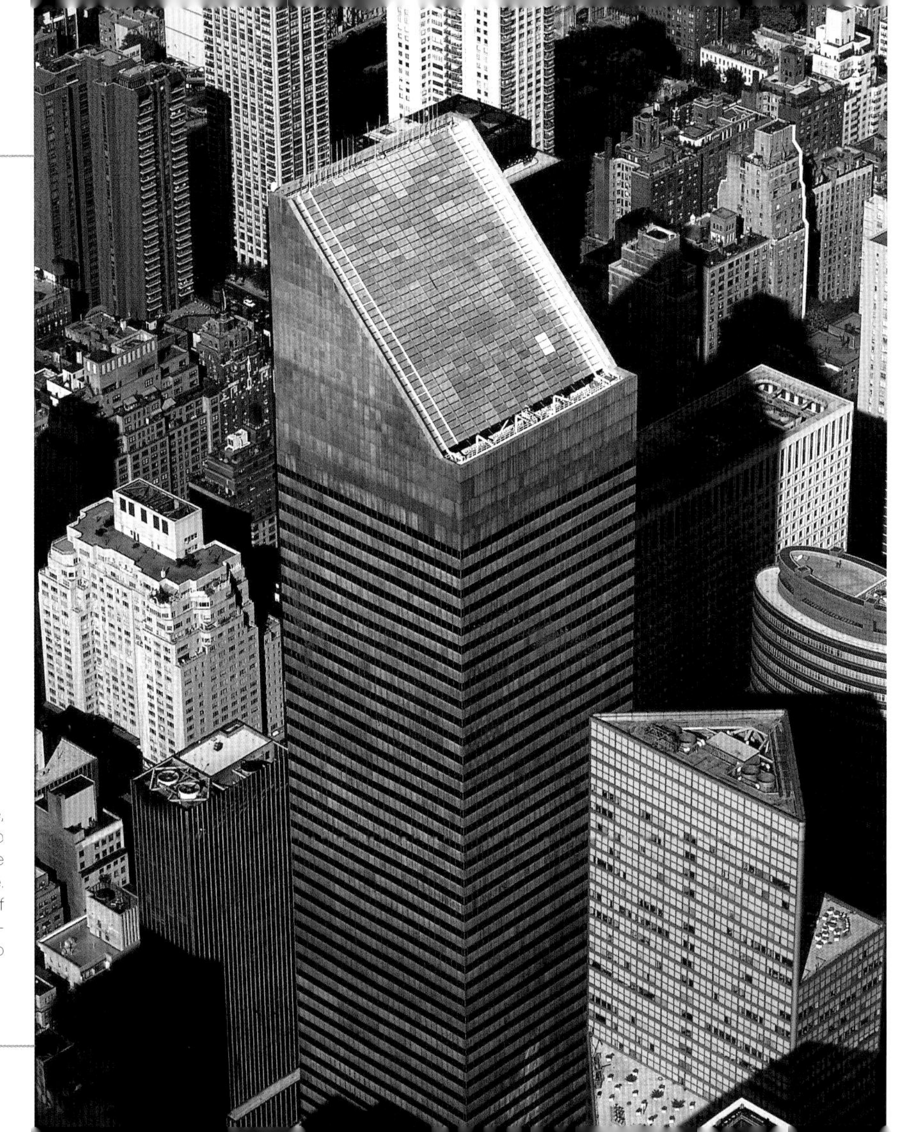

90

Located at 601 Lexington Avenue, the Citicorp Center is one of the most distinctive and recognizable buildings on the New York skyline. It is famous for its intriguing roof with a slope of 45°, originally intended to contain solar panels to provide energy.

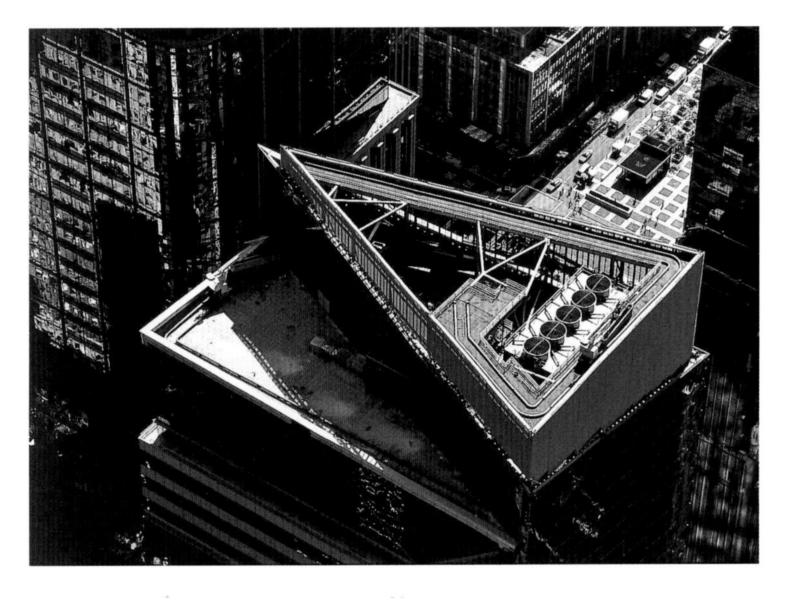

91
Though the roofs of Manhattan's skyscrapers are often used to hold elevator systems or air conditioners, this does not detract from the extraordinary visual impact of these modern works of art.

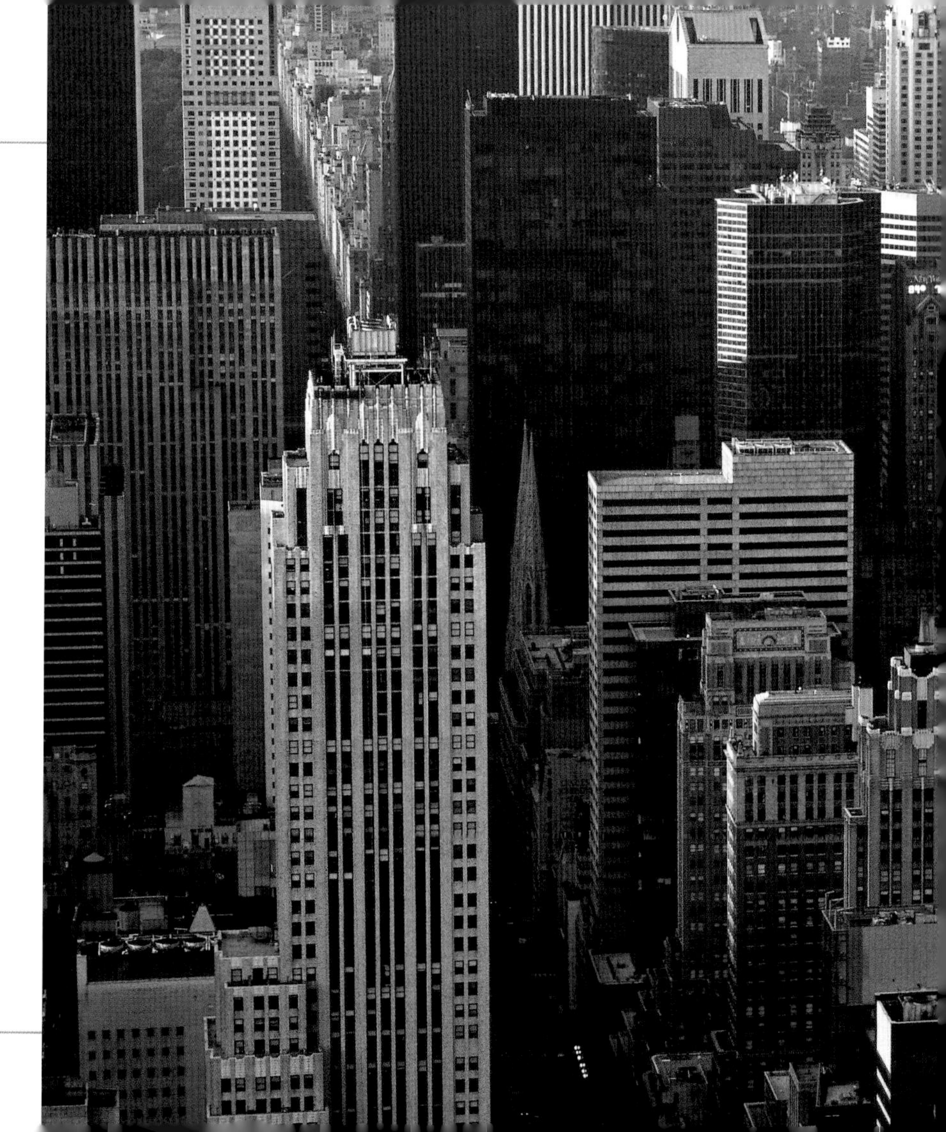

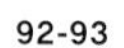

92-93
The octagonal Bear Stearns Headquarters (center) reflects the angles of the MetLife Building that rises above Grand Central Station.

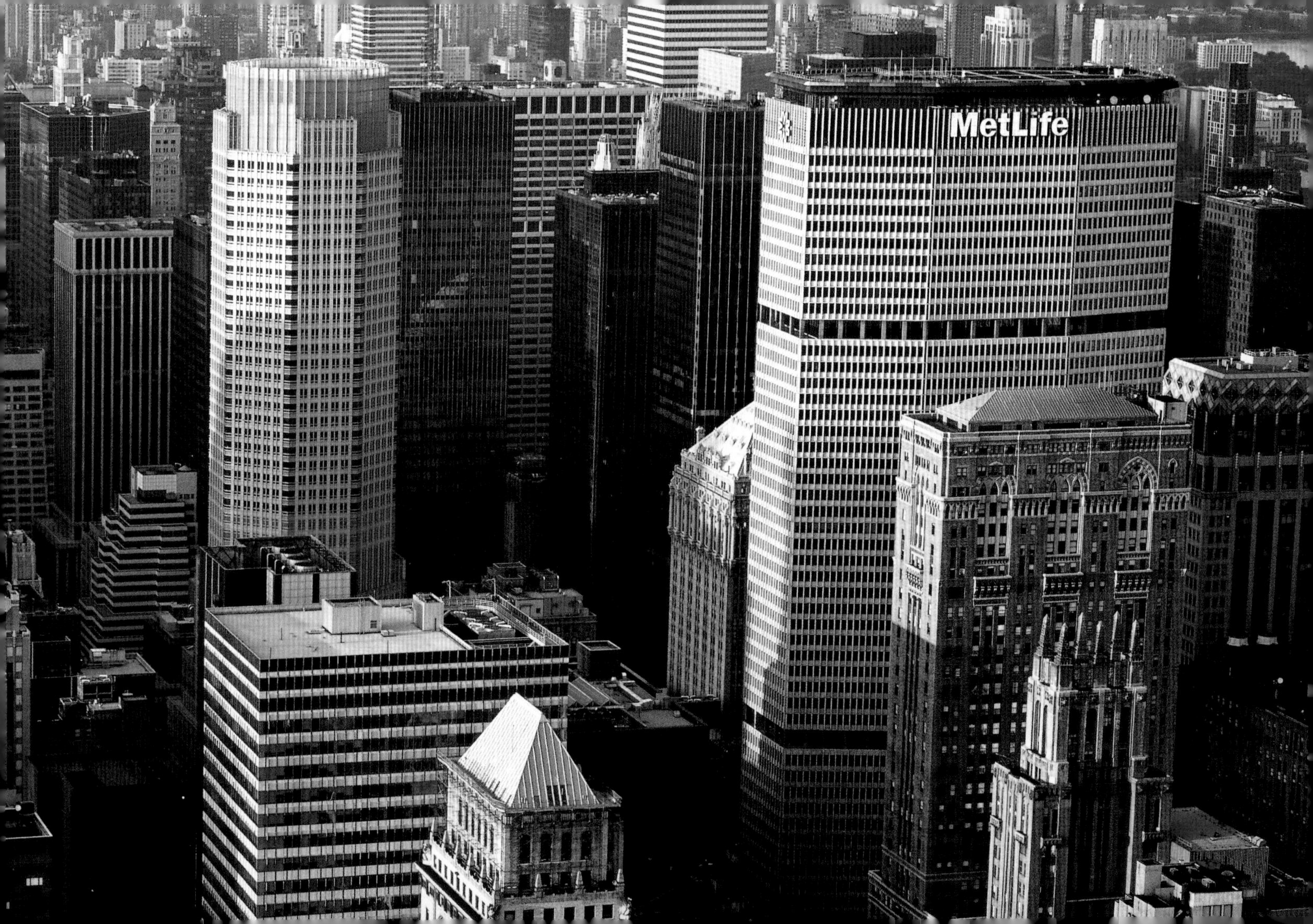
MetLife

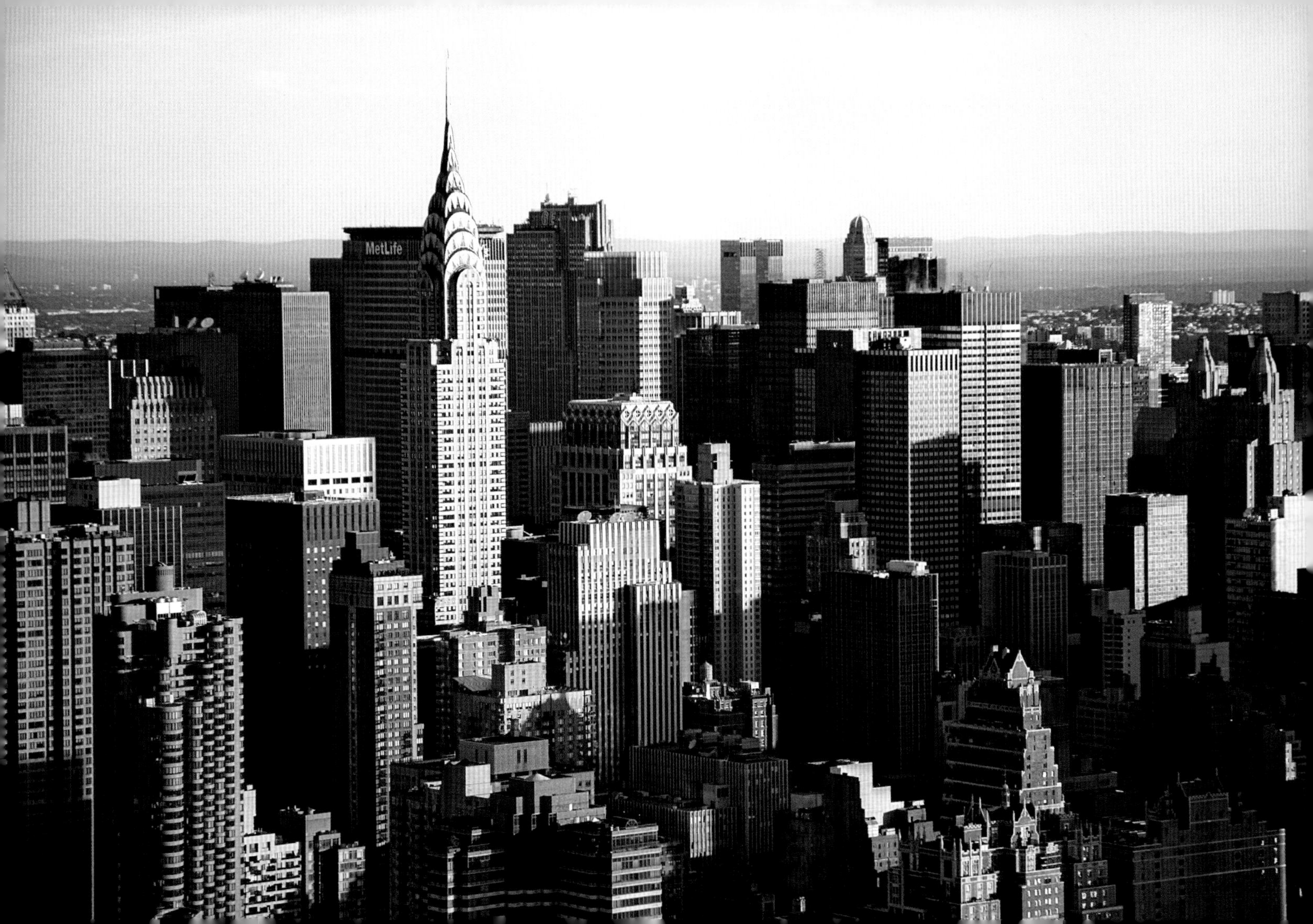
MetLife

94
Tudor City, an historic "city within a city" apartment and retail complex, is dwarfed by midtown landmarks like the Chrysler and MetLife buildings.

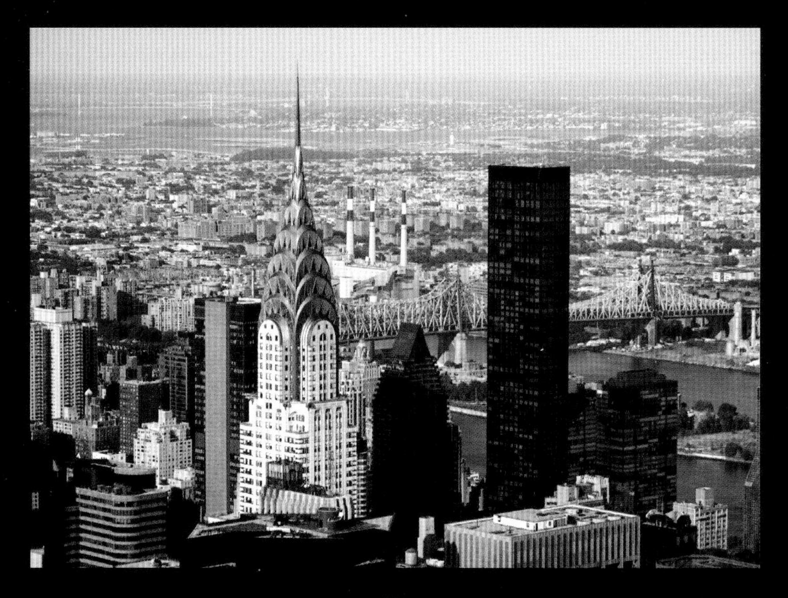

96
The graceful arches of the Chrysler Building are a dramatic counter-point to the stark, black Trump World Tower.

97
One of the most beloved skyscrapers in New York, the Chrysler Building, stands near one of the most criticized, the MetLife Building.

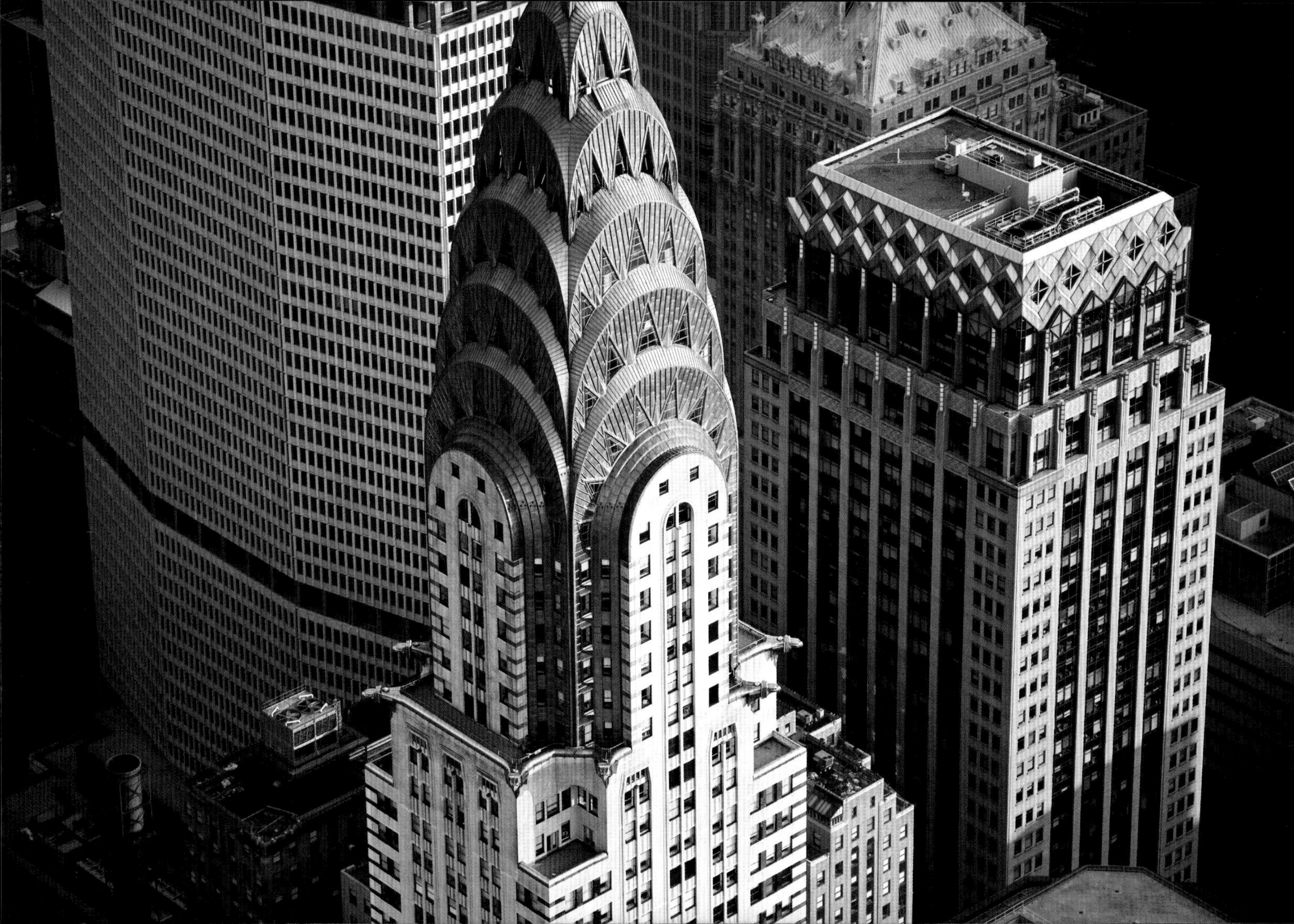

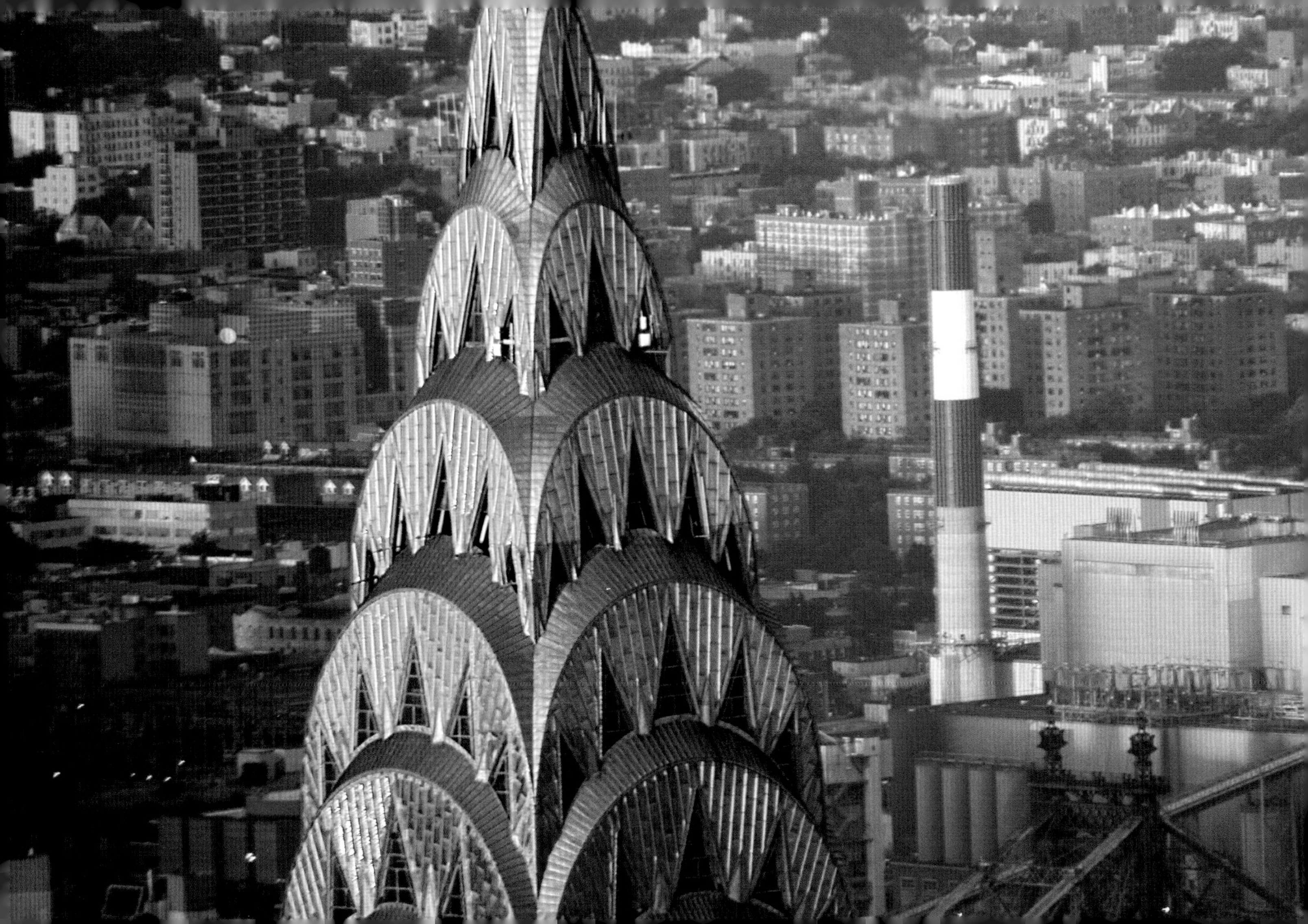

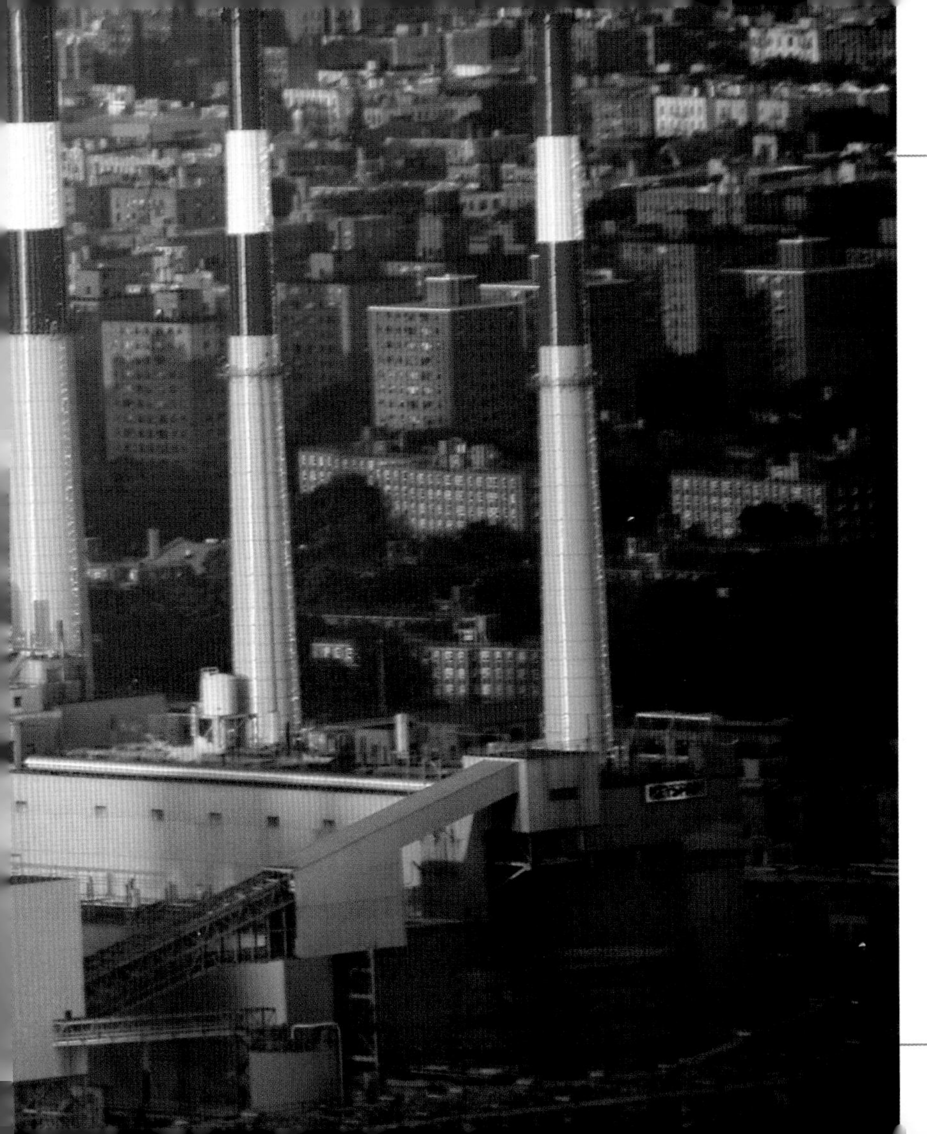

98-99

The stainless steel of the Chrysler Building reflects the bright red of the ConEd power plant in the borough of Queens across the East River.

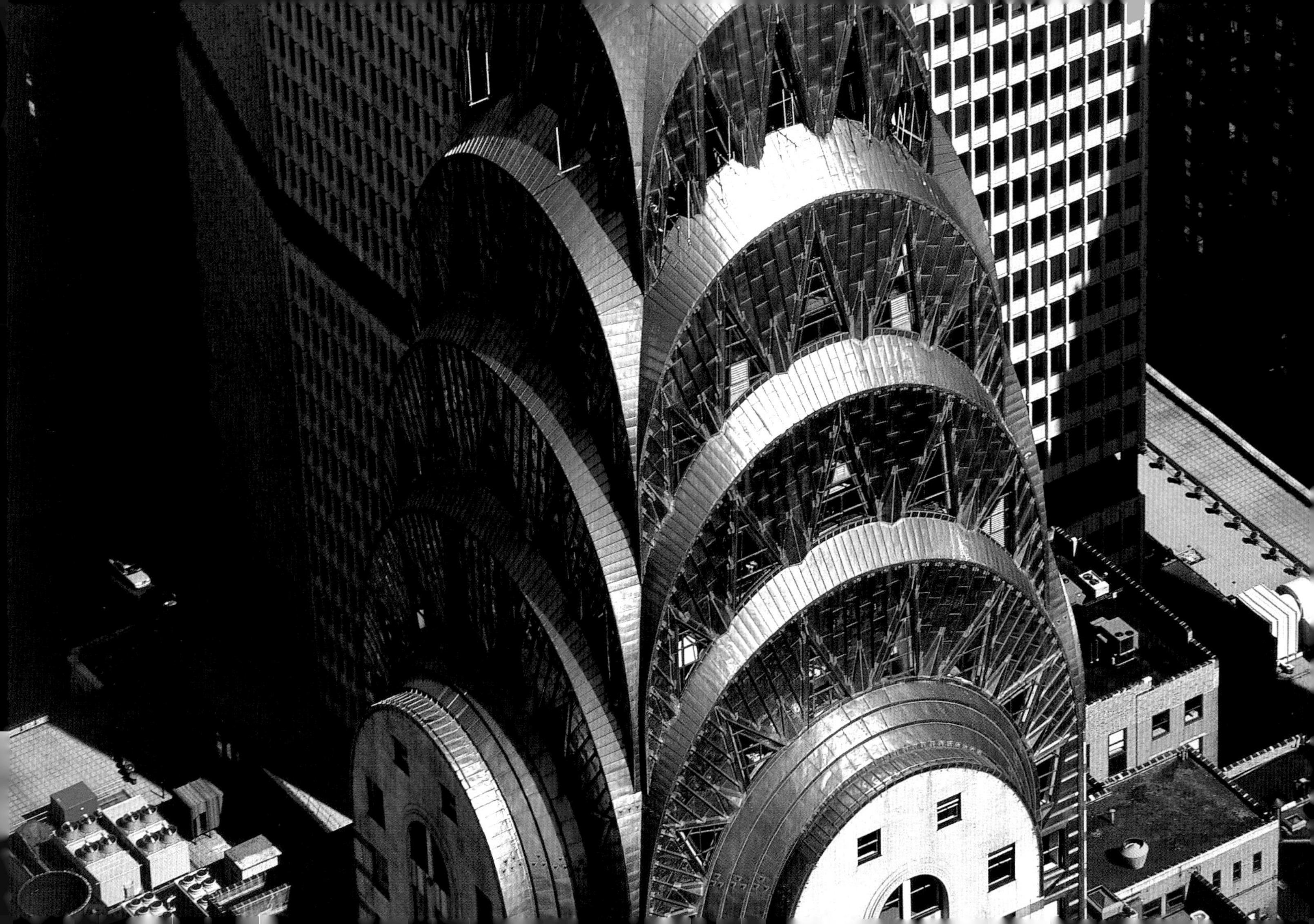

FLYING HIGH NEW YORK

100
Much of the detail of the Chrysler Building is only visible from the sky.

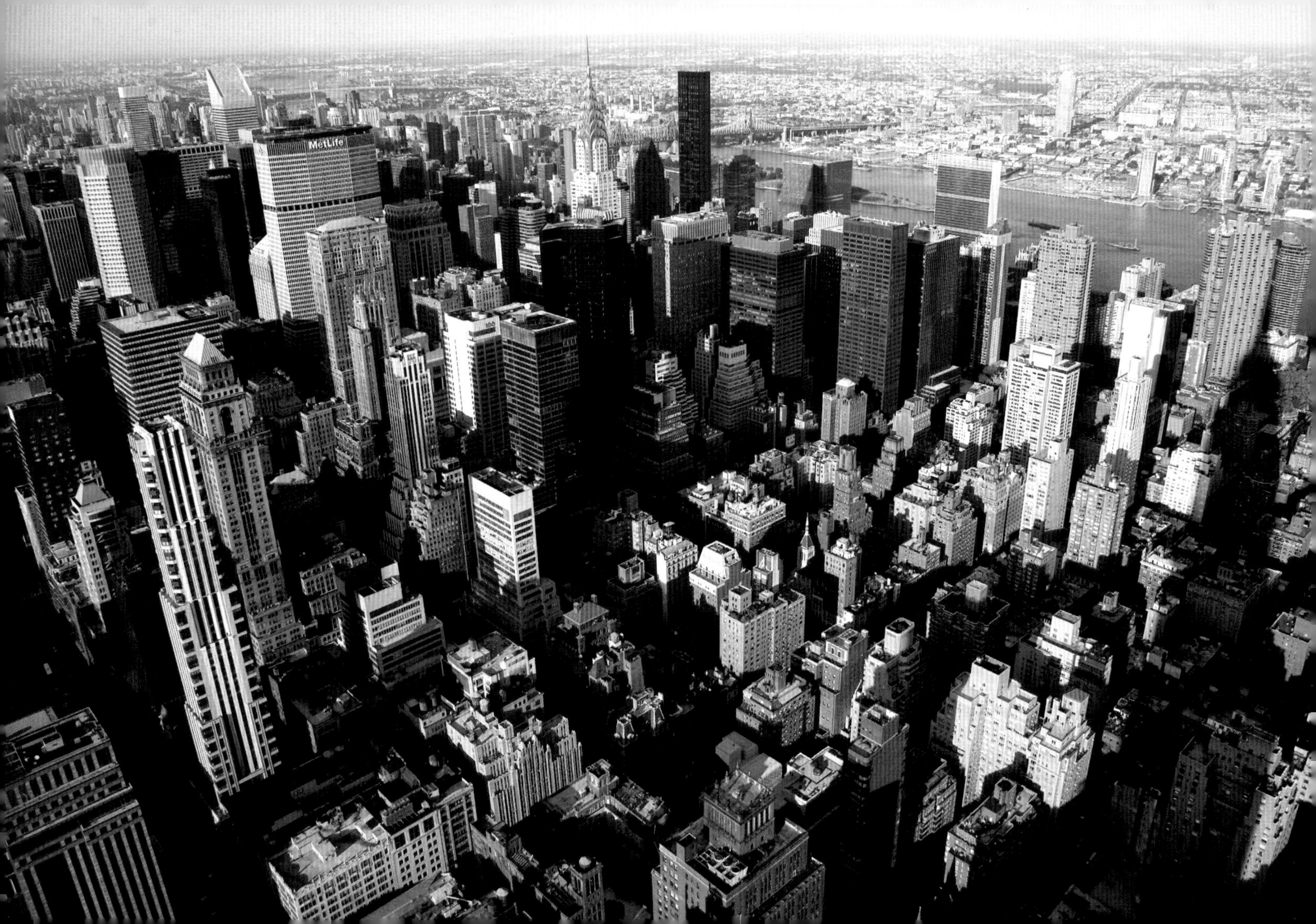
MetLife

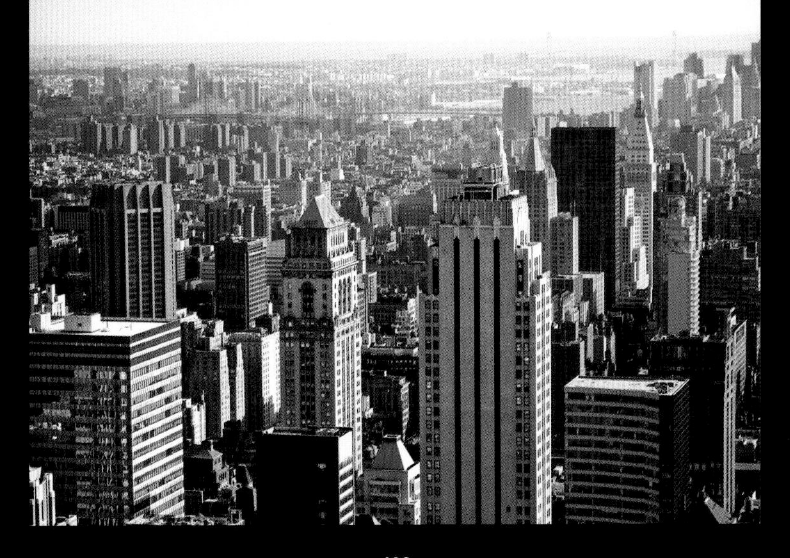

102
The low-rise buildings of Murray Hill and Kips Bay give way to the sky-scrapers of Midtown.

103
Looking south, towards Murray Hill and downtown Manhattan, the scale of buildings decreases.

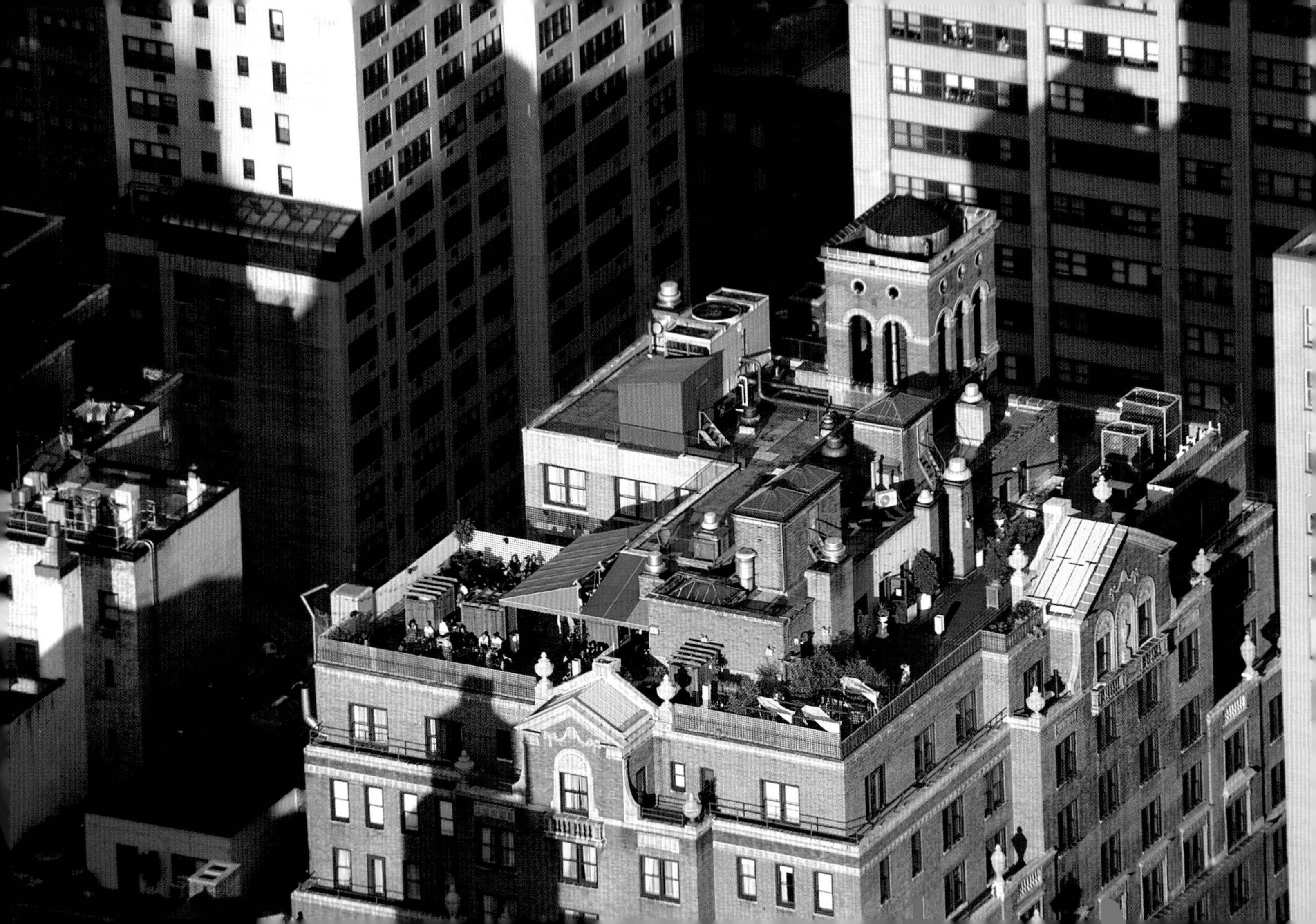

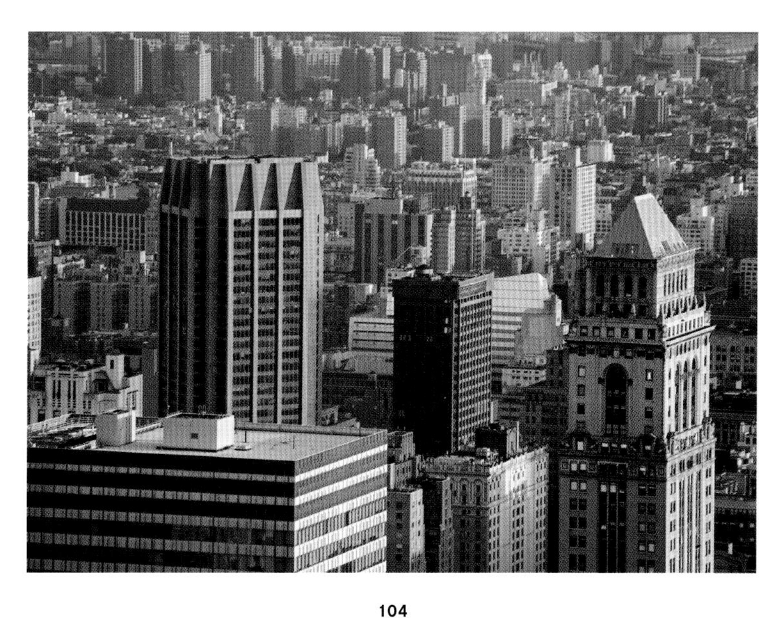

104
A rooftop garden in Murray Hill is the perfect place for an after-work refreshment.

105
Tucked between Art Deco and Post-Modern buildings is the dramatic white facade of Baruch College's Vertical Campus.

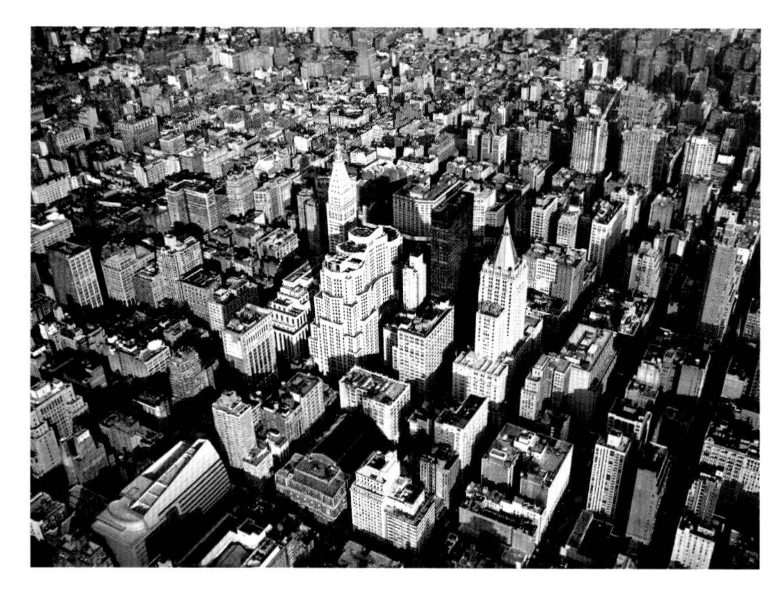

106
The spires of the New York Life and Metropolitan Life Towers rise above Madison Square Park, near the Flatiron District.

107
The bottom part of the photo shows the south edge of Madison Square Park, the former site of Madison Square Garden, with the towering triangular Flatiron Building.

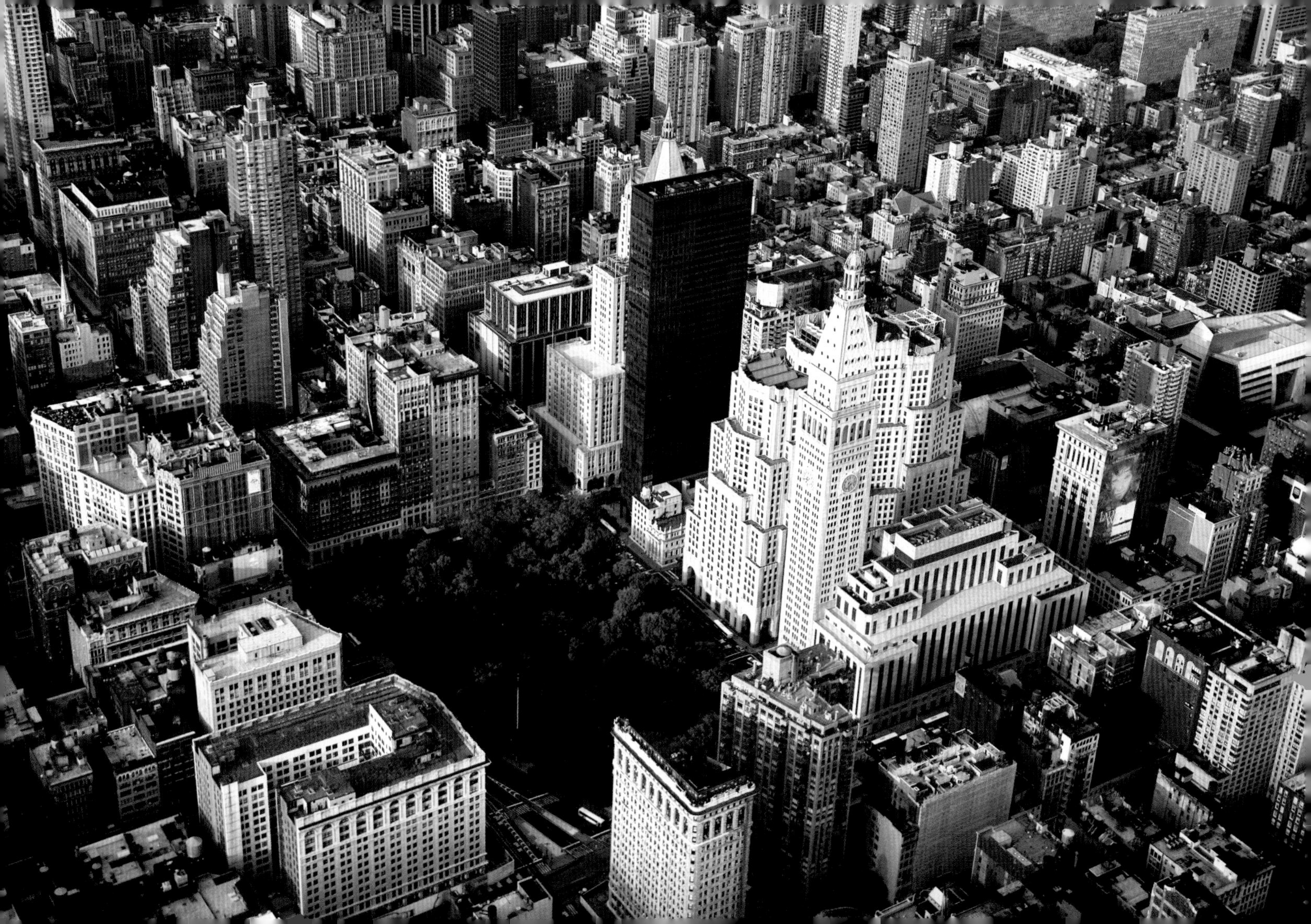

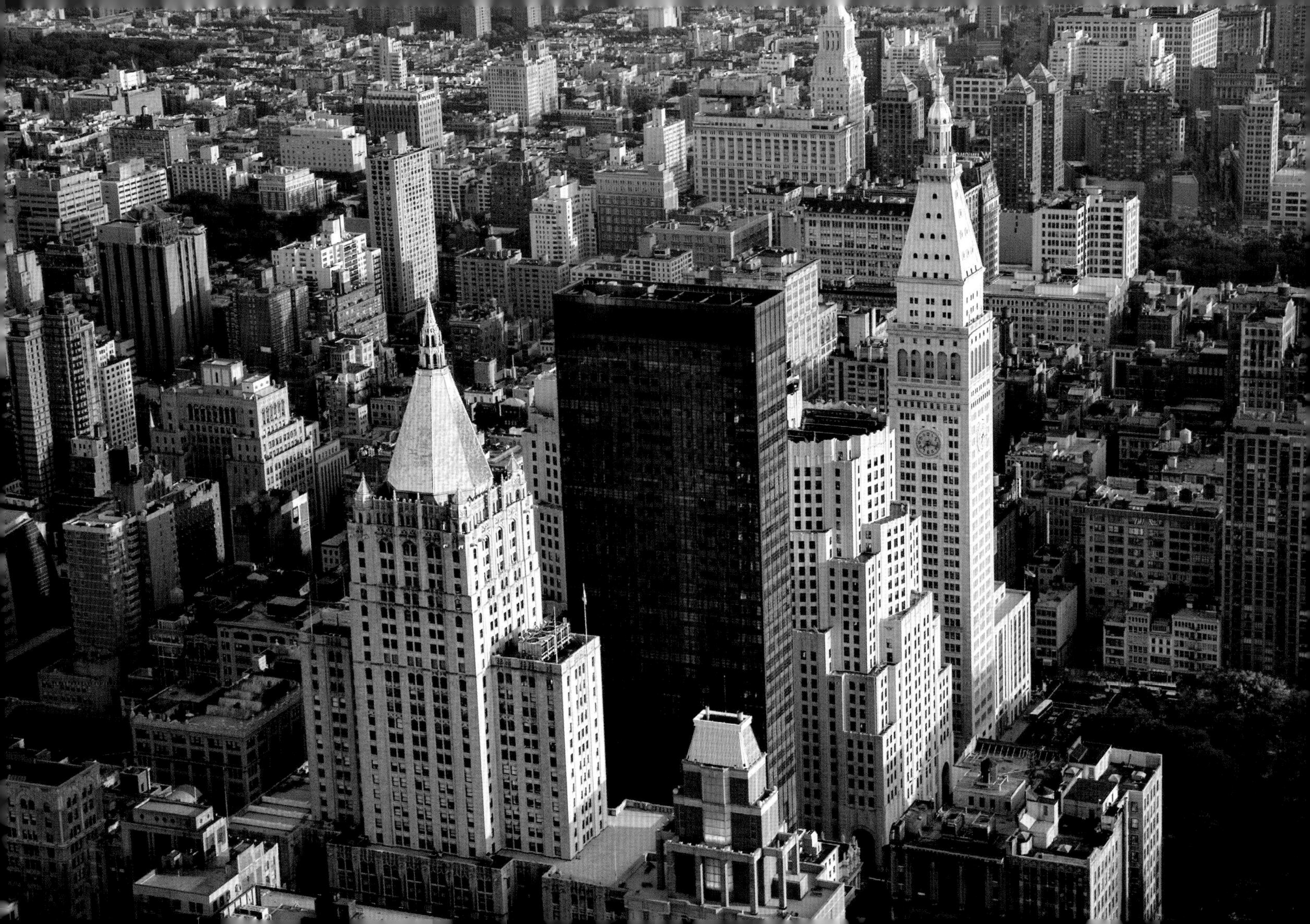

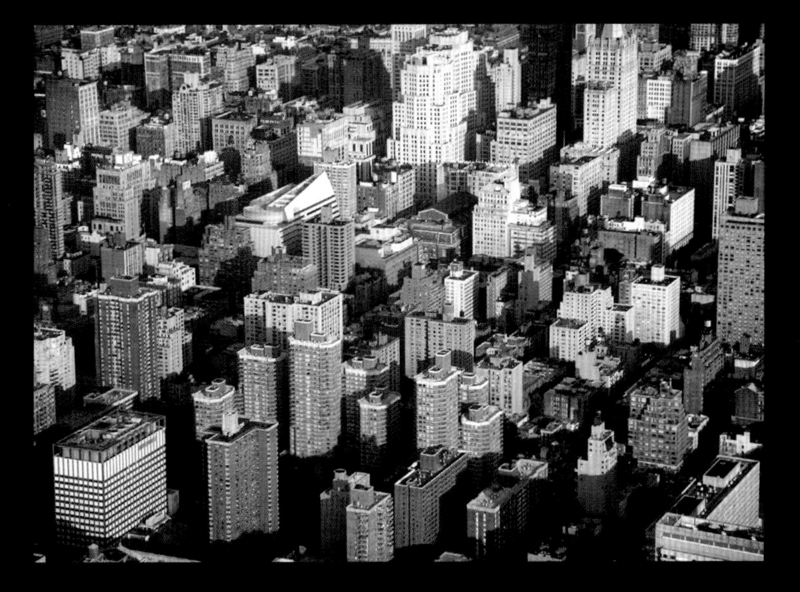

108

The gold-spired New York Life Building and the clocktower of the Metropolitan Life Insurance Building, modeled after the *campanile* at St. Mark's Square in Venice, both overlook Madison Square Park.

109

The Upper East Side stretches from 59th Street to 96th Street, between Central Park and the East River and is renowned for its world-famous museums, such as the Metropolitan Museum of Art, the Guggenheim Museum, the Jewish Museum and the Museum of the City of New York.

111
The Brutalist bulk of the MetLife Building overpowers the gothic-arched Lincoln Building across 42nd Street.

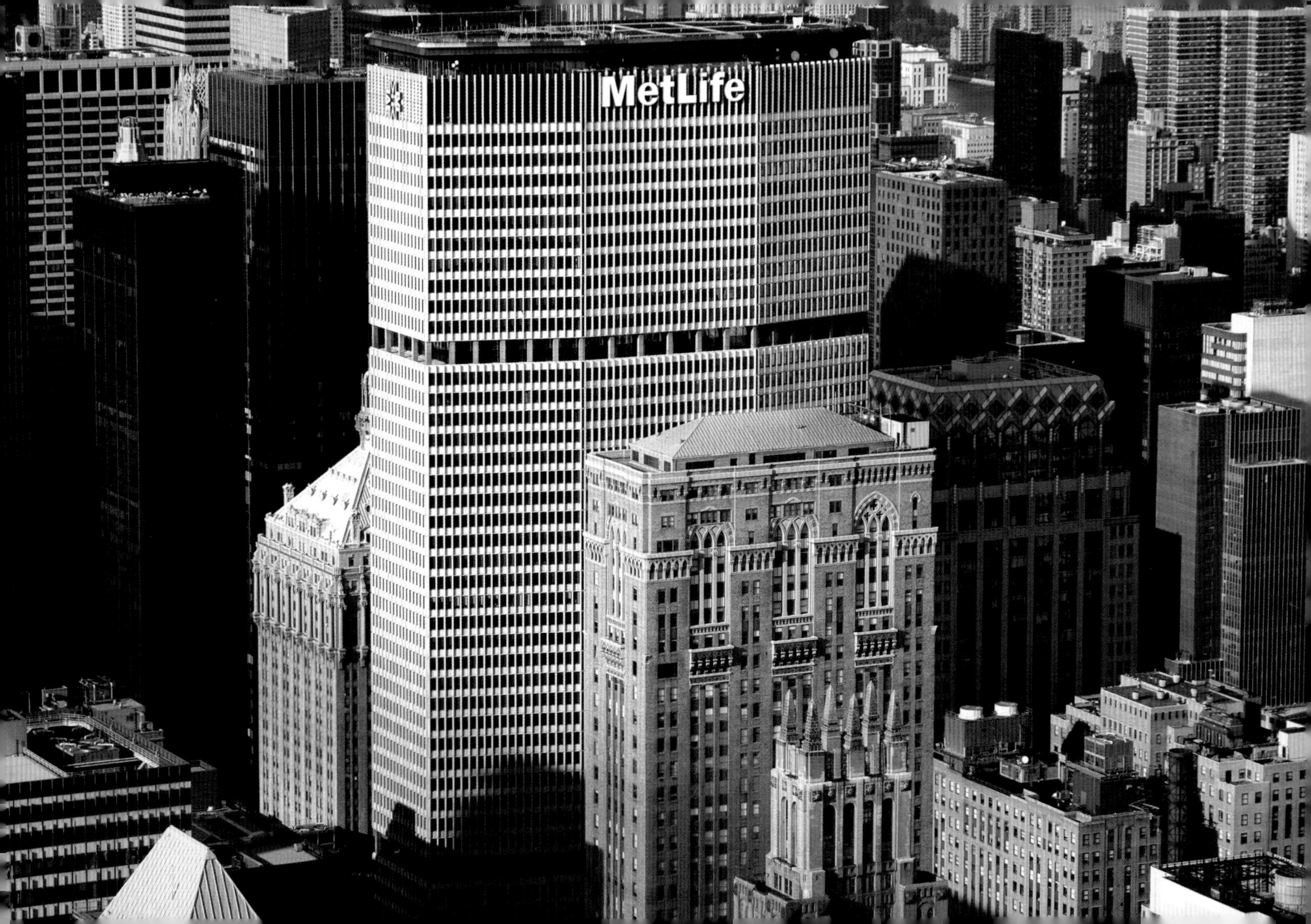
MetLife

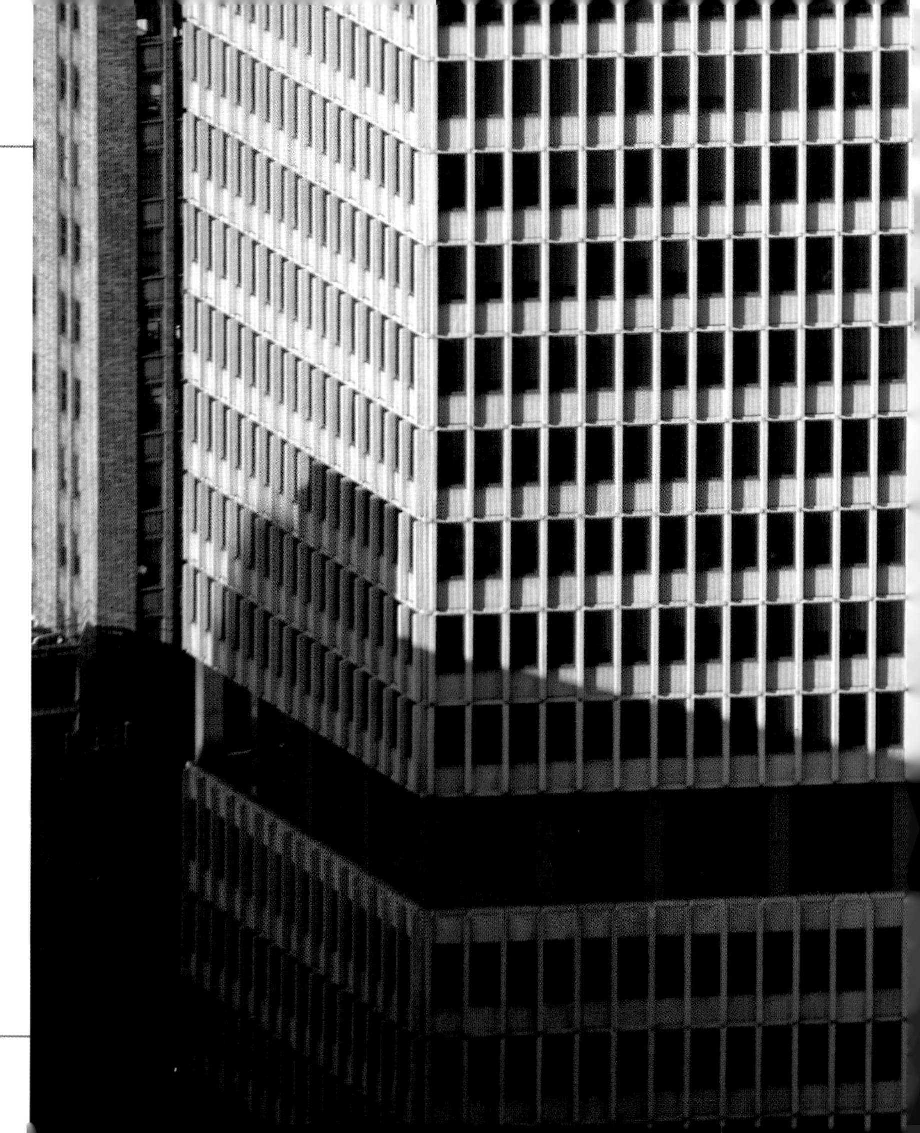

112-113
Two major examples of Art Deco architecture built in the early 20th-Century, the Lincoln Building and 295 Madison Avenue flaunt adornments, unlike the stark, angular MetLife Building.

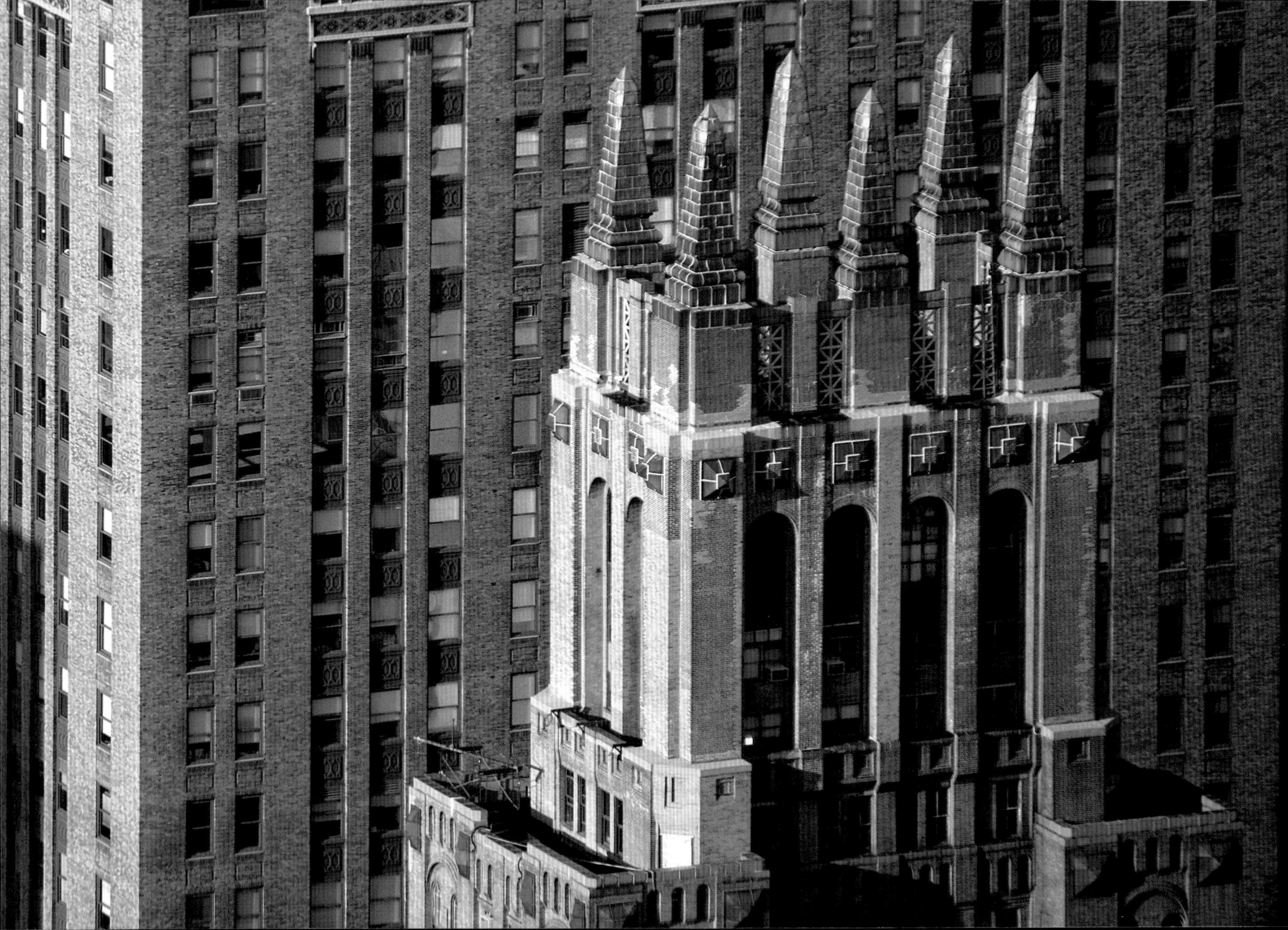

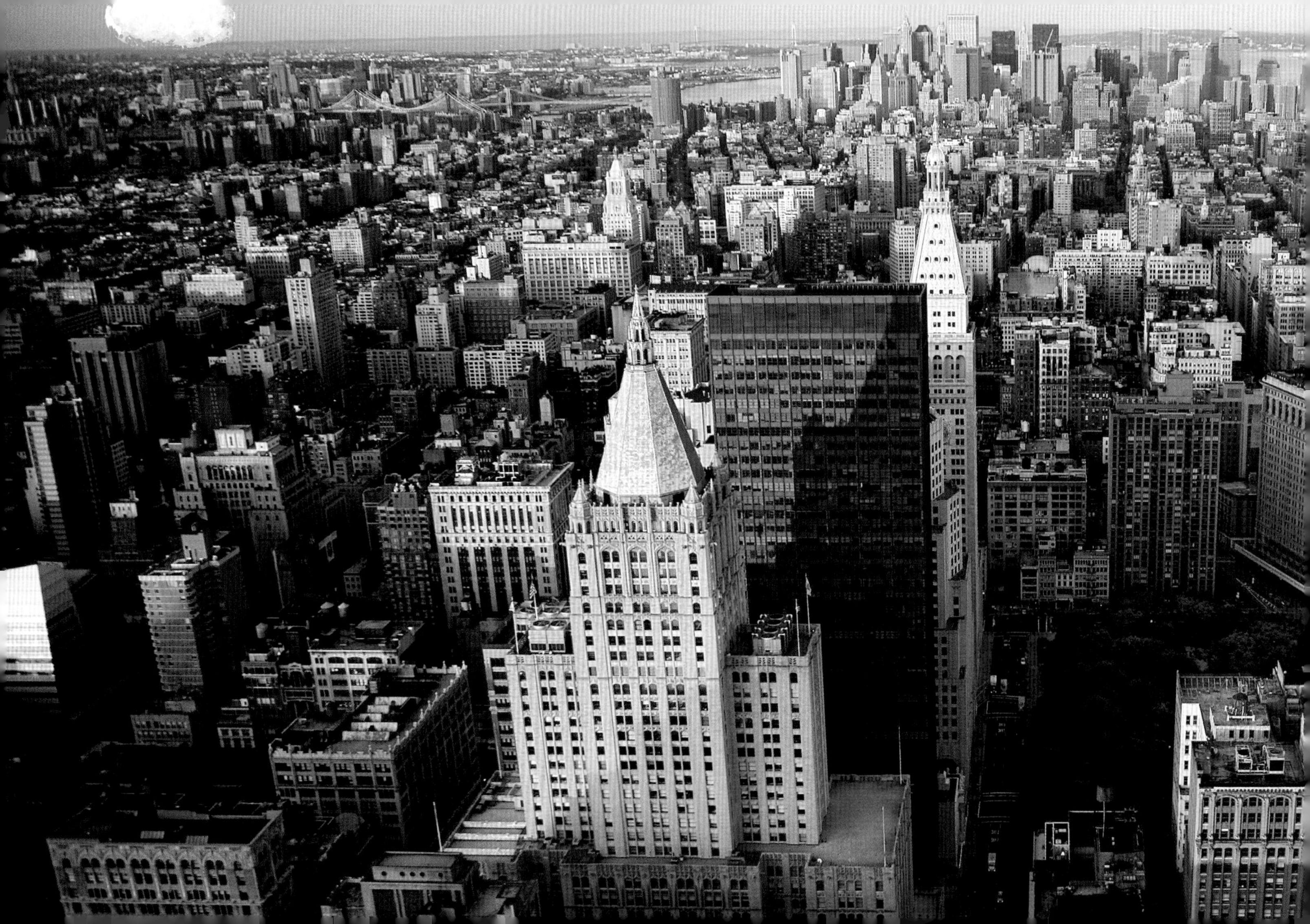

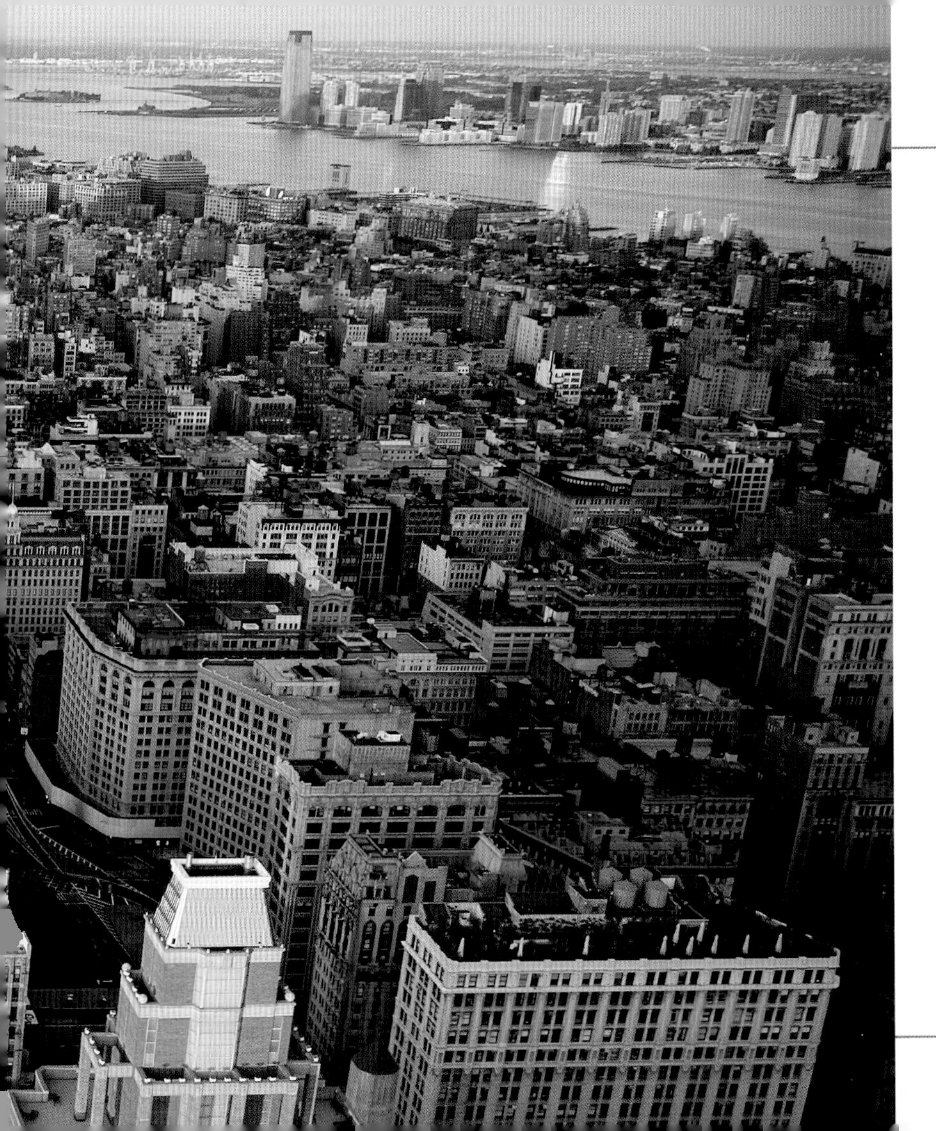

114-115

The Flatiron Building, which is situated on the southeast corner of Madison Square Park, where Broadway and Fifth Avenue cross, is the oldest skyscraper of Manhattan.

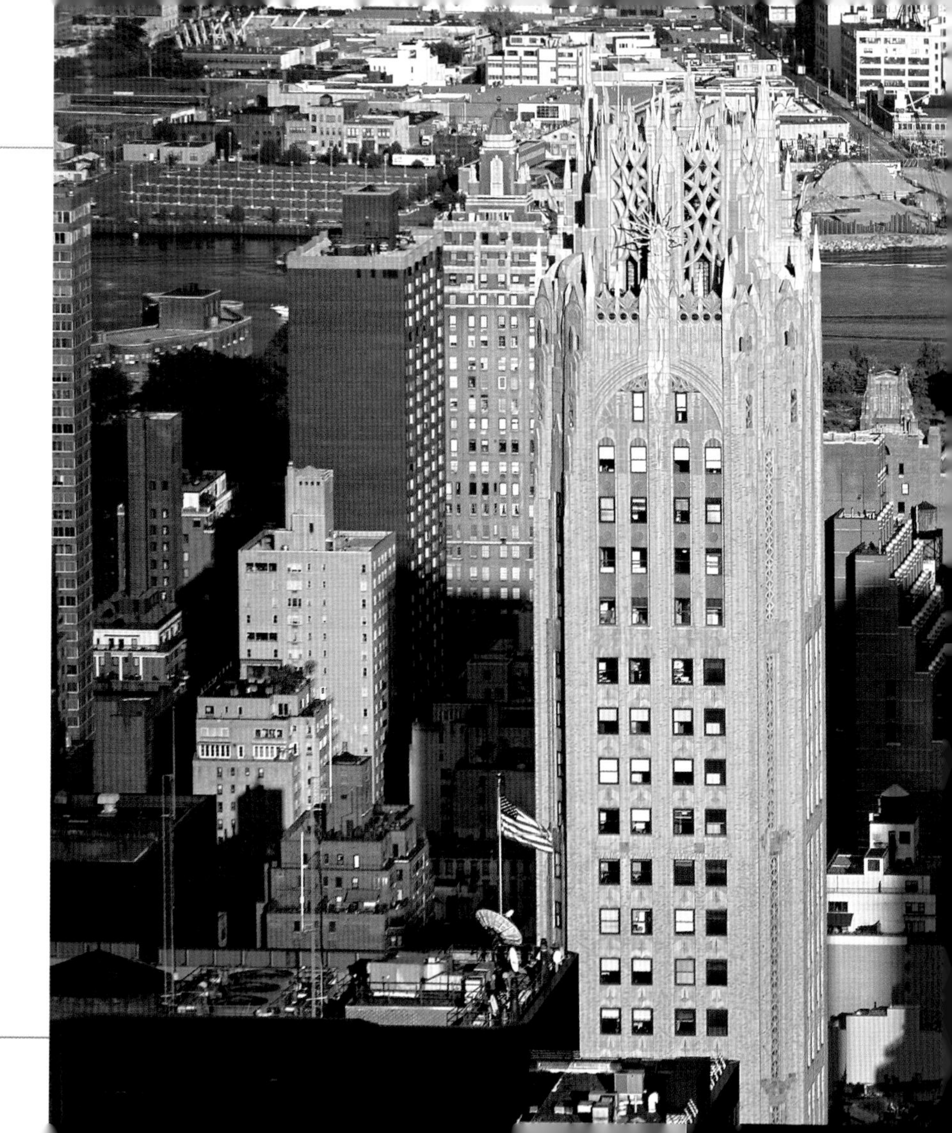

116-117
The rose-colored granite of the General Electric Tower on Lexington Avenue complements the verdigris towers of the Waldorf Astoria Hotel.

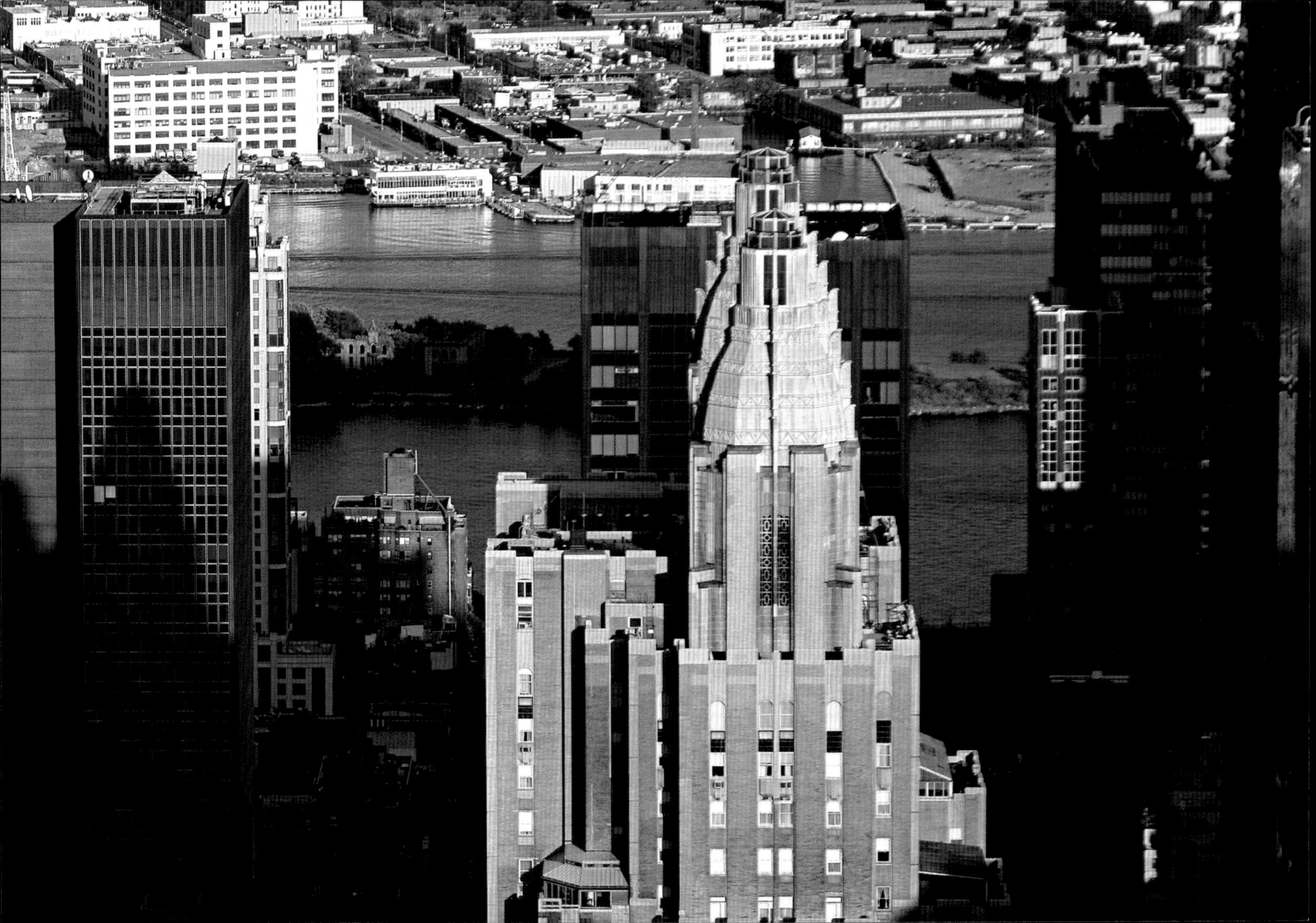

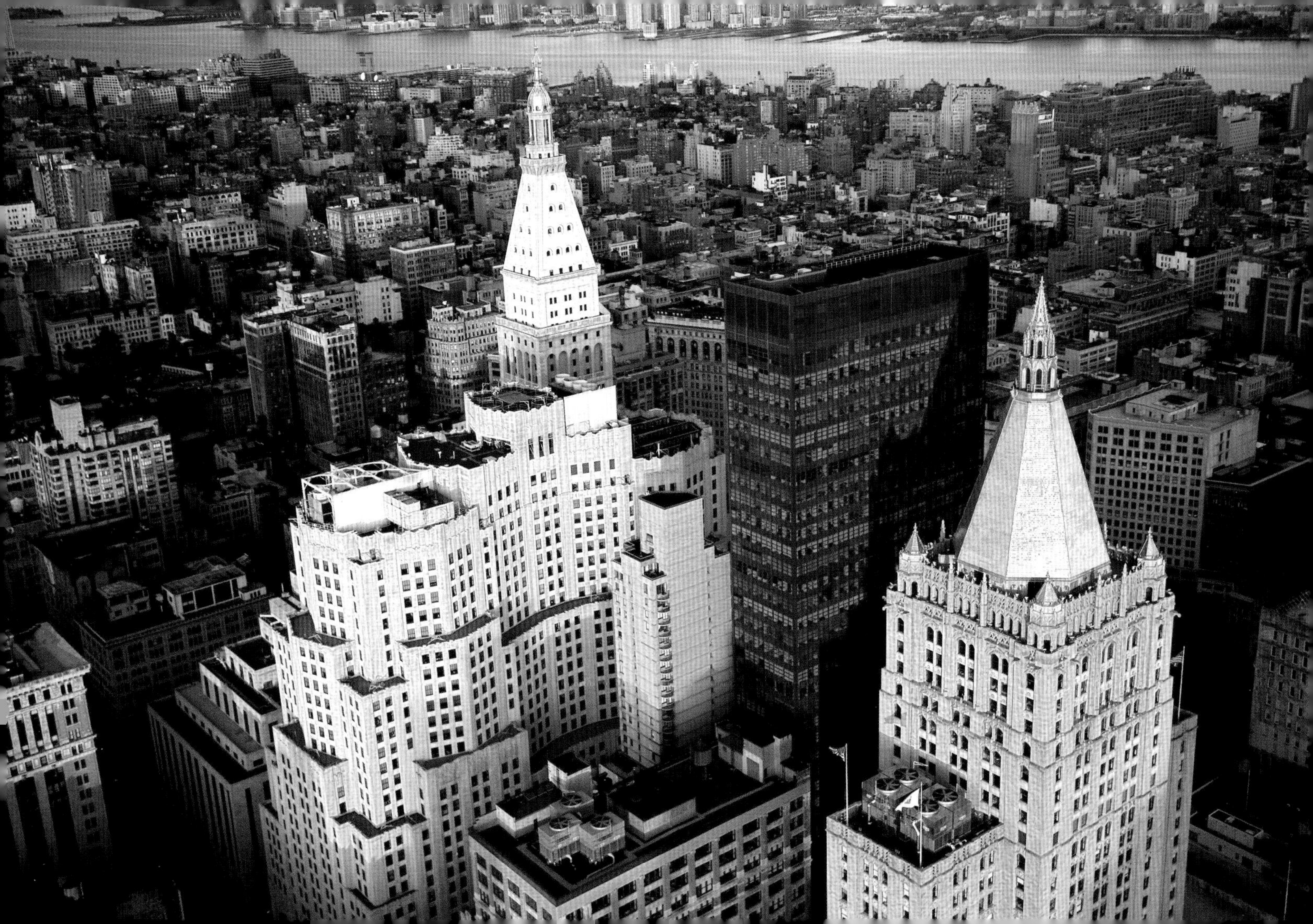

118
With an octagonal pinnacle some say is too small for its massive base, the New York Life Insurance Building at Madison Square Park is one of architect Cass Gilbert's most recognized works.

119
The 102-story Empire State Building and the 77-story Chrysler Building, here perfectly aligned, are Art Deco icons in Manhattan.

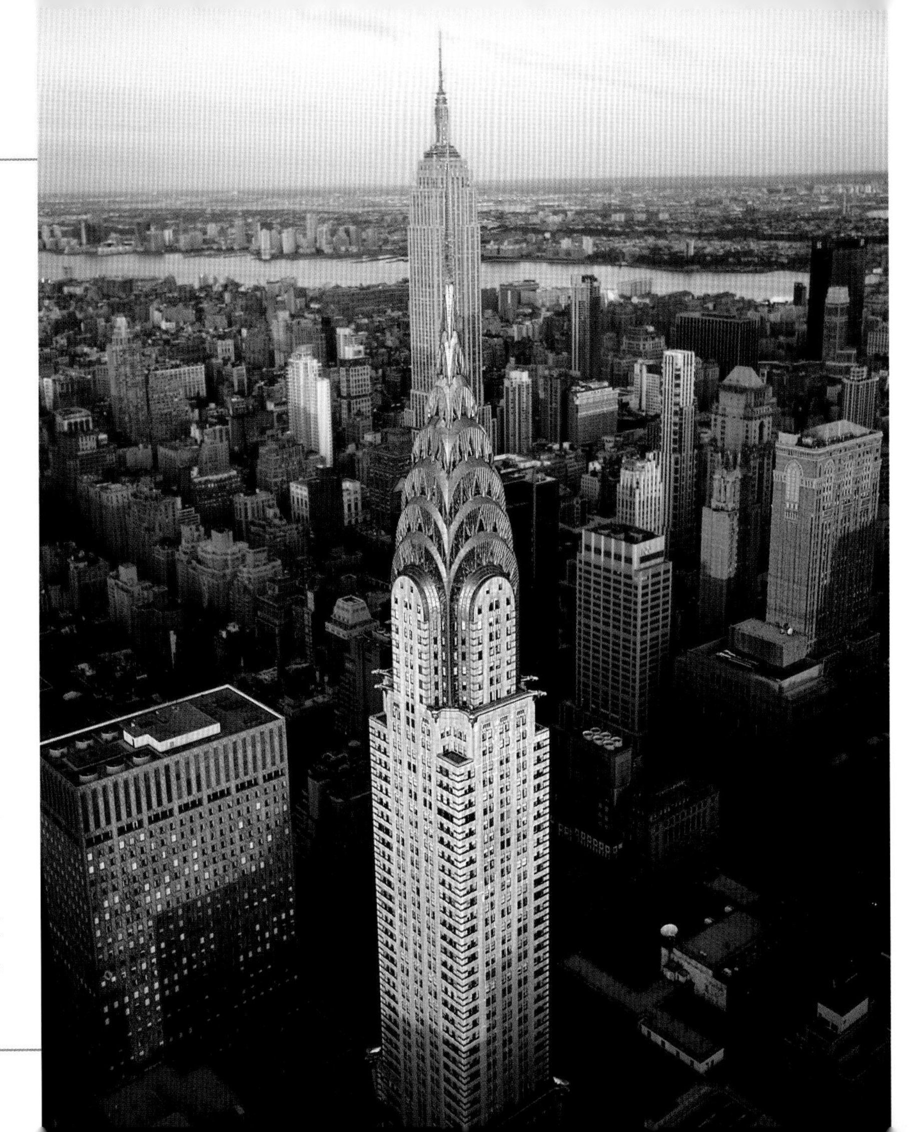

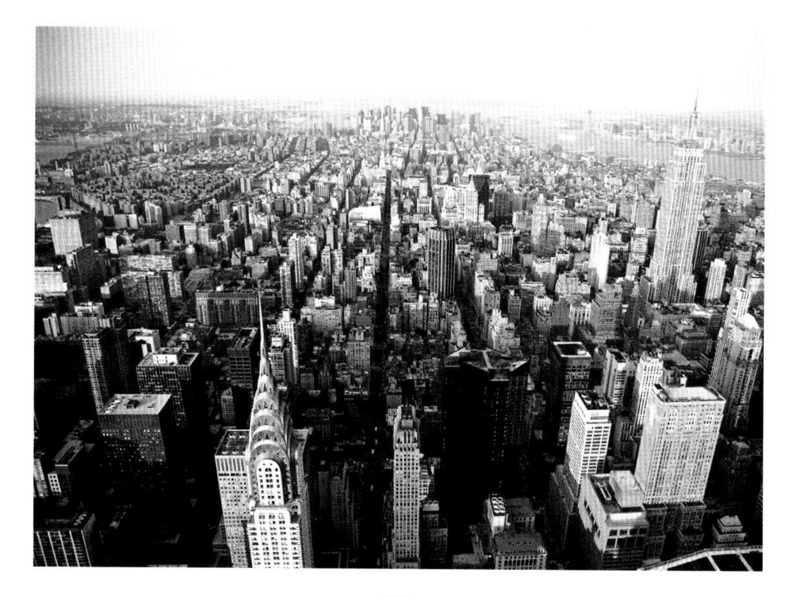

120
Looking south down Lexington Avenue, the grid pattern with its north/south thoroughfares makes order out of the mass of high-rises.

121
Across 34th Street, east of the Empire State Building, the New York University Medical Center and Belleview Hospital overlook the East River.

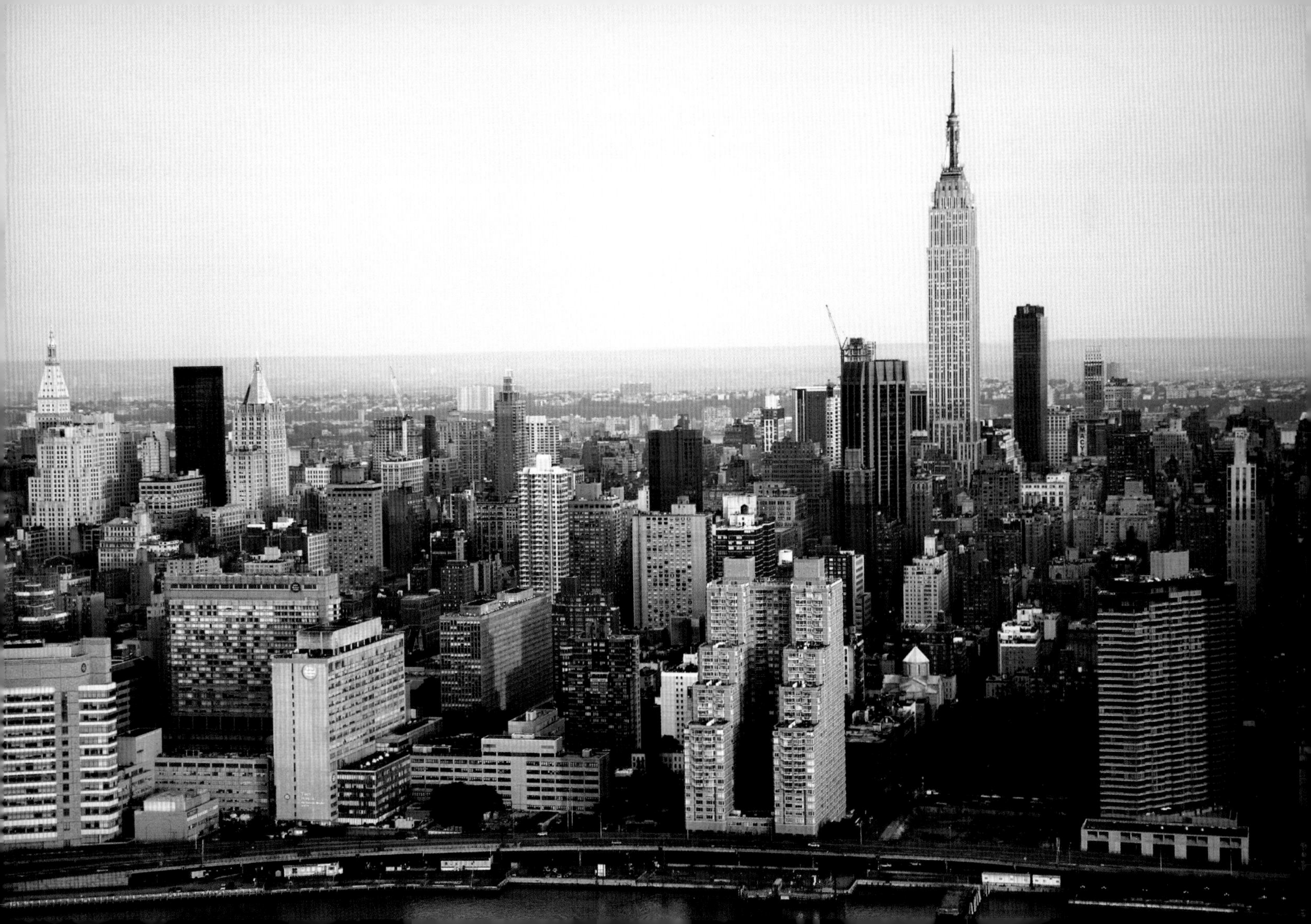

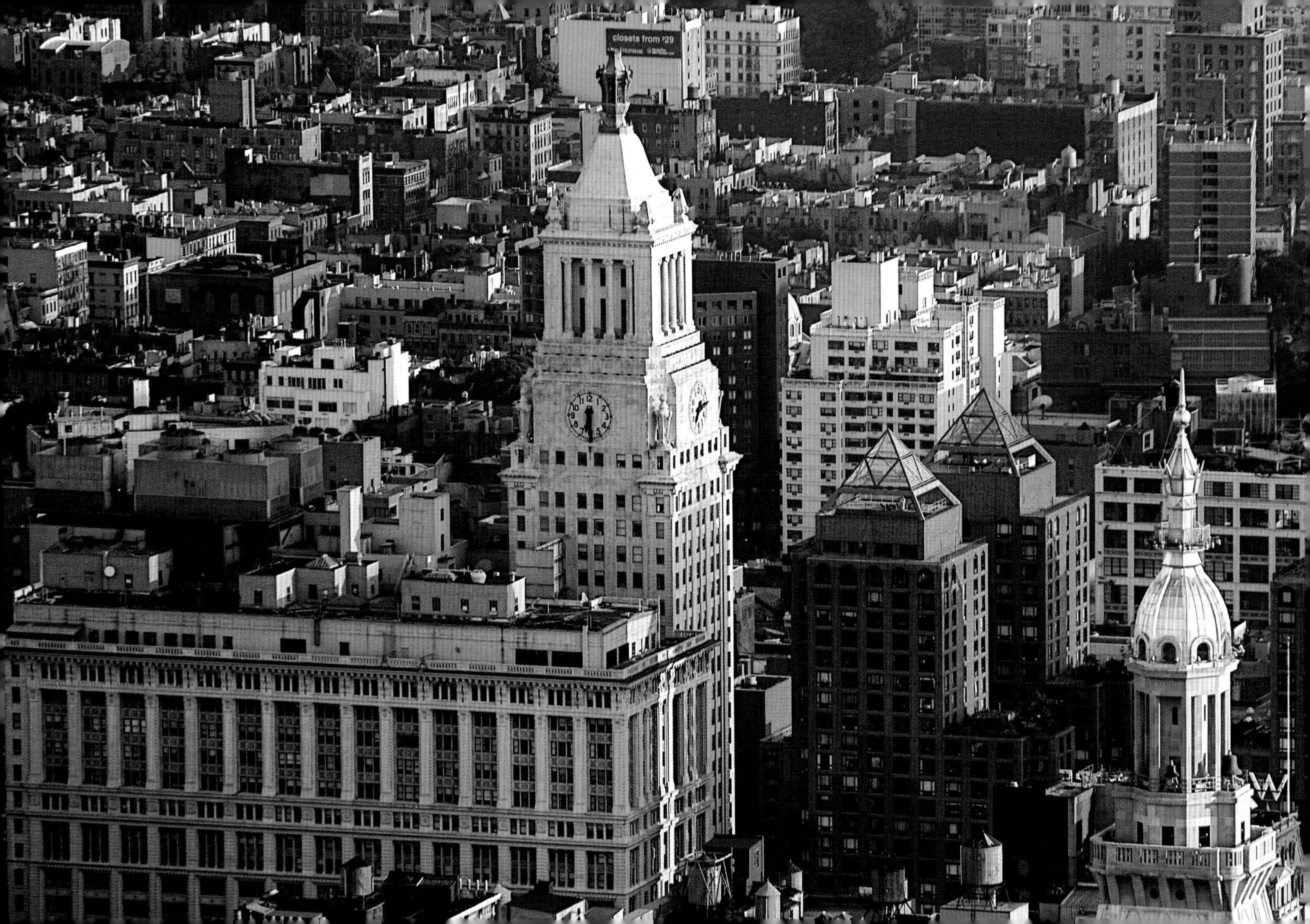
closets from $29

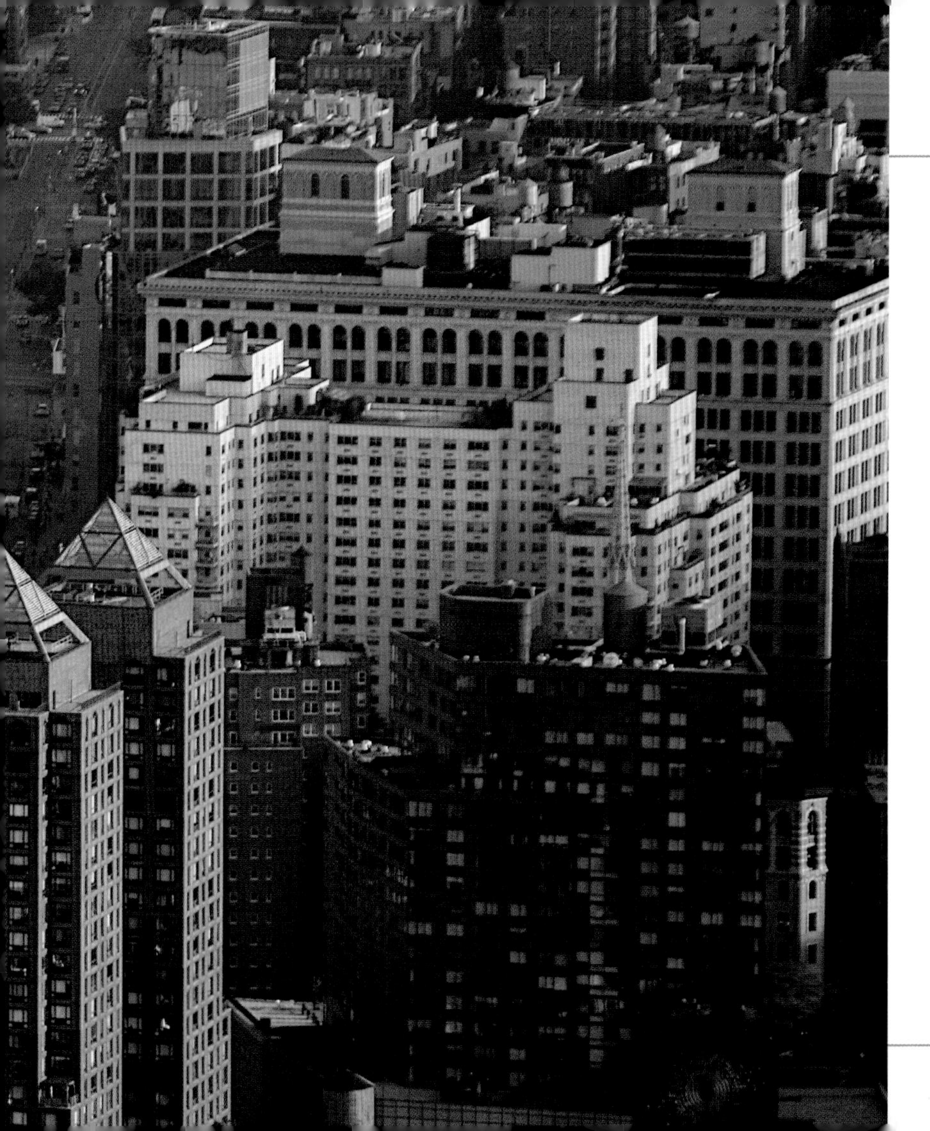

122-123
The four pyramids atop Union Square's Zeckendorf Towers echo the four urns on the Consolidated Edison Building's Irving Plaza Tower.

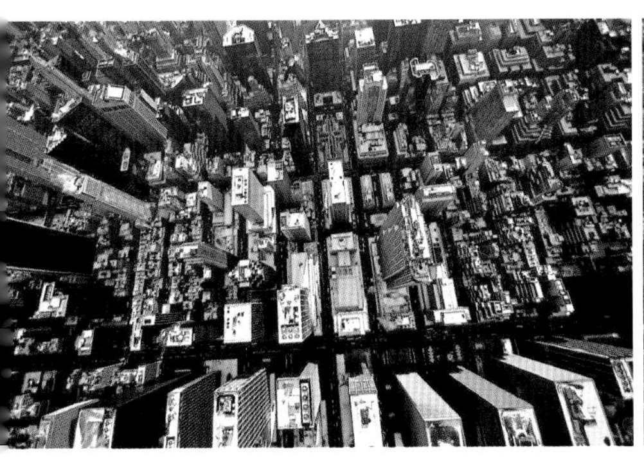

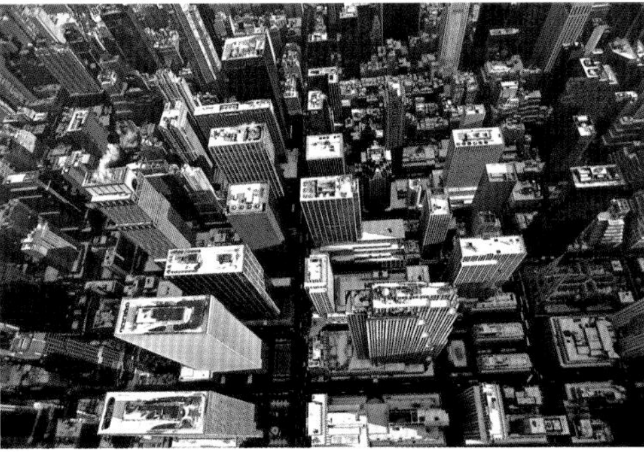

124
From above the buildings of midtown look like a child's box of blocks.

125
The Empire State Building, with its 102 floors, is the heart of midtown, between Fifth Avenue and Broadway on 34th Street.

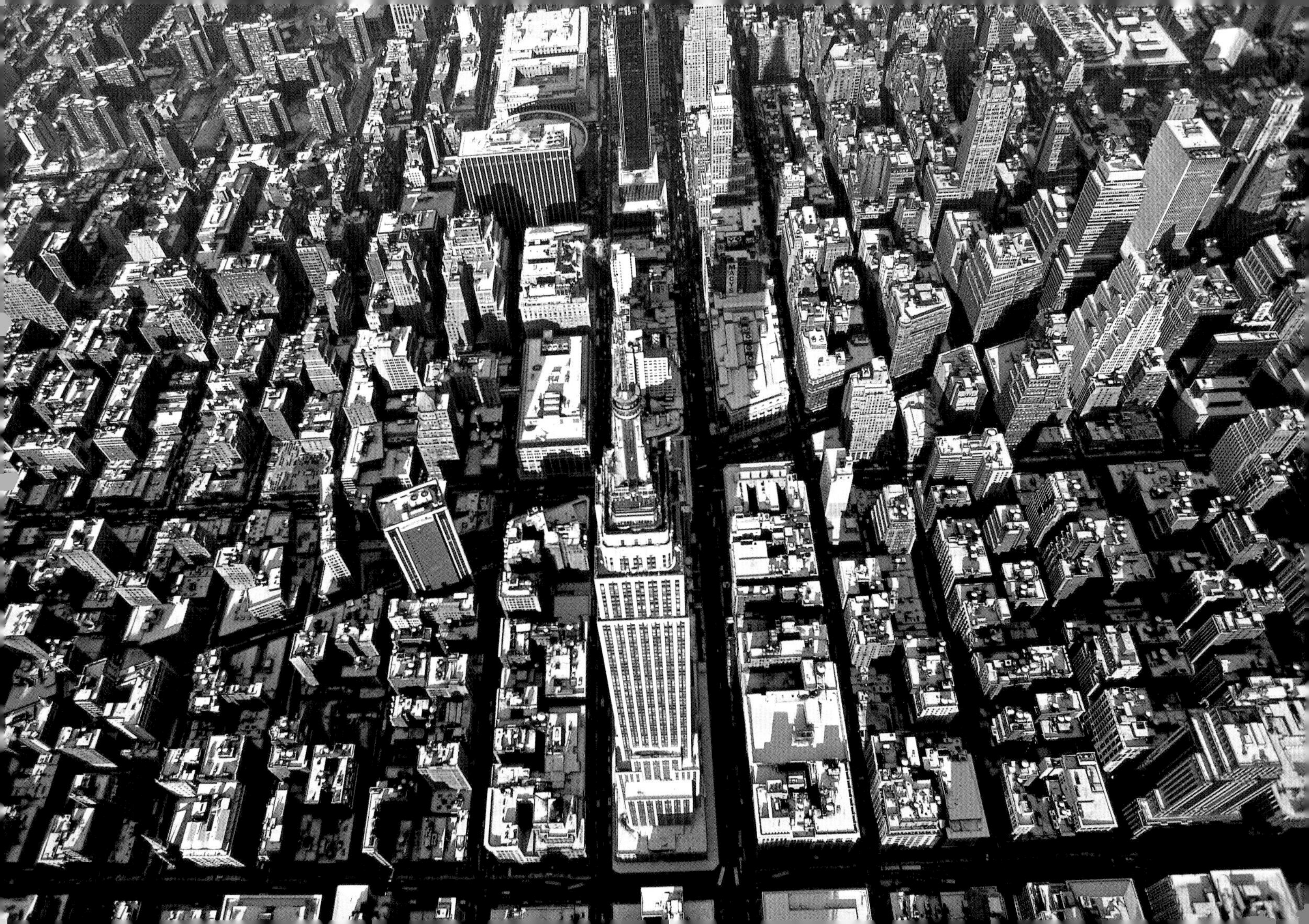
MACYS

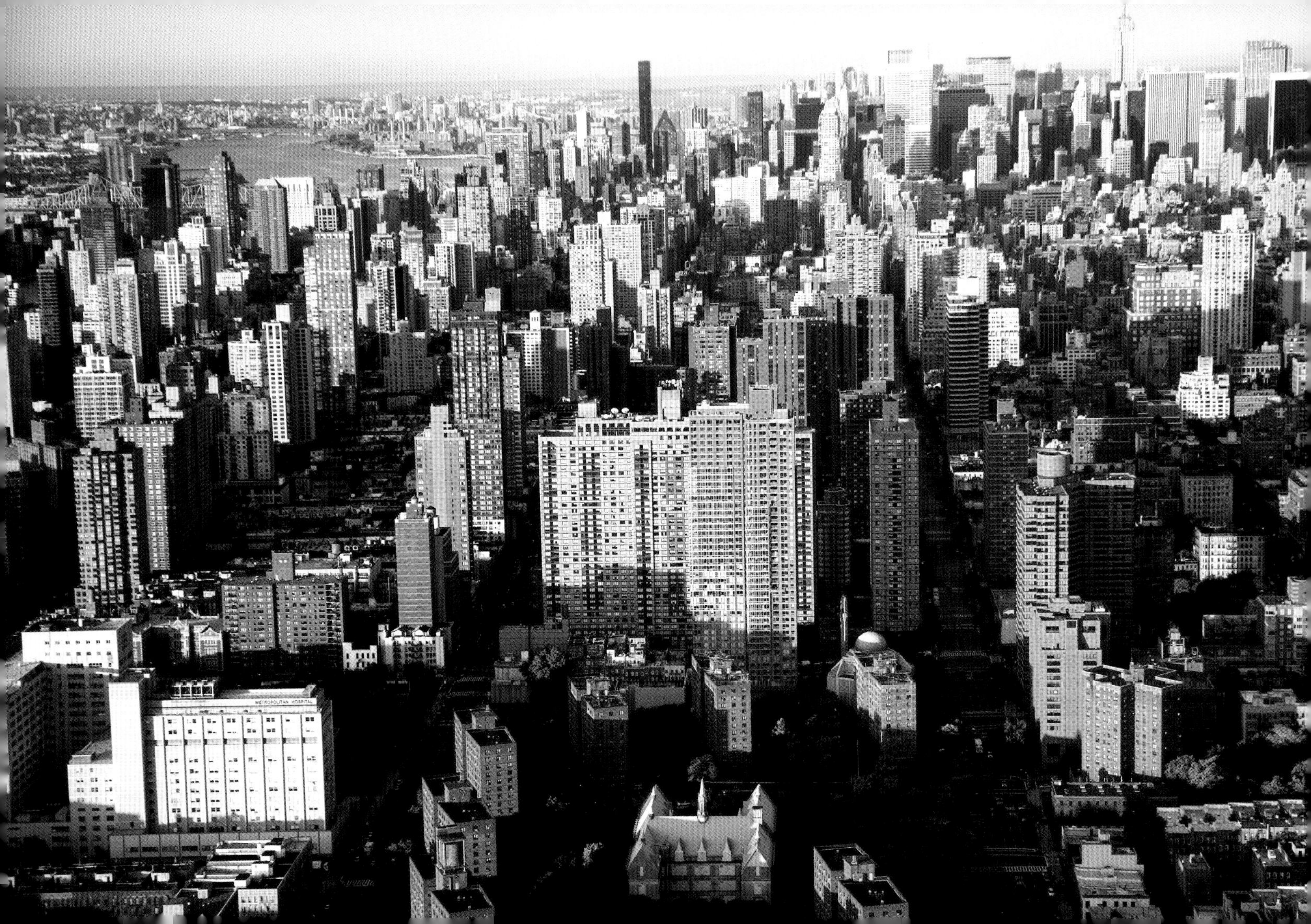
METROPOLITAN HOSPITAL

126

The small hemispheric cupola shown in the center of the photo is part of the Islamic Cultural Center, the first mosque to be built in New York City. The Metropolitan Hospital Center is on the building's left, in the middle of Carnegie Hill in East Harlem.

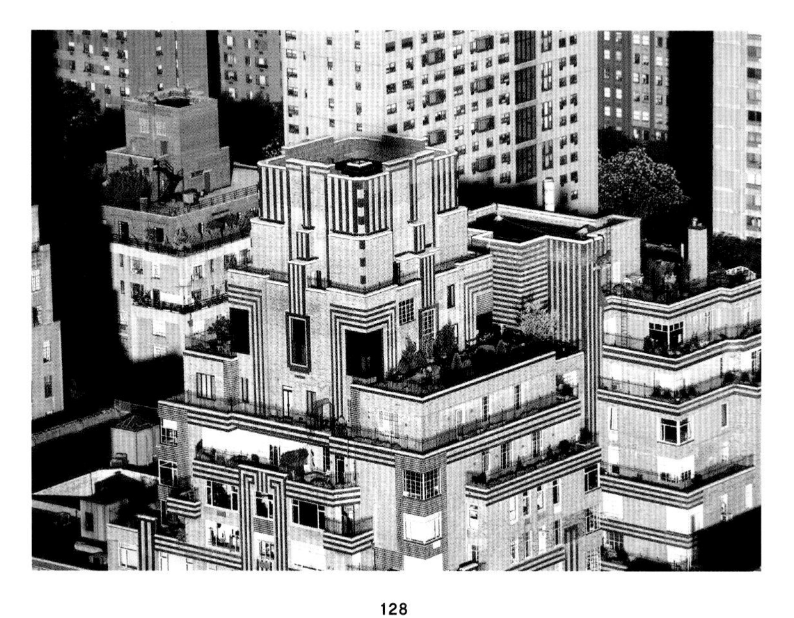

128

The elaborate ornamentation seen during the Art Deco period fell from favor during the latter 20th century, but made a comeback with Post-Modernism.

129

Tile work and setbacks to maximize light and openness distinguished Art Deco architecture in Manhattan.

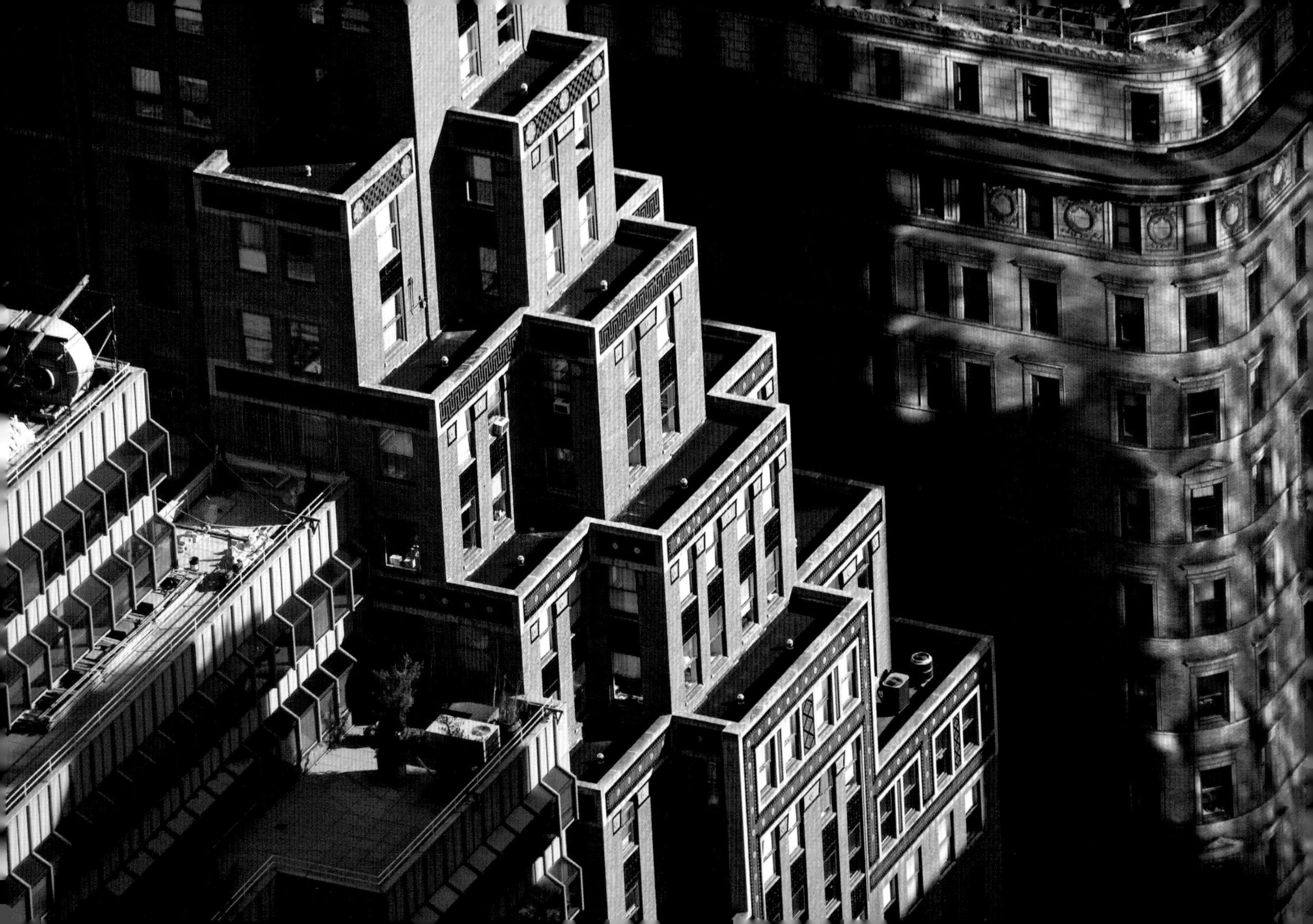

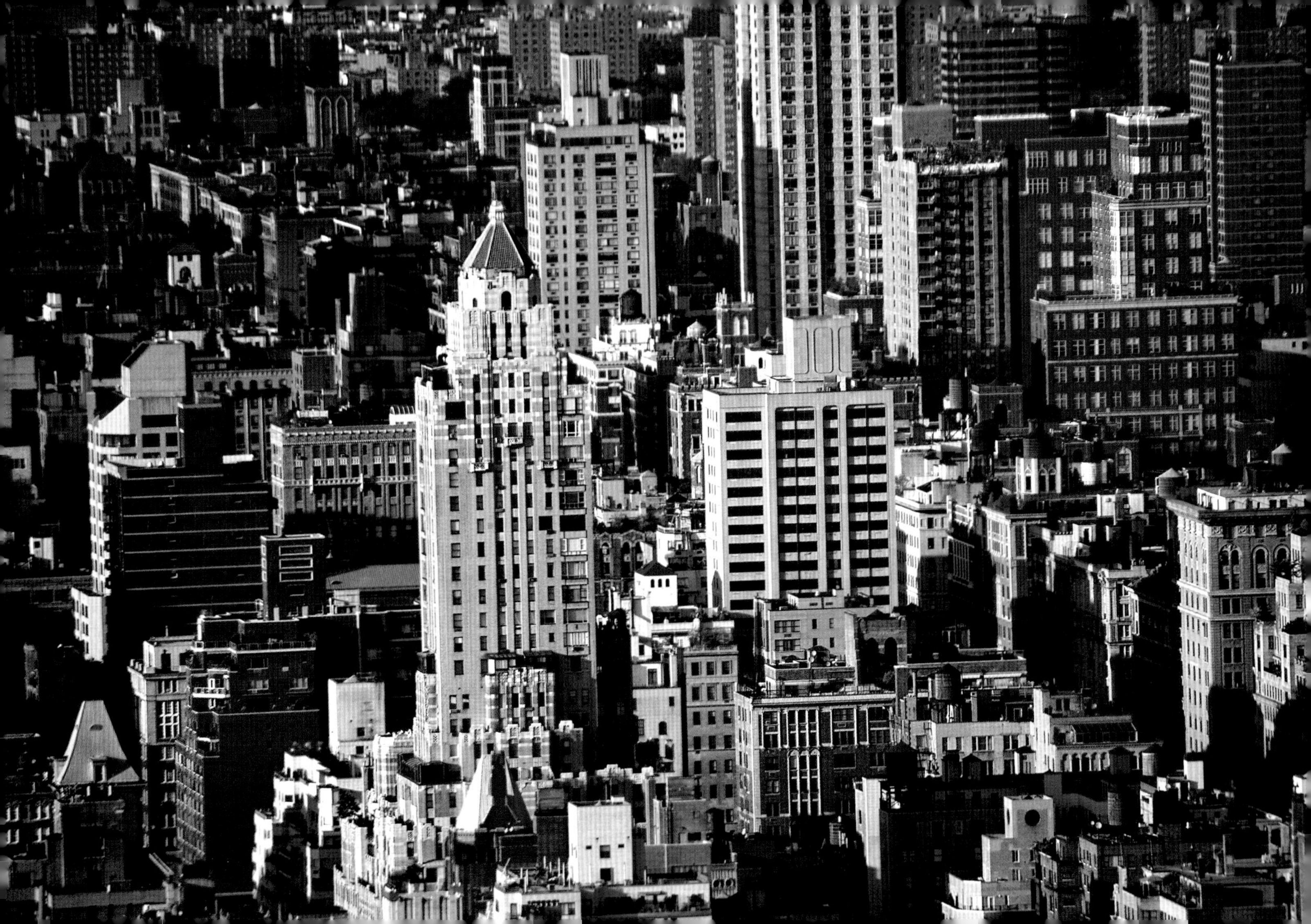

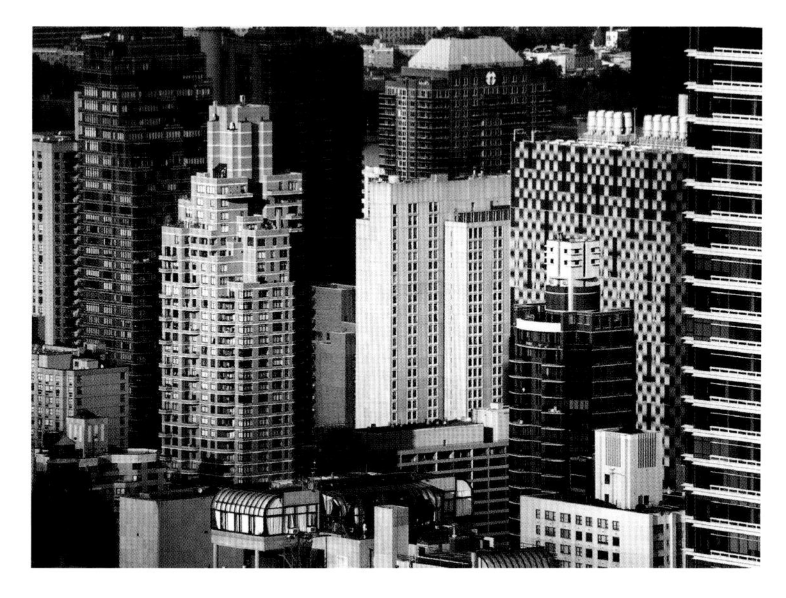

130
One of the most elegant and stately hotels on the Upper East Side, the 75-year-old Carlyle, rises above exclusive residences on Madison Avenue.

131
Upper East Side high-rise developers and tenants prize that elusive commodity: a room with a view of the East River.

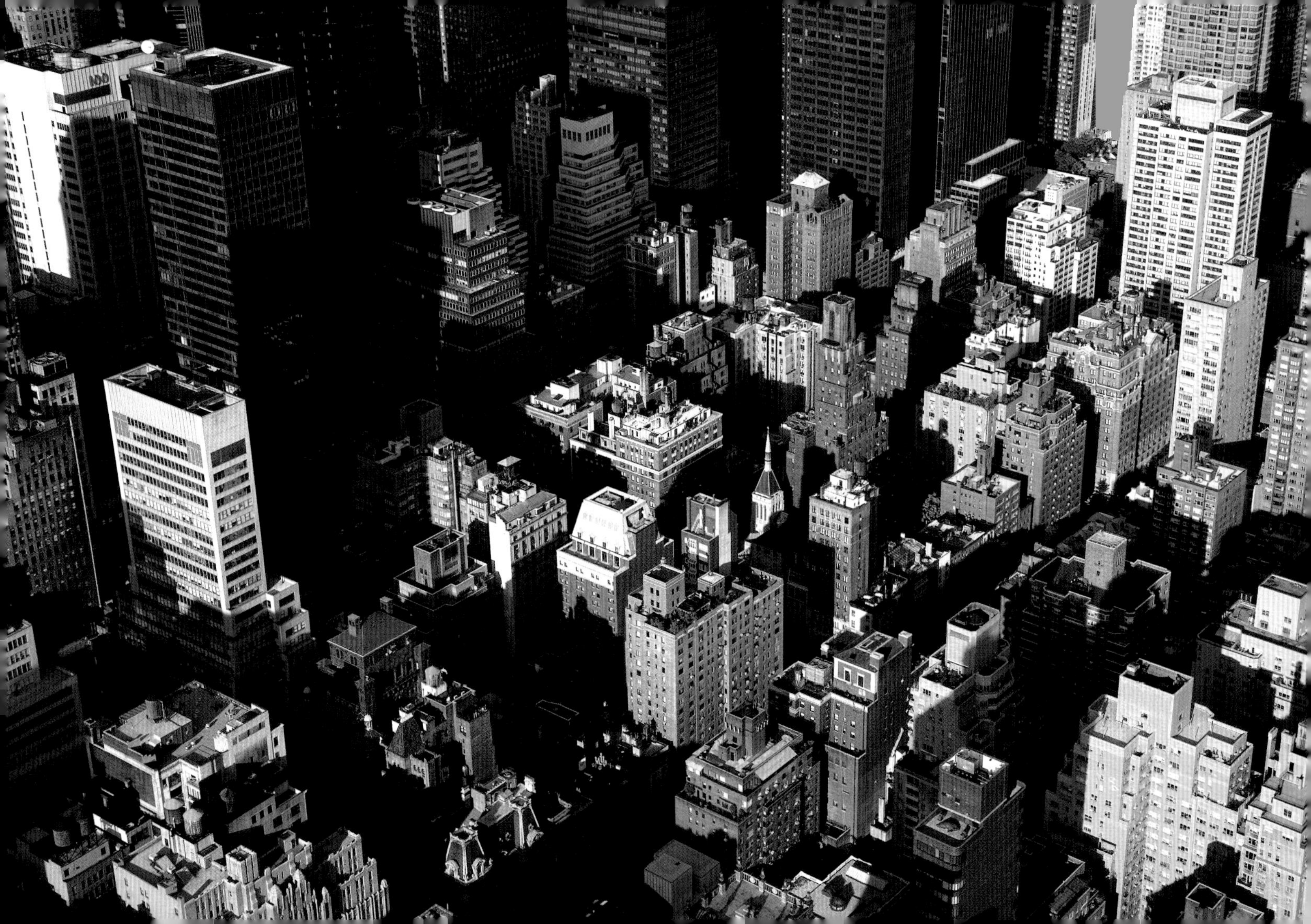

132
Below 34th Street, the size and scale of buildings shifts dramatically.

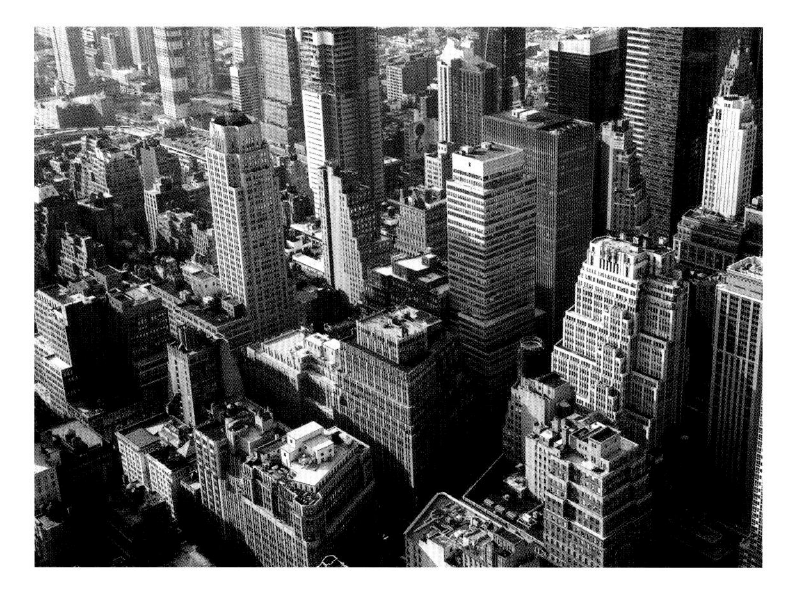

134

Though no longer a prime manufacturing center, the Garment District is still the heart of the New York fashion world.

135

The distinctive pyramidal roof of 10 East 40th Street (center) and the low-lying New York Public Library (left) stand out amidst the flat tops of midtown high-rises.

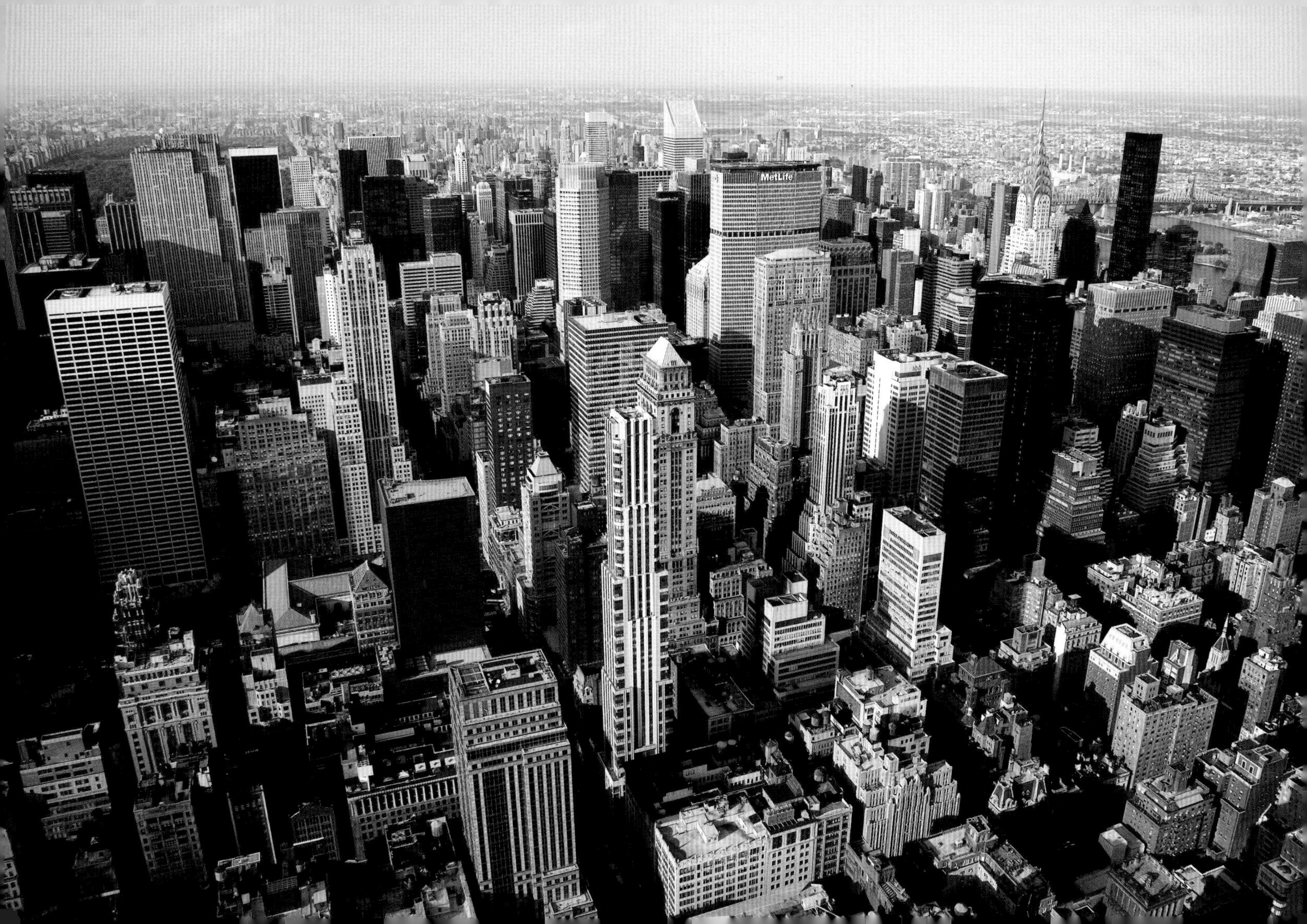
MetLife

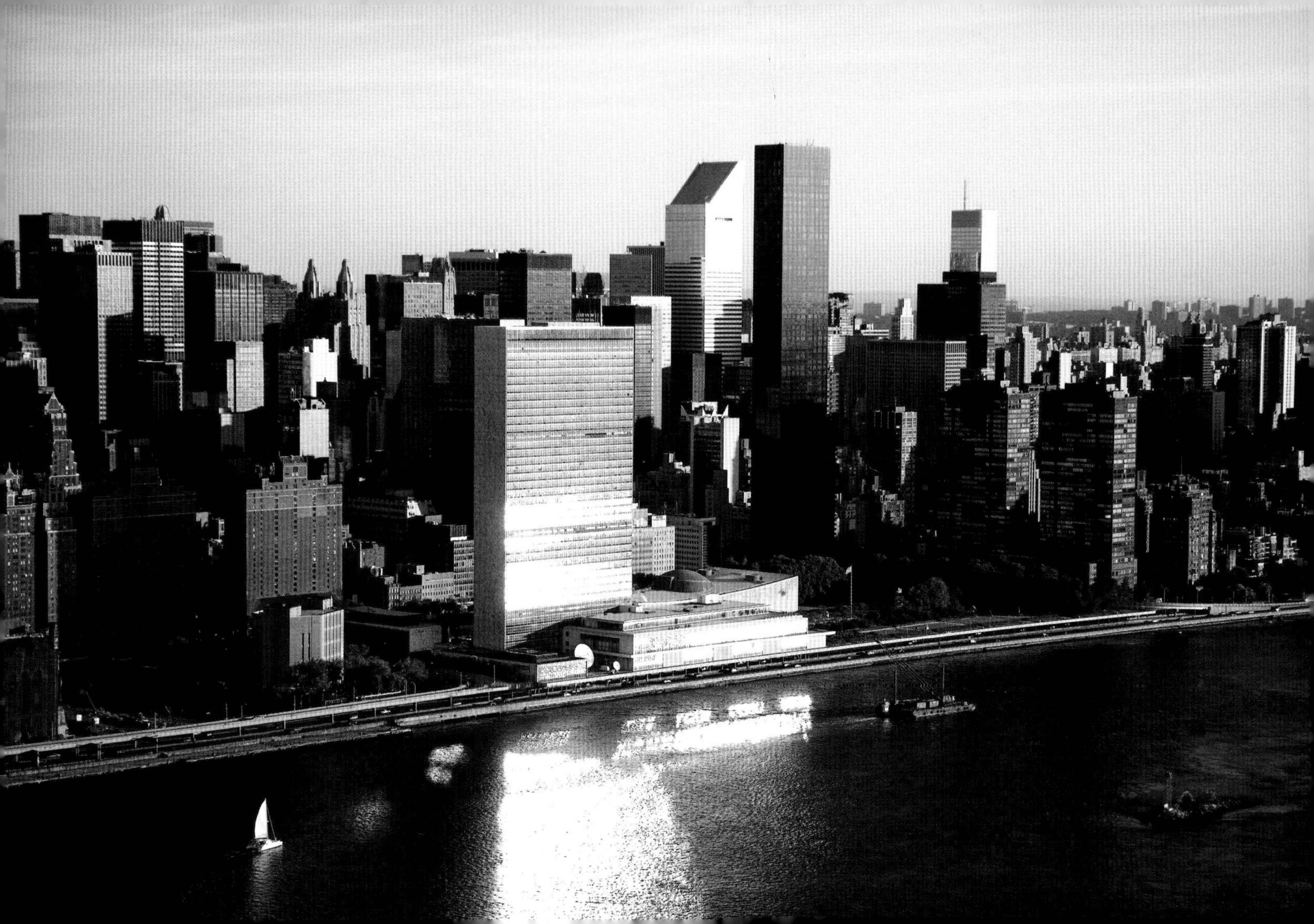

136
Midtown, along the East River, is a modernist vision, with the Secretariat of the United Nations, Citigroup Center and Trump World Tower reflecting the rising sun.

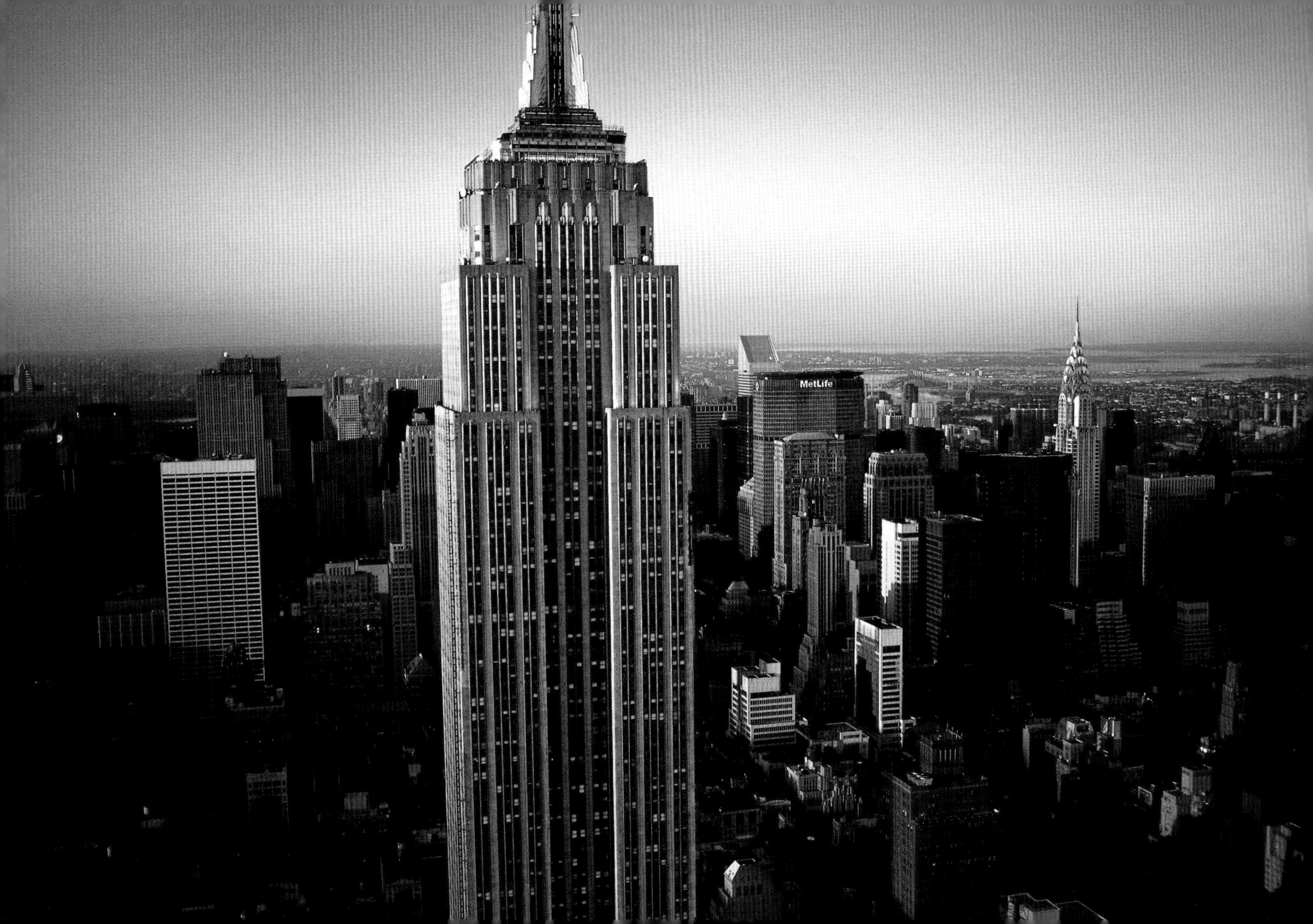
MetLife

138
The Empire State Building towers over Manhattan, dwarfing many other historical and famous buildings.

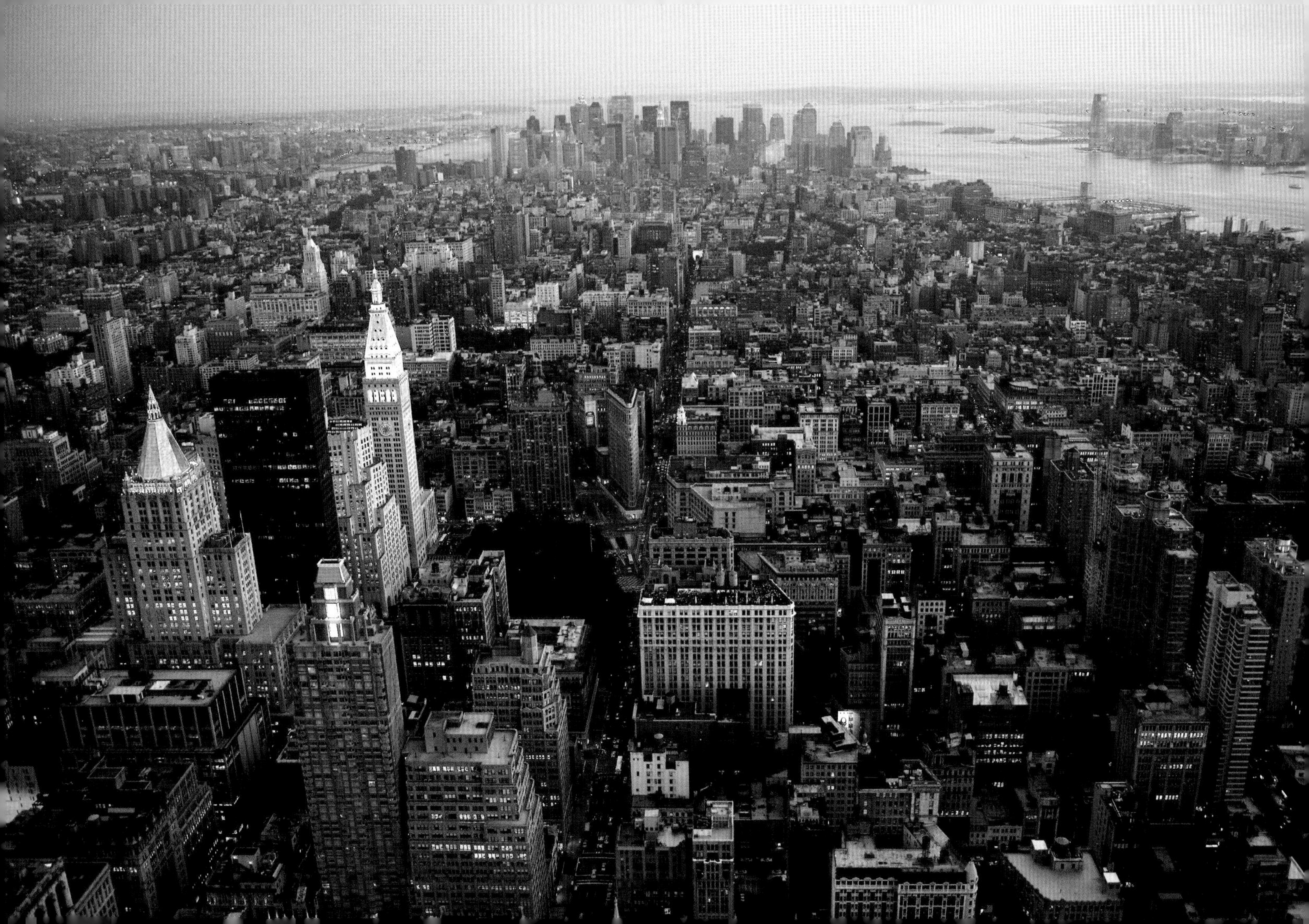

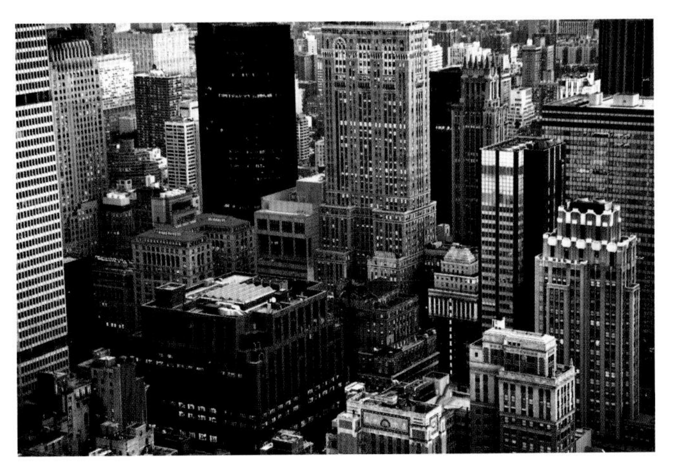

140
This spectacular view of Manhattan shows the powerful upward thrust that has characterized the city since the early 20th century.

141
Forty-second Street has some of New York's most distinctive architecture: (from left to right) the Brutalist MetLife Building, the Art Deco Chanin Building, the Historicist Lincoln Building and (lower right) the Babylonian-inspired Fred French Building.

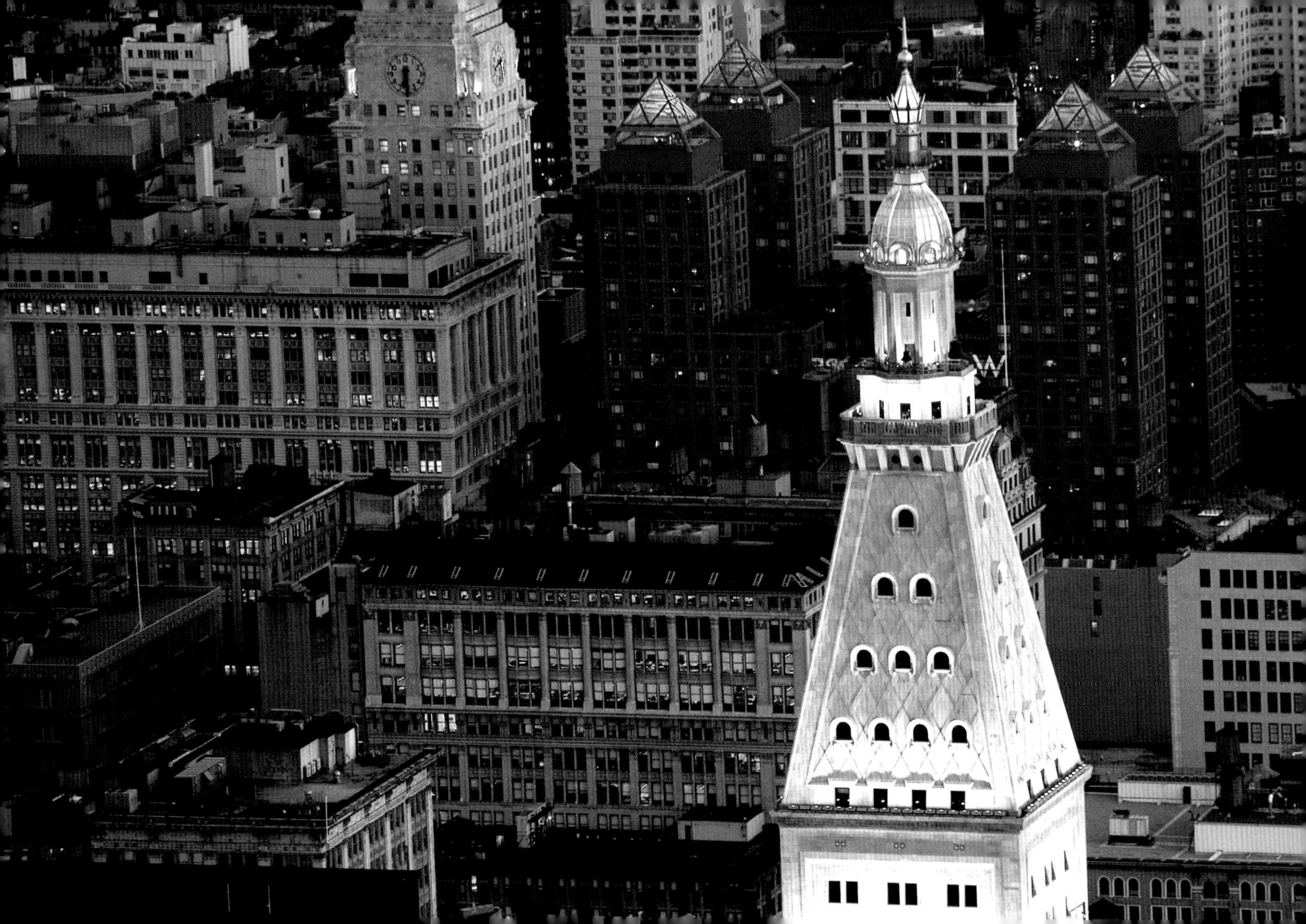
W

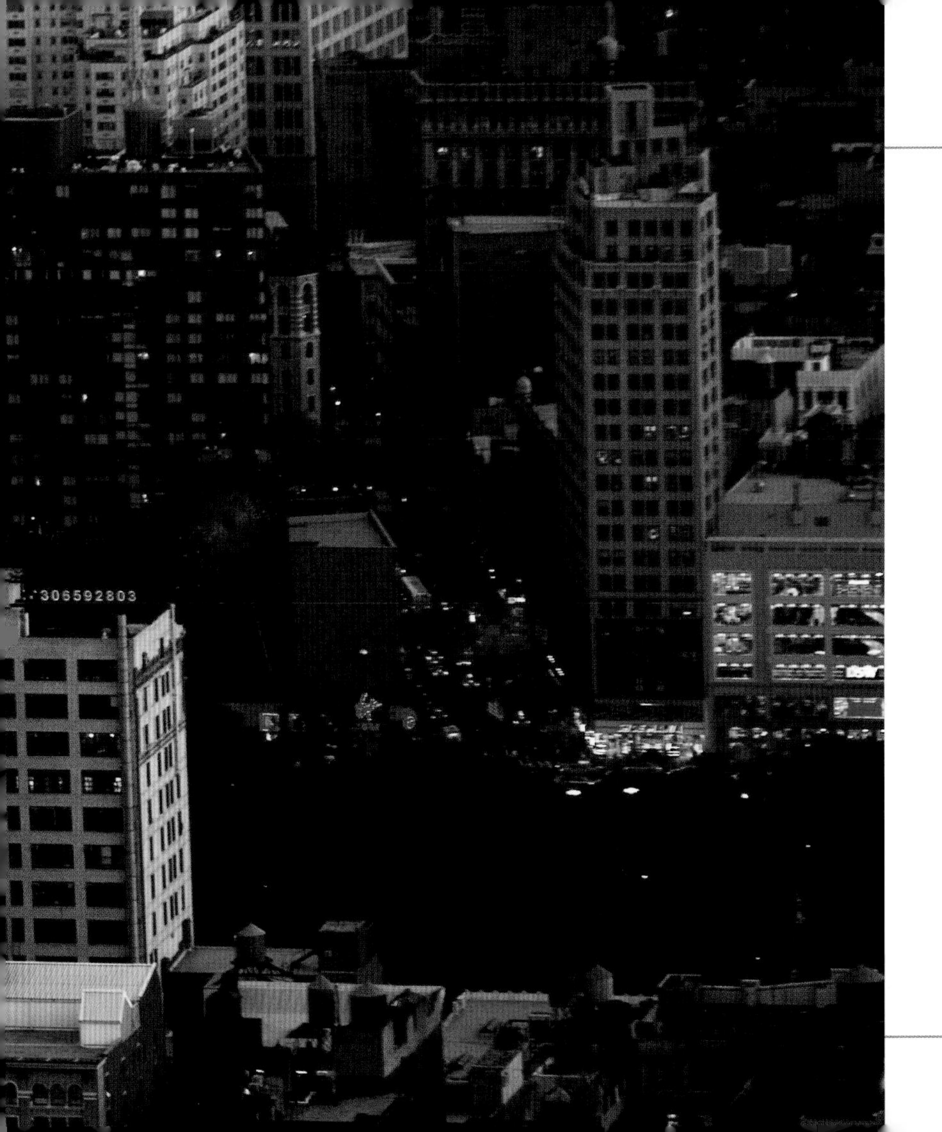

142-143

Pyramids are a recurrent theme in New York architecture, from the post-modern Zeckendorf Towers to the pinnacle of the Metropolitan Life Building.

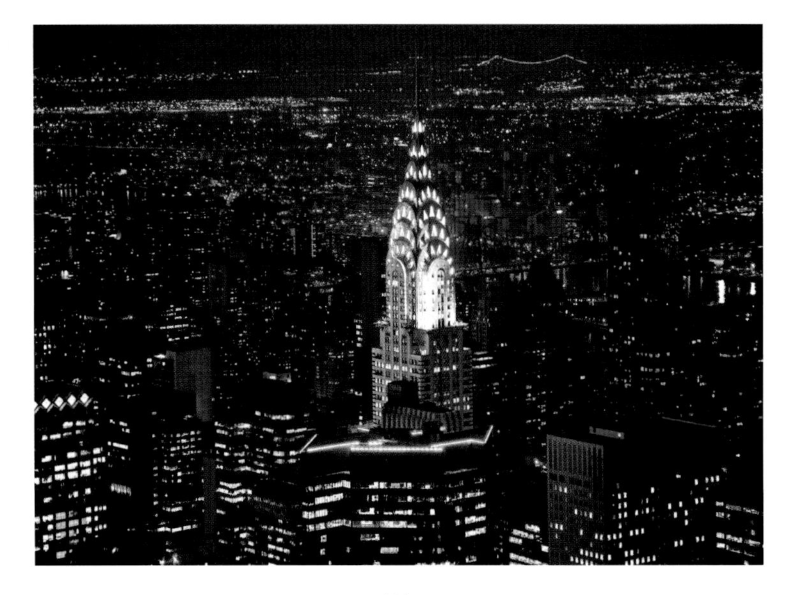

144

The Chrysler Building lights up the surrounding landscape of Midtown.

145

The late-20th century building boom in midtown produced landmark skyscrapers: (from left to right) 712 Fifth Avenue, the General Motors Bldg., the Sony Building (with its perforated façade), and the most recent one, the Bloomberg Tower (highlighted with a red light).

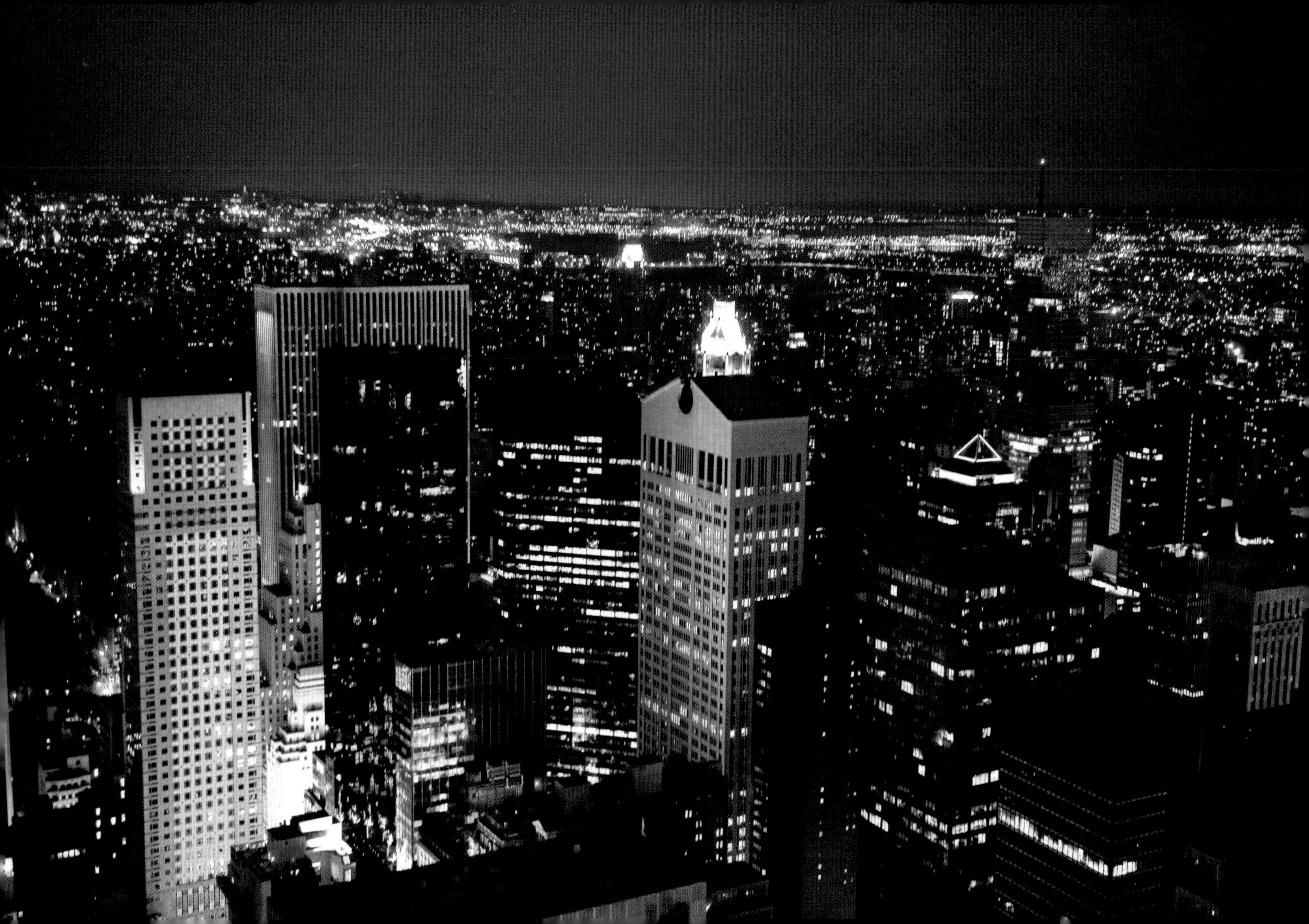

147

Fifth Avenue (left), New York's east/west dividing line, shines with luxury stores along its exclusive retail corridor from 34th to 60th Street.

148-149

The Empire State Building was inaugurated on May 1st, 1931 when the President of the USA, Herbert Hoover, turned on the lights only 14 months after construction began.

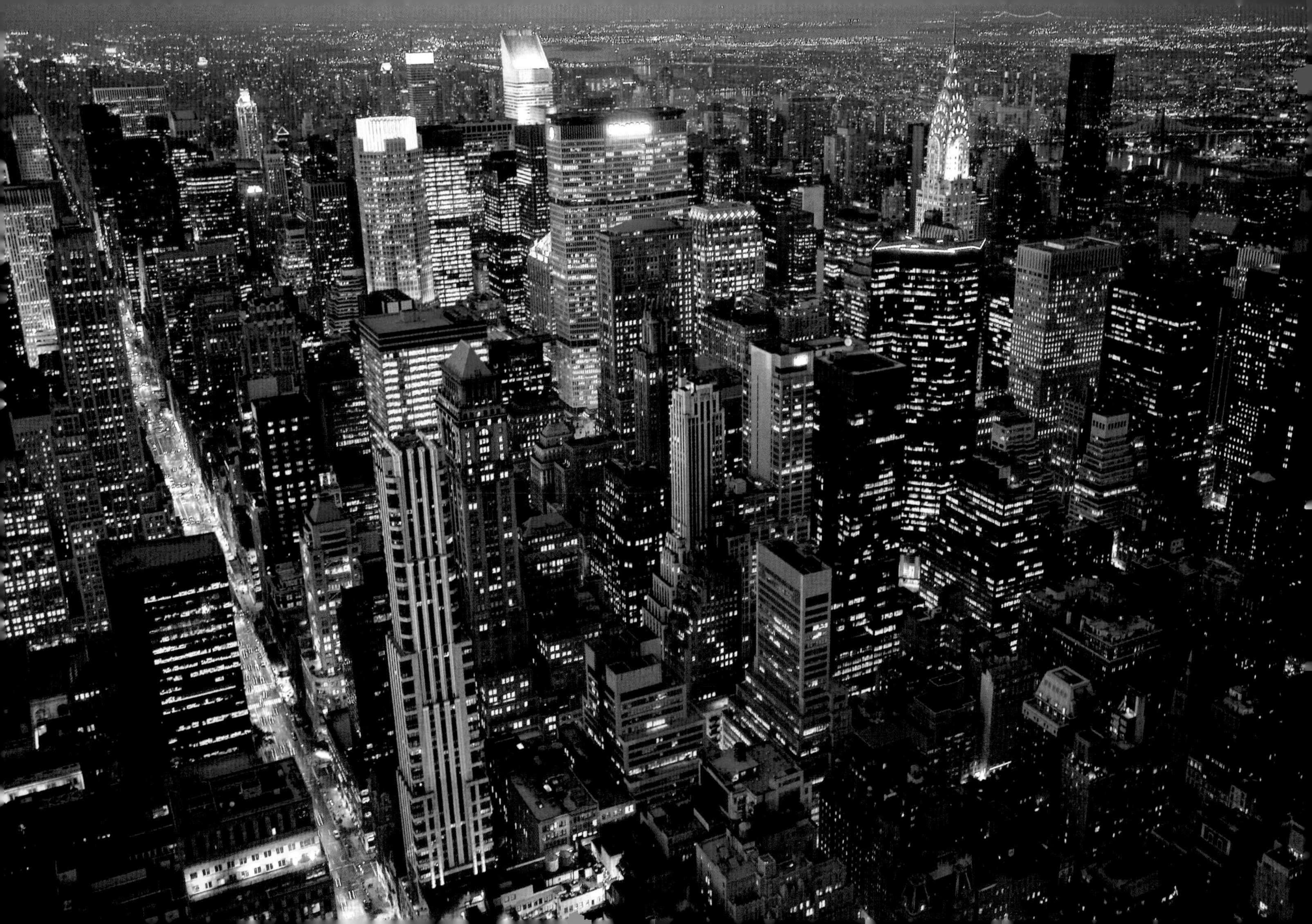

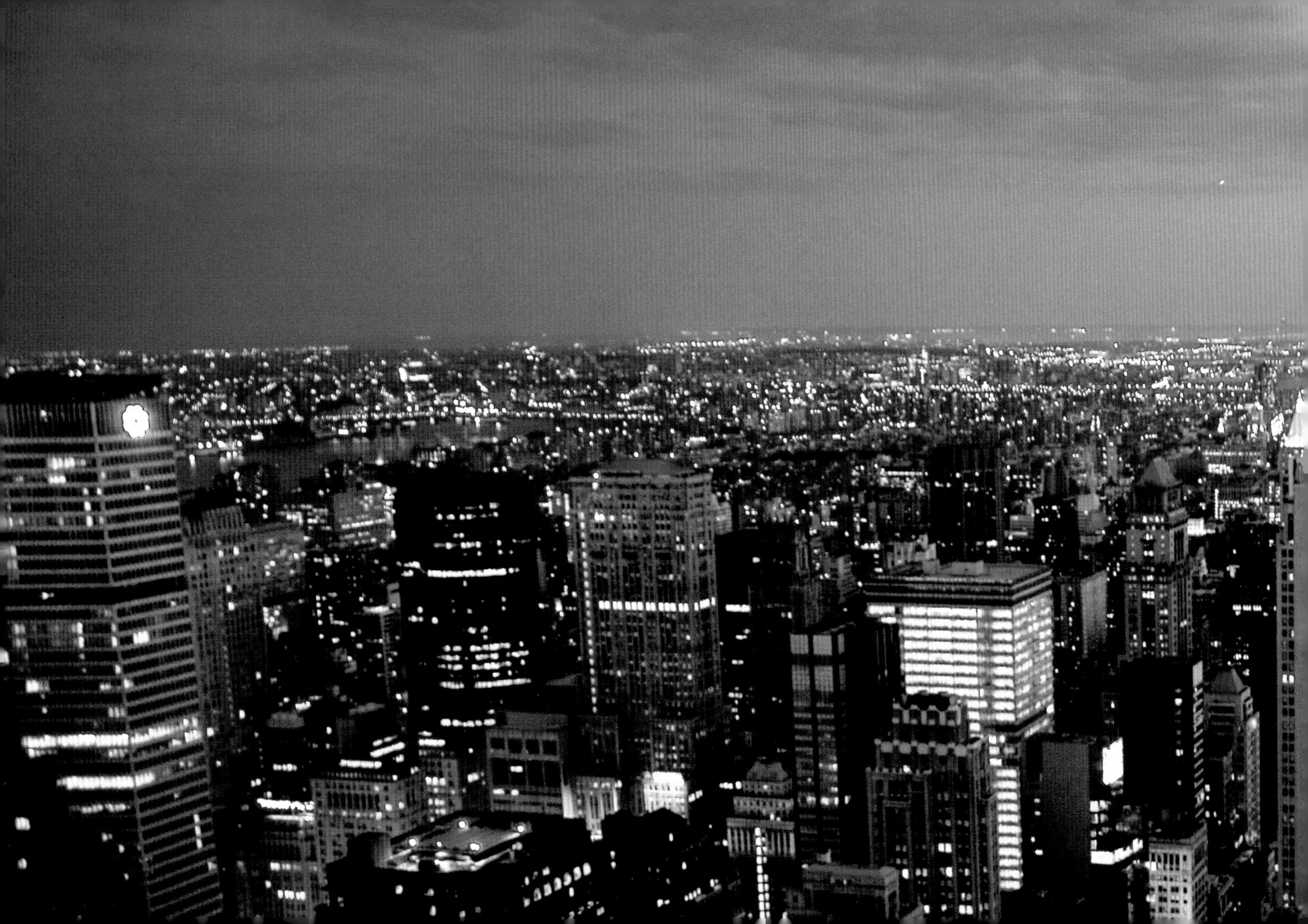

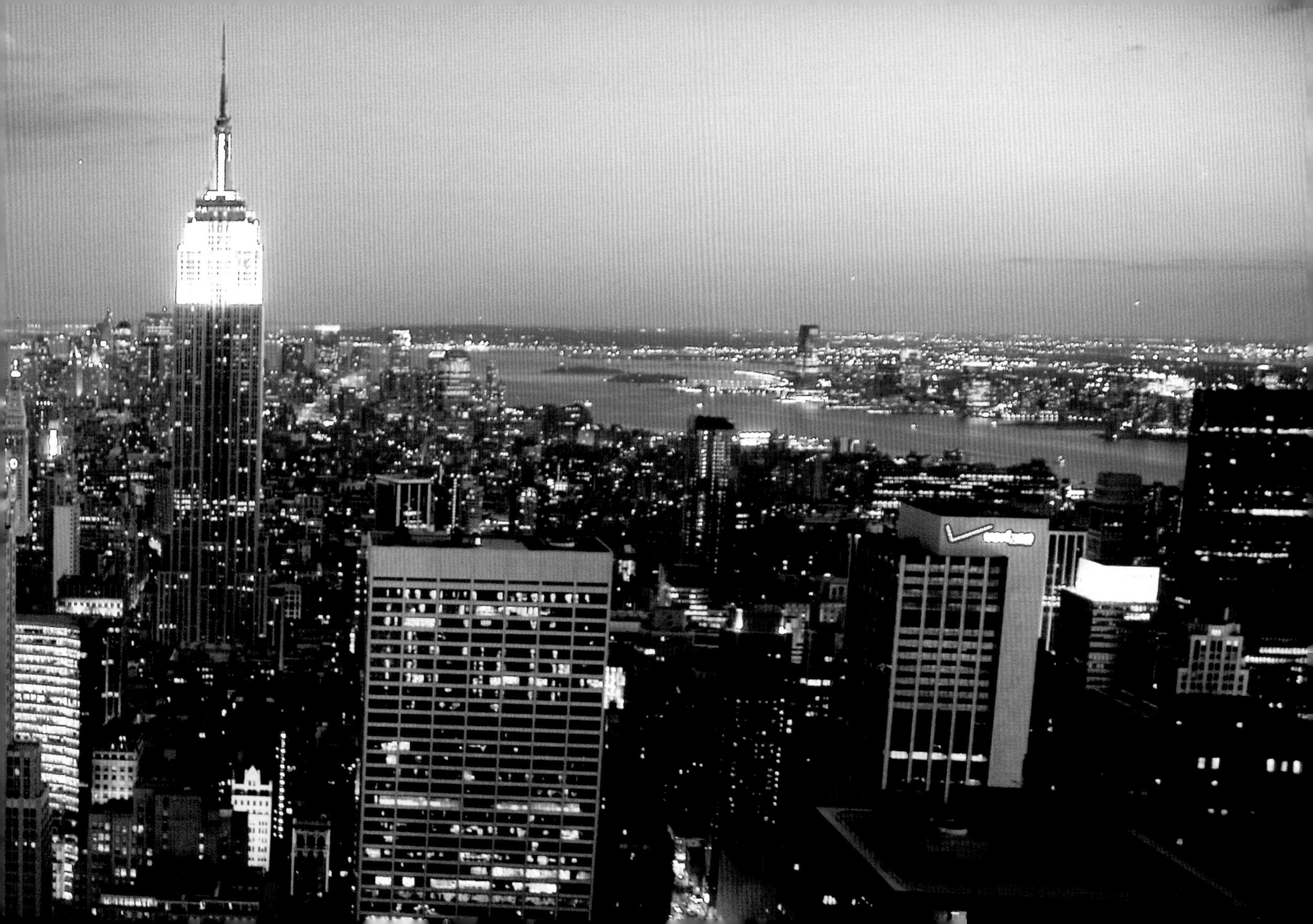

UPTOWN WEST

DINOSAURS, DEANS AND DRAMA

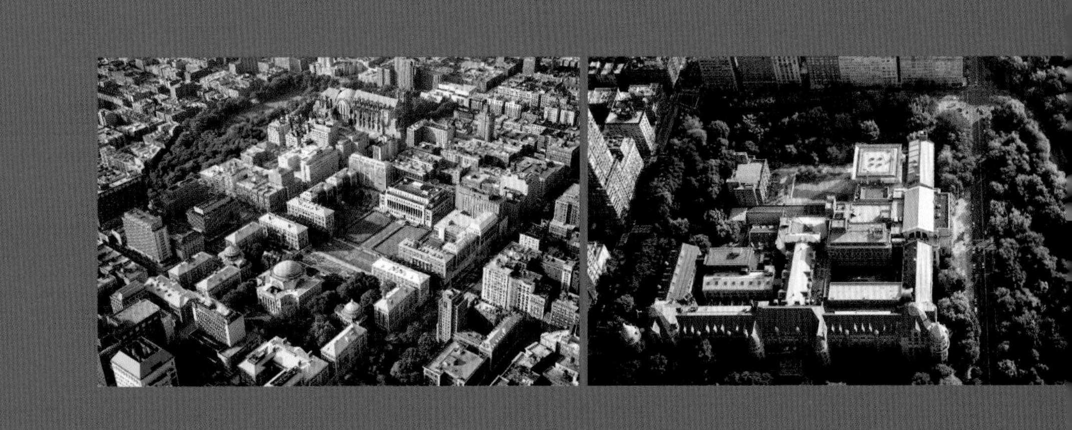

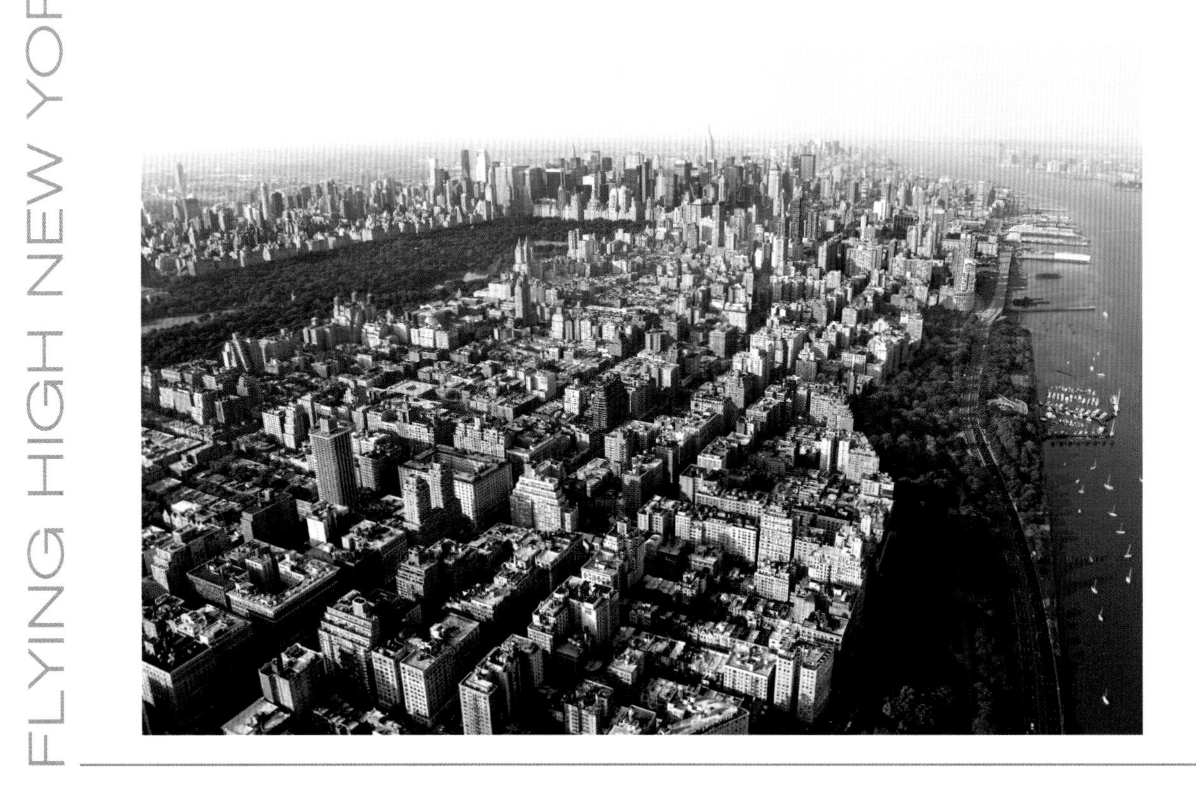

151
Columbia University (left) and the American Museum of Natural History (right) are two of the treasures of New York's west side.

The West Side of New York, much like the American West, began as a wilderness, and those who settled it had similar pioneering spirits. In the early Dutch days, it seemed remote and far from the center of commerce at the southern tip of Manhattan. Gradually, though, the area north of what is now 23rd Street and extending to the current 125th Street, grew, as wealthy landowners and merchants built grand homes and estates. A number of prosperous villages were established, supported by a thriving tobacco industry. The largest of these villages was Bloomingdale (Bloemendal, or "valley of the flowers"). Through it ran Bloomingdale Road, which was later named the Boulevard and was later to become an extension of Broadway. In the 18th and 19th centuries, the area was the preserve of the affluent; by the mid-19th century, a mix of classes had settled there. The arrival of the railroad in the 1830s, as well as the extension of subway lines made it accessible to a variety of people, including squatters who had been displaced after the development of Central Park in 1853.

Central Park became, in essence, the dividing line between east and west in New York, and it was along the west side of the park that some of the city's most flamboyant buildings rose. Developers took advantage of the ample space on the west side, constructing apartment buildings where grand estates once stood. One prominent example is the Dakota, at West 72nd Street and Central Park West, which was designed by architect Henry J. Hardenbergh (who also designed the Plaza Hotel) in 1864. Because the building was situated farther north than most of the other apartments along Central Park West, some observers at the time were said to have commented that the building might as well have been in Dakota, hence the name.

The first true luxury apartment building in the city, the Dakota is only one of a number of striking structures

152
The west side is sandwiched between two of New York's most famous parks, Central and Riverside.

Uptown West
Dinosaurs, Deans and Drama

along Central Park West. Part of what makes the skyline of the west side so distinct is the quintet of twin-towered apartment buildings built along Central Park West. All constructed in the early 20th century they include the Century (southernmost of the five), the Majestic (which replace the 19th-century, sumptuous Majestic Hotel), the San Remo (with towers topped by cupolas) and the Beresford (which actually has three towers.)

Not only the architecture of Uptown West is dramatic; the entire area tends toward the theatrical. In fact, much of the city's rich cultural life happens west of Central Park. The area is home to many actors, dancers and writers, both established and aspiring.

The name Broadway defines not just the major thoroughfare angling through the area, but also New York's primary professional theatre district. Clustered in the booming Times Square area, 39 Broadway theatres currently offer top-caliber dramas, comedies and musicals. Once notorious as a seedy and dangerous neighborhood, especially for unsuspecting tourists, the Times Square area has revived and is now jammed with visitors 24 hours a day. Soaring new office and residential towers, many of which are cutting-edge examples of "green" engineering, like the Conde Nast building, are employing the latest in environmentally and self-sustaining technology. Benefiting from the Times Square boom, the surrounding residential area to the west, once known as Hell's Kitchen, and now referred to as Clinton or Midtown West, has also experienced revitalization. Restaurants and condominiums are replacing flophouses and porn theaters in the district.

The West Side also is home to a number of New York's major cultural and educational institutions. The famed "temple of sound," Carnegie Hall, to the east of Times Square, at West 57th and Seventh Avenue, now sits beneath a towering new high-rise, Carnegie Towers. A bit farther north lies Lincoln Center for the Performing Arts, between West 62nd and 66th streets at Broadway, now undergoing a massive renovation. Home to 12 arts companies, including the Metropolitan Opera, the New York Philharmonic and the New York State Theater, the center is a focal point of New York's culture scene. And

Uptown West
Dinosaurs, Deans and Drama

at the northern end of Manhattan's west side is The Cloisters, in Fort Tryon Park, housing the medieval collection of the Metropolitan Museum of Art.

The American Museum of Natural History occupies its own park, Manhattan Square, from West 79th to West 81st Streets, across from Central Park. Built in 1869, the venerable institution showcases a stunning collection of dinosaurs and other wonders of the natural world, as well as the Rose Center for Earth and Space.

Columbia University, too, commands its own large chunk of the Upper West Side. Bounded by West 114th and West 121st streets between Broadway and Amsterdam Avenues, Columbia's plan and most of its buildings were designed by the noted firm of McKim, Mead and White. Planned as an "urban academic village," the campus brings the Ivy League into the heart of the city.

The west side's topography was originally one of hills and valleys, much of which has been graded to allow for development. But the bluffs remaining offer some of the best views of the other defining geographic landmark on the west side – the Hudson River. Piers, docks and ferry slips line the shore, along which runs Riverside Park. At the 79th Street Boat Basin, many New Yorkers trade high-rise living for life on the river. Parallel to the Hudson is Riverside Drive, lined with elegant apartment buildings, which offer stunning sunset views of the palisades of New Jersey to the west.

North of the Columbia University, on Riverside Drive and Seminary Rd., sits the imposing monument dedicated to General Ulysses S. Grant, civil war general and 18th president of the United States. The monument, where Grant and his wife are entombed, is the largest mausoleum in North America.

Farther south along the river, at West 46th Street, is the site Intrepid Sea-Air-Space Museum, home to the Intrepid aircraft carrier, the submarine, the USS Growler and the world's fastest commercial airliner, the Concorde. The Intrepid is currently on leave for repairs and is in dry-dock across the river in Bayonne, NJ. The entire complex is also closed for repairs, slated to reopen in 2008. Two blocks farther north are three passenger ship terminals, built to accommodate large ocean liners and

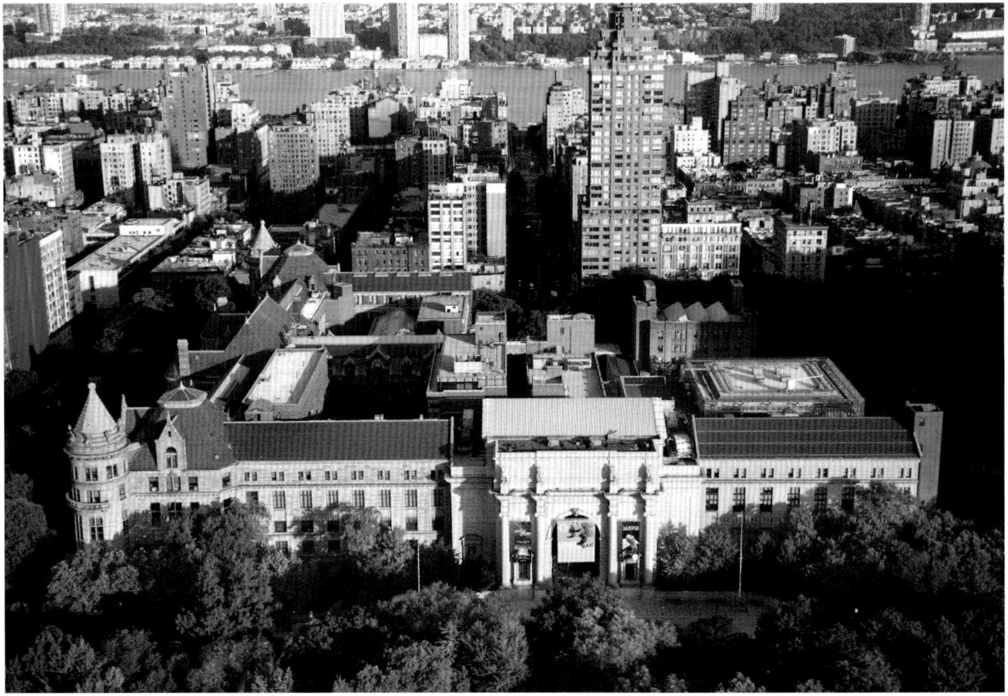

156
The American Museum of Natural History is one of the most visited museums in New York, and Dinosaur Hall is one of its most popular exhibits.

cruise ships. While the western midtown area of New York is a mix of commercial and cultural pursuits, including Rockefeller Center, a complex of 19 commercial buildings – including Radio City Music Hall, most of the Upper West Side north of 59th street is residential. To service the faithful who live there, the area is filled with many noteworthy houses of worship. The massive Cathedral of St. John the Divine is on Amsterdam Avenue at West 112th Street in the Morningside Heights section. Begun in 1892, construction on the church is still not finished, but when it is, it will be the largest Neo-Gothic cathedral in the world.

Farther north and west, at 120th Street and Riverside Drive, the ecumenical Riverside Church was built with funds donated by wealthy members, including John D. Rockefeller. Nearby are the Union Theological Seminary and the Jewish Theological Seminary, founded in 1886. Across Cathedral Parkway into west Harlem, churches also abound, over 400 in all. Since the founding of the Abyssinian Baptist Church in 1808, which was the first African-American Baptist Church in America, churches have provided the cornerstones of the African-American community, which thrived in Harlem after the turn of the 20th century. Farther up the Hudson, past Morningside and Hamilton Heights, the George Washington Bridge links upper Manhattan to Fort Lee, New Jersey. The bridge, known simply as the GWB, celebrated its 75th birthday in 2006. Built in 1931, it is still the busiest bridge for vehicles in the world. The view from the bridge is a spectacular panorama of the west side of the city.

Washington Heights, the neighborhood into which traffic from the bridge flows, is named for Fort Washington, the site of a revolutionary war fortification. Situated at the highest point in the city (265 feet above sea level), the fort no longer stands, but the house where George Washington himself headquartered during the fall of 1776, still does. The oldest remaining house in Manhattan, Morris-Jumel mansion gives a glimpse of 18th-century life in New York, amidst the non-stop pace and growth of the city around it.

From the oldest to the newest, the one constant of the Upper West Side, in fact, of all New York, is change.

159

The Morningside Heights neighborhood is an educational mecca that includes Columbia University, Barnard College, the Jewish Theological Seminary, Teachers College, and the Union Theological Seminary.

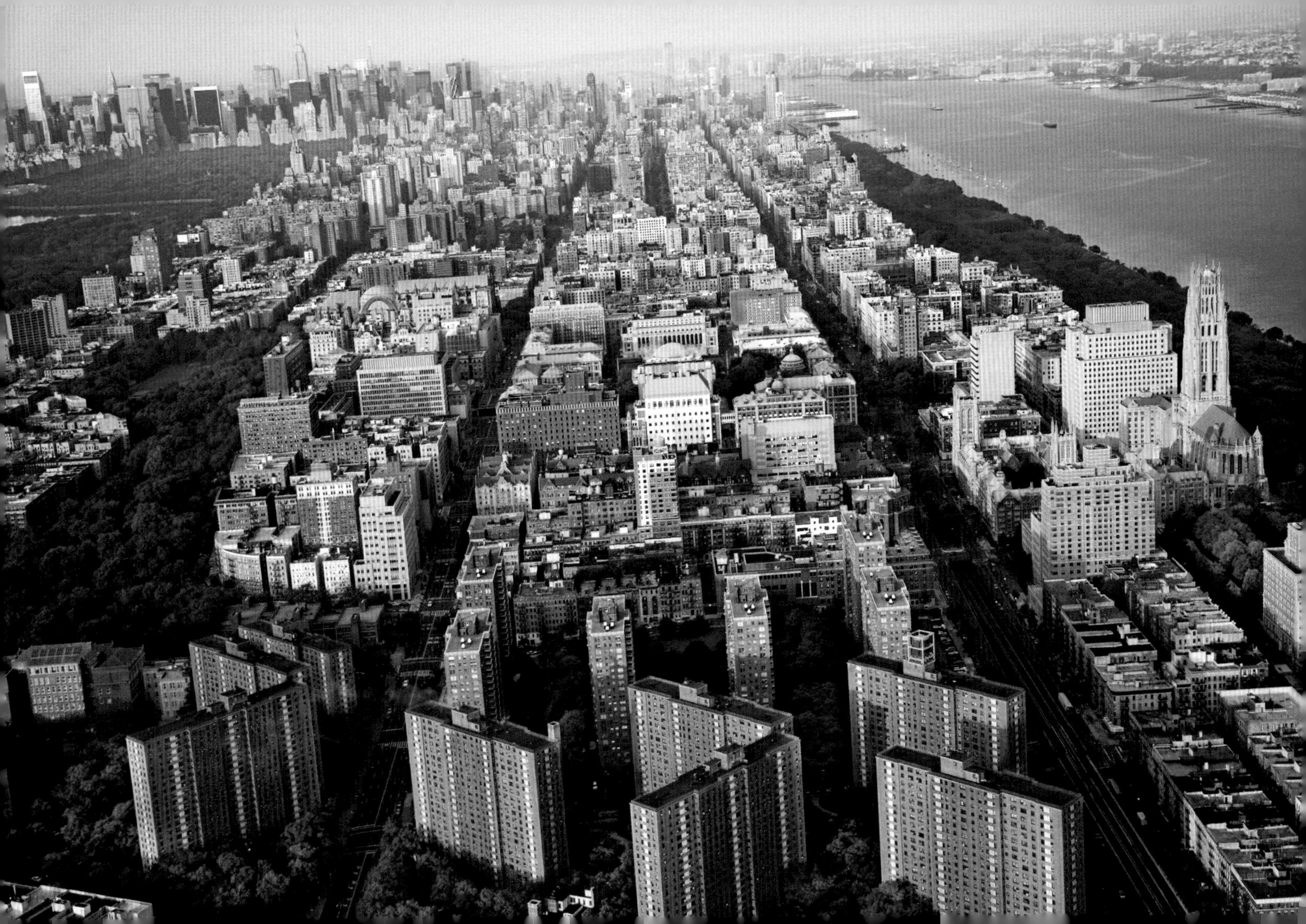

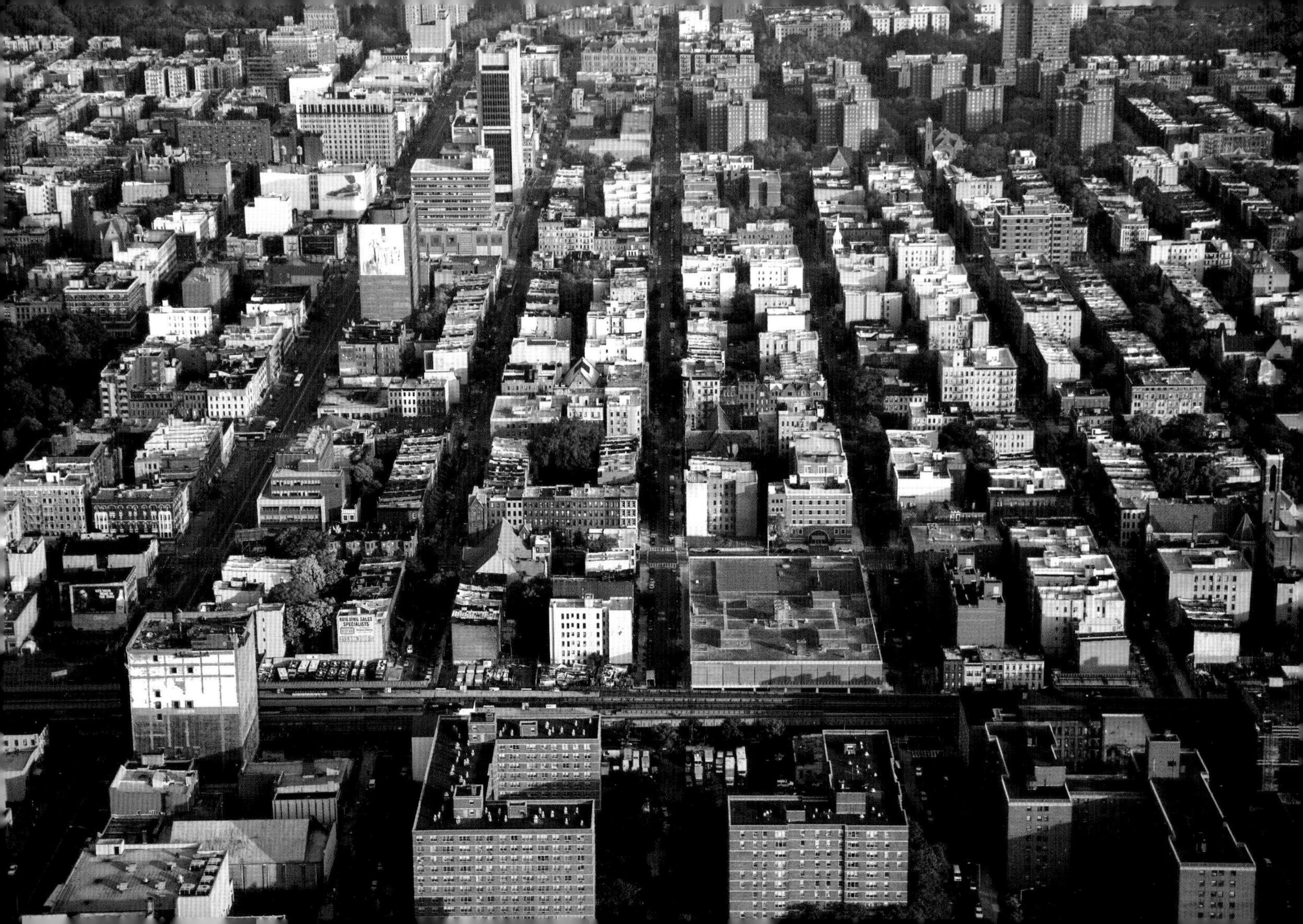
BUILDING SALES
SPECIALISTS

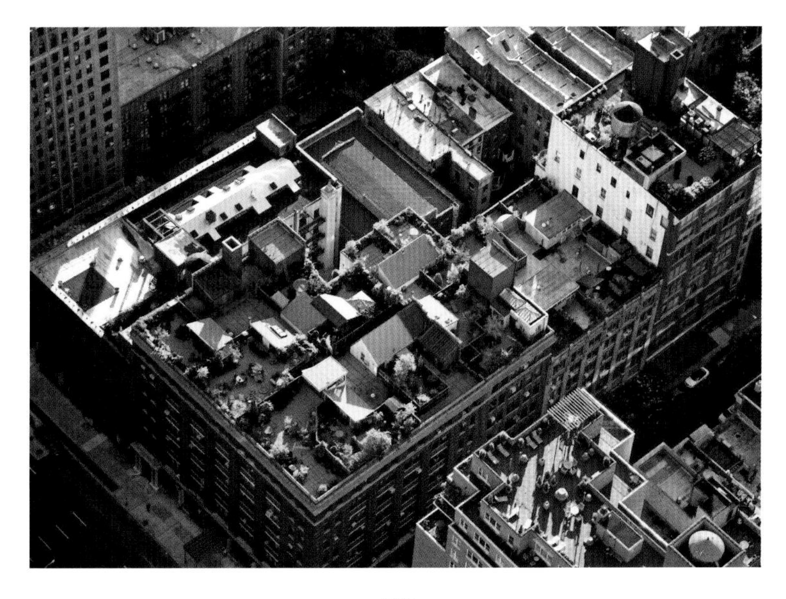

160
The scale of buildings on the Upper West Side is more modest than the skyscraper jungle of Midtown.

161
Rooftops in New York are used for everything from mechanical equipment and water-tanks to elegant gardens and patios.

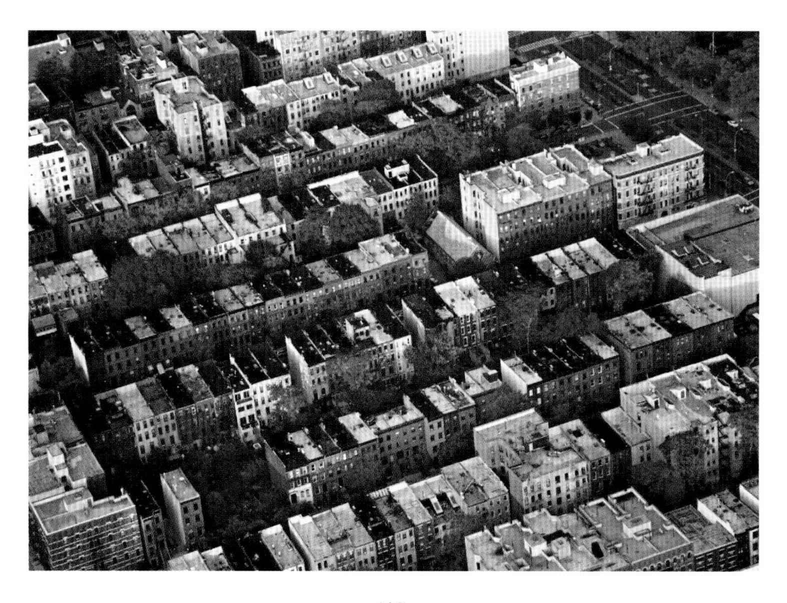

162

Before the age of the skyscraper, densely packed row houses, no more than four or five stories tall, were the order of the day.

163

City University, in Harlem, with its landmark Neo-Gothic architecture, is the oldest free public educational institution in the United State.

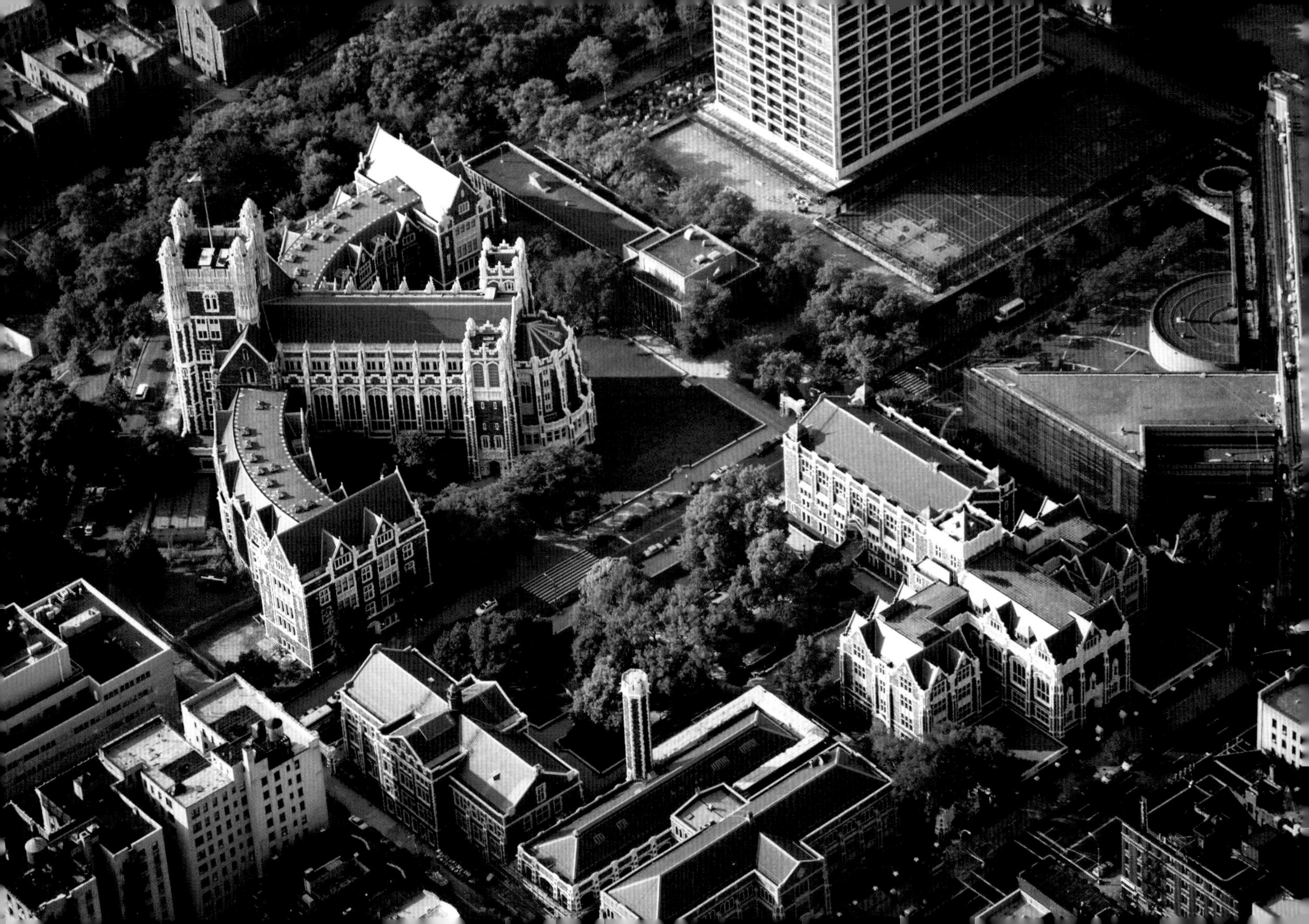

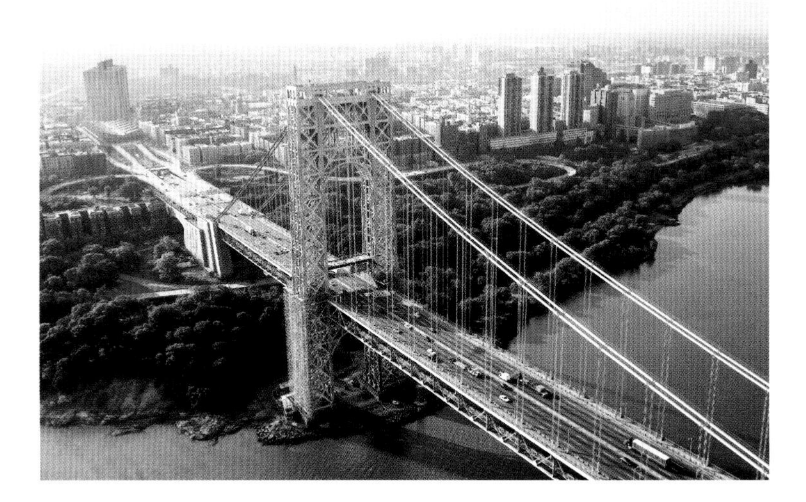

164
The tiny "Litte Red Lighthouse," made famous in a children's book, is tucked under the base of the George Washington Bridge.

165
The George Washington Bridge links New Jersey to the Washington Heights neighborhood and upper Manhattan.

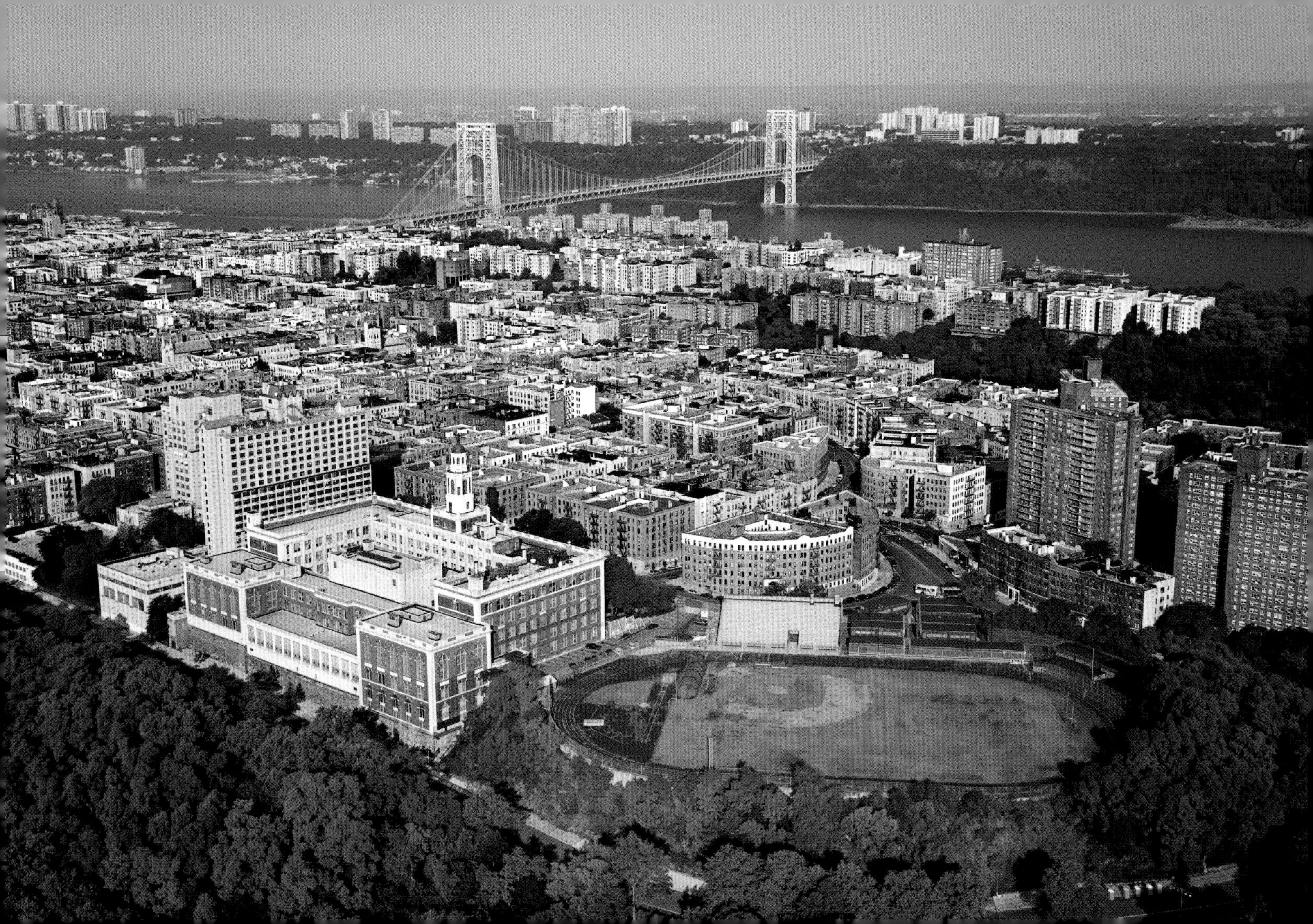

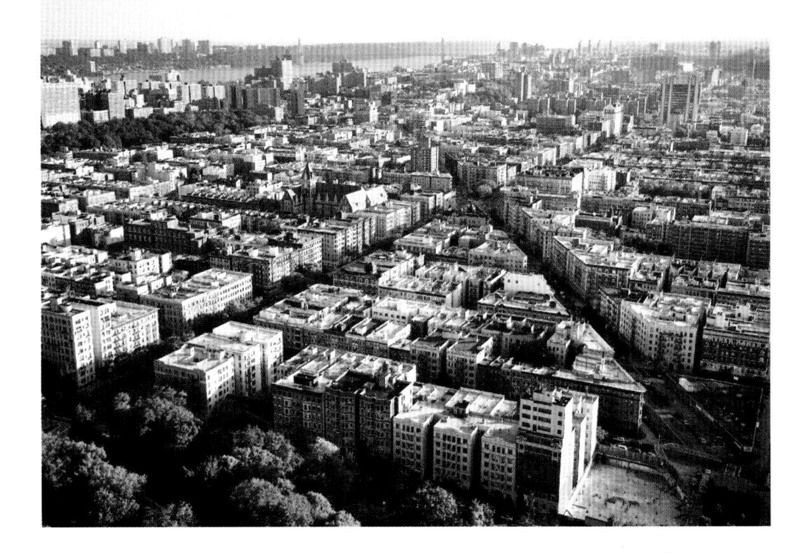

166
The northwest neighborhoods of Manhattan include parks, row houses, wide thoroughfares and views of the Hudson River.

167
The apartments along Central Park West, with their dramatic towers and turrets, tend to be more flamboyant than the more sedate Fifth Avenue counterparts.

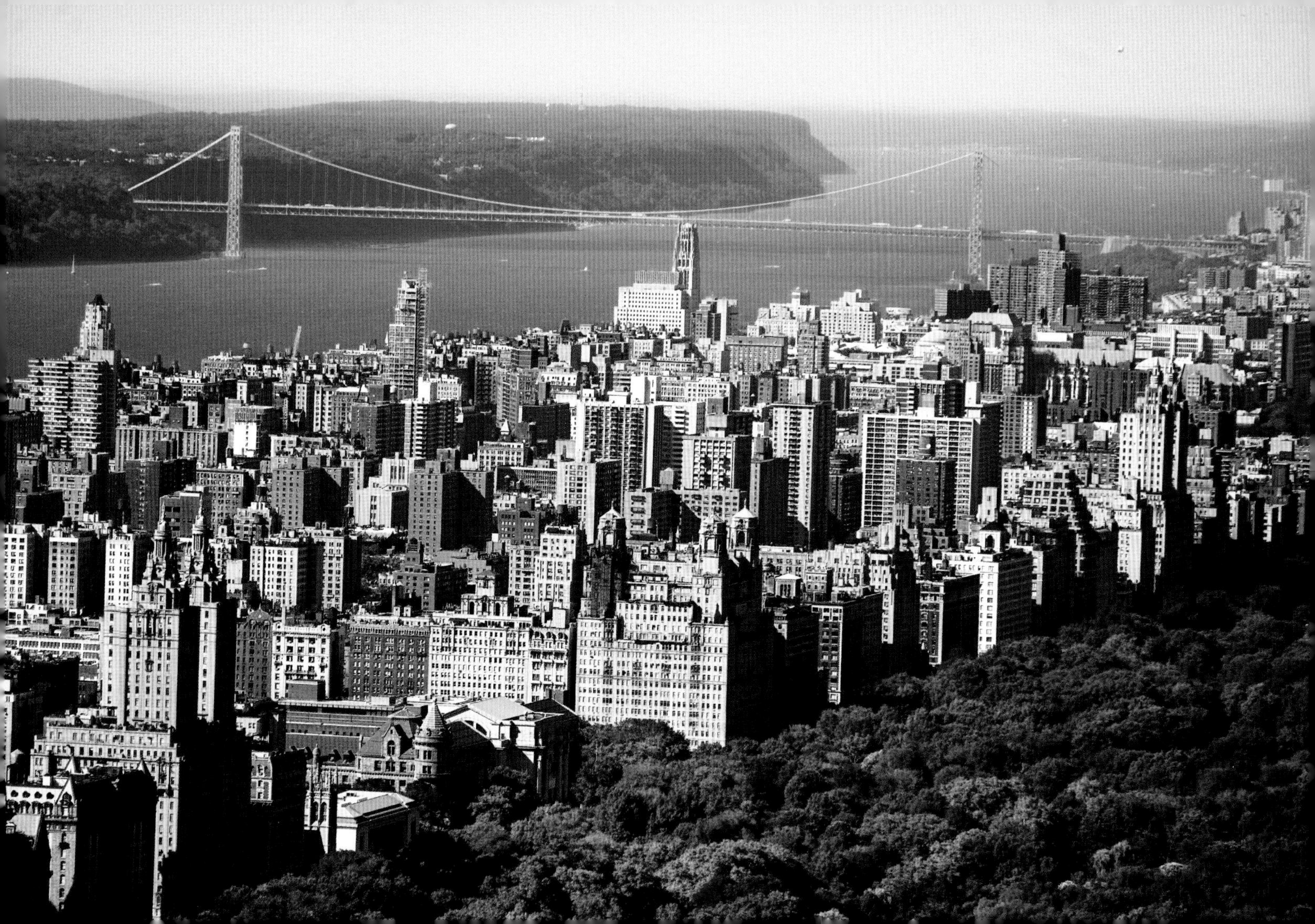

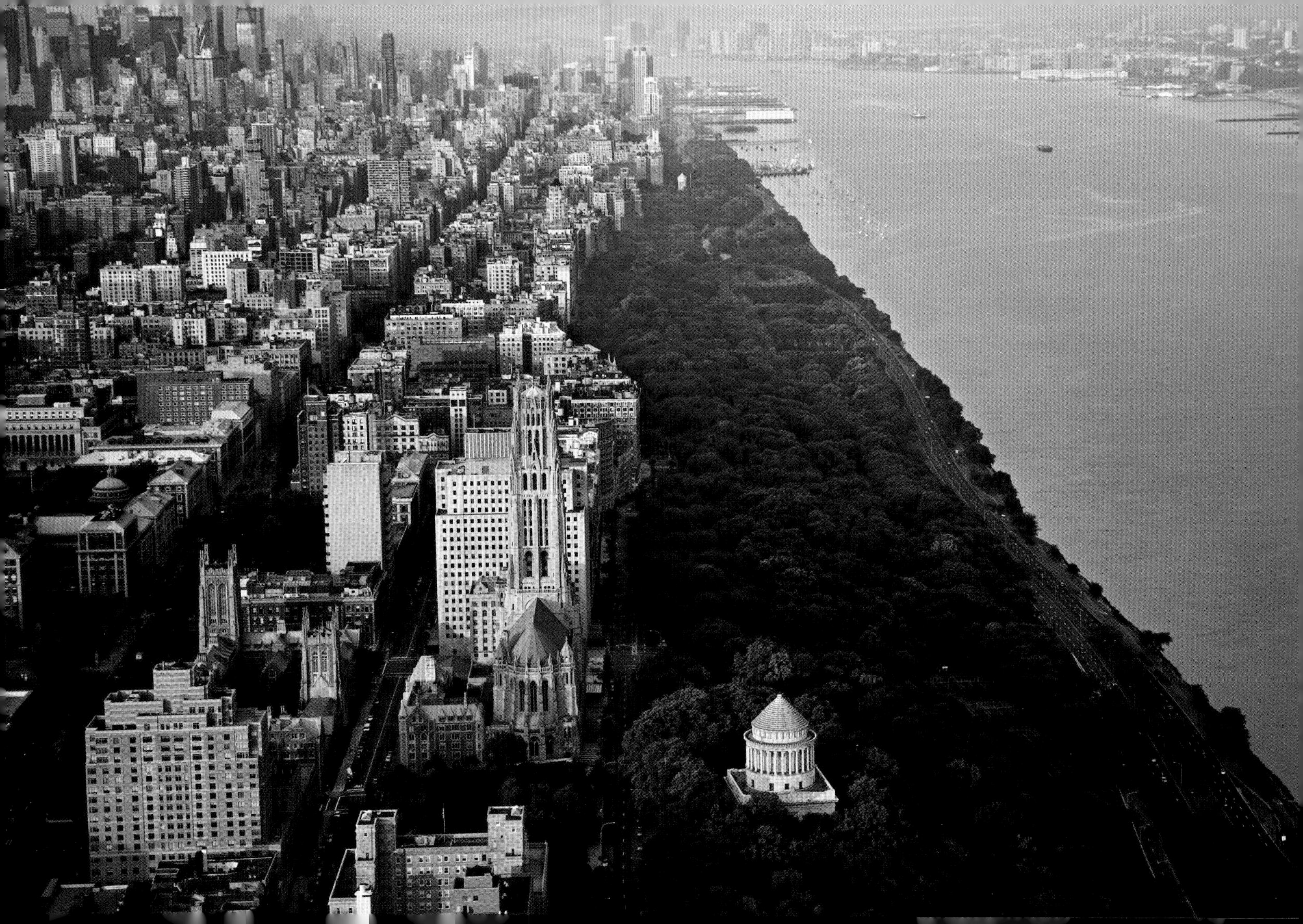

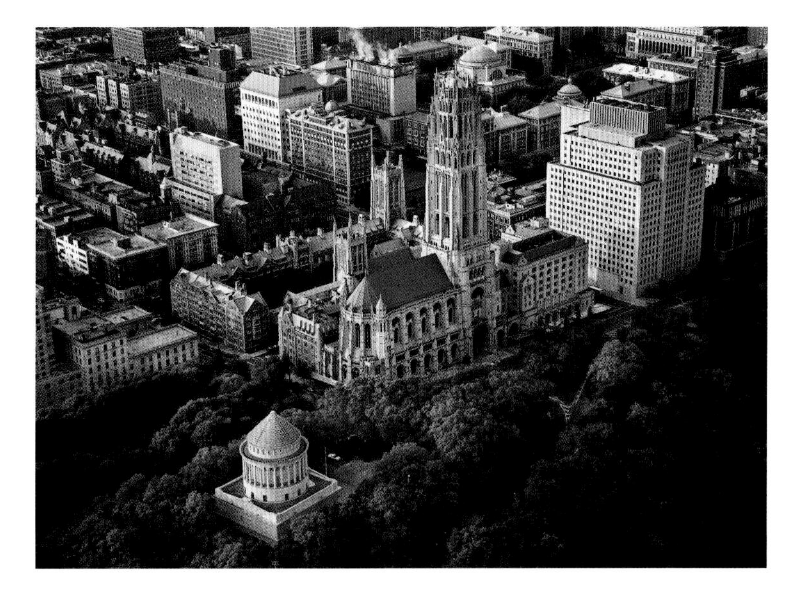

168
Grants Tomb, which holds the remains of President Ulysses Grant and his wife, is nestled amidst the trees of Riverside Park, across from Riverside Church, with its single massive gothic spire.

169
Riverside Church was founded by wealthy benefactors, including John D. Rockefeller, and was modeled after French cathedrals.

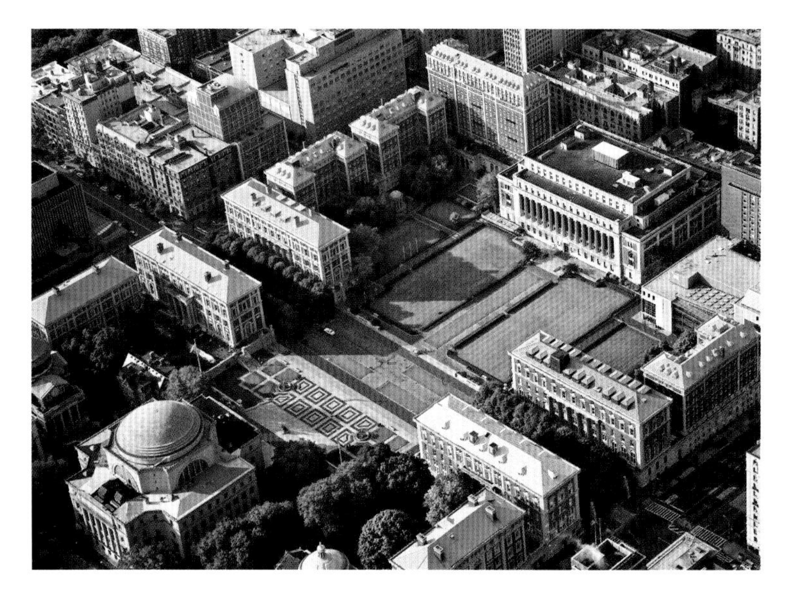

170

Columbia University, with its distinctive green rooftops, dominates Morningside Heights, and its two libraries, Lowe and Butler, are the focal points of the campus.

171

Columbia University stretches from 114th to 121st Street, between Broadway and Amsterdam, and is a neighbor to Teachers College, Barnard College, Union Theological Seminary, the Jewish Theological Seminary, and Riverside Church.

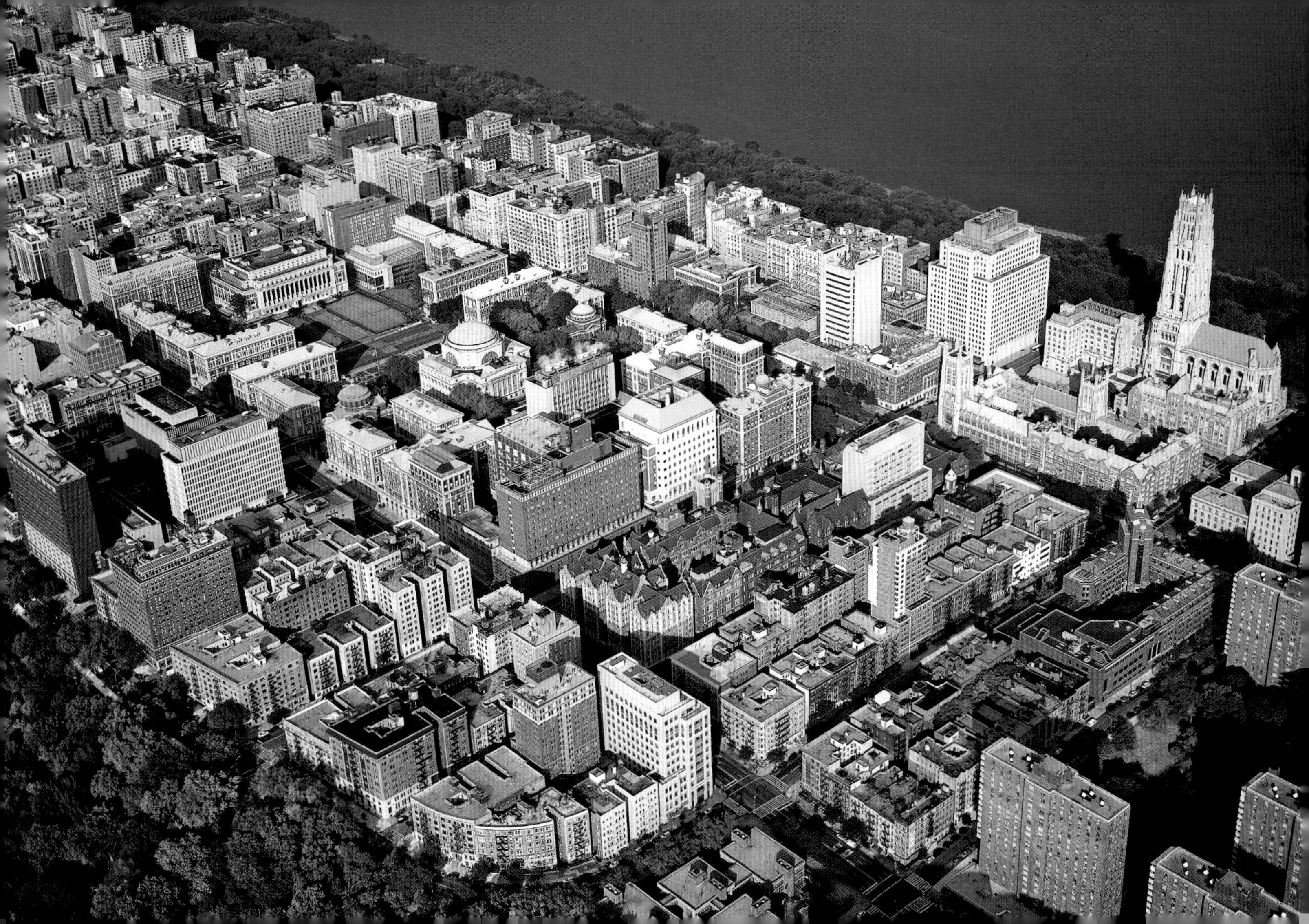

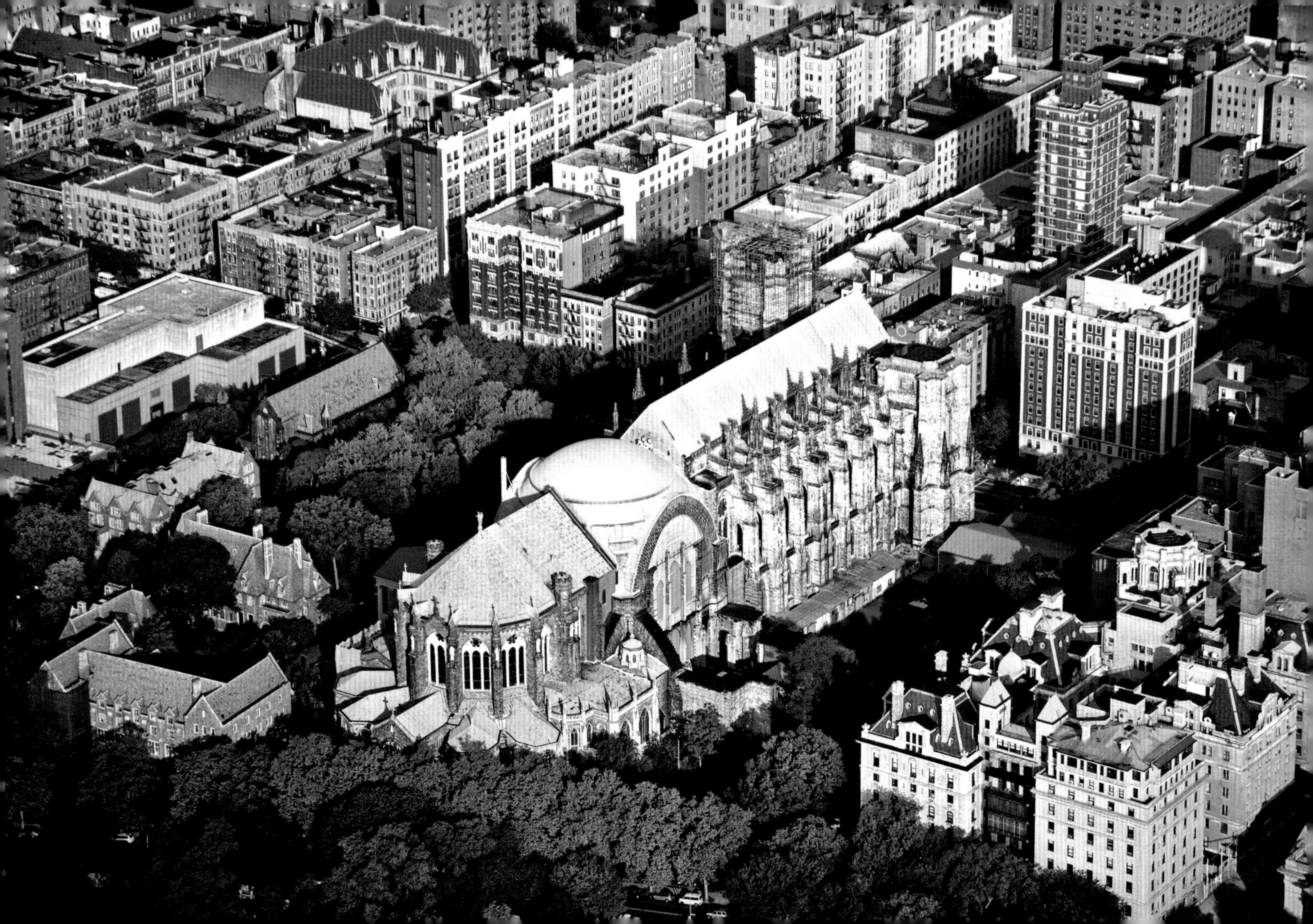

172
The Episcopal Cathedral of St. John the Divine will be the largest Neo-Gothic cathedral in the world when it is completed. Construction was begun in 1892.

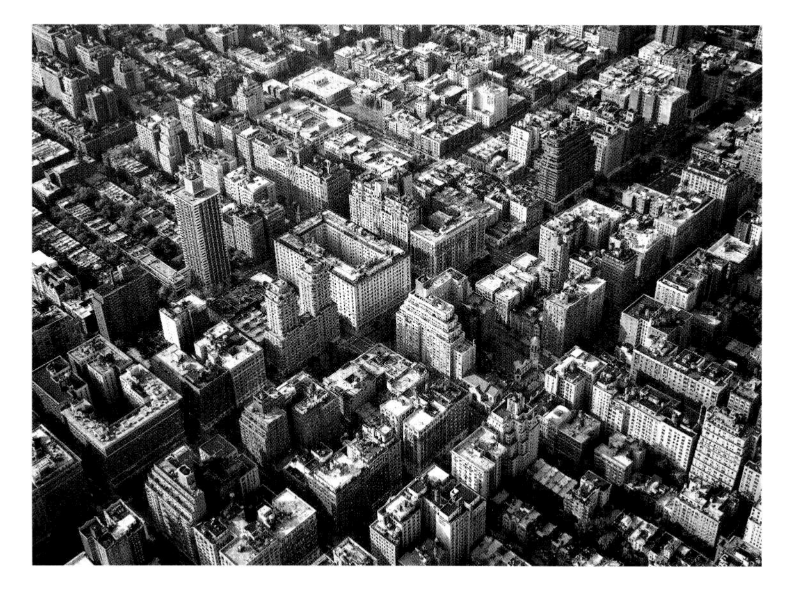

174
The Upper West Side has many apartments built around a central courtyard; the most massive of these is the Belnord at 86th Street and Broadway.

175
455 Central Park West has recently been converted to luxury condominium apartments; it was originally built as a cancer hospital in 1887.

176-177
The grand multi-towered apartment buildings along Central Park West command the choicest views of the massive park.

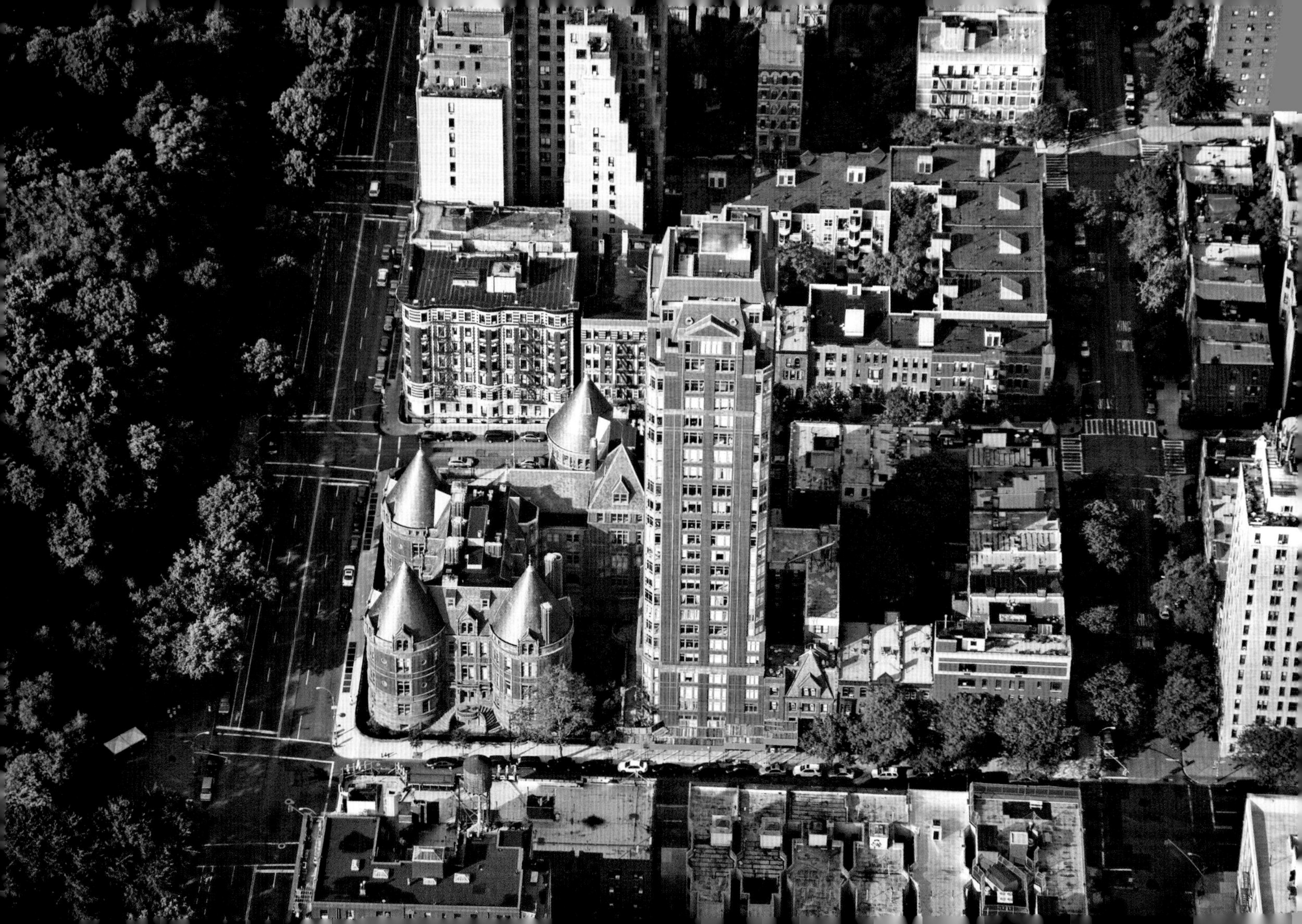

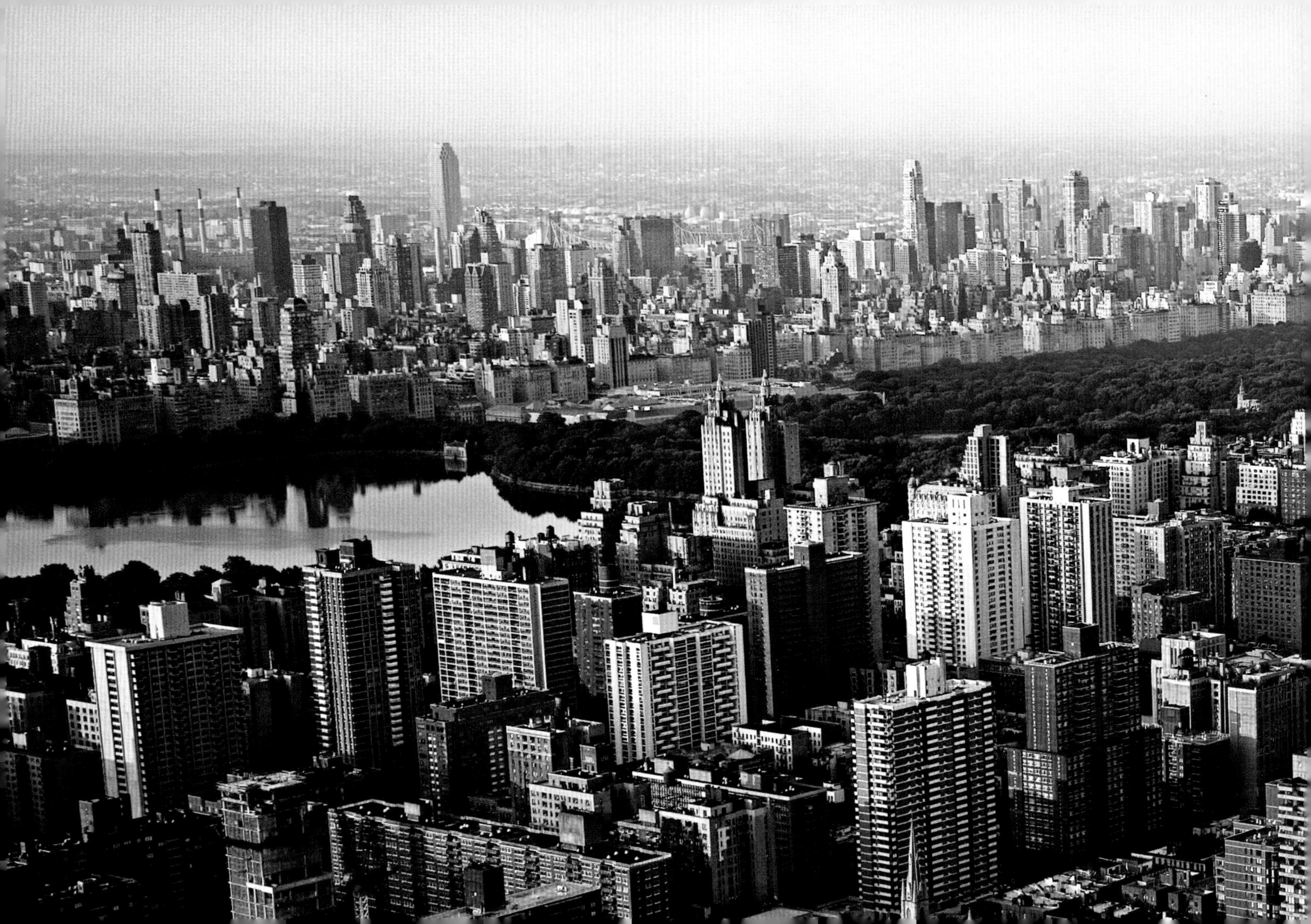

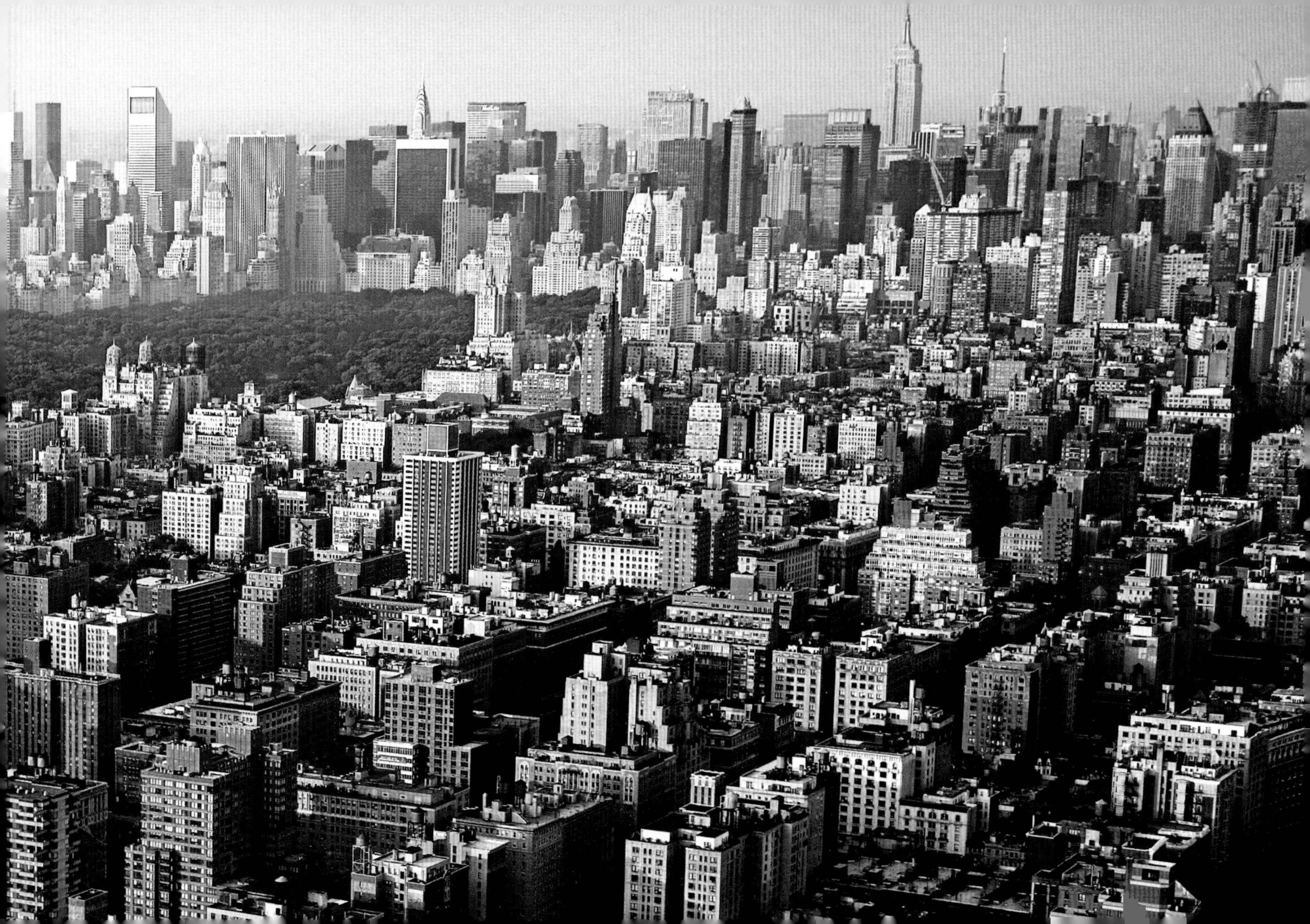

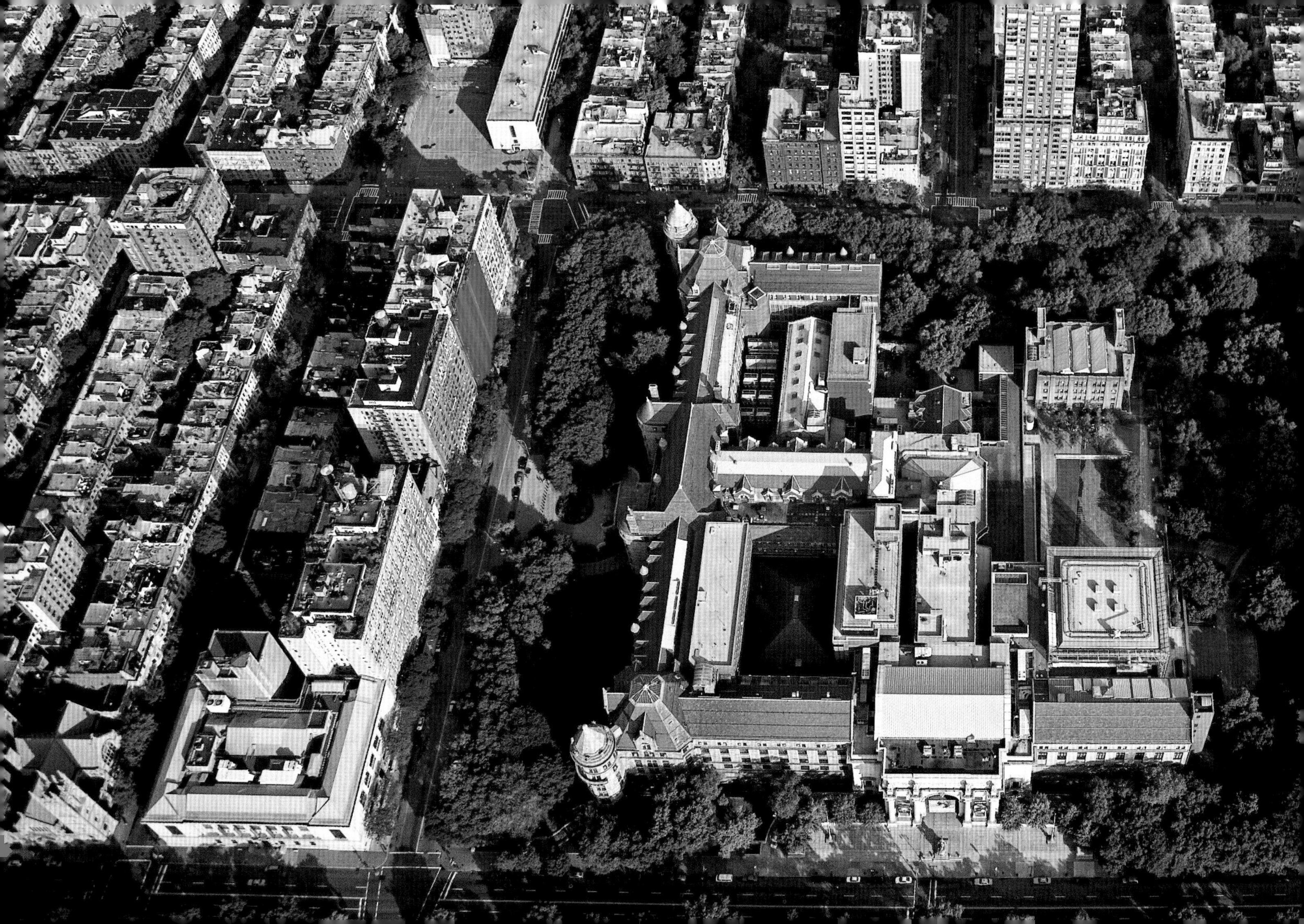

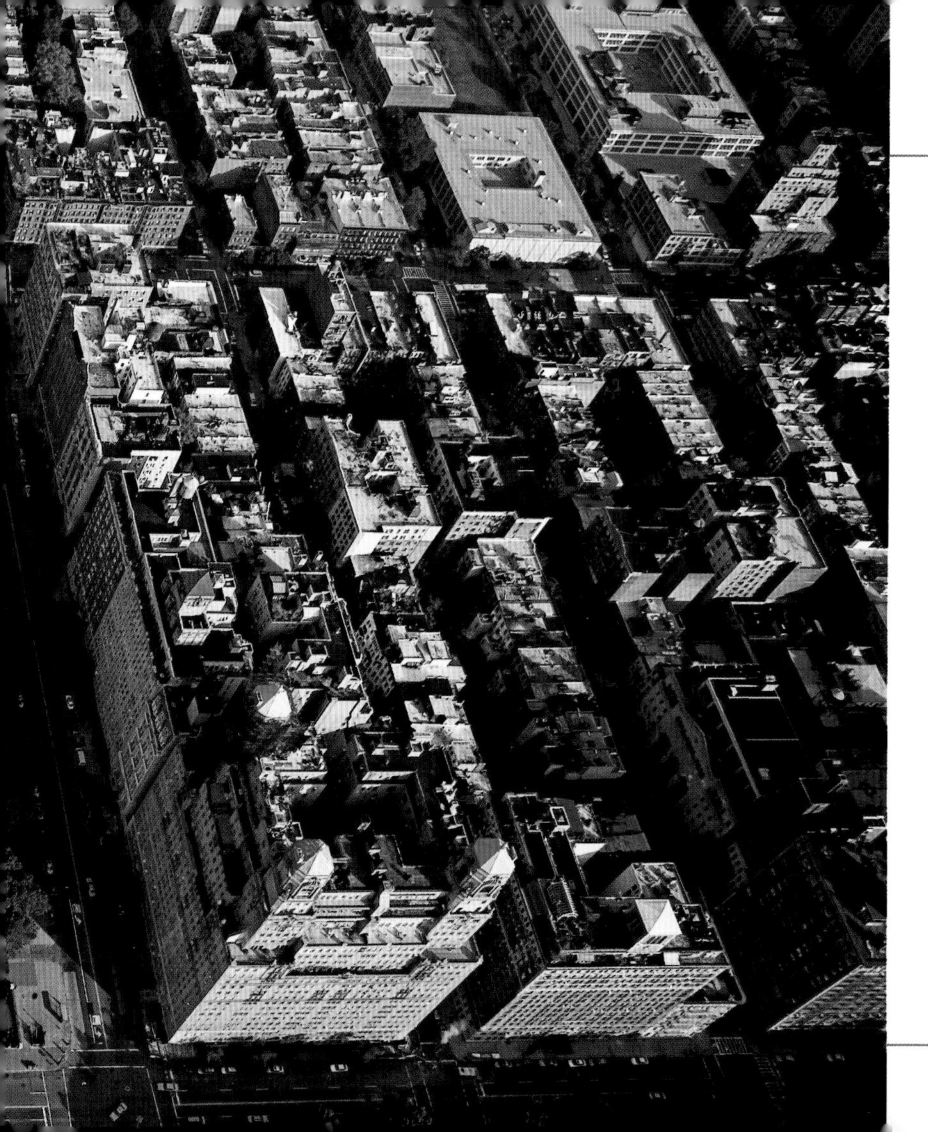

178-179
The American Museum of Natural History dominates the block, between West 77th and West 81st Streets. The New York Historical Society and the Beresford Apartments flank it.

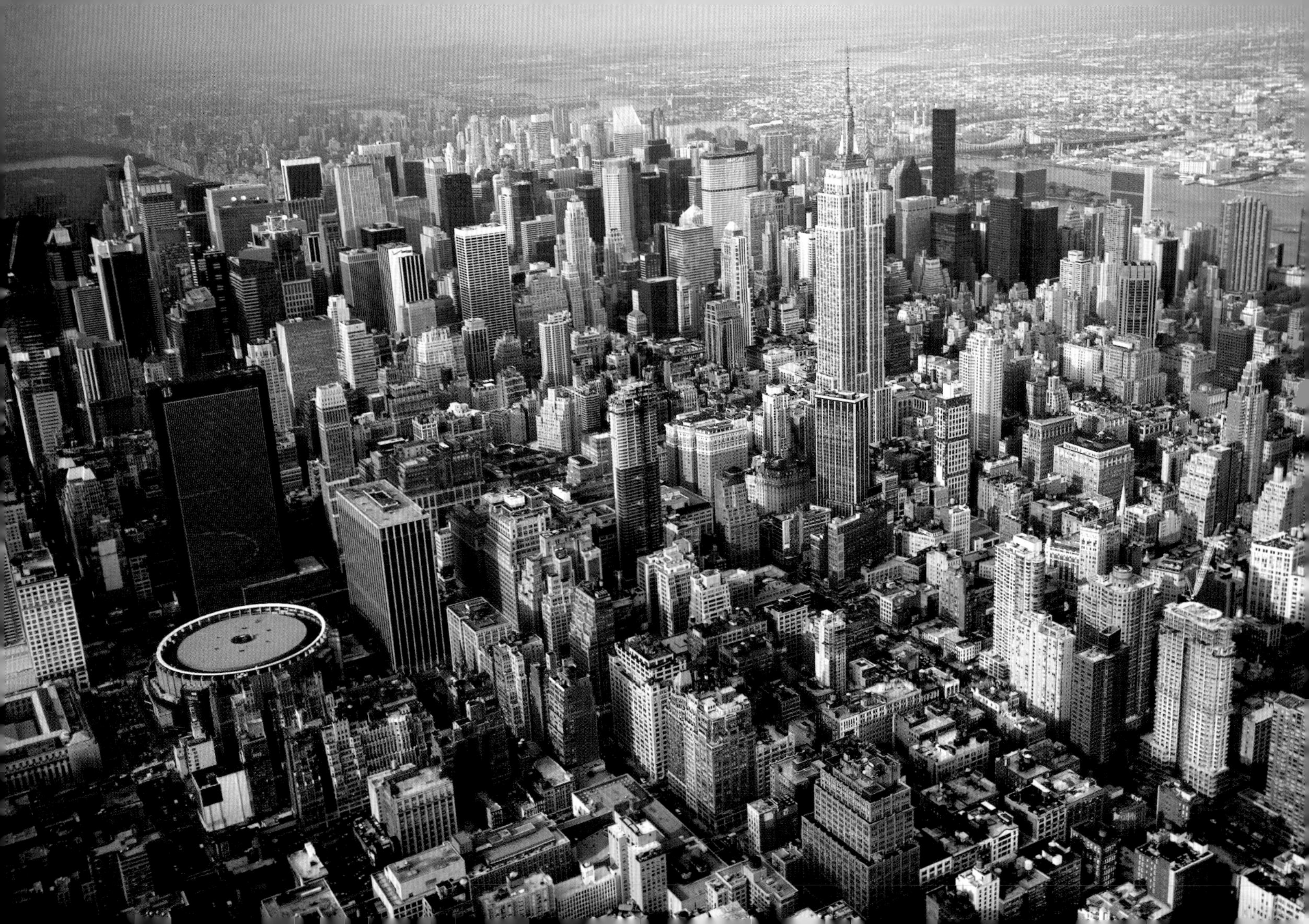

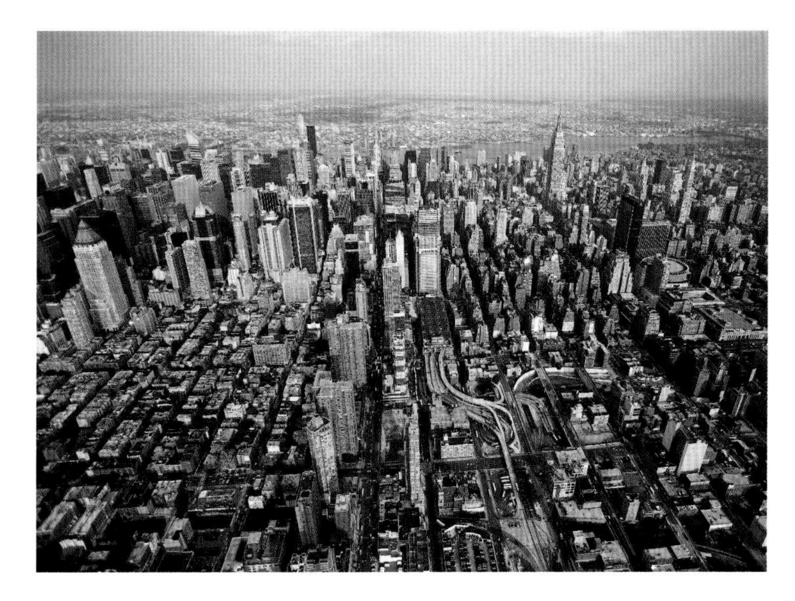

180

Madison Square Garden sits above Pennsylvania Station, which is to get a new entrance across the street in the landmarked former General Post Office building.

181

The Port Authority Bus Terminal (center) between West 40th and West 42nd Streets, is the main gateway for interstate buses and serves 58 million passengers a year.

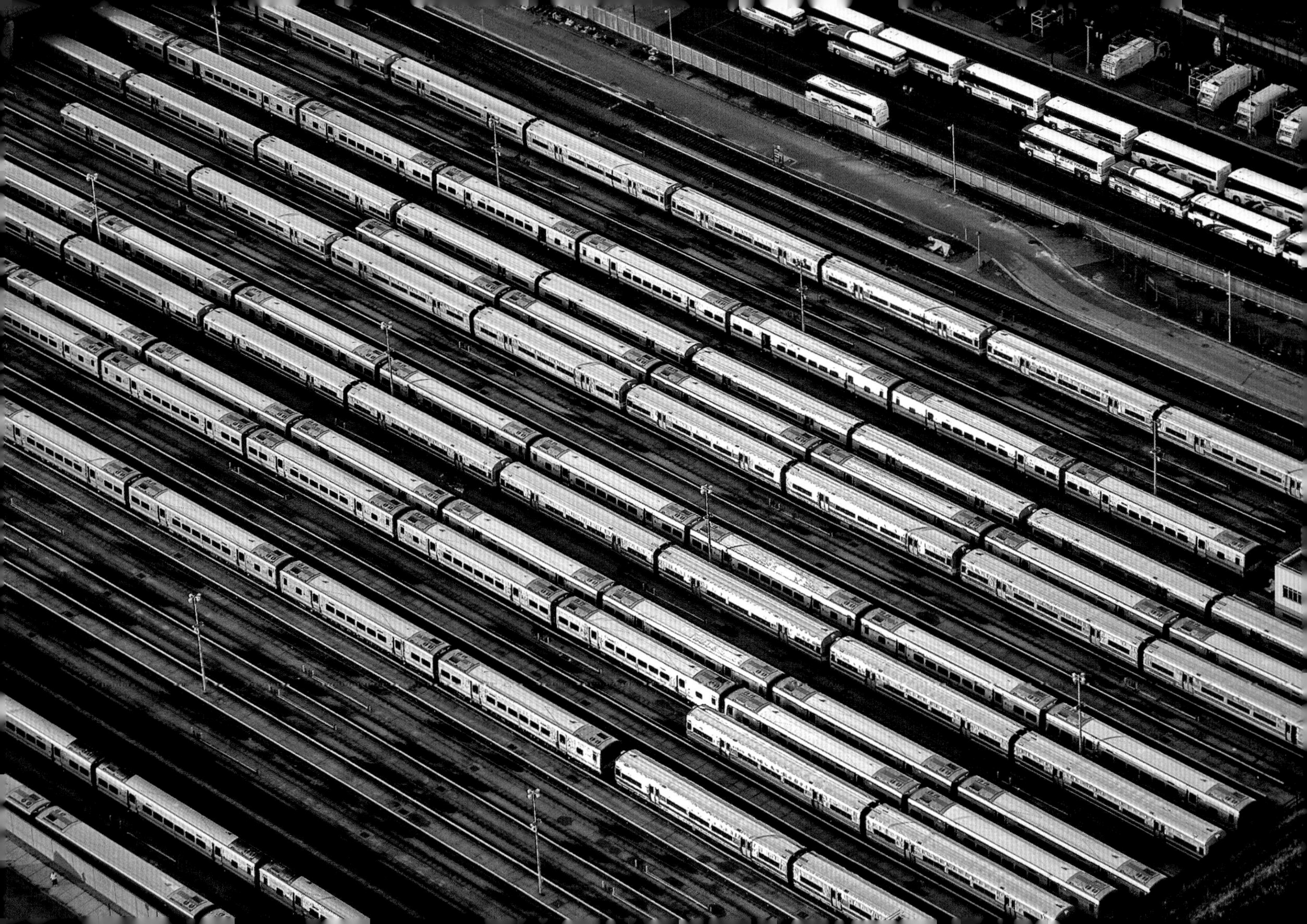

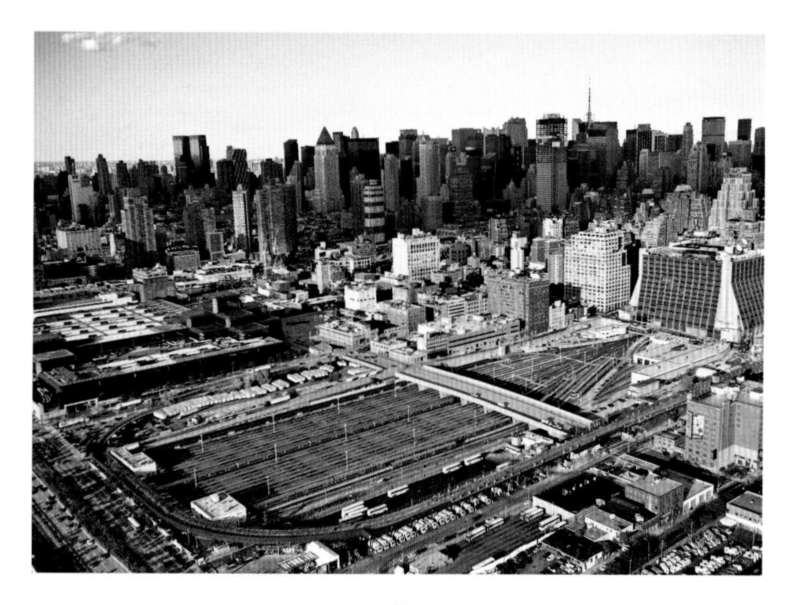

182

Amtrak and New Jersey Transit trains service rail passengers arriving in or departing from Manhattan's west side.

183

The Westside railyards, once considered by the New York officials as a site for a football stadium, will instead be developed into a high-rise office and residential district.

185
The area called Hell's Kitchen has become gentrified and is now also known as Clinton; Worldwide Plaza, with its pyramidal top, marks its eastern edge.

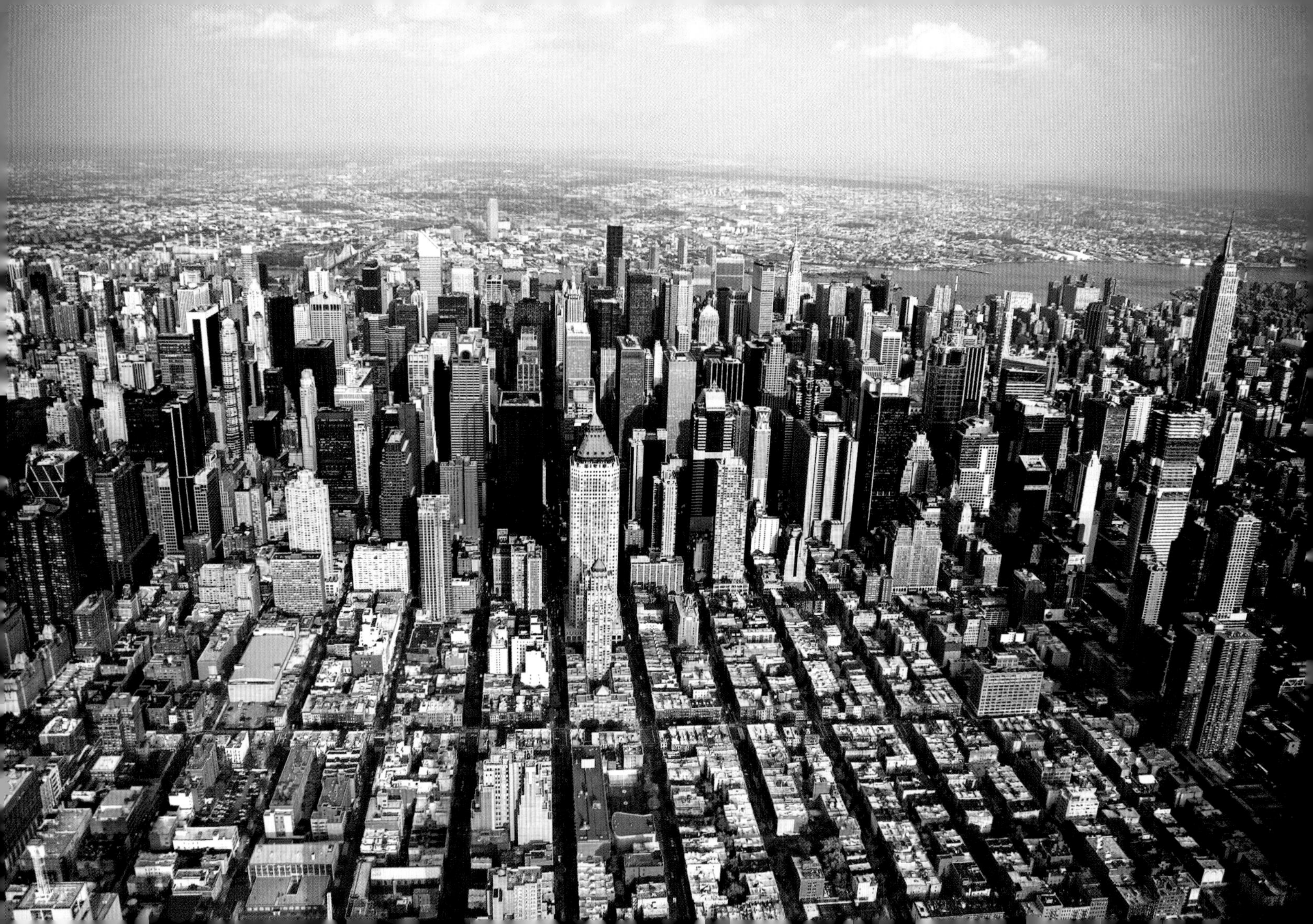

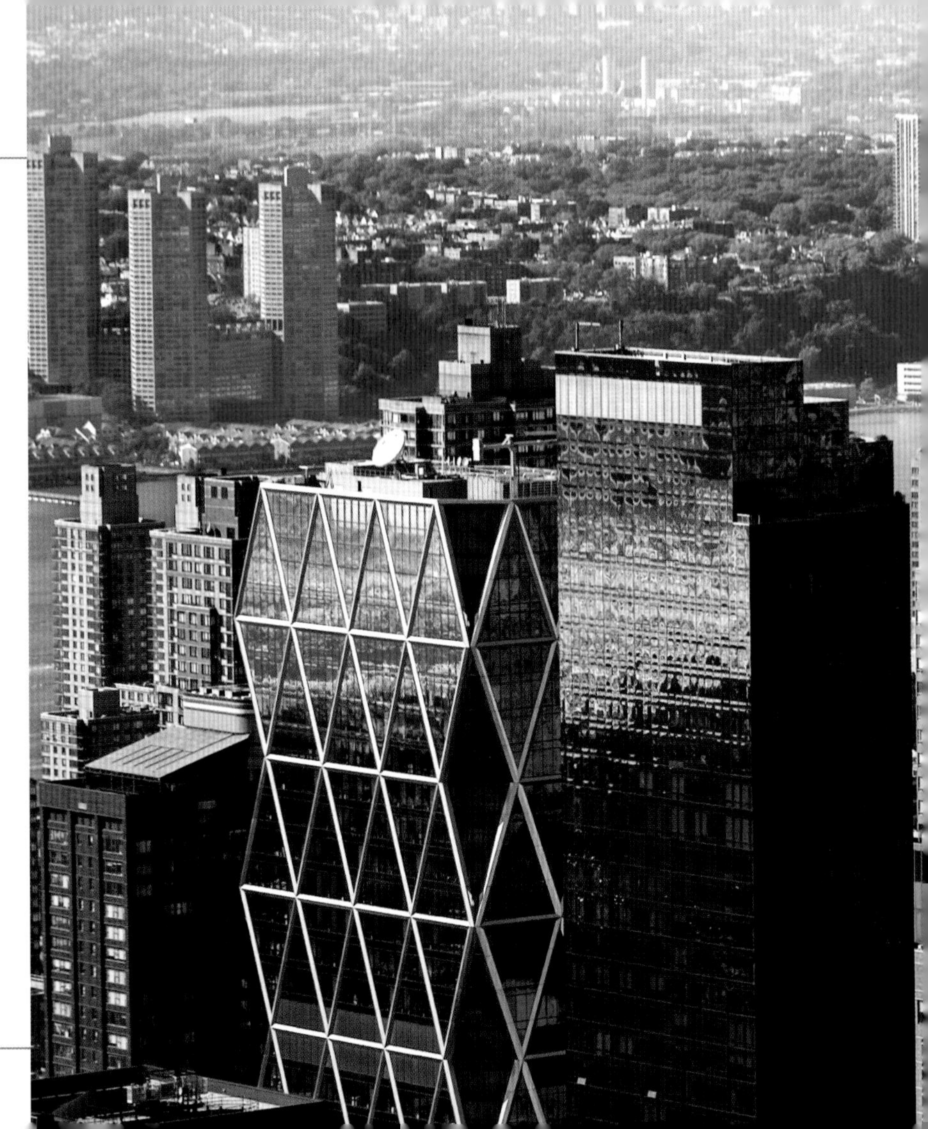

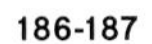

186-187
The Hearst Building, with its unique faceted frame, and the Time Warner towers (center) are part of a recent revival of the Columbus Circle area.

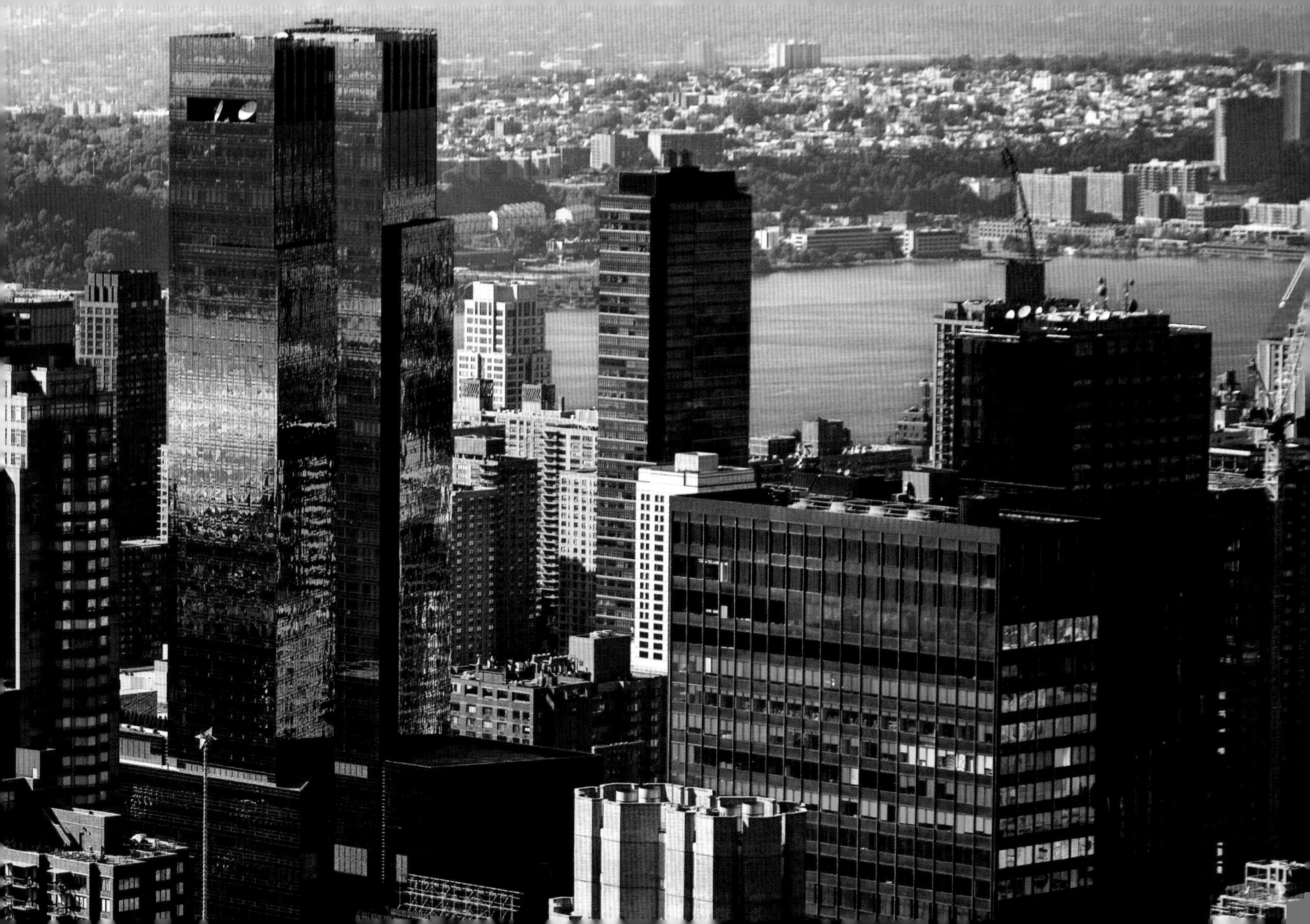

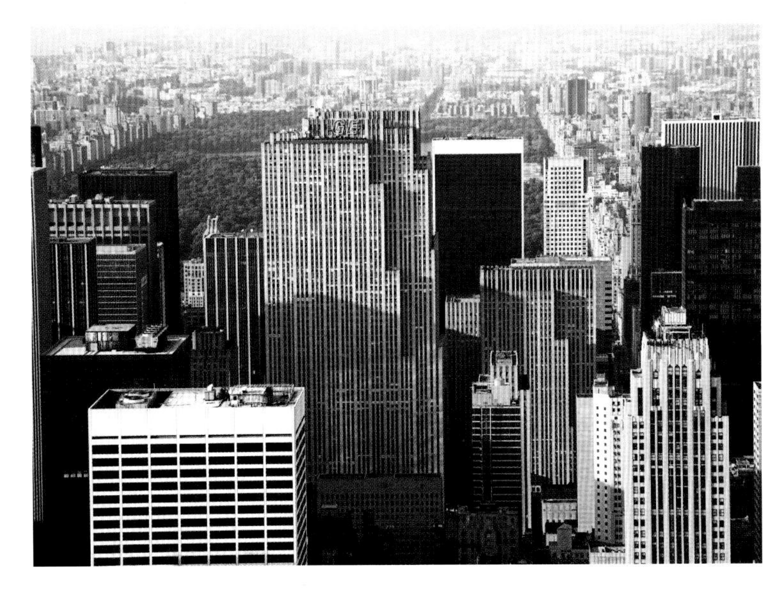

188

The former Grace Building at 1114 Avenue of the Americas (lower left) and the Solow Building (upper middle) both have sloping lower facades designed by Gordon Bunschaft.

189

The serenity of the pool and gardens on the roof of the British Empire Building is not disturbed by the bustle along Fifth Avenue below.

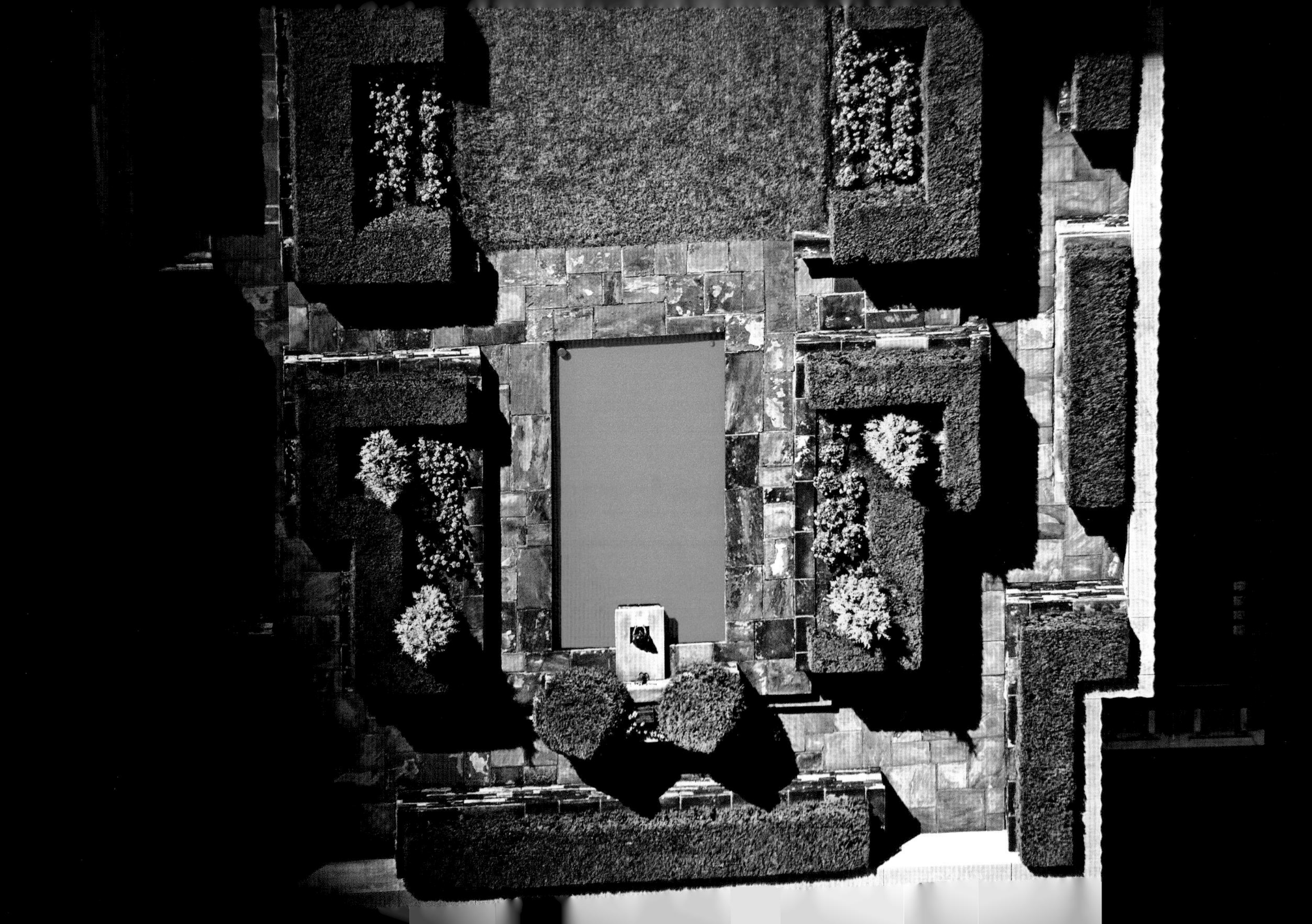

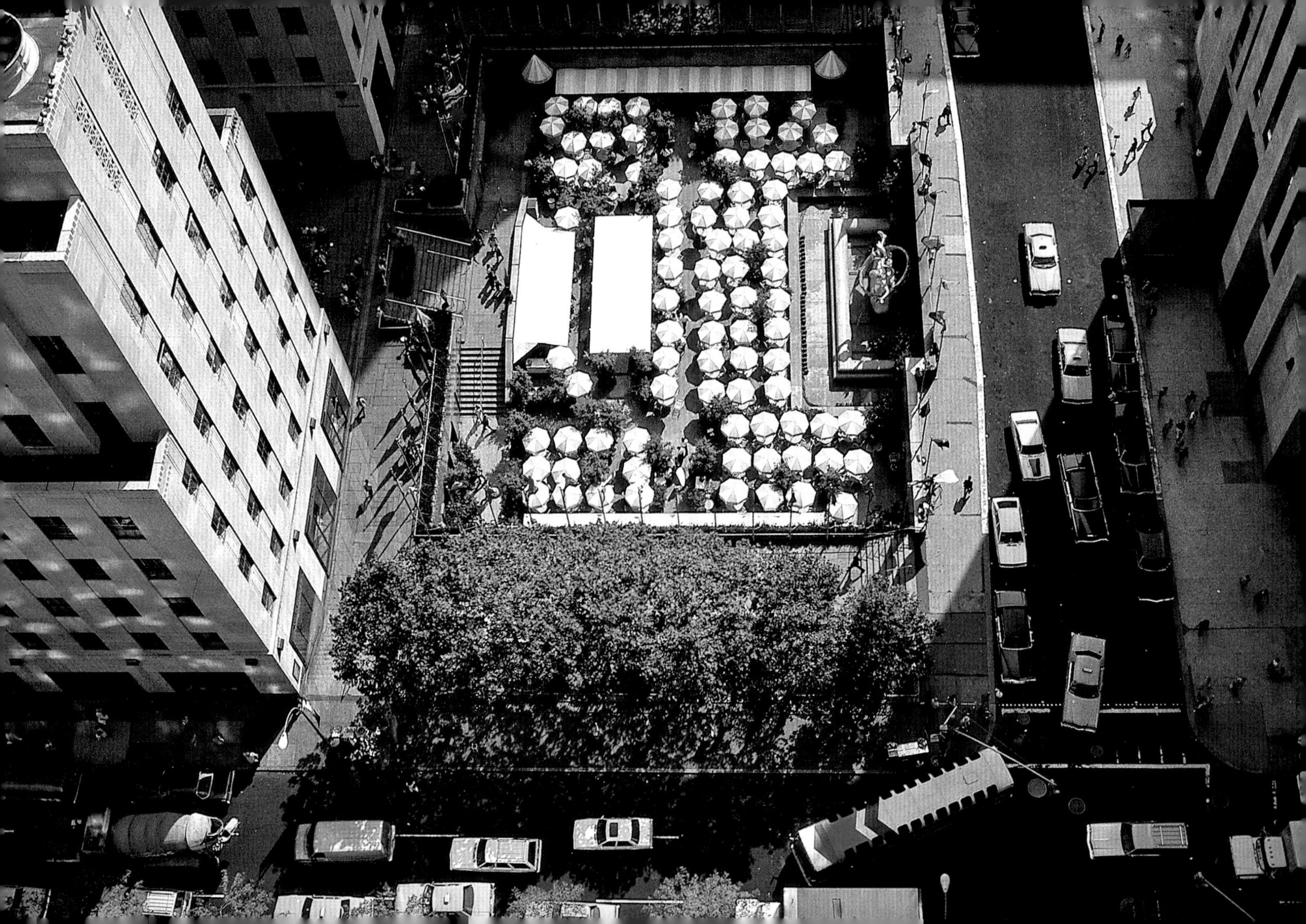

190
The sunken plaza of Rockefeller Center is a café in summer and is transformed into a skating rink in the winter.

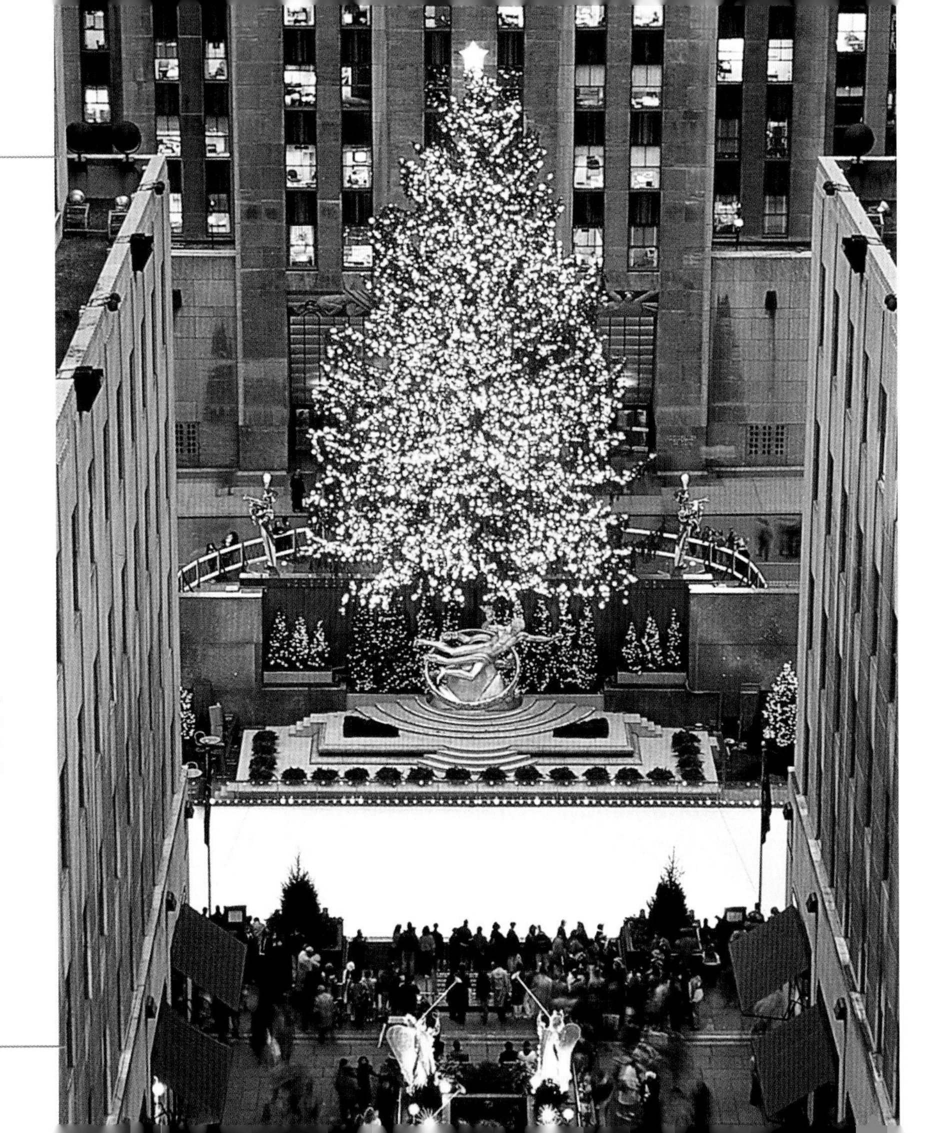

192

Visiting the Christmas tree (always a minimum of 65 feet tall) and ice rink at Rockefeller Center is a holiday ritual for both New Yorkers and tourists.

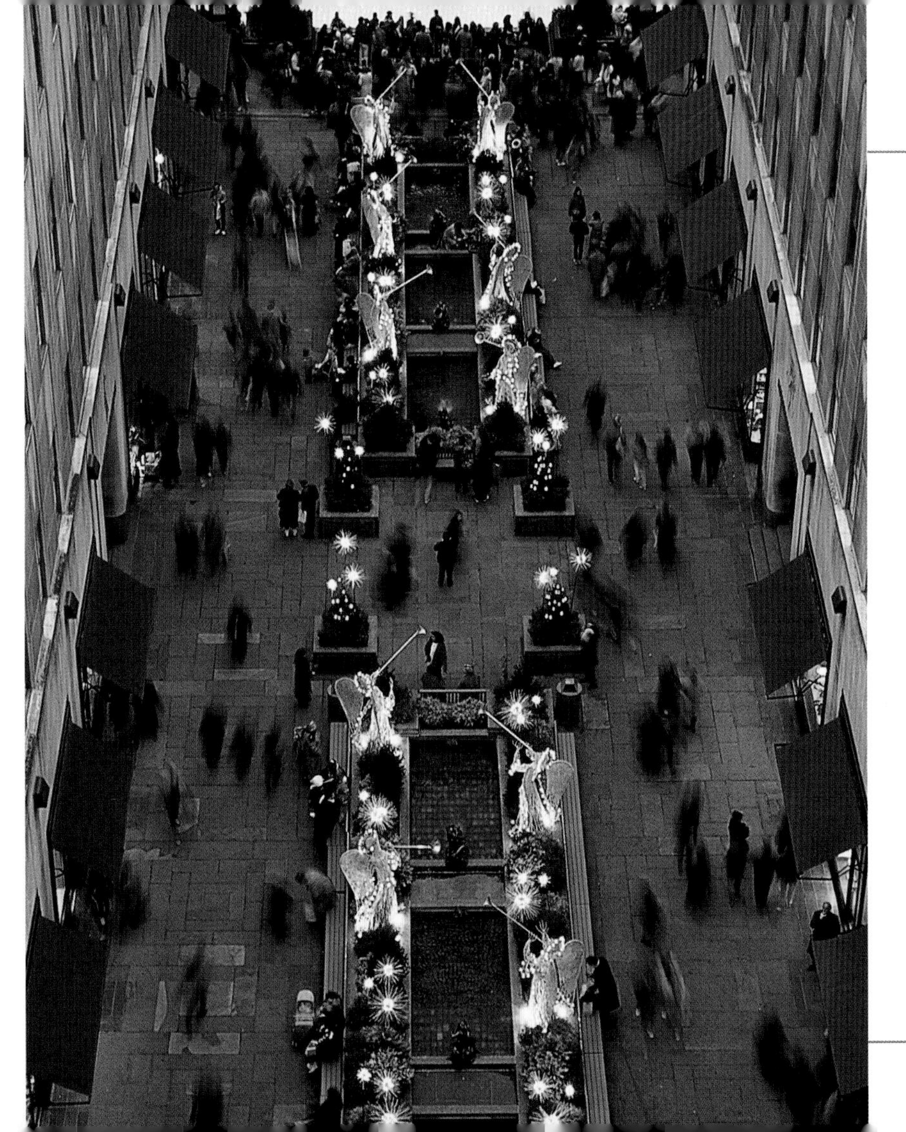

193
Celestial trumpeters herald the holiday season along the arcade approach to Rockefeller Center.

194-195
Remnants of the neighborhood's seedier days, like the bargain-rate Hotel Carter, are not far from the high-gloss glamour of the "new" Times Square.

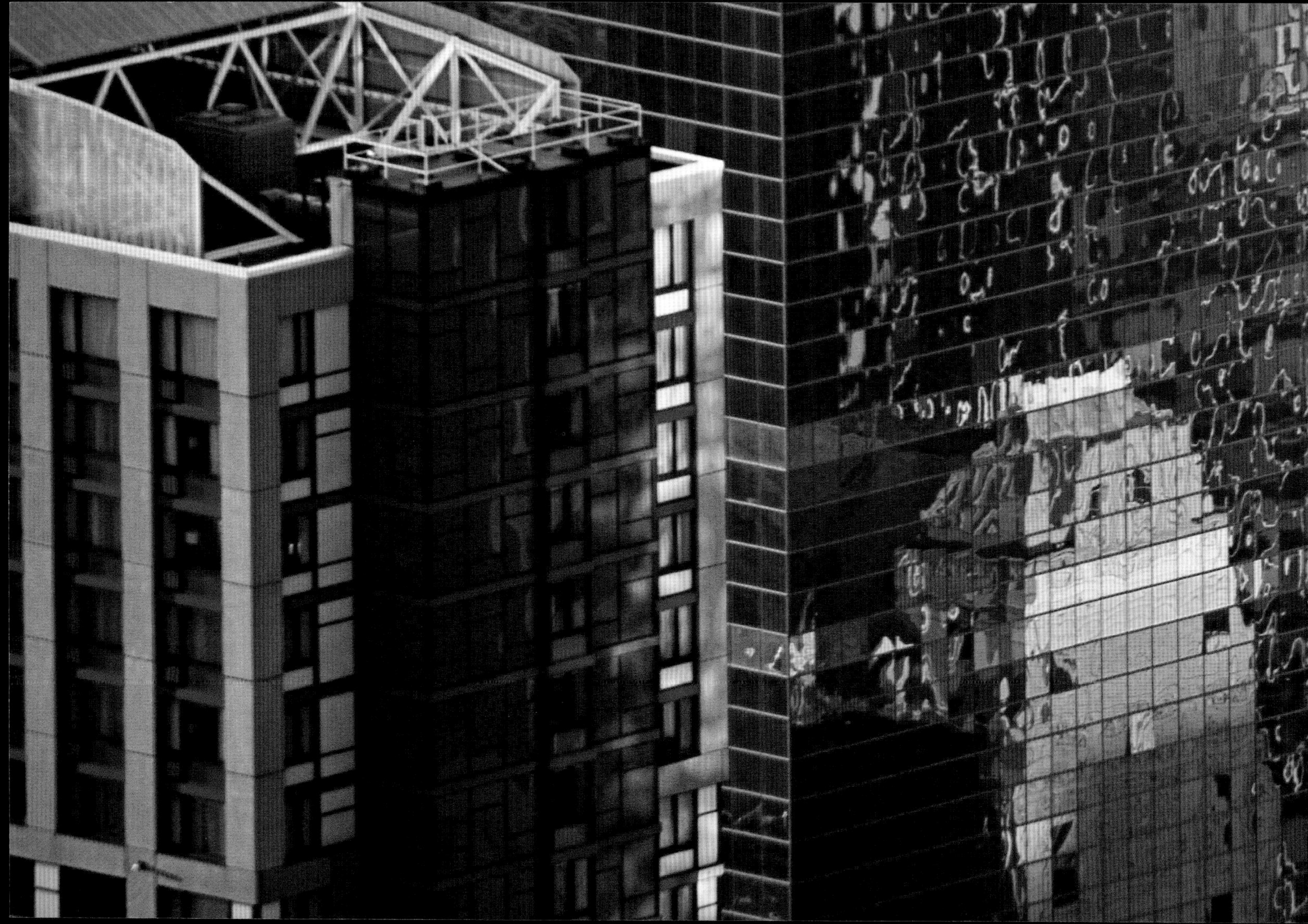

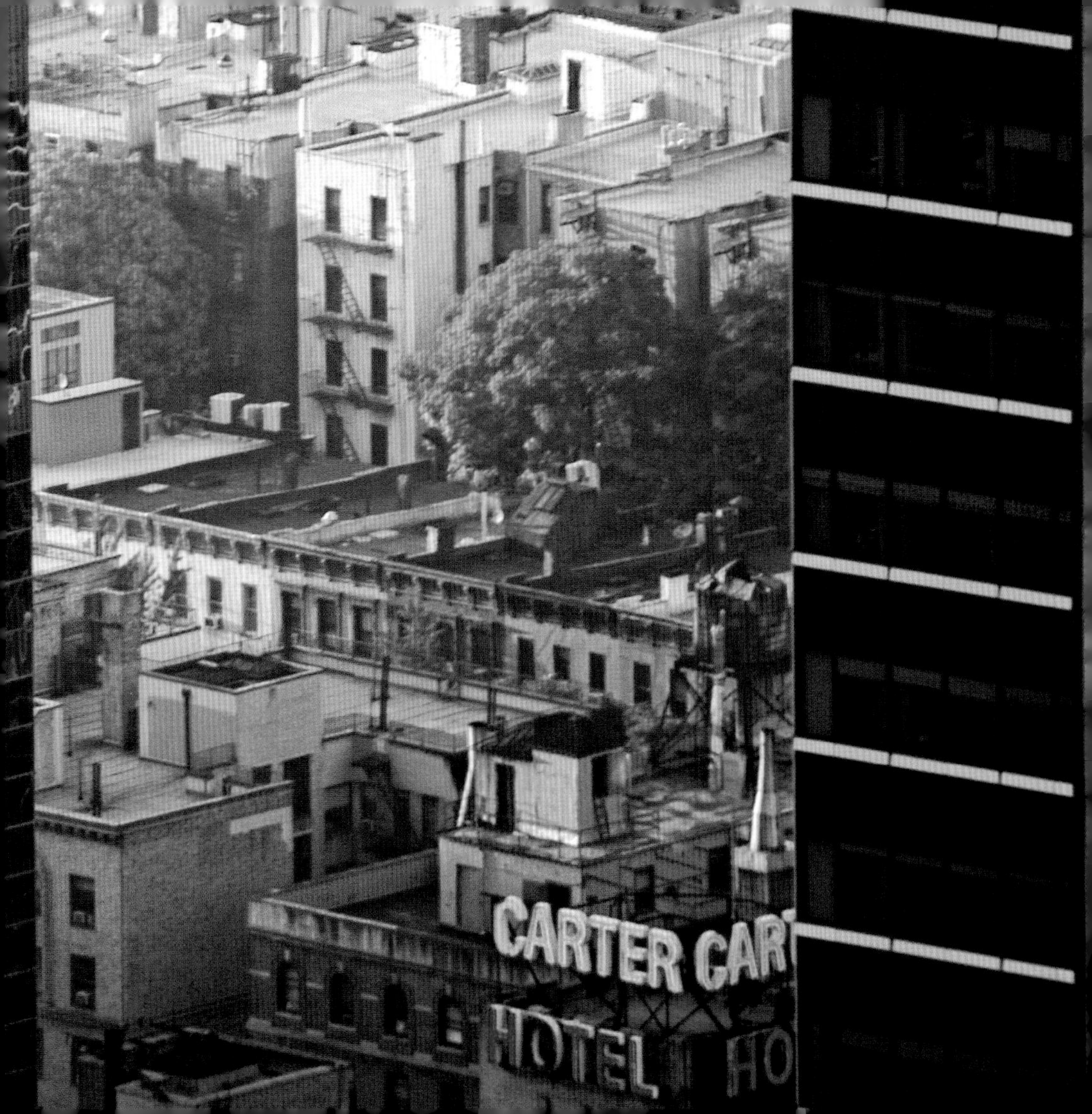
CARTER
HOTEL

197

The growing interest in cruising has revived the Passenger Ship Terminals on the Hudson River. A Carnival cruise ship anchors near the Intrepid Sea, Air, Space Museum.

198-199 and 200-201

The aircraft carrier *USS Intrepid*, moored on the Hudson River, is a great tourist attraction that draws 700,000 visitors a year. Its deck holds a number of U.S. fighter planes.

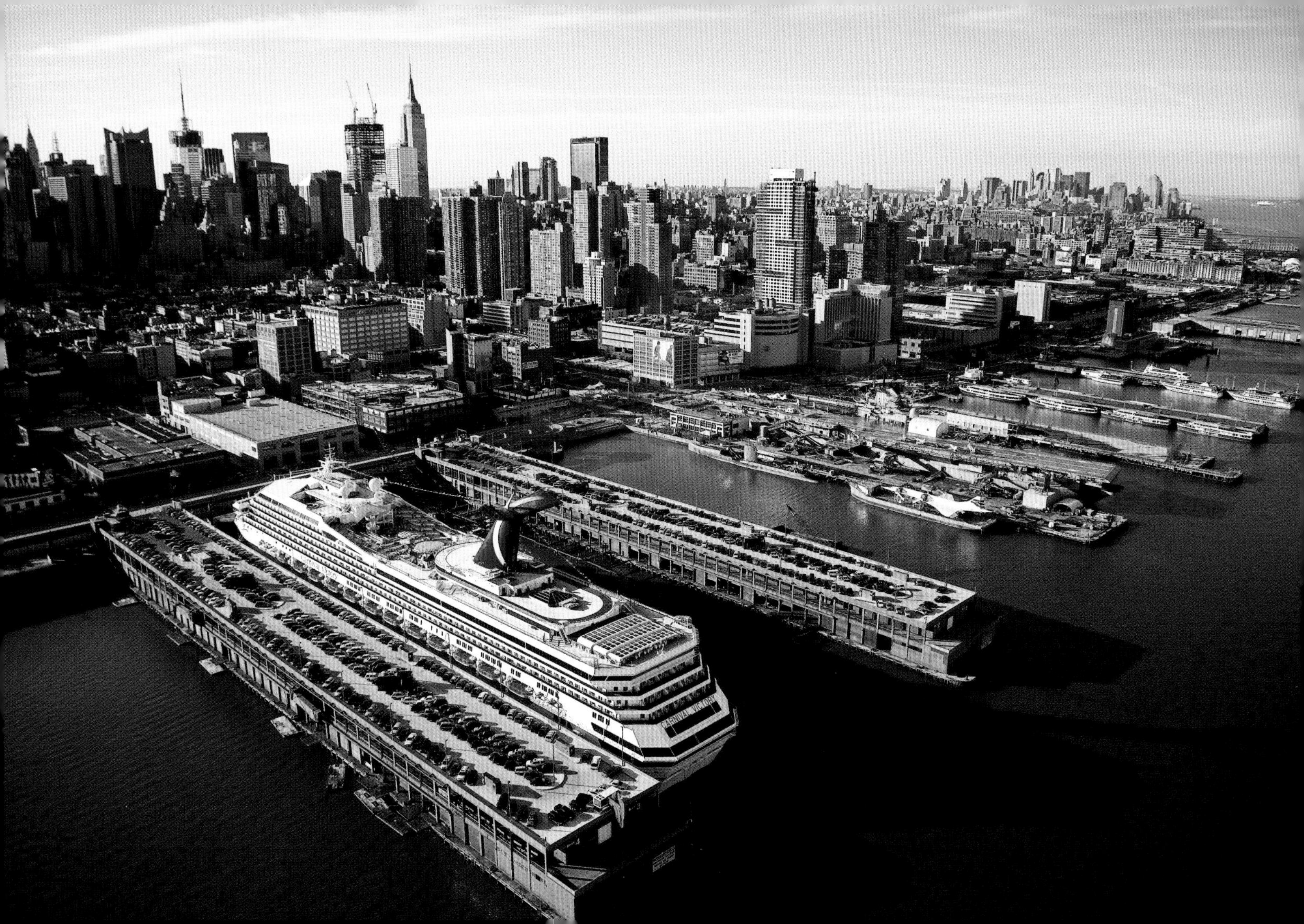
CARNIVAL VICTORY

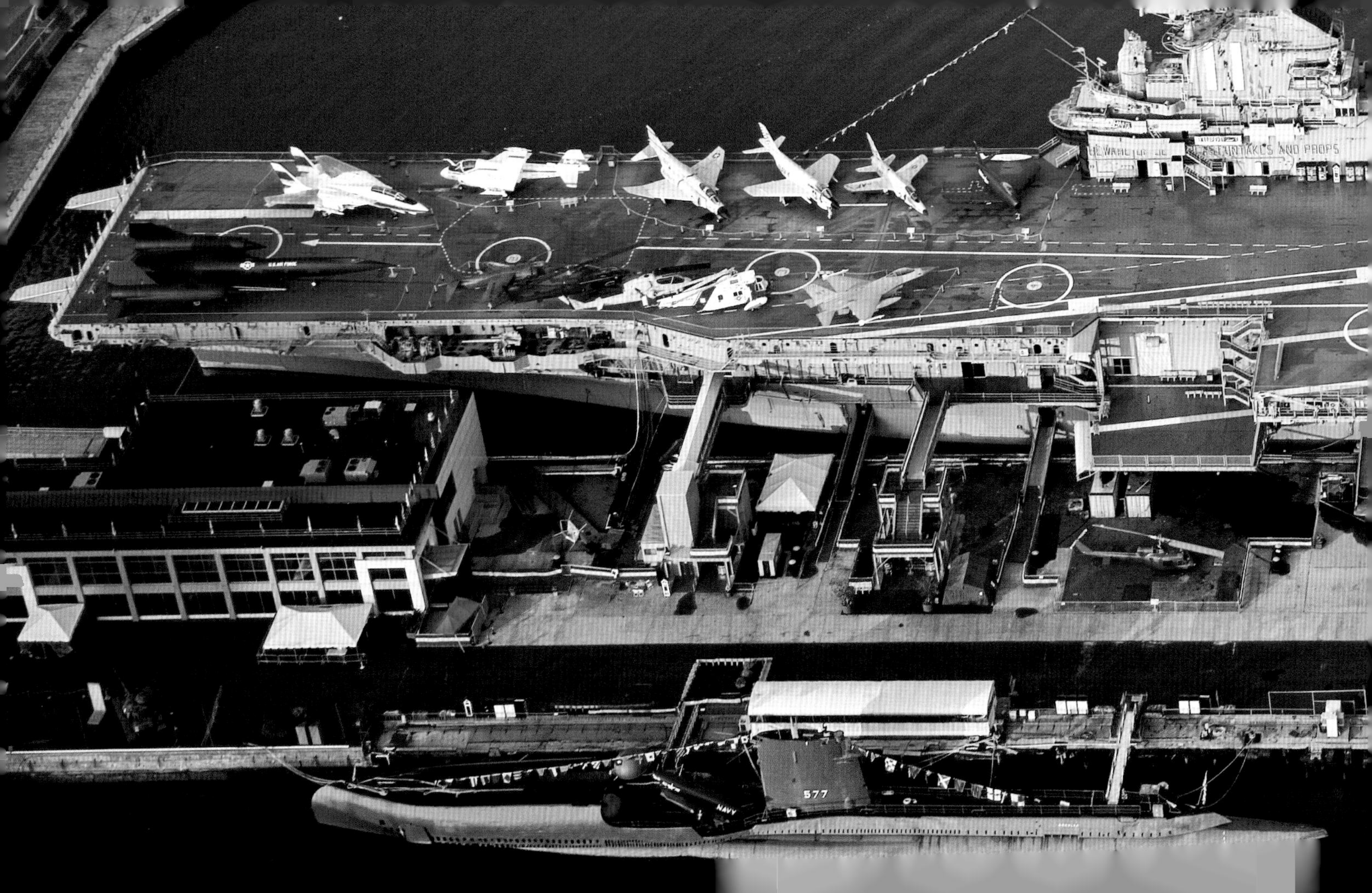
AND PROPS
577
NAVY

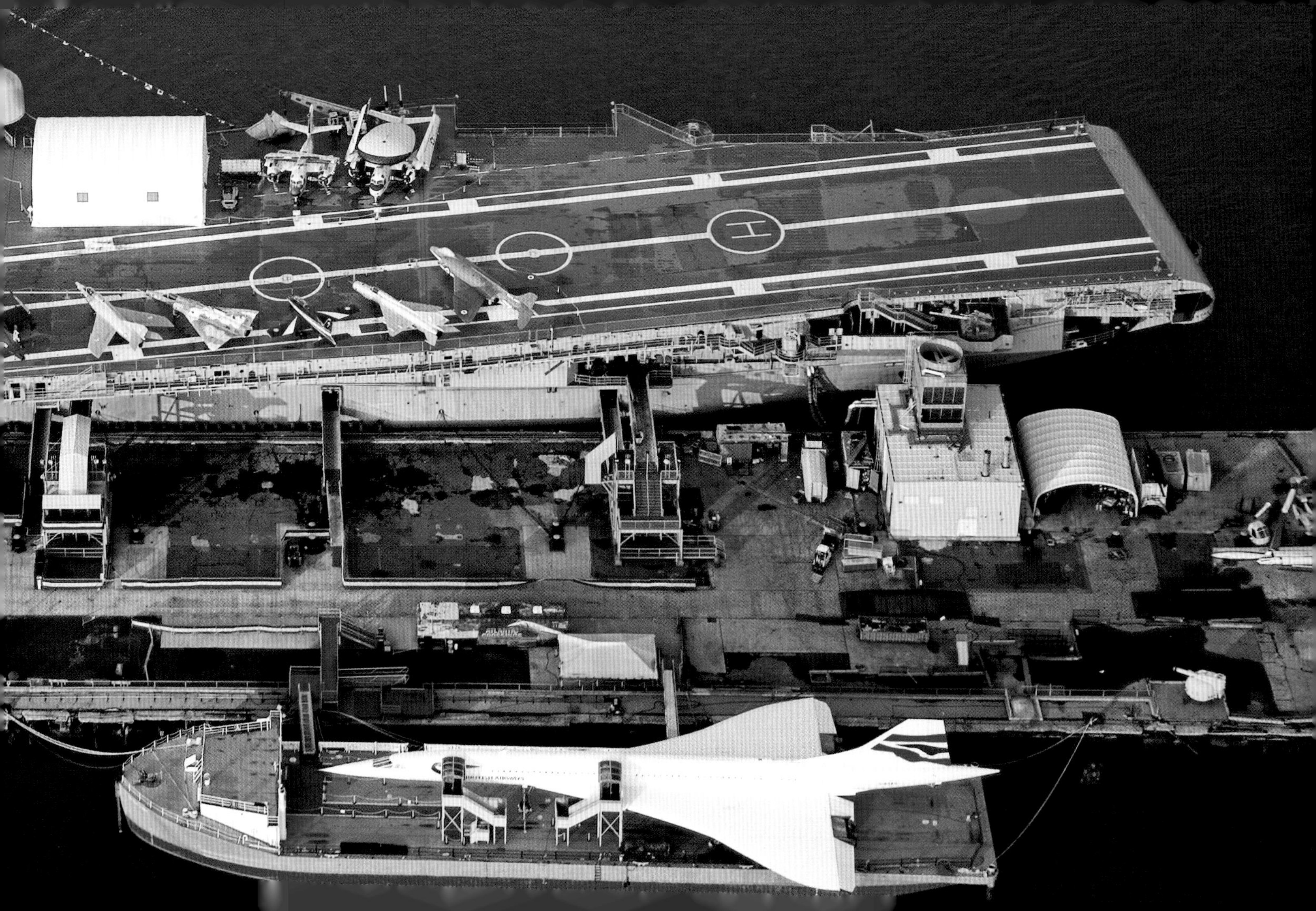

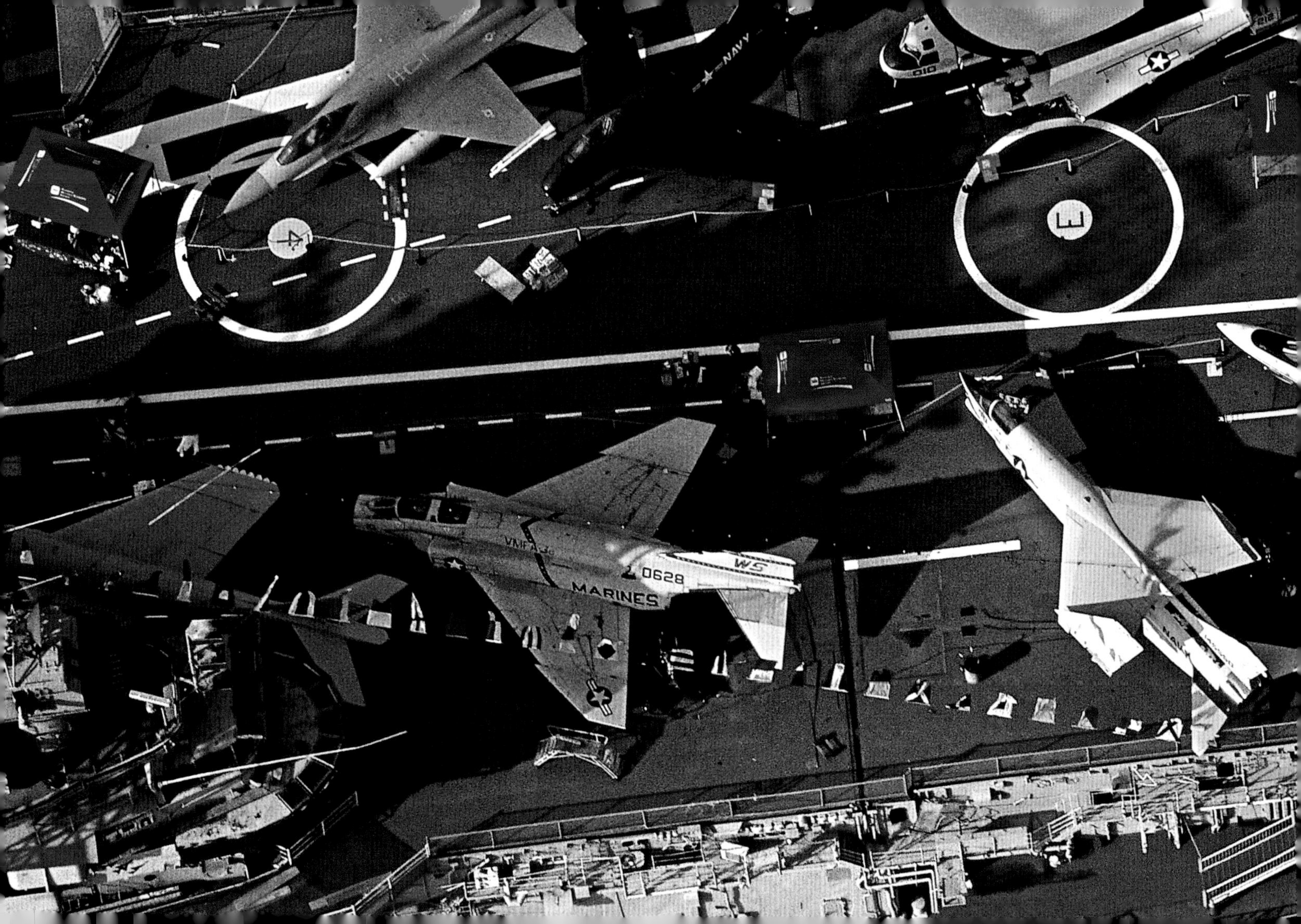
NAVY
MARINES
0628

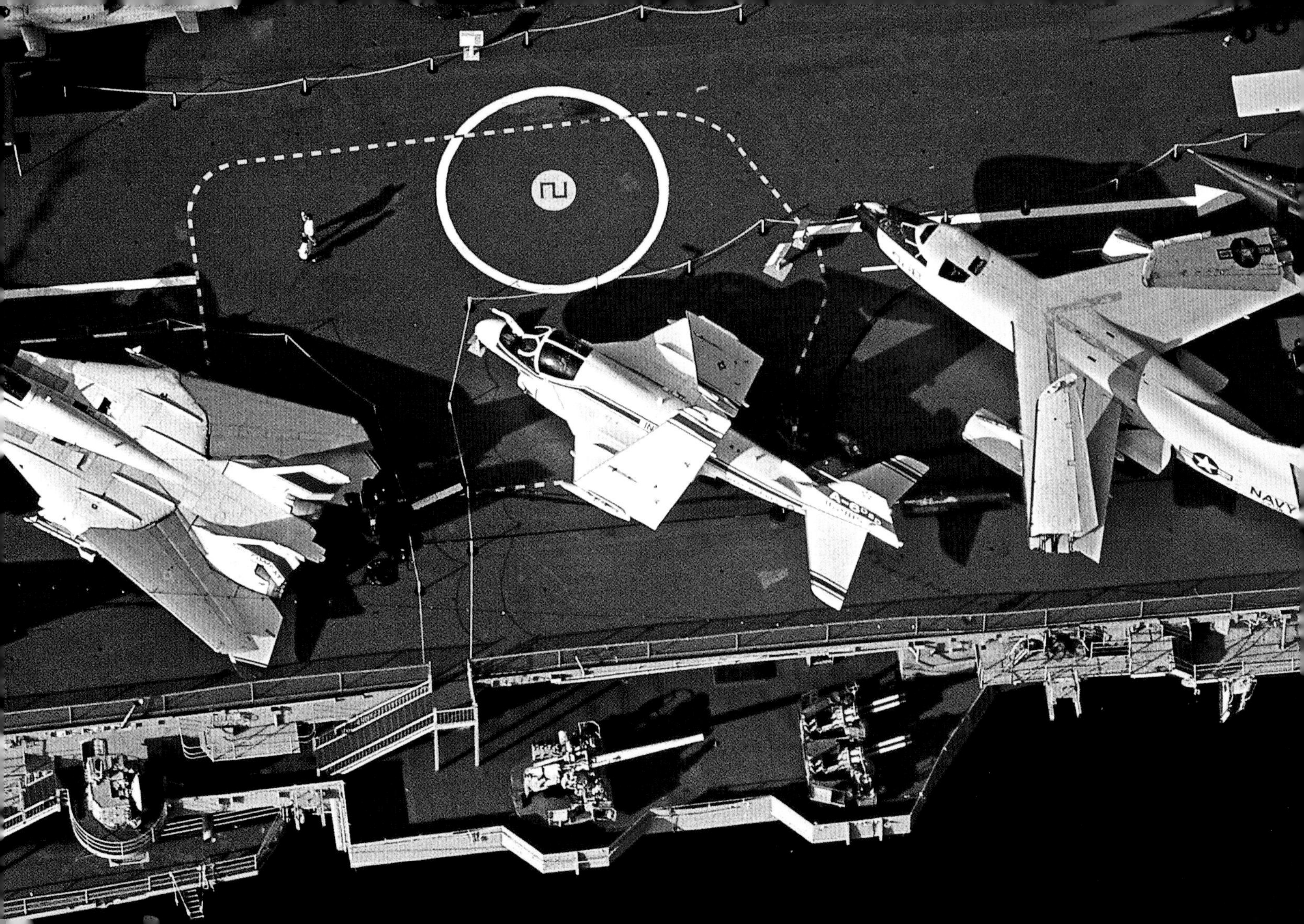
NAVY

203

The abandoned wharves on the Hudson River, seen here from the west, are being transformed into recreation centers

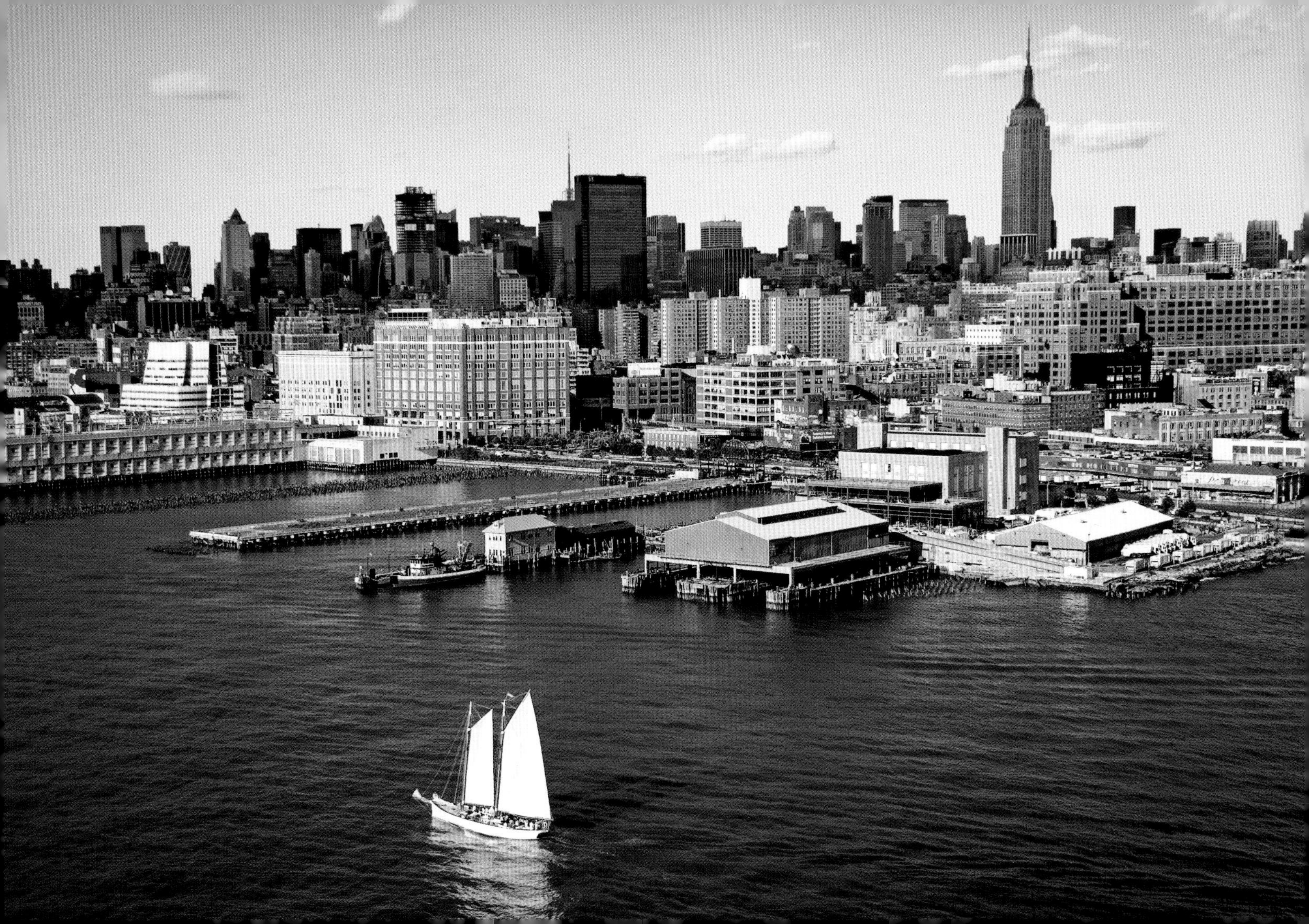

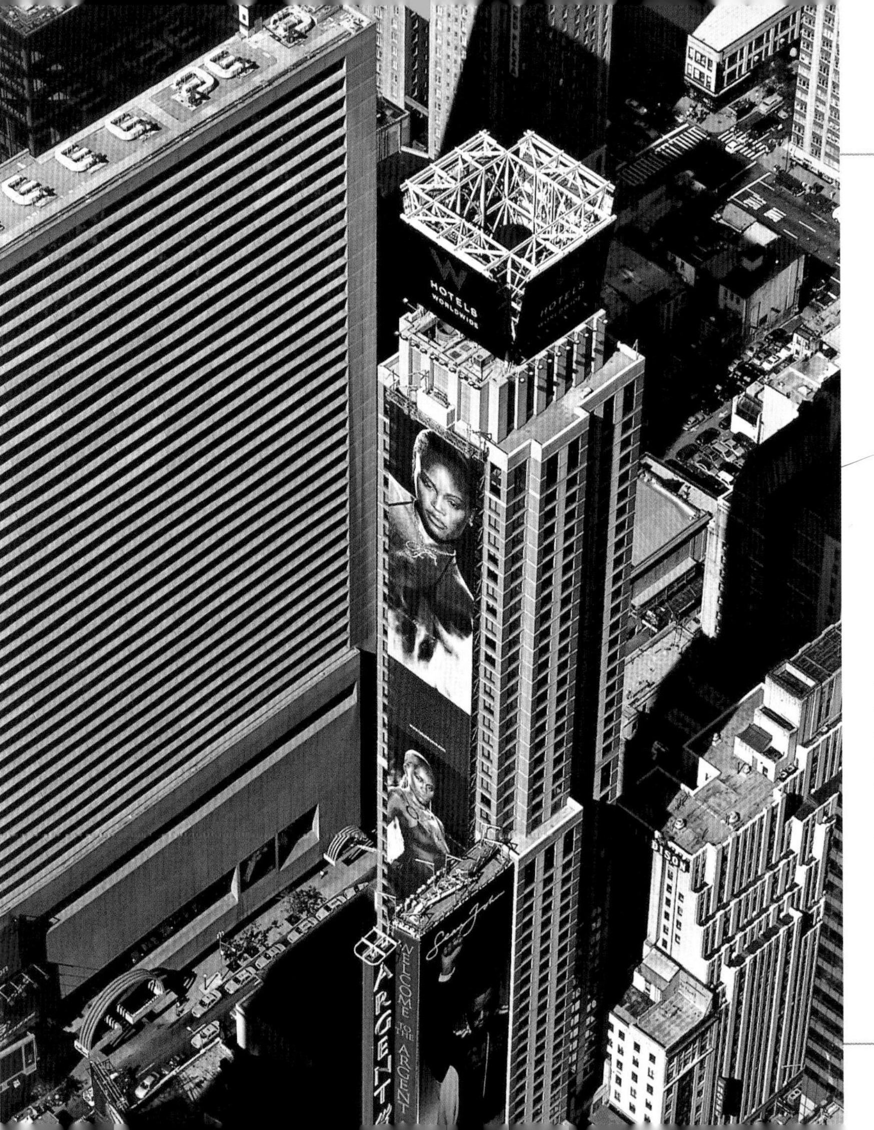

204

The quintessential symbol of New York City, Times Square is famed for the spectacular atmosphere created by neon signs, billboards and eclectic architecture.

205

The New Yorker Hotel, built in the Art Deco style popular in the Twenties and Thirties, was the biggest hotel in New York for many years. Its list of illustrious guests includes Spencer Tracy, Joan Crawford and Fidel Castro.

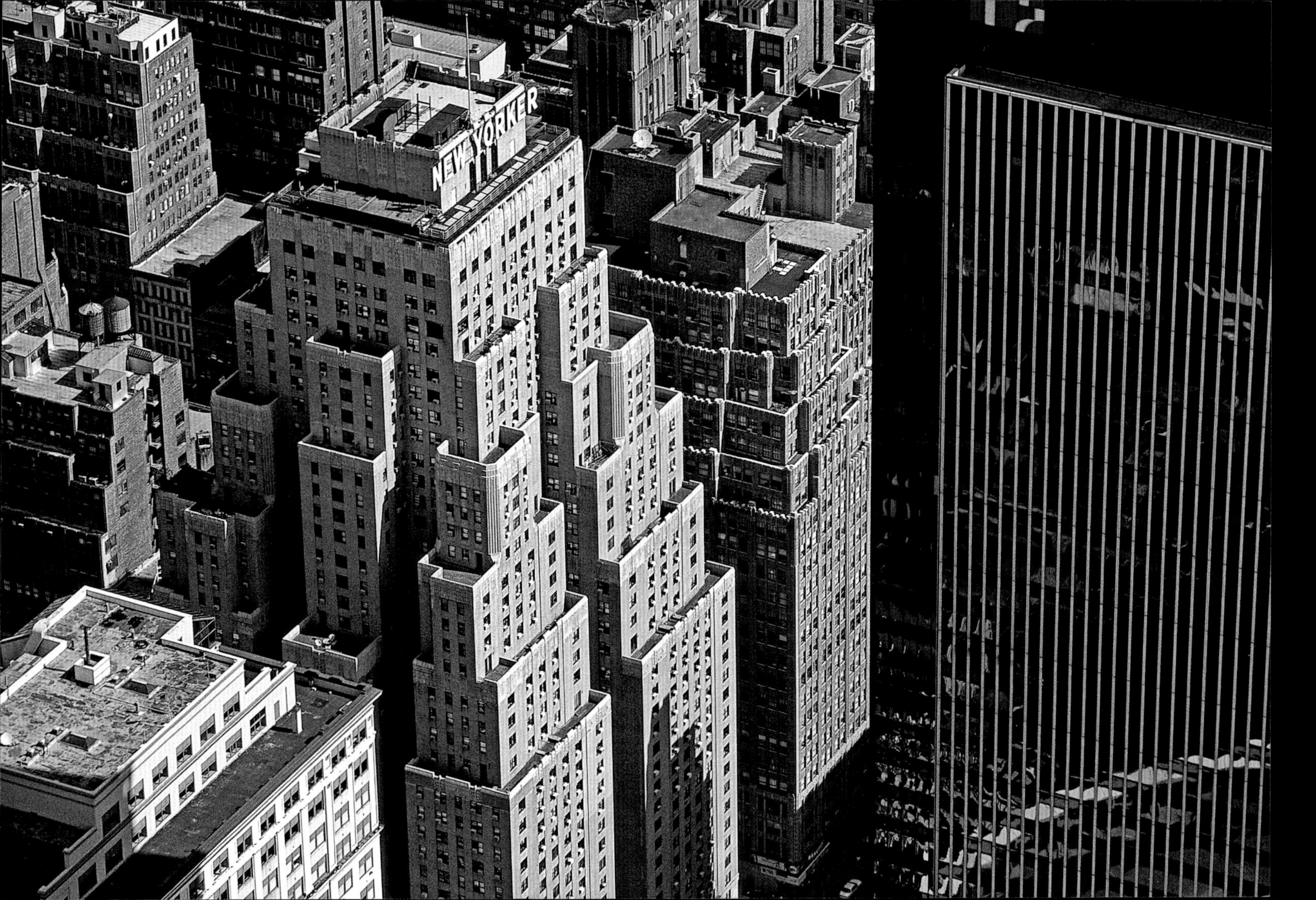
NEW YORKER

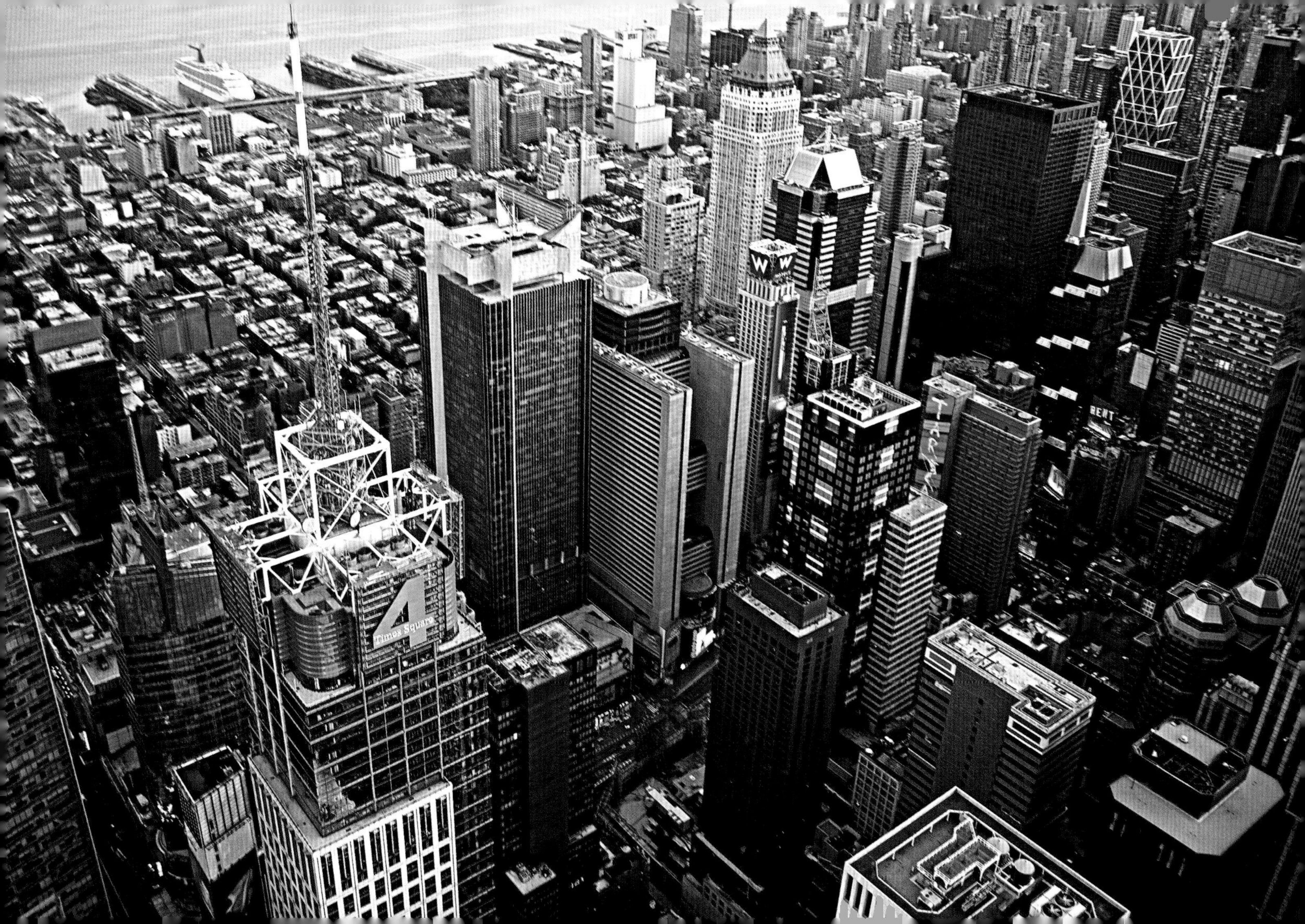
4
Times Square
RENT

206
4 Times Square, the Conde Nast headquarters, built in 1995, was one of the first large-scale buildings to make use of energy efficient "green" technology.

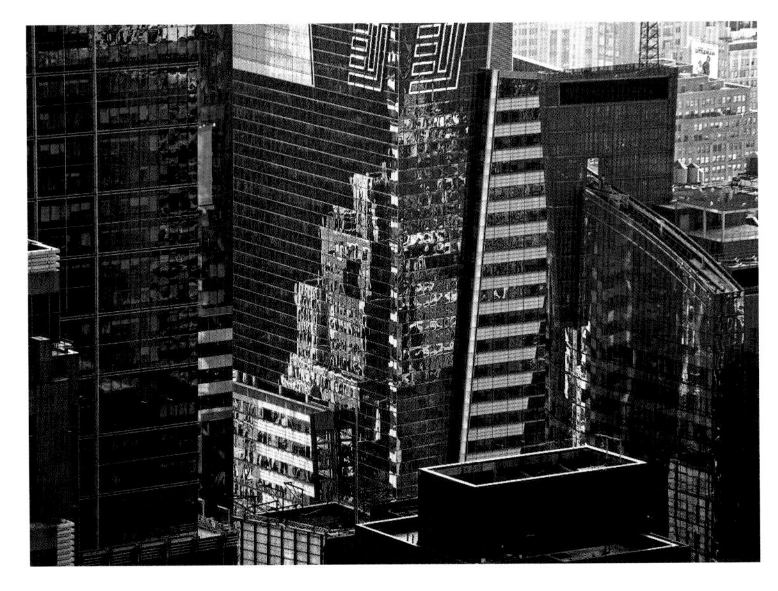

208

Times Square, the heart of Manhattan, has experienced a surge in cutting-edge architecture, like the modernist Ernst and Young Headquarters at 5 Times Square.

209

In the midst of exciting new design, the classic Art Deco Paramount Building still commands attention at Broadway and 43rd Street.

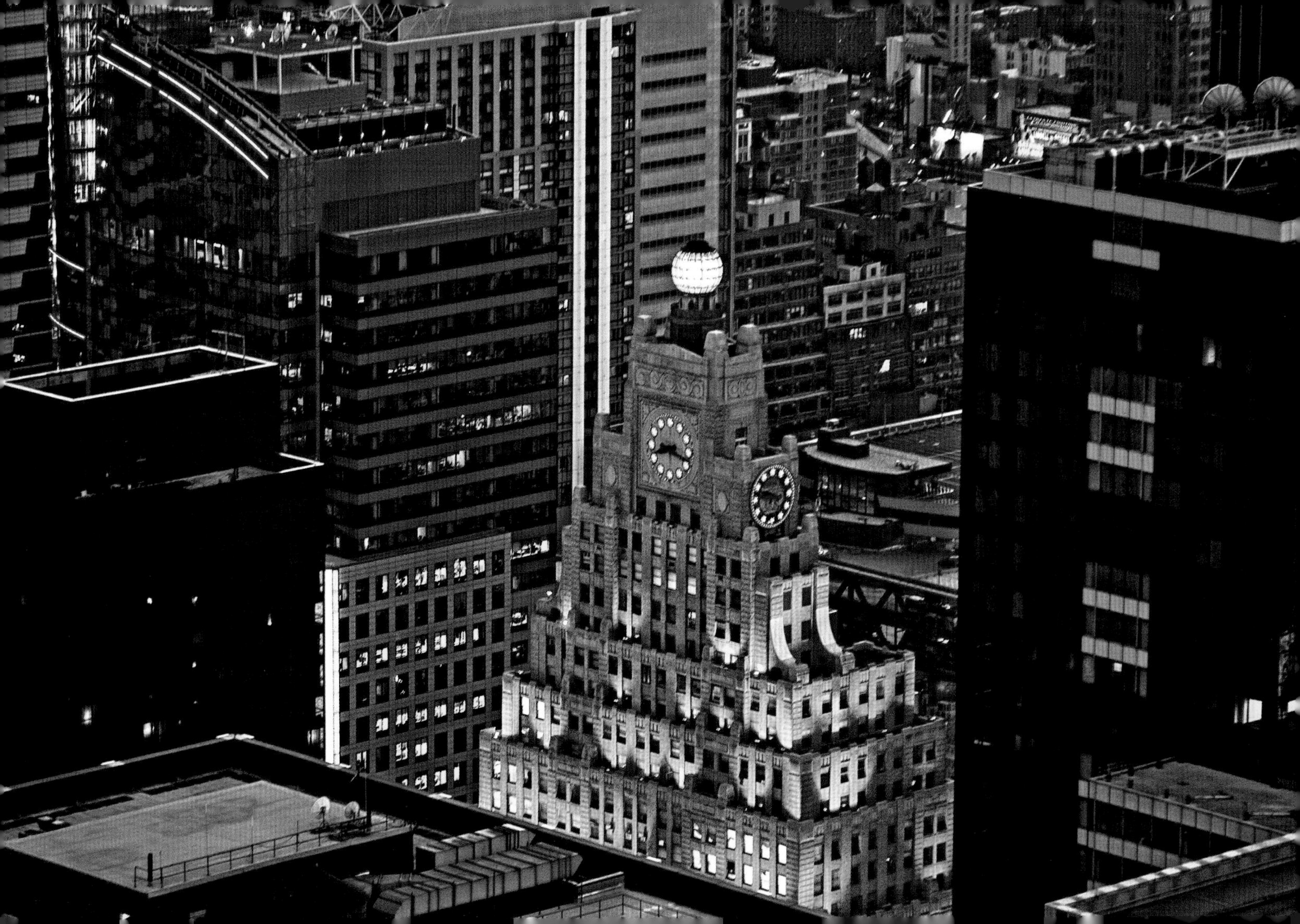

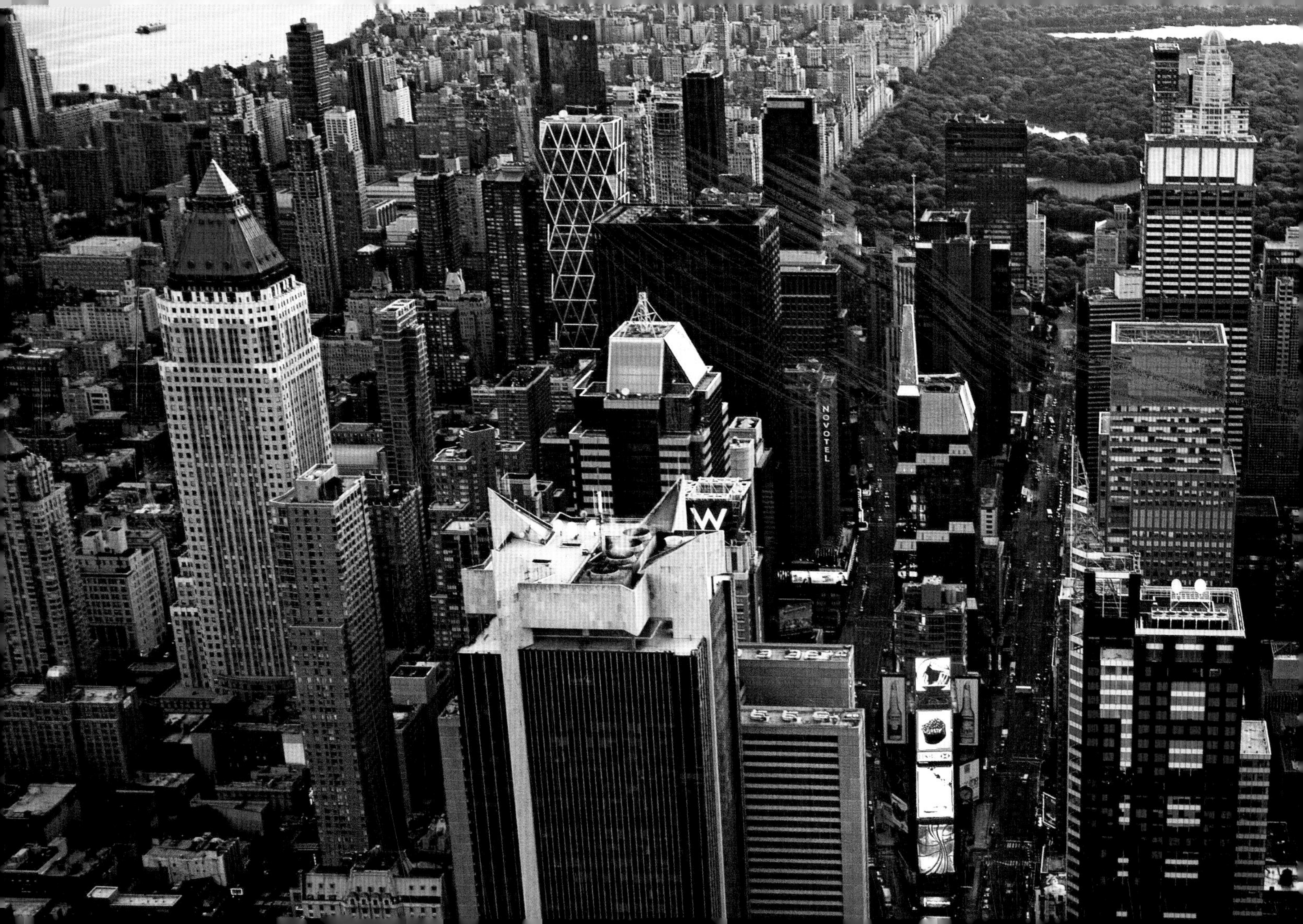
NOVOTEL
W

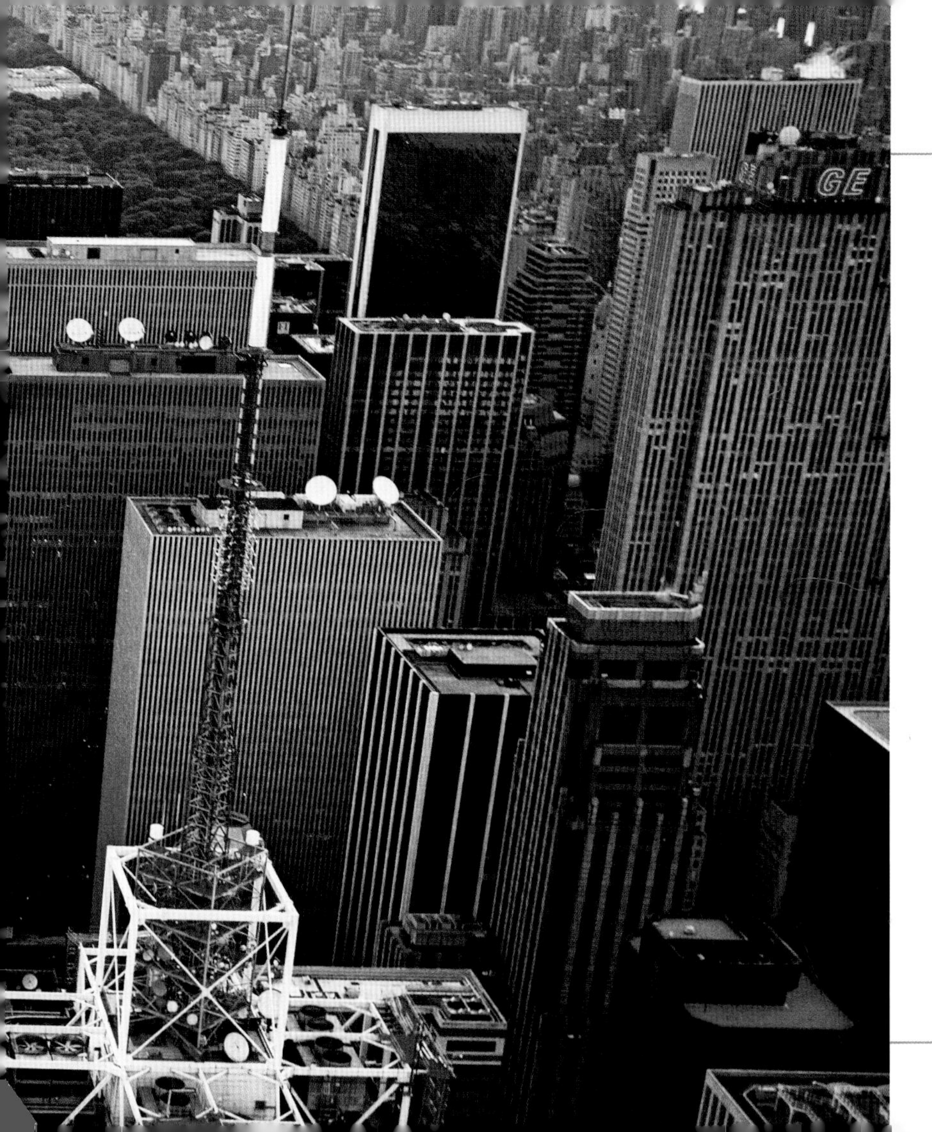

210-211
Seventh Avenue and Broadway merge at Times Square, the center of New York's theatrical district.

212-213
At night, the Times Square area dazzles, from the eccentric crownlike spikes of the Astor Plaza to the pyramid of the World-wide Plaza and the clock tower of the Paramount Building. The GW Bridge twinkles in the distance.

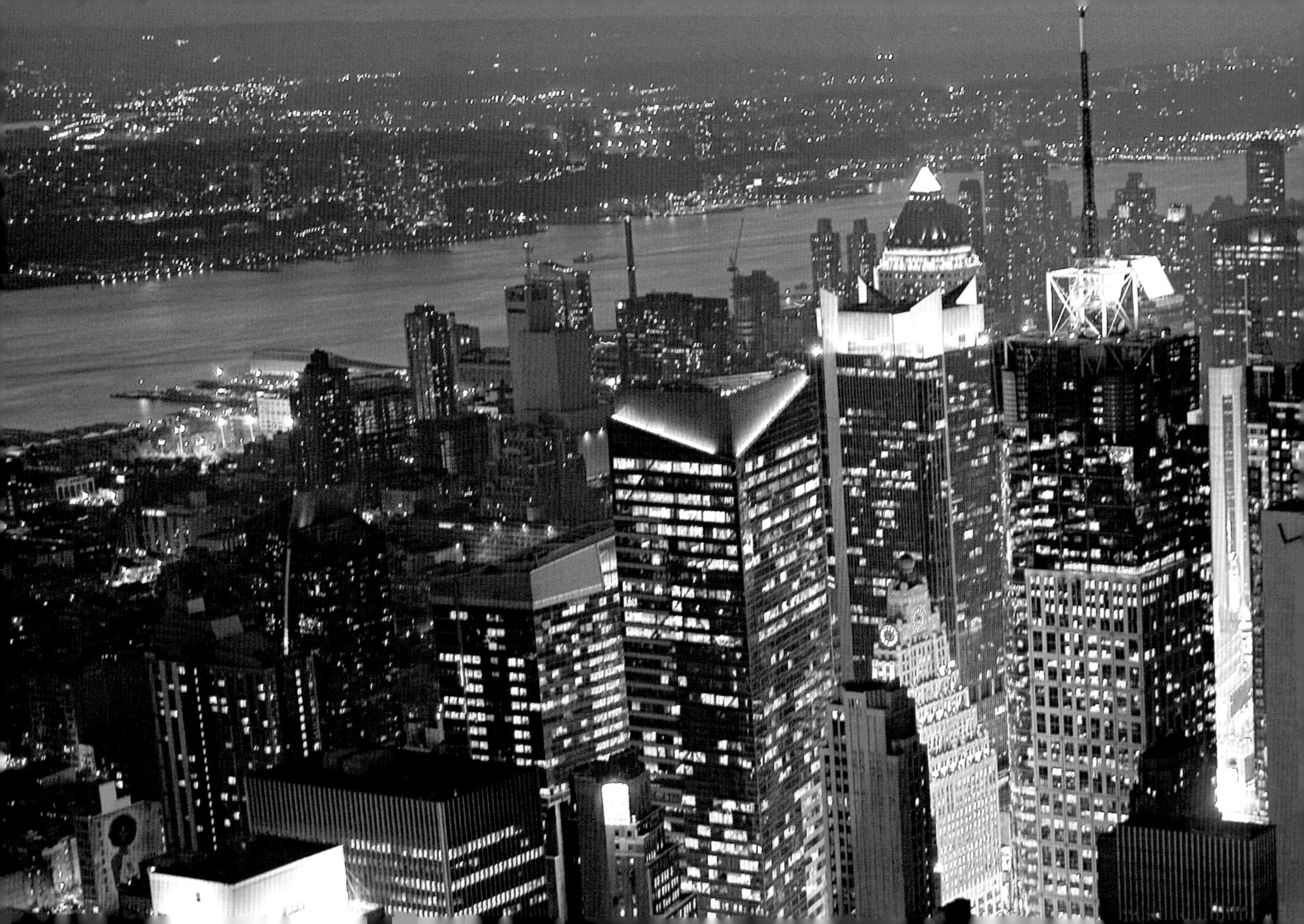

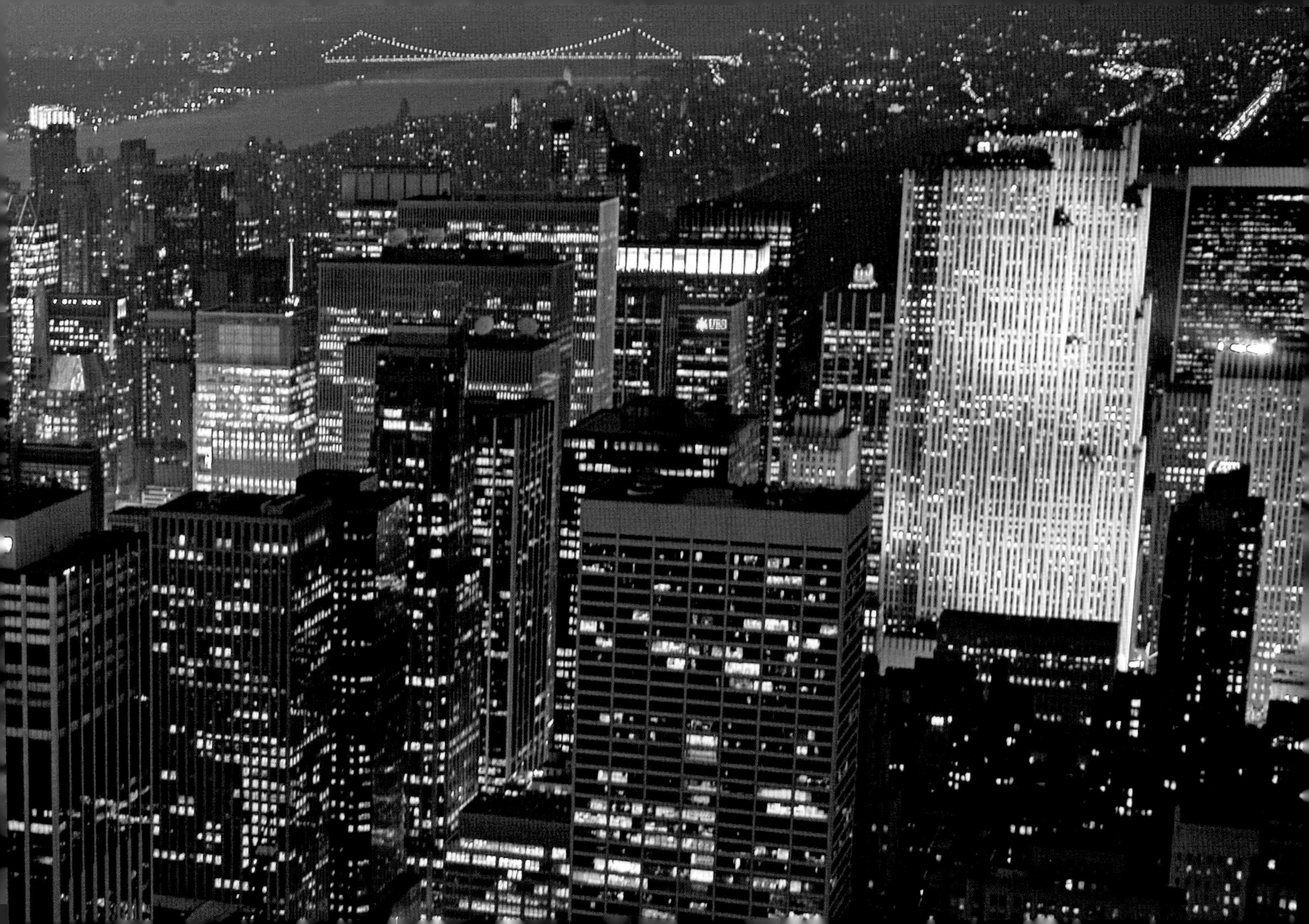

THE PARKS
GREEN OASES AMONG THE CANYONS

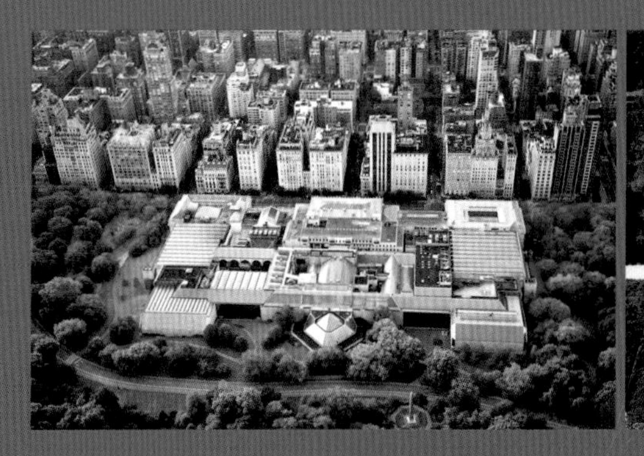

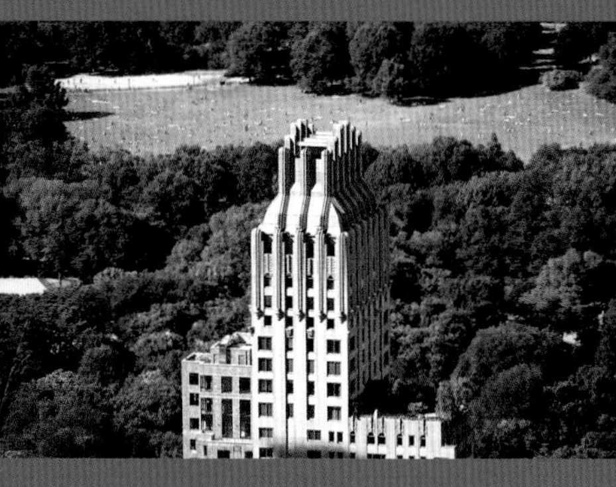

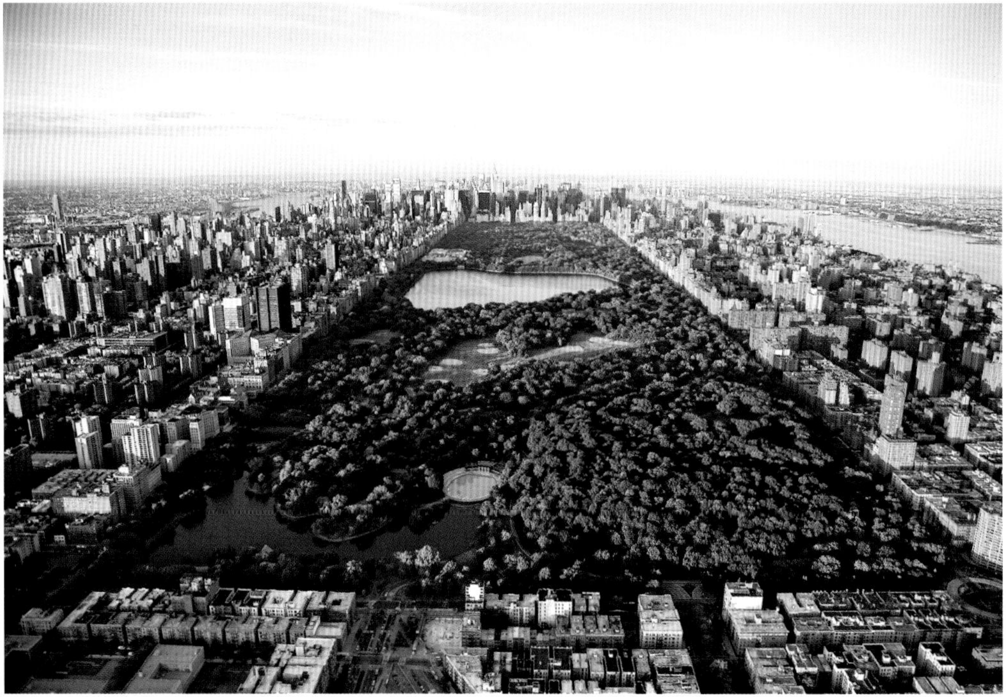

215
The Metropolitan Museum of Art (left) and Trump Parc Condominiums on Central Park South (right).

New York may be the "city that never sleeps," but New Yorkers nevertheless occasionally need a break from the fast-paced life of Manhattan. What is true today was just as true in the 19th century, when New York was growing into the largest commercial center in the country. In 1850, 500,000 people were crammed into New York, most of them living below 39th Street. But the city was woefully lacking open space, as there were virtually no parks, public squares or plazas included in the grid plan of 1811.

Open spaces in New York originally came in the form of parade grounds, battlefields and graveyards. Wealthy landowners were able to escape to the countryside for fresh air, trees and grass, but for the thousands crammed into the city's tenements, there was no relief from urban life. Battery Park and City Hall Park were delineated and protected during the 1700s, but were not considered to be recreational; in fact, public hangings were common at City Hall Park. The first official park in the city was dedicated in 1733 – Bowling Green Park, a green respite from the densely packed commercial area extending northward. But from the mid-18th until the mid-19th century, New York continued to grow with little regard for providing spaces for public recreation.

By 1850, crusading politicians, social activists and journalists set out to remedy the situation. The solution was to create an immense open space of

216
The 844 acres of Central Park are the heart and lungs of Manhattan.

The Parks
Green Oases Among the Canyons

over 700 acres to be situated in the center of the island. Ranging from 59th Street to 106th, and later extended to 110th Street, Central Park has become one of the most familiar, and most visited, parks in the world, with a total area of 843 acres.

In 1858, Frederick Law Olmsted and Calvert Vaux were selected, from a field of 33 competitors, to design what was to become one of New York's most celebrated landmarks. Olmsted and Vaux called their plan "Greensward," envisioning a park in the tradition of English pastoral design. Their concept was to tame the landscape without destroying it. The team intended to create a bucolic haven away from the stresses of city life, free and open to all classes of people. Central Park became the first landscaped park in the United States, and helped give birth to the field of "landscape architecture" in America. Today, the park has lakes, ponds, meadows and lawns, meandering trails and rugged outcroppings, as well as a wildlife sanctuary, tennis courts, skating rinks and ballparks.

The northern end of the park was intended to be the wilder, more naturalistic section; the southeast corner was designed to offer more activities for children. In between, activities in the park range from concerts of the New York Philharmonic to free performances of Shakespeare's plays at the Delacourte Theatre. Joggers stay fit running around the Jacqueline Kennedy Onassis reservoir between East 86th and East 96th streets, and each year over 30,000 runners finish the last leg of the New York Marathon in the park.

In an example of "if you build it they will come," as voiced in the movie Field of Dreams, the creation of Central Park produced some of the most desirable real estate on the entire Island of Manhattan. Grand homes and apartment buildings sprouted along the borders of the park, which gave their tenants glorious views of lakes, lawns and trees. While the well-to-do migrated toward these desirable new residences, hundreds of squatters and immigrants were displaced and forced to move to more mar-

The Parks
Green Oases Among the Canyons

ginal locations. In 1873, Frederick Law Olmsted delivered plans for yet another extensive park, this time on a hilly ridge overlooking the Hudson. Riverside Park, extending four miles from West 72nd to West 158th Street, offers panoramic vistas of the Hudson. Park Drive snakes through the park and is edged by a tree-lined promenade on its west side and grand apartments on its east. An extension of the park, Riverside South, is being added from West 72nd to West 59th Street on the old Penn Central Railroad yards.

Despite the scarcity of land on the island, and the tendency for developers to gobble up the little that does exist, there is a renewed interest in preserving and creating more parkland on the island. A plan to create an "emerald necklace" of bike paths, esplanades and parks around the island of Manhattan is in high gear, with the Greenway project well on the way to completing the last links in the chain.

The Greenway starts at Battery Park, and will eventually wrap around the tip of the island on both sides. On the west, it will continue past Battery Park City through the Hudson River Park, which incorporates 13 public piers, to Riverside South and Riverside Parks, all the way to the Harlem River Greenway. On the east, the Greenway will eventually extend along the East River, from South Street Seaport up to Highbridge Park.

One of the most prominent features of the Greenway project is the emphasis on the waterfront. As is so apparent from above, though not always so clear at street-level, Manhattan is surrounded by water. Even though the city was once a thriving and bustling port, the city's waterfront fell into decline with the coming of large container ships and air transport. The Greenway, as well as a number of private recreational concerns, like Chelsea Piers, is putting the city's unused and dilapidated piers to good use – with golf and tennis players replacing stevedores on the docks.

In addition to using abandoned piers, one of the

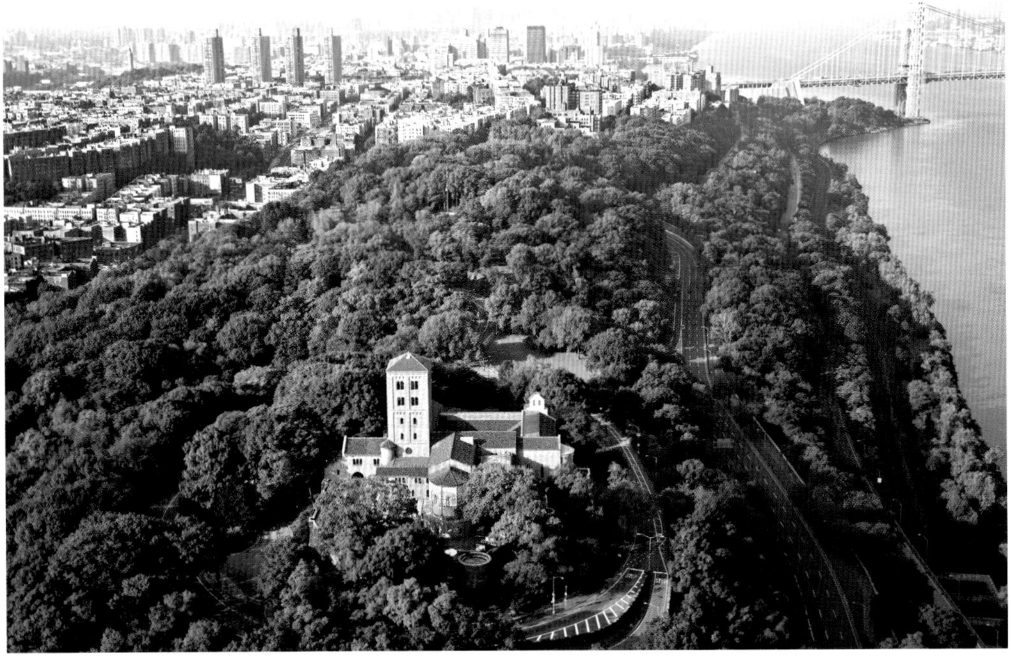

220
The dozens of species of trees which thrive in Manhattan's parks (here, we see Fort Tyron Park) are all part of a fragile ecosystem.

most creative locations for a park in Manhattan is Riverbank State Park. It is a 28-acre park complex built on top of a sewage treatment plant. It has a pool, skating park, theater, restaurant and carousel. The only state park within Manhattan, it runs from West 137th to West 145th Street along the West Side Highway.

The High Line Park will use deserted elevated railroad tracks that run along the West Side from the historic Meatpacking District up to the Jacob Javits Convention Center and the Hudson Railroad Yards. Inspired by projects such as the Promenade Plantee in Paris, the High Line will create a park in place of an eyesore.

Although the earliest parks on the island were downtown, some of the most historically significant are at the other end of Manhattan. Fort Tryon, with the Metropolitan Museum's medieval collection at the Cloisters, Fort Washington Park, with its Little Red Lighthouse tucked under the George Washington Bridge, and Inwood Hill Park at the north end of Manhattan.

But back in Lower Manhattan, where New York's first park was dedicated, one of the city's most awaited, and also one of its most contested, parks is still on the drawing boards. The memorial at Ground Zero, to be located on the footprint of the World Trade Center, is part of a massive reconstruction project planned for much of the downtown area that was damaged or destroyed on September 11, 2001. Though the memorial will be a somber reminder of that day, a short walk to the waterfront will give another perspective, one of hope and inspiration, as visitors gaze out at the symbols of freedom and self-determination in the New York harbor – the Statue of Liberty National Monument and Ellis Island.

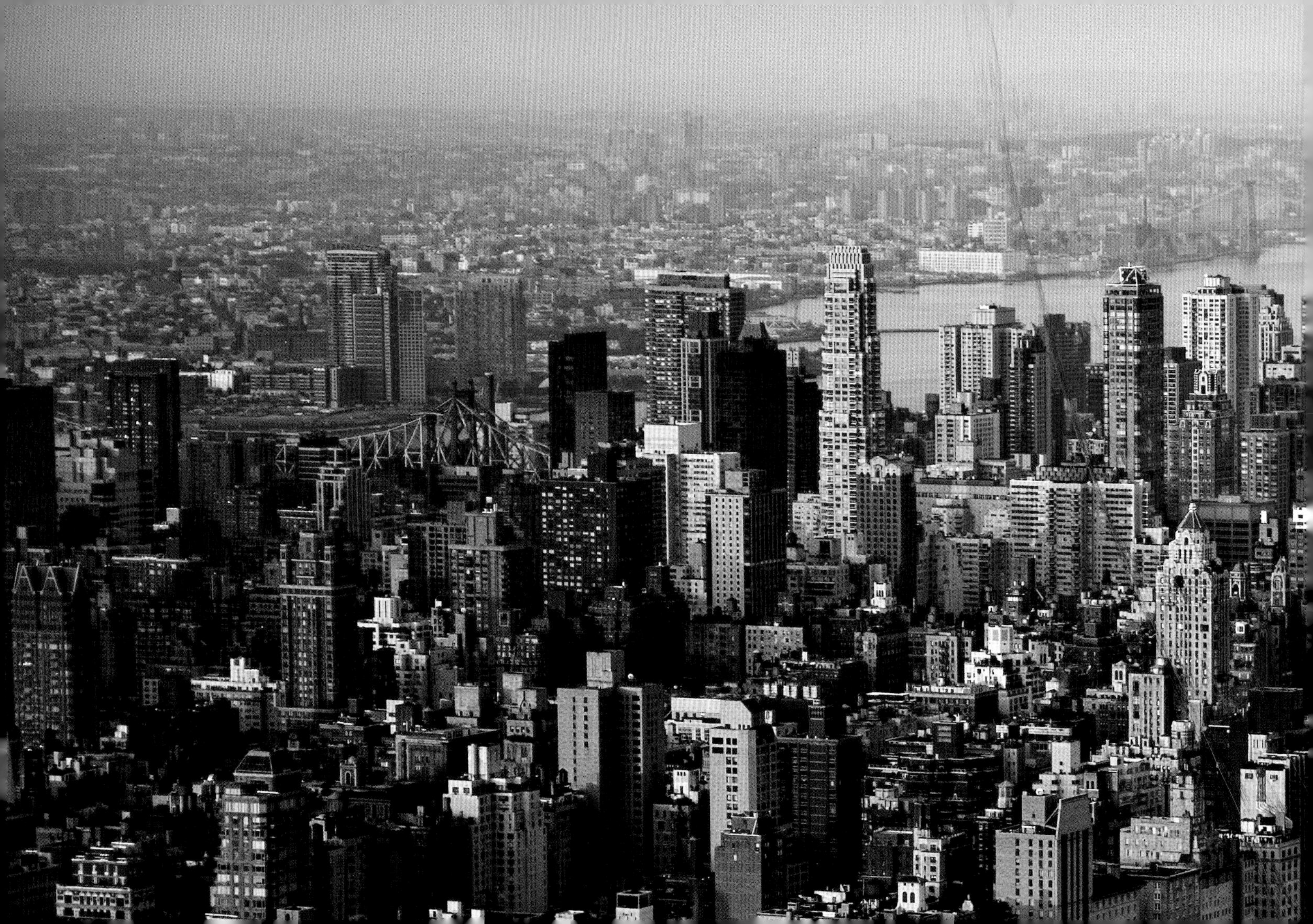

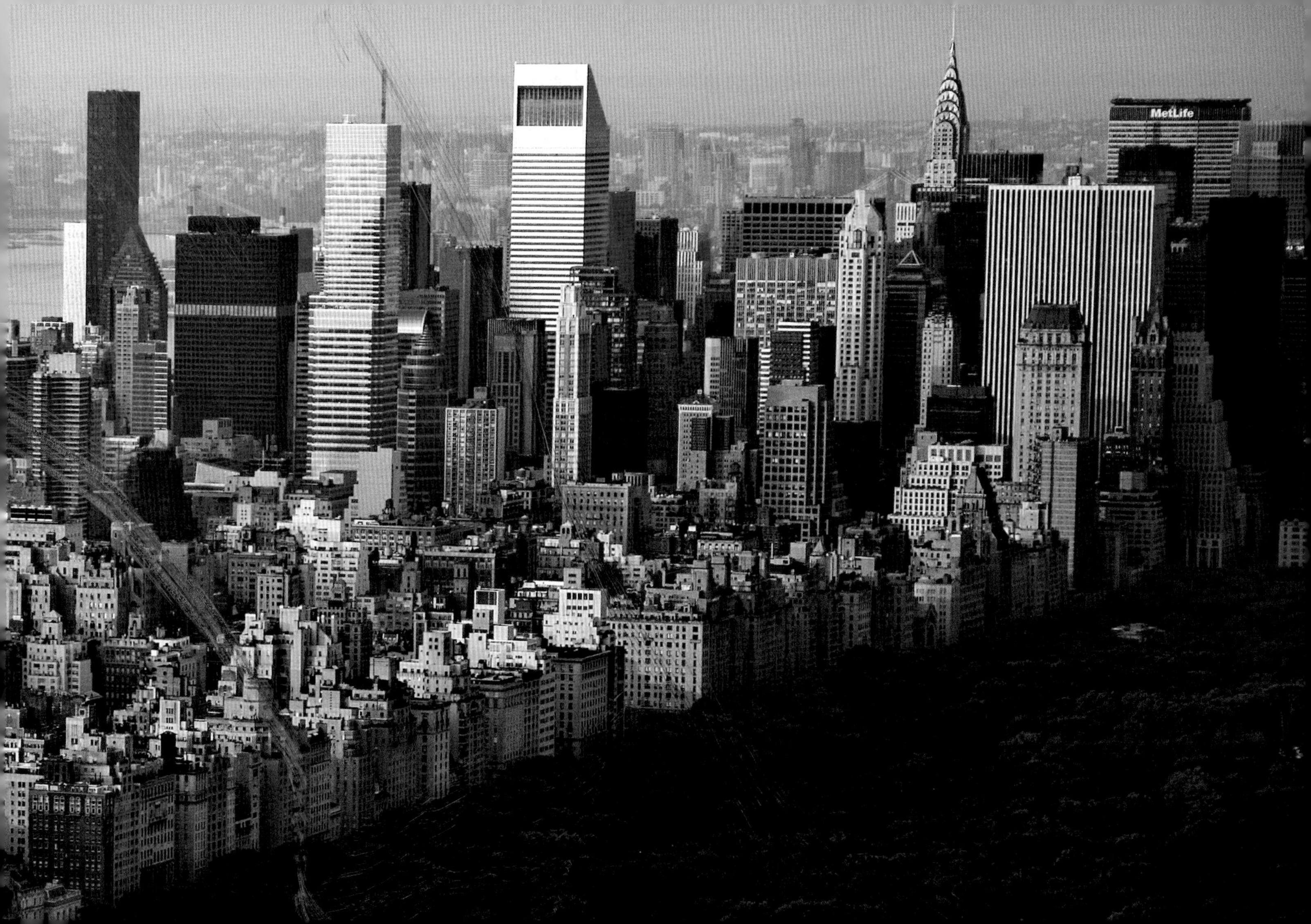
MetLife

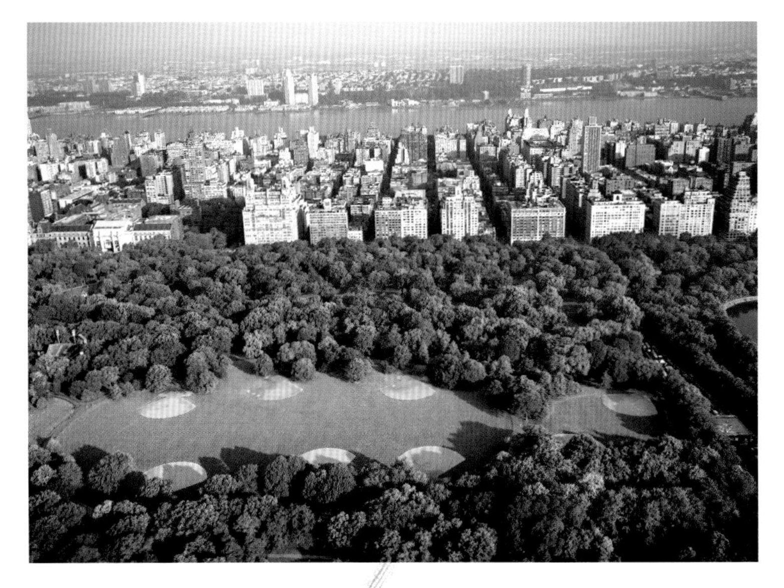

222-223

Between a green oasis and the East River, elegant apartment buildings edge Fifth Avenue along Central Park.

224

New Yorkers take time out from commerce to play ball: Central Park has 26 ball fields – eight are on the Great Lawn.

225

The recently renovated North Meadow, just above the Jacqueline Onassis Reservoir, has had baseball fields since the 1870s.

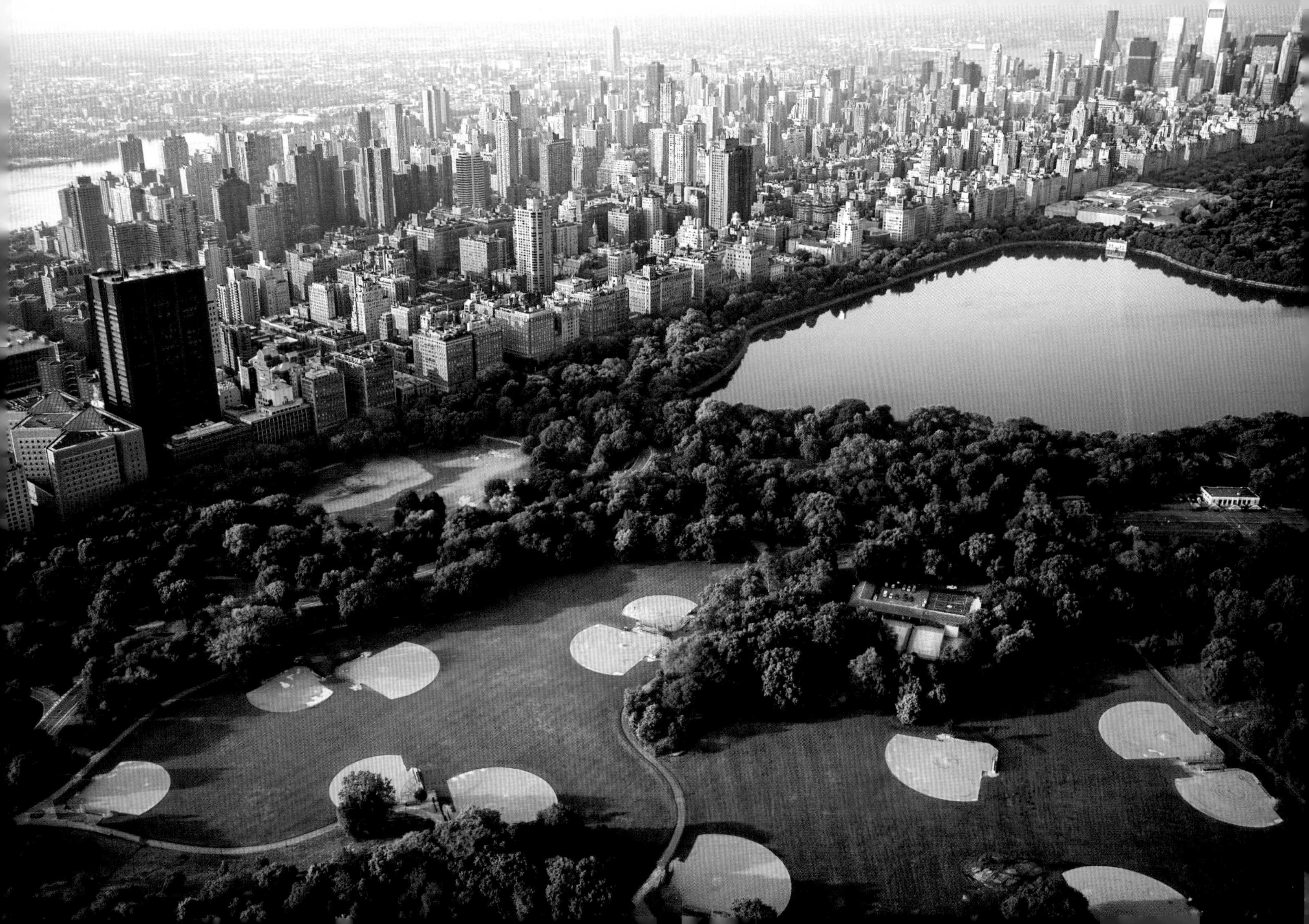

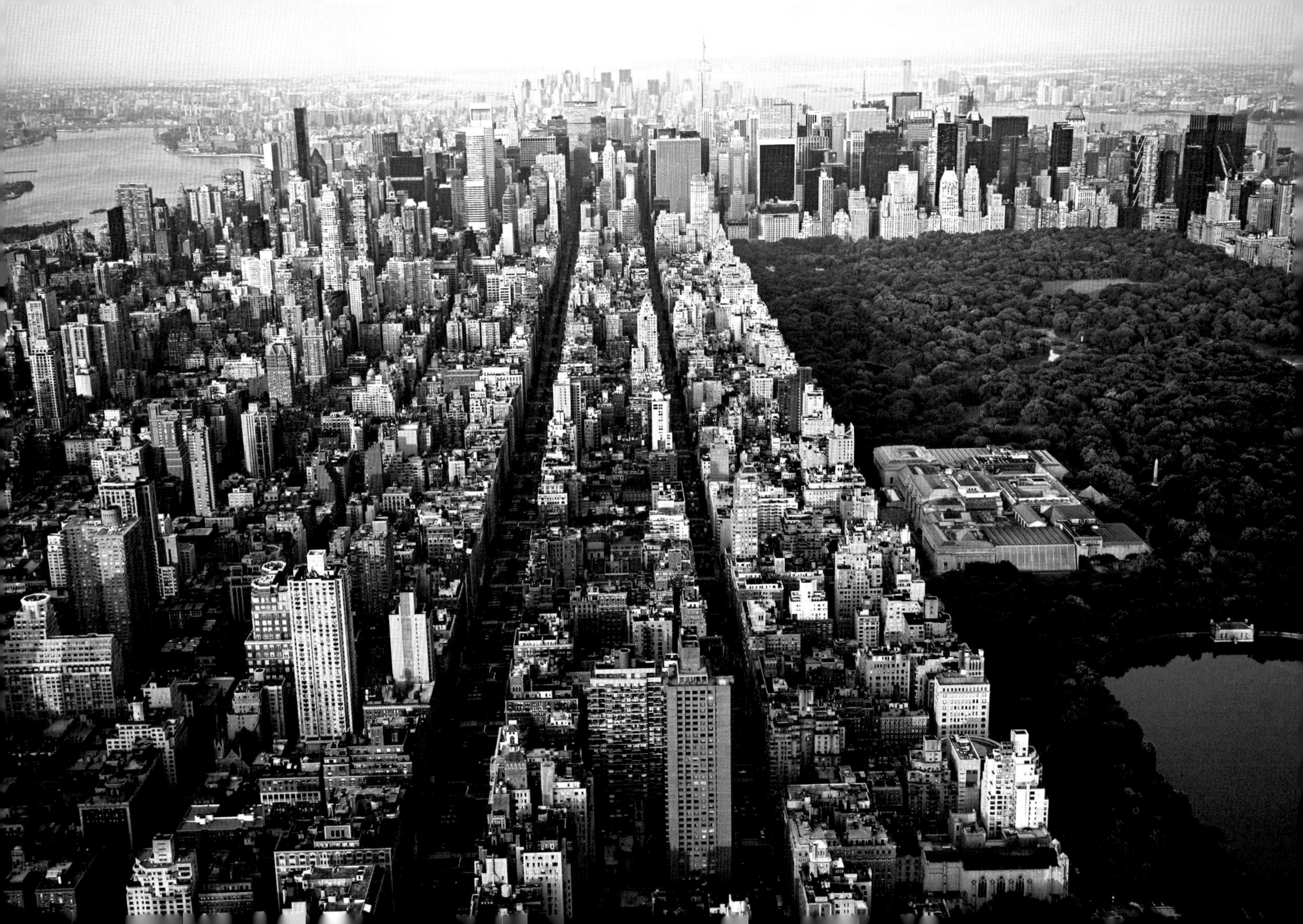

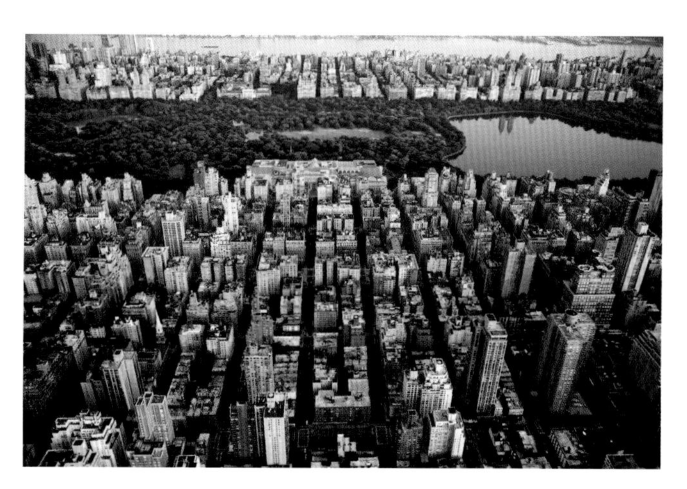

226

Park Avenue, has its landscaped center islands, and Madison Avenue has upscale boutiques, but Fifth Avenue has the Museum Mile and Central Park vistas.

227

Proximity to Central Park is part of what has made the Upper East Side a desirable and exclusive residential neighborhood.

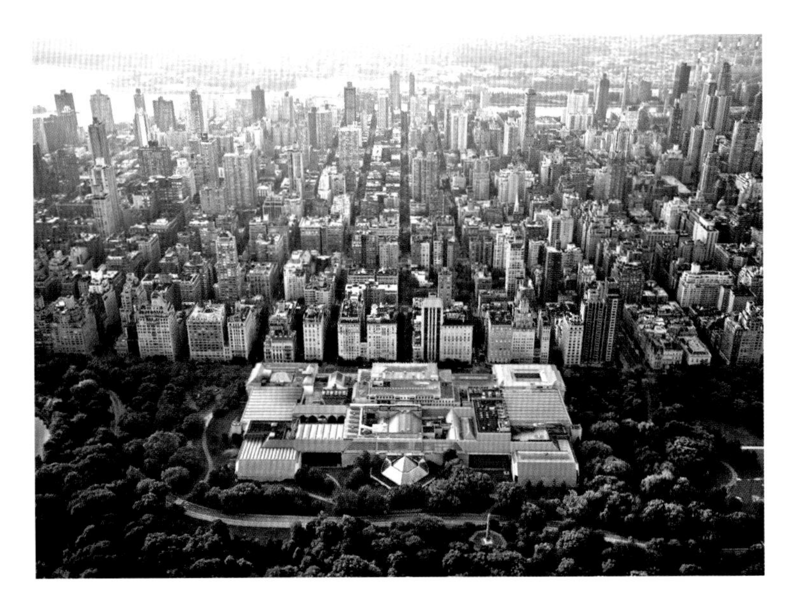

228

Central Park designer Frederick Olmsted once said he regretted allowing The Metropolitan Museum of Art to extend into the great green space, but the museum and the park have coexisted happily since 1880.

229

The Metropolitan Museum of Art commands a prominent spot on the east side of Central Park; from its roof garden, the views of the park are spectacular.

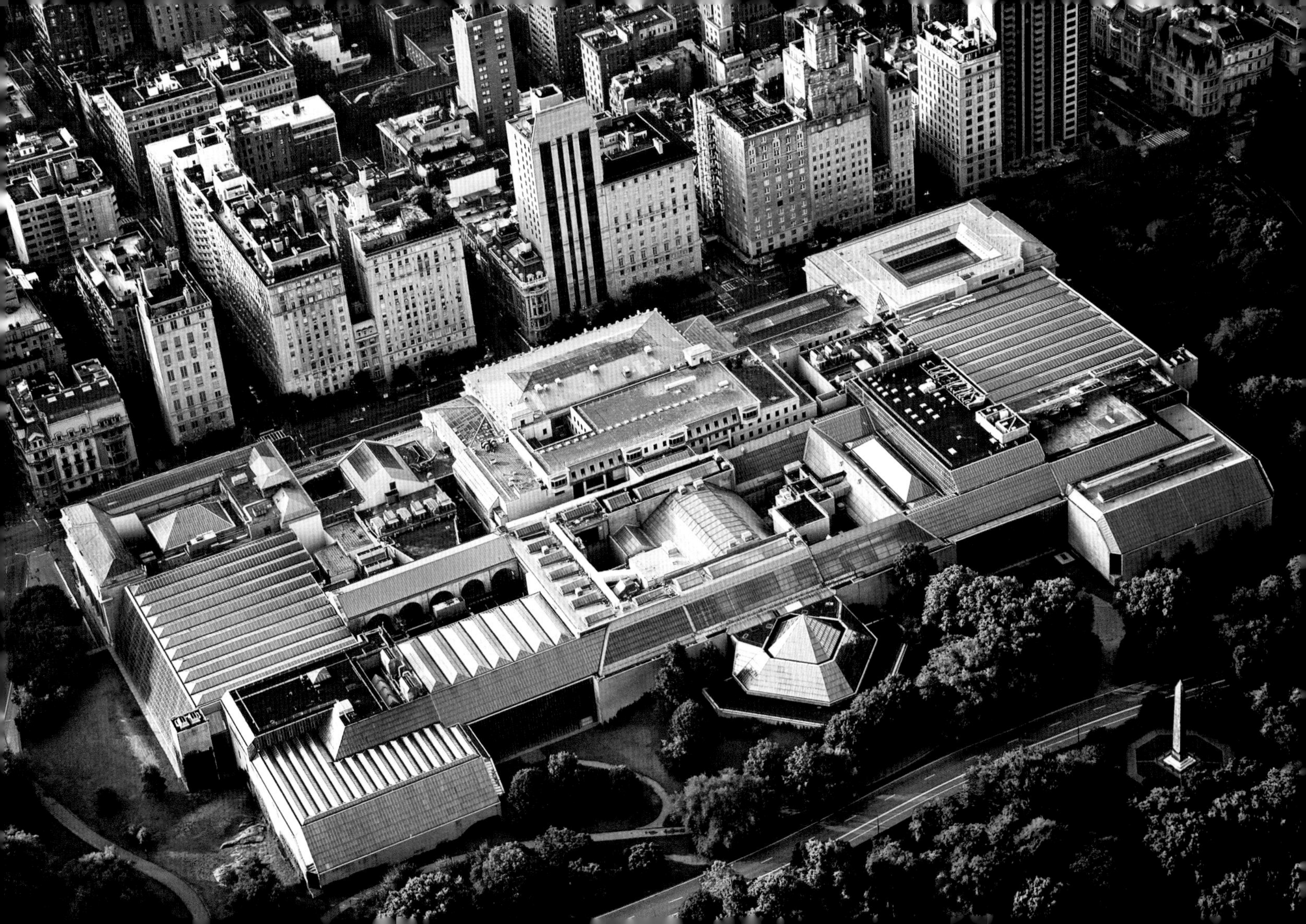

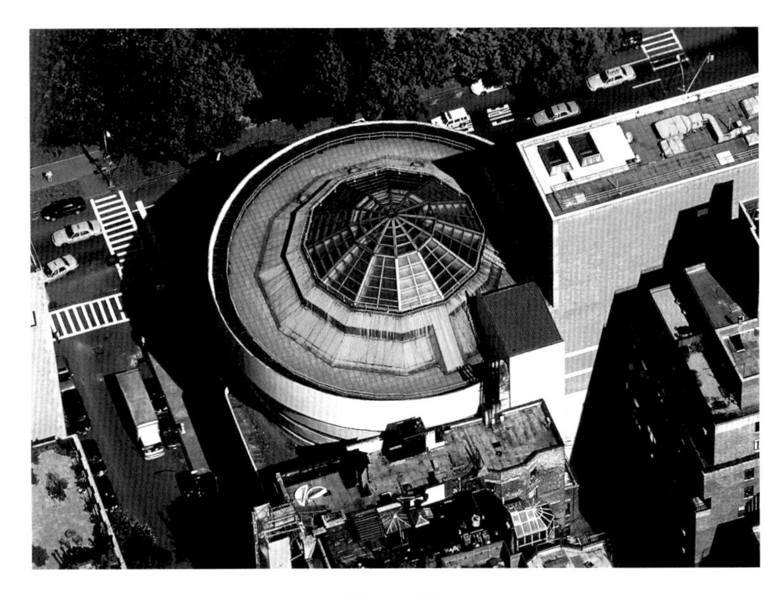

230 and 231
Central Park was a major inspiration for Frank Lloyd Wright, the designer of the Guggenheim Museum on Fifth Avenue and 89th Street.

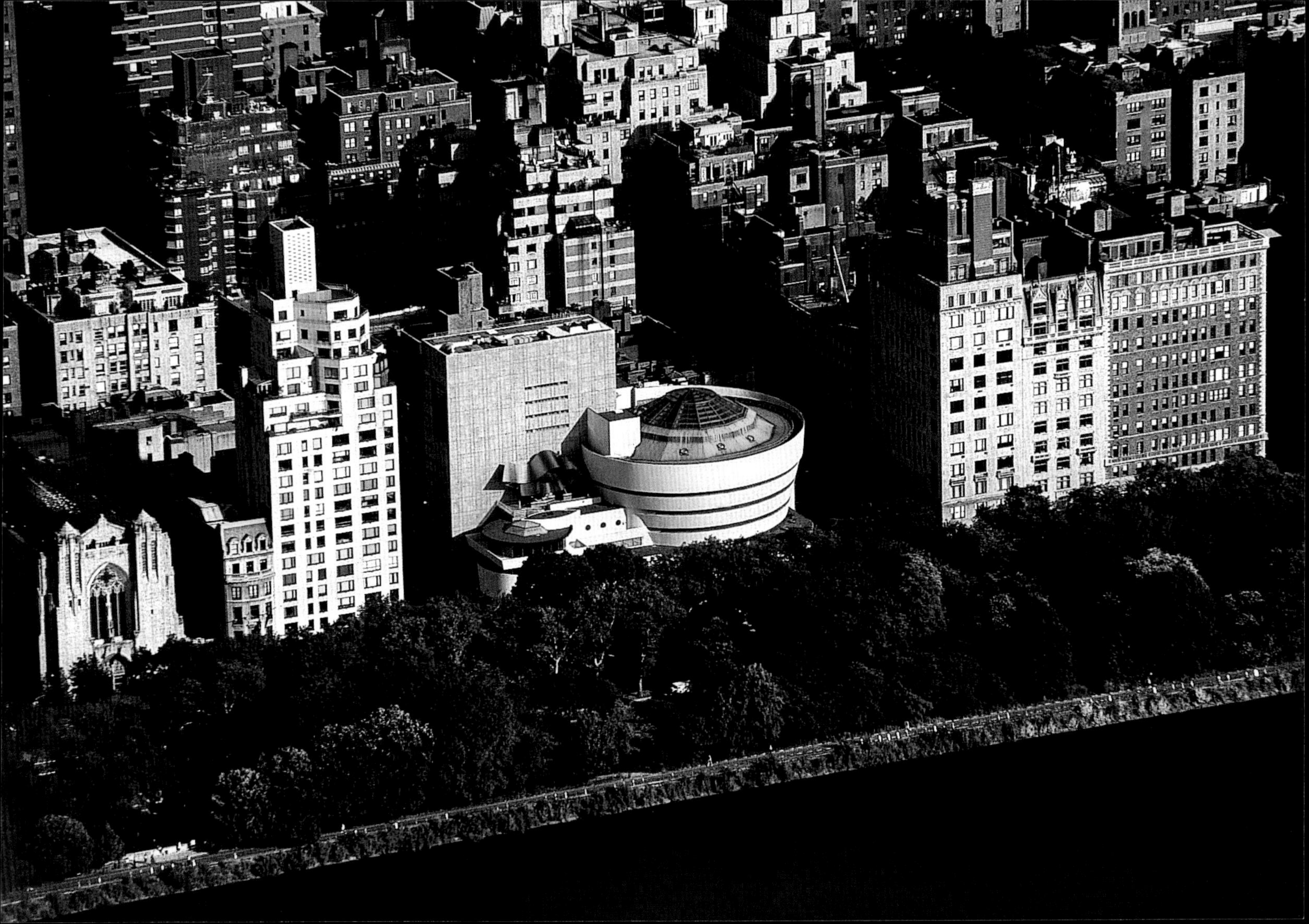

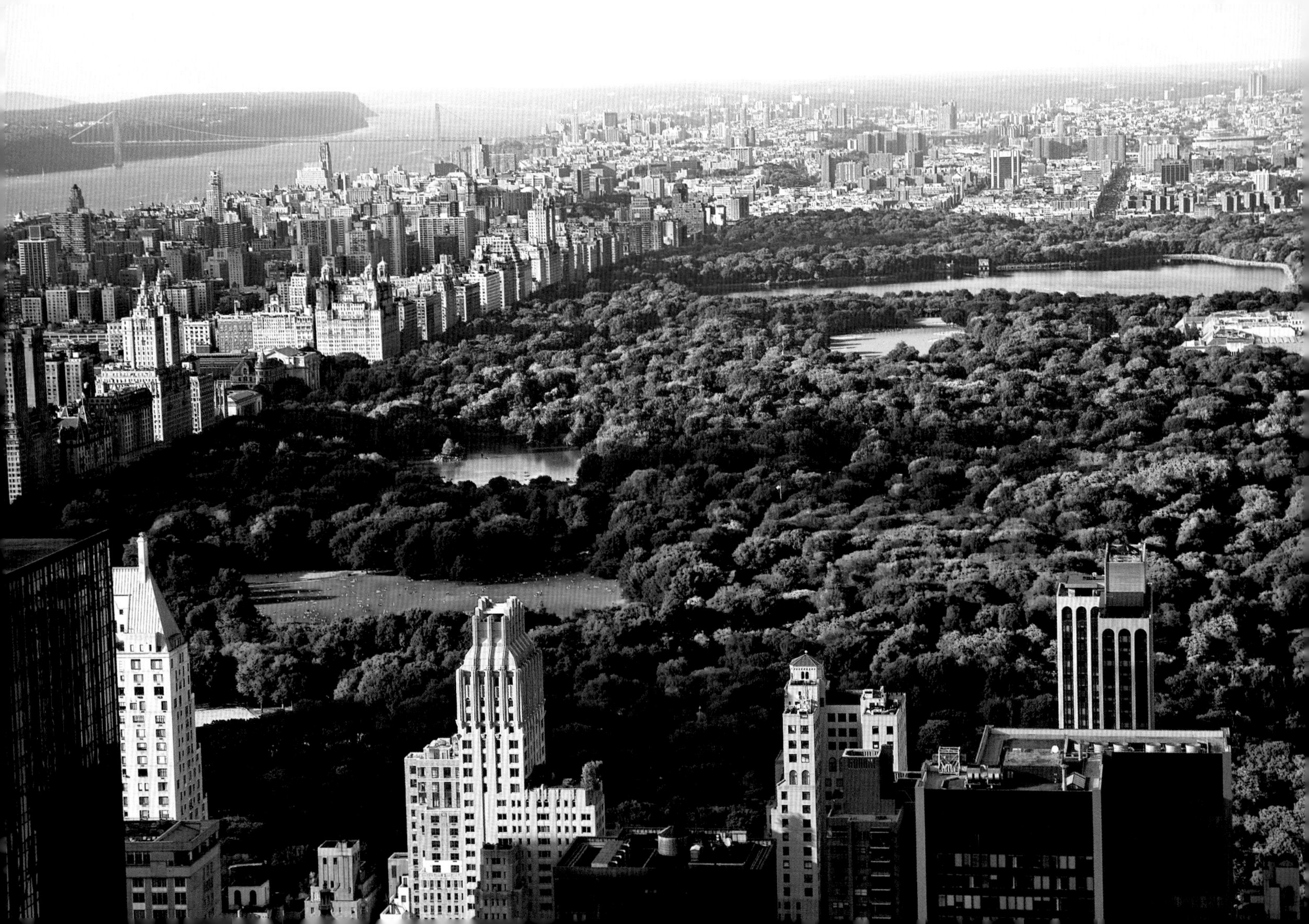

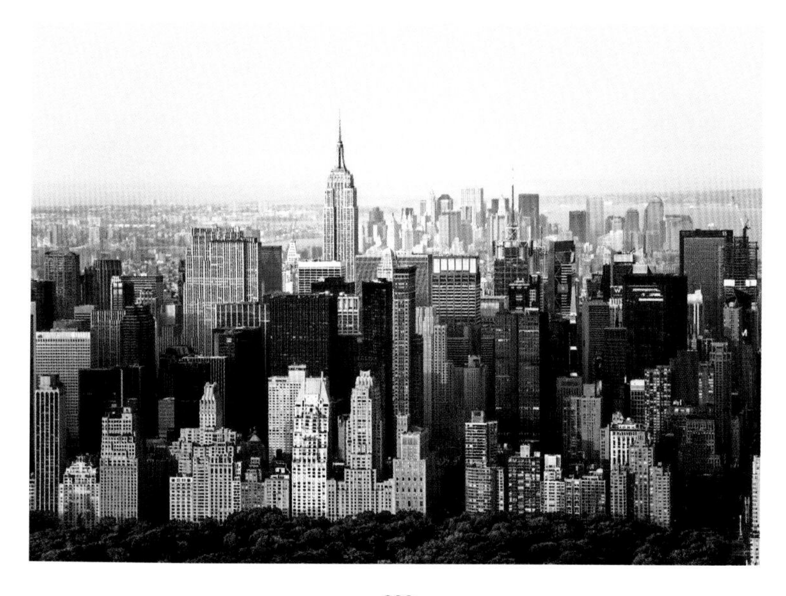

232

The view from Central Park South extends from the Sheep Meadow, past the Jacqueline Onassis Reservoir, and beyond the park's northern border at 110th Street (Cathedral Parkway).

233 and 234-235

Though tall and stately, the apartments and hotels of Central Park South allow their even taller neighbors to the south to enjoy grand views of the park as well. Some of the most exclusive real estate in the world is sited opposite Central Park, including the Plaza and Pierre hotels.

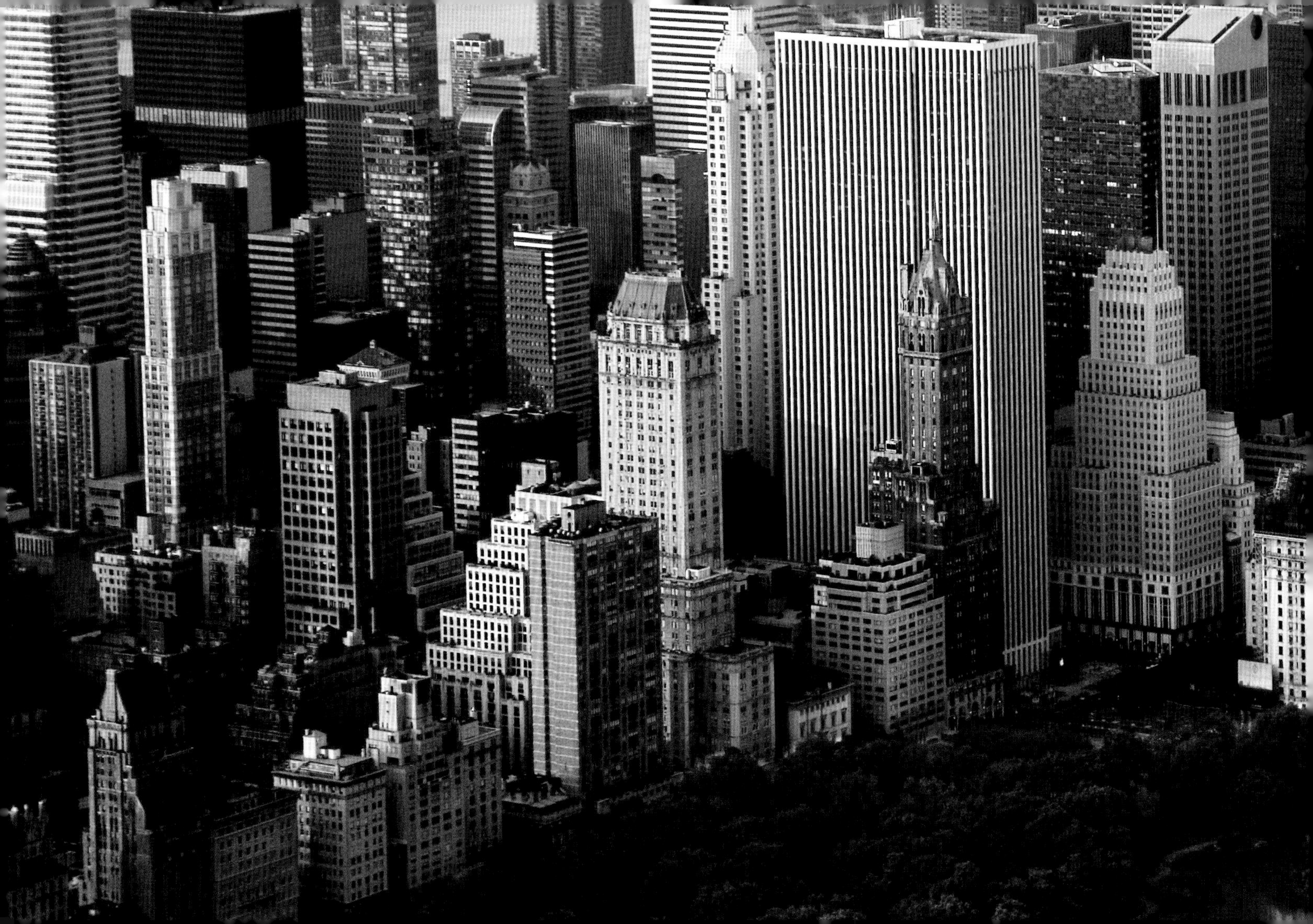

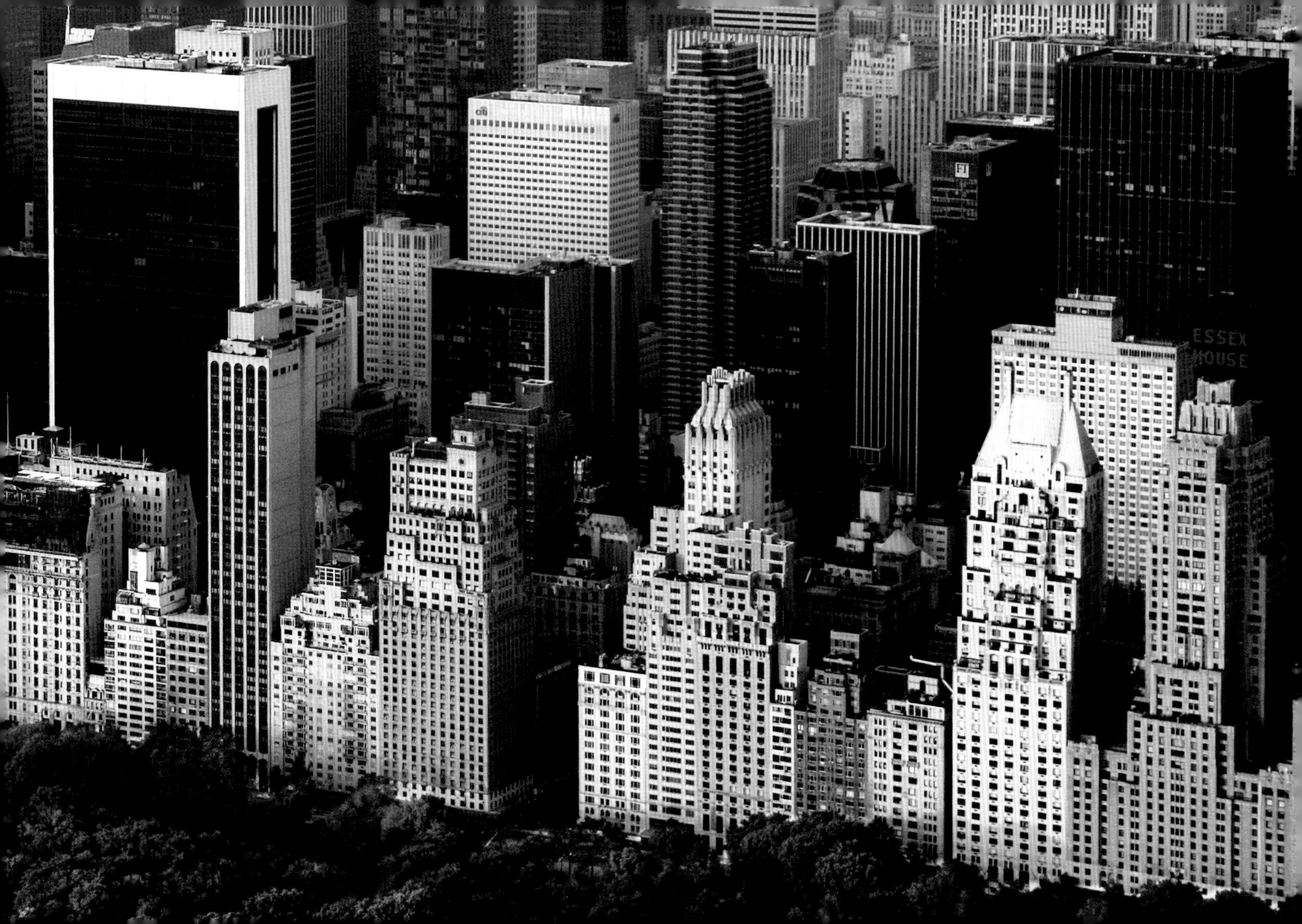
ESSEX
HOUSE

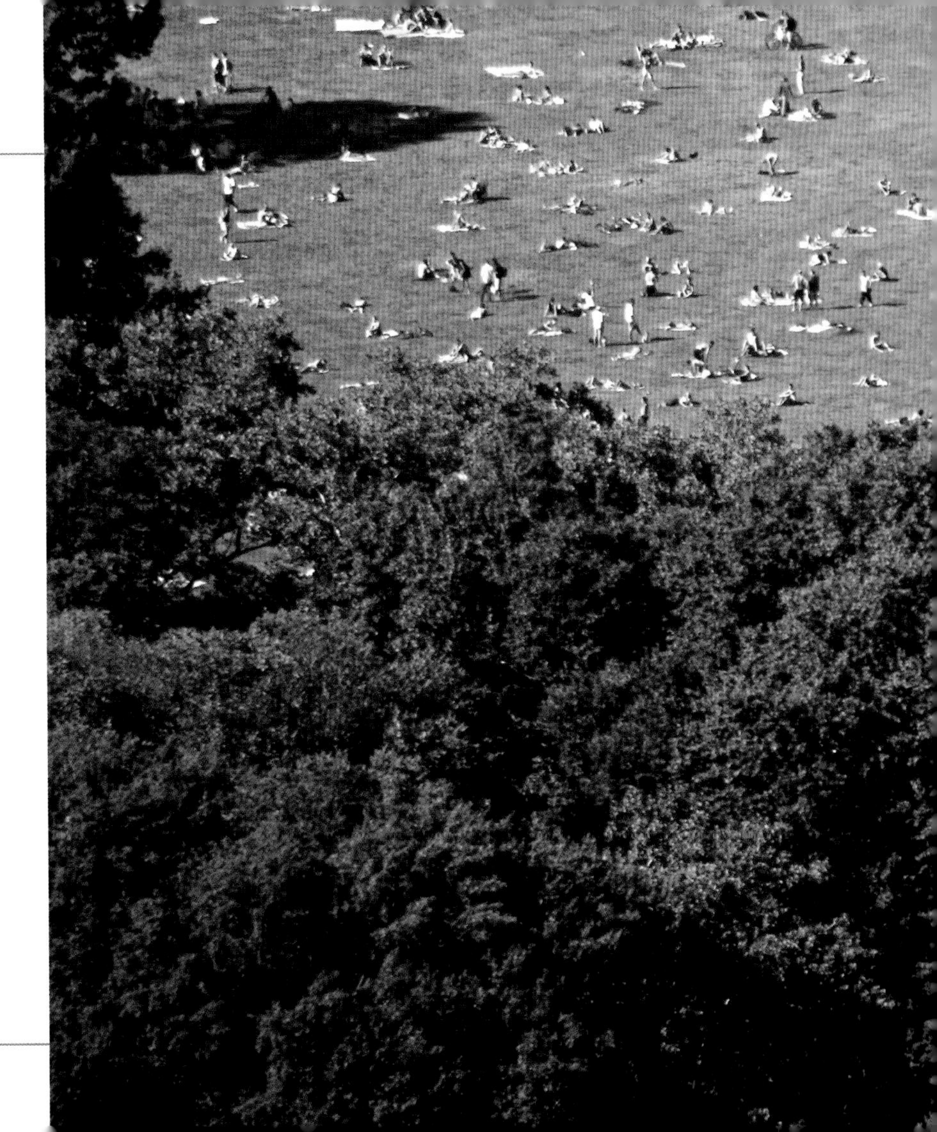

236-237
On any given summer afternoon, sunbathers and picnickers find their ways to the Sheep Meadow, where flocks of sheep grazed until 1934. (The Art Deco Trump Park Condominium is lower right.)

238-239
Located at what was once the far-reaches of Manhattan at West 90th St., and Central Park West, the twin-towered El Dorado has full-floor apartments that have views of both river and Central Park.

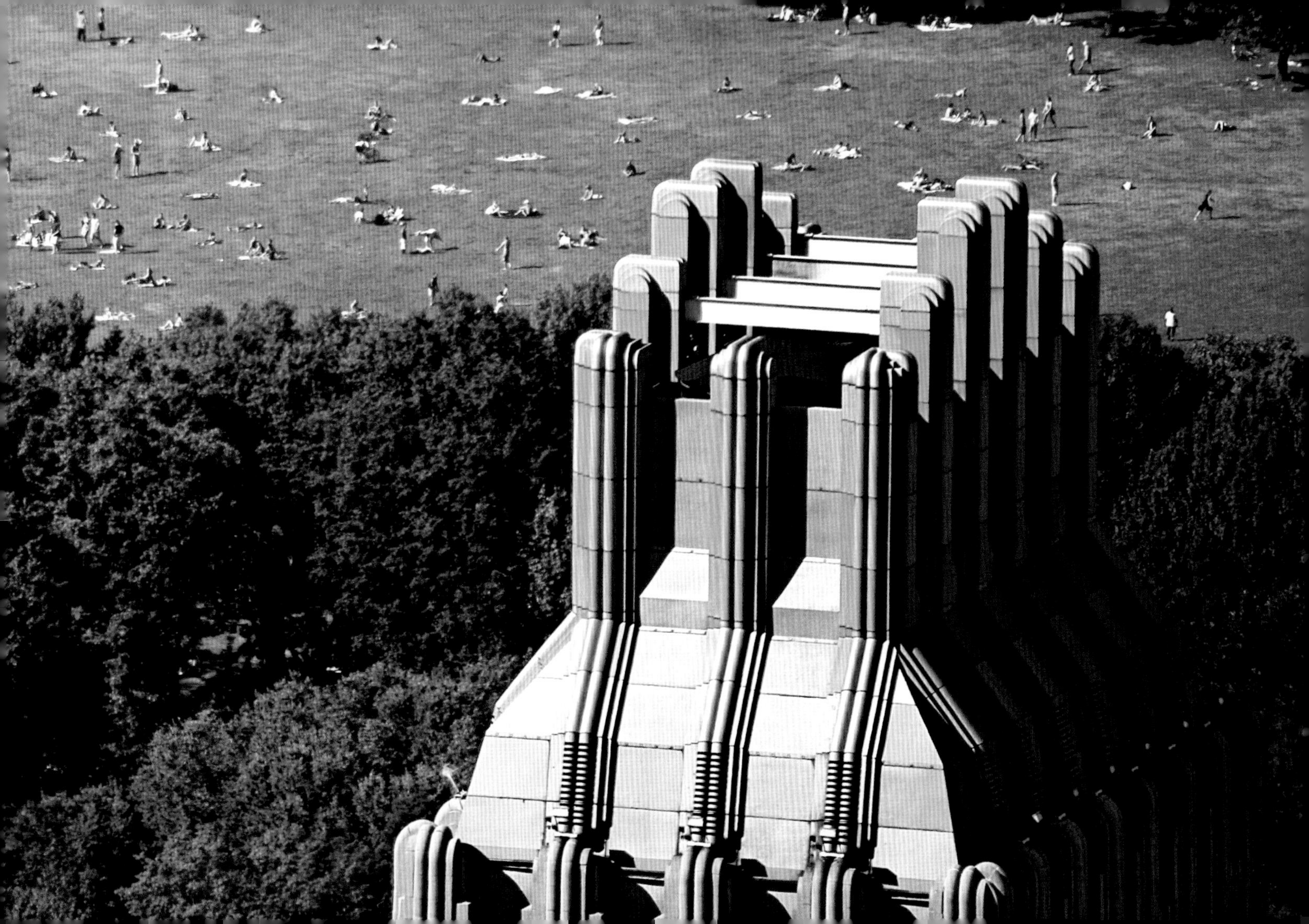

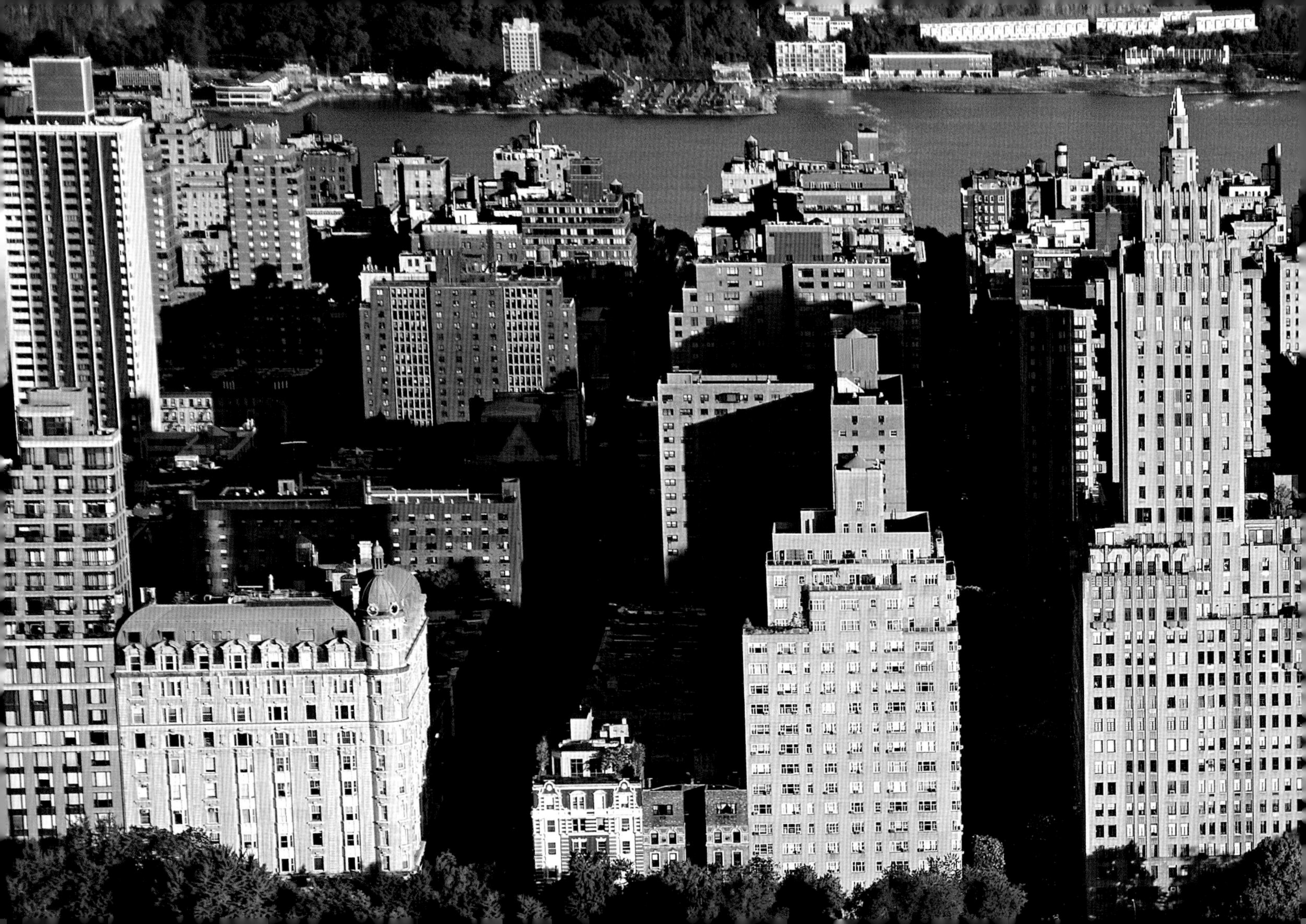

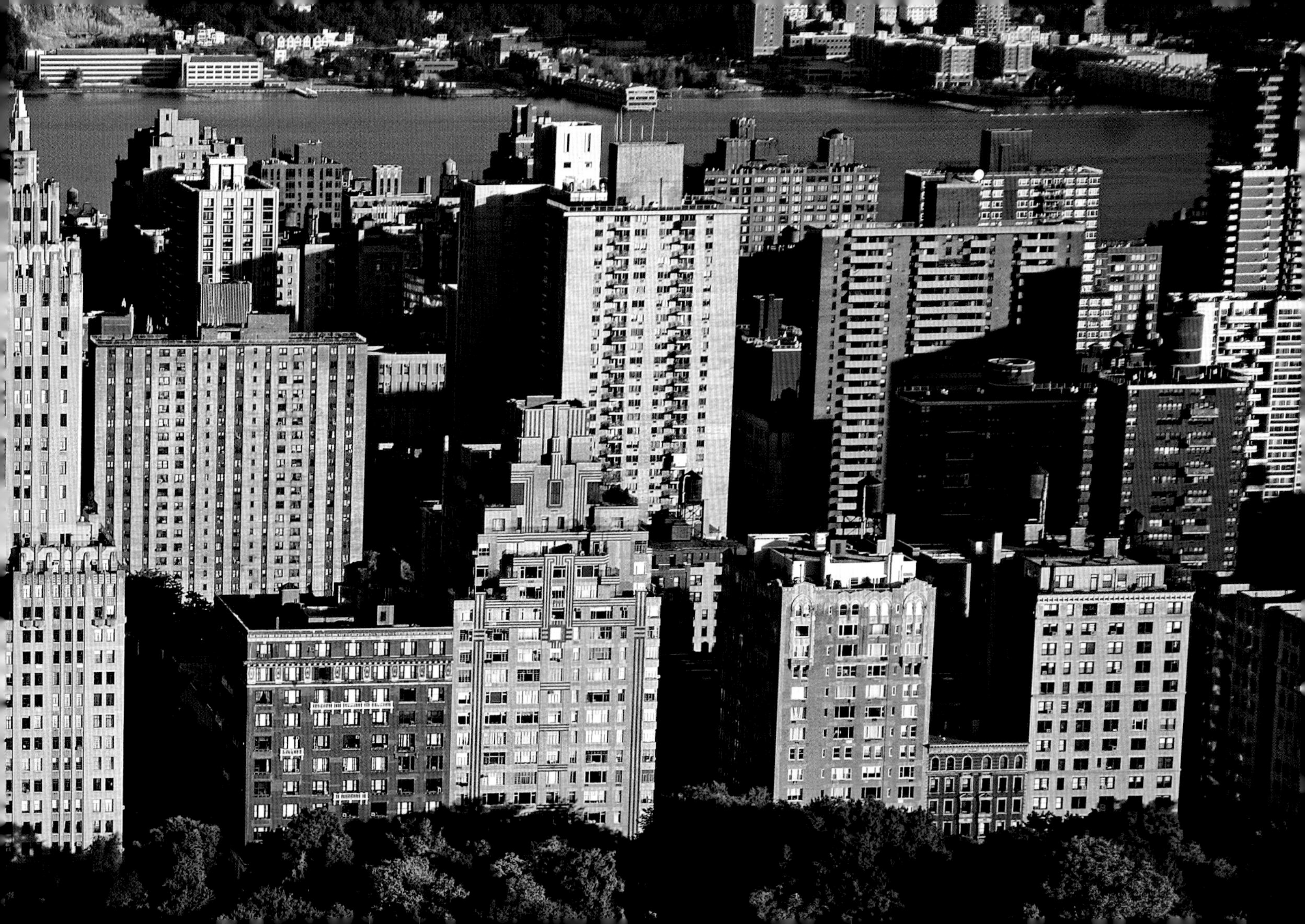

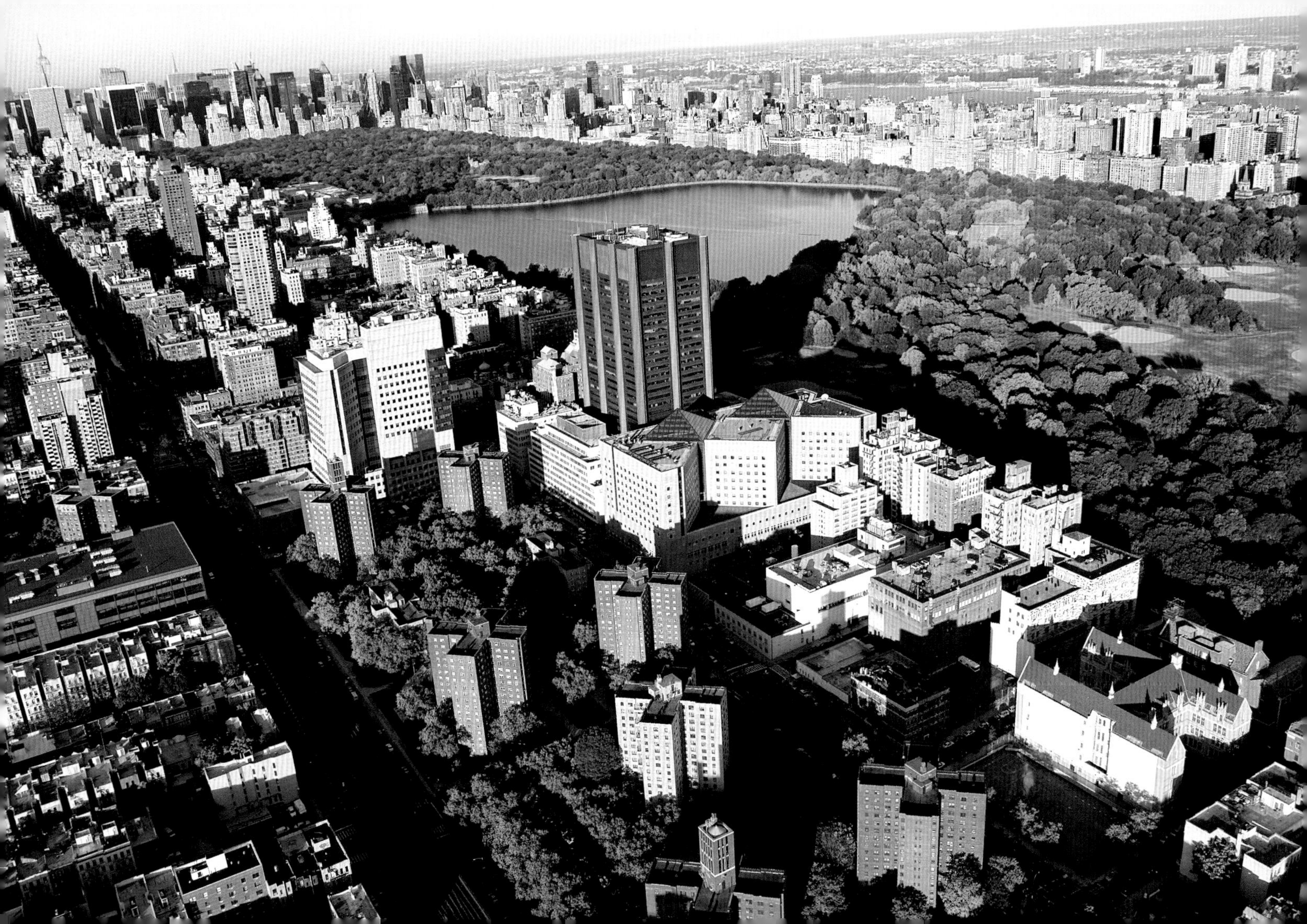

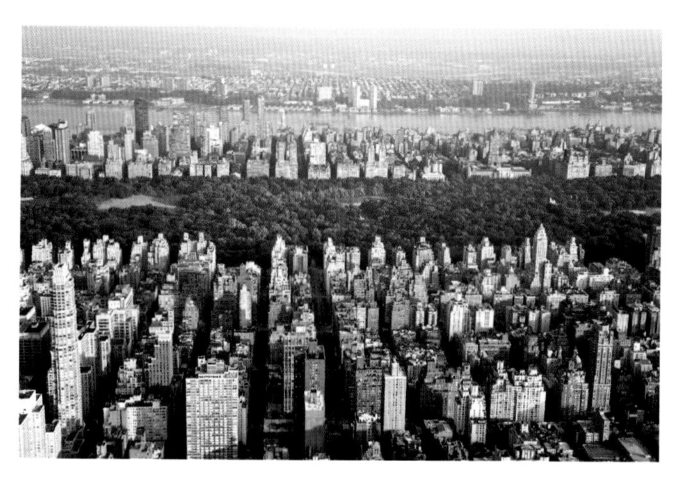

240
Many patients at the Mount Sinai Hospital Medical Center, at the northwest corner of Central Park, have the benefit of a soothing view of the park and the reservoir.

241
The blue of the Hudson River and green of Central Park help restore a sense of nature to the high-rise canyons of New York.

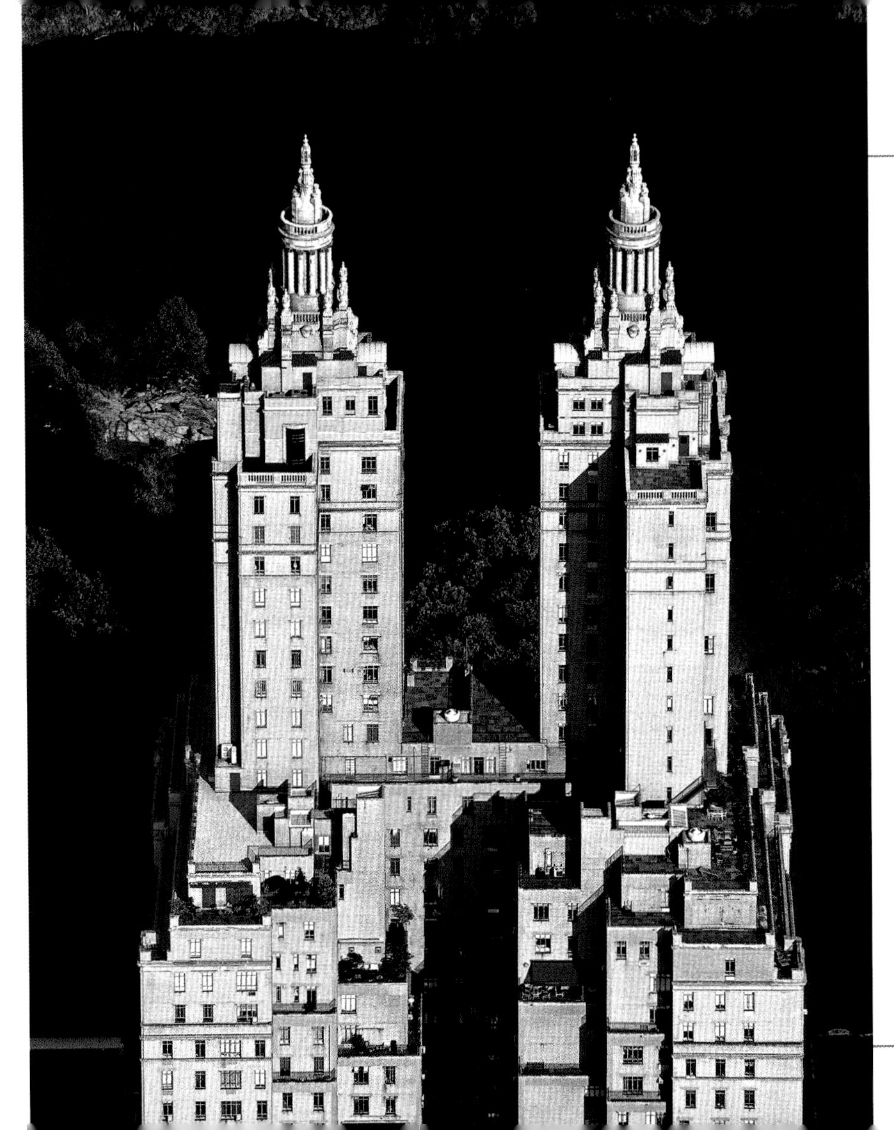

242
One of Central Park West's classic twin-towered apartment buildings, the San Remo overlooks Strawberry Fields, dedicated to the memory of John Lennon.

243
At the Central Park Reservoir, along E. 96th St. we see the cupola of the Islamic Cultural Center.

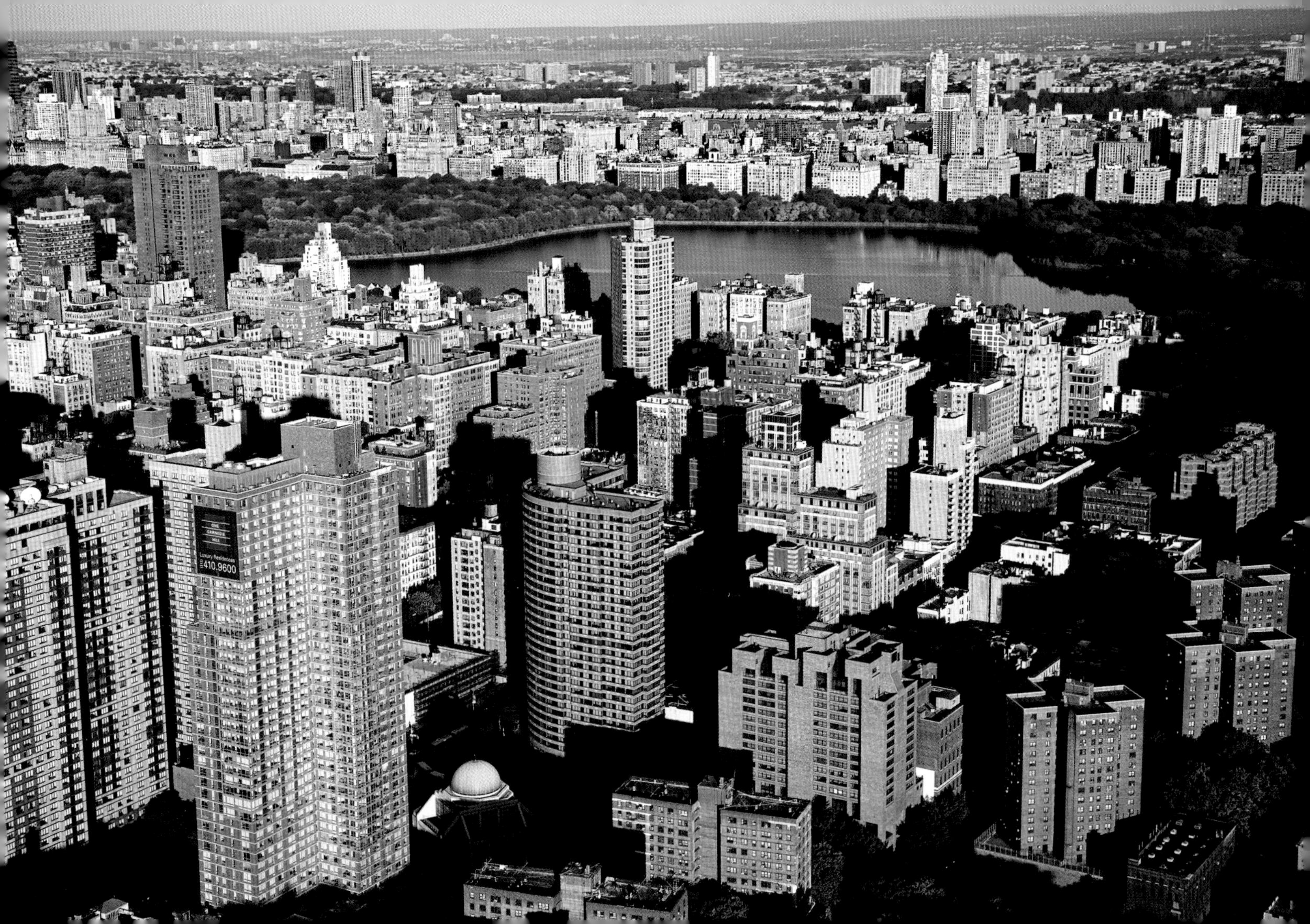
Luxury Residences
410.9600

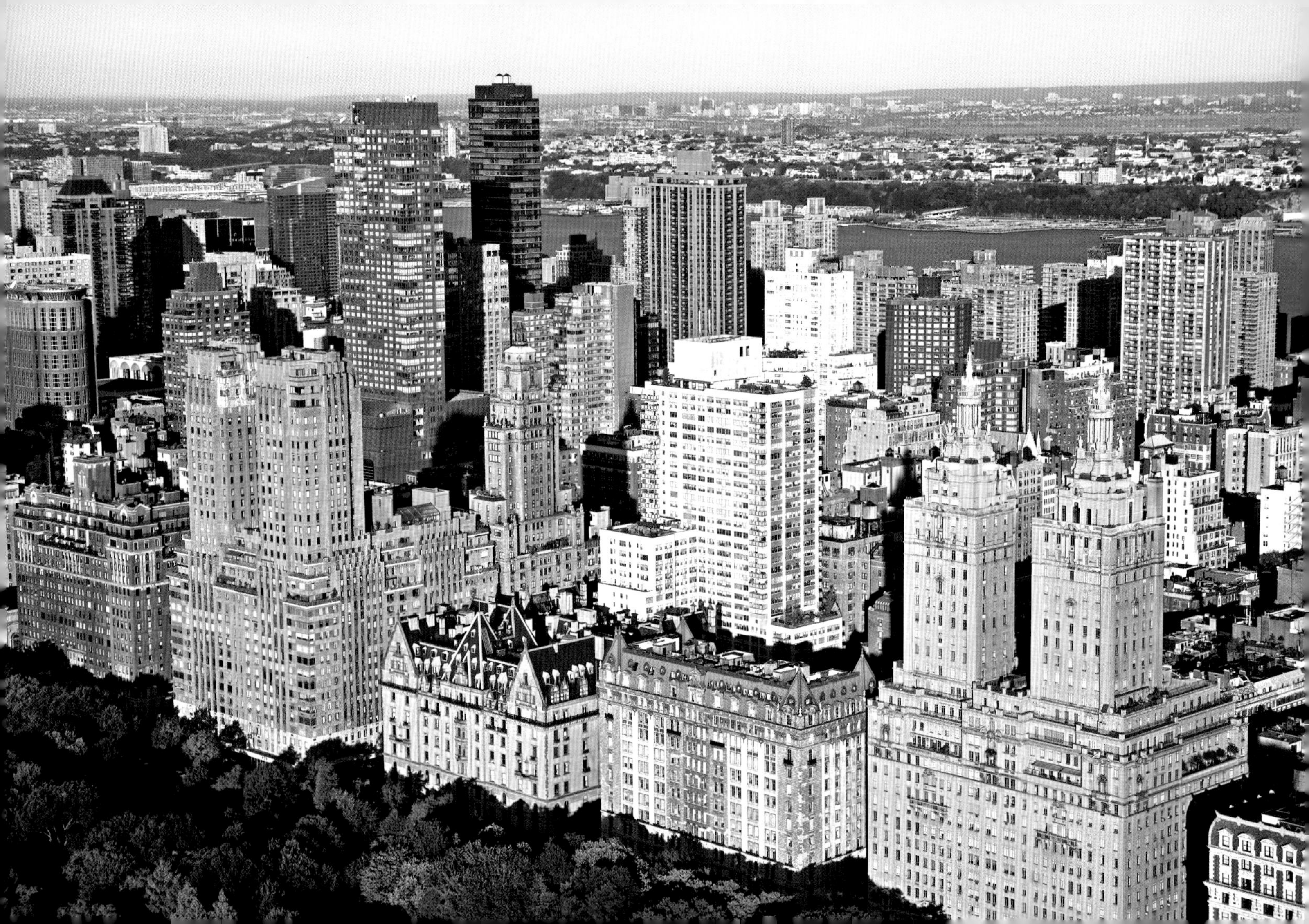

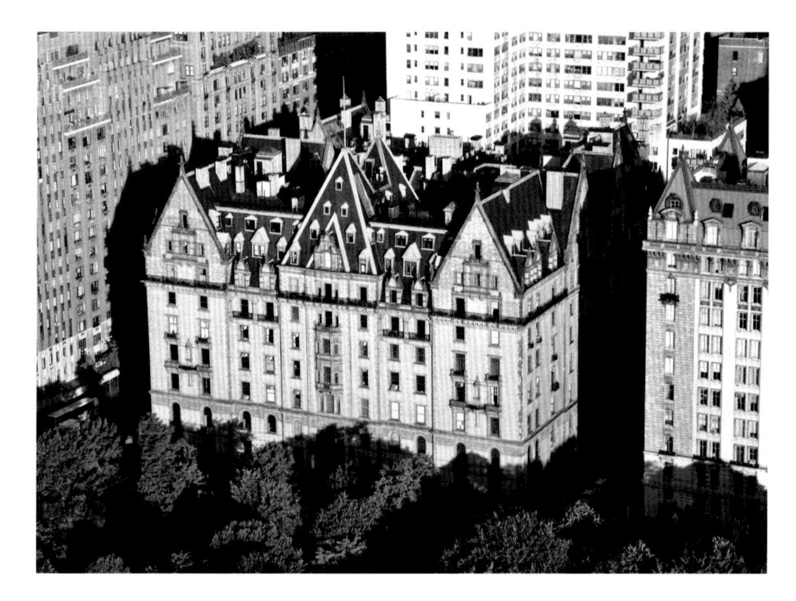

244
The high-gabled neighbor of the twin-spired San Remo, the Dakota, at the corner of West 72nd and Central Park West, is well-known for its celebrity residents, including John Lennon, who was shot in the building's courtyard.

245
Designed by the same architect who built the Plaza Hotel, the Dakota is across from the Central Park Lake and Strawberry Fields - a location once thought to be as remote as the Dakota territory.

247

From the steel and glass of Midtown East, the Yorkville section of the Upper East Side reflects the calm of Central Park. The Church of St. Jean Baptiste (lower right), still uses Latin in some services, to accommodate the many Europeans who live in the area.

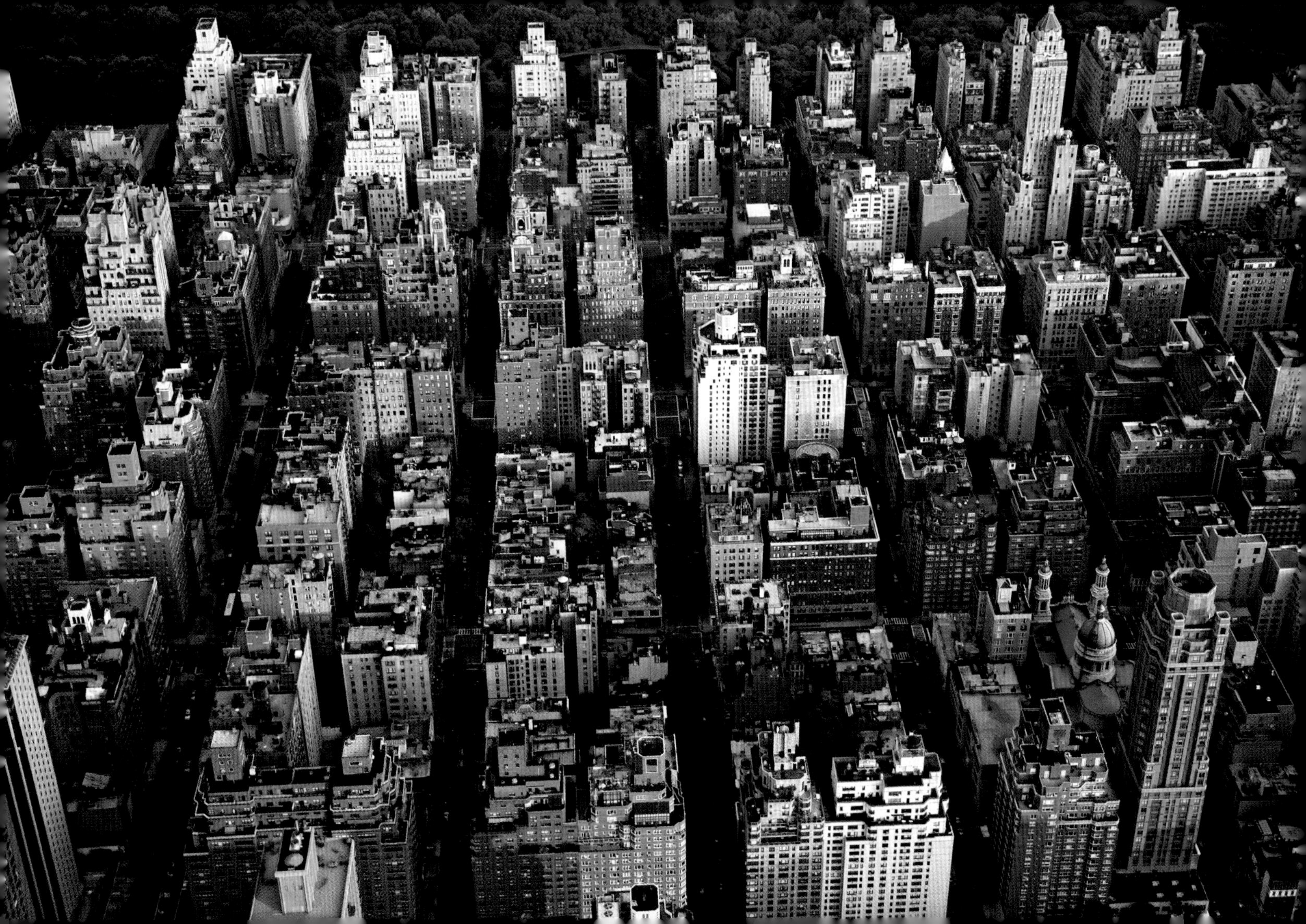

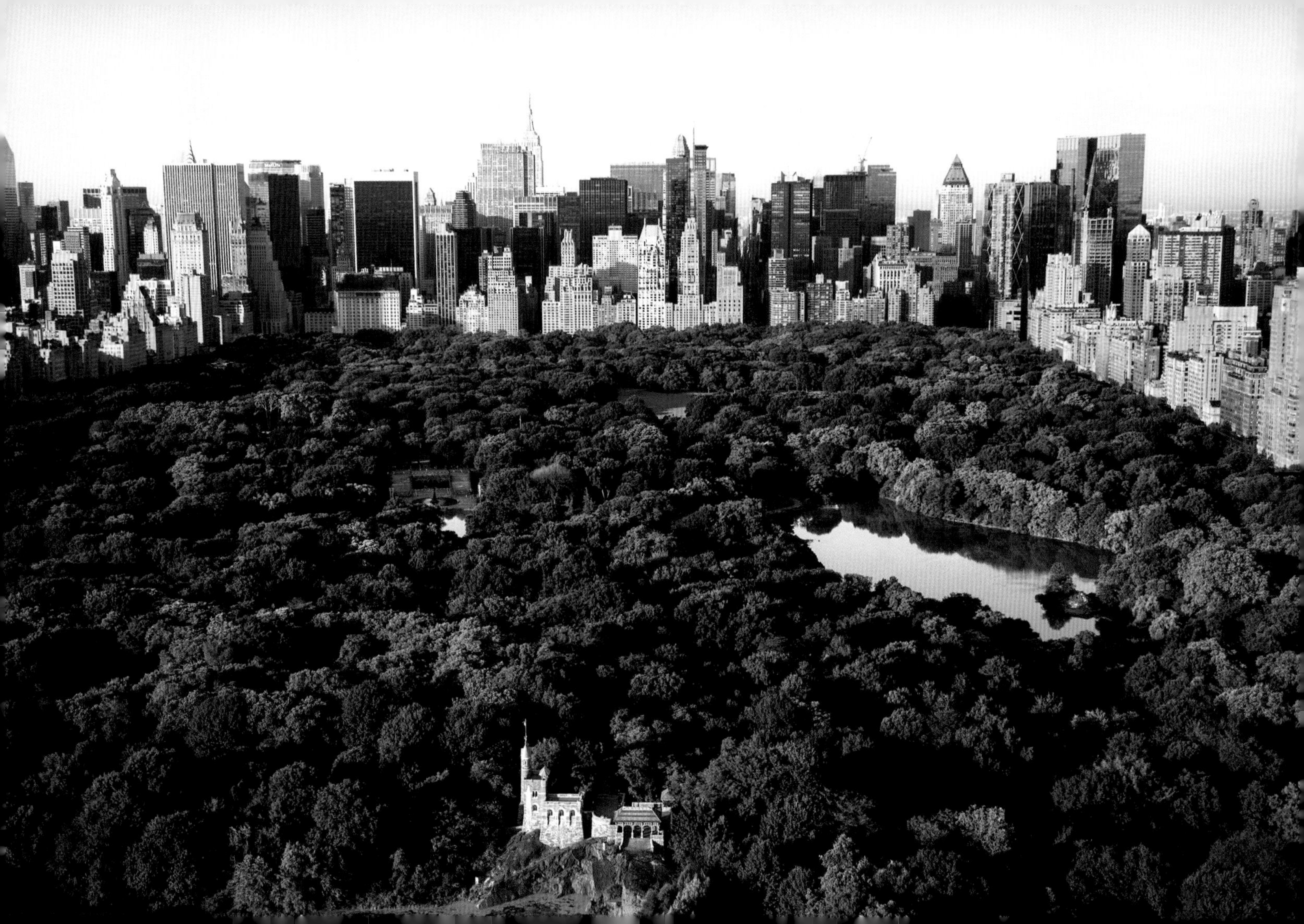

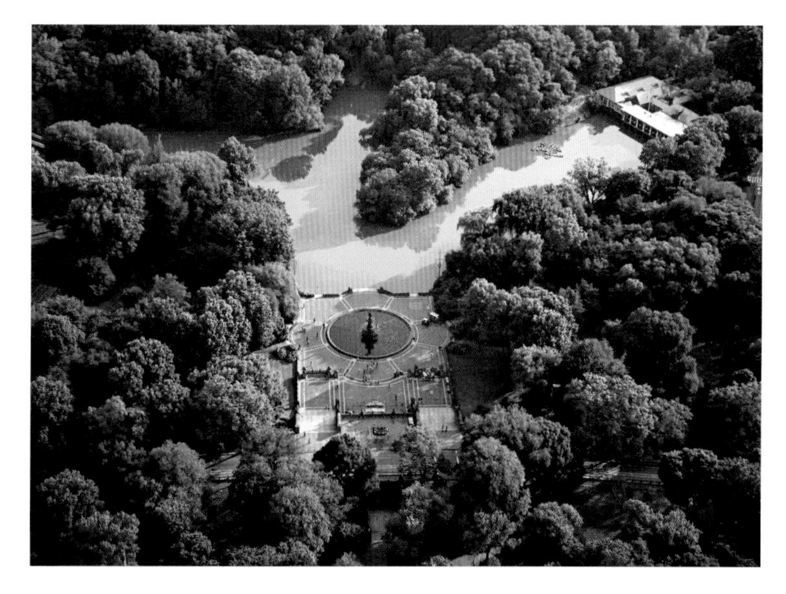

248

Belvedere Castle, which rises out of Vista Rock, the second highest natural elevation in Central Park, was designed as a Victorian folly and was empty inside; today it houses the Henry Luce Nature Observatory.

249

The Angel of the Lake fountain, located on Bethesda Terrace overlooking the lake in Central Park, is one of the most photographed fountains in the world.

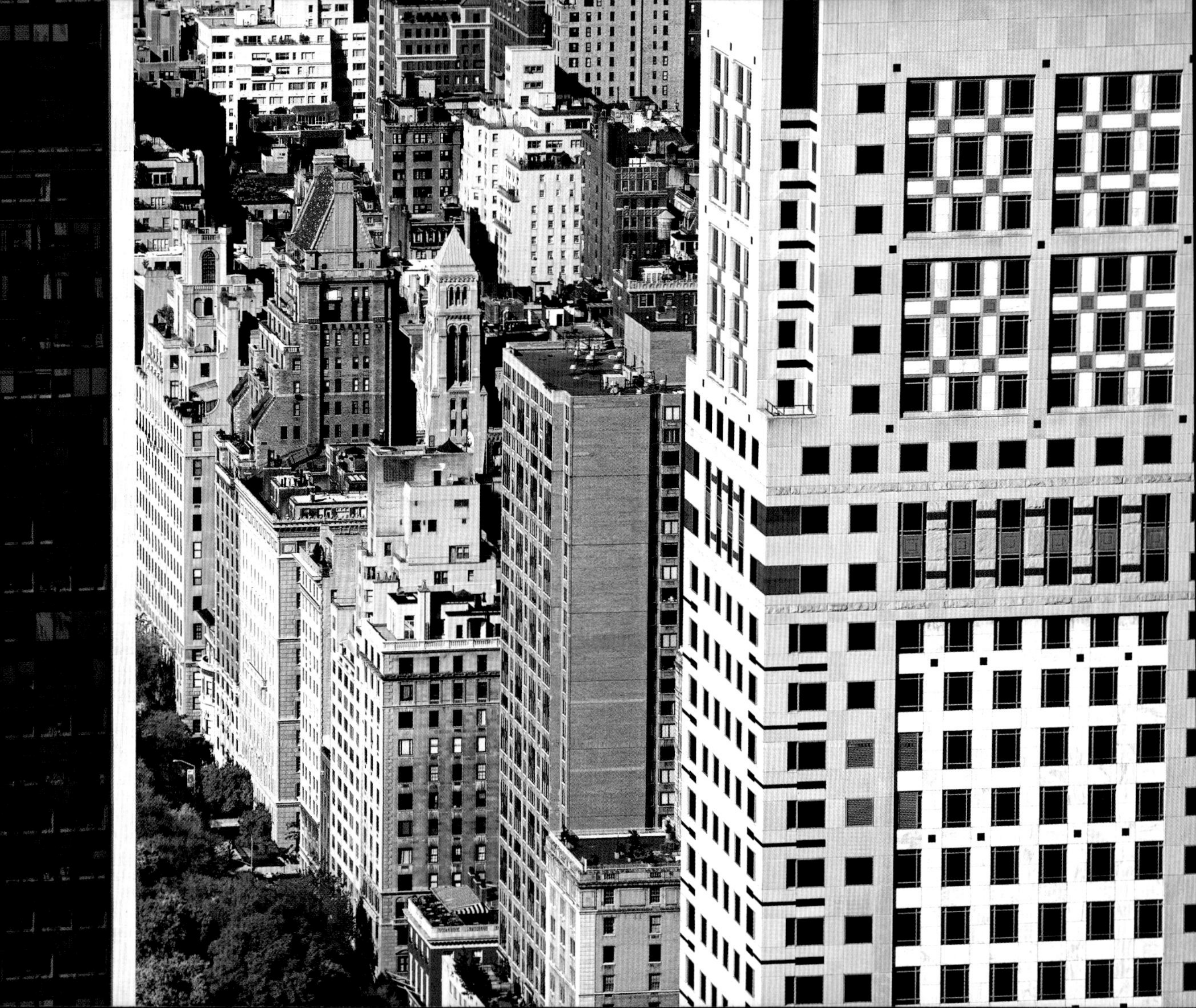

250
A peek around the corner of 9 West 57th Street reveals a hint of Central Park.

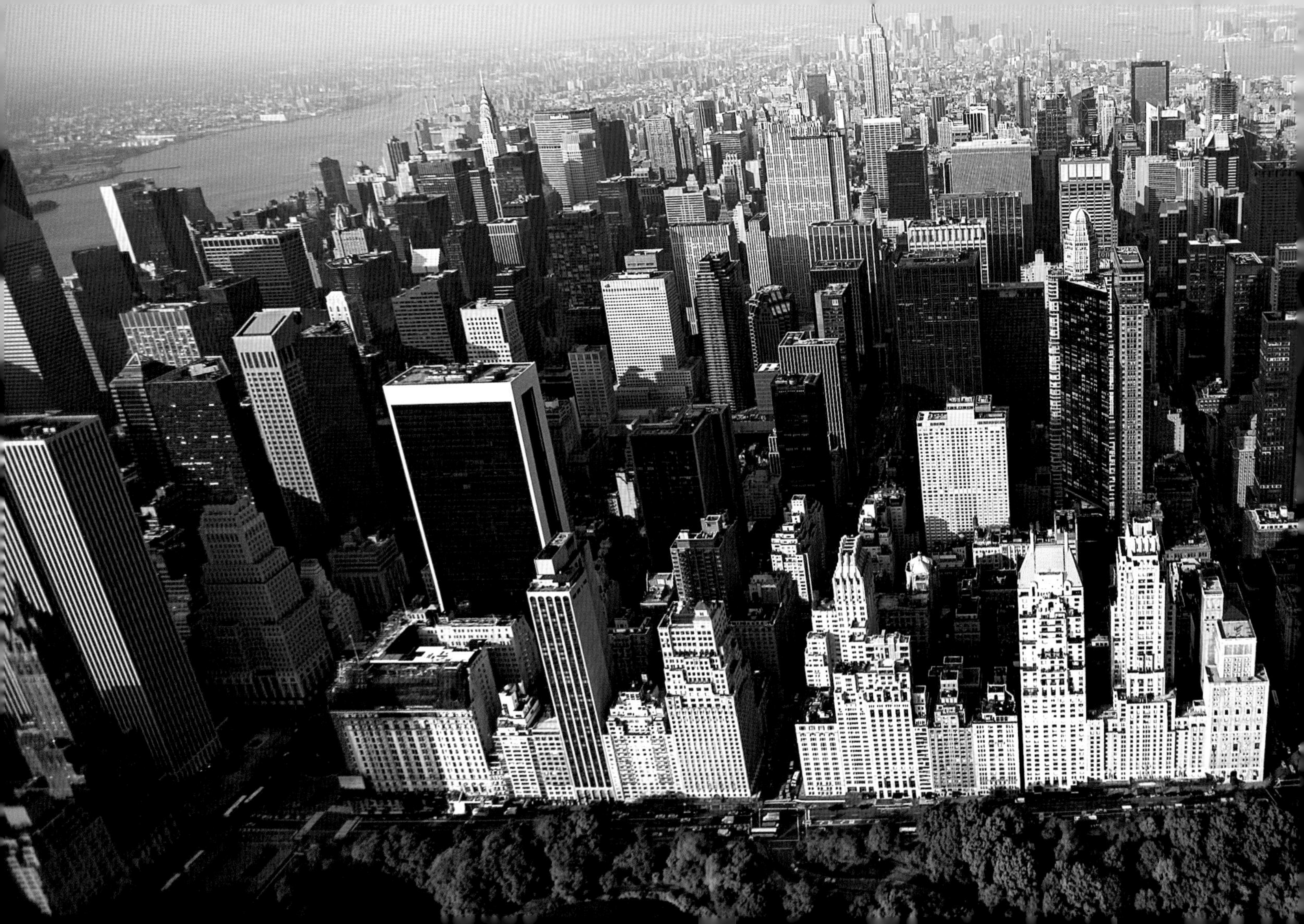

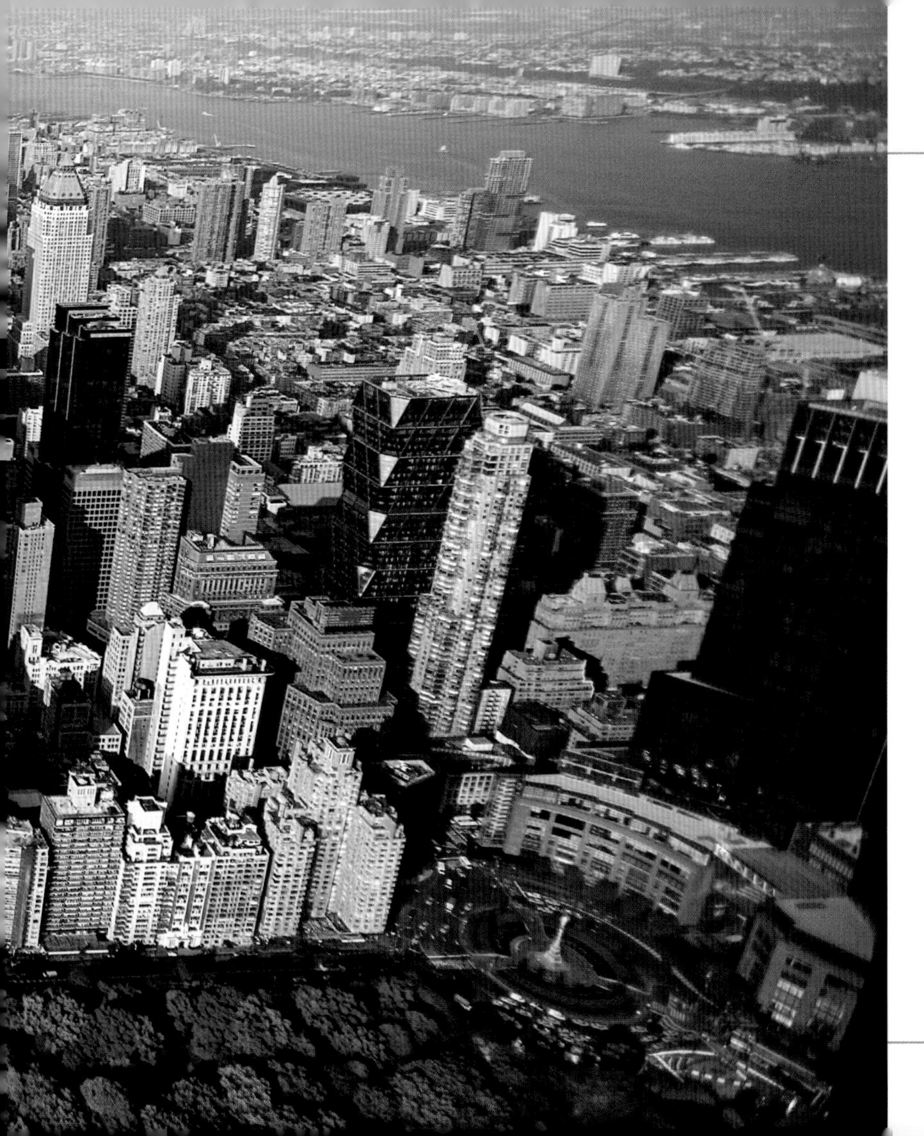

252-253
A main entrance to Central Park is at Columbus Circle (lower right), the crossroads of Broadway, Central Park West, Central Park South and Eighth Avenue. The shimmering Time Warner Towers rise above the monument to Columbus in the center.

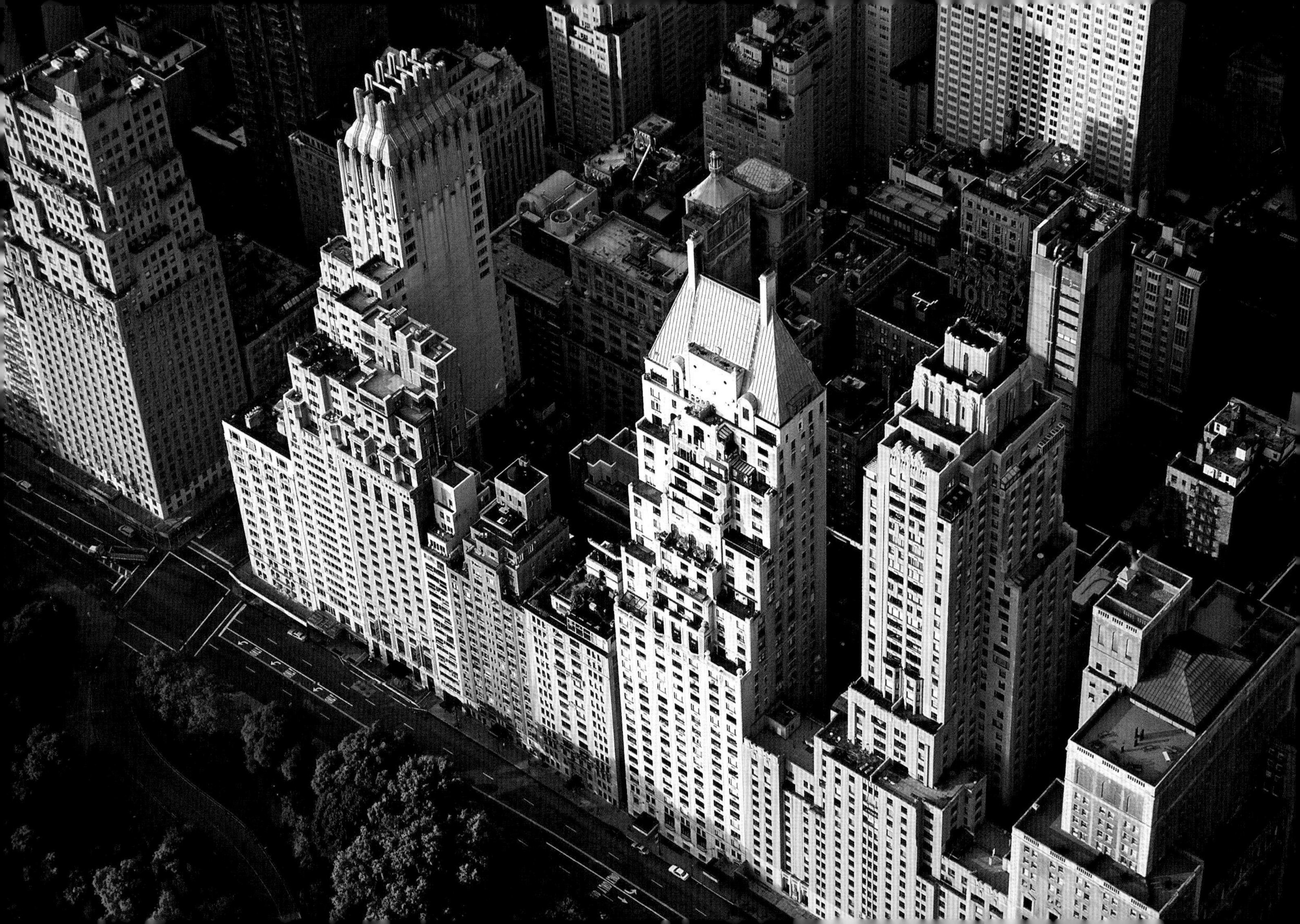

254

Long the tallest building on Central Park South, Hampshire House Hotel's two chimneys are barely two meters taller than the roof of the neighboring Jumeirah Essex House hotel.

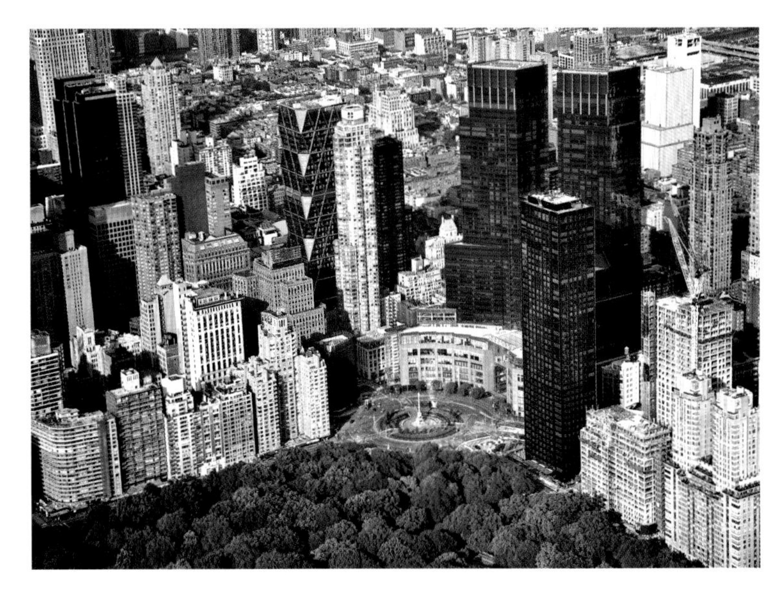

256

The Time Warner Center anchors the western corner of Columbus Circle, dwarfing the elegantly scaled buildings of Central Park South, and even the high-rise Trump International Hotel and Tower.

257

Columbus Circle is a major traffic hub and gateway to Central Park; the monument in the center is dedicated to Christopher Columbus. The Merchant's Gate entrance to the park, dominated by the gilded bronze Maine Monument, is in the lower foreground.

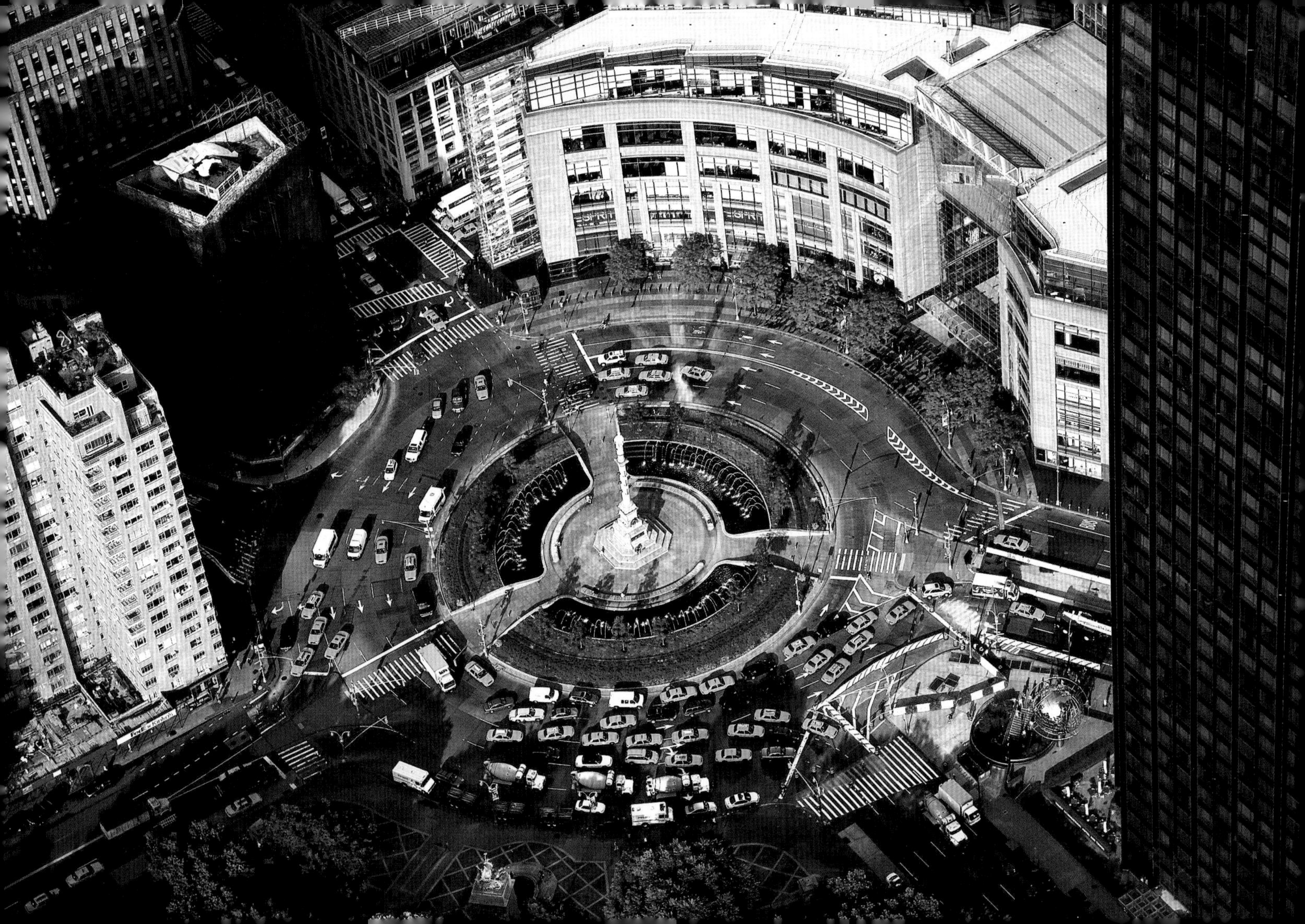
FedEx Kinko's

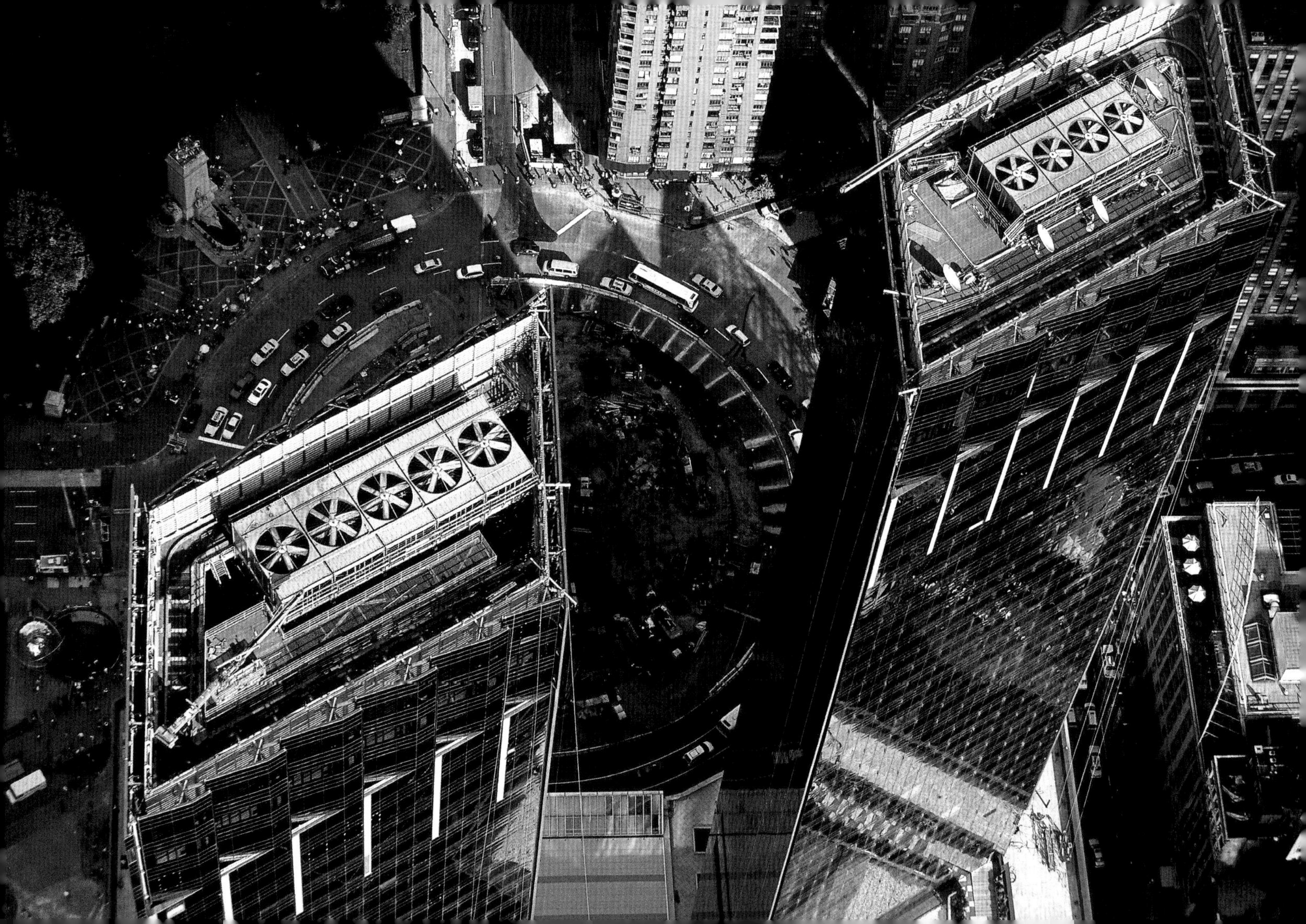

258

Designed by David Childs of Skidmore, Owings & Merrill, the twin towers of the Time Warner Center were completed in 2004. Over 750 feet tall, the towers dominate Columbus Circle.

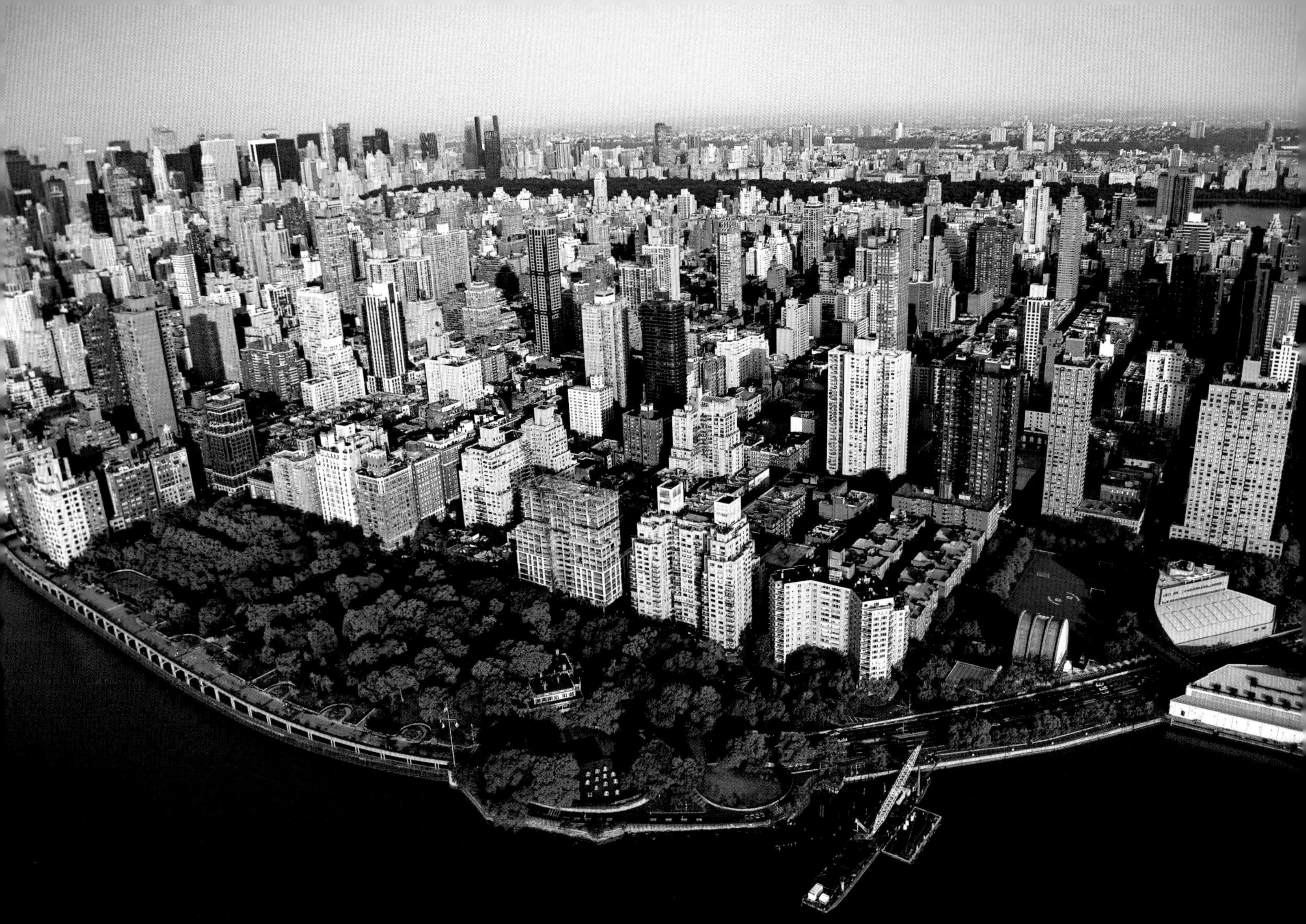

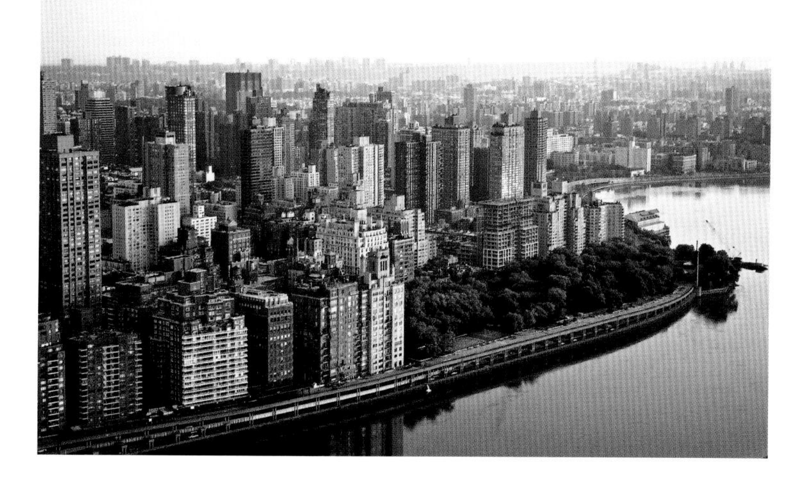

260
Gracie Mansion, the residence of New York's mayor, is located in Carl Schurz Park on the Upper East Side.

261
The Franklin Delano Roosevelt Highway wraps around Carl Schurz Park, along the East River.

263
Barges in the East River get sunrise views of Carl Schurz Park and Asphalt Green Fitness Center with the city's only 50-meter Olympic standard swimming pool.

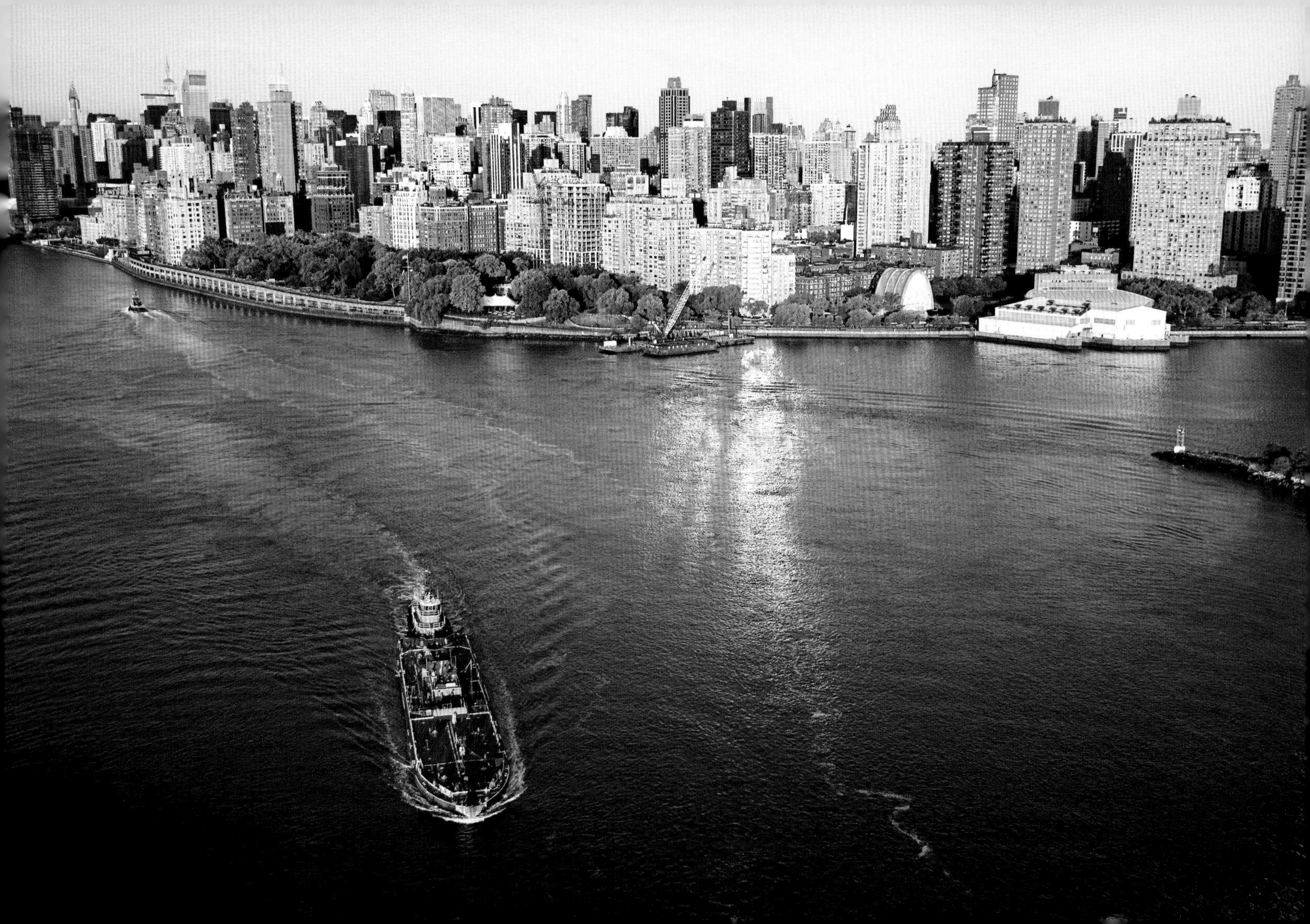

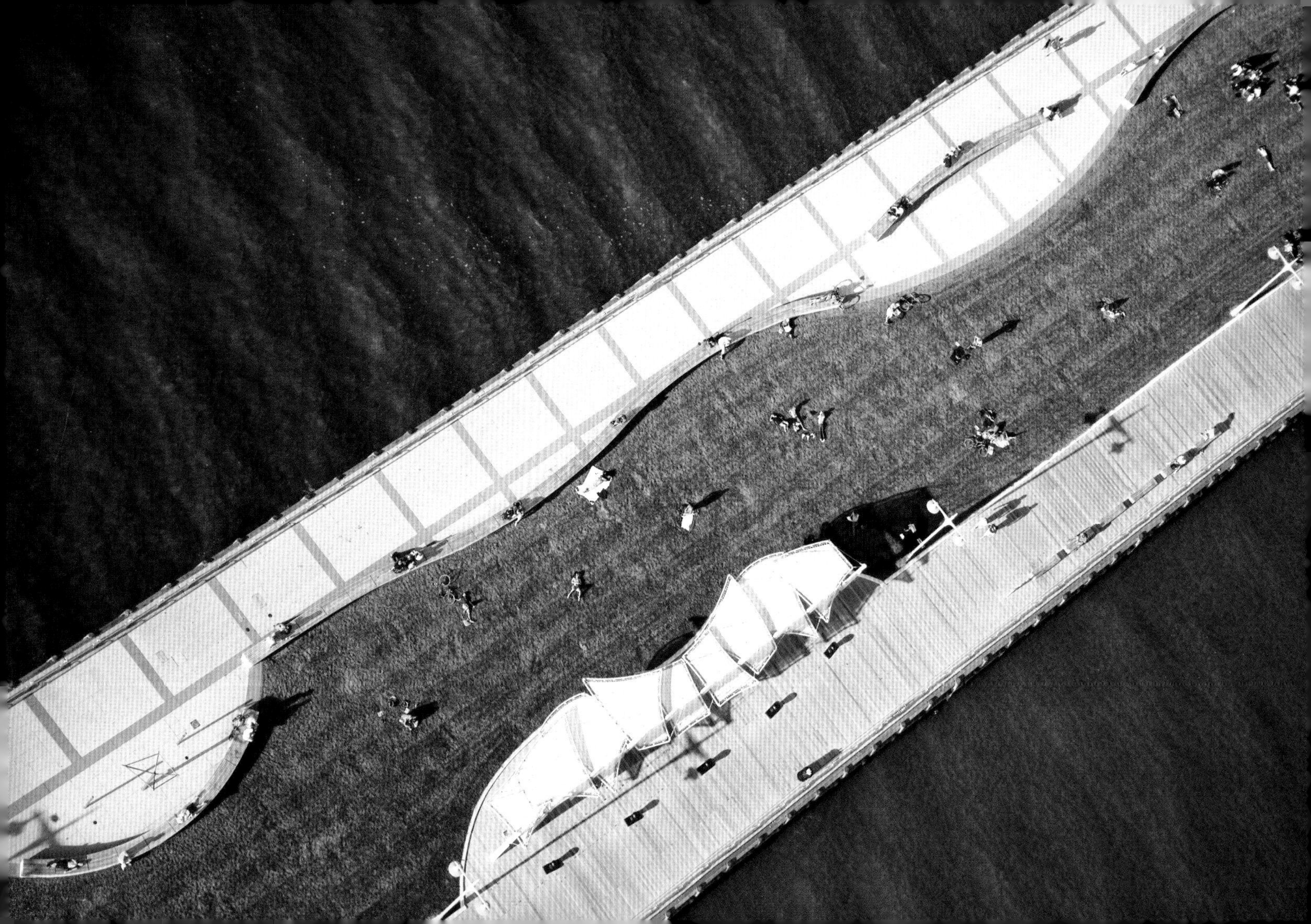

264
The 550-acre Hudson River Park has revived abandoned and neglected piers, creating the largest open space project in Manhattan since Central Park.

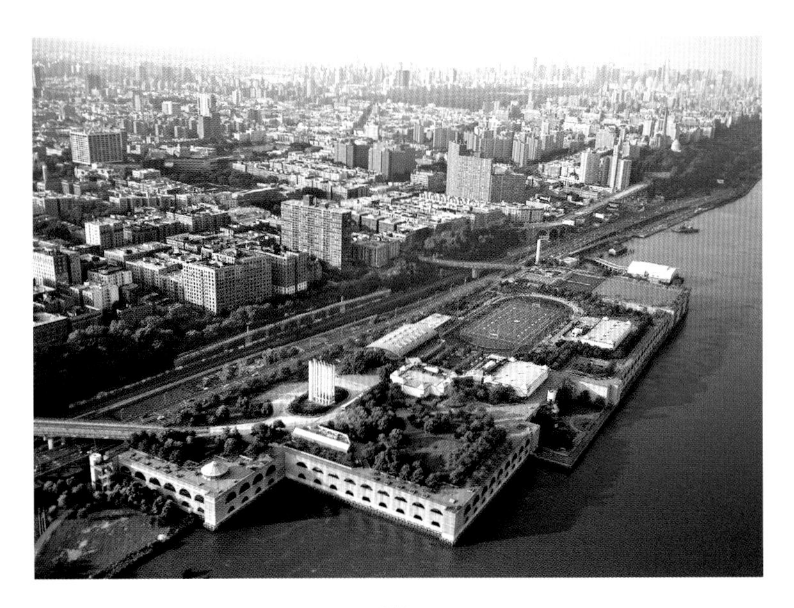

266

Ever resourceful, given its limited open space, New York even has a 28-acre state park, Riverbank State Park, rising 69 feet above the Hudson River, built above a residential wastewater treatment center.

267 and 268-269

Chelsea Piers, on the Hudson River, has found new uses for a once-forgotten waterfront, including golf and skateboarding.

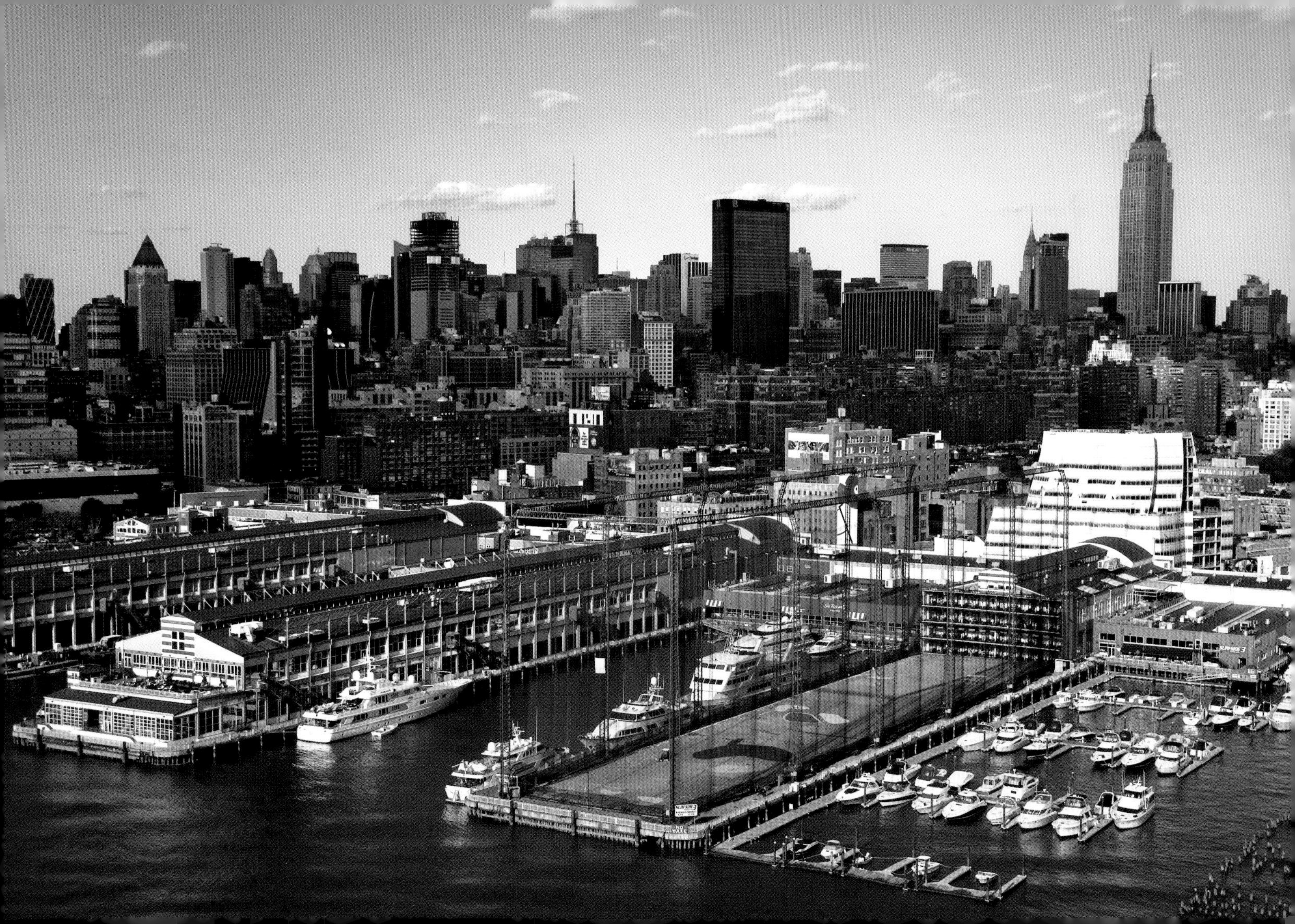

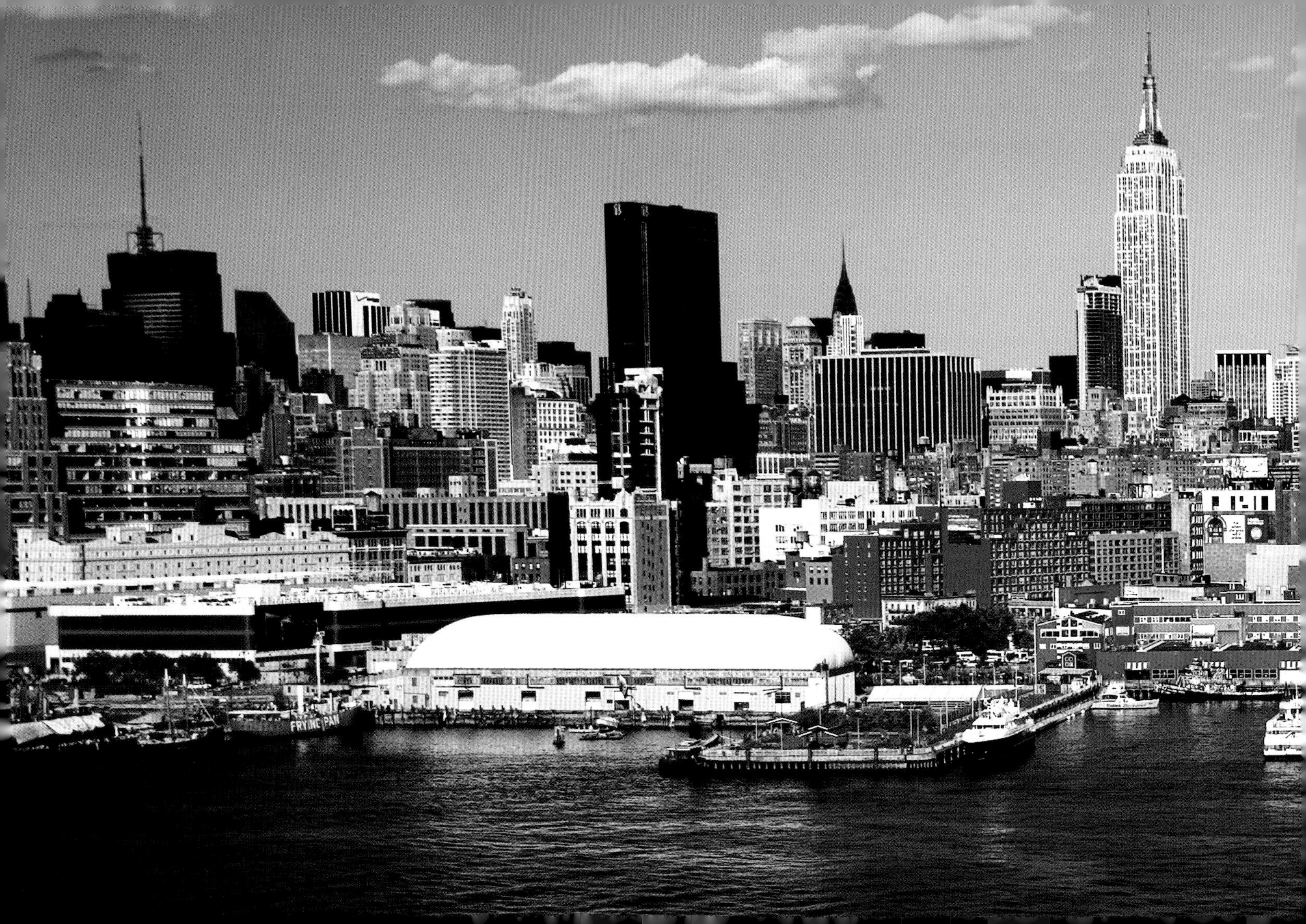
FRYING PAN

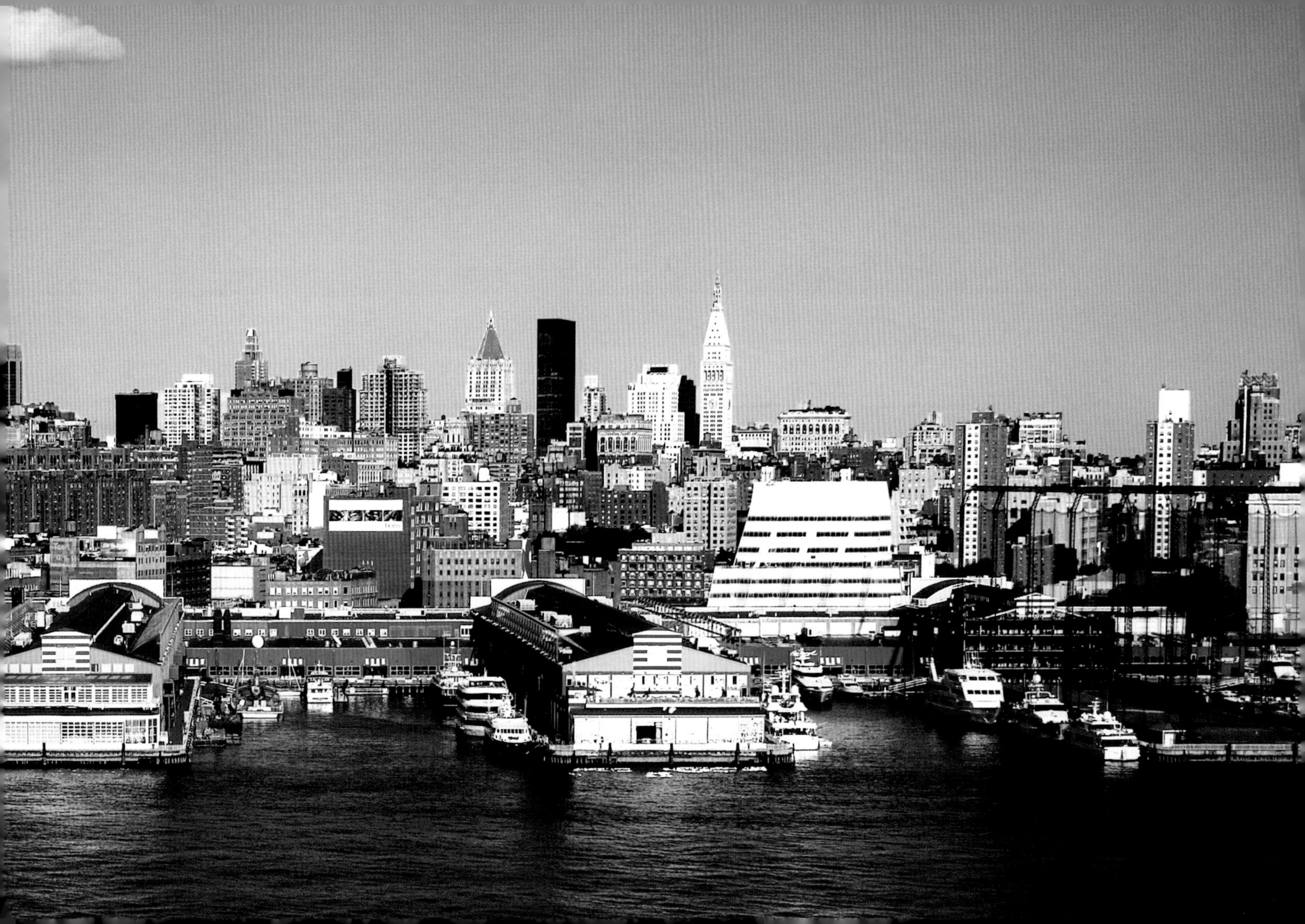

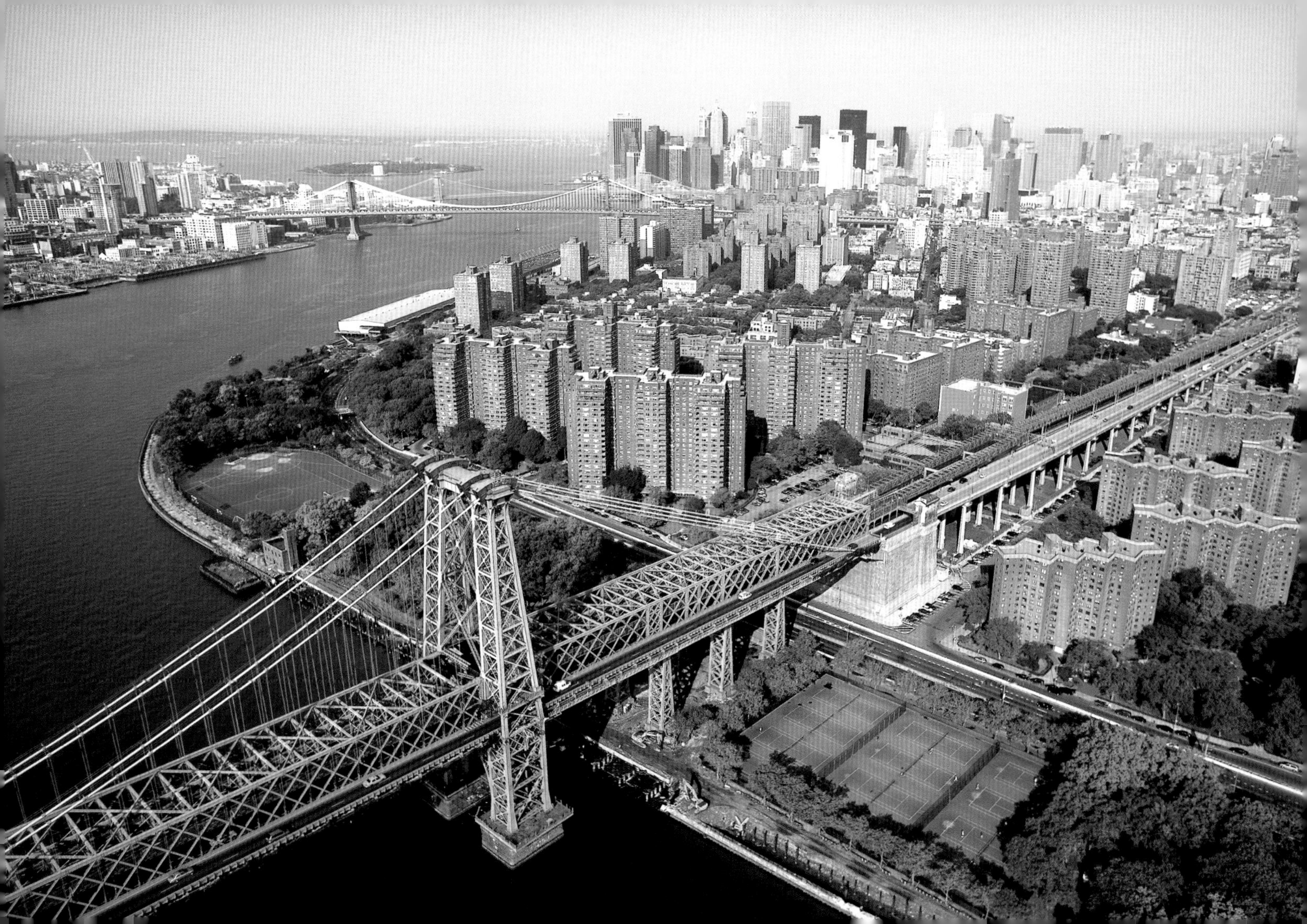

270
Once an area of factories, tenements and slaughterhouses, the East River Park now offers a riverside promenade alongside a running track.

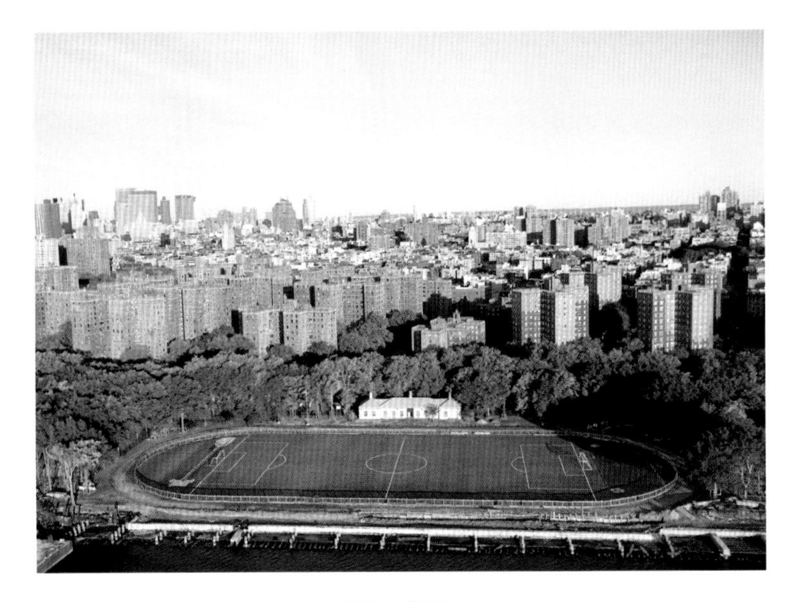

272 and 273

Areas along the East River that were home to the poorest immigrants until the Thirties and Forties are now dotted with playing fields and landscaped areas.

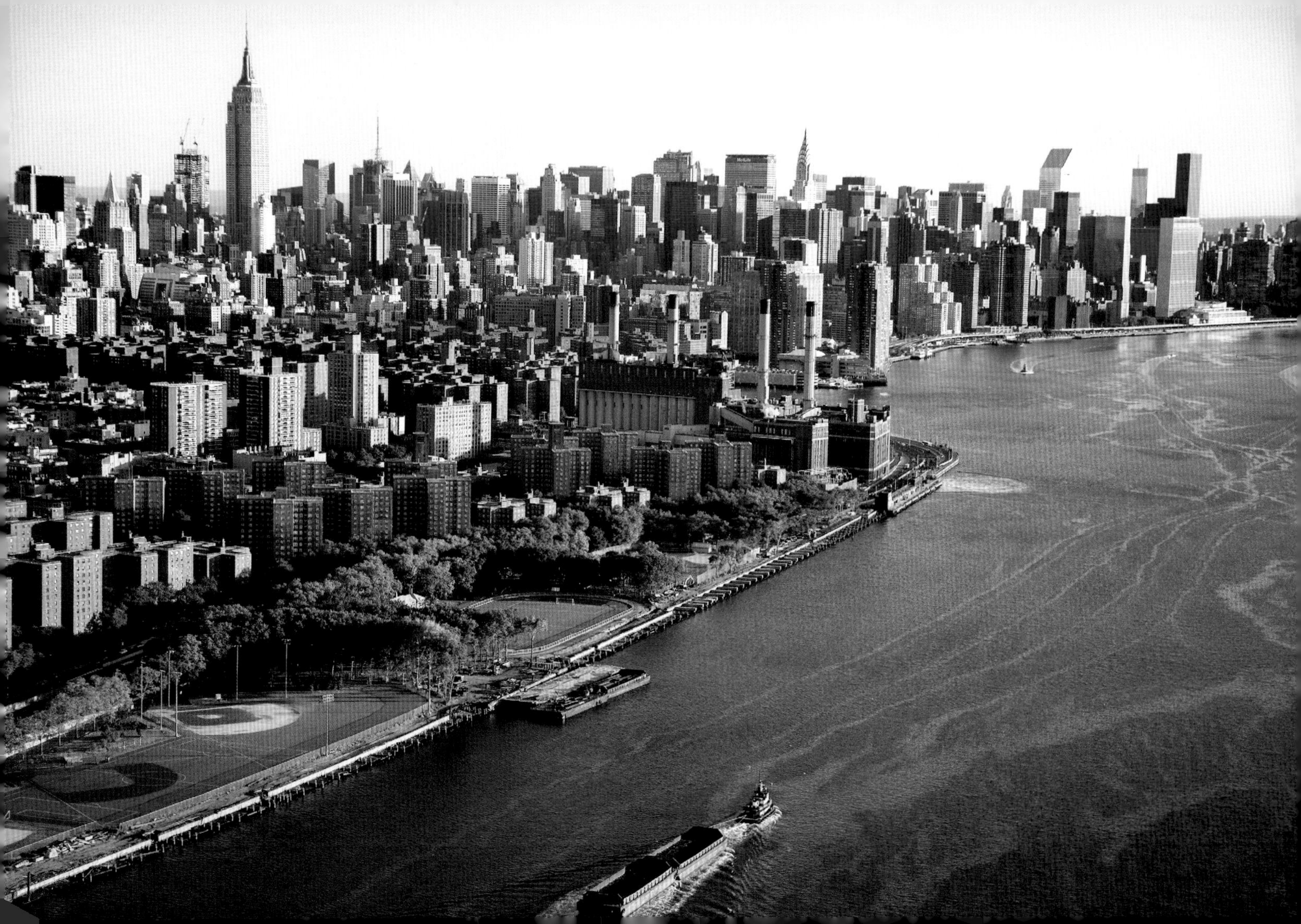

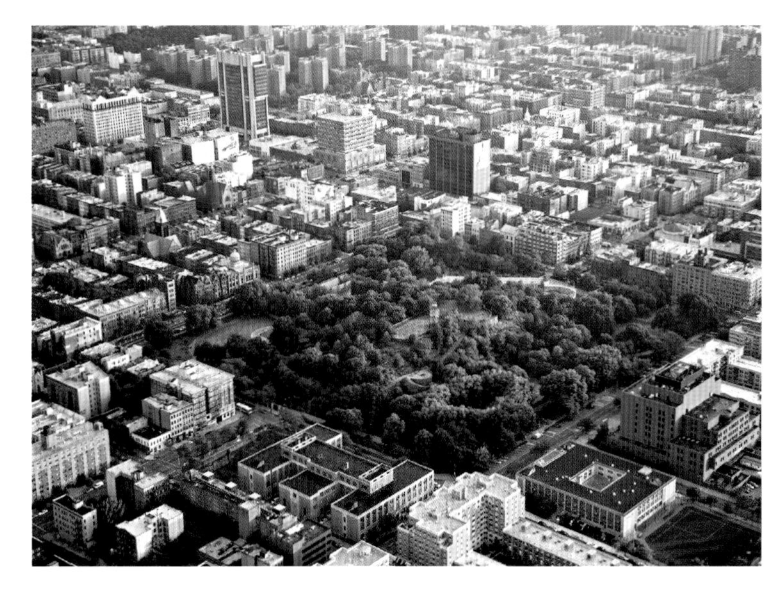

274

Northeast of Central Park is the Marcus Garvey Memorial Park in Harlem, named for a black nationalist leader prominent in the 1920s.

275

Features of the Marcus Garvey Park, in addition to its pool and playgrounds, include an amphitheater and a landmark cast-iron fire watch-tower, the only one of its kind in the United States.

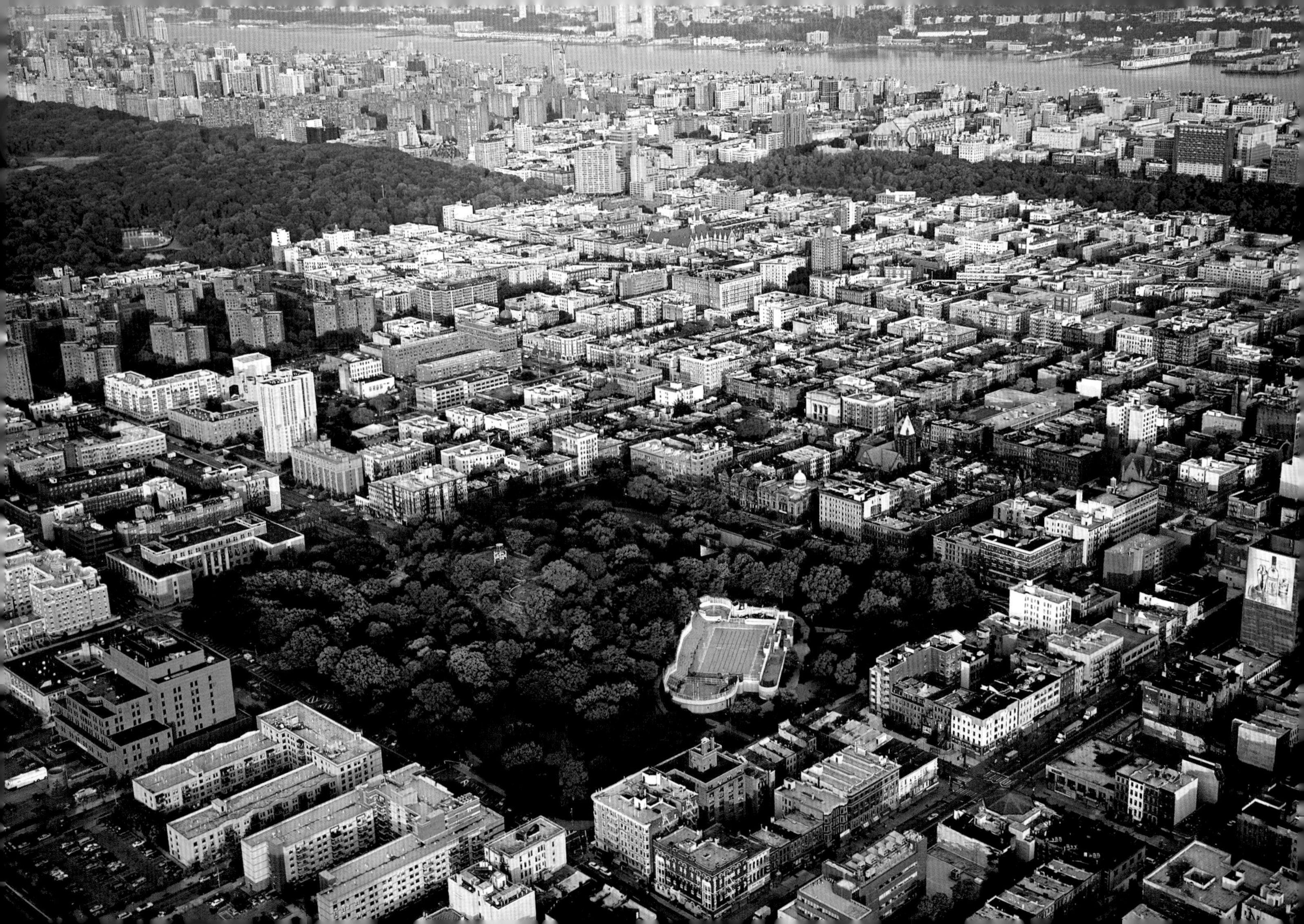

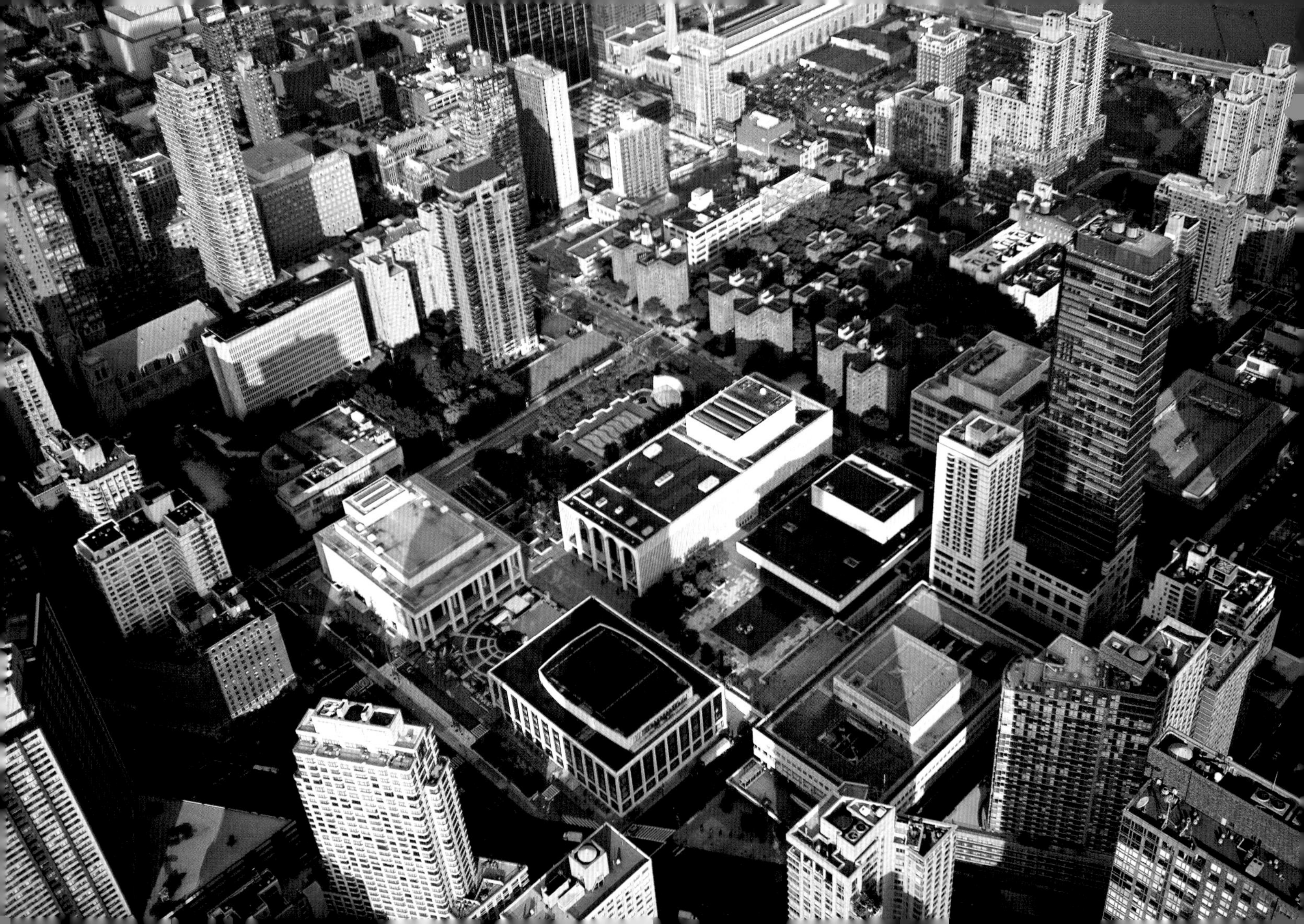

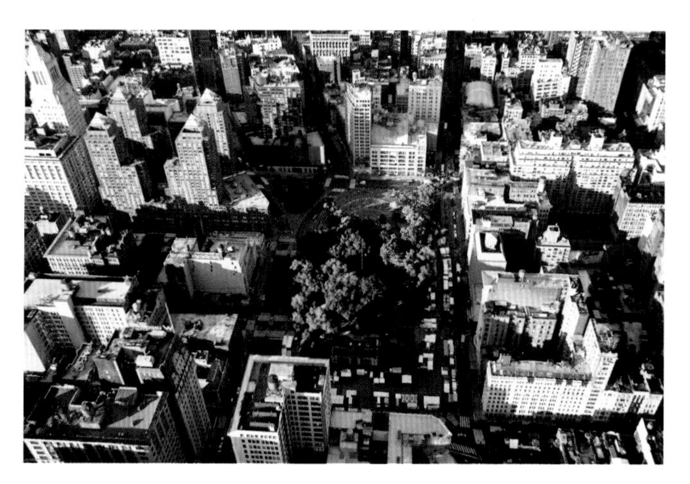

276
Lincoln Center for the Performing Arts, hosts many outdoor recreational events, including open-air dancing on the front plaza, circuses and concerts.

277
Washington Square Park has had a varied history, serving once as a Potter's Field, a parade ground and a public gallows, as well as a fashionable address.

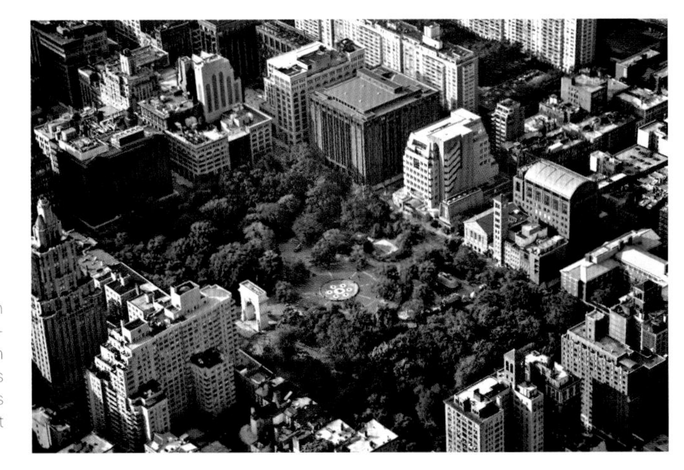

278 and 279

Since the beginning of the 19th century, Washington Square Park – among New York's best-known and most frequented parks – has been one of the city's cultural hubs and the meeting place for great artists and writers.

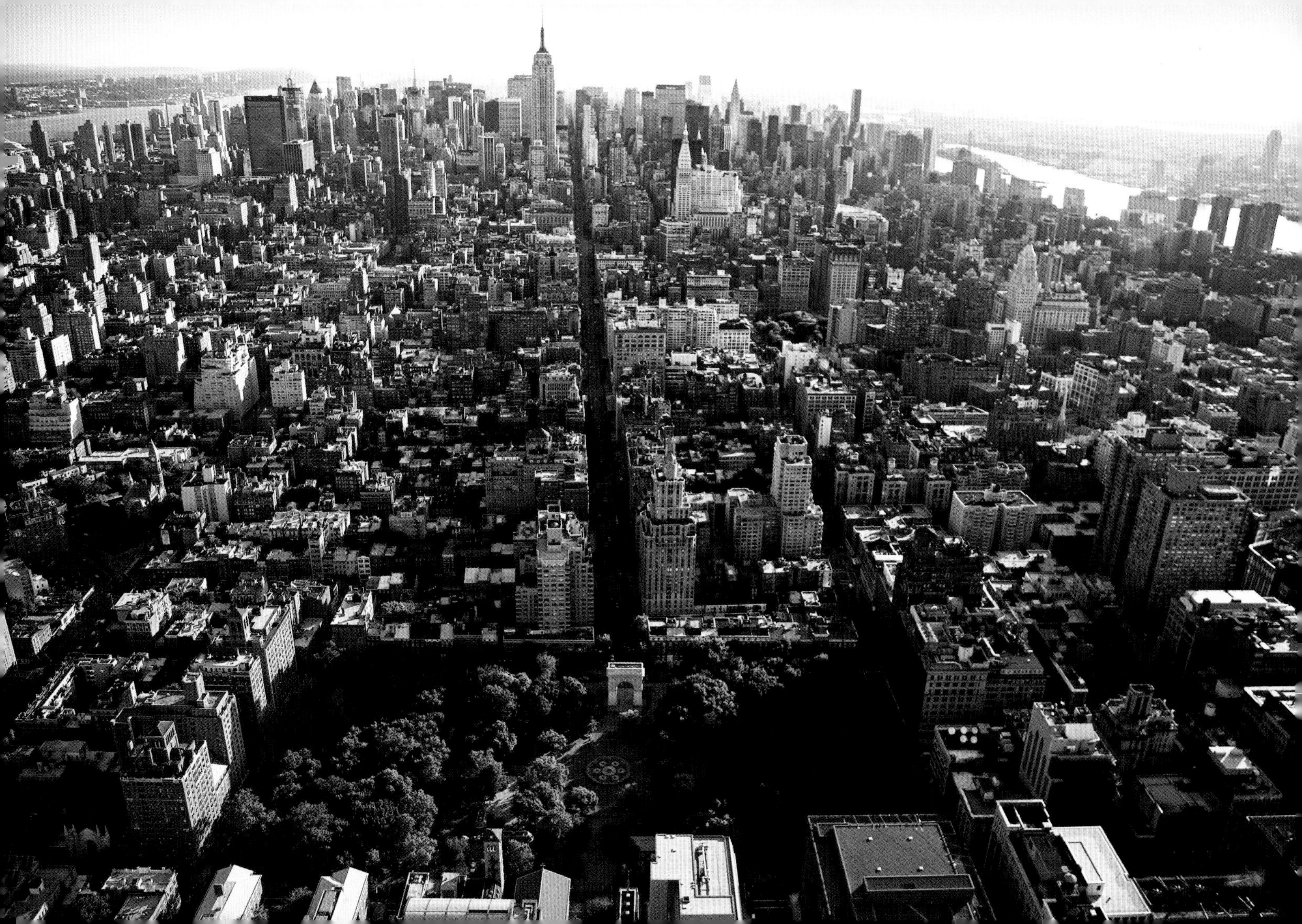

DOWNTOWN EAST
PAGODAS, PASTA AND PUNKS

FLYING HIGH

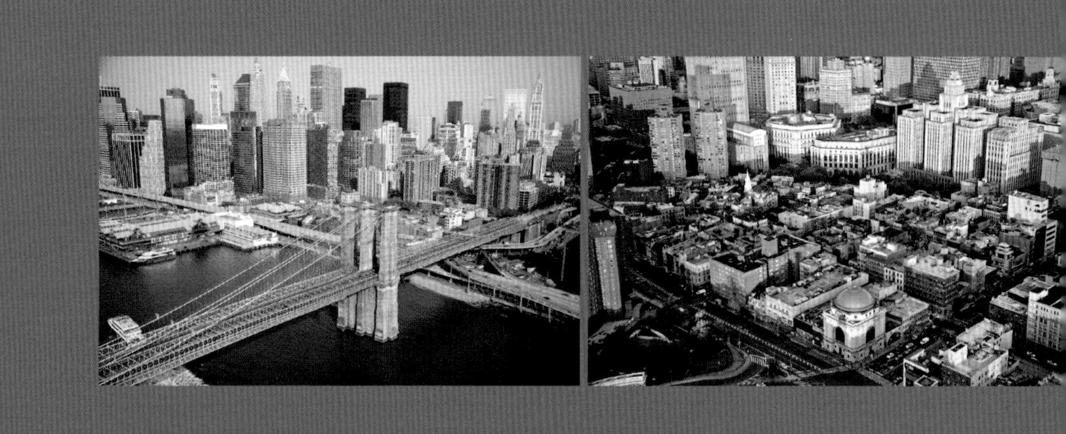

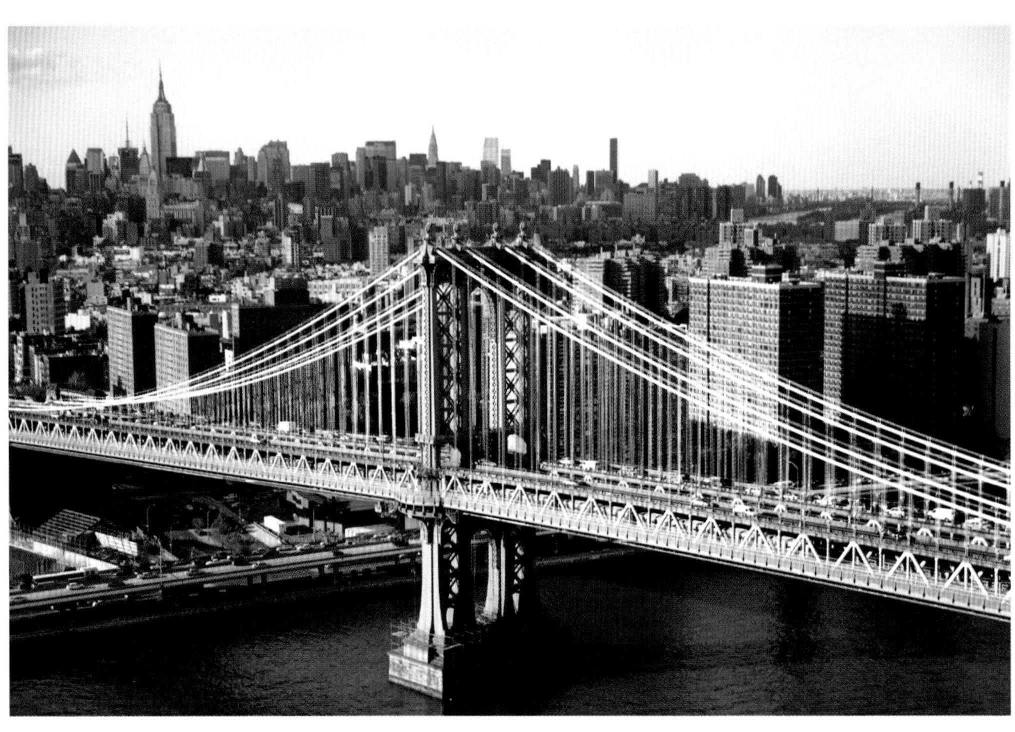

281
The Brooklyn Bridge (left) and the entrance to the Manhattan Bridge (right), a gateway into Chinatown and the Lower East Side.

Since New York grew from the bottom up, the neighborhoods below 14th Street are a maze of living history, despite a flurry of dazzling new construction projects underway there. This is especially apparent from the air. In fact, the only real way to see the buildings clustered tightly in Lower Manhattan, especially east of Broadway, is to fly above them – it's impossible to see their tops from street-level. The curving streets, tapering shoreline and densely packed buildings are far different from the orderly crosshatched grid of streets and avenues that stretches above 14th Street.

A hint of the city's earliest days comes from the street names of the area. Wall Street, named for the wall erected by the Dutch to provide fortifications for its early settlement; Pearl Street, a nod to New York's once abundant oyster beds; Stone Street, for the first paved thoroughfare in New York, built in the 1660s. Some streets, like Canal and Broad, are paved over versions of their earlier incarnations as waterways. Today, aside from street names and monuments to their memory, almost nothing remains from the days of the Dutch settlement.

Although the British presided over the next 120 years of growth in New York – until American colonists won their independence from the Crown in 1783 – they were generally tolerant of the Dutch and their ways, including their language and religion. But even before the English arrived, New Amsterdam had been a magnet for a multitude of ethnicities and cultures: French Huguenots, German Protestants, Jewish refugees from Europe and South America, Scottish and Irish, as well as African-Americans, who came both as settlers and slaves. Each different cultural and ethnic group made its mark on the city,

282
Completed in 1883, the Brooklyn Bridge opened downtown Manhattan to the growing city of Brooklyn across the East River.

Downtown East
Pagodas, Pasta and Punks

which became known for its pluralism, and its landmarks and architecture, especially downtown, exemplify this. By the mid-18th century, lower Manhattan was a densely populated complex of windy streets, drainage ditches used to dry out marshy areas, canals and piers. It was blessed with a supply of fresh water from Collect Pond, a small lake just north of Wall Street. By 1817, the pond had silted up due to pollution from nearby breweries, tanneries and slaughterhouses. In its place grew the notorious, crime-ridden slum called Five Points, depicted in Martin Scorsese's 2002 film, *Gangs of New York*. As an example of the layering-on of history in New York, it is now the current site of Foley Square, which sits in the midst of the city's municipal complex.

Today the eastern part of lower Manhattan is a jumble of architectural styles and periods, at once home to the 18th-century Fraunces Tavern and Federal Hall, where George Washington took his oath of office as president of the newly formed United States, as well as to the modern Liberty Tower and the post-modern horizontal strips of 60 Wall Street. The district from above is a hodgepodge of ornate decorative rooftops and sleek modern towers, all easily missed from below.

New York's fast-growing fortunes fueled a push skyward with architects vying to erect the tallest building in the world. The city's drive for the biggest and the best took shape in the nation's earliest skyscrapers, with the Neo-Gothic marvel, the Woolworth Building, grabbing center stage in 1913.

Downtown Manhattan is often equated with the world of finance, and Wall Street has grown to symbolize that world. The New York Stock Exchange had its beginnings on that street, where traders gathered under a sycamore tree in the shadow of the wall, which the Dutch had constructed for protection from unfriendly Native Americans and the British.

A little farther north, past the distinctive verdigris pyramidal top of 40 Wall Street and the Chase Manhattan Building straddling two city blocks, sits City Hall and its park, flanked by the ornate Gothic won-

Downtown East
Pagodas, Pasta and Punks

der, the Woolworth Building, the Municipal Building with its columns and cupola, and the curved front of the Javits Federal Building. Across the park, Park Row, where the earliest newspapers were published, leads to the entrance to the Brooklyn Bridge, one of five spans linking New York with Long Island.

The Brooklyn Bridge, built in 1883, was the first bridge to connect Lower Manhattan to the city of Brooklyn, replacing a fleet of ferry boats that carried 50 million people a year back and forth across the East River. Followed 20 years later by the Williamsburg Bridge, and in 1909, by the Manhattan Bridge, the spans helped to satisfy the demands of a growing city, bursting at the seams.

Piers once dotted the shore, which over the years has been extended with landfill. Water Street was originally the easternmost thoroughfare in lower Manhattan; now it is well inland. On what is today the eastern shore of lower Manhattan lies South Street Seaport, a living museum of New York's maritime roots, complete with restored sailing vessels anchored at its piers. With almost every square inch of space filled within the original borders of the city, the affluent and the ambitious, seeking cleaner air and more space, pushed farther north into the lands where the Dutch had established large farms, or bouweries. The estate of Peter Stuyvesant, New Amsterdam's last Director-General, was situated at the end of the street now known as Bowery.

Beyond the entrance to the Brooklyn Bridge and north of New York's municipal complex lie neighborhoods that became home to the millions of immigrants who poured into New York. Chinatown grew as Chinese workers who had worked on the railroads out west headed east to look for work and soon became an enclave for Asian immigrants from around the world. At the eastern end of Canal Street, once an actual canal cutting across the island, sits Confucius Square, next to the grand colonnaded entrance to the Manhattan Bridge. To the north of Chinatown, lies Little Italy, which like its neighbor, was settled by immigrants, in this case, Italian. Like the Chinese, the Ital-

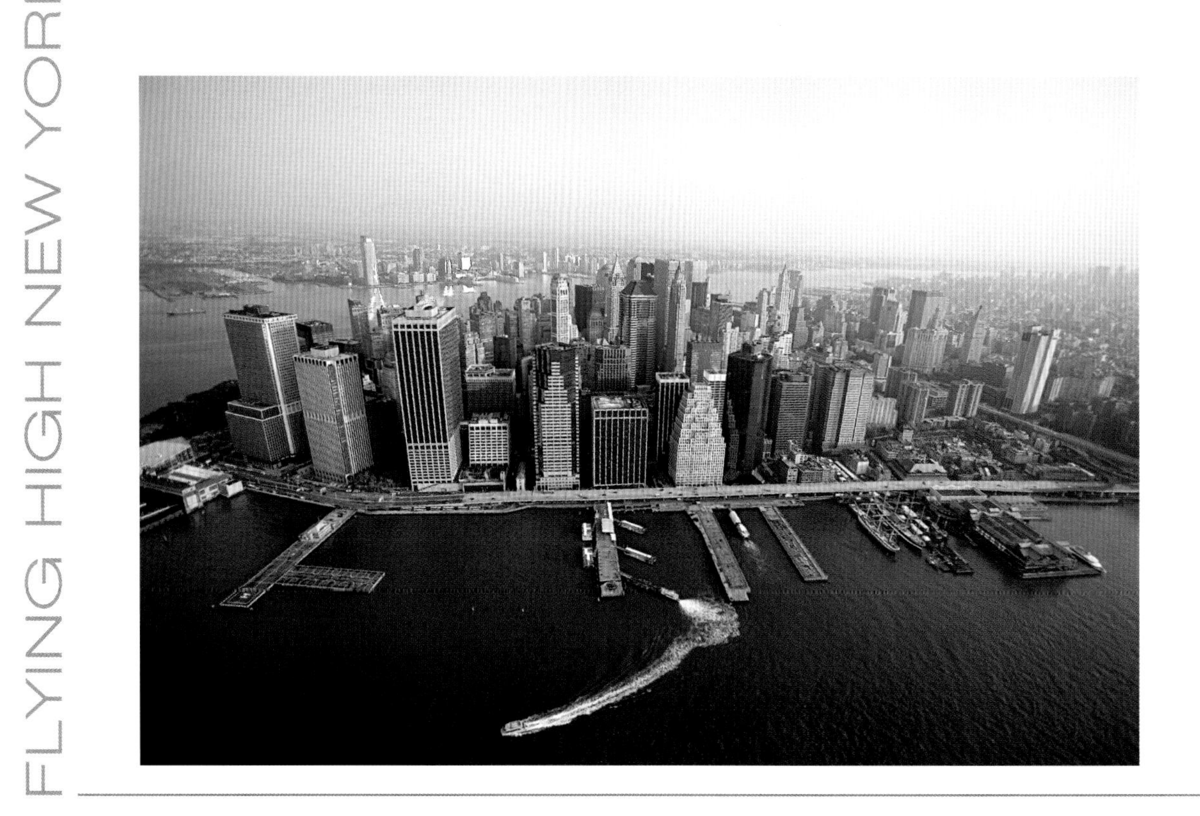

South Street Seaport, on the East River, recreates the days when downtown New York was a bustling shipping center.

ians established their own businesses, restaurants, markets and even festivals. North of Canal Street is a neighborhood dubbed the Lower East Side, a densely packed community that has been in continual flux since its establishment. Once a bastion of immigrants of every nationality and ethnicity, the area gained a reputation in the late 19th and early 20th centuries as a boisterous neighborhood filled with overcrowded tenements and often dire living conditions, but with a vibrant mix of cultures and influences. Though many immigrant groups settled in the Lower East Side, it is often thought of as the cradle of the Jewish experience in America. More than half a million eastern European Jews, fleeing oppression and pogroms, found their way to this four-mile section of New York in the late 19th and early 20th centuries, establishing schools, synagogues and newspapers.

The energy and zest for commerce that every new group has brought to New York for all of its 300+ history continues today. Though shaken by terror and loss after the collapse of the World Trade Towers in the attacks of September 11, 2001, downtown Manhattan has rebounded with a sense of optimism and commerce, with $10-billion in construction projects underway. A renewed desire to celebrate history by preserving the landmarks of earlier eras, with renovation projects and museums, is palpable in lower Manhattan. From the Smithsonian's National Museum of the American Indian in the former Customs House Building to the Skyscraper Museum, the move is on to celebrate the old as well as the new.

Commercial development is also expanding throughout lower Manhattan. Since 9/11 tk buildings have been built or are on the drawing board. Another sign of the neighborhood's revitalization is the increase in residential construction. The canyons of downtown, once deserted after the close of business every day, are being transformed with the restoration of former commercial buildings into residential condominiums and hotels. But always, along with downtown's relish for expansion and growth, a profound sense of history and tradition remain.

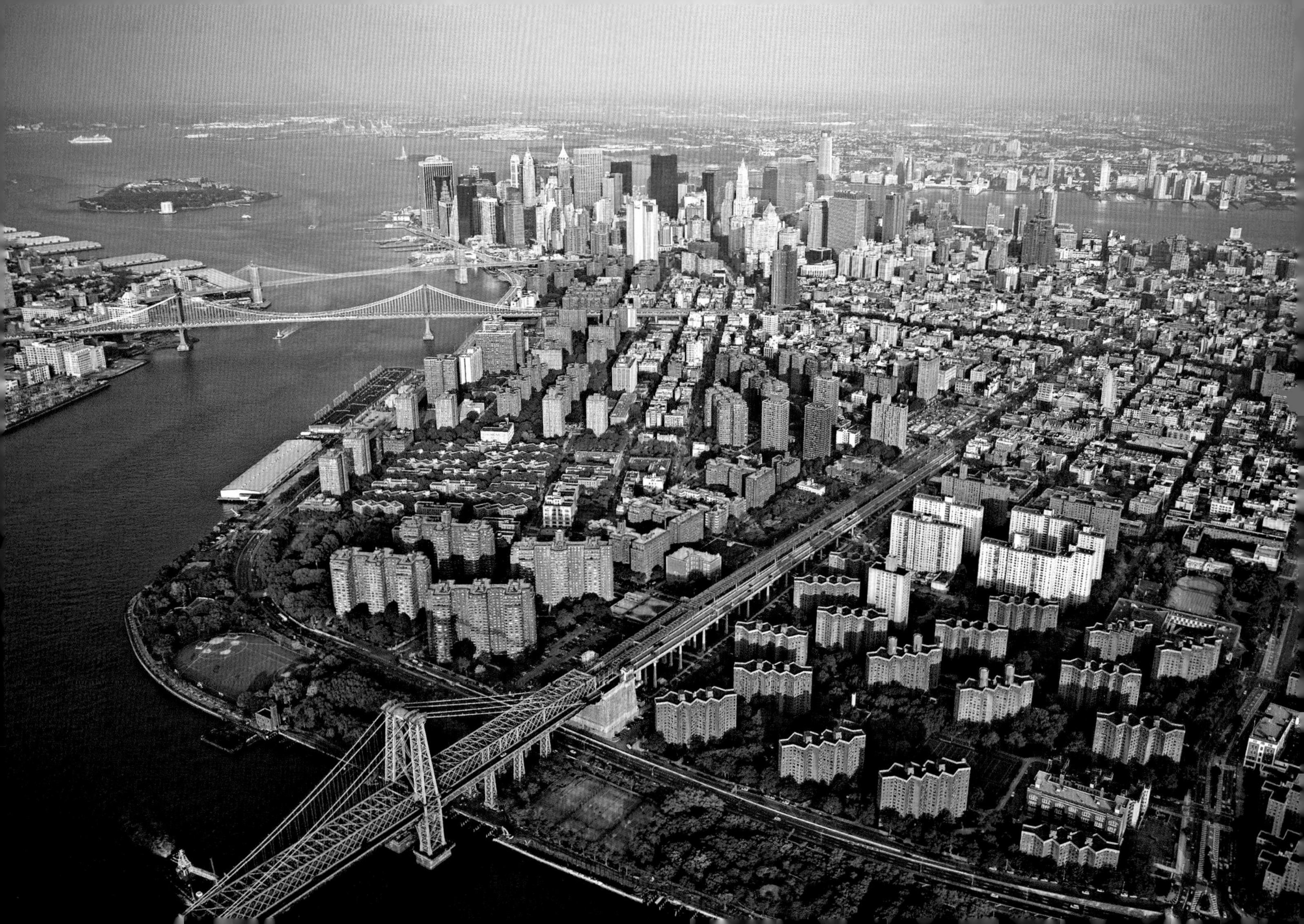

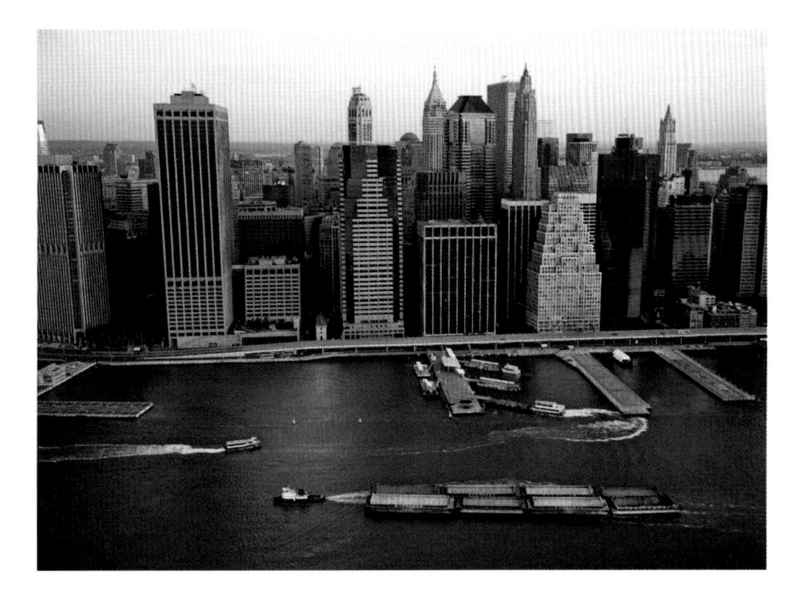

288

The Williamsburg Bridge entrance cuts through the Baruch Houses, Manhattan's largest housing project, and follows Delancey Street, the unofficial northern border of Chinatown.

289

The East River, where shipping thrived from the 18th to the 20th centuries, is now the eastern border of the financial district. The "wedding cake" style 120 Wall Street was the earliest high-rise (1931) to be built on the river.

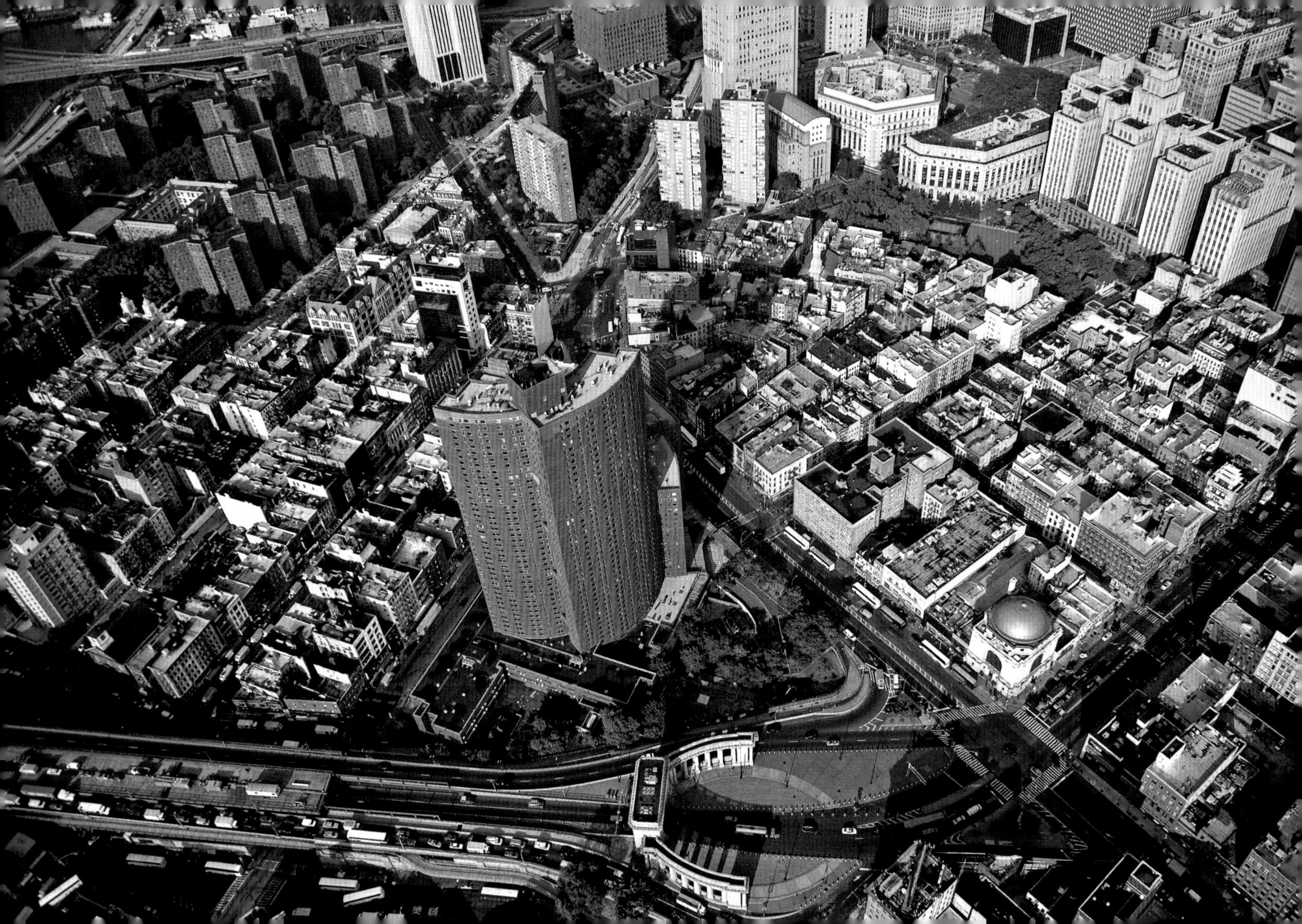

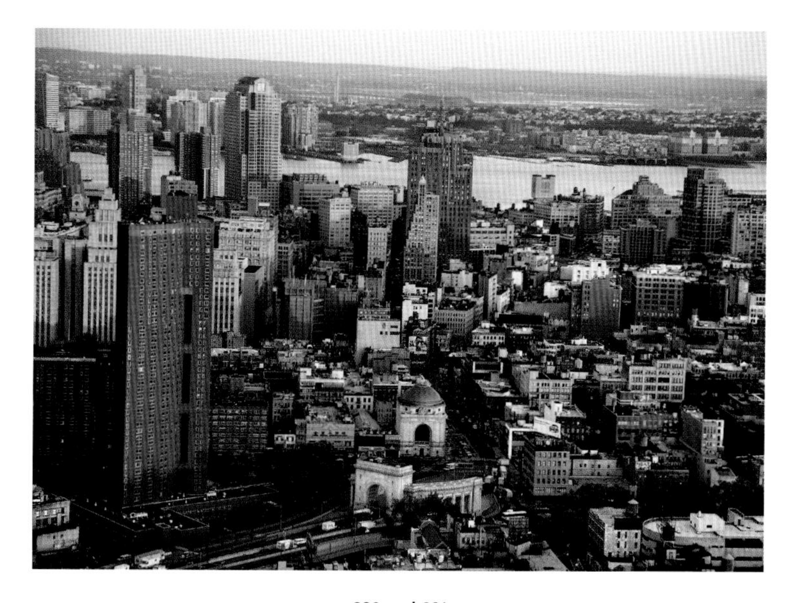

290 and 291

The 44-story Confucius Plaza, a subsidized housing cooperative in Chinatown, rises above the colonnade leading to the Manhattan Bridge, at Canal Street and Park Row.

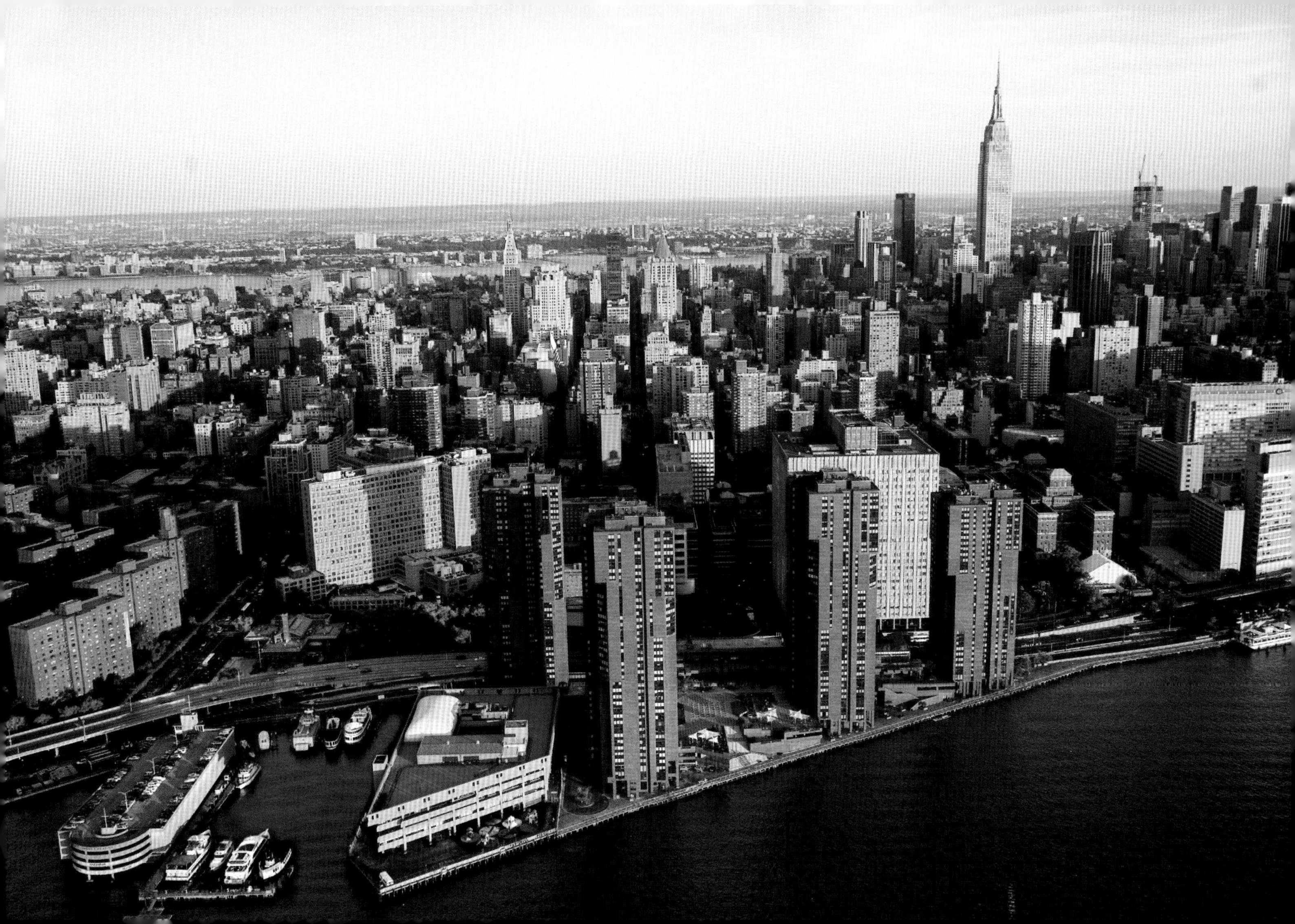

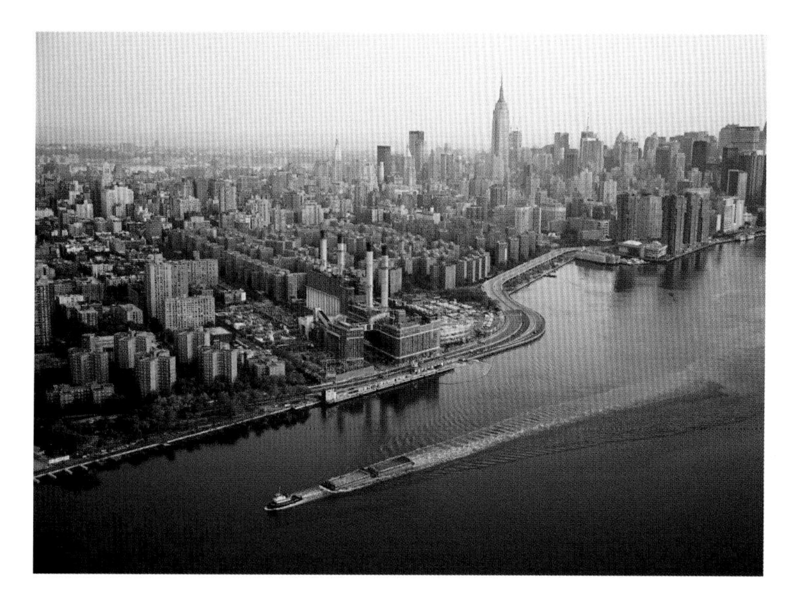

292
The four red-brick apartment towers of Waterside Plaza are built on a platform over the East River. On the southern tip is the United Nations International School.

293
Peter Stuyvesant, New Amsterdam's first governor, built his estate along this stretch of the East River; today, Stuyvesant Town apartments and Stuyvesant Cove Park occupy the land.

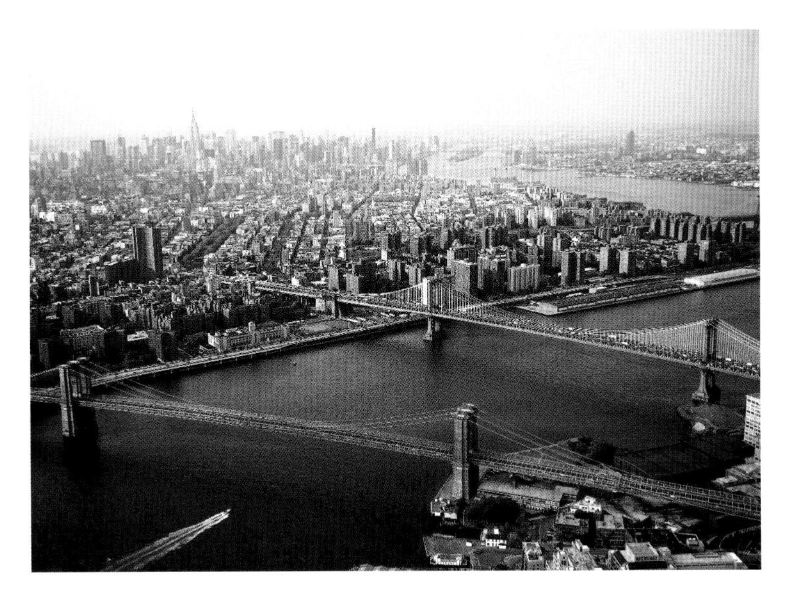

294

The Manhattan Bridge and the Brooklyn Bridge carry not only cars, but also pedestrians and bicyclists; subways run across the Manhattan Bridge, as well.

295

Built a quarter-century apart, the designs of the Brooklyn and the Manhattan Bridges are radically different.

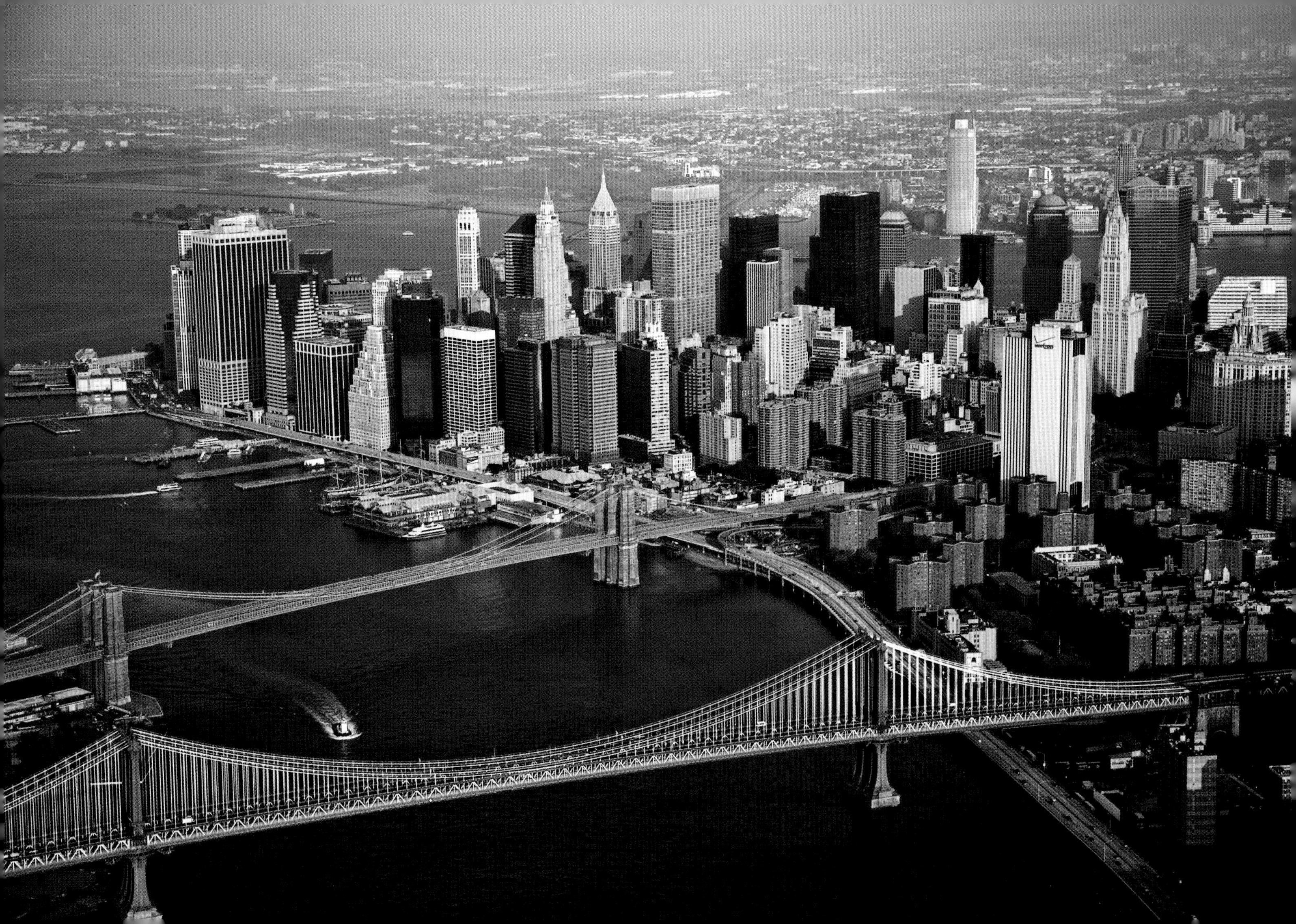

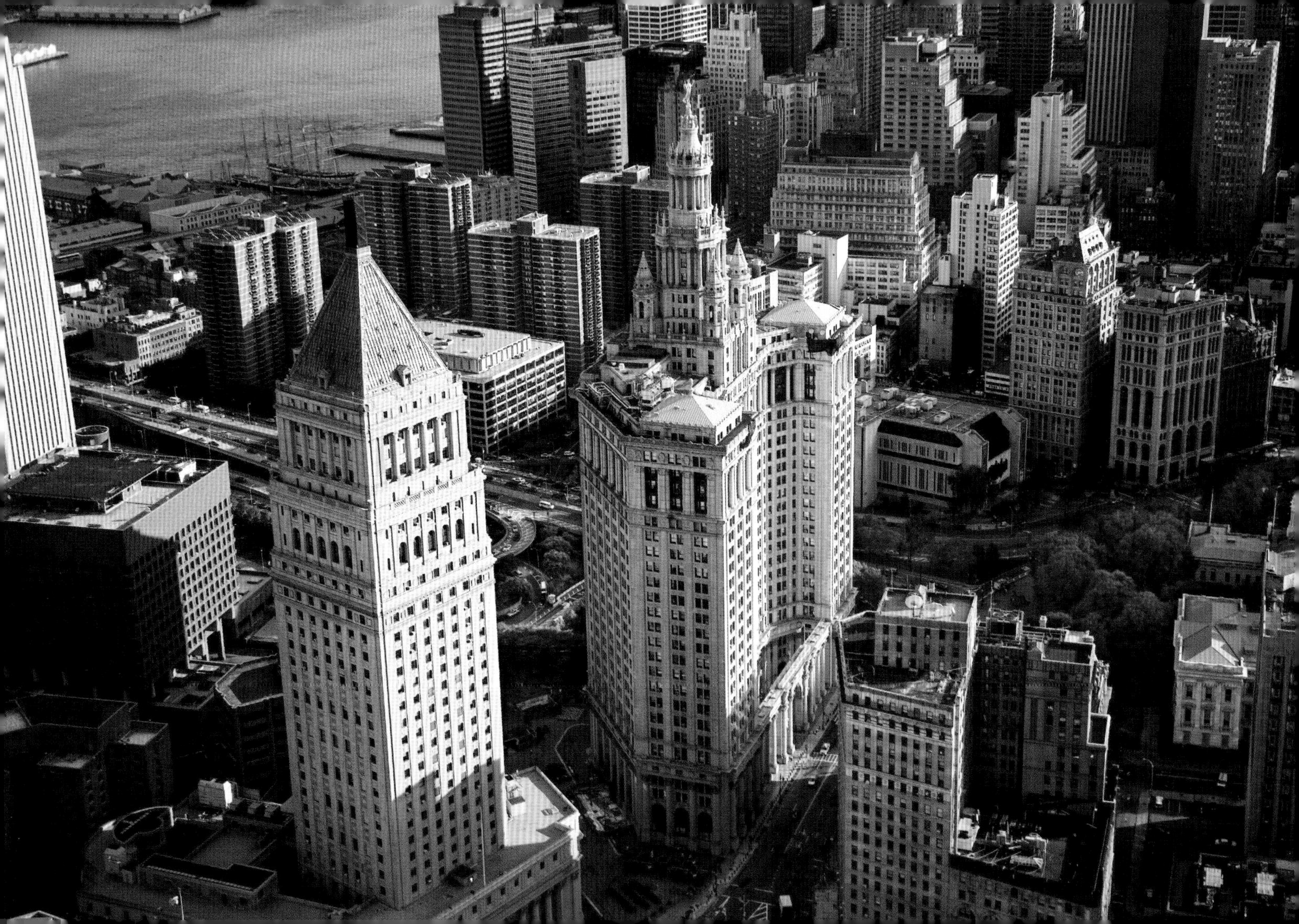

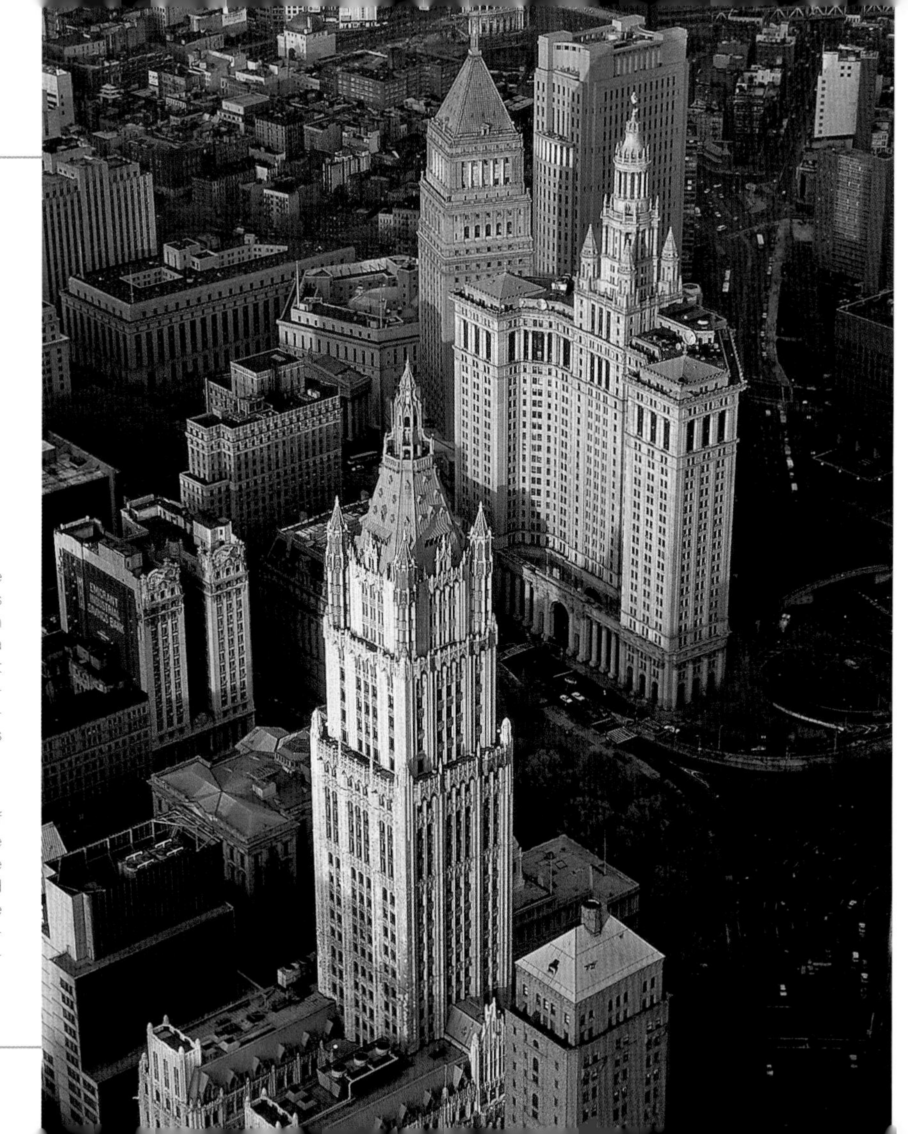

296

The US Courthouse (left) was the last of noted designer Cass Gilbert's New York buildings, with a temple-like base topped by a 24-story tower with gilded roof. It complements the Municipal Building, with four turrets on top symbolizing the four other boroughs linked to Manhattan.

297

Situated at the intersection of Chambers and Centre Streets, the Municipal Building is one of the largest civic buildings in the world and is characterized by a large Corinthian colonnade along the entrance, inspired by Bernini's colonnade in St. Peter's Square.

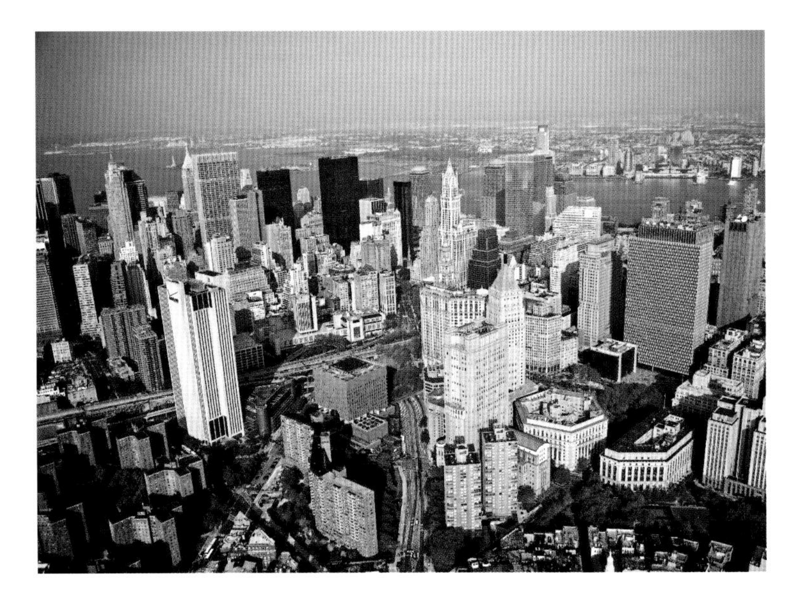

298

The area around City Hall, equidistant to the Hudson and the East Rivers, is America's second largest administrative complex (next to Washington DC) of courts, offices and jails. Park Row, to the south of City Hall, was once known as "Newspaper Row" for the many newspapers based there.

299

The hexagonal New York County Courthouse was modeled after a Corinthian temple, with a circular center linked to each of the six wings by hallways.

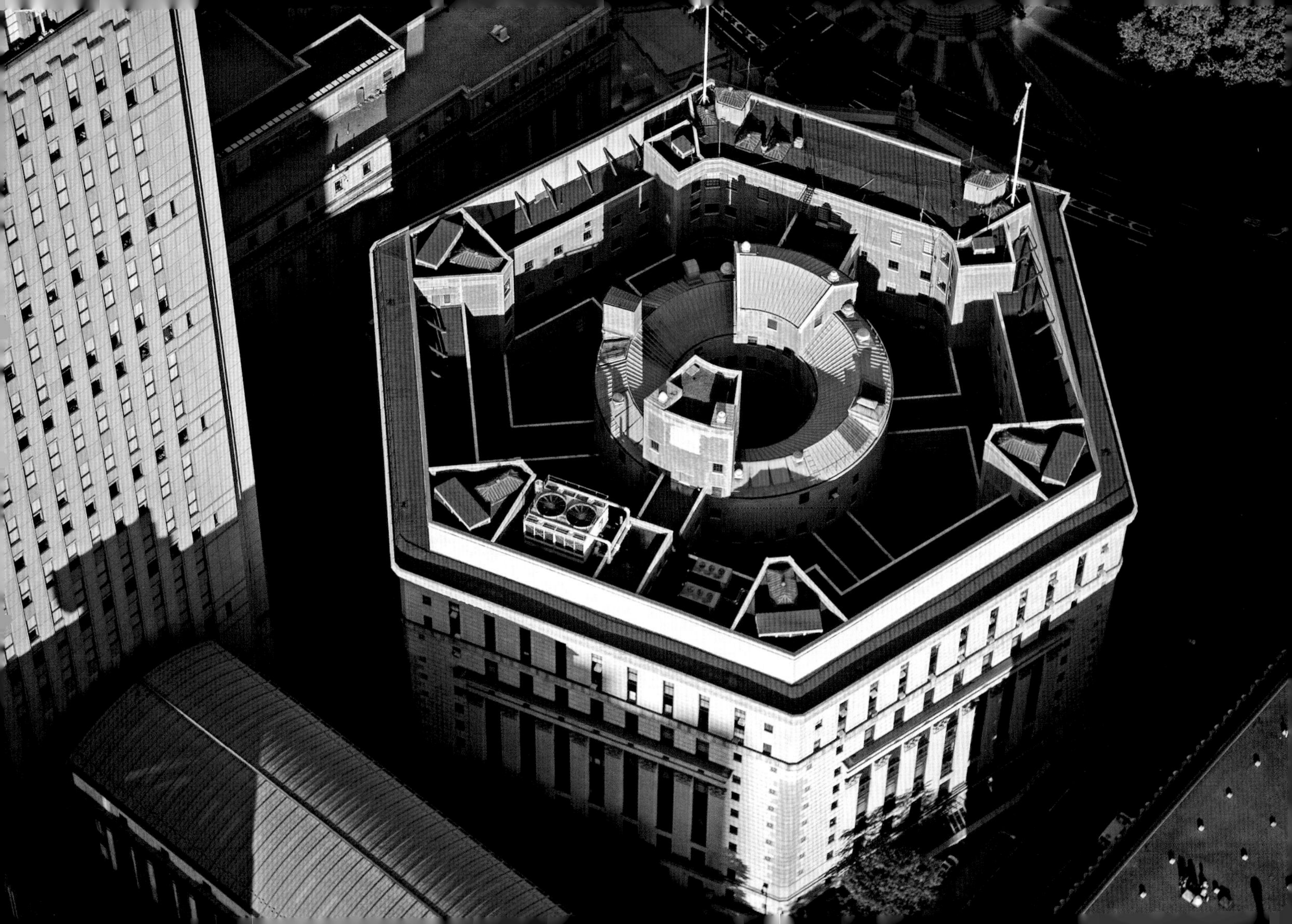

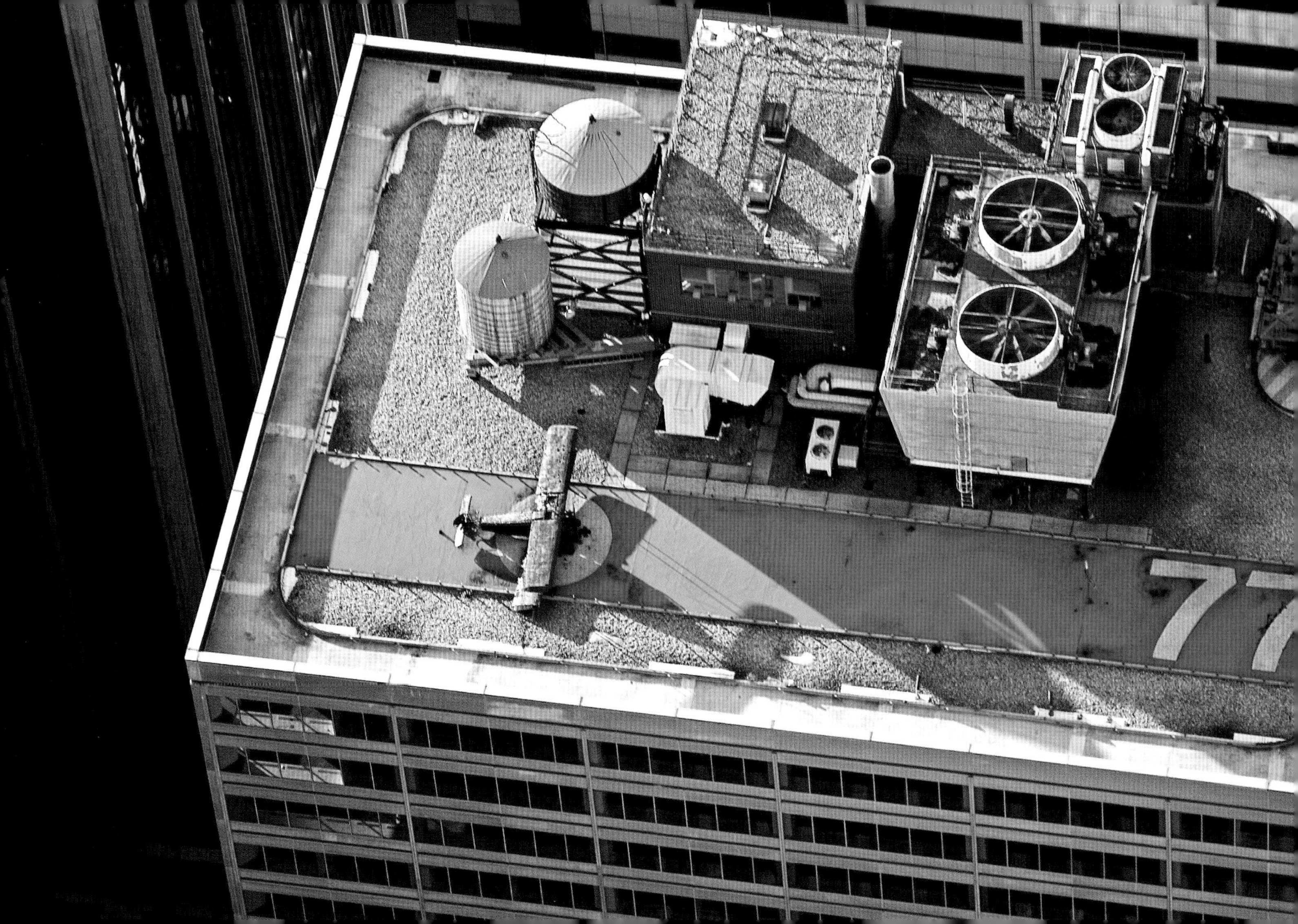
77

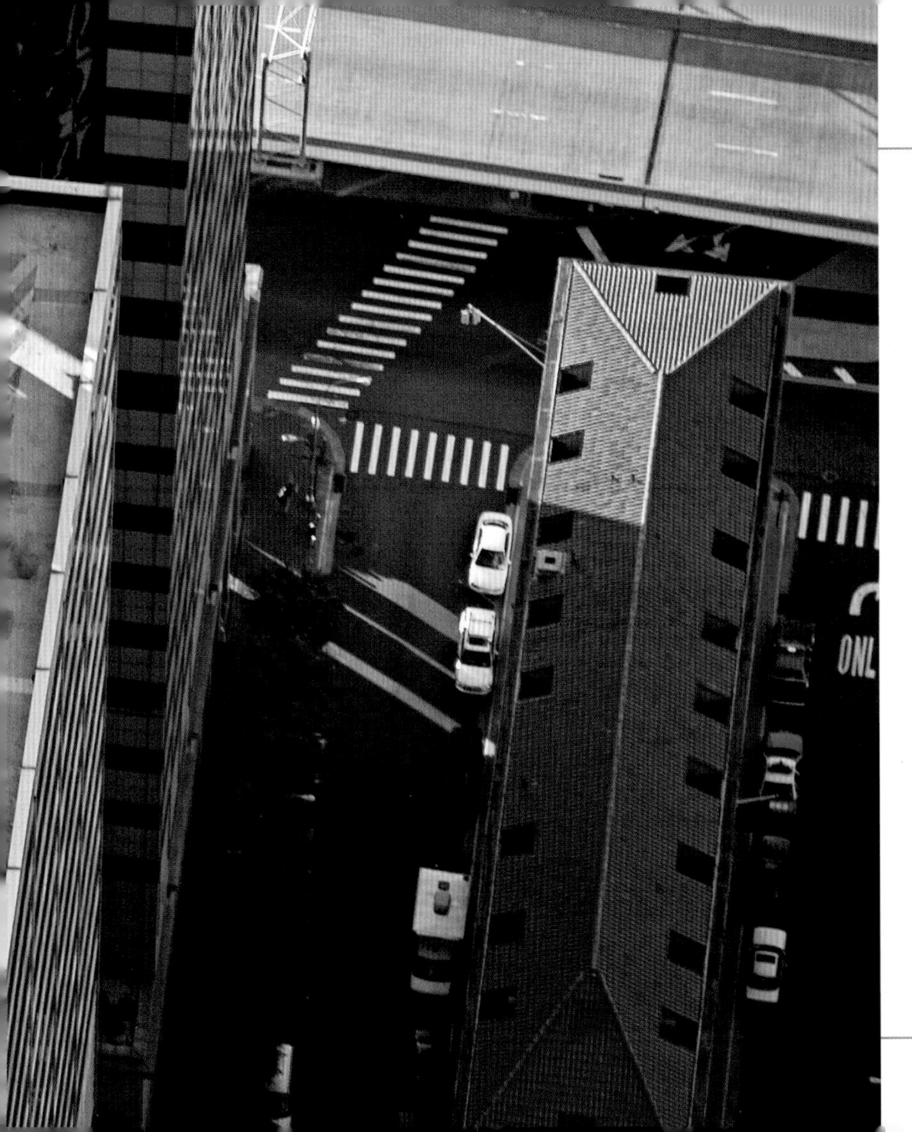

300-301
A replica of a World War 1 Sopwith Camel biplane is poised for a flight of fancy atop 77 Water Street, in the insurance district of lower Manhattan. The sculpture is said to have been placed there for the amusement of workers in neighboring skyscrapers.

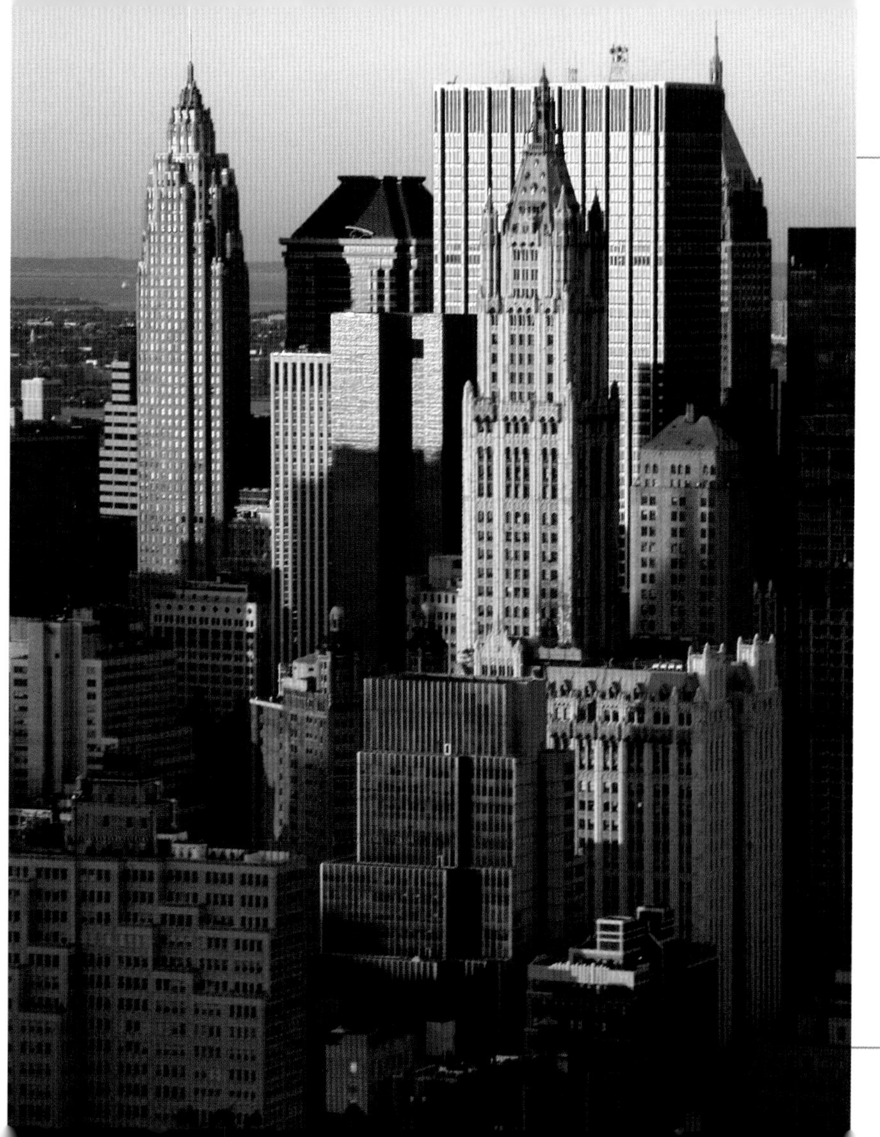

302
The Gothic wonder of the white terracotta-clad Woolworth Building (right) appears pink in the sunlight and is a more ornate cousin of the pyramidal top of 70 Pine Street.

303
The New York rooftops are often home to hanging gardens or, as in this case, children's playgrounds.

304-305
Buildings along the East River in Lower Manhattan were built on land that used to be water, using fill from construction sites.

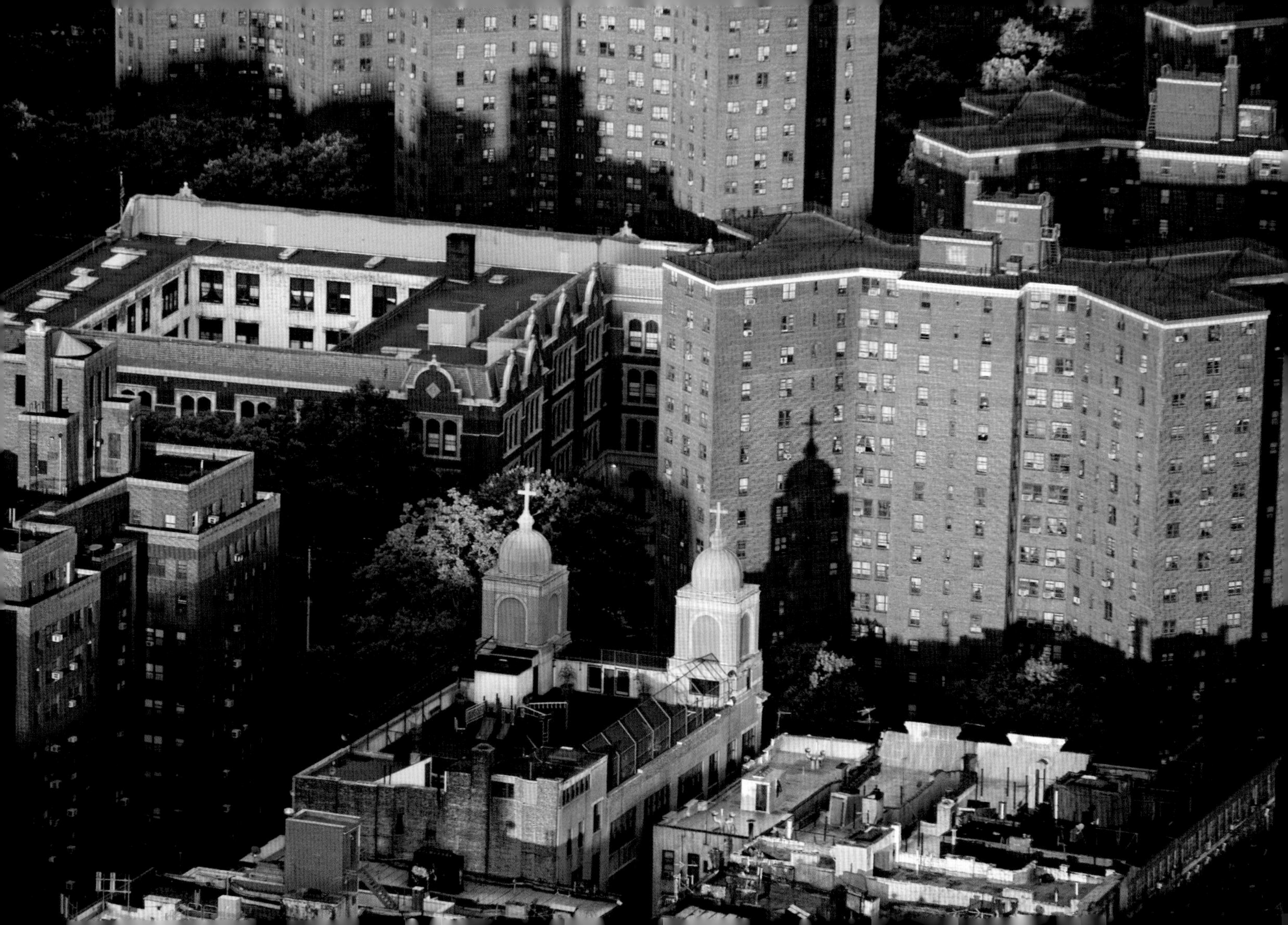

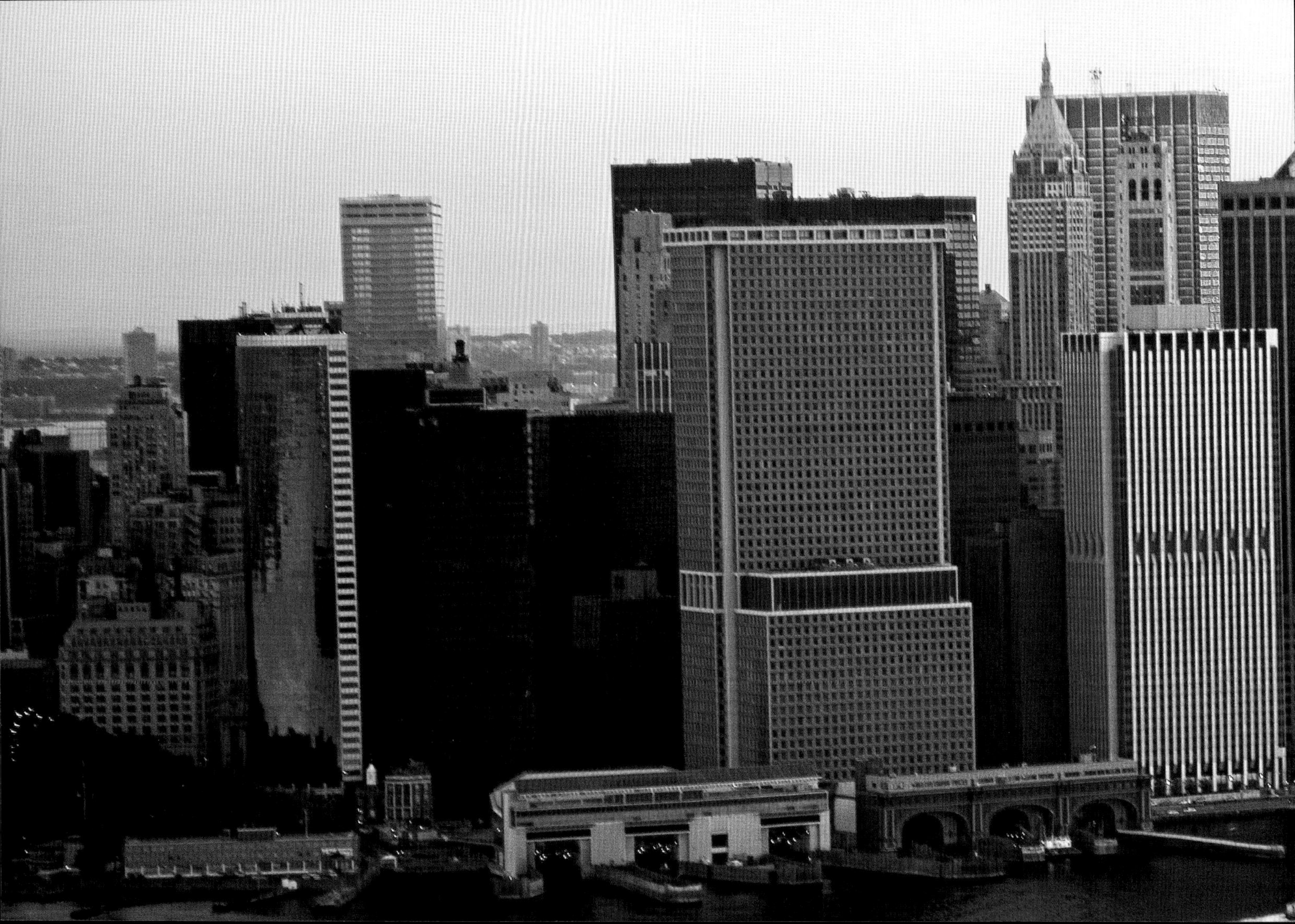

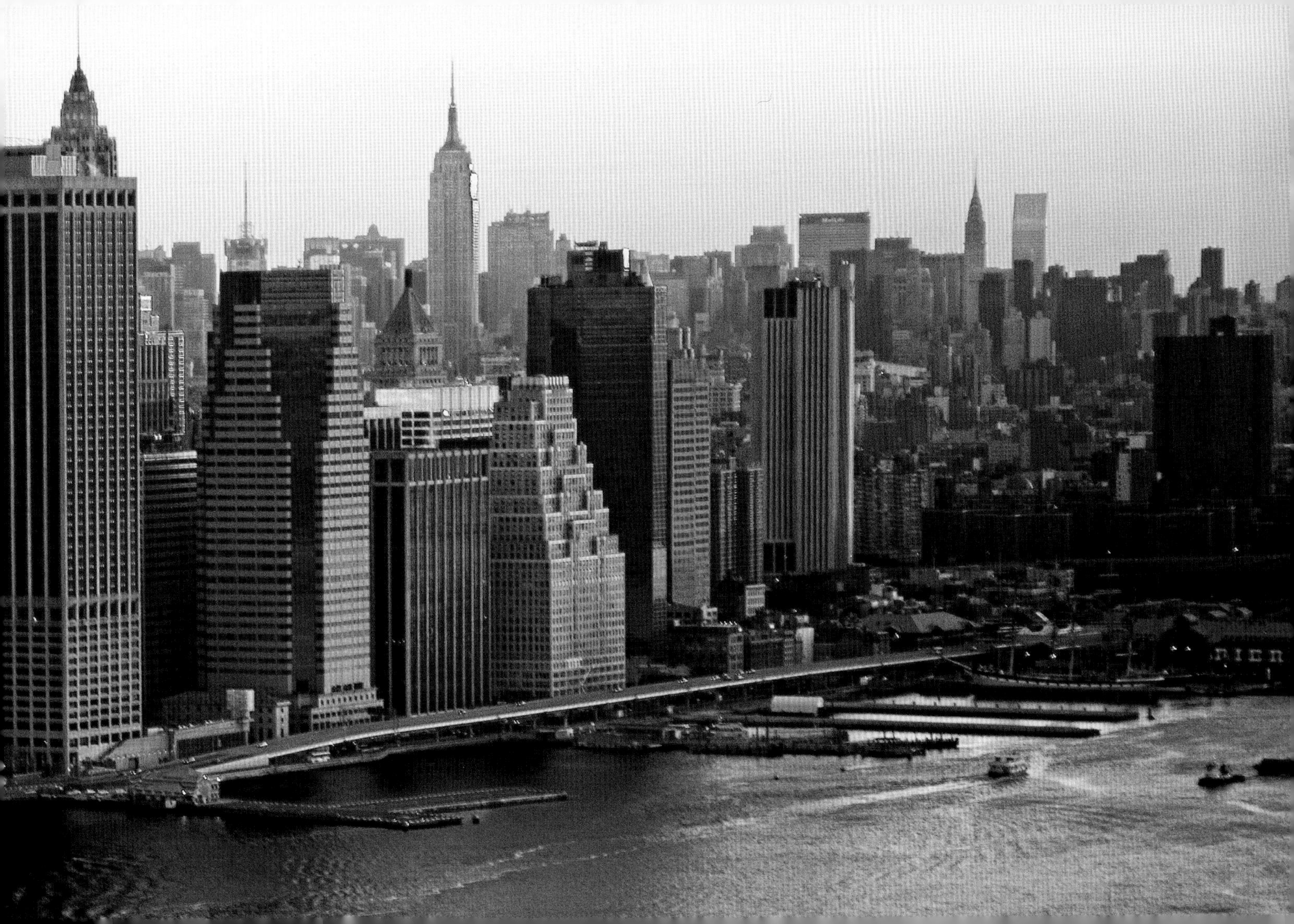

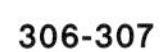

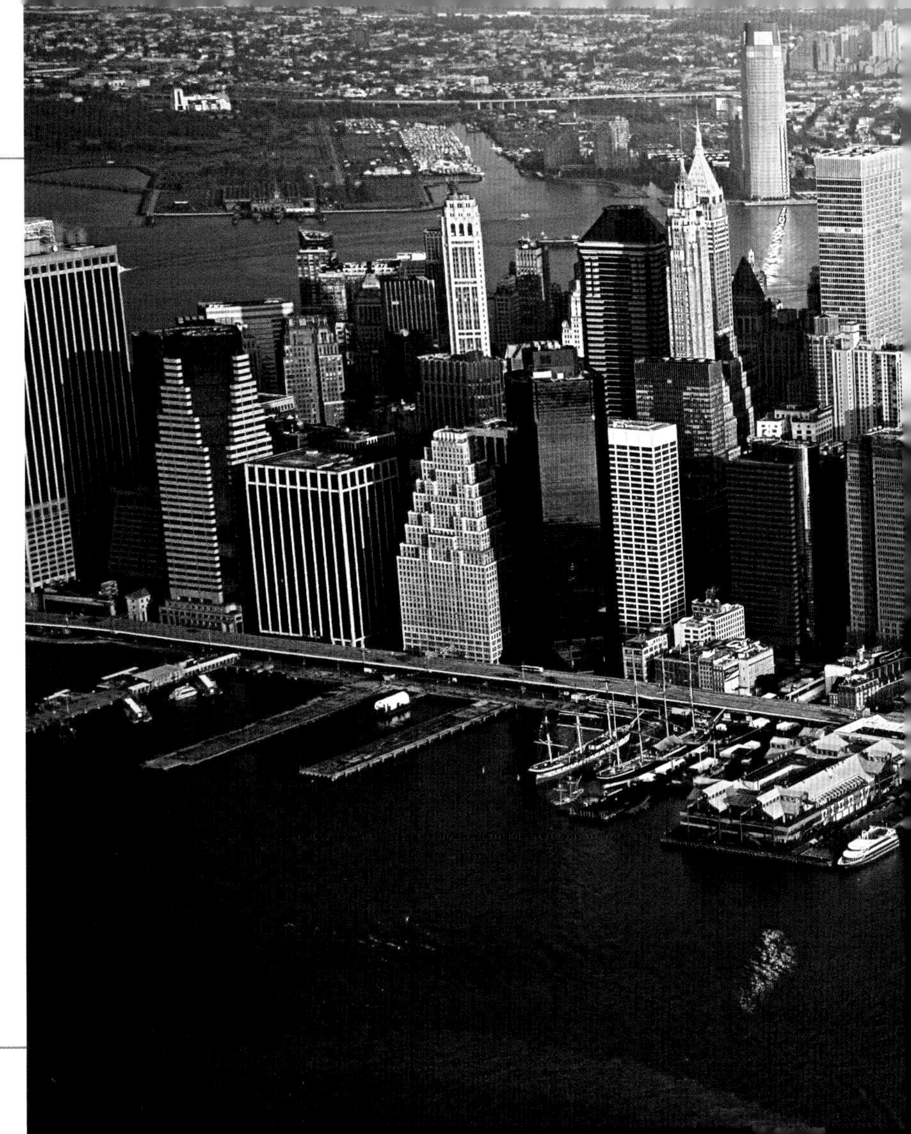

306-307
The Brooklyn Bridge leads from Brooklyn to lower Manhattan, where some of New York's oldest structures can be found alongside some of its newest.

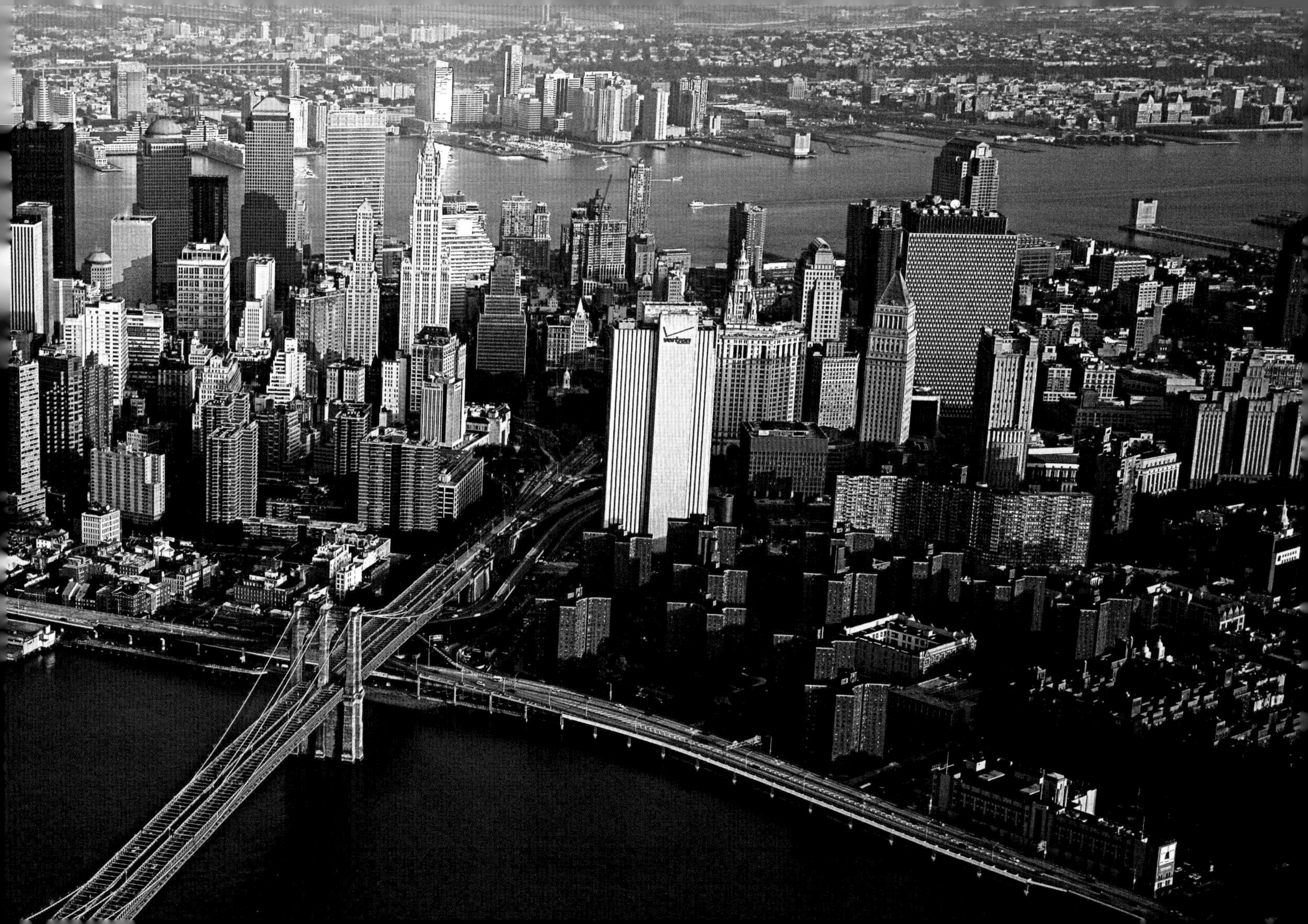

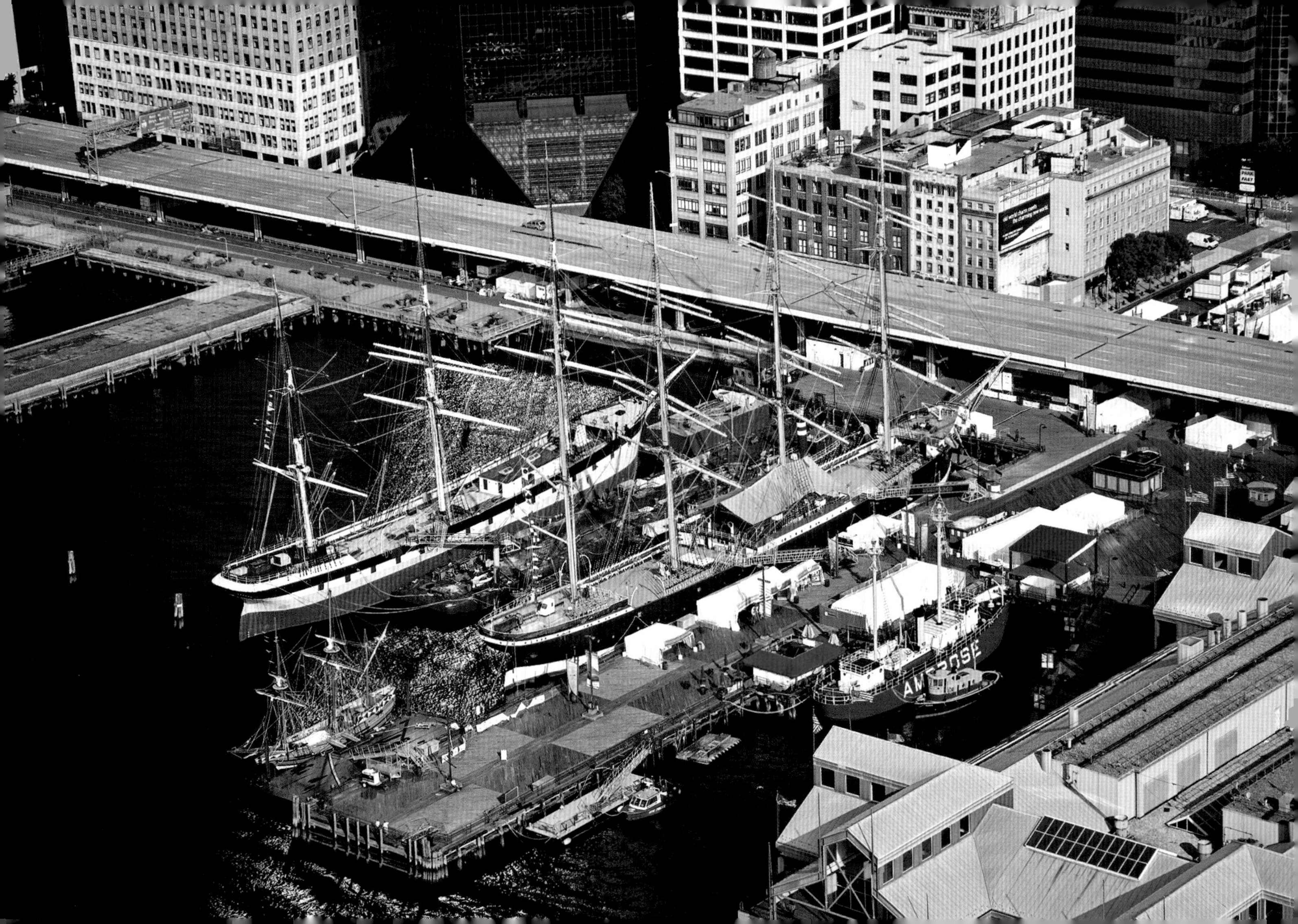

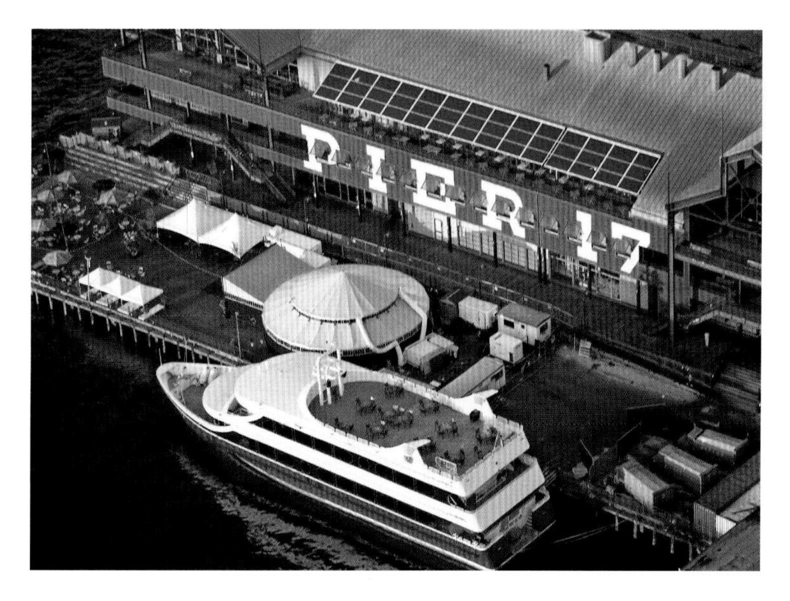

308

The fleet at the South Street Seaport Museum includes three historic ships that are open to the public: the *Peking*, the *Wavetree* and the *Ambrose*. Other vessels offer training and trips of the harbor.

309

Pier 17 is at the heart of New York's 19th-century seaport, and now holds three floors of shops and restaurants, as wells as breathtaking views of the Brooklyn Bridge and East River.

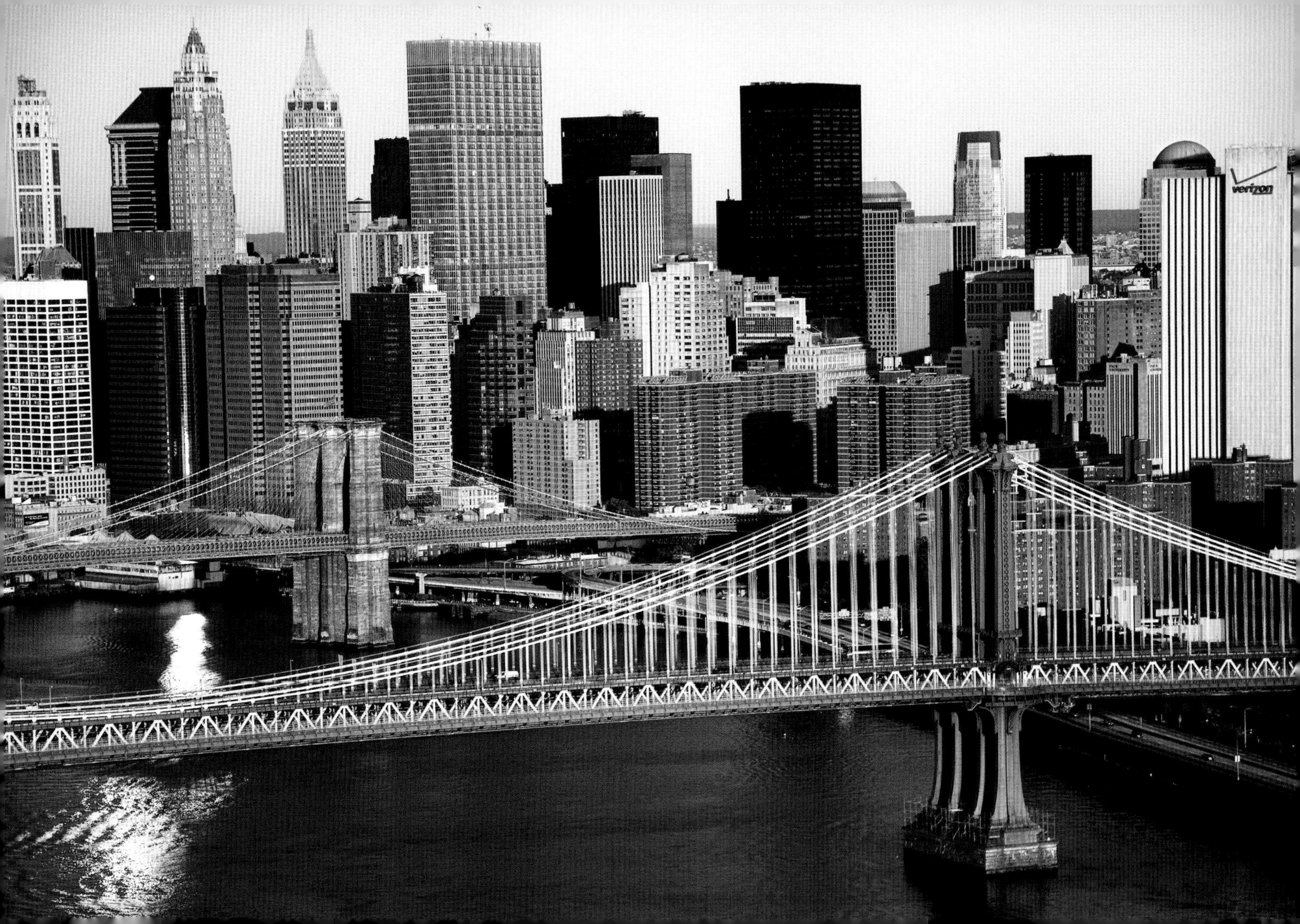
verizon

310

The Manhattan Bridge has a two-dimensional profile to its towers, as compared to the rigid, three-dimensional towers on the Brooklyn Bridge.

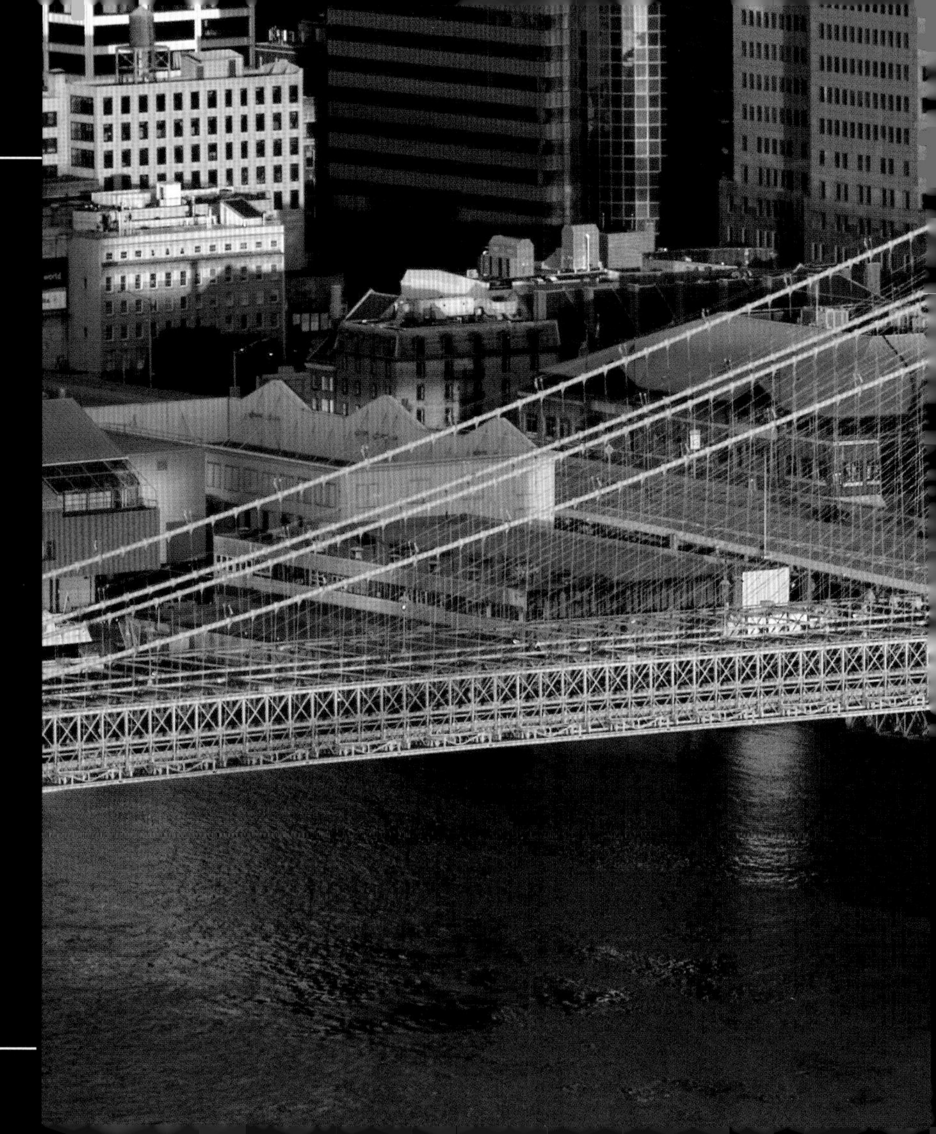

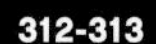

312-313

The solidity of the Brooklyn Bridge's towers makes its suspension cables seem almost delicate by comparison.

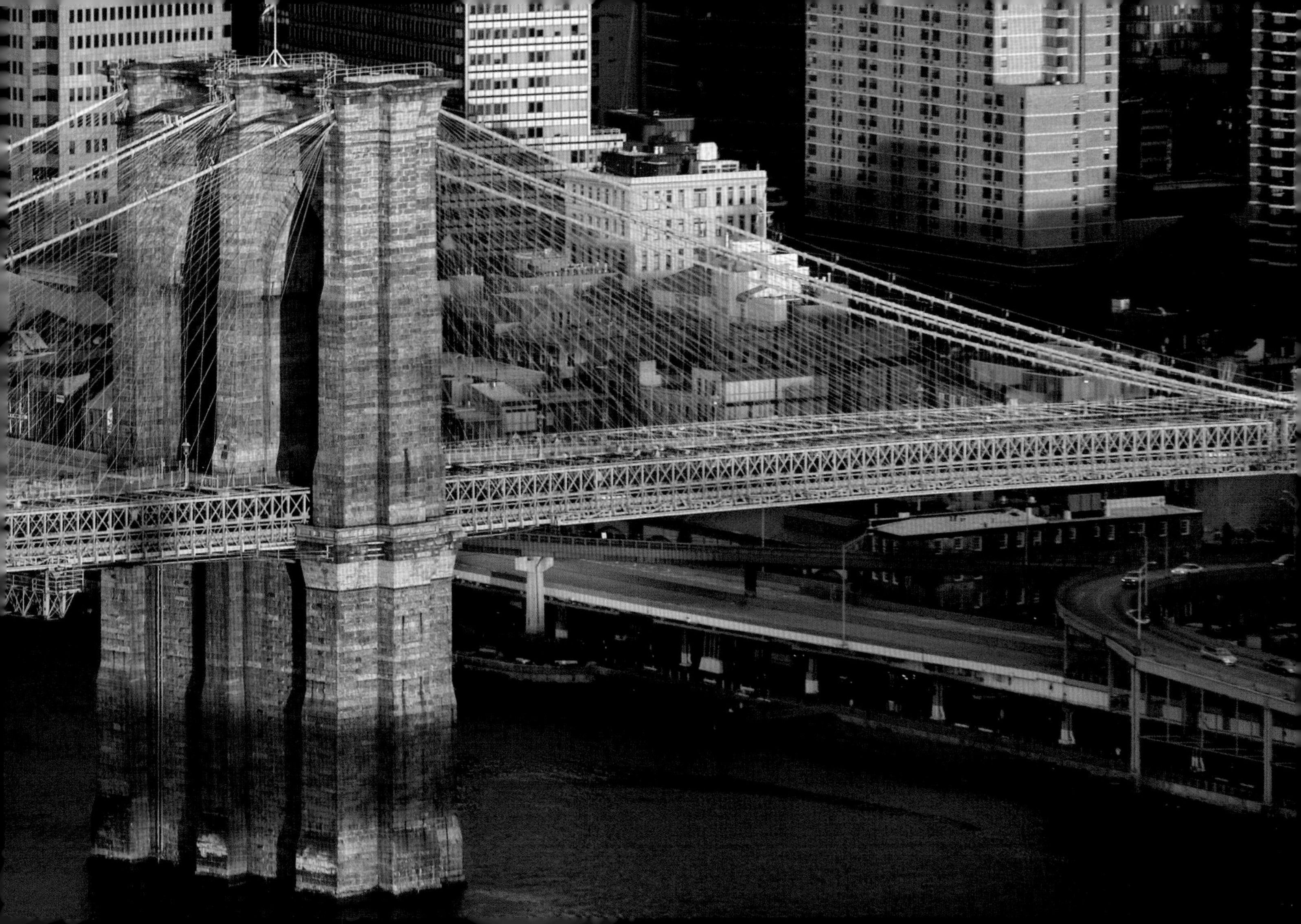

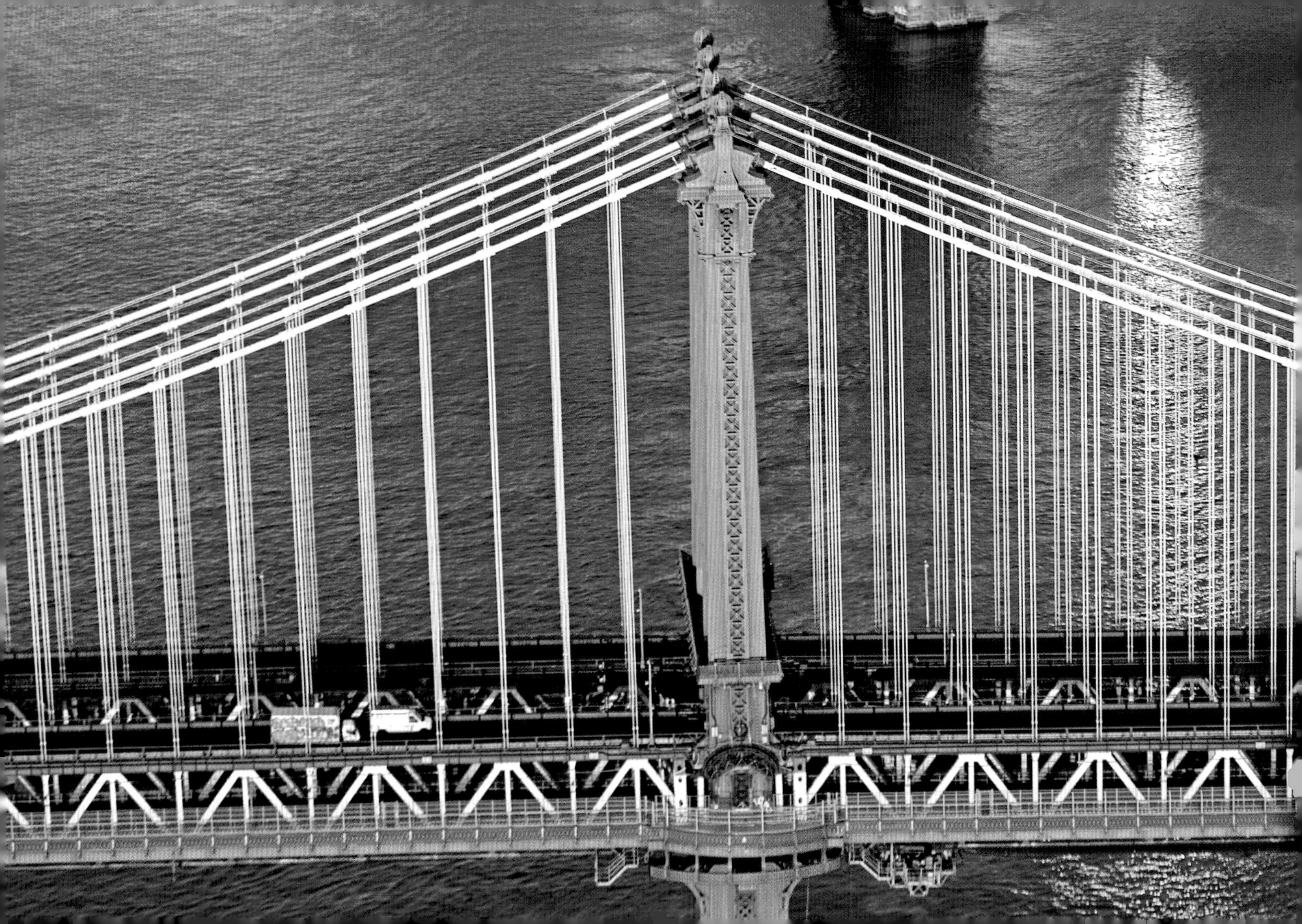

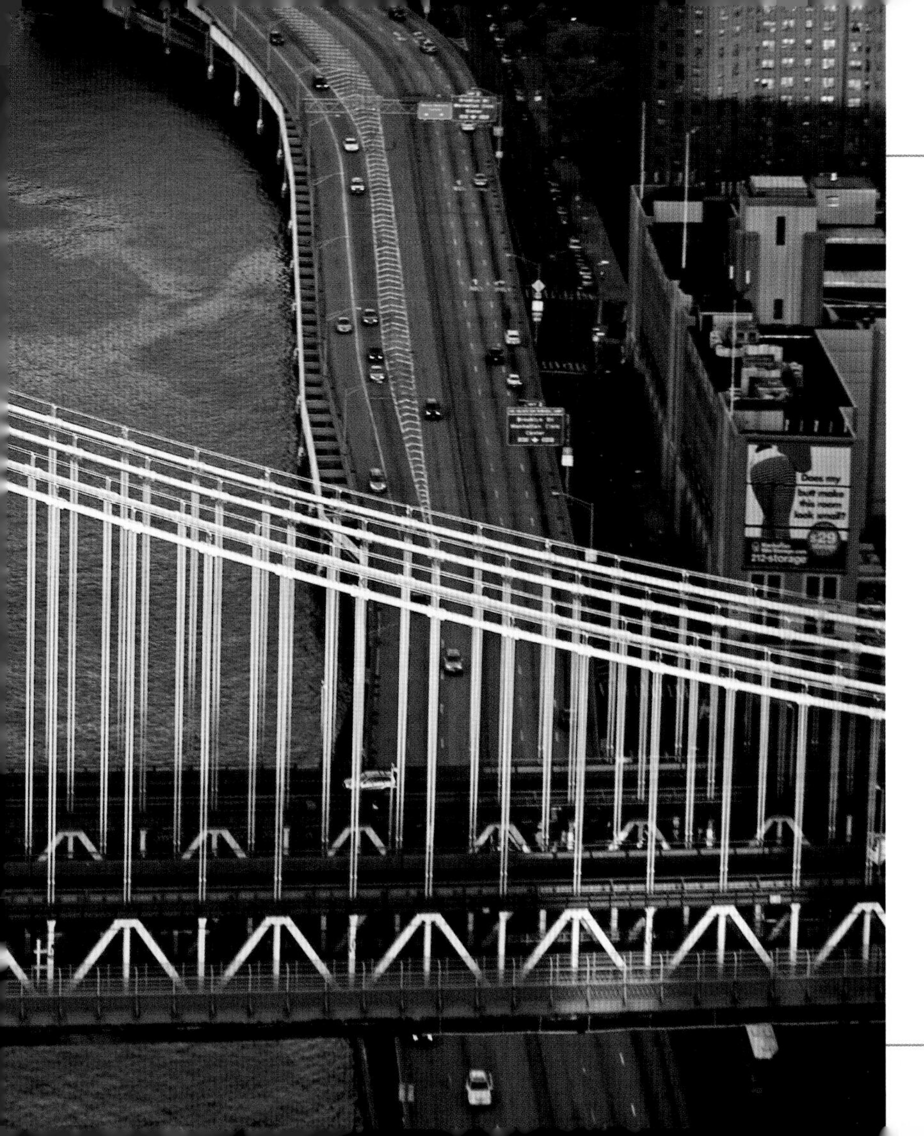

314-315
The Manhattan Bridge is one of two suspension bridges in New York that carry both vehicular and rail traffic; four subway tracks run on the lower level.

317

Immediately after the 9/11/2001 terrorist attacks, we see the American flag waving high on top of Brooklyn Bridge.

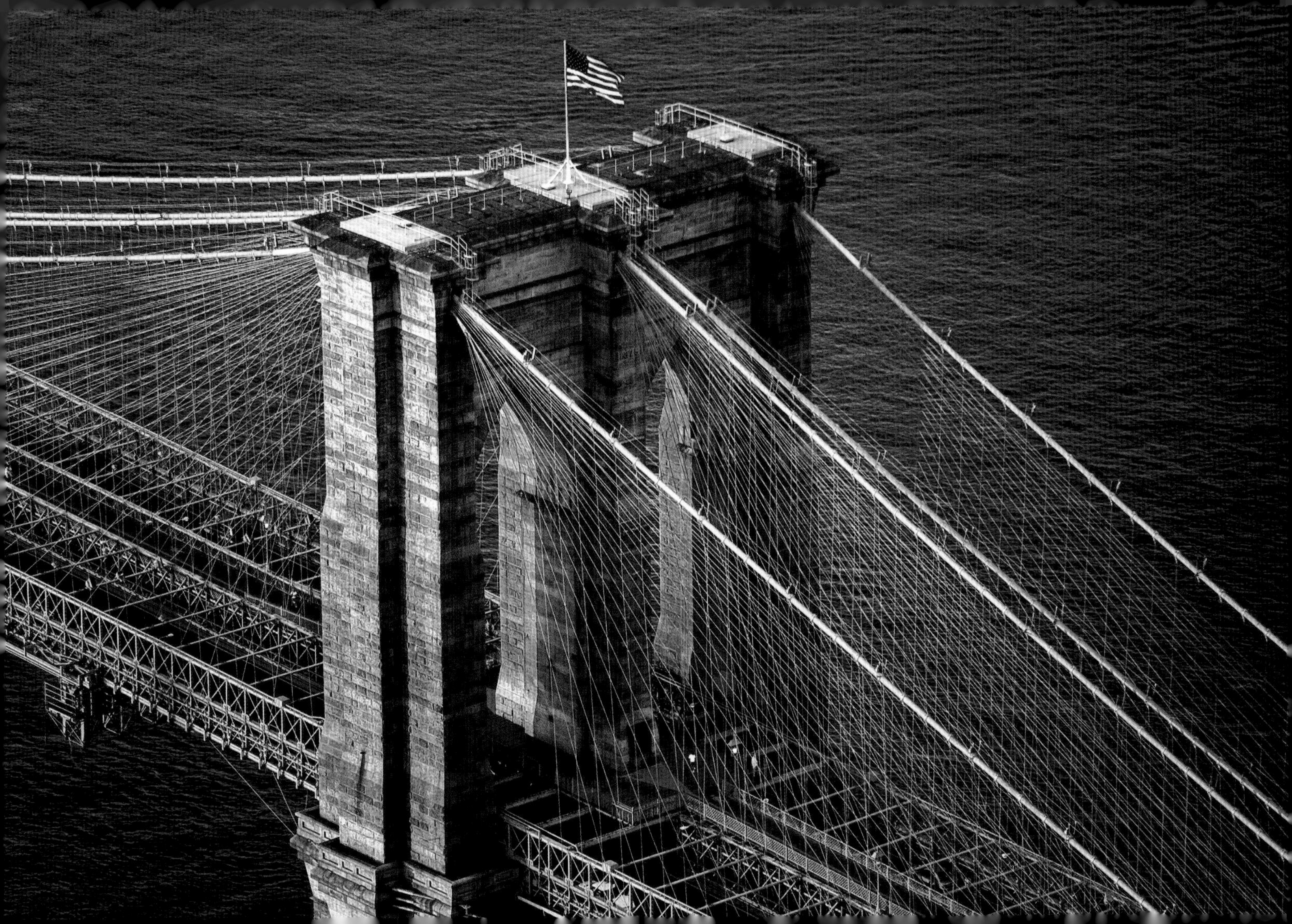

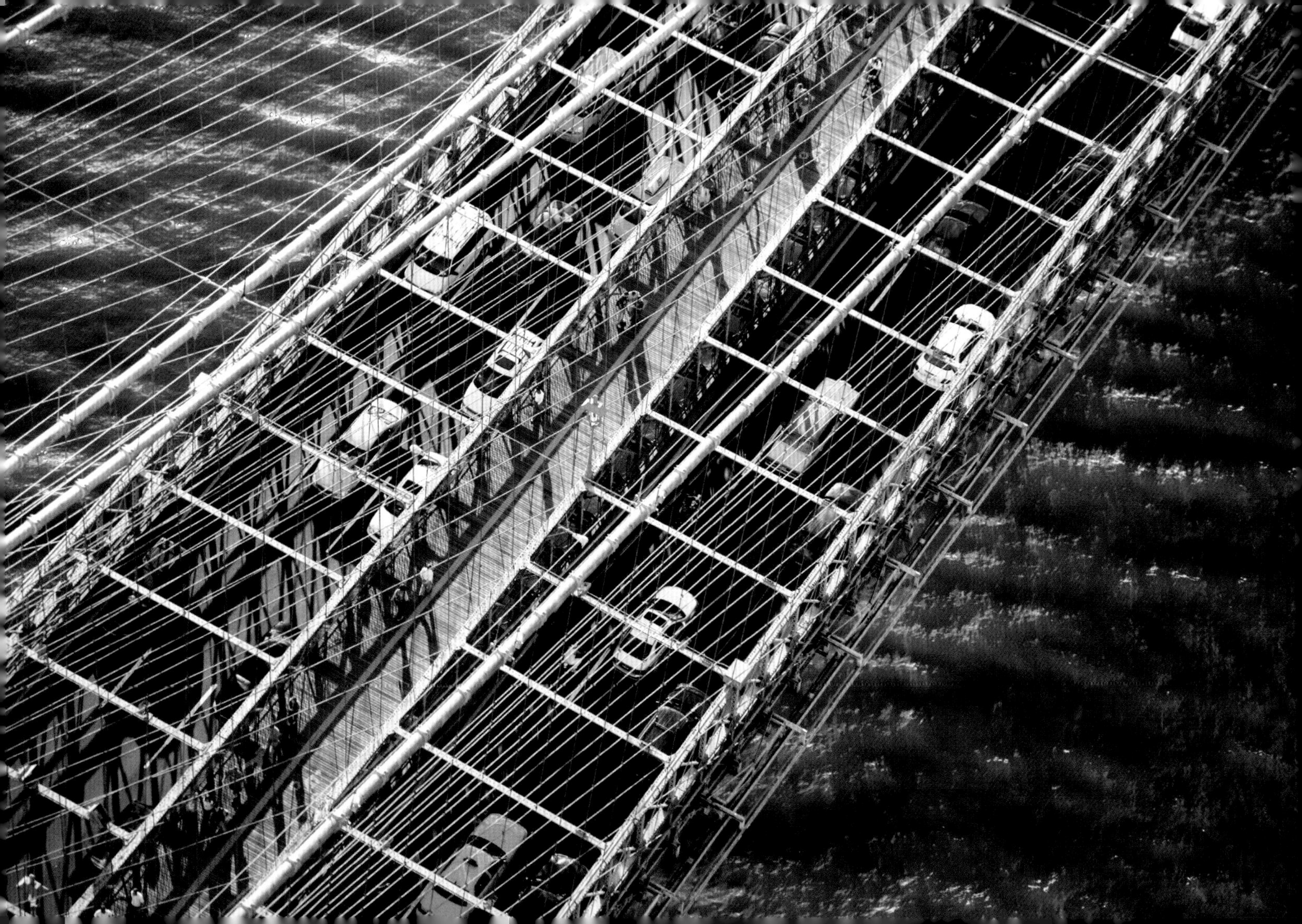

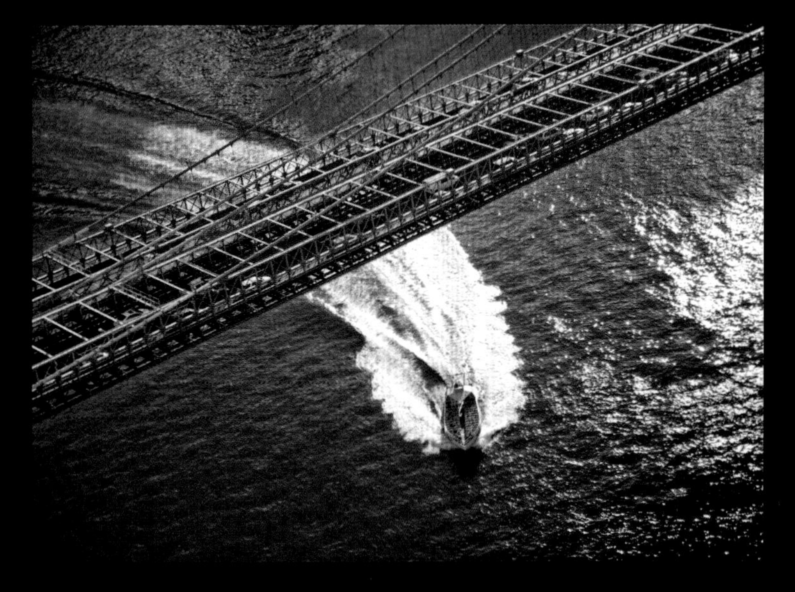

318

In 1884, showman P.T. Barnum herded 21 elephants across the Brooklyn Bridge; today 150,000 cars and thousands of pedestrians cross daily.

319

The Brooklyn Bridge has a clearance at its center of 135 feet above the East River.

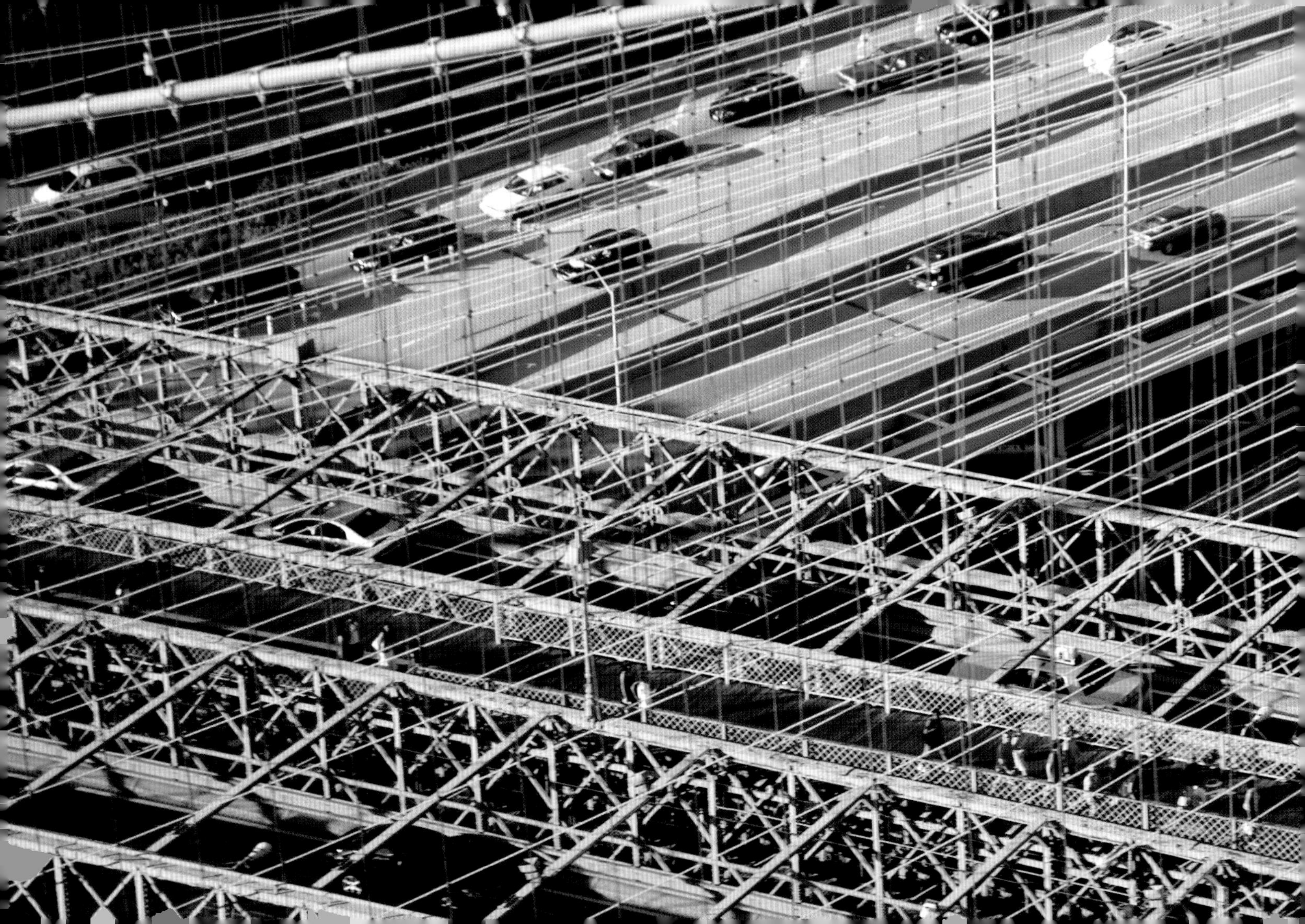

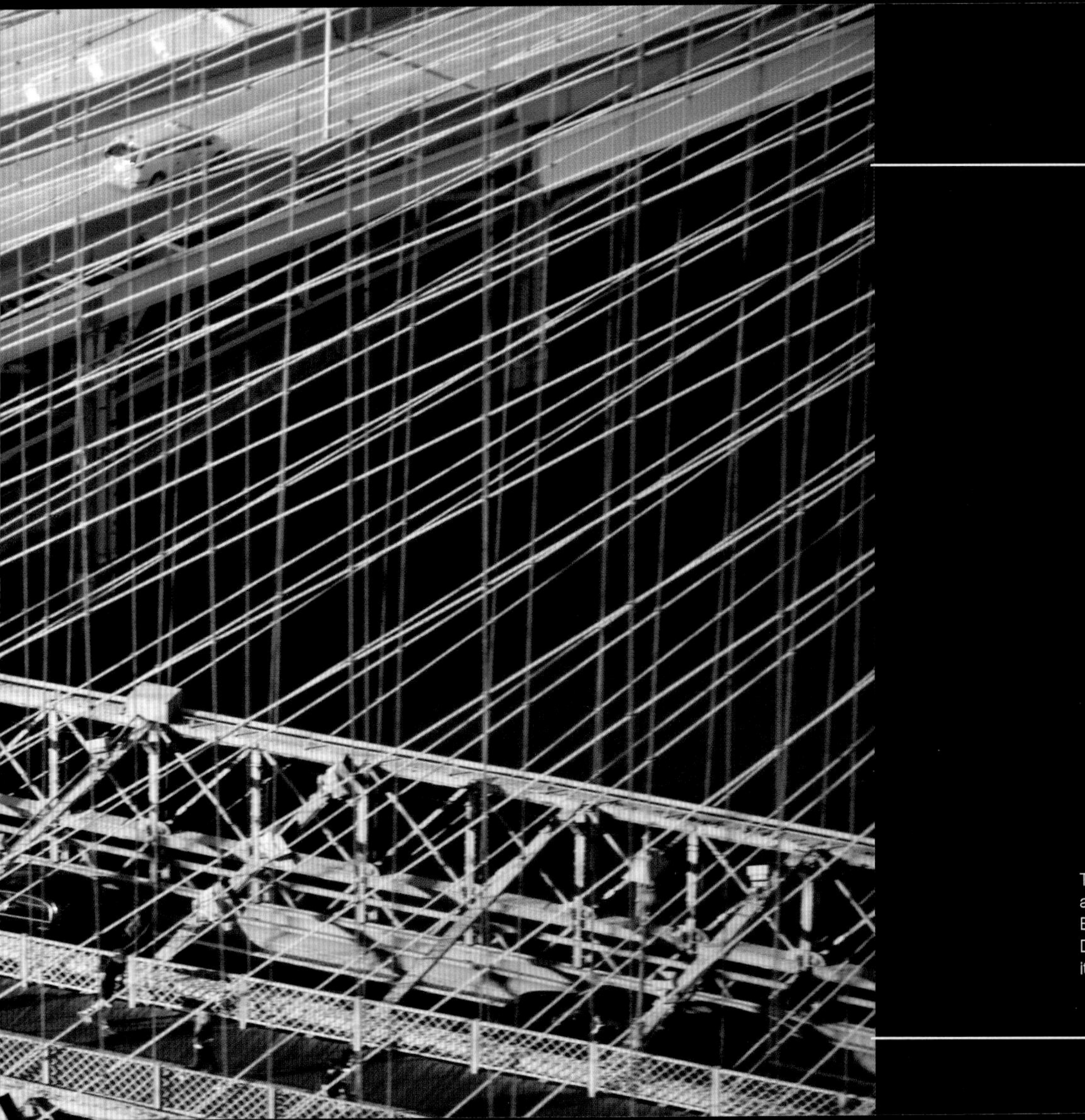

320-321 ◦
The maze of cars and pedestrians traversing the Brooklyn Bridge crosses over the FDR Drive, which passes underneath its Manhattan approach.

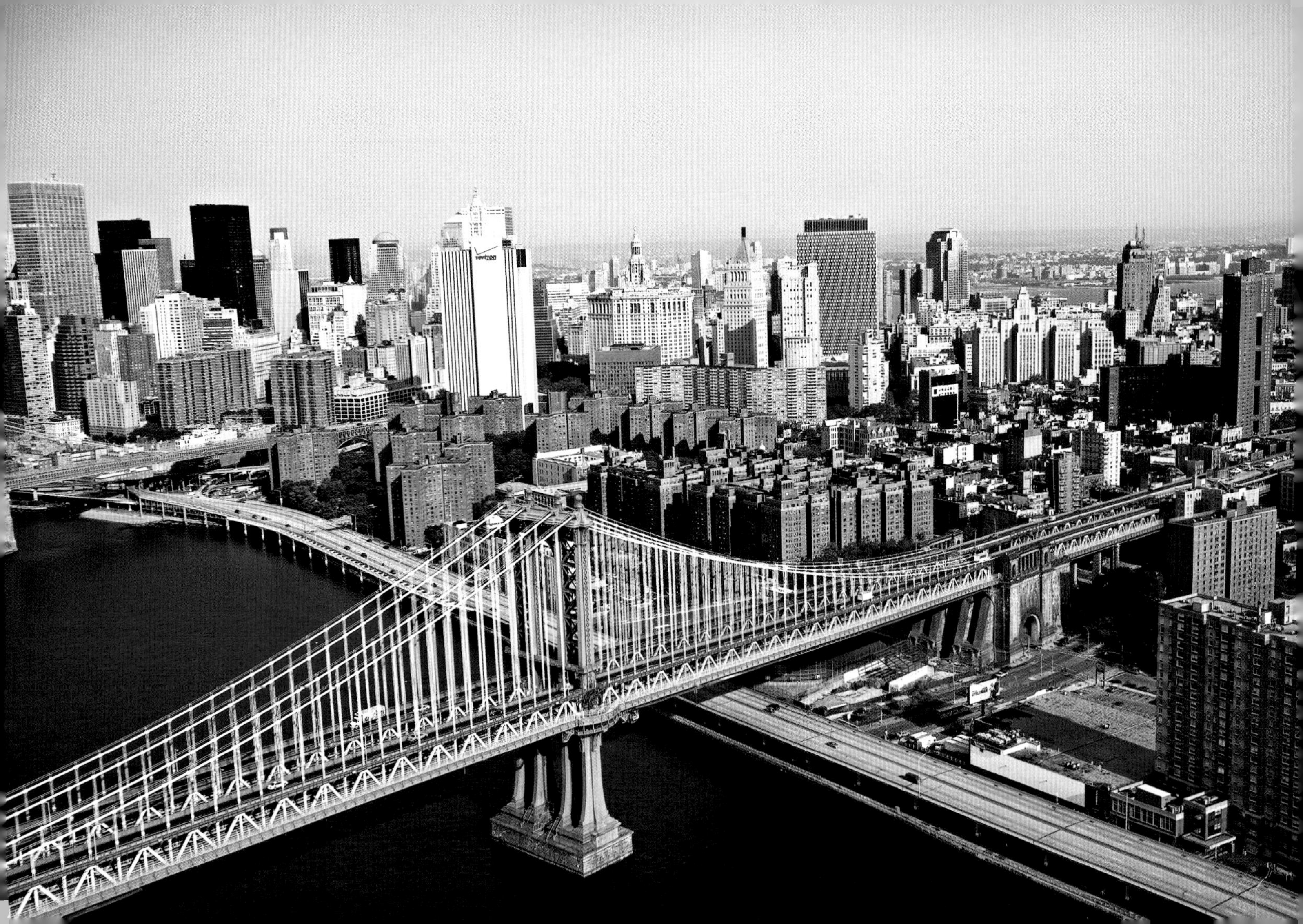
verizon

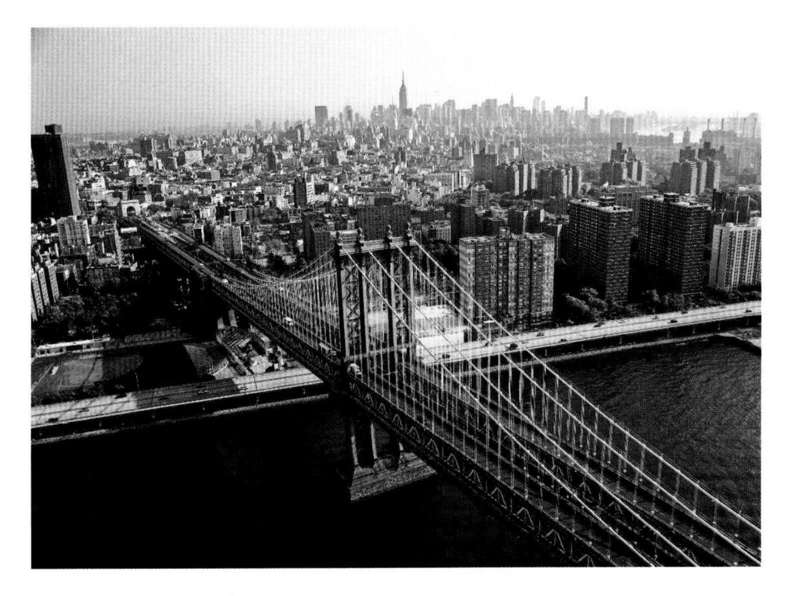

322 and 323

Once one of the busiest ports in the world, the area surrounding the Manhattan Bridge was formerly the northern-most edge of the city.

324-325

The pylons of Manhattan Bridge are periodically repainted an attractive bright blue color, as if to match the color of the waters of the East River.

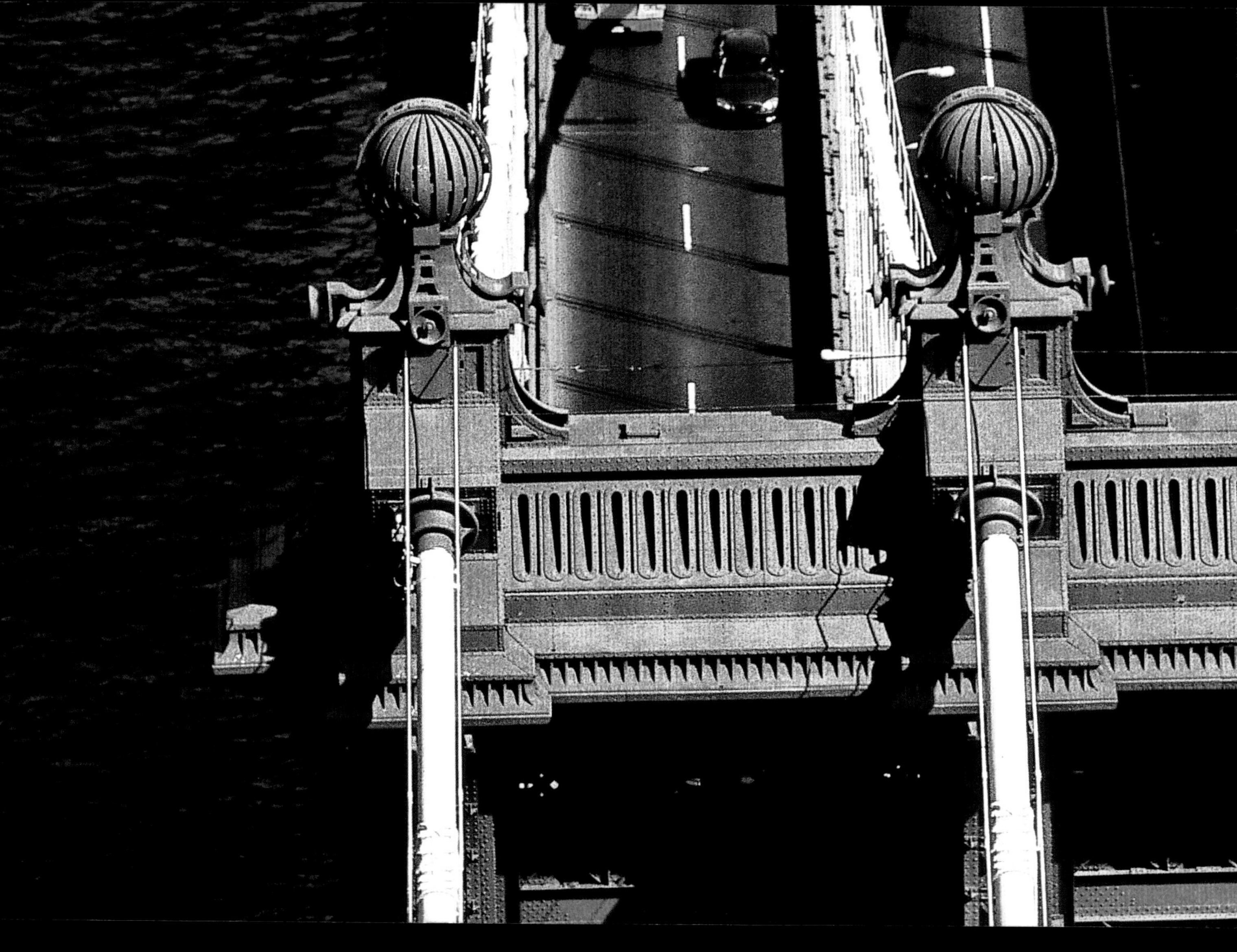

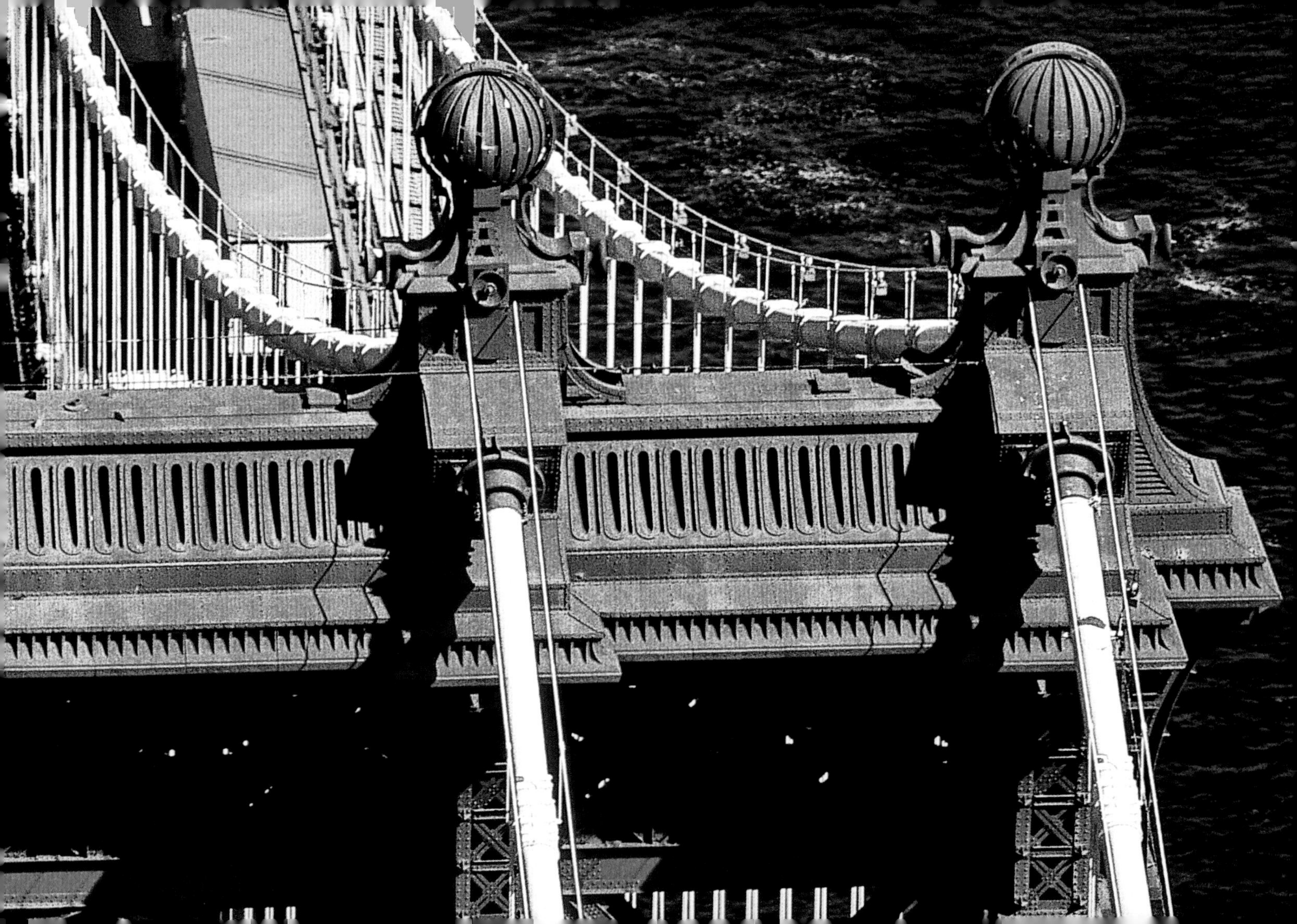

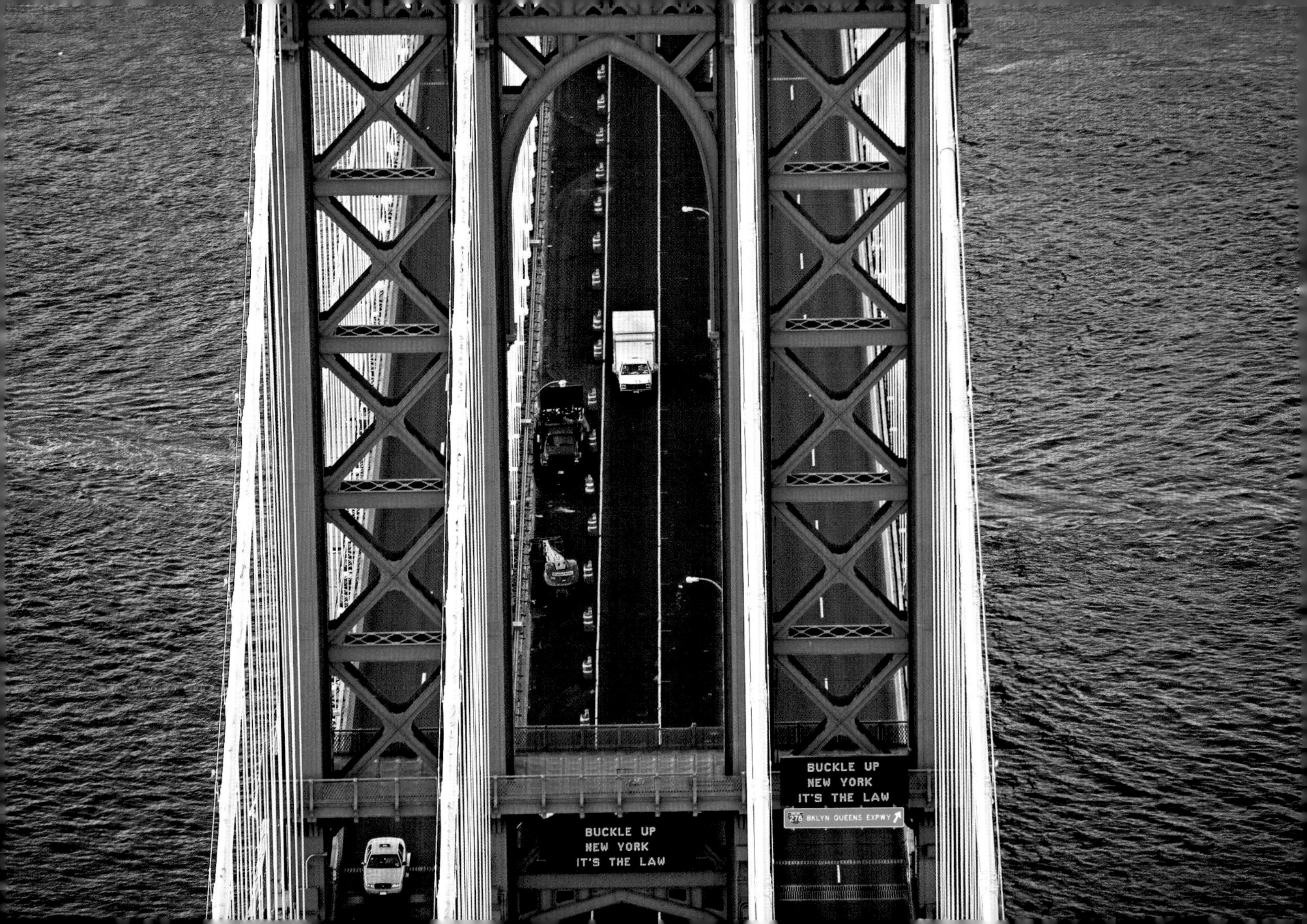
BUCKLE UP
NEW YORK
IT'S THE LAW
278 BKLYN QUEENS EXPWY
BUCKLE UP
NEW YORK
IT'S THE LAW

326

The Manhattan Bridge carries seven lanes of roadways and four subway tracks, as well as pedestrians and cyclists.

328-329

Though eclipsed in fame by its older neighbor, the Brooklyn Bridge, the Manhattan Bridge is the busiest of the East River crossings.

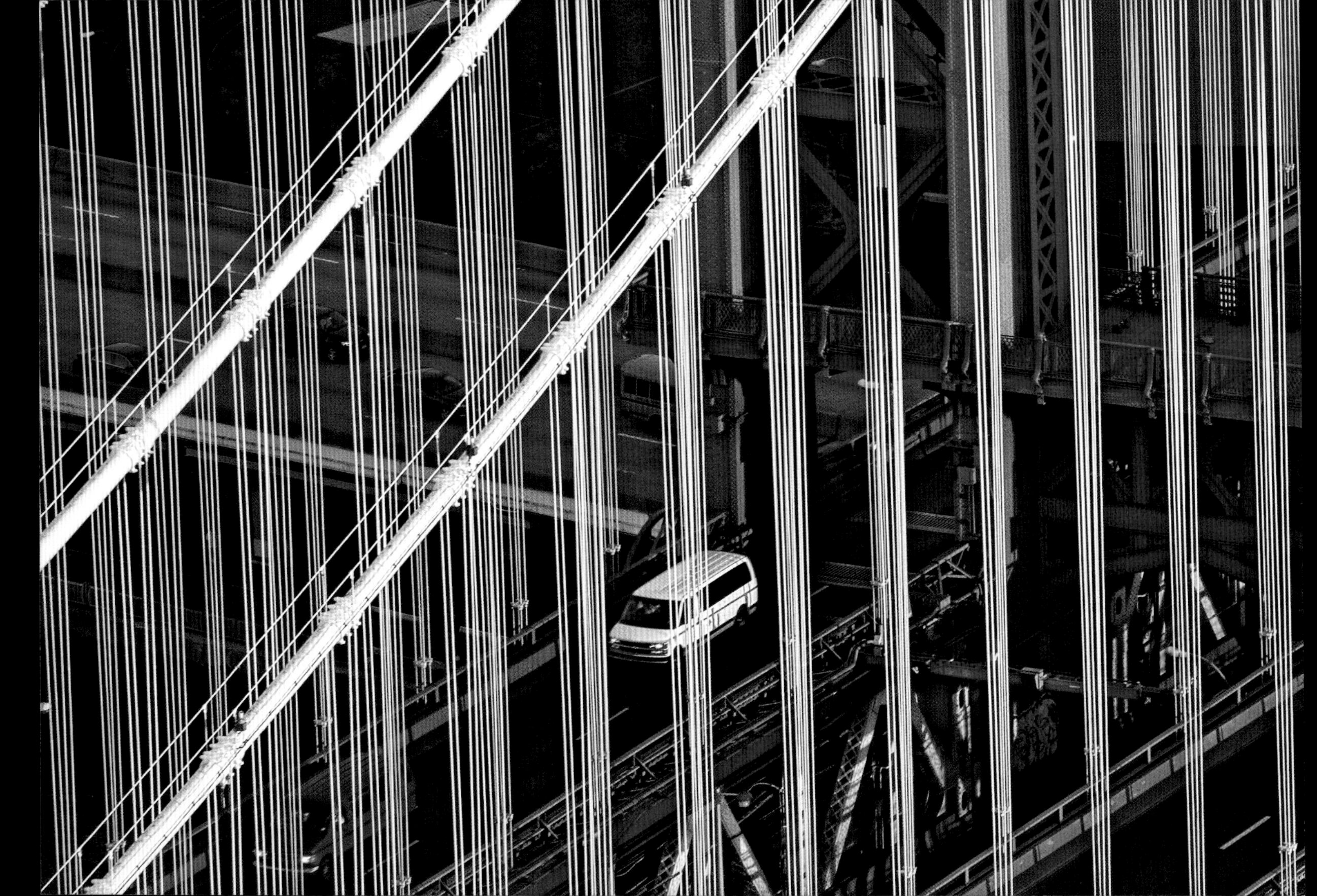

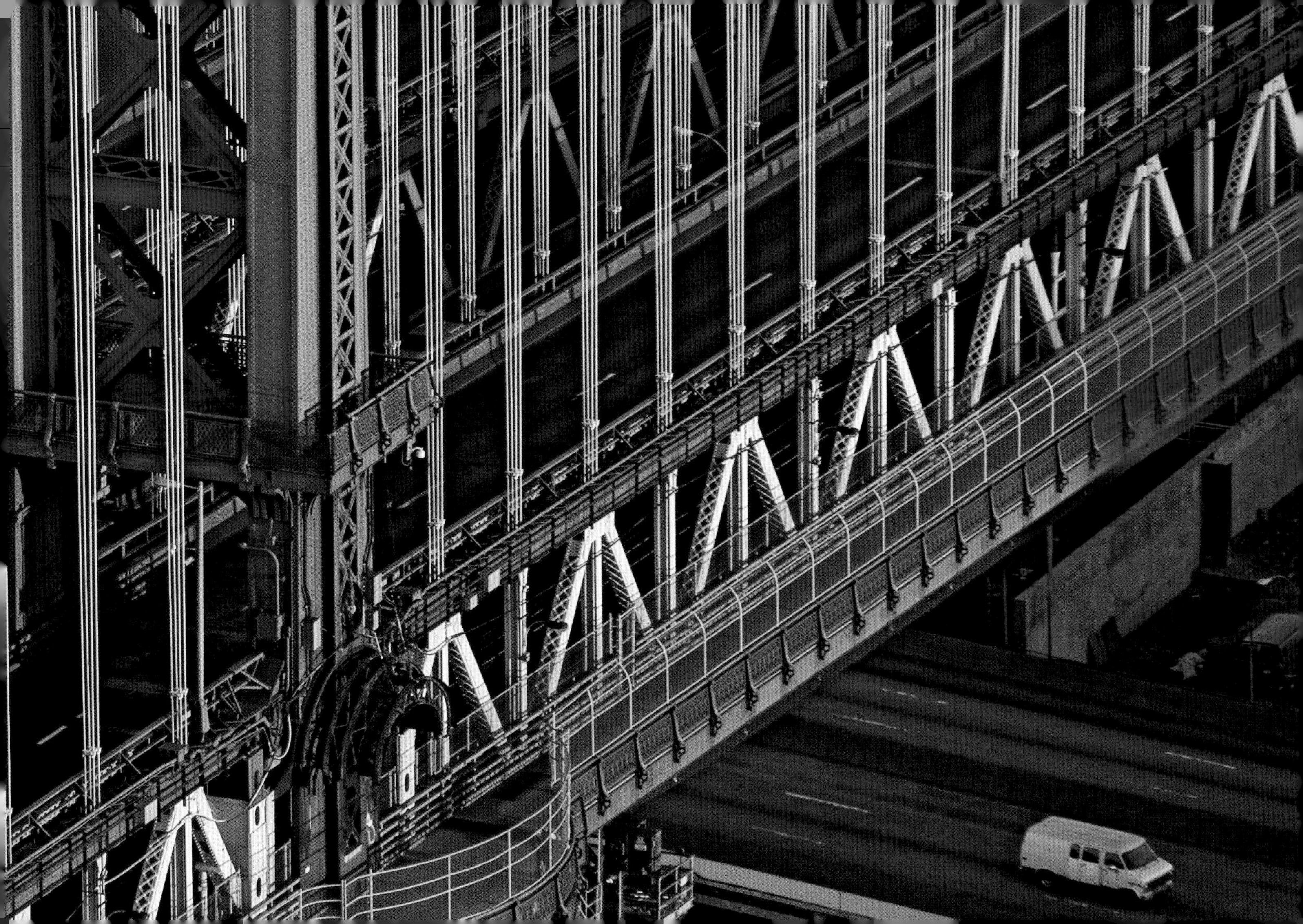

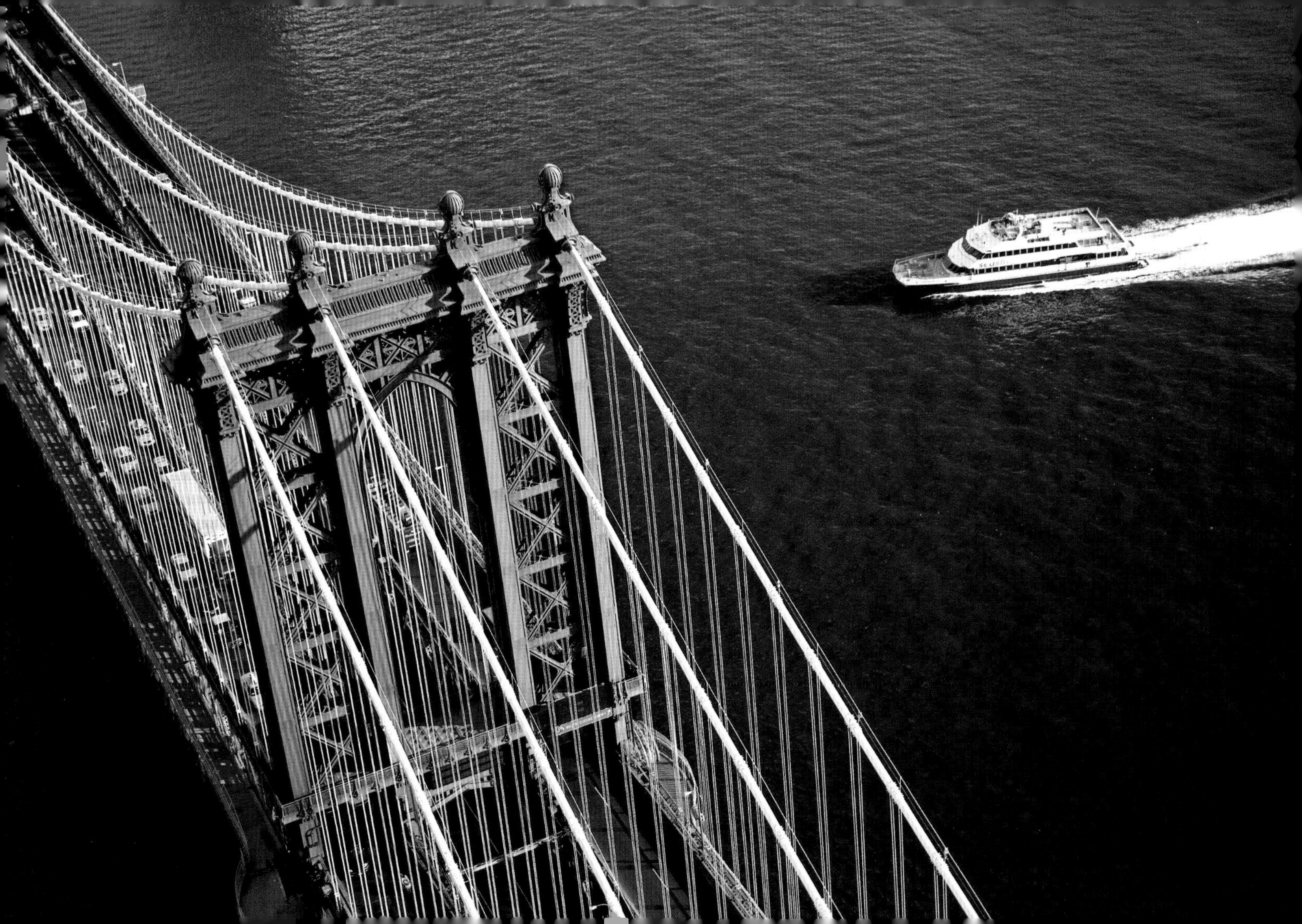

330

A sightseeing cruiser approaches the Manhattan Bridge, topped by four decorative spheres on each of its towers.

332-333

The solid granite buttresses of the Brooklyn Bridge and the graceful blue-tinted towers of the Manhattan Bridge link burgeoning sections of Manhattan and Brooklyn.

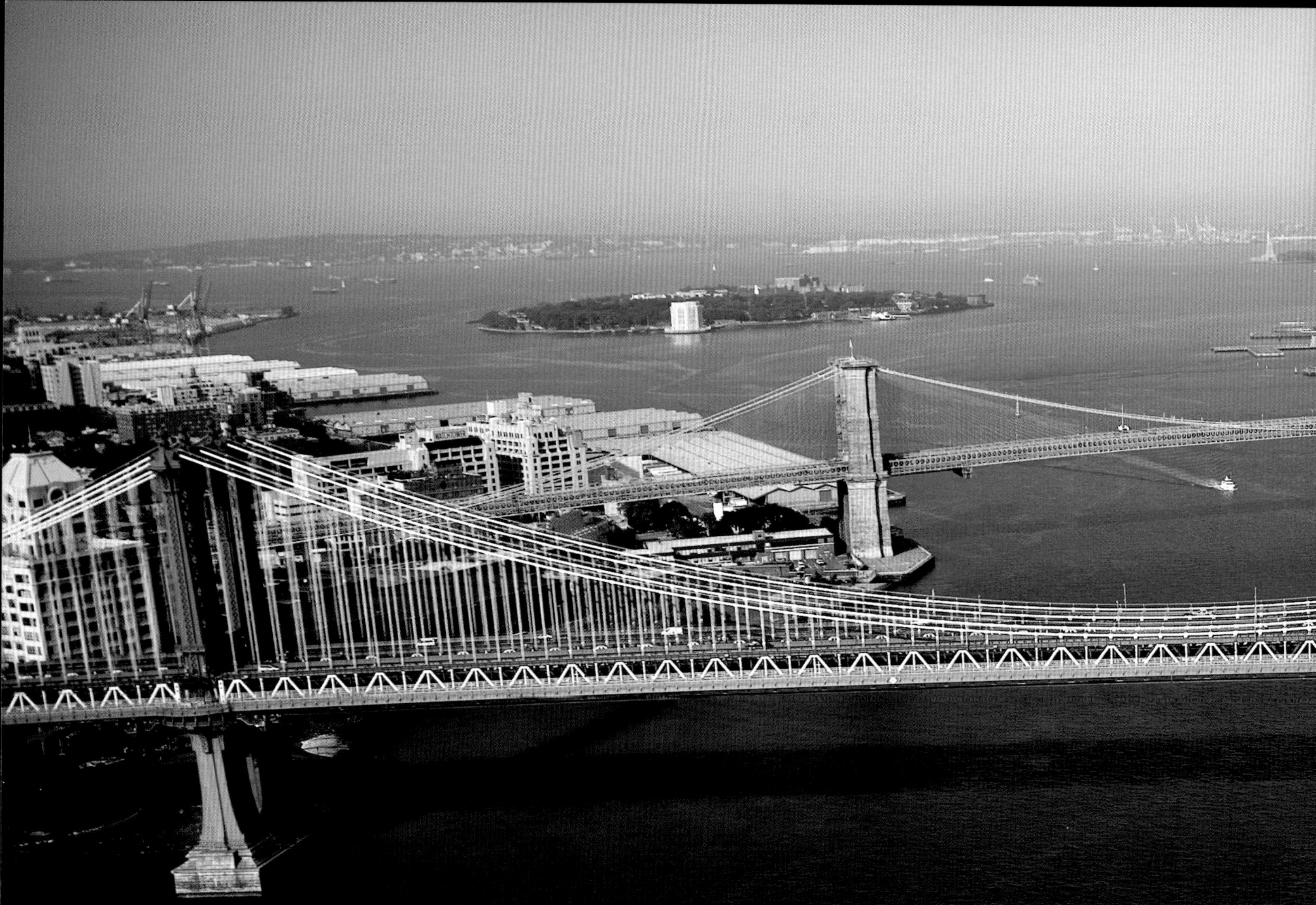

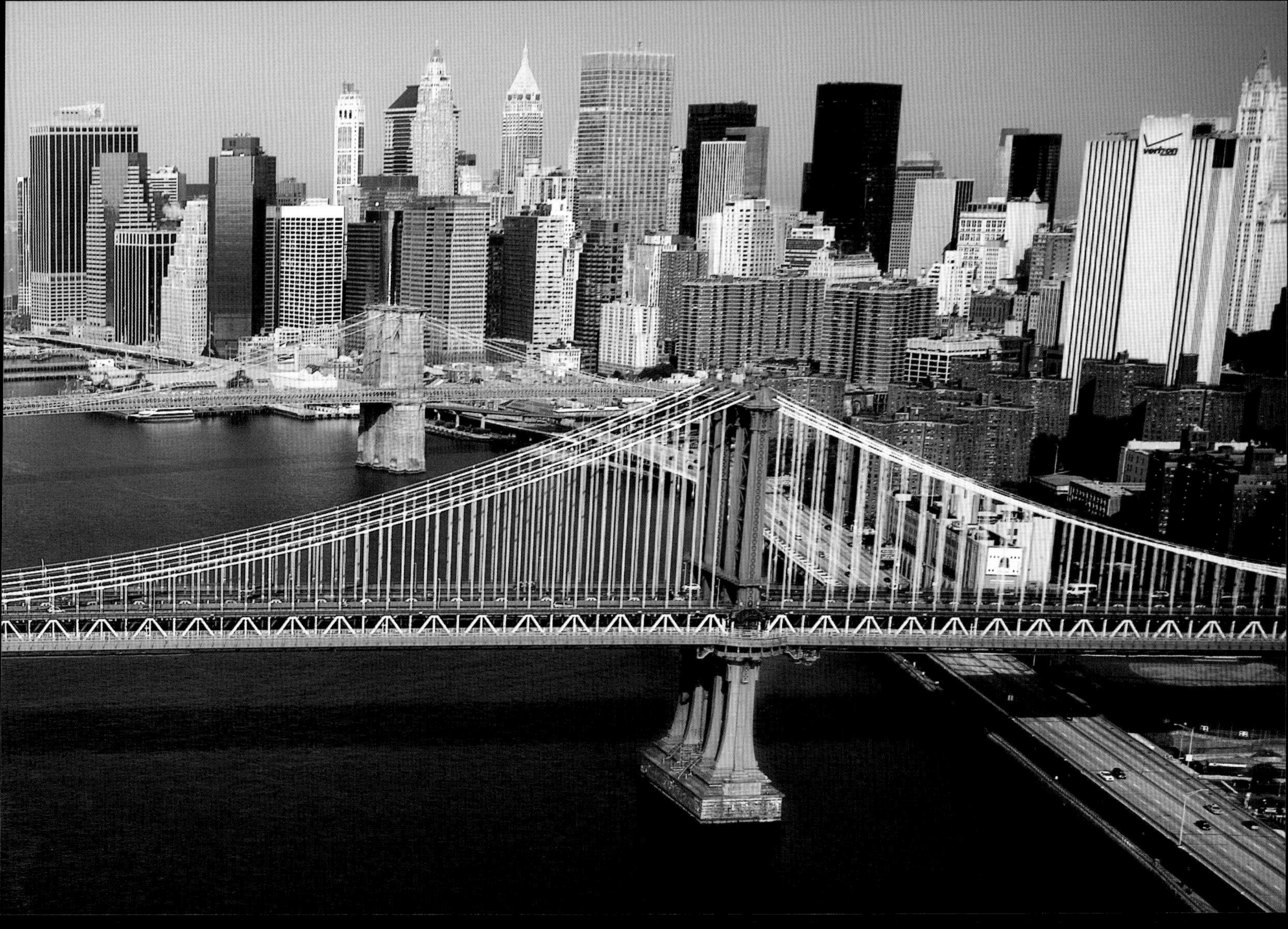

DOWNTOWN WEST
COBBLESTONES AND COMMERCE

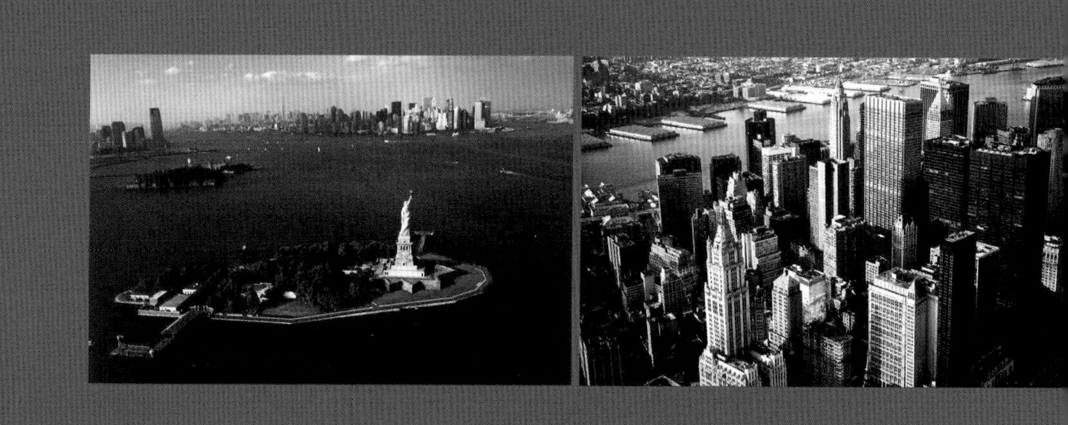

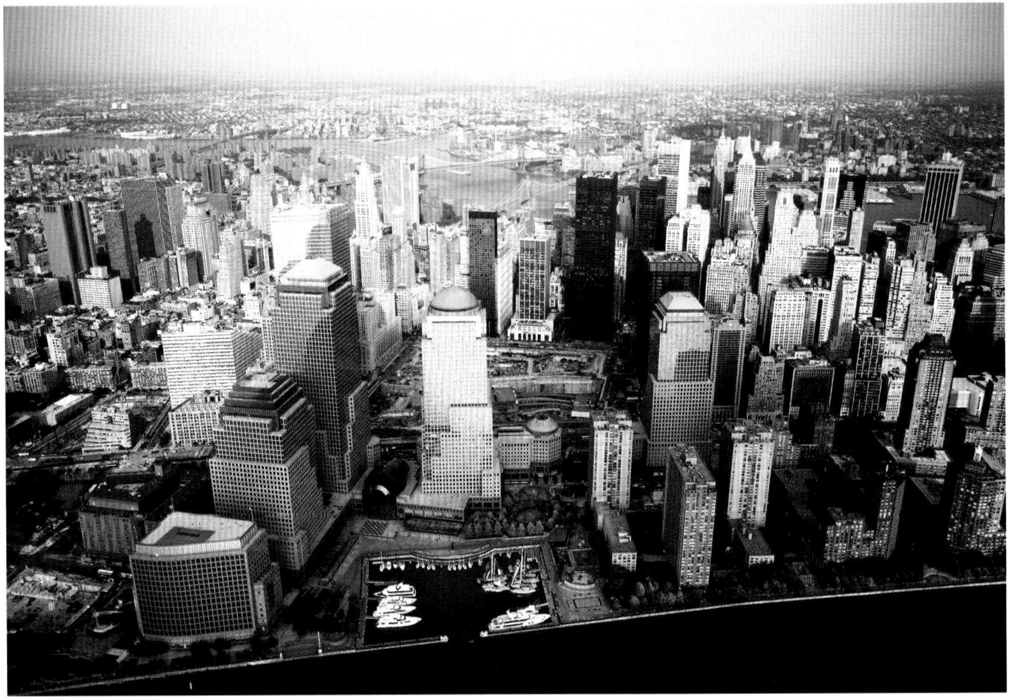

335
The Statue of Liberty holds her torch high (left), the Financial District is located at the southern end of Manhattan (right).

Below Times Square, the high-rise hubbub of midtown begins to spread out, and soon more sky than skyscraper is evident. Though many of the city's most notable high-rises are below 42nd Street, including the Empire State Building at 34th Street and Fifth Avenue, and more are being built or planned every day, there is a distinct feel of openness downtown that is not part of the uptown experience.

Walking south from Times Square, through what is known as the Garment or Fashion District, skyscrapers are replaced by densely packed loft buildings, housing warehouses and workshops, once home to clothing manufacturers. Though clothes manufacturing has largely moved overseas, the area around Seventh Avenue, from 42nd to 34th Streets, is still known as the heart of the fashion industry in America.

The Fashion District is bordered by the Javits Convention Center to the west, Pennsylvania Station and Madison Square Garden to the south and the Empire State Building to the East – each a landmark of the area in its own right. Beyond Penn Station lie the 350-acre Hudson Railyards. In a city where dreams and ambitions are limitless, land is not, and so plans are on the drawing board to cover over the railyards and add more convention, office and residential space above them. A number of waterfront parks are also slated, and are expected to connect with another proposed park project, the re-use of

336
The attack and collapse of the World Trade Towers – which once soared above the World Financial Center – left a gaping hole in Lower Manhattan

Downtown West
Cobblestones and Commerce

the former High-Line elevated railway in Chelsea, the neighborhood south of the Javits Center.

Reclaiming the waterfront characterizes much of what is happening in downtown New York. Where an active shipping trade once thrived on the Hudson River, many piers were later abandoned and fell into decay, prompting a move in the 1980s to establish new uses for the land along the river and the West Side Highway that runs along it. In addition to green spaces and parks, the Chelsea Piers sports and entertainment complex between 23rd Street and 18th Street made creative use of former docks. With everything from skateboarding, swimming to open-air golf and tennis, brings health and fitness to stressed-out urban dwellers. It has also revived a once forgotten area of the waterfront.

The neighborhood around Chelsea Piers has also revived, and has challenged Soho, to the south, as a thriving gallery scene. Once an estate belonging to a single family, Chelsea is now a trendy collection of galleries, lofts, restaurants and boutiques. The area, bounded by 29th and 14th streets, has also become a bastion of upscale gay life, like the West Village just below it.

While its identification with the bohemian lifestyle dates from the early 20th century, Greenwich Village, which includes the West Village and East Village, is one of the oldest areas of Manhattan. Growing from a rural hamlet that developed separately and more slowly from Lower Manhattan, the area south of 14th Street and bounded by the Hudson to the west and Broadway to the east was, and still is in many ways, an actual village. Its distinctiveness is seen even in its street layout and architecture; as it was already established when the 1811 numbered grid system was incorporated, Greenwich Village was allowed to keep its angled street patterns as well as street names. Zoning regulations and the efforts of dedicated preservationists have kept the Village's unique character, complete with cobblestone streets and brick and clapboard town houses. Central to Greenwich Village is Washington Square; in fact, the entire

Downtown West
Cobblestones and Commerce

area was once known as Washington Square. The terminus of Fifth Avenue, the park is a central meeting place in the Village, with New York University's library at its southern border.

Houston (pronounced How-stun) Street is the east-west divider between Greenwich Village and the rest of Lower Manhattan. Below Houston is the neighborhood that takes its name from its location, SoHo (south of Houston). Once rural, then a chic residential area, SoHo became a commercial and industrial center in the 1800s, and was noted for its many cast-iron buildings that housed manufacturing and warehouse operations. By the 1930s, manufacturing moved elsewhere and the district was deserted. Discovered in the 1960s by artists seeking space and low rents, SoHo became synonymous with cutting edge art and design; fashion soon followed, and the area went from being called the Hell's Hundred Acres to become one of the priciest neighborhoods in Manhattan.

Driven out by high rates and crowds of art and fashion loving tourists, the artists moved south, to Tribeca, the triangle below Canal Street, making it now one of the choicest residential addresses in New York. It, too, had been a farming community when New Amsterdam was being established, and it remained residential until the mid-nineteenth century. But as commercial interests began to move in, residents moved north, and the area soon became a neighborhood of vast warehouses and lofts. The western edge of Tribeca was known as Washington Market, and was the center of the wholesale food trade.

Tribeca borders an area that didn't even exist when the Dutch arrived on Manhattan – Battery Park City, a 90-acre planned residential, commercial and open-space development that was built on landfill and opened in 1976. Once a thriving port area, by the 1950s, the piers along the southwestern edge of Manhattan had become decrepit and rundown slums; in the 1960s, plans were announced to rebuild the area, literally from the ground up.

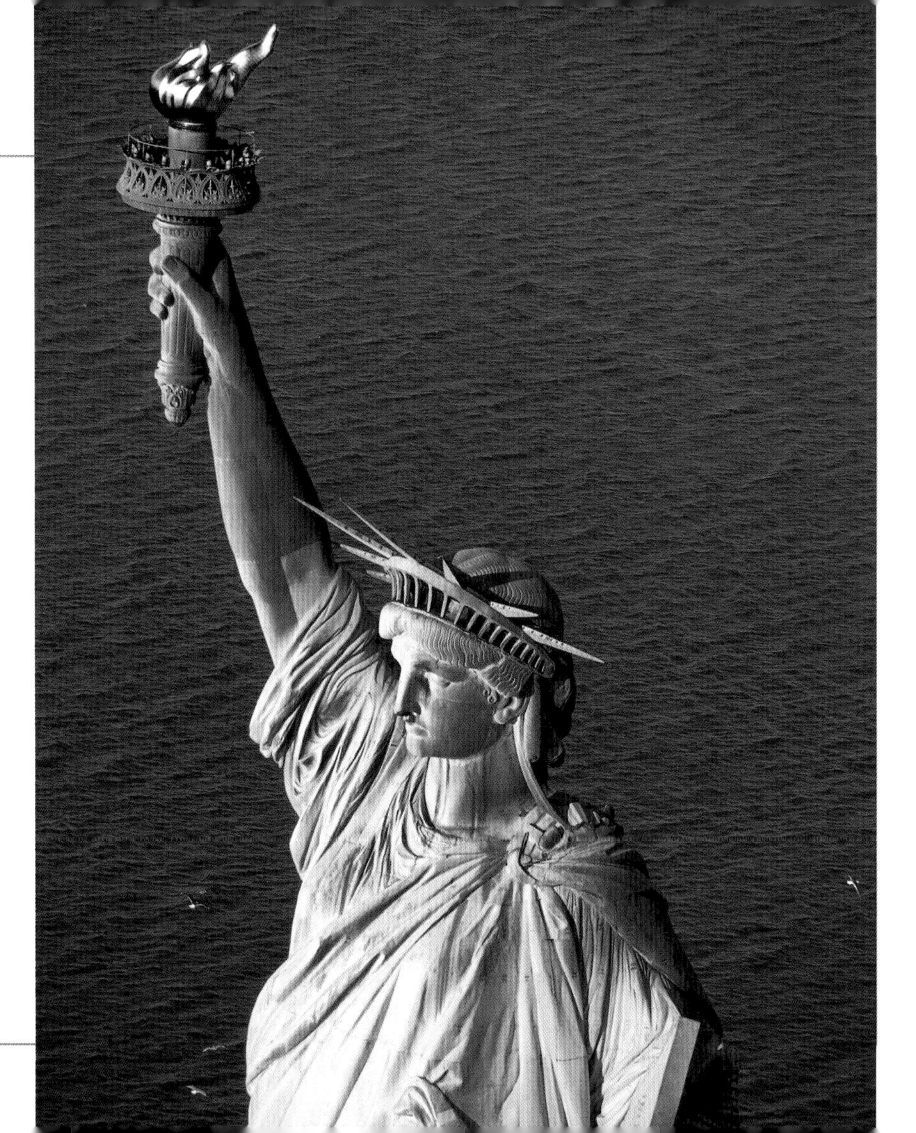

340
A gift from the people of France to the people of the United States in 1886, the Statue of Liberty's torch represents enlightenment to all who see her.

The elite Stuyvesant High School sits on the northern end of Battery Park City, and the actual Battery Park (not part of the complex) is at its southern border. The Esplanade, a park with meandering walkways and lawns runs the entire length of the development.

The World Financial Center is at the nexus of Battery Park City, with its four distinctive tours and glass-enclosed Winter Garden. The entire complex, both residential and commercial, grew up, quite literally, in the shadow of the World Trade Center, and will be forever identified with it. The gaping hole to the east of the World Financial Center is all that is left of the Twin Towers, once the tallest structures in the world.

After the terrorist attacks of September 11, 2001, the character of this area of New York was forever changed. A new dedication to the neighborhood and its rebuilding has emerged since those events. A new Freedom Tower is slated to rise where the Twin Towers once stood, as well as a memorial to all those who lost their lives in the tragedy. Battery Park City is home to other memorials – the Jewish Heritage Museum, the Irish Hunger Memorial and appropriately, the Skyscraper Museum. Though the view from the eastern side of the buildings of Battery Park City and the WFC is of the footprint of the World Trade Center and the ongoing reconstruction surrounding it, to the west, the view is of Ellis Island and the Statue of Liberty, long seen as welcoming beacons of hope for a new life, a new start in a new land.

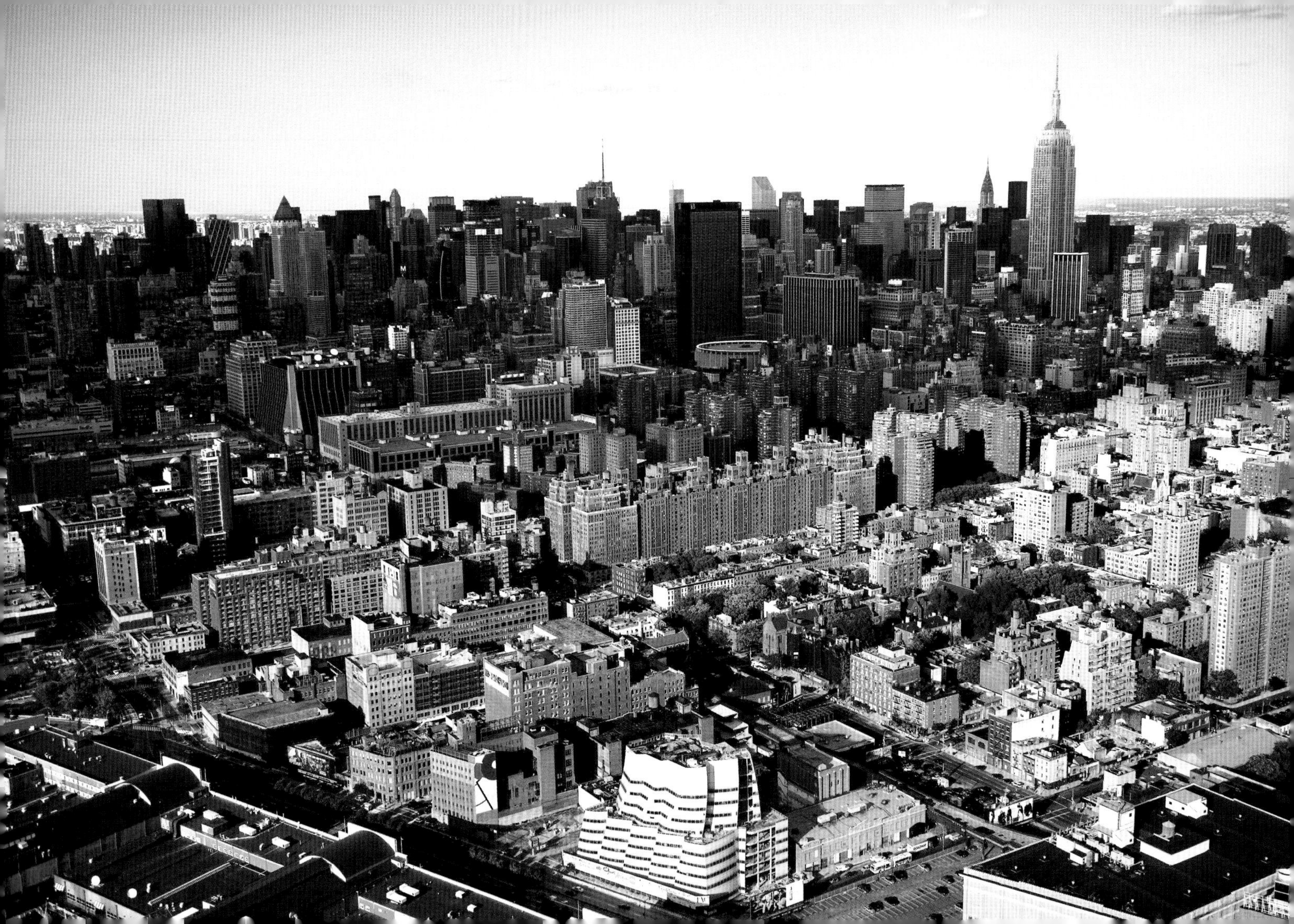

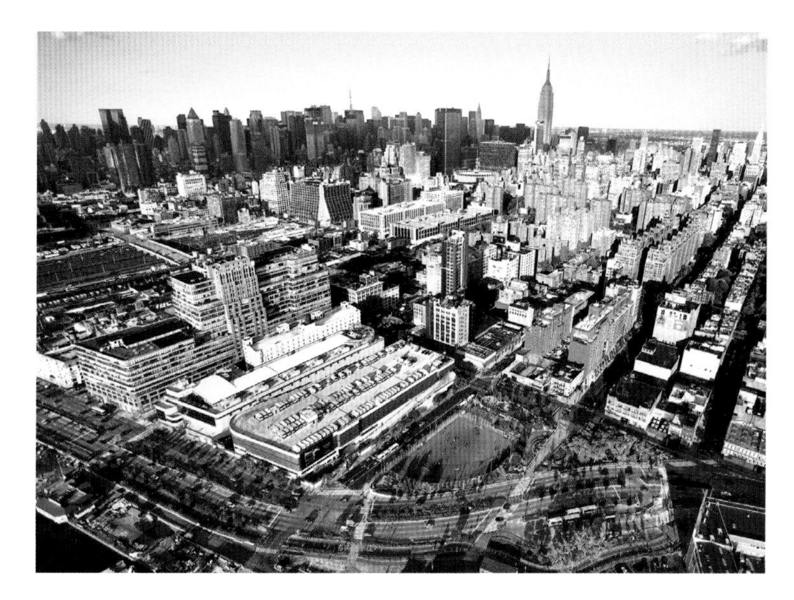

342 and 343
From Chelsea to Battery Park the corridor formed by Downtown West is an excellent example of successful urban development and undoubtedly offers the best leisure opportunities in the entire city, with numerous art galleries, trendy stores and top-class restaurants.

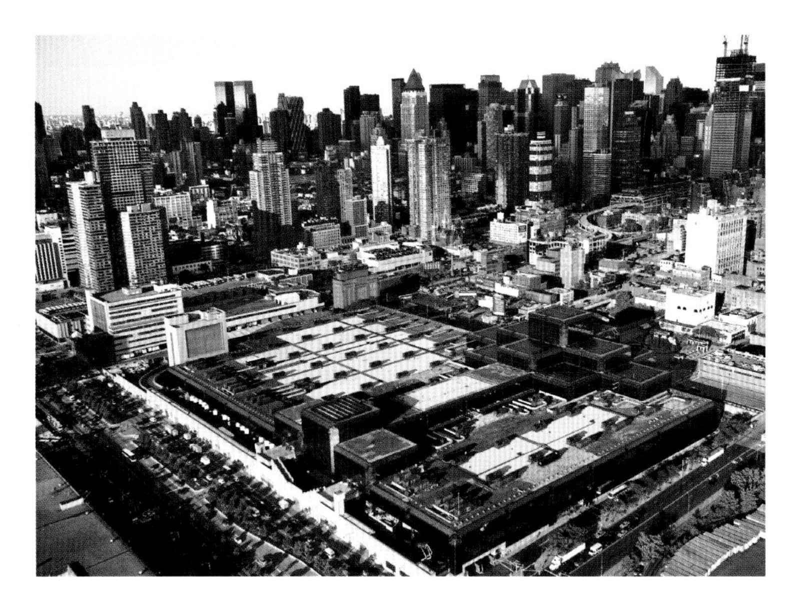

344 and 345

The Jacob Javits Convention Center was designed by I.M. Pei and built in 1986. It is the centerpiece of a major reconstruction on Manhattan's west side, an area long neglected after the demise of the shipping along the Hudson.

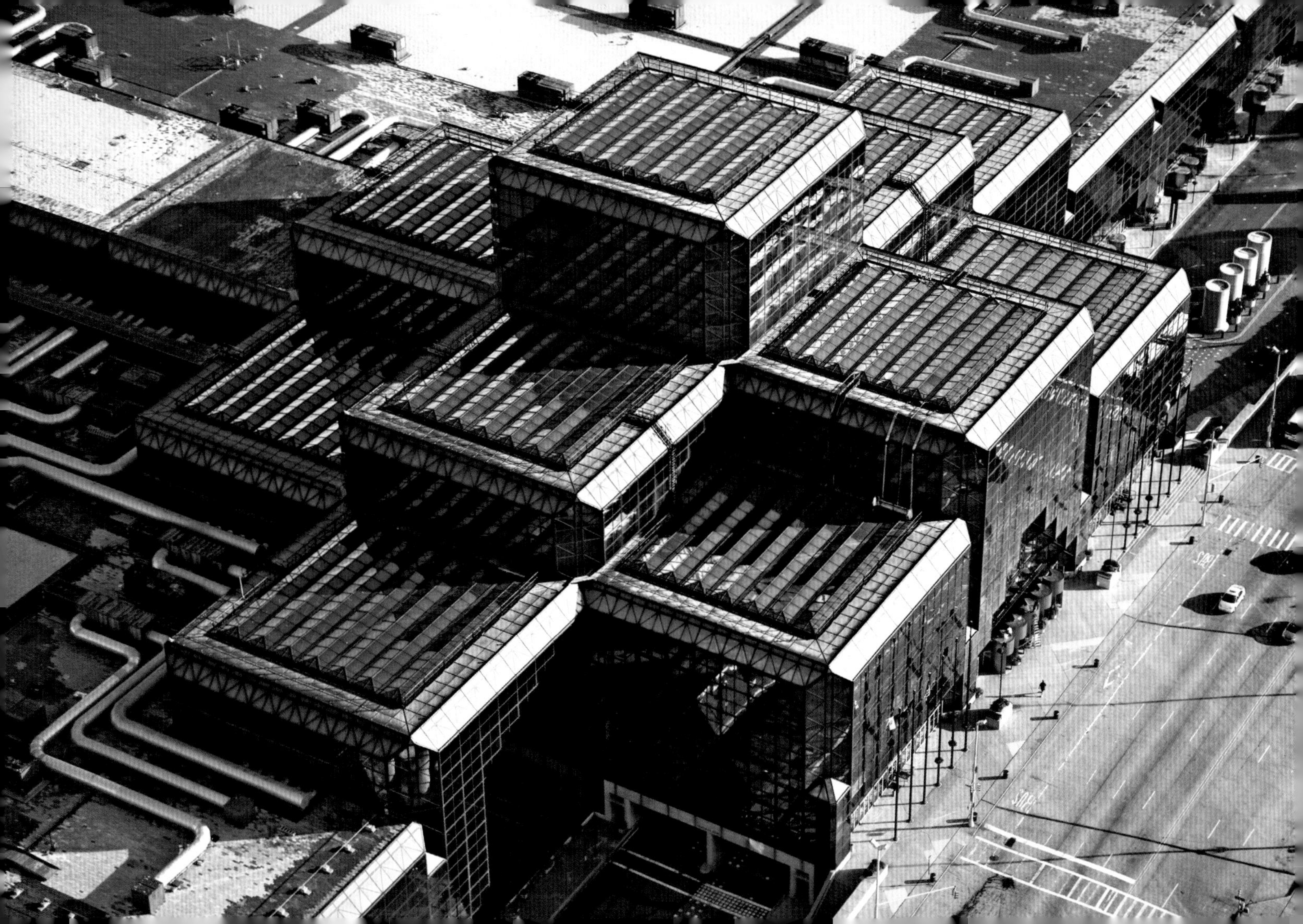

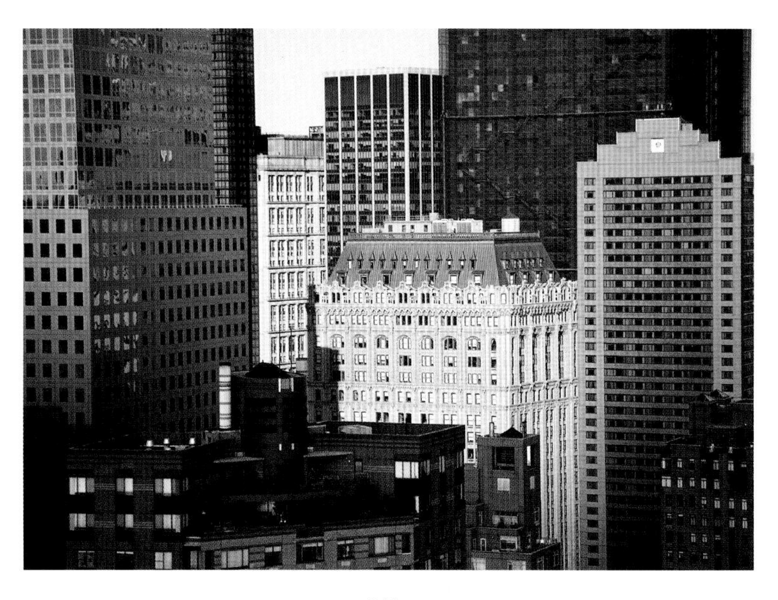

346
Hanging gardens create areas of greenery in the Manhattan sky.

347
A view of Tribeca: cars loop around the exit leading from the Holland Tunnel at the convergence of Hudson Street and Canal. The brick building, lower left, is the headquarters of AT&T.

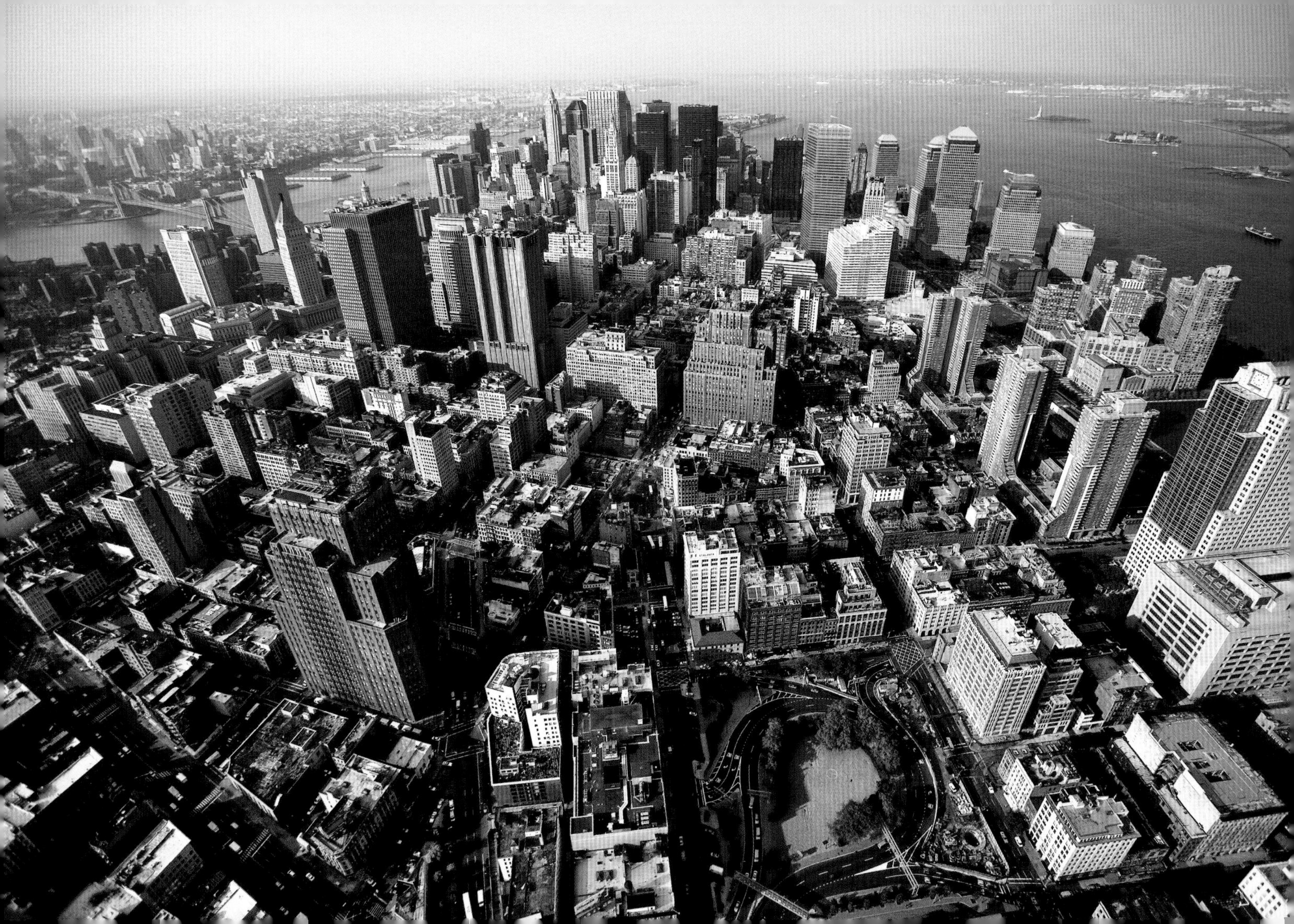

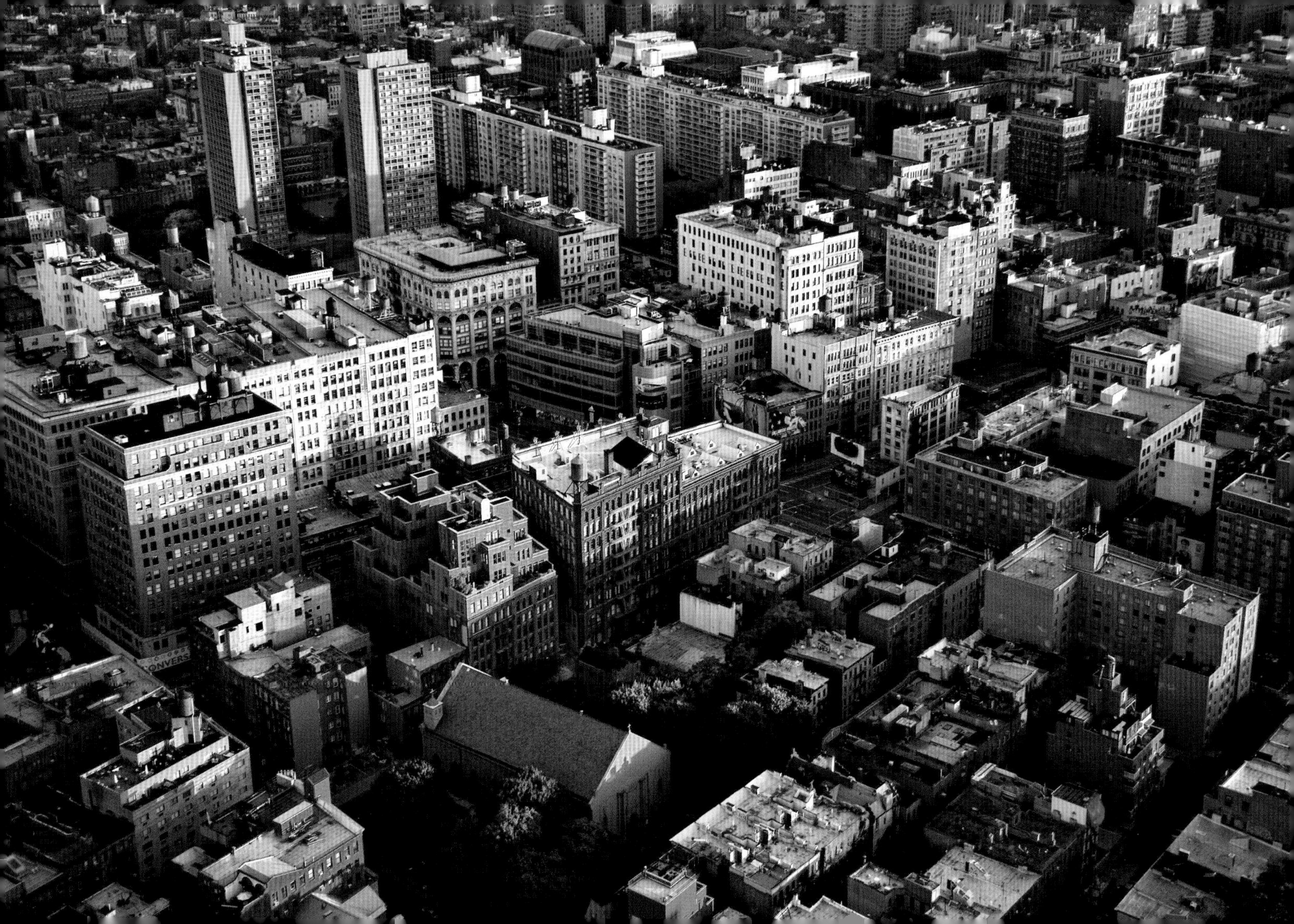

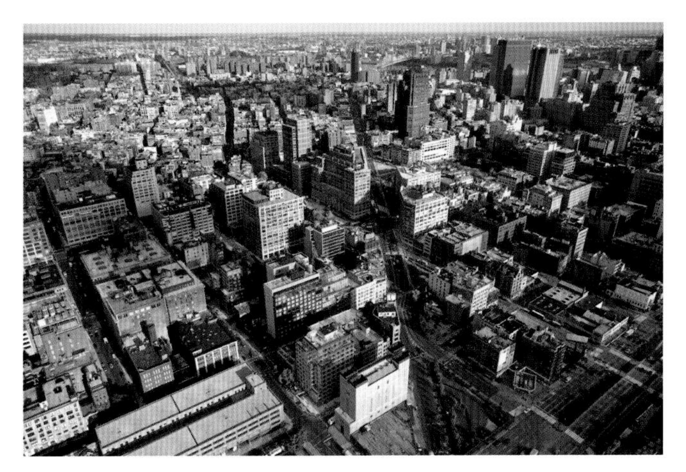

348
Tucked between Greenwich Village and the East Village, the newly designated neighborhoods of Noho and Nolita are populated by filmmakers and fashionistas in renovated tenements.

349
Architect Philip Johnson's last residential commission, the Urban Glass House (center foreground), at Spring and Washington, sits on the northern border of Tribeca, the Triangle Below Canal.

351

The High Line, a 1.5 mile, abandoned elevated railway that runs from West 34th Street through the now-trendy Meatpacking District, over and often through buildings, is slated to become a landscaped park.

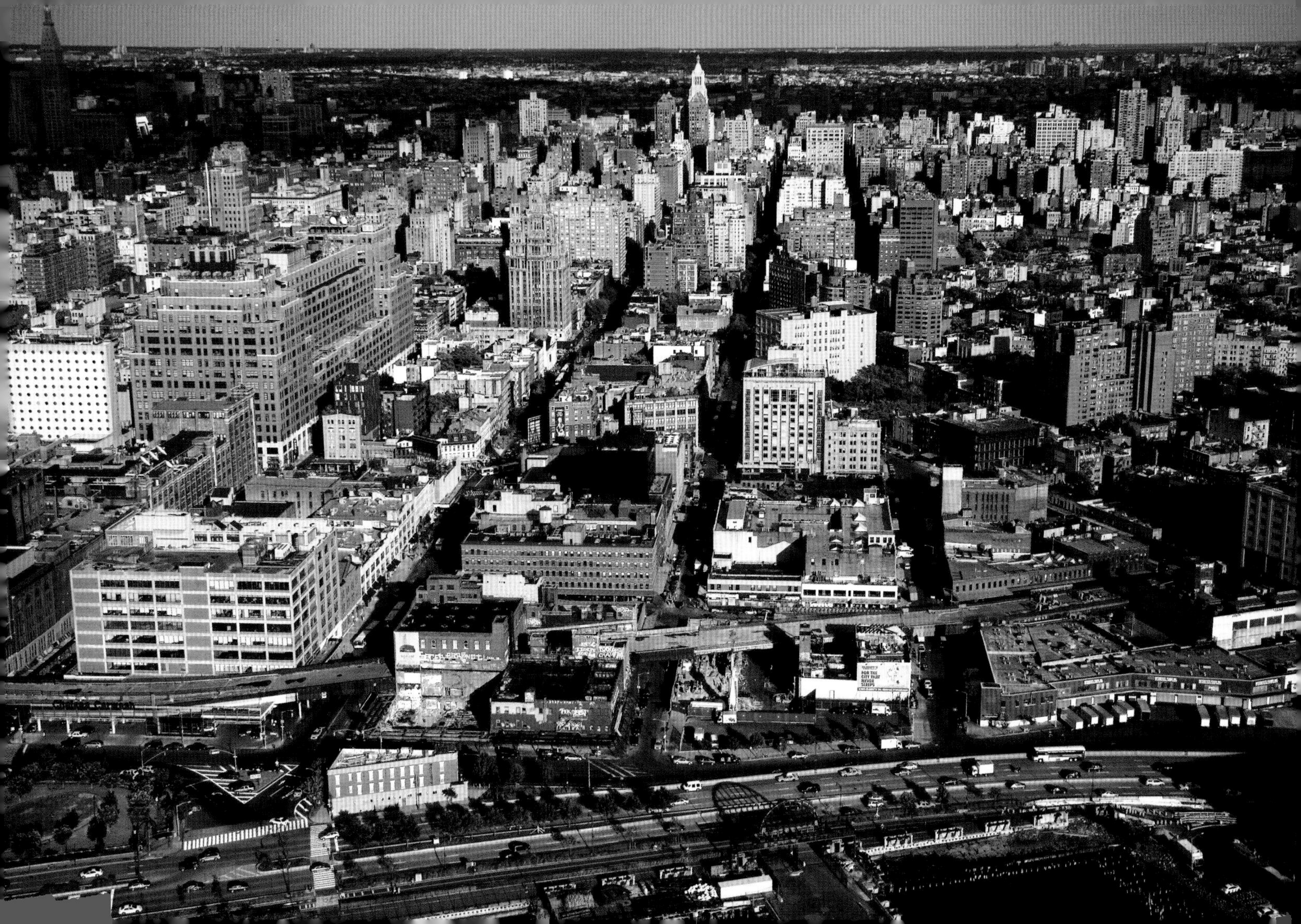
FOR THE CITY THAT NEVER SLEEPS

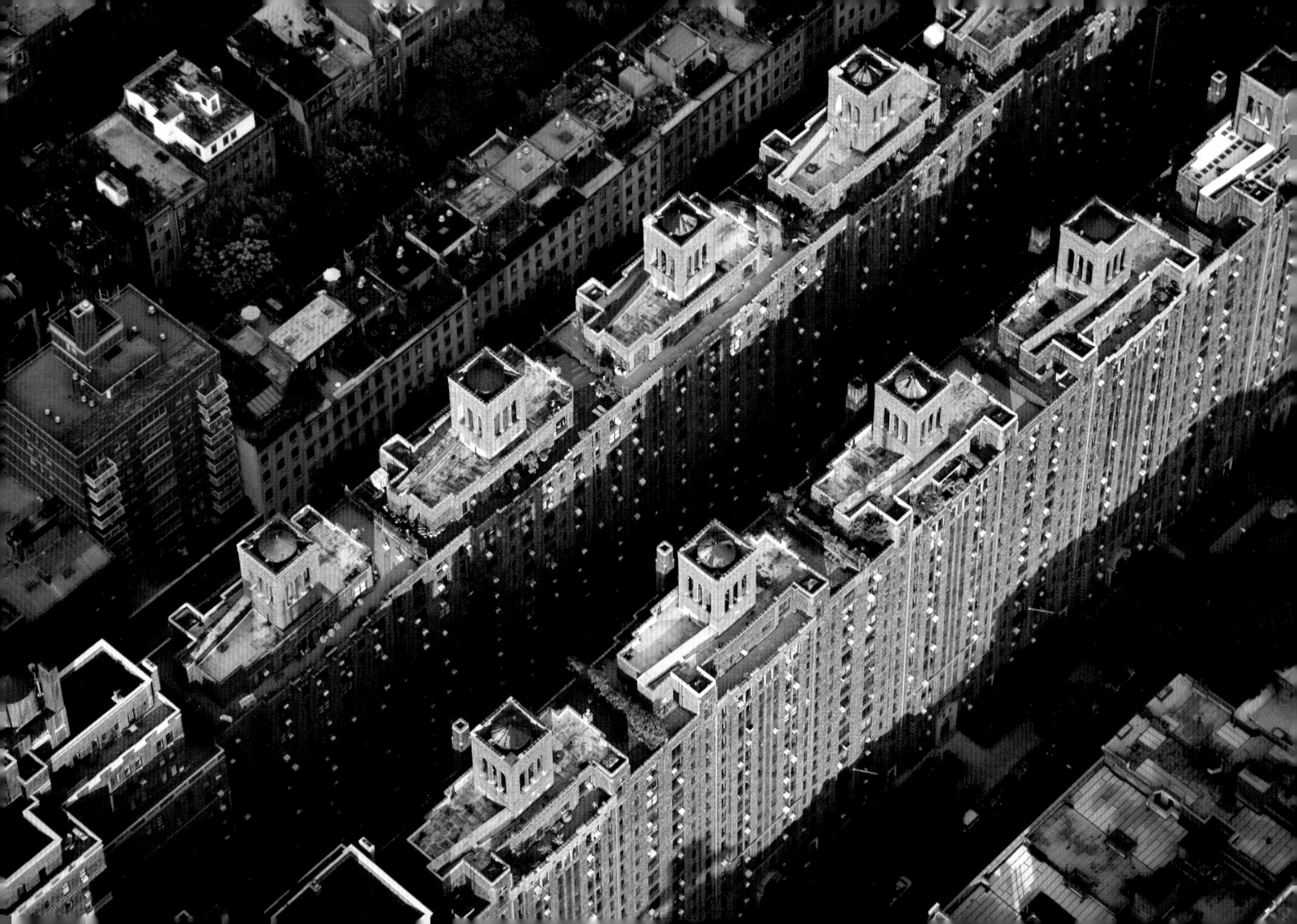

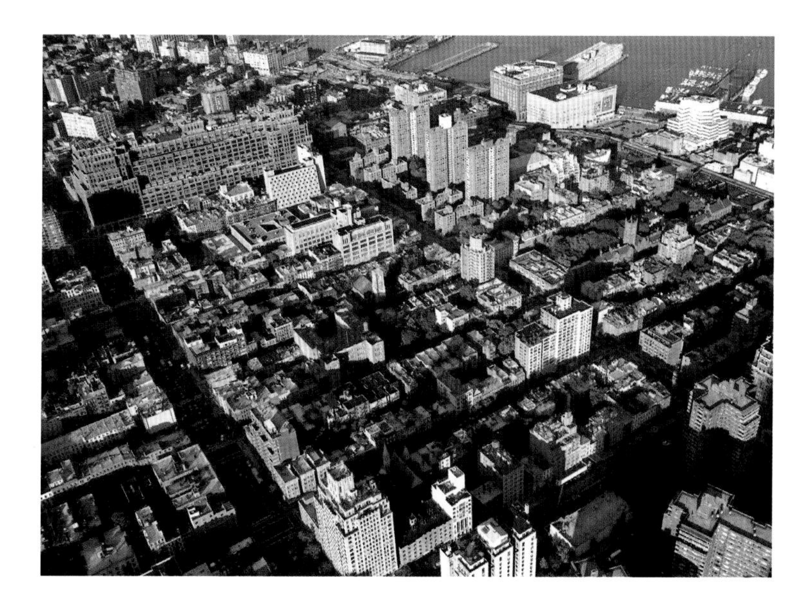

352

London Terrace, with 1665 units filling an entire block at West 23rd Street and Tenth Avenue, was the largest apartment building New York had ever seen when it was constructed in 1930.

353

Chelsea, once home to stately townhouses and later to longshoremen, now rivals Soho as a center for art galleries expensive lofts.

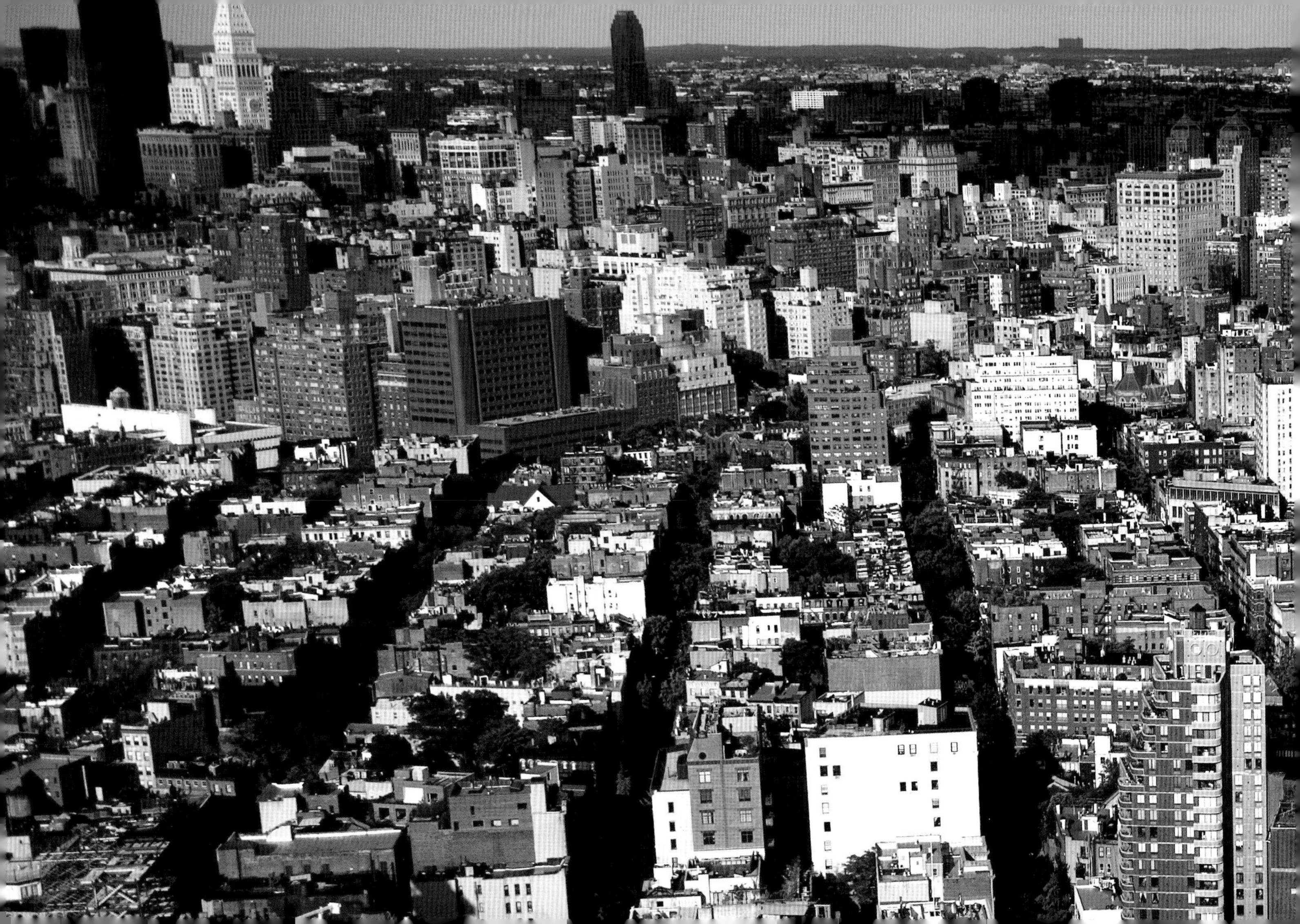

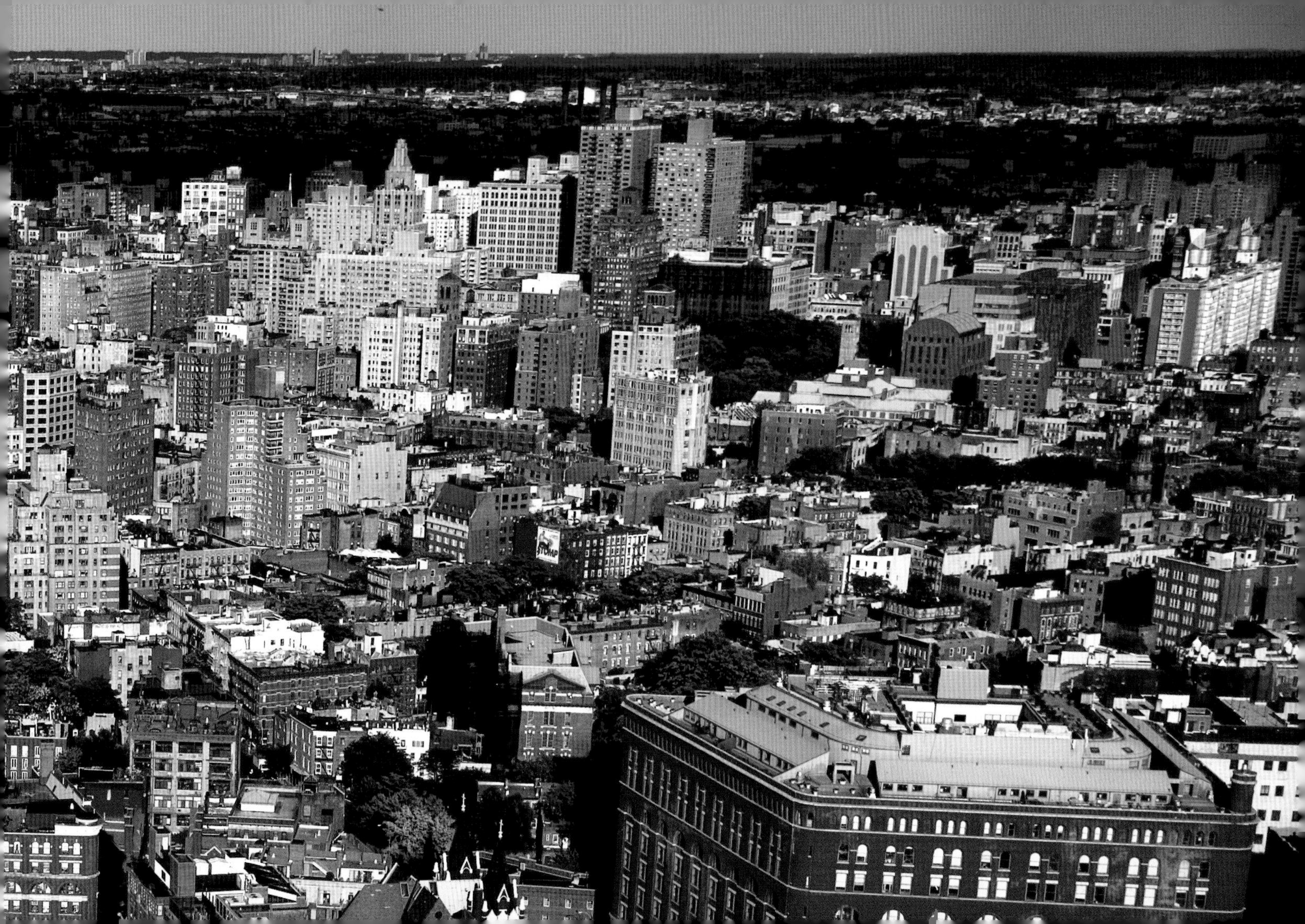
STOMP

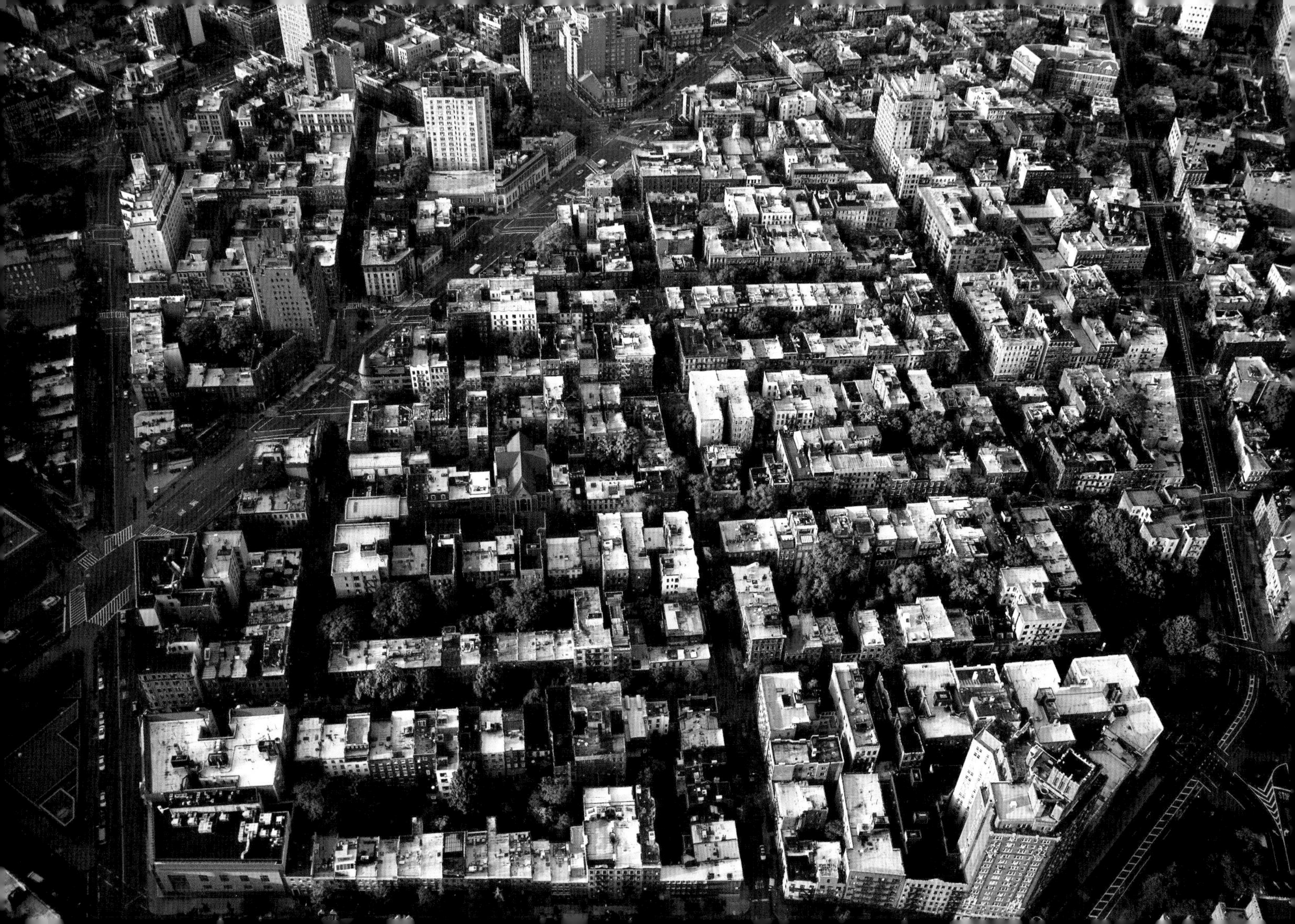

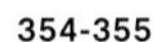

354-355

Once a rural hamlet, Greenwich Village retains its low-rise character, though wedged between the skyscrapers of midtown and downtown Manhattan.

356

Greenwich Village is one of the few places in Manhattan that does not conform to the grid pattern, with streets and alleys that cut across blocks at many odd angles.

357

The Victorian Gothic Jefferson Market, on Sixth Avenue at West 10th Street, was once a courthouse and is now a public library. The clock tower originally served as a fire lookout.

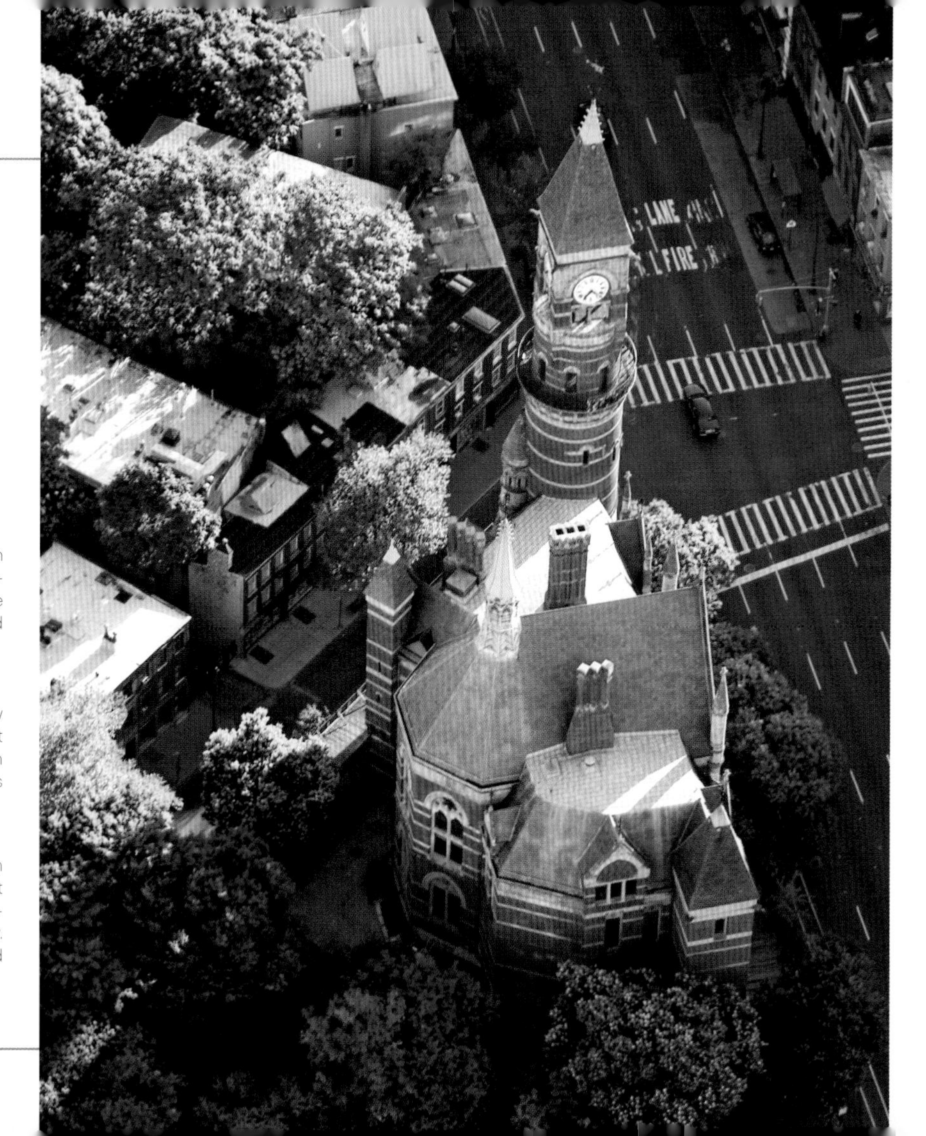

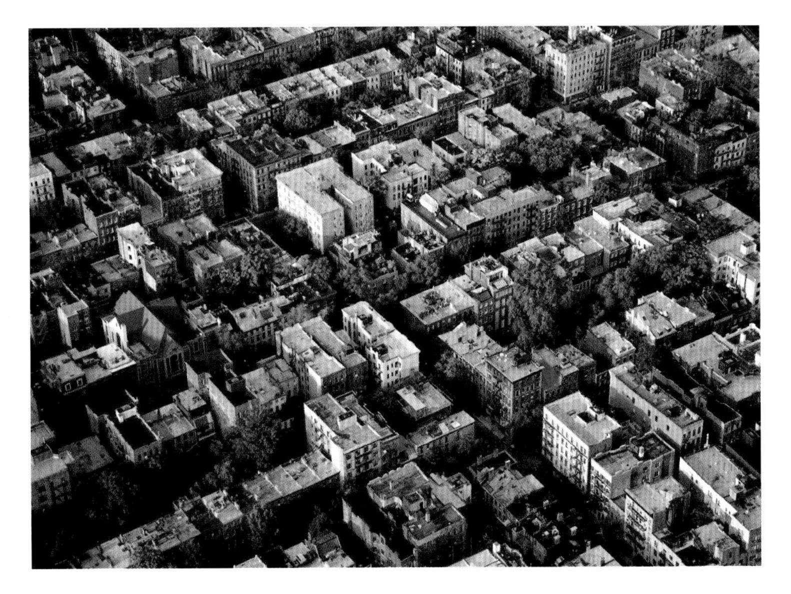

358

In addition to charming cobblestone streets and historic townhouses, Greenwich Village is also one of the greener areas of New York. Trees and community gardens are abundant.

359

The Archives, a luxury condominium and office complex, was once the U.S. Federal Archives Building. Across Christopher Street is St. Veronica's Church, built in 1889–90 to serve Catholic longshoremen.

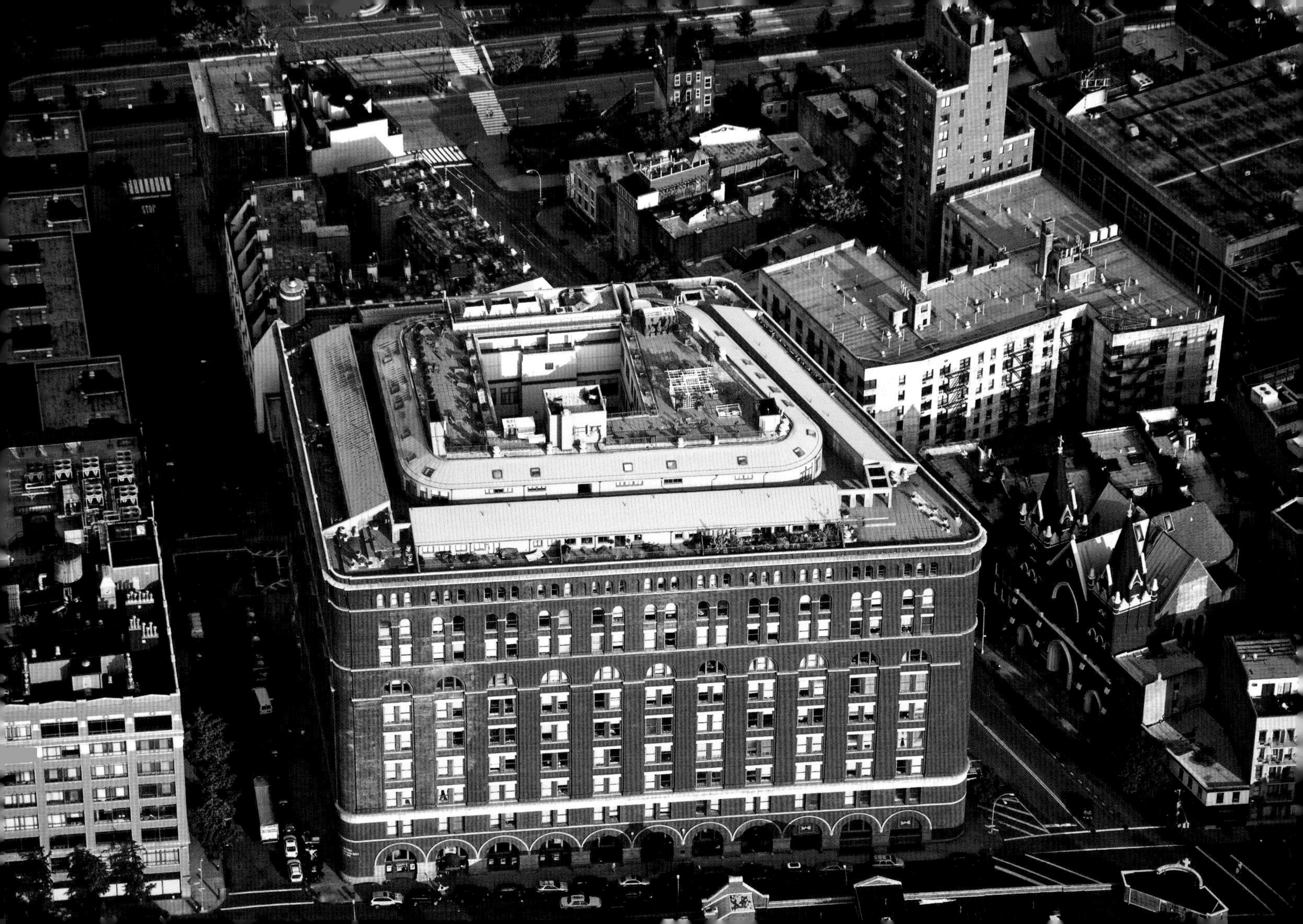

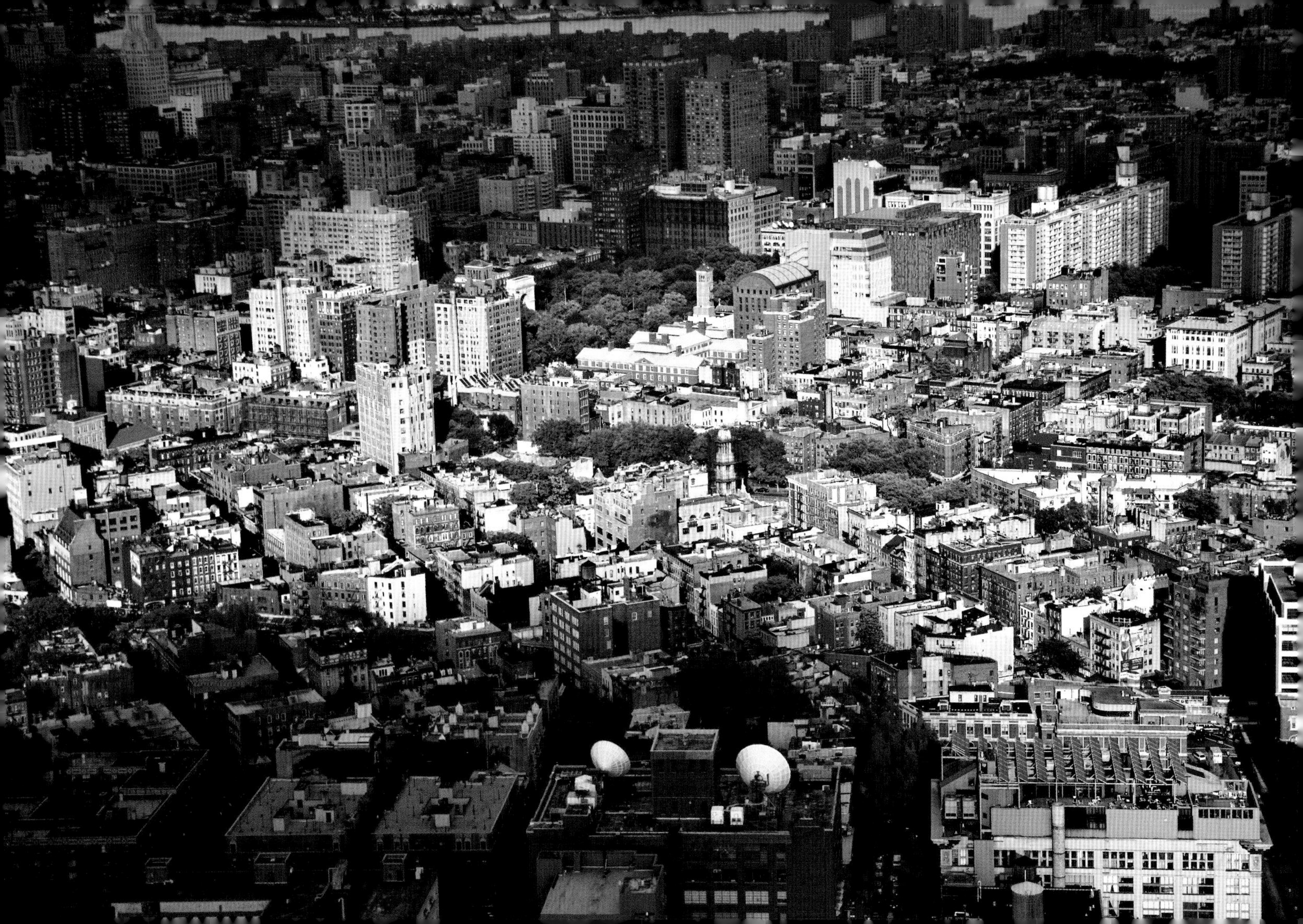

360
New York University buildings and dorms dominate much of Greenwich Village surrounding Washington Square.

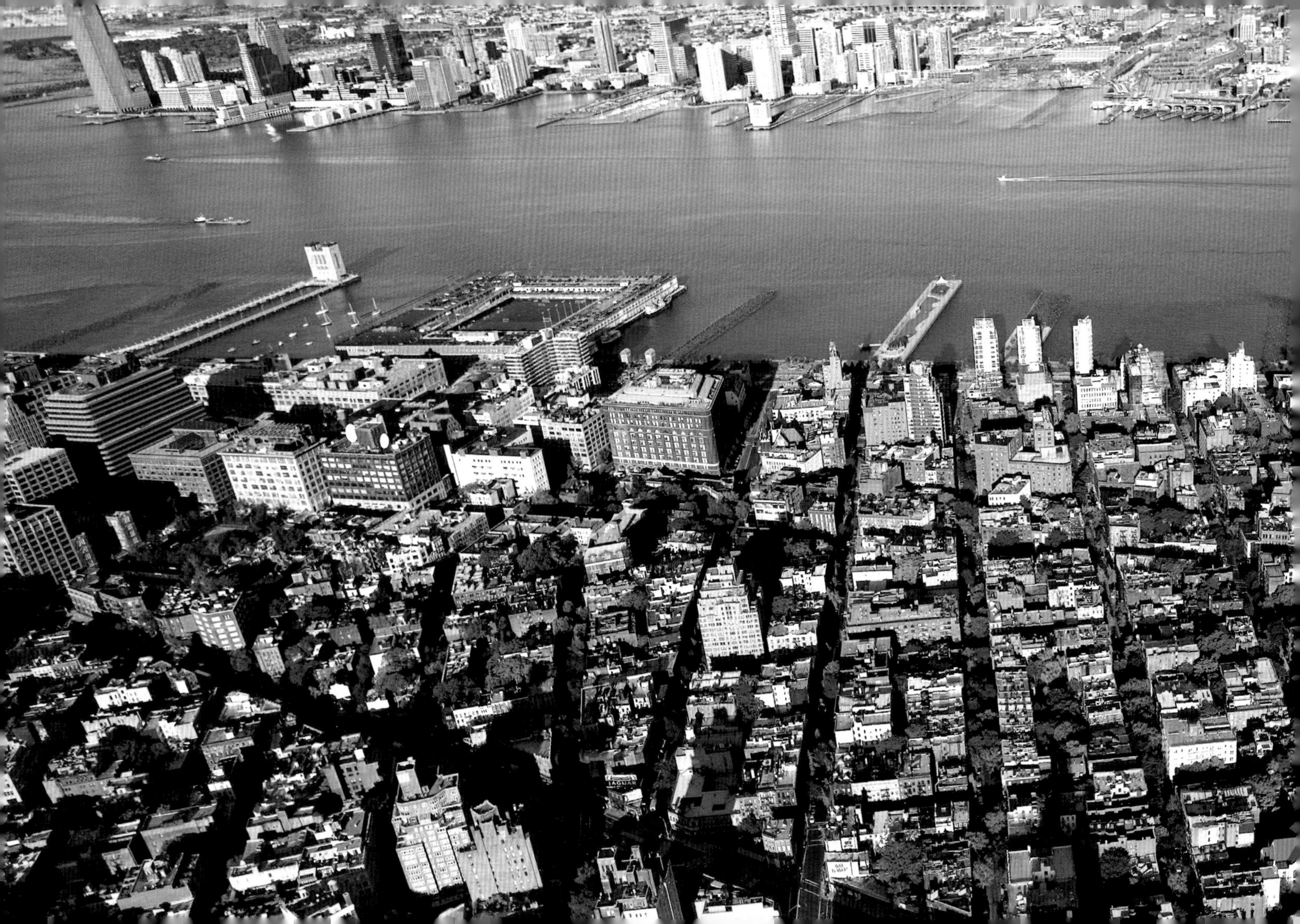

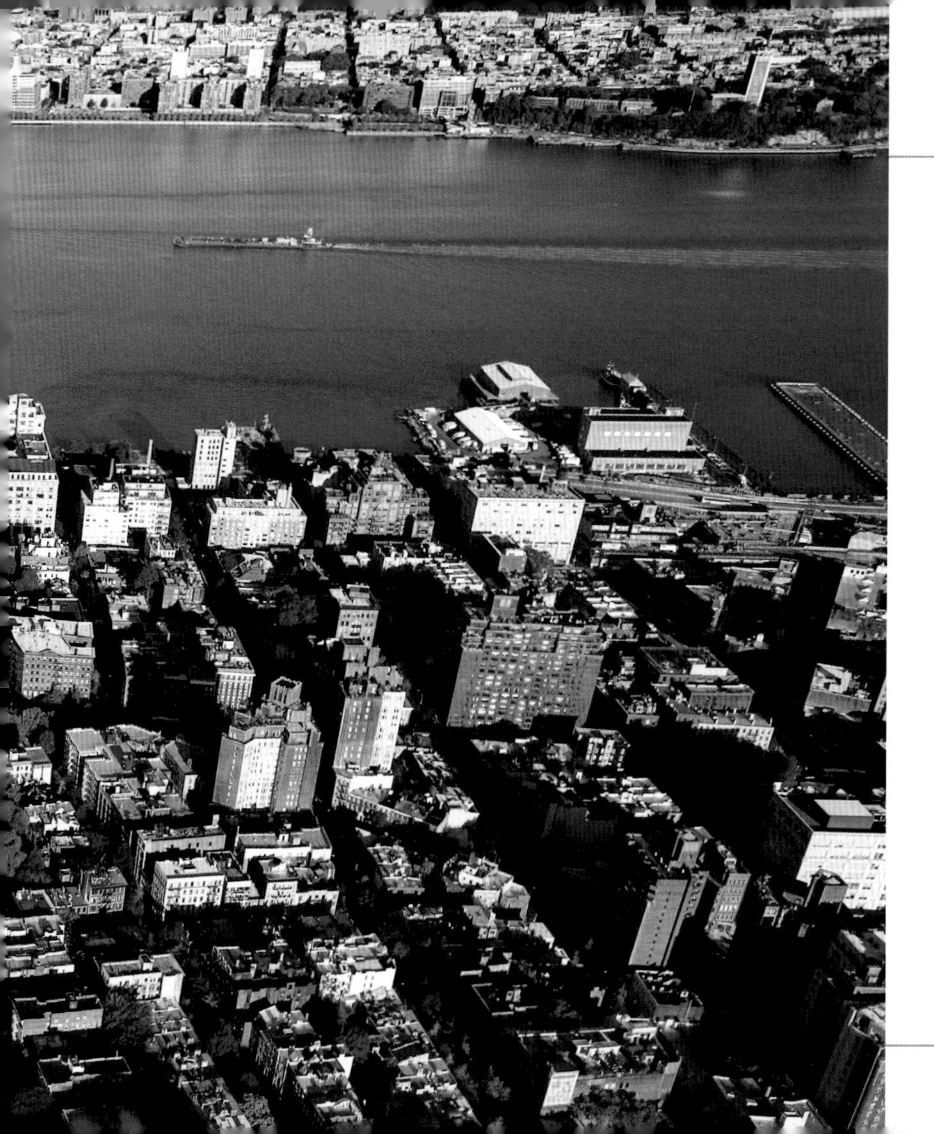

362-363
Abandoned and derelict twenty years ago, the Hudson riverfront has been reborn as a vital and exciting place to live and play, from the Chelsea Piers to Pier 40 at Houston Street, with indoor and outdoor athletic fields.

365

Pier 40, at West Houston Street and the Hudson River, houses the Pier Park and Playground Association, as well as fields for soccer, baseball, football, rugby and lacrosse. The athletes share space with a long-term parking garage.

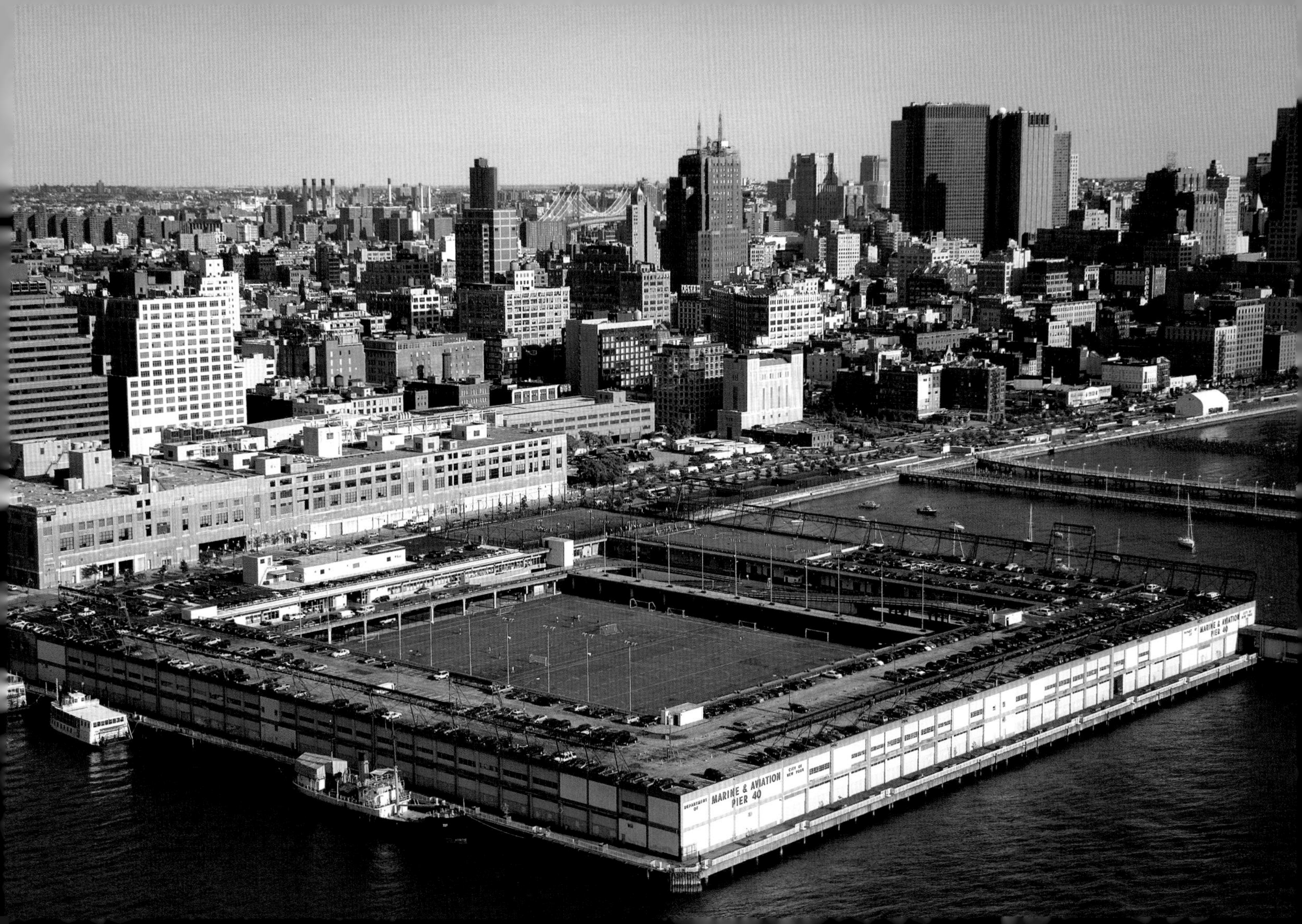
MARINE & AVIATION
PIER 40

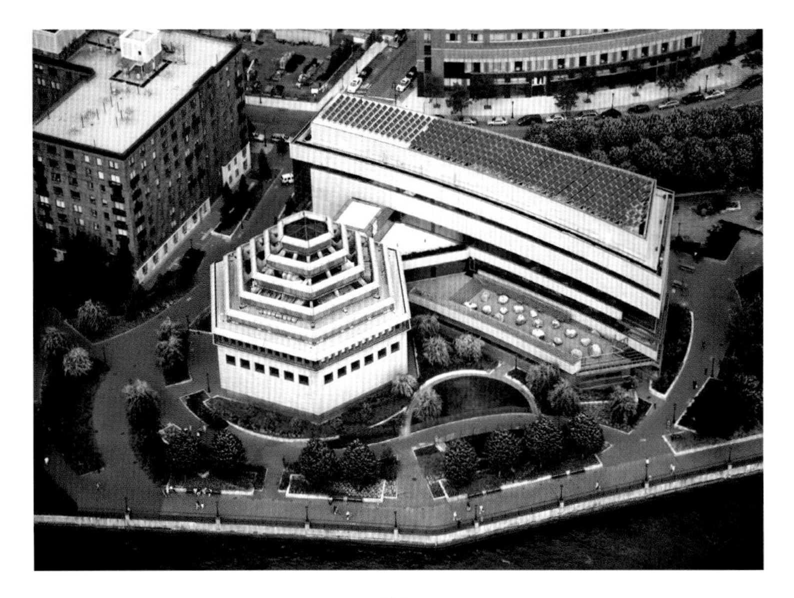

366

The Museum of Jewish Heritage is a living memorial to the Holocaust, located at the southern end of Battery Park City. Its six-sided shape symbolizes the Star of David and the six million Jews who died in the Holocaust.

367

The tip of the island is where New York began; its area has increased since the Dutch first settled here, thanks to landfill extending Battery Park and the shores of the Hudson and East Rivers.

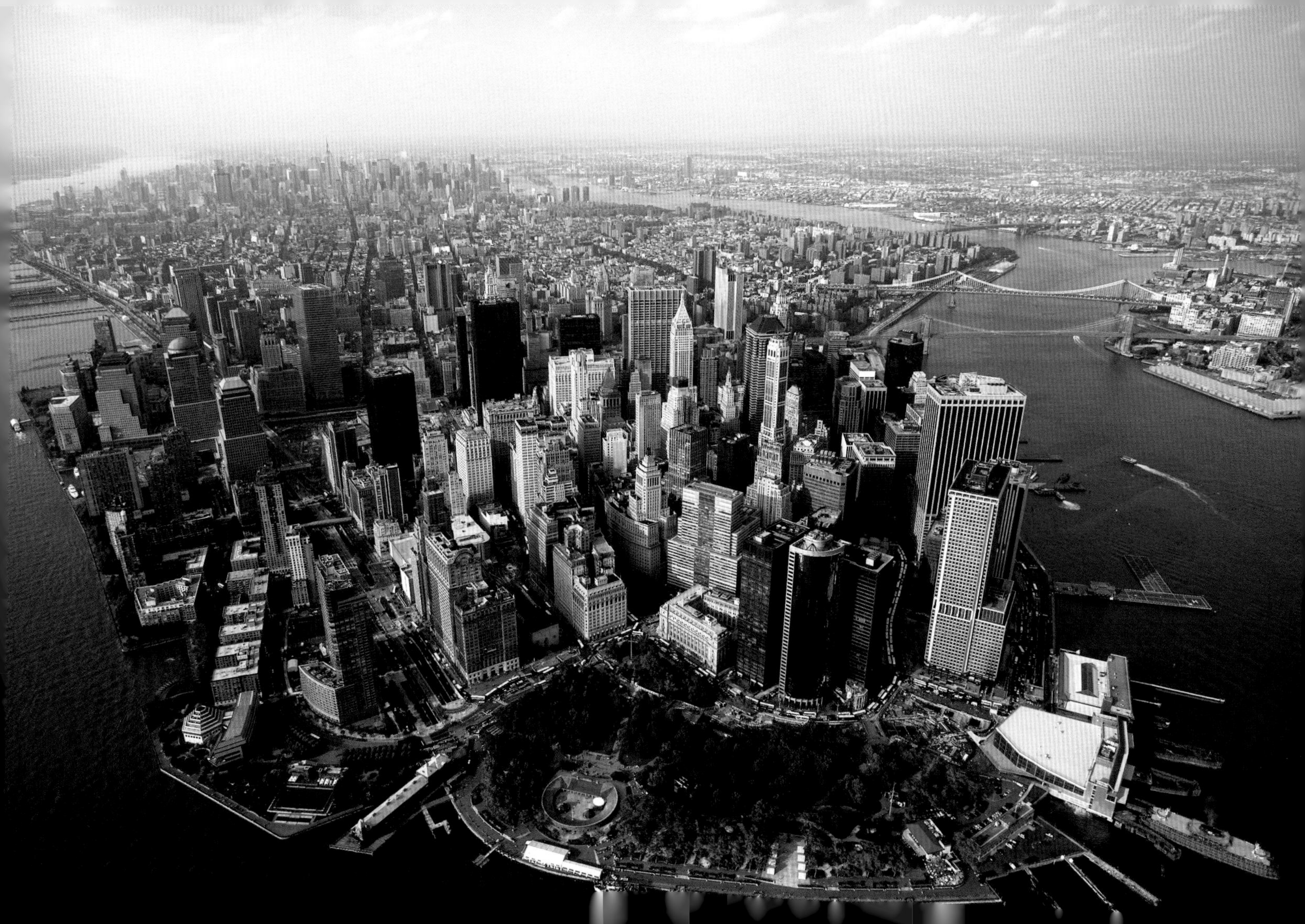

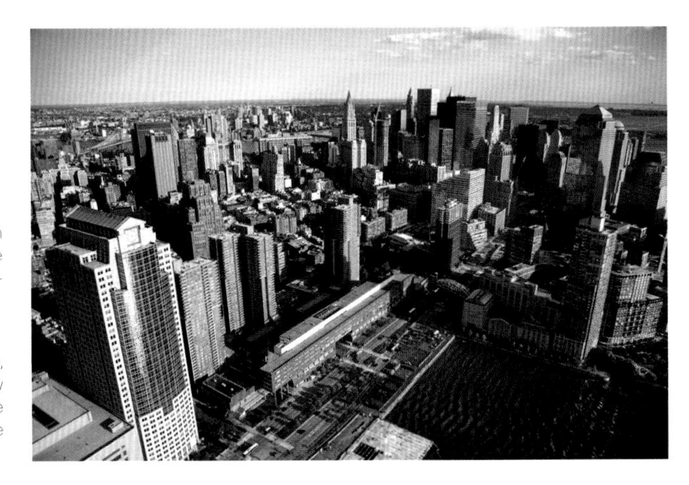

368
The low-slung modern Borough of Manhattan Community College is perpendicular to the North Esplanade of Battery Park City.

369
The former U.S. Customs House, a u-shaped building just below Bowling Green, is now the home of the National Museum of the American Indian.

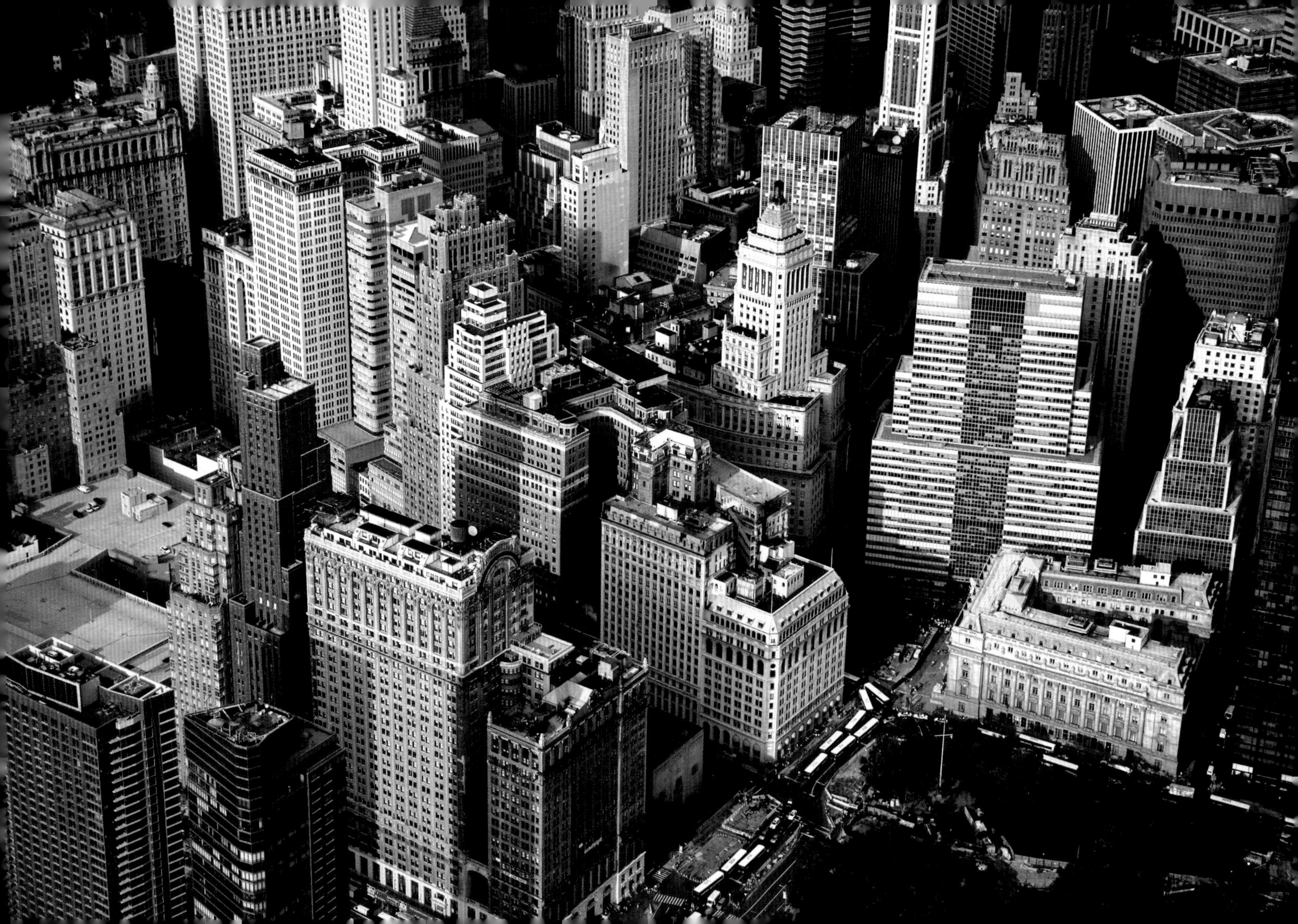

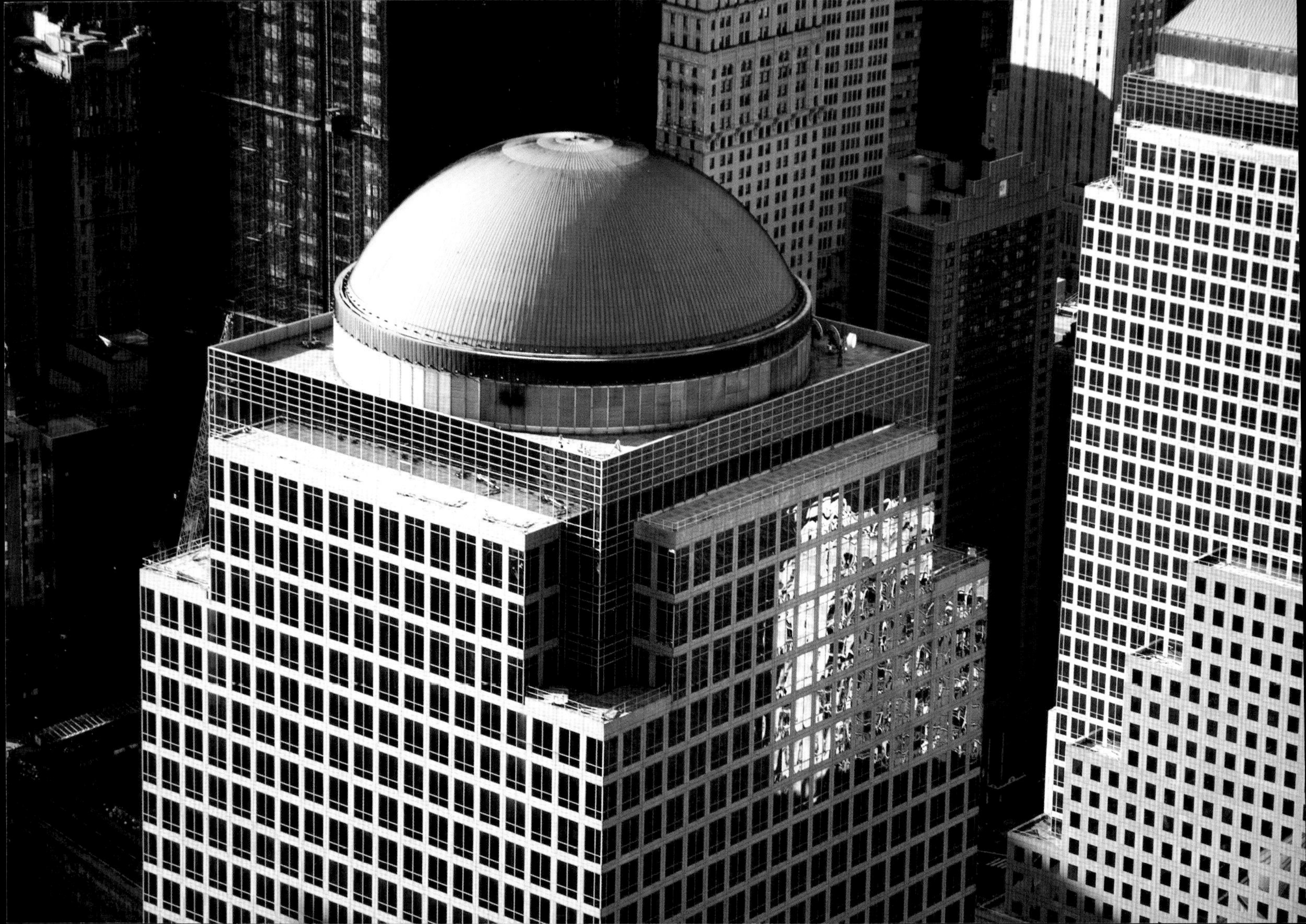

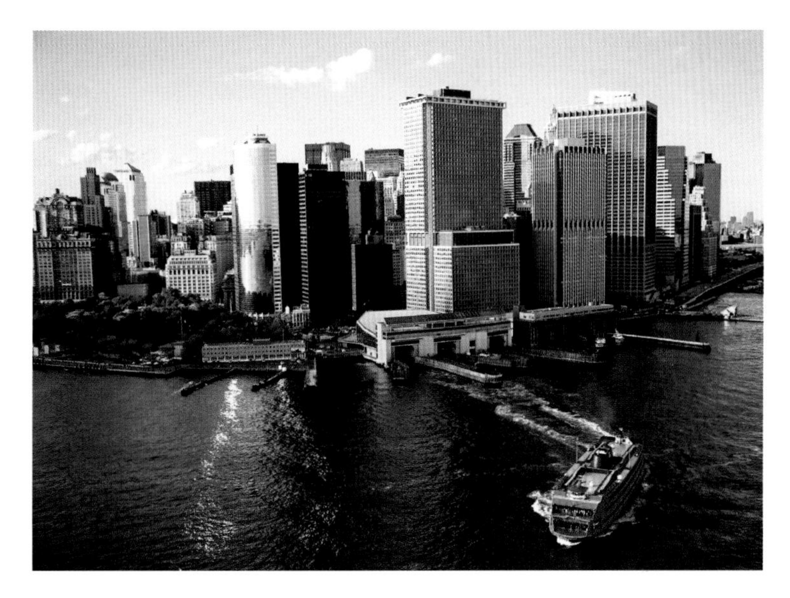

370

The Cesar Pelli-designed domed tower of 2 World Financial Center is home to Merrill Lynch, and is part of a complex of offices, restaurants and retail spaces, overlooking Battery Park City's North Cove marina.

371

The ferry at the southern tip of the island is free of charge and has carried commuters to and from Manhattan and Staten Island since 1817, and also offers one of the best views of New York harbor.

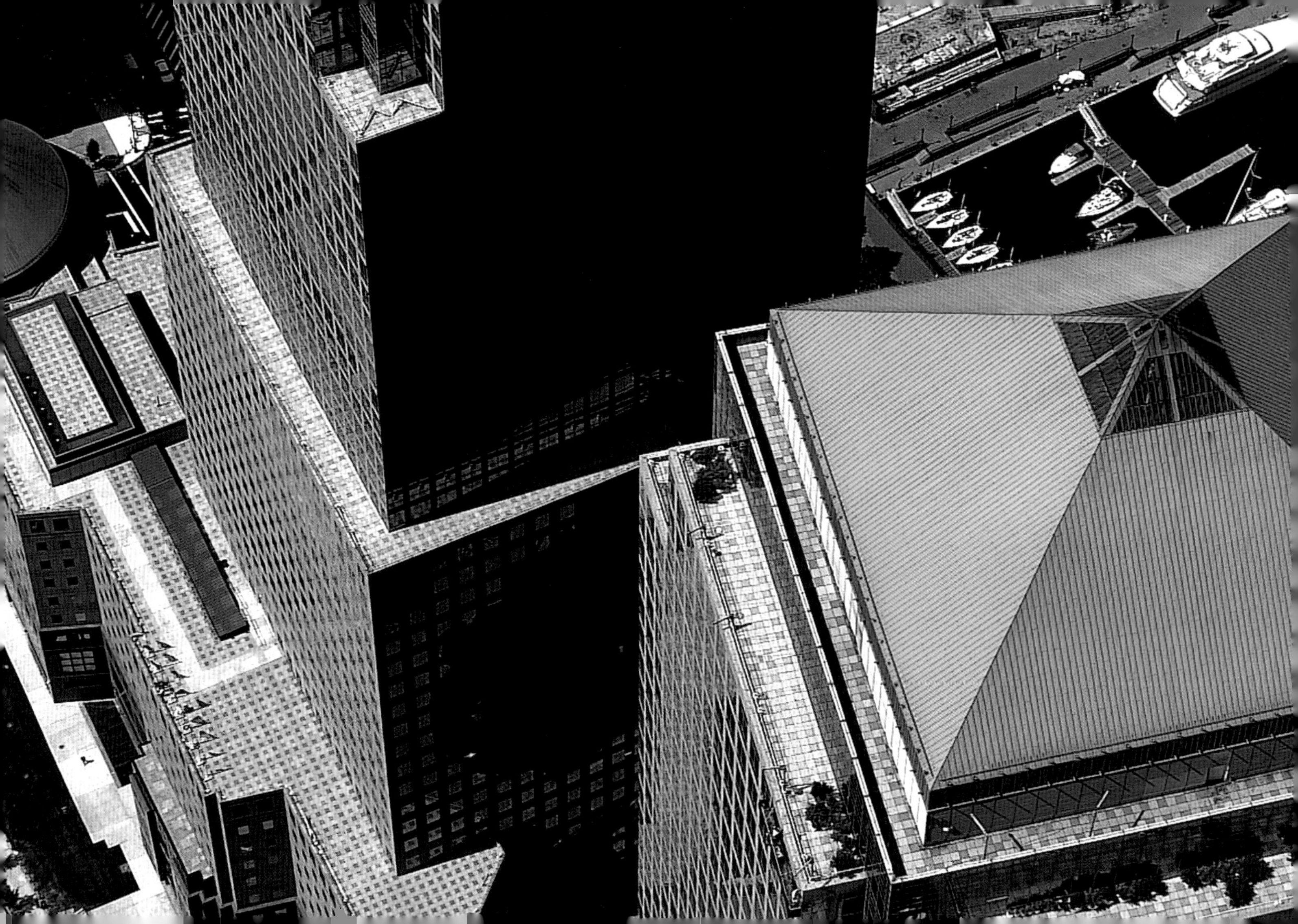

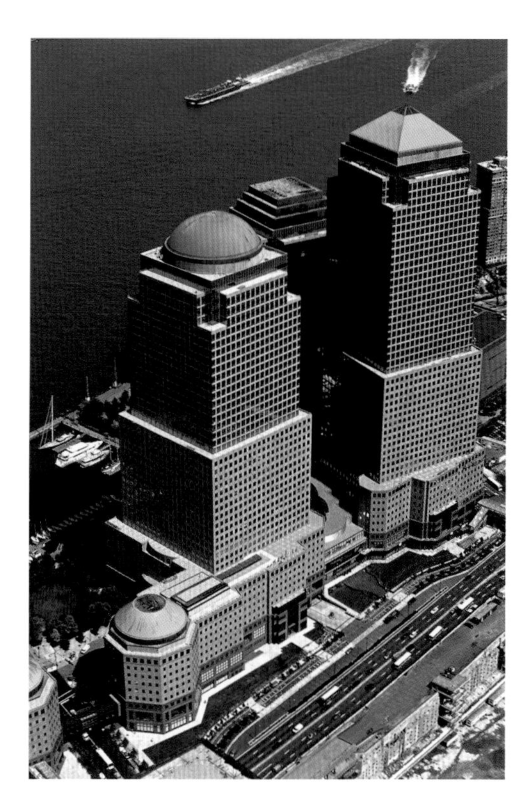

372 and 373
The World Financial Center is a complex of commercial buildings designed by César Pelli. Major companies such as Merrill Lynch, American Express, Dow Jones & Company and Deloitte & Touch have offices here.

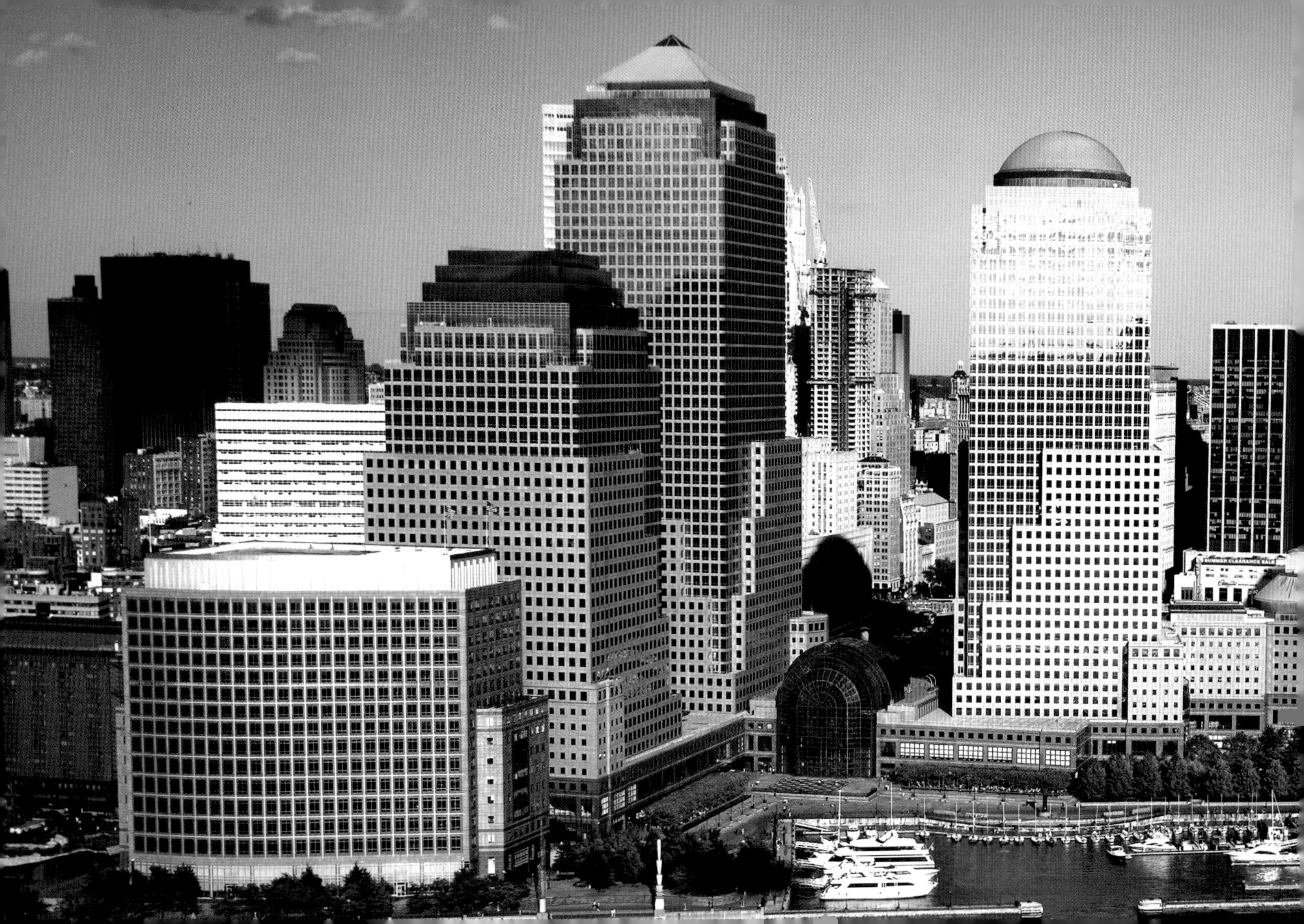
SUMMER CLEARANCE SALE

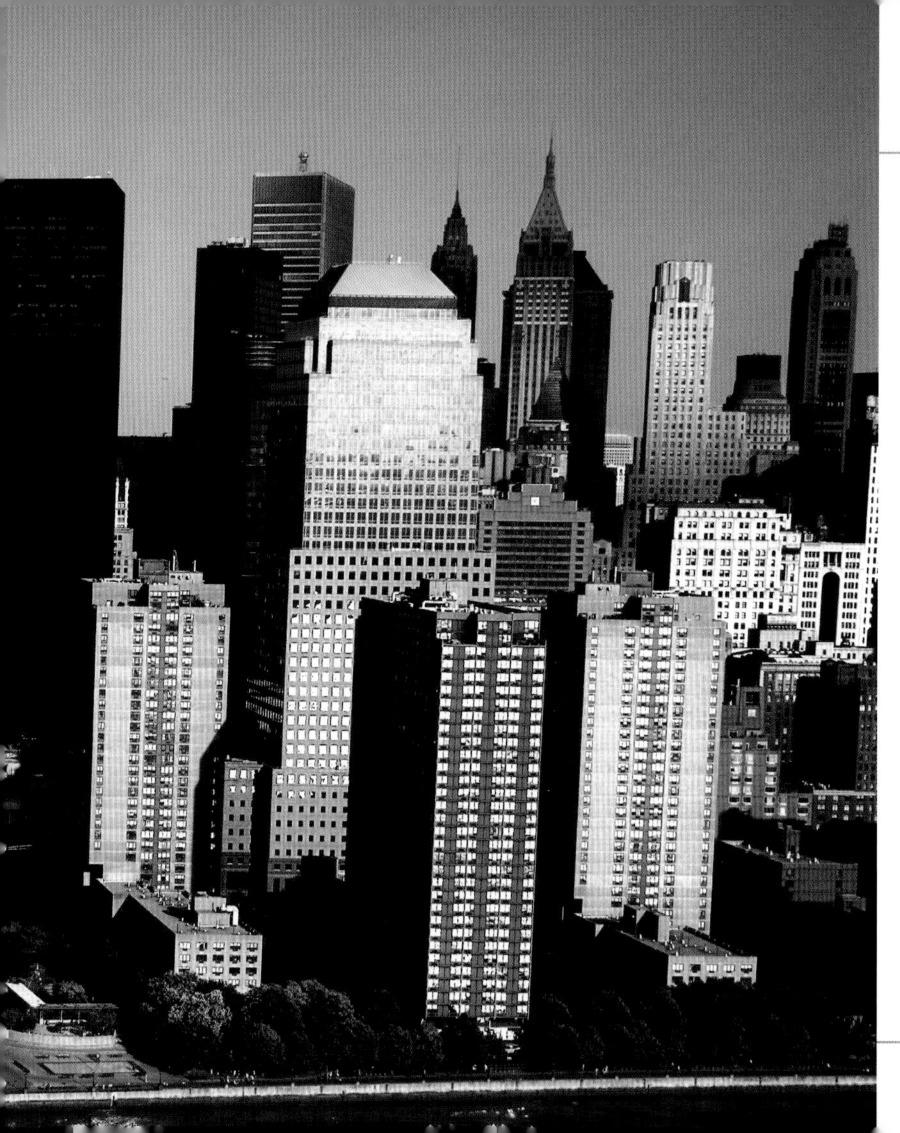

374-375
The distinctive copper roof tops of the four World Financial Center Towers include a dome, a solid pyramid, a cut pyramid and a stepped pyramid. Though heavily damaged in the September 11, 2001 attacks, the center underwent extensive renovation and reopened in 2002.

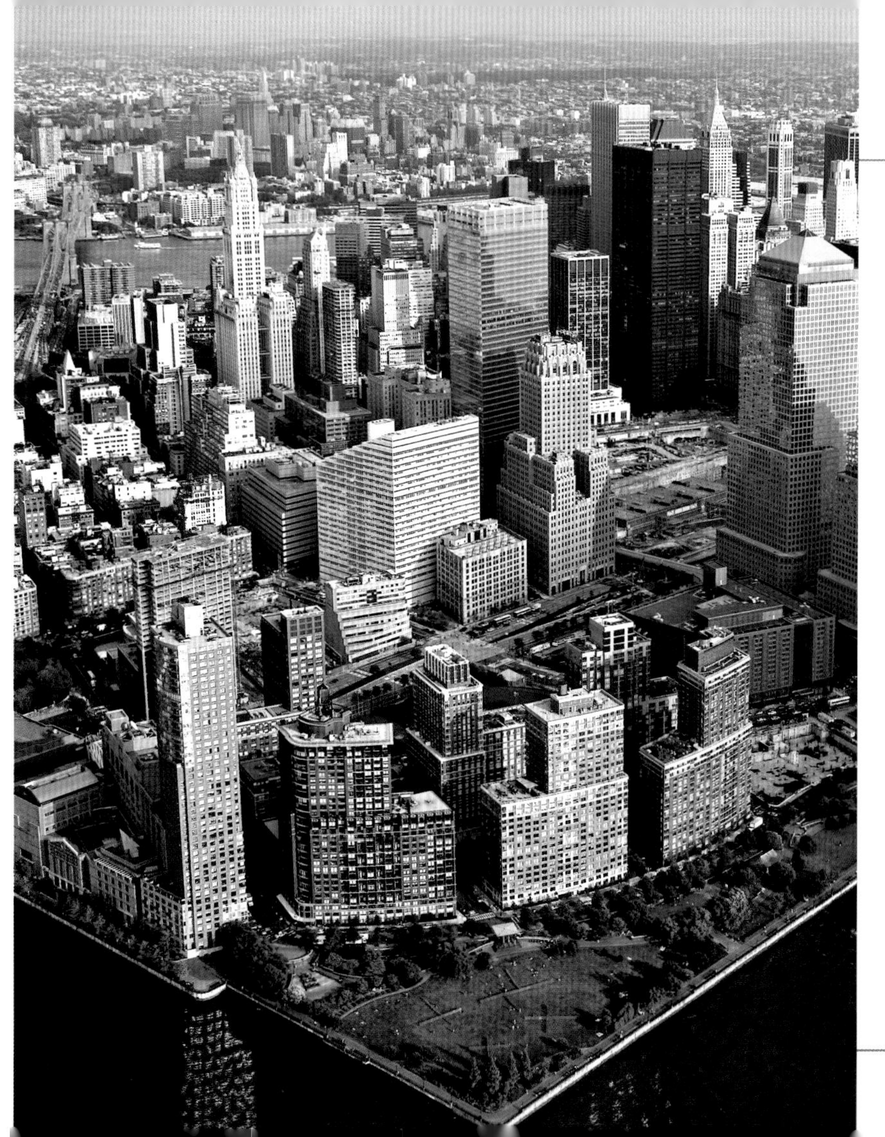

376

Ever resourceful, New Yorkers have created land where once there was river; Battery Park City, with grassy lawns and a riverfront esplanade, was built on fill from the excavation of the foundation for the World Trade Center.

377

Rockefeller Park sits at the northwestern corner of Battery Park City, a 90-acre planned community of apartments, parks, offices and stores.

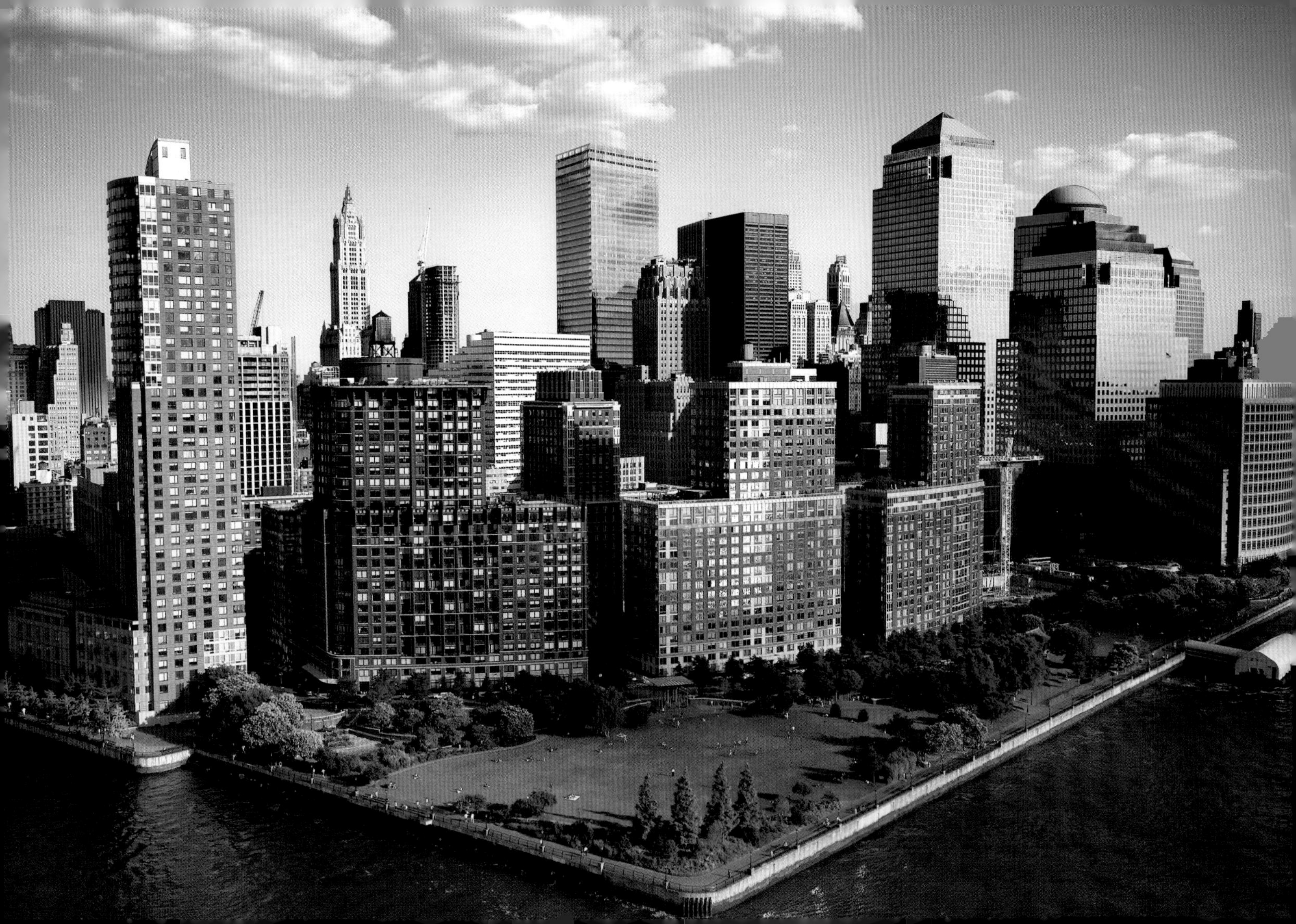

379
The gaping 16-acre space left after the destruction of the World Trade Center is a visible sign of dramatic impact of the terrorist attacks; plans are underway to rebuild the area, with the 415-meter Freedom Tower as its centerpiece.

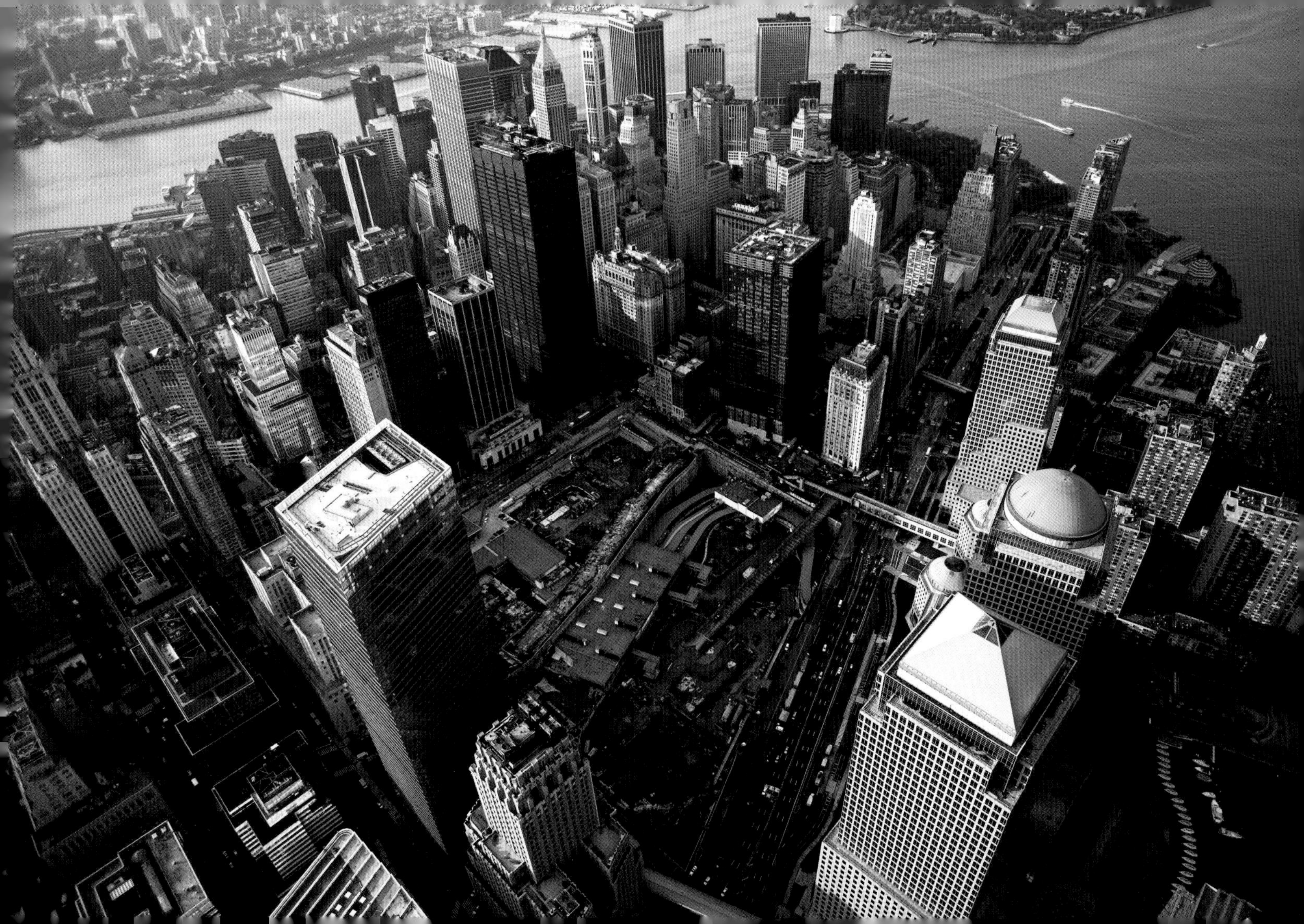

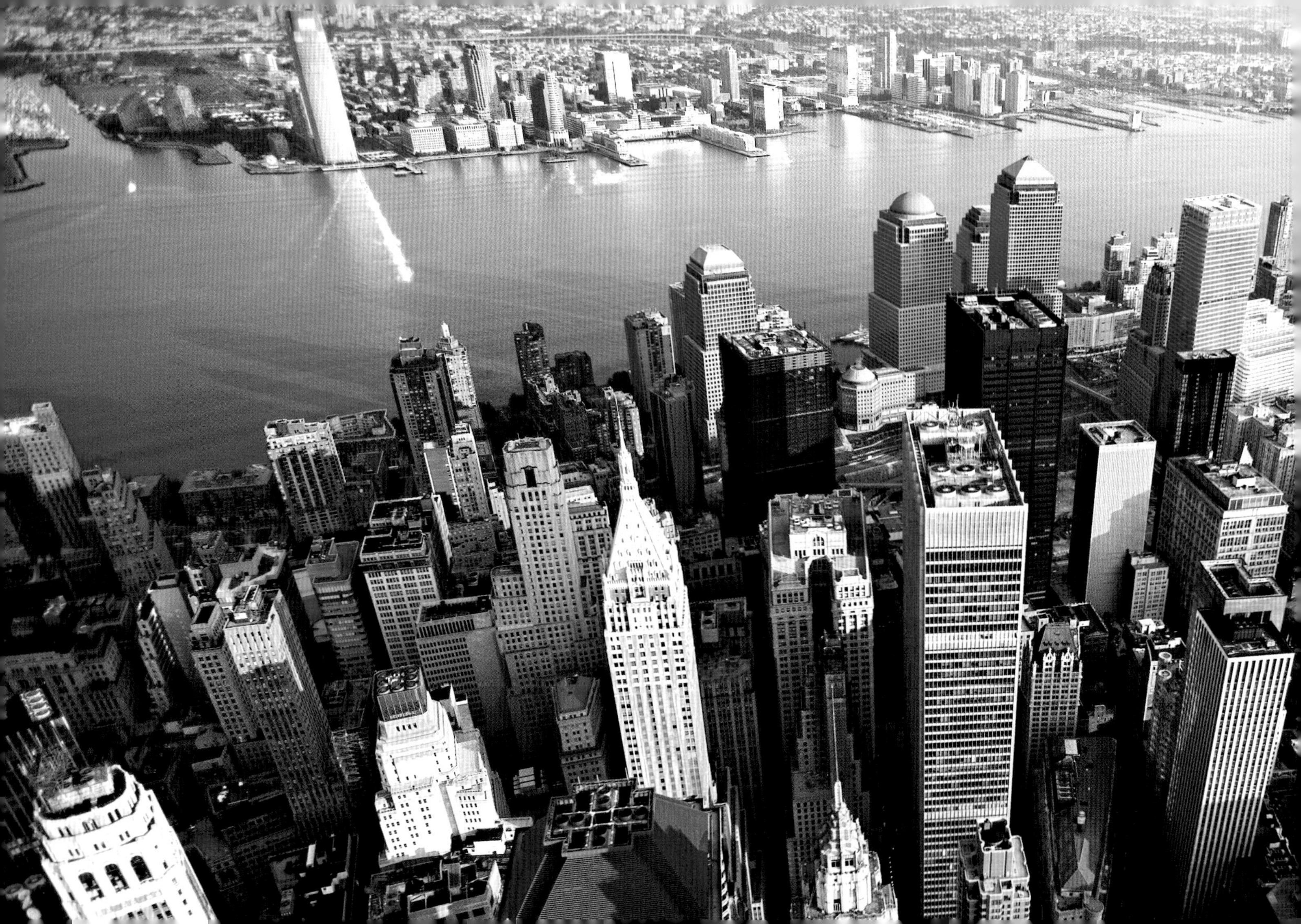

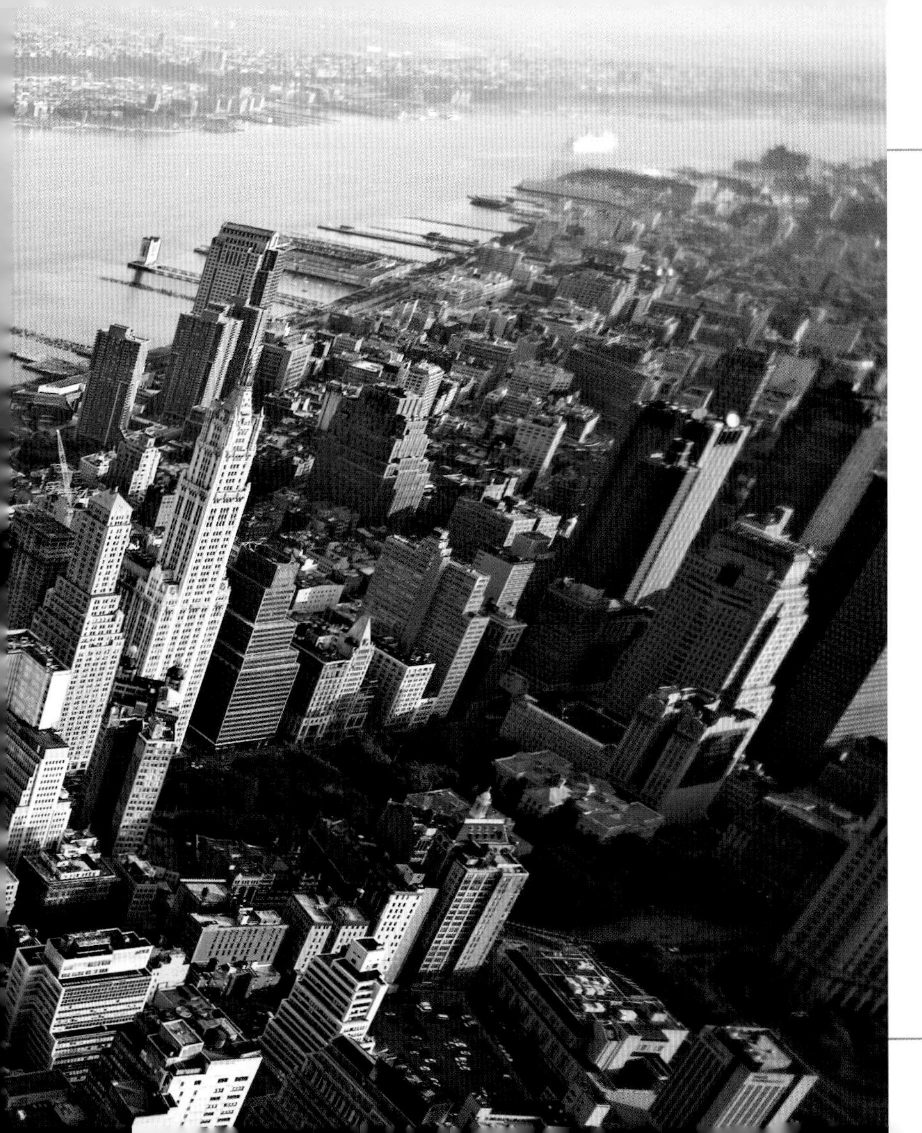

380-381
Power and high finance are concentrated in Wall Street and the surrounding areas. From left to right it is possible to recognize Exchange Place (in the foreground), 40 Wall Street with its distinctive green pinnacle, and the imposing One Chase Manhattan Plaza, one of New York City's ten highest skyscrapers.

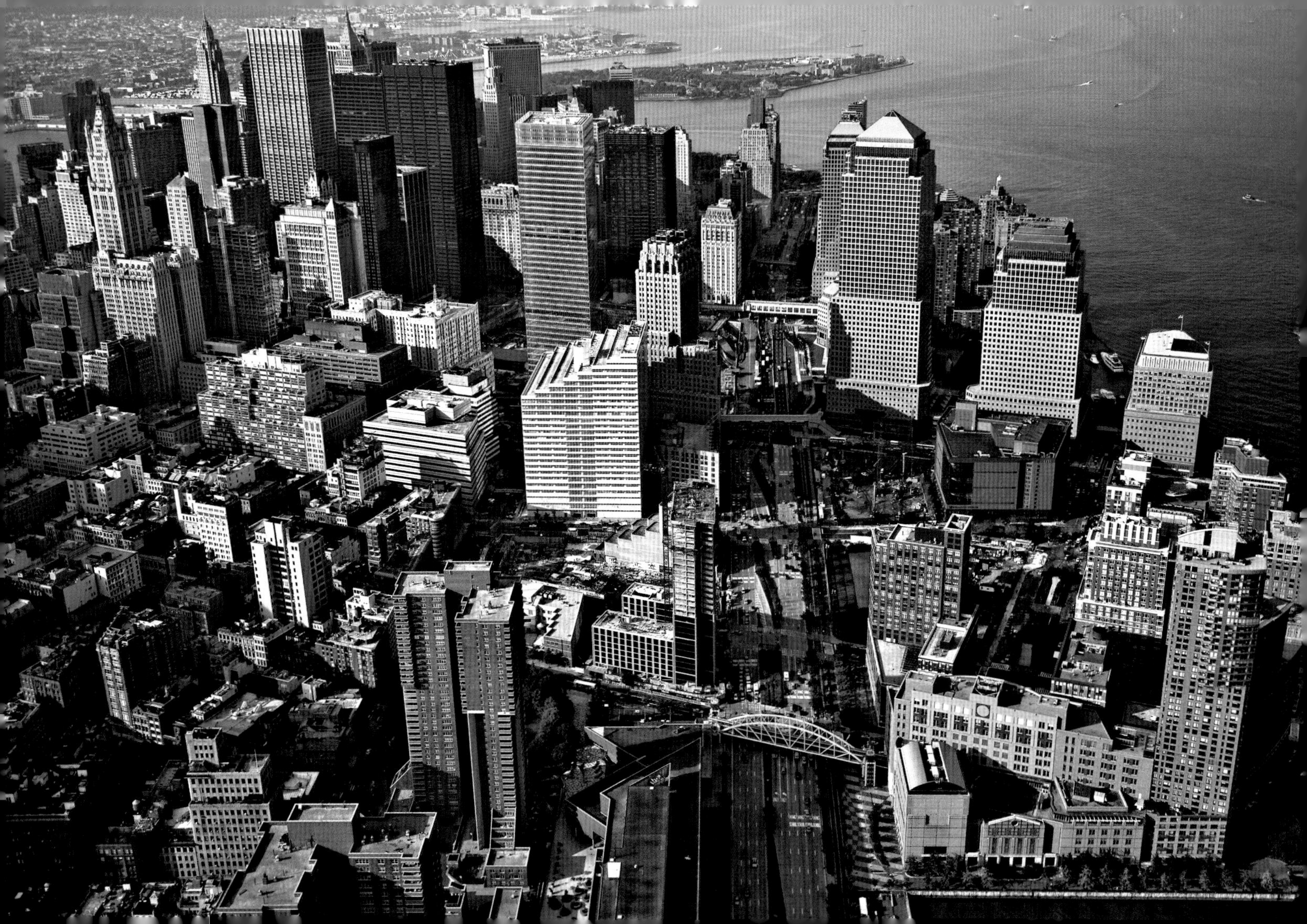

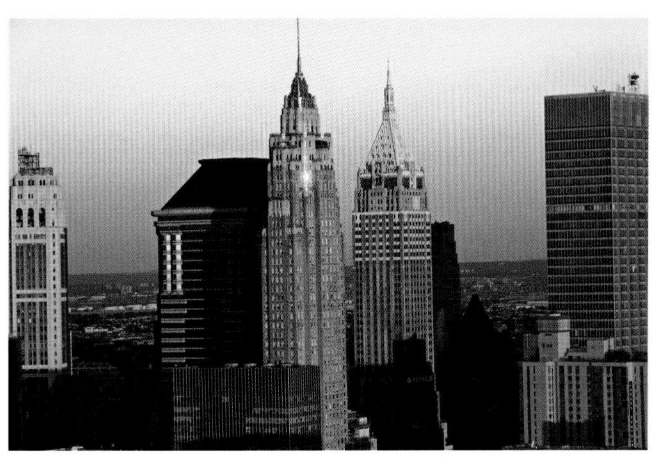

382
Stuyvesant High School (lower right) is one of Manhattan's most competitive public schools.

383
The AIG Building and the Trump Building were the second-generation of Financial District skyscrapers.

384-385
Chase Manhattan Building, One Liberty Plaza, the Morgan Bank and the World Financial Center buildings surround 40 Wall Street and 70 Pine Street.

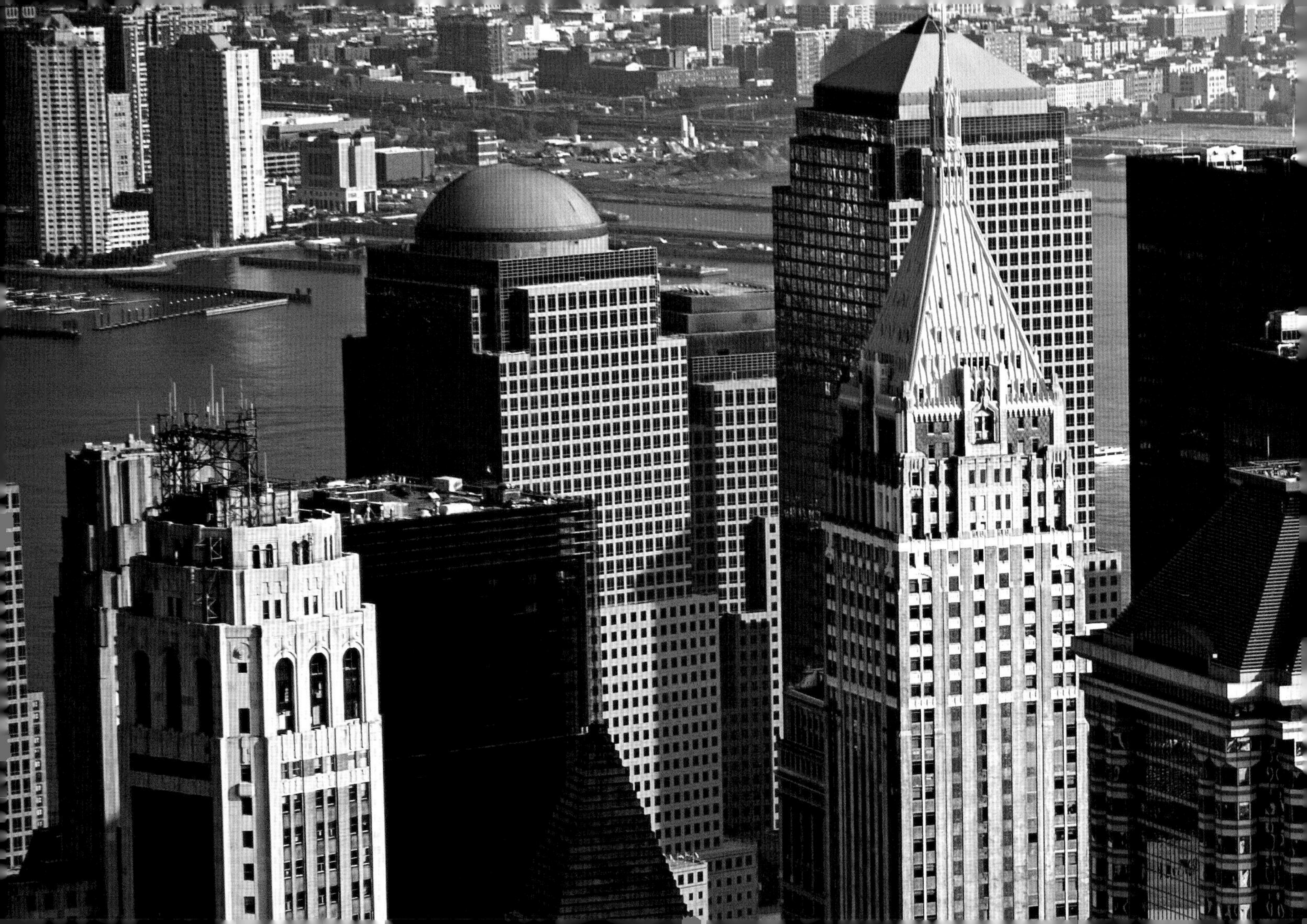

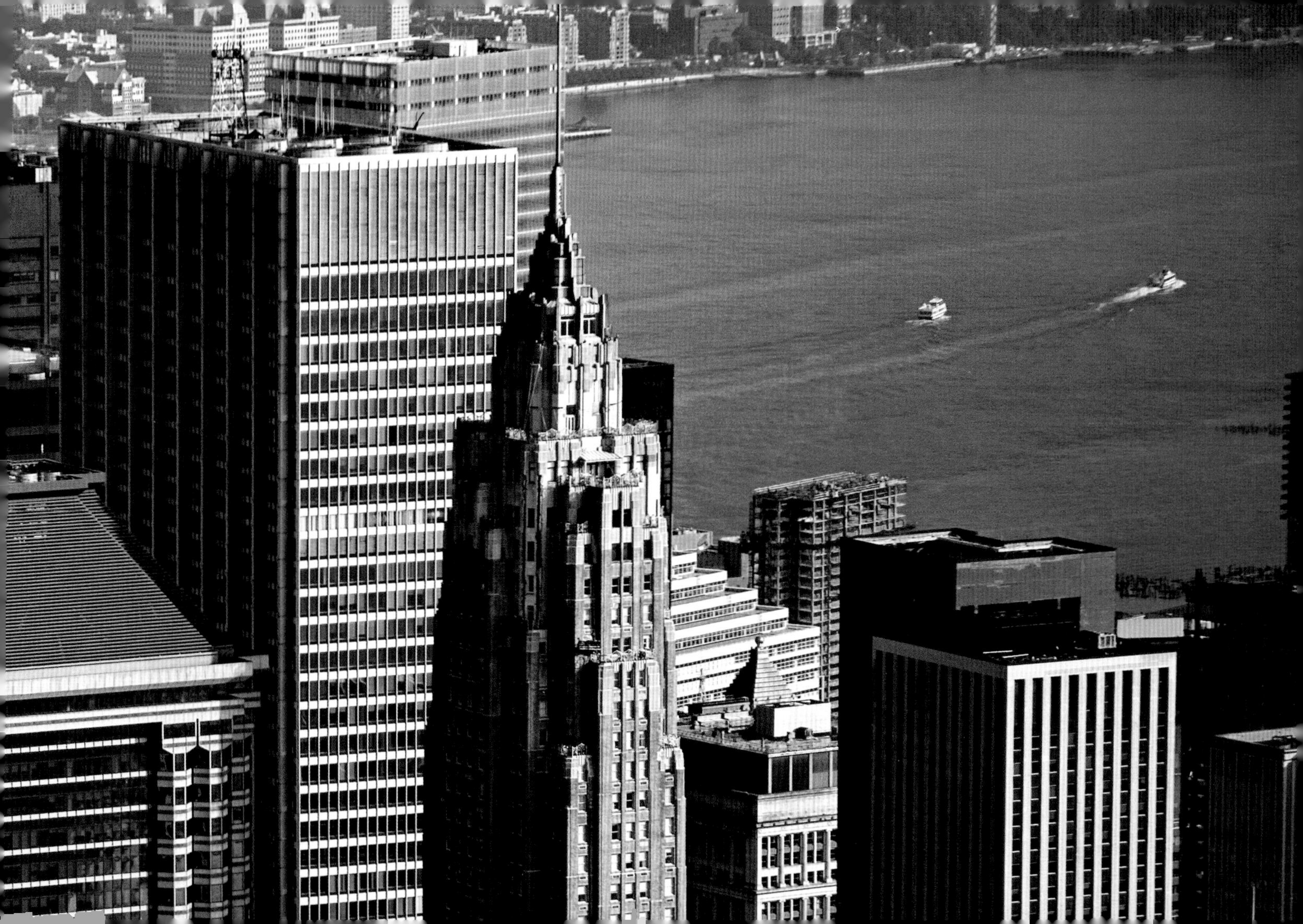

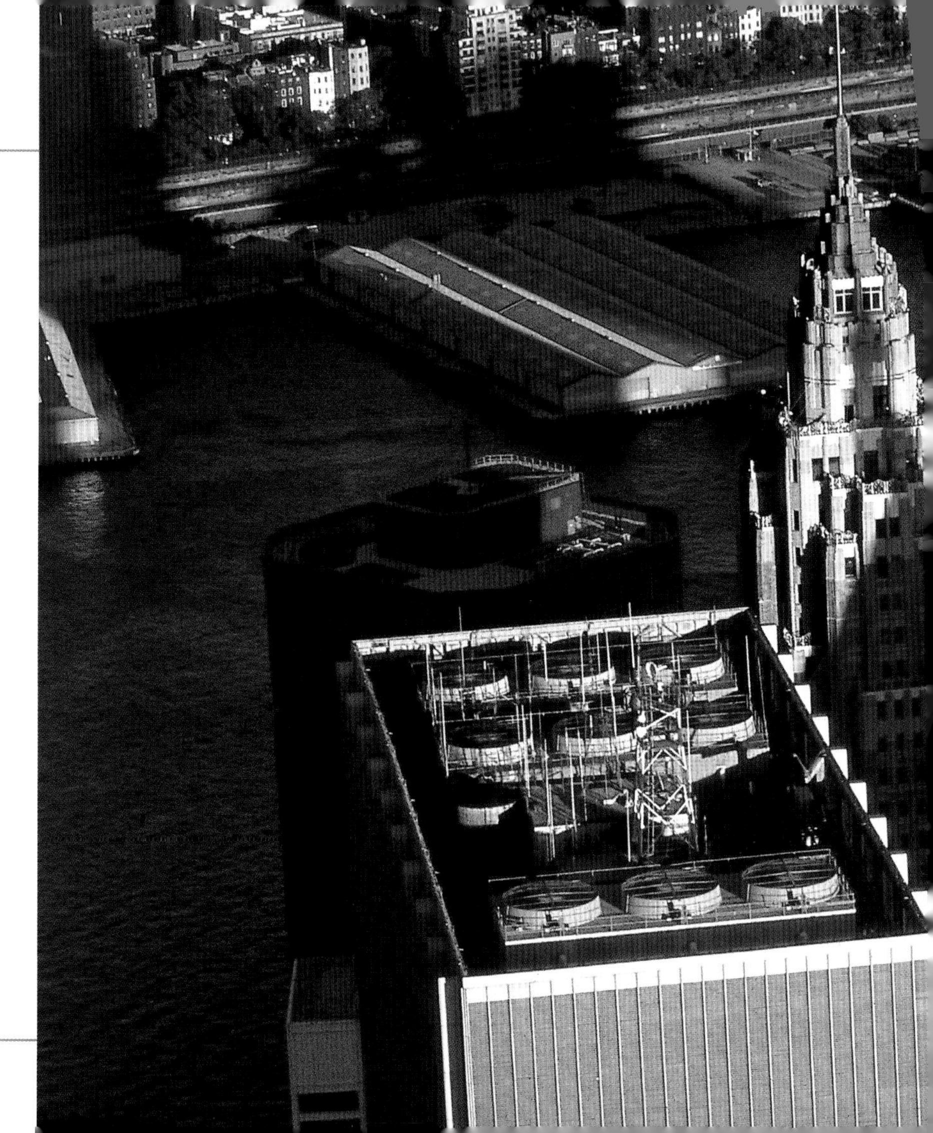

386-387
The spires of the Trump Building (right) and the American International Building (left), with their distinctively Neo-Gothic style, evoke the splendor of France's medieval chateaux and are considered among the most beautiful buildings in the world.

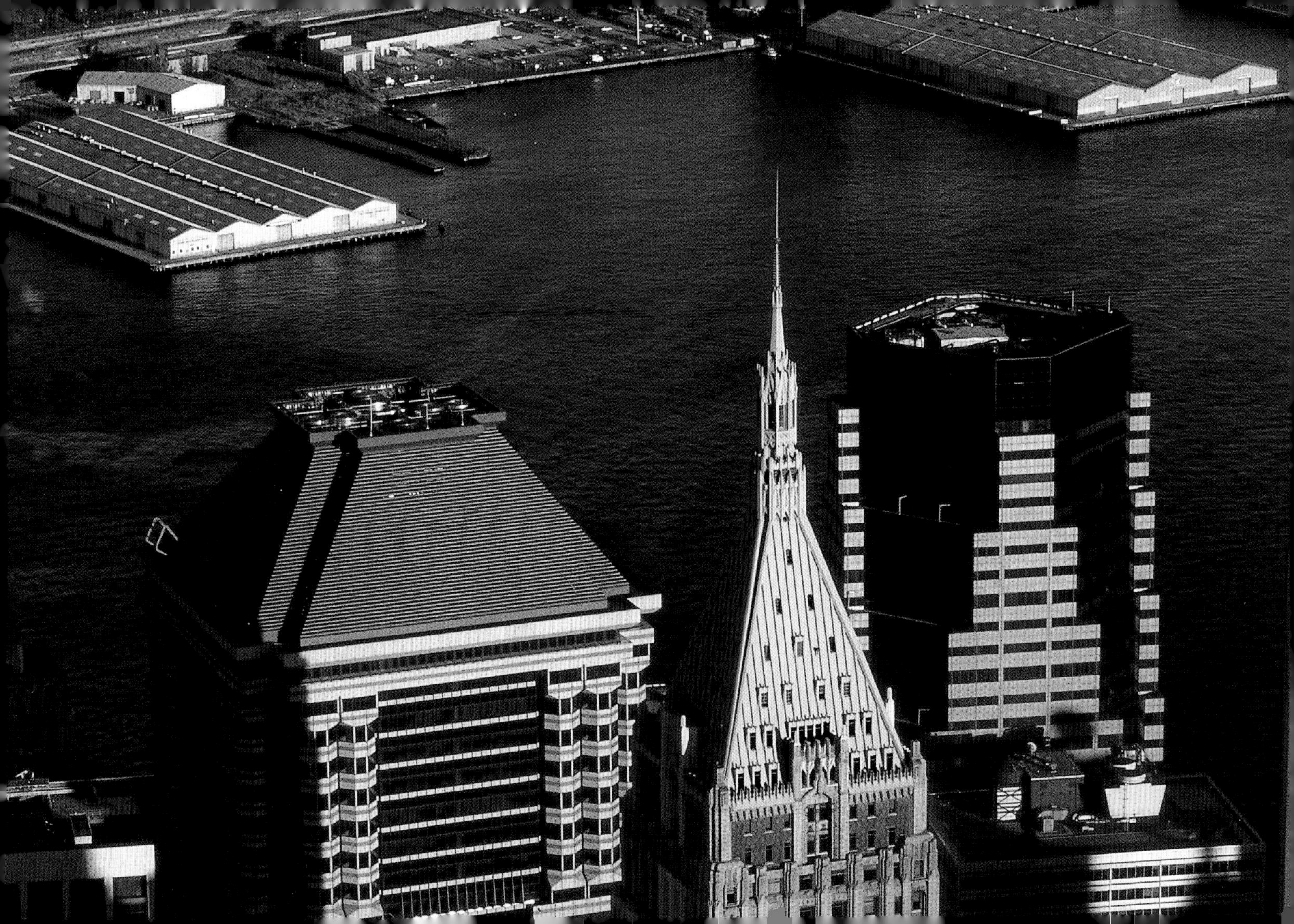

389
Thanks to a solid foundation of granite bedrock, lower Manhattan can accommodate the jumble of skyscrapers at its tip, though the topography and street plan often call for creative architectural and engineering feats.

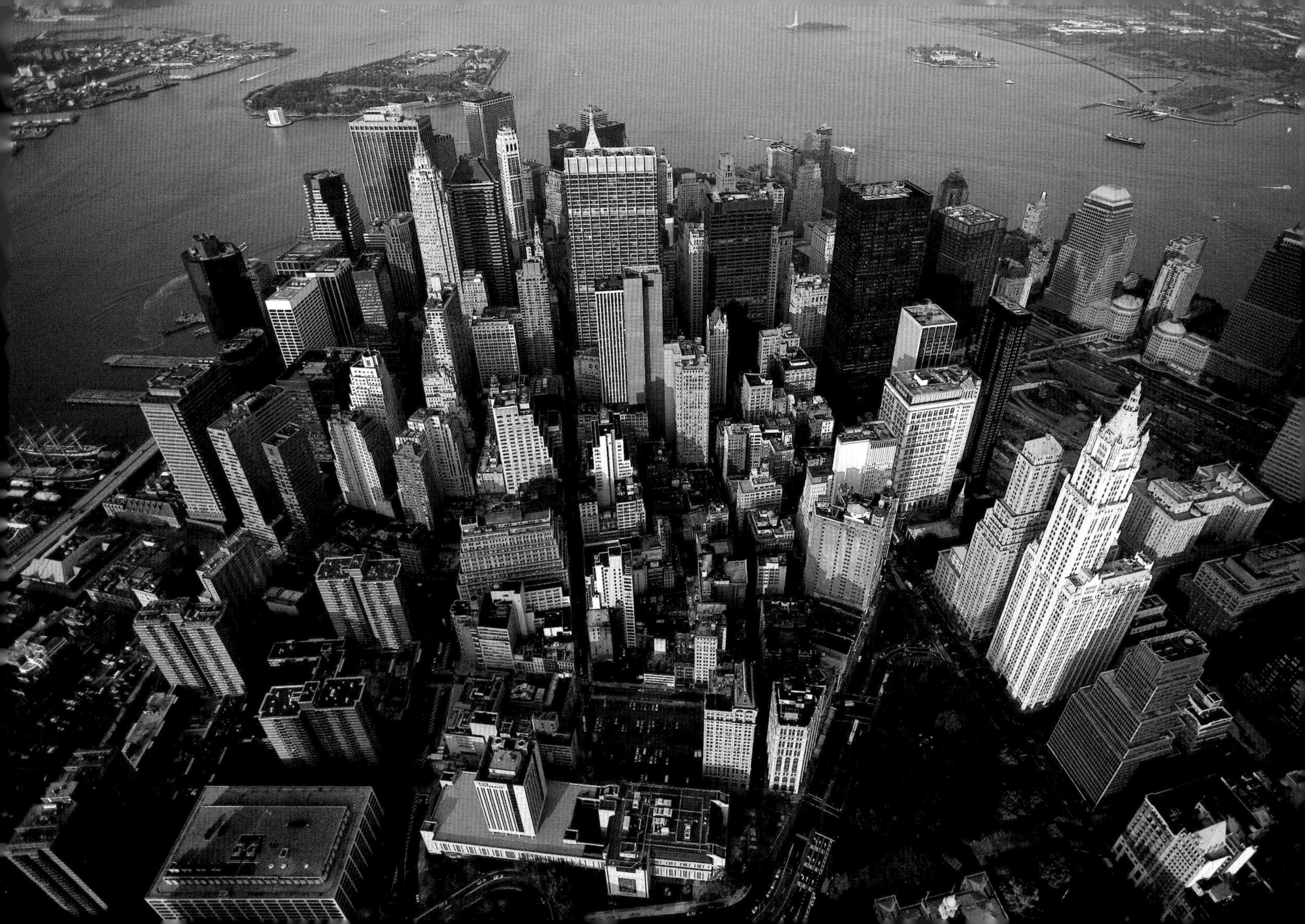

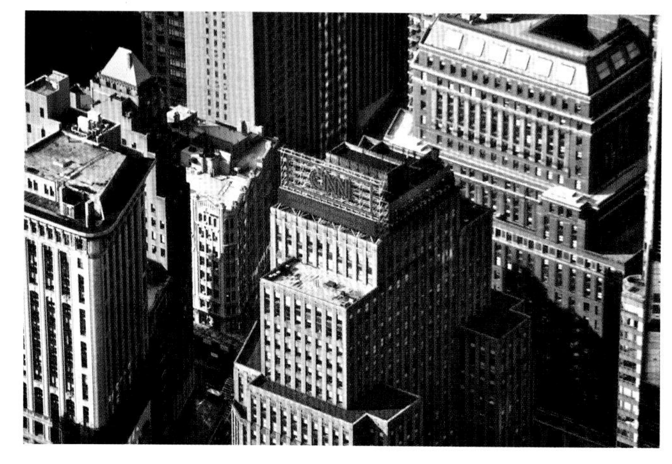

390
A big neon sign advertises CNN, the television network that has come to symbolize New York and the United States around the world.

391
Lower Manhattan competes with Downtown Chicago for the record for the first forest of skyscrapers in the world.

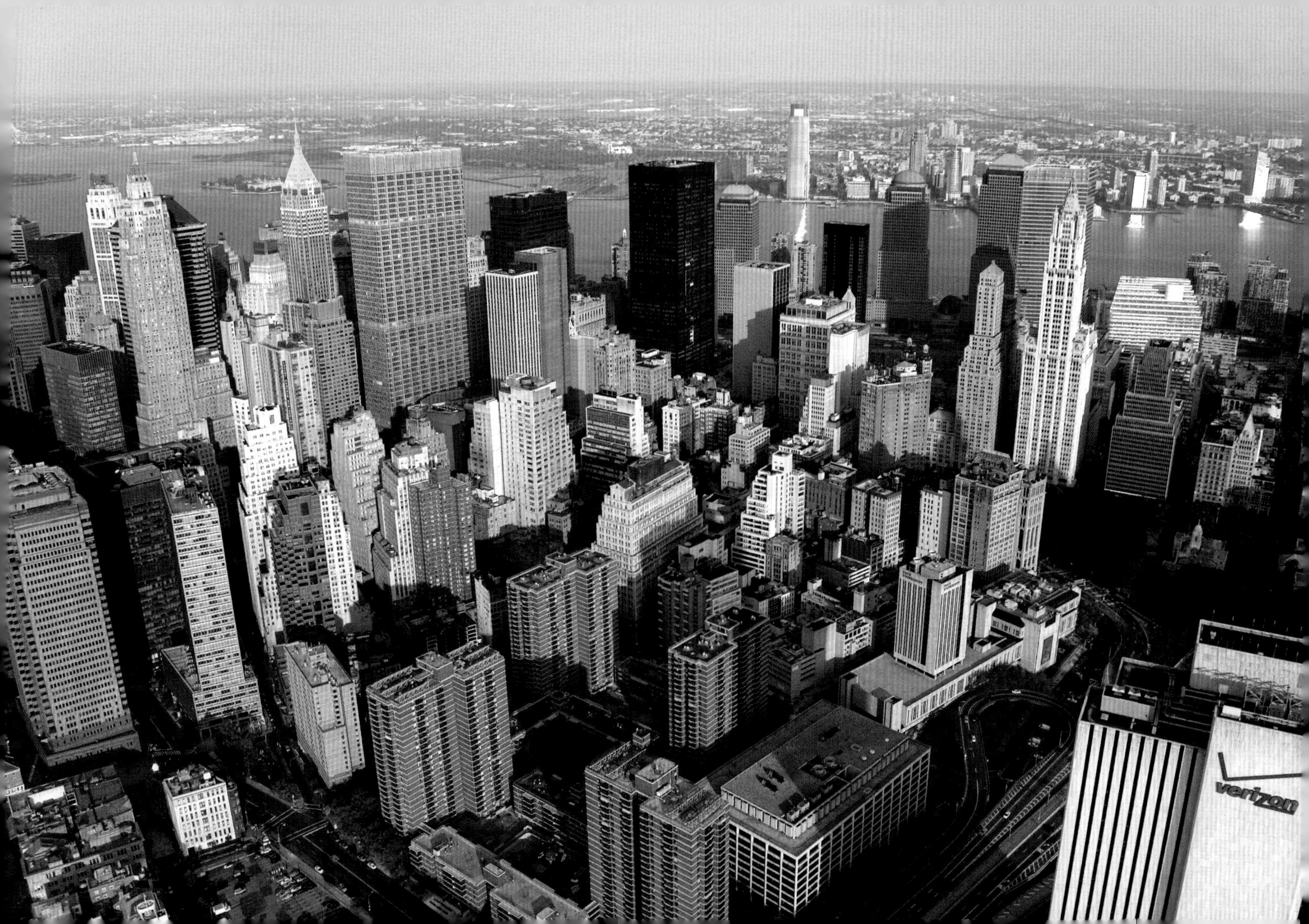
verizon

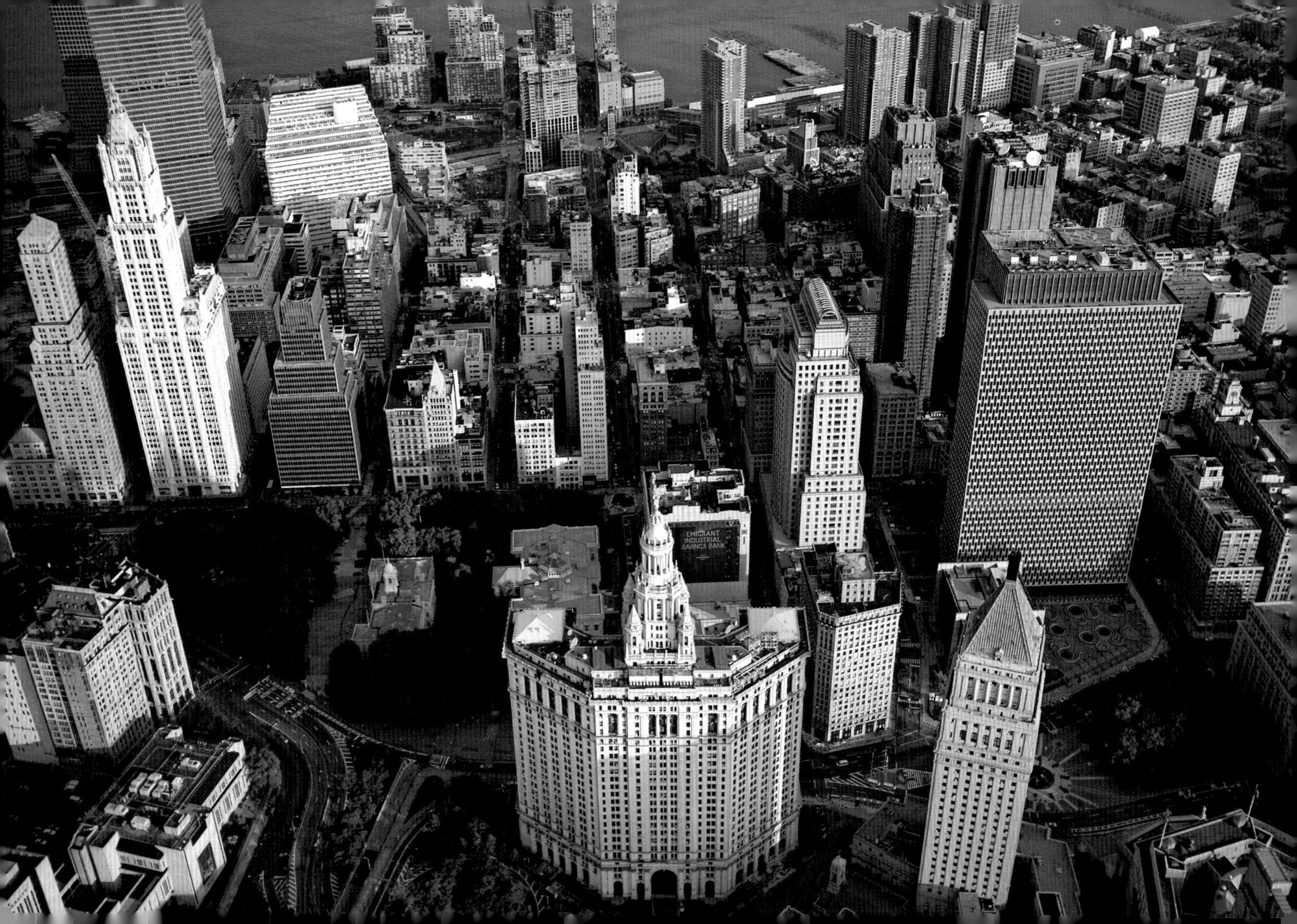
EMIGRANT
INDUSTRIAL
SAVINGS BANK

392

The McKim, Mead and White-designed Municipal Building inspired the designers of the Stalinist-era skyscrapers of Moscow with its Corinthian pilasters and columns. The US Courthouse, with a pyramidal roof, is to the right, and to the left is the 17th-century City Hall. The Woolworth Building, designed by noted architect Cass Gilbert, is on the upper left. The modern rectangular building is the Javits Federal Office Building.

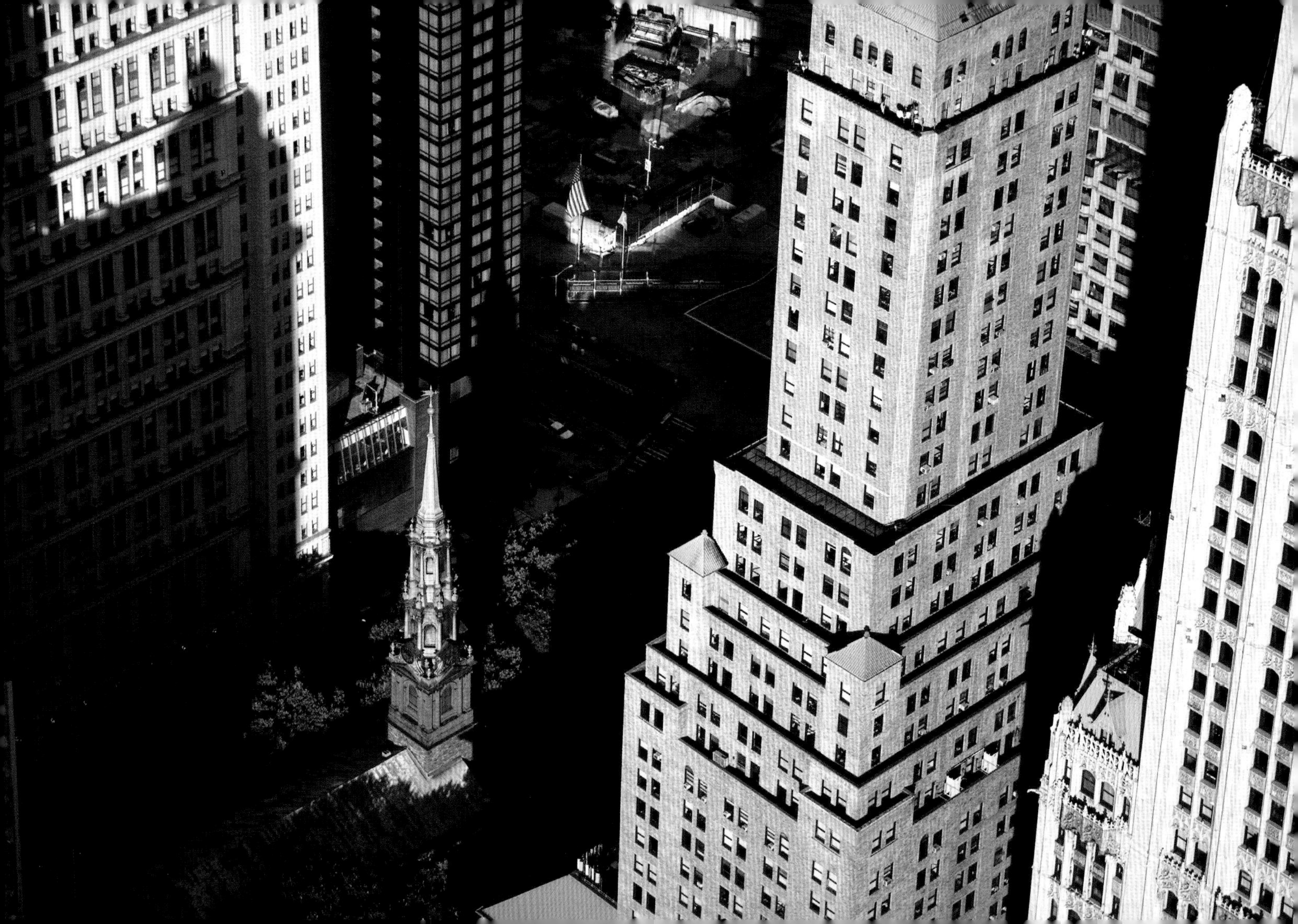

394

St. Paul's Chapel is the oldest church in Manhattan and pre-dates the American Revolution. It has survived fires, wars and the collapse of the World Trade Center, directly across Church Street. The historic chapel served as a meeting place for the teams of volunteers and firefighters who spent almost a year searching for survivors and clearing the site.

397
A ferry heads for Liberty Island, which is situated off the southwest tip of New York in New York harbor.

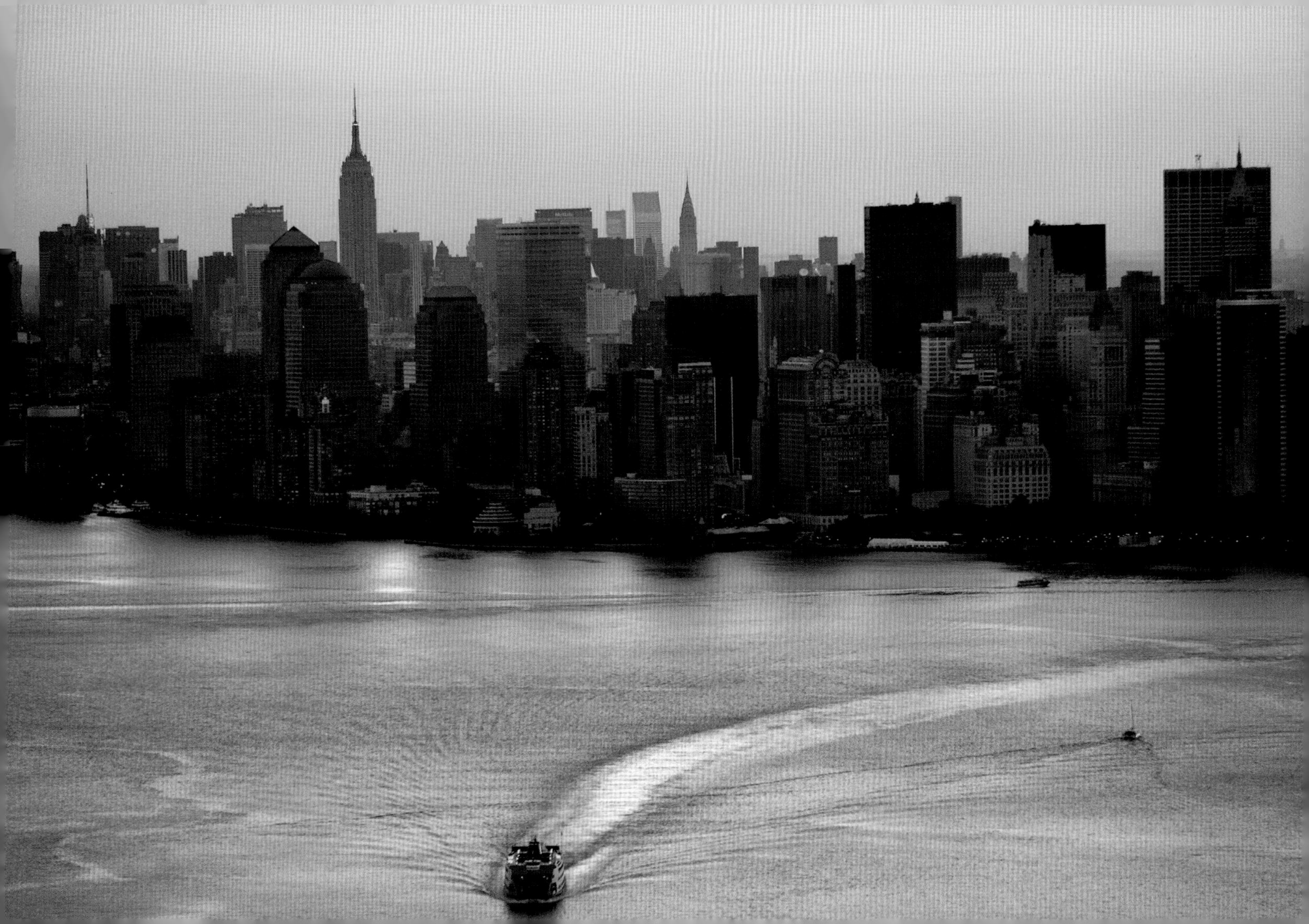

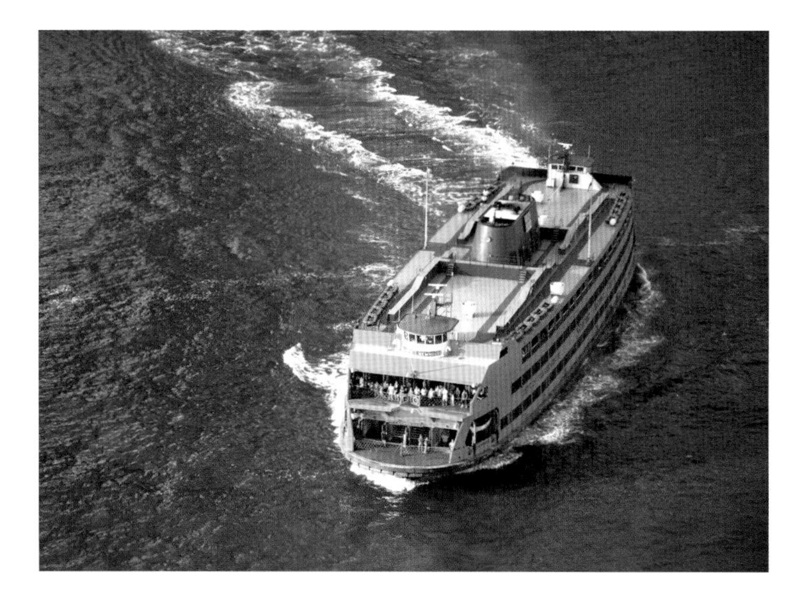

398 and 399

Ferries carry tourists to Ellis Island, where between 1890 and 1954, 12 million immigrants were processed after arriving on ships. Once a tiny 3-acre tract called Pearl Island by the Dutch Settlers, for its abundant oyster beds, today's Ellis Island is now a 27-acre National Park and Museum.

400-401

The Lady of Liberty, a gift to the US from the people of France in 1886 holds her torch aloft on her perch on Liberty Island.

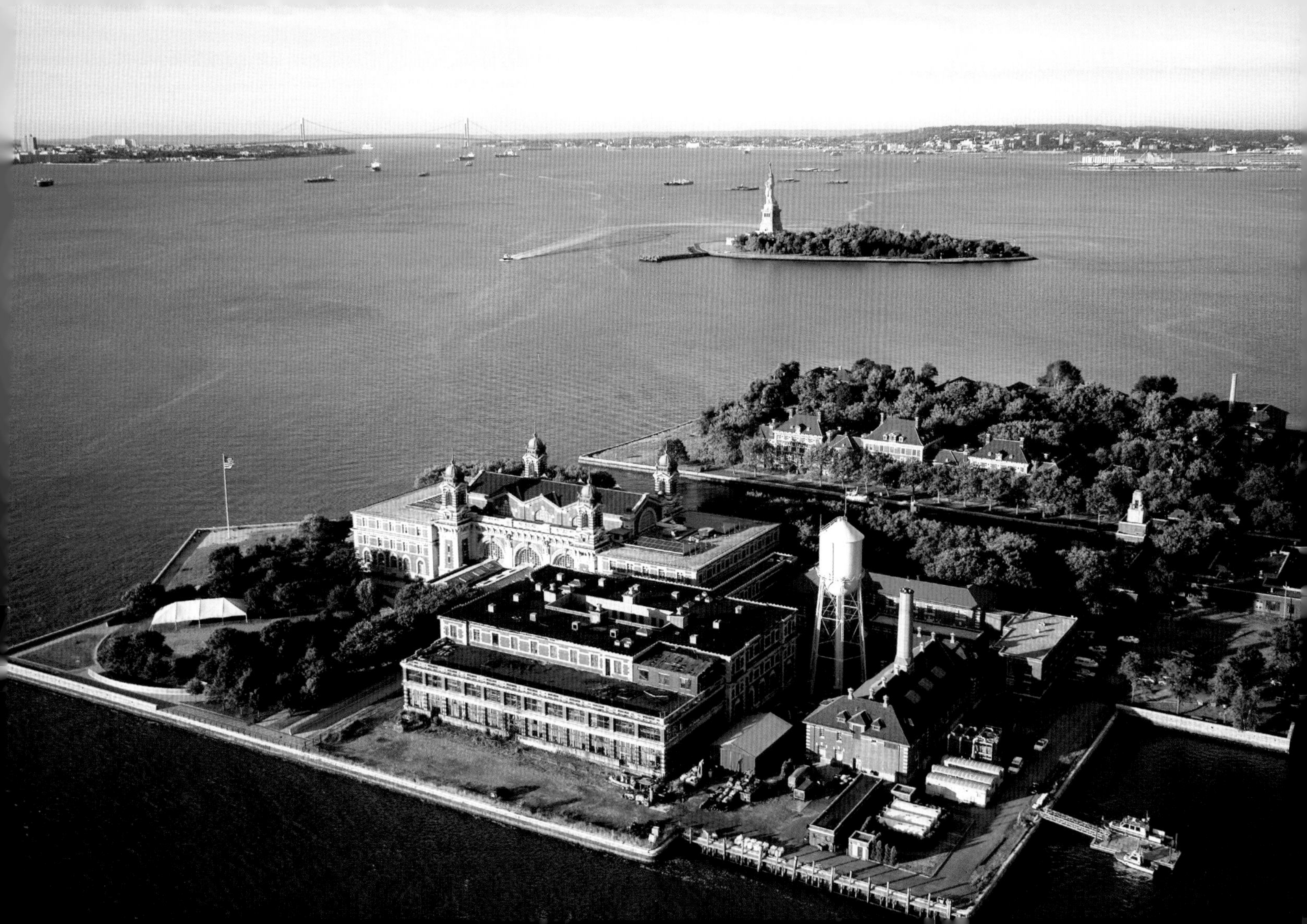

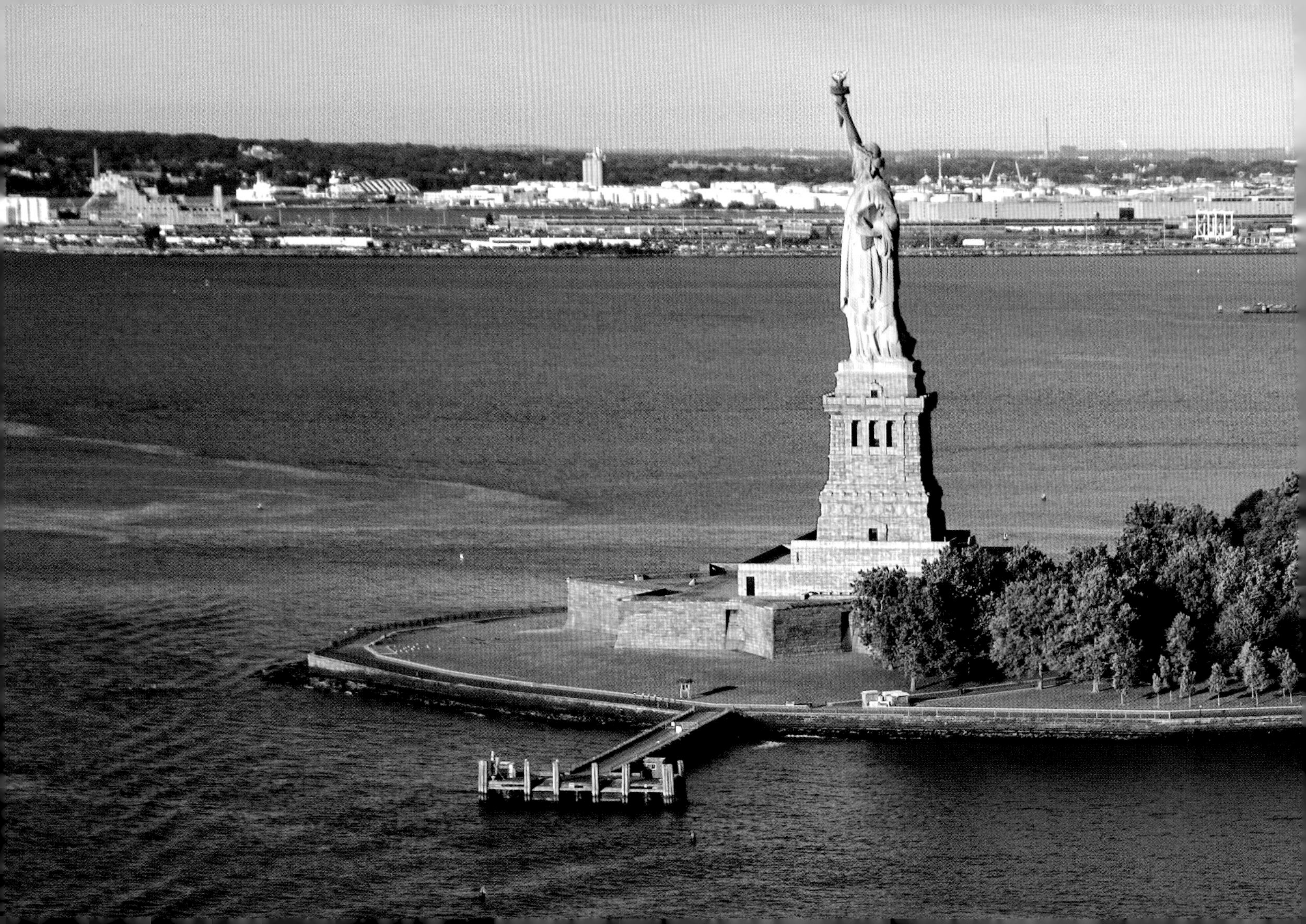

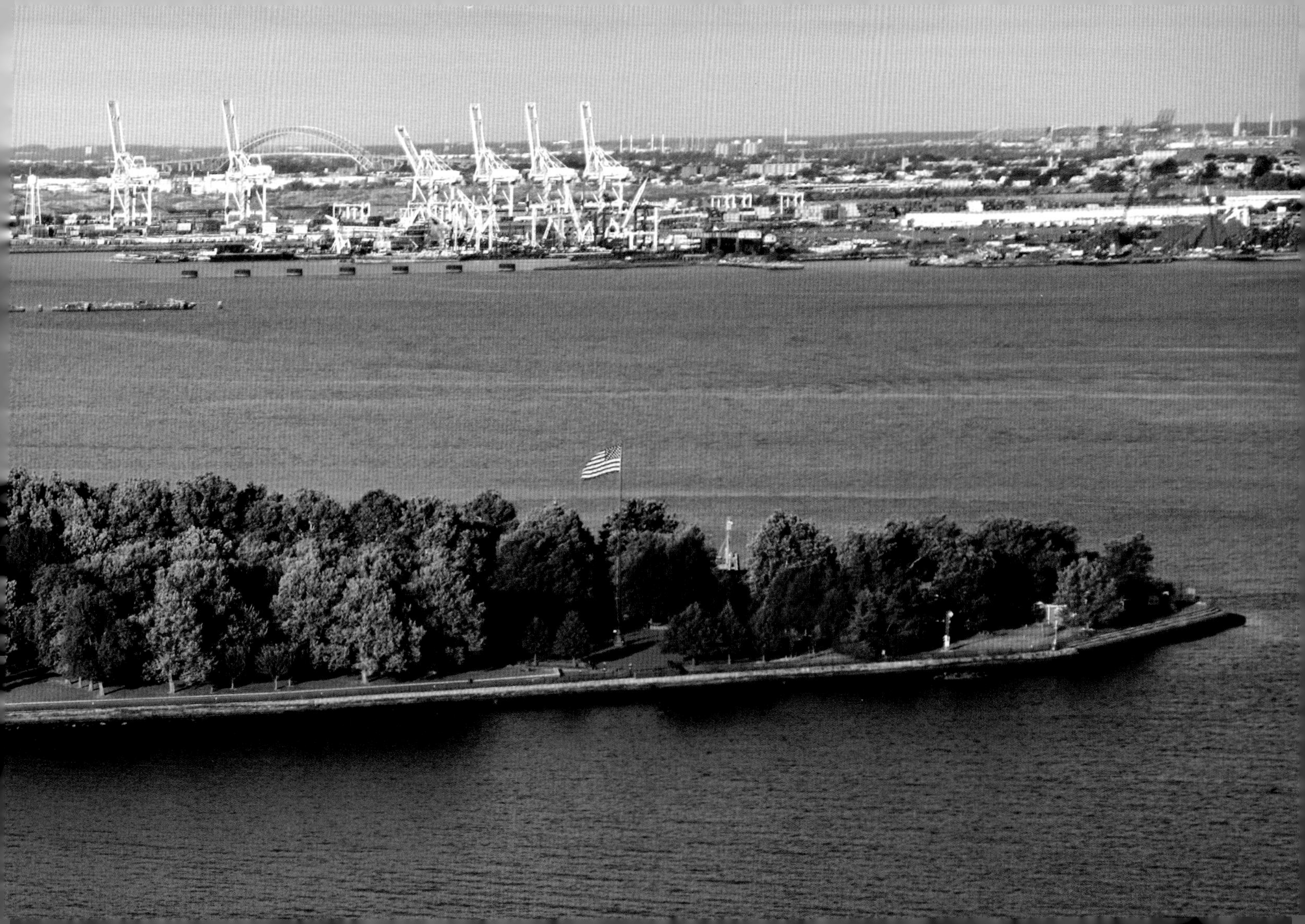

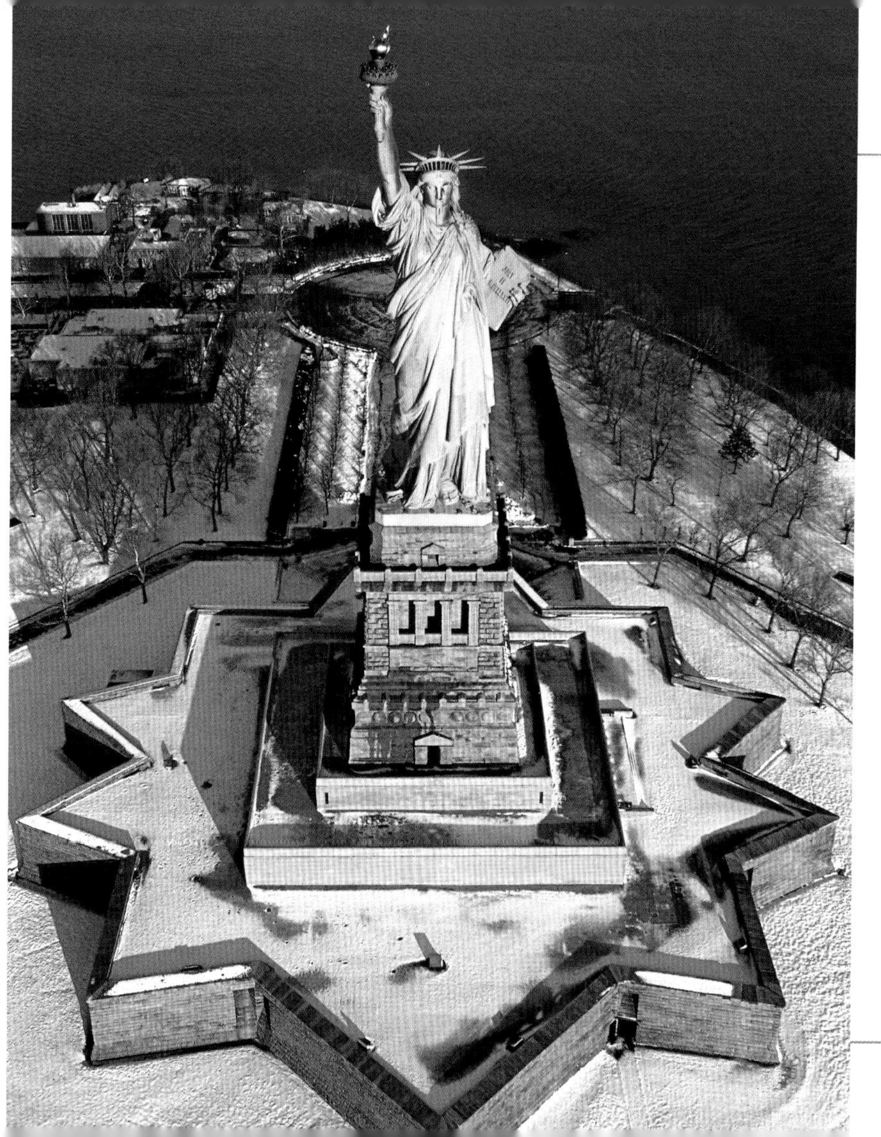

402

In summer's heat and winter's snow, the Statue of Liberty's torch gleams gold, and as Edouard-Rene Laboulaye, the man who conceived of the idea of the statue once said, it is "not an incendiary torch, but one that lights the way."

403

With a face said to have been modeled after the mother of her sculptor, Frederic Bartholdi, the Statue of Liberty wears a crown with seven rays, symbolizing the seven seas and seven continents.

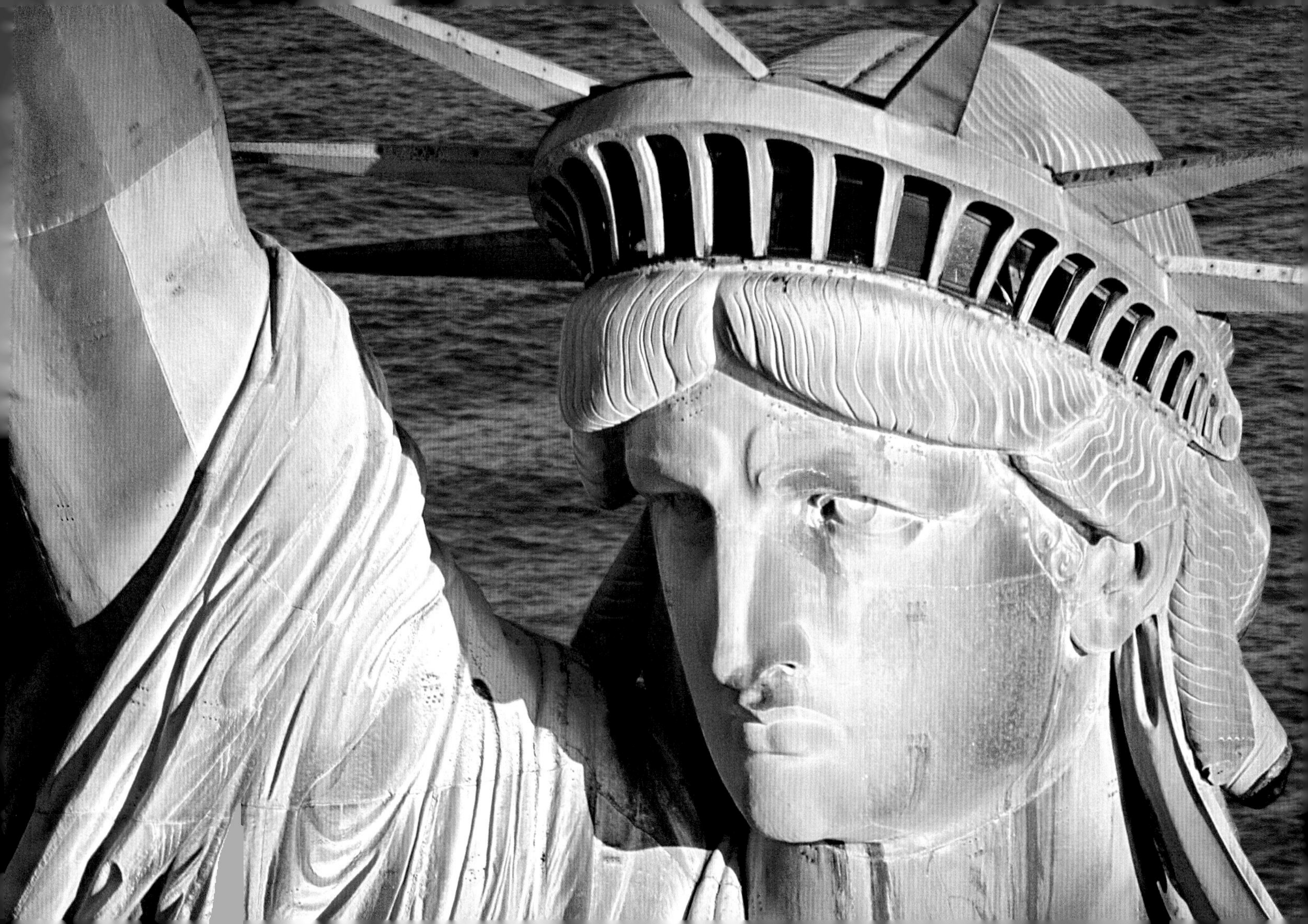

Index

c = caption

Index

Index

ELIZABETH BIBB IS A WRITER AND EDITOR WHO WORKS IN BOTH MAGAZINE AND BOOK PUBLISHING. SHE HAS WRITTEN FOR MAGAZINES AND NEWSPAPERS, INCLUDING *COSMOPOLITAN*, *SEVENTEEN* AND *NEW YORK*, AS WELL AS THE *LOS ANGELES TIMES* AND THE *DALLAS TIMES HERALD*. SHE WAS THE FOUNDING EDITOR OF *CAREERS*, A MAGAZINE FOR YOUNG ADULTS; SENIOR EDITOR OF CONDÉ NAST'S *MADEMOISELLE* MAGAZINE, EDITORIAL CONSULTANT FOR TIME-WARNER MAGAZINE DEVELOPMENT AND EDITOR-IN-CHIEF OF *AMERICAN HEALTH* MAGAZINE'S SPONSORED PUBLICATIONS DEPARTMENT. SHE IS ALSO THE AUTHOR OF TWO BOOKS, *IN THE JAPANESE GARDEN* AND *WOMB FOR RENT*, AND IS ACTIVE IN PLAY- AND SCREENWRITING WORKSHOPS IN NEW YORK. SHE IS A FOUNDING MEMBER OF THE NEW JERSEY SCREENWRITERS GROUP AND HAS SERVED AS DRAMATURGE FOR THE T. SCHREIBER STUDIO IN NEW YORK. SHE HAS ALSO EDITED PREVIOUS WORKS BY MICHAEL YAMASHITA, INCLUDING *ZHENG HE* AND *MEKONG: MOTHER OF WATERS*.

Photo Credits

All photographs are by Michael Yamashita except the following:
Antonio Attini /Archivio White Star: pages 12-13, 90, 91, 100,138, 200-201, 204, 205, 230, 231, 242, 258, 324-325, 335 left, 372, 373, 386-387
Ira Block: page 18

Via Candido Sassone, 22-24
13100 Vercelli - Italy
WWW.WHITESTAR.IT

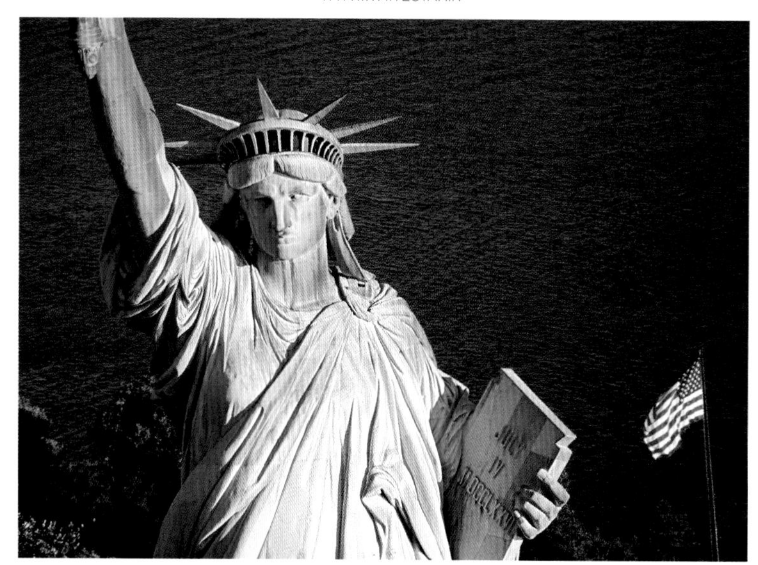

408
Though it is no longer possible to climb to the torch of the Statue of Liberty, her crown is accessible for those willing to make the 354-step ascent.

ISBN 978-88-544-0194-5

Reprints: 1 2 3 4 5 6 11 10 09 08 07

Printed in Thailand
Color separation: Chiaroscuro and Fotomec, Turin